Semi-Supervised Learning

Semi-Supervised Learning

Olivier Chapelle
Bernhard Schölkopf
Alexander Zien

The MIT Press
Cambridge, Massachusetts
London, England

First MIT Press paperback edition, 2010

©2006 Massachusetts Institute of Technology

Typeset by the authors using LATEX 2_ε
Printed and bound in the United States of America

Library of Congress Cataloging-in-Publication Data
Semi-supervised learning / edited by Olivier Chapelle, Bernhard Schölkopf, Alexander Zien.
    p. cm. – (Adaptive computation and machine learning)
Includes bibliographical references.
ISBN 978-0-262-03358-9 (hc. : alk. paper)—978-0-262-51412-5 (pb. : alk. paper)
1. Supervised learning (Machine learning) I. Chapelle, Olivier. II. Schölkopf, Bernhard. III. Zien, Alexander. IV. Series.
Q325.75.S42 2006   006.3'1–dc22   2006044448

10 9 8 7 6 5 4 3

Contents

Series Foreword   xi

Preface   xiii

1 Introduction to Semi-Supervised Learning   1
1.1 Supervised, Unsupervised, and Semi-Supervised Learning 1
1.2 When Can Semi-Supervised Learning Work? 4
1.3 Classes of Algorithms and Organization of This Book 8

I Generative Models   13

2 A Taxonomy for Semi-Supervised Learning Methods   15
Matthias Seeger
2.1 The Semi-Supervised Learning Problem 15
2.2 Paradigms for Semi-Supervised Learning 17
2.3 Examples 22
2.4 Conclusions 31

3 Semi-Supervised Text Classification Using EM   33
Kamal Nigam, Andrew McCallum, Tom Mitchell
3.1 Introduction 33
3.2 A Generative Model for Text 35
3.3 Experimental Results with Basic EM 41
3.4 Using a More Expressive Generative Model 43
3.5 Overcoming the Challenges of Local Maxima 49
3.6 Conclusions and Summary 54

4 Risks of Semi-Supervised Learning   57
Fabio Cozman, Ira Cohen
4.1 Do Unlabeled Data Improve or Degrade Classification Performance? 57
4.2 Understanding Unlabeled Data: Asymptotic Bias 59
4.3 The Asymptotic Analysis of Generative Semi-Supervised Learning . 63
4.4 The Value of Labeled and Unlabeled Data 67
4.5 Finite Sample Effects 69

4.6   Model Search and Robustness   70
4.7   Conclusion   71

5   Probabilistic Semi-Supervised Clustering with Constraints   73
Sugato Basu, Mikhail Bilenko, Arindam Banerjee, Raymond Mooney
5.1   Introduction   74
5.2   HMRF Model for Semi-Supervised Clustering   75
5.3   HMRF-KMEANS Algorithm   81
5.4   Active Learning for Constraint Acquisition   93
5.5   Experimental Results   96
5.6   Related Work   100
5.7   Conclusions   101

II   Low-Density Separation   103

6   Transductive Support Vector Machines   105
Thorsten Joachims
6.1   Introduction   105
6.2   Transductive Support Vector Machines   108
6.3   Why Use Margin on the Test Set?   111
6.4   Experiments and Applications of TSVMs   112
6.5   Solving the TSVM Optimization Problem   114
6.6   Connection to Related Approaches   116
6.7   Summary and Conclusions   116

7   Semi-Supervised Learning Using Semi-Definite Programming   119
Tijl De Bie, Nello Cristianini
7.1   Relaxing SVM Transduction   119
7.2   An Approximation for Speedup   126
7.3   General Semi-Supervised Learning Settings   128
7.4   Empirical Results   129
7.5   Summary and Outlook   133
       Appendix: The Extended Schur Complement Lemma   134

8   Gaussian Processes and the Null-Category Noise Model   137
Neil D. Lawrence, Michael I. Jordan
8.1   Introduction   137
8.2   The Noise Model   141
8.3   Process Model and Effect of the Null-Category   143
8.4   Posterior Inference and Prediction   145
8.5   Results   147
8.6   Discussion   149

9   Entropy Regularization   151

Yves Grandvalet, Yoshua Bengio

9.1 Introduction 151
9.2 Derivation of the Criterion 152
9.3 Optimization Algorithms 155
9.4 Related Methods 158
9.5 Experiments 160
9.6 Conclusion 166
       Appendix: Proof of Theorem 9.1 166

10 Data-Dependent Regularization   **169**
Adrian Corduneanu, Tommi Jaakkola
10.1 Introduction 169
10.2 Information Regularization on Metric Spaces 174
10.3 Information Regularization and Relational Data 182
10.4 Discussion 189

III   Graph-Based Methods   **191**

11 Label Propagation and Quadratic Criterion   **193**
Yoshua Bengio, Olivier Delalleau, Nicolas Le Roux
11.1 Introduction 193
11.2 Label Propagation on a Similarity Graph 194
11.3 Quadratic Cost Criterion 198
11.4 From Transduction to Induction 205
11.5 Incorporating Class Prior Knowledge 205
11.6 Curse of Dimensionality for Semi-Supervised Learning 206
11.7 Discussion 215

12 The Geometric Basis of Semi-Supervised Learning   **217**
Vikas Sindhwani, Misha Belkin, Partha Niyogi
12.1 Introduction 217
12.2 Incorporating Geometry in Regularization 220
12.3 Algorithms 224
12.4 Data-Dependent Kernels for Semi-Supervised Learning 229
12.5 Linear Methods for Large-Scale Semi-Supervised Learning . . 231
12.6 Connections to Other Algorithms and Related Work 232
12.7 Future Directions 234

13 Discrete Regularization   **237**
Dengyong Zhou, Bernhard Schölkopf
13.1 Introduction 237
13.2 Discrete Analysis 239
13.3 Discrete Regularization 245
13.4 Conclusion 249

14 Semi-Supervised Learning with Conditional Harmonic Mixing   251
Christopher J. C. Burges, John C. Platt
14.1 Introduction 251
14.2 Conditional Harmonic Mixing 255
14.3 Learning in CHM Models 256
14.4 Incorporating Prior Knowledge 261
14.5 Learning the Conditionals 261
14.6 Model Averaging 262
14.7 Experiments 263
14.8 Conclusions 273

IV   Change of Representation   275

15 Graph Kernels by Spectral Transforms   277
Xiaojin Zhu, Jaz Kandola, John Lafferty, Zoubin Ghahramani
15.1 The Graph Laplacian 278
15.2 Kernels by Spectral Transforms 280
15.3 Kernel Alignment 281
15.4 Optimizing Alignment Using QCQP for Semi-Supervised Learning . 282
15.5 Semi-Supervised Kernels with Order Constraints 283
15.6 Experimental Results 285
15.7 Conclusion 289

16 Spectral Methods for Dimensionality Reduction   293
Lawrence K. Saul, Kilian Q. Weinberger, Fei Sha, Jihun Ham, Daniel D. Lee
16.1 Introduction 293
16.2 Linear Methods 295
16.3 Graph-Based Methods 297
16.4 Kernel Methods 303
16.5 Discussion 306

17 Modifying Distances   309
Sajama, Alon Orlitsky
17.1 Introduction 309
17.2 Estimating DBD Metrics 312
17.3 Computing DBD Metrics 321
17.4 Semi-Supervised Learning Using Density-Based Metrics 327
17.5 Conclusions and Future Work 329

V   Semi-Supervised Learning in Practice   331

18 Large-Scale Algorithms   333

Olivier Delalleau, Yoshua Bengio, Nicolas Le Roux
18.1 Introduction 333
18.2 Cost Approximations 334
18.3 Subset Selection 337
18.4 Discussion 340

19 Semi-Supervised Protein Classification
Using Cluster Kernels **343**
Jason Weston, Christina Leslie, Eugene Ie, William Stafford Noble
19.1 Introduction 343
19.2 Representations and Kernels for Protein Sequences 345
19.3 Semi-Supervised Kernels for Protein Sequences 348
19.4 Experiments 352
19.5 Discussion 358

20 Prediction of Protein Function from
Networks **361**
Hyunjung Shin, Koji Tsuda
20.1 Introduction 361
20.2 Graph-Based Semi-Supervised Learning 364
20.3 Combining Multiple Graphs 366
20.4 Experiments on Function Prediction of Proteins 369
20.5 Conclusion and Outlook 374

21 Analysis of Benchmarks **377**
21.1 The Benchmark 377
21.2 Application of SSL Methods 383
21.3 Results and Discussion 390

VI   Perspectives **395**

22 An Augmented PAC Model for Semi-Supervised Learning **397**
Maria-Florina Balcan, Avrim Blum
22.1 Introduction 398
22.2 A Formal Framework 400
22.3 Sample Complexity Results 403
22.4 Algorithmic Results 412
22.5 Related Models and Discussion 416

23 Metric-Based Approaches for Semi-
Supervised Regression and Classification **421**
Dale Schuurmans, Finnegan Southey, Dana Wilkinson, Yuhong Guo
23.1 Introduction 421
23.2 Metric Structure of Supervised Learning 423

23.3 Model Selection 426
23.4 Regularization 436
23.5 Classification 445
23.6 Conclusion 449

**24 Transductive Inference and
Semi-Supervised Learning**   **453**
Vladimir Vapnik
24.1 Problem Settings 453
24.2 Problem of Generalization in Inductive and Transductive Inference . 455
24.3 Structure of the VC Bounds and Transductive Inference 457
24.4 The Symmetrization Lemma and Transductive Inference 458
24.5 Bounds for Transductive Inference 459
24.6 The Structural Risk Minimization Principle for Induction and Trans-
     duction 460
24.7 Combinatorics in Transductive Inference 462
24.8 Measures of the Size of Equivalence Classes 463
24.9 Algorithms for Inductive and Transductive SVMs 465
24.10 Semi-Supervised Learning 470
24.11 Conclusion: Transductive Inference and the New Problems of Infer-
      ence 470
24.12 Beyond Transduction: Selective Inference 471

25 A Discussion of Semi-Supervised Learning and Transduction   **473**

References   **479**

Notation and Symbols   **499**

Contributors   **503**

Index   **509**

Series Foreword

The goal of building systems that can adapt to their environments and learn from their experience has attracted researchers from many fields, including computer science, engineering, mathematics, physics, neuroscience, and cognitive science. Out of this research has come a wide variety of learning techniques that have the potential to transform many scientific and industrial fields. Recently, several research communities have converged on a common set of issues surrounding supervised, unsupervised, and reinforcement learning problems. The MIT Press series on Adaptive Computation and Machine Learning seeks to unify the many diverse strands of machine learning research and to foster high-quality research and innovative applications.

Thomas Dietterich

Preface

During the last years, semi-supervised learning has emerged as an exciting new direction in machine learning reseach. It is closely related to profound issues of how to do inference from data, as witnessed by its overlap with *transductive inference* (the distinctions are yet to be made precise).

At the same time, dealing with the situation where relatively few labeled training points are available, but a large number of unlabeled points are given, it is directly relevant to a multitude of practical problems where is it relatively expensive to produce labeled data, e.g., the automatic classification of web pages. As a field, semi-supervised learning uses a diverse set of tools and illustrates, on a small scale, the sophisticated machinery developed in various branches of machine learning such as kernel methods or Bayesian techniques.

As we work on semi-supervised learning, we have been aware of the lack of an authoritative overview of the existing approaches. In a perfect world, such an overview should help both the practitioner and the researcher who wants to enter this area. A well researched monograph could ideally fill such a gap; however, the field of semi-supervised learning is arguably not yet sufficiently mature for this. Rather than writing a book which would come out in three years, we thus decided instead to provide an up-to-date edited volume, where we invited contributions by many of the leading proponents of the field. To make it more than a mere collection of articles, we have attempted to ensure that the chapters form a coherent whole and use consistent notation. Moreover, we have written a short introduction, a dialogue illustrating some of the ongoing debates in the underlying philosophy of the field, and we have organized and summarized a comprehensive *benchmark* of semi-supervised learning.

Benchmarks are helpful for the practitioner to decide which algorithm should be chosen for a given application. At the same time, they are useful for researchers to choose issues to study and further develop. By evaluating and comparing the performance of many of the presented methods on a set of eight benchmark problems, this book aims at providing guidance in this respect. The problems are designed to reflect and probe the different assumptions that the algorithms build on. All data sets can be downloaded from the book web page, which can be found at `http://www.kyb.tuebingen.mpg.de/ssl-book/`.

Finally, we would like to give thanks to everybody who contributed towards the success of this book project, in particular to Karin Bierig, Sabrina Nielebock, Bob Prior, to all chapter authors, and to the chapter reviewers.

1   Introduction to Semi-Supervised Learning

1.1   Supervised, Unsupervised, and Semi-Supervised Learning

In order to understand the nature of semi-supervised learning, it will be useful first to take a look at supervised and unsupervised learning.

1.1.1   Supervised and Unsupervised Learning

Traditionally, there have been two fundamentally different types of tasks in machine learning.

unsupervised learning

The first one is *unsupervised learning*. Let $X = (x_1, \ldots, x_n)$ be a set of n examples (or points), where $x_i \in \mathcal{X}$ for all $i \in [n] := \{1, \ldots, n\}$. Typically it is assumed that the points are drawn i.i.d. (independently and identically distributed) from a common distribution on $\mathcal{X}$. It is often convenient to define the $(n \times d)$-matrix $\mathbf{X} = (x_i^\top)_{i \in [n]}^\top$ that contains the data points as its rows. The goal of unsupervised learning is to find interesting structure in the data X. It has been argued that the problem of unsupervised learning is fundamentally that of estimating a density which is likely to have generated X. However, there are also weaker forms of unsupervised learning, such as quantile estimation, clustering, outlier detection, and dimensionality reduction.

supervised learning

The second task is *supervised learning*. The goal is to learn a mapping from x to y, given a training set made of pairs (x_i, y_i). Here, the $y_i \in \mathcal{Y}$ are called the labels or targets of the examples x_i. If the labels are numbers, $\mathbf{y} = (y_i)_{i \in [n]}^\top$ denotes the column vector of labels. Again, a standard requirement is that the pairs (x_i, y_i) are sampled i.i.d. from some distribution which here ranges over $\mathcal{X} \times \mathcal{Y}$. The task is well defined, since a mapping can be evaluated through its predictive performance on test examples. When $\mathcal{Y} = \mathbb{R}$ or $\mathcal{Y} = \mathbb{R}^d$ (or more generally, when the labels are continuous), the task is called regression. Most of this book will focus on classification (there is some work on regression in chapter 23), i.e., the case where y takes values in a finite set (discrete labels). There are two families of algorithms for supervised learning. *Generative* algorithms try to model the class-conditional

generative methods

[handwritten margin note: Given a Target what is the Probability density that the data points are generated from?]

density $p(x|y)$ by some unsupervised learning procedure.[1] A predictive density can then be inferred by applying Bayes theorem:

$$p(y|x) = \frac{p(x|y)p(y)}{\int_y p(x|y)p(y)dy}.$$ (1.1)

discriminative methods

In fact, $p(x|y)p(y) = p(x,y)$ is the joint density of the data, from which pairs (x_i, y_i) could be generated. *Discriminative* algorithms do not try to estimate how the x_i have been generated, but instead concentrate on estimating $p(y|x)$. Some discriminative methods even limit themselves to modeling whether $p(y|x)$ is greater than or less than 0.5; an example of this is the support vector machine (SVM). It has been argued that discriminative models are more directly aligned with the goal of supervised learning and therefore tend to be more efficient in practice. These two frameworks are discussed in more detail in sections 2.2.1 and 2.2.2.

1.1.2   Semi-Supervised Learning

standard setting of SSL

Semi-supervised learning (SSL) is halfway between supervised and unsupervised learning. In addition to unlabeled data, the algorithm is provided with some supervision information – but not necessarily for all examples. Often, this information will be the targets associated with some of the examples. In this case, the data set $X = (x_i)_{i \in [n]}$ can be divided into two parts: the points $X_l := (x_1, \ldots, x_l)$, for which labels $Y_l := (y_1, \ldots, y_l)$ are provided, and the points $X_u := (x_{l+1}, \ldots, x_{l+u})$, the labels of which are not known. This is "standard" semi-supervised learning as investigated in this book; most chapters will refer to this setting.

SSL with constraints

Other forms of partial supervision are possible. For example, there may be constraints such as "these points have (or do not have) the same target" (cf. Abu-Mostafa, 1995). This more general setting is considered in chapter 5. The different setting corresponds to a different view of semi-supervised learning: In chapter 5, SSL is seen as unsupervised learning guided by constraints. In contrast, most other approaches see SSL as supervised learning with additional information on the distribution of the examples x. The latter interpretation seems to be more in line with most applications, where the goal is the same as in supervised learning: to predict a target value for a given x_i. However, this view does not readily apply if the number and nature of the classes are not known in advance but have to be inferred from the data. In contrast, SSL as unsupervised learning with constraints may still remain applicable in such situations.

transductive learning

inductive learning

A problem related to SSL was introduced by Vapnik already several decades ago: so-called *transductive learning.* In this setting, one is given a (labeled) training set and an (unlabeled) test set. The idea of transduction is to perform predictions only for the test points. This is in contrast to *inductive learning,* where the goal is to

---

1. For simplicity, we are assuming that all distributions have densities, and thus we restrict ourselves to dealing with densities.

output a prediction function which is defined on the entire space $\mathcal{X}$. Many methods described in this book will be transductive; in particular, this is rather natural for inference based on graph representations of the data. This issue will be addressed again in section 1.2.4.

1.1.3 A Brief History of Semi-Supervised Learning

self-learning

Probably the earliest idea about using unlabeled data in classification is self-learning, which is also known as self-training, self-labeling, or decision-directed learning. This is a wrapper-algorithm that repeatedly uses a supervised learning method. It starts by training on the labeled data only. In each step a part of the unlabeled points is labeled according to the current decision function; then the supervised method is retrained using its own predictions as additional labeled points. This idea has appeared in the literature already for some time (e.g., Scudder (1965); Fralick (1967); Agrawala (1970)).

An unsatisfactory aspect of self-learning is that the effect of the wrapper depends on the supervised method used inside it. If self-learning is used with empirical risk minimization and 1-0-loss, the unlabeled data will have no effect on the solution at all. If instead a margin maximizing method is used, as a result the decision boundary is pushed away from the unlabeled points (cf. chapter 6). In other cases it seems to be unclear what the self-learning is really doing, and which assumption it corresponds to.

transductive
inference

Closely related to semi-supervised learning is the concept of transductive inference, or transduction, pioneered by Vapnik (Vapnik and Chervonenkis, 1974; Vapnik and Sterin, 1977). In contrast to inductive inference, no general decision rule is inferred, but only the labels of the unlabeled (or test) points are predicted. An early instance of transduction (albeit without explicitly considering it as a concept) was already proposed by Hartley and Rao (1968). They suggested a combinatorial optimization on the labels of the test points in order to maximize the likelihood of their model.

mixture of
Gaussians

It seems that semi-supervised learning really took off in the 1970s when the problem of estimating the Fisher linear discriminant rule with unlabeled data was considered (Hosmer, 1973; McLachlan, 1977; O'Neill, 1978; McLachlan and Ganesalingam, 1982). More precisely, the setting was in the case where each class-conditional density is Gaussian with equal covariance matrix. The likelihood of the model is then maximized using the labeled and unlabeled data with the help of an iterative algorithm such as the expectation-maximization (EM) algorithm (Dempster et al., 1977). Instead of a mixture of Gaussians, the use of a mixture of multinomial distributions estimated with labeled and unlabeled data has been investigated in (Cooper and Freeman, 1970).

Later, this one component per class setting has been extended to several components per class (Shahshahani and Landgrebe, 1994) and further generalized by Miller and Uyar (1997).

Learning rates in a probably approximately correct (PAC) framework (Valiant,

theoretical
analysis

1984) have been derived for the semi-supervised learning of a mixture of two Gaussians by Ratsaby and Venkatesh (1995). In the case of an *identifiable* mixture, Castelli and Cover (1995) showed that with an infinite number of unlabeled points, the probability of error has an exponential convergence (w.r.t. the number of labeled examples) to the Bayes risk. Identifiable means that given $P(\mathbf{x})$, the decomposition in $\sum_y P(y)P(\mathbf{x}|y)$ is unique. This seems a relatively strong assumption, but it is satisfied, for instance, by mixtures of Gaussians. Related is the analysis in (Castelli and Cover, 1996) in which the class-conditional densities are known but the class priors are not.

text applications

Finally, the interest in semi-supervised learning increased in the 1990s, mostly due to applications in natural language problems and text classification (Yarowsky, 1995; Nigam et al., 1998; Blum and Mitchell, 1998; Collins and Singer, 1999; Joachims, 1999).

Note that, to our knowledge, Merz et al. (1992) were the first to use the term "semi-supervised" for classification with both labeled and unlabeled data. It has in fact been used before, but in a different context than what is developed in this book; see, for instance, (Board and Pitt, 1989).

1.2   When Can Semi-Supervised Learning Work?

A natural question arises: is semi-supervised learning meaningful? More precisely: in comparison with a supervised algorithm that uses only labeled data, can one hope to have a more accurate prediction by taking into account the unlabeled points? As you may have guessed from the size of the book in your hands, in principle the answer is "yes." However, there is an important prerequisite: that the distribution of examples, which the unlabeled data will help elucidate, be relevant for the classification problem.

In a more mathematical formulation, one could say that the knowledge on $p(x)$ that one gains through the unlabeled data has to carry information that is useful in the inference of $p(y|x)$. If this is not the case, semi-supervised learning will not yield an improvement over supervised learning. It might even happen that using the unlabeled data degrades the prediction accuracy by misguiding the inference; this effect is investigated in detail in chapter 4.

smoothness
assumption

One should thus not be too surprised that for semi-supervised learning to work, certain *assumptions* will have to hold. In this context, note that plain supervised learning also has to rely on assumptions. In fact, chapter 22 discusses a way of formalizing assumptions of the kind given below within a PAC-style framework. One of the most popular such assumptions can be formulated as follows.

Smoothness assumption of supervised learning:[2] If two points x_1, x_2 are close, then so should be the corresponding outputs y_1, y_2.

Clearly, without such assumptions, it would never be possible to generalize from a finite training set to a set of possibly infinitely many unseen test cases.

1.2.1   The Semi-Supervised Smoothness Assumption

semi-supervised
smoothness
assumption

We now propose a generalization of the smoothness assumption that is useful for semi-supervised learning; we thus call it the "semi-supervised smoothness assumption". While in the supervised case according to our prior beliefs the output varies smoothly with the distance, we now also take into account the density of the inputs. The assumption is that the label function is smoother in high-density regions than in low-density regions:

Semi-supervised smoothness assumption: If two points x_1, x_2 in a high-density region are close, then so should be the corresponding outputs y_1, y_2.

Note that by transitivity, this assumption implies that if two points are linked by a path of high density (e.g., if they belong to the same cluster), then their outputs are likely to be close. If, on the other hand, they are separated by a low-density region, then their outputs need not be close.

Note that the semi-supervised smoothness assumption applies to both regression and classification. In the next section, we will show that in the case of classification, it reduces to assumptions commonly used in SSL. At present, it is less clear how useful the assumption is for regression problems. As an alternative, chapter 23 proposes a way to use unlabeled data for model selection that applies to both regression and classification.

1.2.2   The Cluster Assumption

cluster
assumption

if homogeneous

Suppose we knew that the points of each class tended to form a cluster. Then the unlabeled data could aid in finding the boundary of each cluster more accurately: one could run a clustering algorithm and use the labeled points to assign a class to each cluster. That is in fact one of the earliest forms of semi-supervised learning (see chapter 2). The underlying, now classical, assumption may be stated as follows:

Cluster assumption: If points are in the same cluster, they are likely to be of the same class.

This assumption may be considered reasonable on the basis of the sheer existence

---

2. Strictly speaking, this assumption only refers to continuity rather than smoothness; however, the term *smoothness* is commonly used, possibly because in regression estimation y is often modeled in practice as a smooth function of x.

of classes: if there is a densly populated continuum of objects, it may seem unlikely that they were ever distinguished into different classes.

Note that the cluster assumption does not imply that each class forms a single, compact cluster: it only means that, usually, we do not observe objects of two distinct classes in the same cluster.

The cluster assumption can easily be seen as a special case of the above-proposed semi-supervised smoothness assumption, considering that clusters are frequently defined as being sets of points that can be connected by short curves which traverse only high-density regions.

The cluster assumption can be formulated in an equivalent way:

low density separation

Low density separation: The decision boundary should lie in a low-density region.

The equivalence is easy to see: A decision boundary in a high-density region would cut a cluster into two different classes; many objects of different classes in the same cluster would require the decision boundary to cut the cluster, i.e., to go through a high-density region.

Although the two formulations are conceptually equivalent, they can inspire different algorithms, as we will argue in section 1.3. The low-density version also gives additional intuition why the assumption is sensible in many real-world problems. Consider digit recognition, for instance, and suppose that one wants to learn how to distinguish a handwritten digit "0" against digit "1". A sample point taken exactly from the decision boundary will be between a 0 and a 1, most likely a digit looking like a very elongated zero. But the probability that someone wrote this "weird" digit is very small.

1.2.3 The Manifold Assumption

A different but related assumption that forms the basis of several semi-supervised learning methods is the manifold assumption:

manifold assumption

Manifold assumption: The (high-dimensional) data lie (roughly) on a low-dimensional manifold.

curse of dimensionality

How can this be useful? A well-known problem of many statistical methods and learning algorithms is the so-called curse of dimensionality (cf. section 11.6.2). It is related to the fact that volume grows exponentially with the number of dimensions, and an exponentially growing number of examples is required for statistical tasks such as the reliable estimation of densities. This is a problem that directly affects generative approaches that are based on density estimates in input space. A related problem of high dimensions, which may be more severe for discriminative methods, is that pairwise distances tend to become more similar, and thus less expressive.

If the data happen to lie on a low-dimensional manifold, however, then the learning algorithm can essentially operate in a space of corresponding dimension, thus avoiding the curse of dimensionality.

As above, one can argue that algorithms working with manifolds may be seen as approximately implementing the semi-supervised smoothness assumption: such algorithms use the metric of the manifold for computing geodesic distances. If we view the manifold as an approximation of the high-density regions, then it becomes clear that in this case, the semi-supervised smoothness assumption reduces to the standard smoothness assumption of supervised learning, applied on the manifold.

Note that if the manifold is embedded into the high-dimensional input space in a curved fashion (i.e., it is not just a subspace), geodesic distances differ from those in the input space. By ensuring more accurate density estimates and more appropriate distances, the manifold assumption may be useful for classification as well as for regression.

1.2.4 Transduction

As mentioned before, some algorithms naturally operate in a transductive setting. According to the philosophy put forward by Vapnik, high-dimensional estimation problems should attempt to follow the following principle:

Vapnik's principle: When trying to solve some problem, one should not solve a more difficult problem as an intermediate step.

Consider as an example supervised learning, where predictions of labels y corresponding to some objects x are desired. Generative models estimate the density of x as an intermediate step, while discriminative methods directly estimate the labels.

In a similar way, if label predictions are only required for a given test set, transduction can be argued to be more direct than induction: while an inductive method infers a function $f : \mathcal{X} \to \mathcal{Y}$ on the entire space $\mathcal{X}$, and afterward returns the evaluations $f(x_i)$ at the test points, transduction consists of directly estimating the finite set of test labels, i.e., a function $f : X_u \to \mathcal{Y}$ only defined on the test set. Note that transduction (as defined in this book) is not the same as SSL: some semi-supervised algorithms are transductive, but others are inductive.

Now suppose we are given a transductive algorithm which produces a solution superior to an inductive algorithm trained on the same labeled data (but discarding the unlabeled data). Then the performance difference might be due to one of the following two points (or a combination thereof):

1. transduction follows Vapnik's principle more closely than induction does, or

2. the transductive algorithm takes advantage of the unlabeled data in a way similar to semi-supervised learning algorithms.

There is ample evidence for improvements being due to the second of these points. We are presently not aware of empirical results that selectively support the first point. In particular, the evaluation of the benchmark associated with this book (chapter 21) does not seem to suggest a systematic advantage of transductive methods. However, the properties of transduction are still the topic of debate, and chapter 25 tries to present different opinions.

1.3   Classes of Algorithms and Organization of This Book

Although many methods were not explicitly derived from one of the above assumptions, most algorithms can be seen to correspond to or implement one or more of them. We try to organize the semi-supervised learning methods presented in this book into four classes that roughly correspond to the underlying assumption. Although the classification is not always unique, we hope that this organization makes the book and its contents more accessible to the reader, by providing a guiding scheme.

For the same reason, this book is organized in "parts." There is one part for each class of SSL algorithms and an extra part focusing on generative approaches. Two further parts are devoted to applications and perspectives of SSL. In the following we briefly introduce the ideas covered by each book part.

1.3.1   Generative Models

Part I presents history and state of the art of SSL with generative models. Chapter 2 starts with a thorough review of the field.

Inference using a generative model involves the estimation of the conditional density $p(x|y)$. In this setting, any additional information on $p(x)$ is useful. As a simple example, assume that $p(x|y)$ is Gaussian. Then one can use the EM algorithm to find the parameters of the Gaussian corresponding to each class. The only difference to the standard EM algorithm as used for clustering is that the "hidden variable" associated with any labeled example is actually not hidden, but it is known and equals its class label. It implements the cluster assumption (cf. section 2.2.1), since a given cluster belongs to only one class.

mixture models

This small example already highlights different interpretations of semi-supervised learning with a generative model:

- It can be seen as classification with additional information on the marginal density.

- It can be seen as clustering with additional information. In the standard setting, this information would be the labels of a subset of points, but it could also come in the more general form of constraints. This is the topic of chapter 5.

A strength of the generative approach is that knowledge of the structure of the problem or the data can naturally be incorporated by modeling it. In chapter 3, this is demonstrated for the application of the EM algorithm to text data. It is observed that, when modeling assumptions are not correct, unlabeled data can decrease prediction accuracy. This effect is investigated in depth in chapter 4.

In statistical learning, before performing inference, one chooses a class of functions, or a prior over functions. One has to choose it according to what is known in advance about the problem. In the semi-supervised learning context, if one has some ideas about what the structure of the data tells about the target function, the

data-dependent
priors

choice of this prior can be made more precise after seeing the unlabeled data: one
could typically put a higher prior probability on functions that satisfy the cluster
assumption. From a theoretical point, this is a natural way to obtain bounds for
semi-supervised learning as explained in chapter 22.

1.3.2   Low-Density Separation

Part II of this book aims at describing algorithms which try to directly implement
the low-density separation assumption by pushing the decision boundary away from
the unlabeled points.

The most common approach to achieving this goal is to use a maximum margin
algorithm such as support vector machines. The method of maximizing the margin
for unlabeled as well as labeled points is called the transductive SVM (TSVM).

transductive
SVM (TSVM)

However, the corresponding problem is nonconvex and thus difficult to optimize.

One optimization algorithm for the TSVM is presented in chapter 6. Starting
from the SVM solution as trained on the labeled data only, the unlabeled points are
labeled by SVM predictions, and the SVM is retrained on all points. This is iterated
while the weight of the unlabeled points is slowly increased. Another possibility is
the semi-definite programming SDP relaxation suggested in chapter 7.

Two alternatives to the TSVM are then presented that are formulated in a
probabilistic and in an information theoretic framework, respectively. In chapter
8, binary Gaussian process classification is augmented by the introduction of a null
class that occupies the space between the two regular classes. As an advantage over
the TSVM, this allows for probabilistic outputs.

This advantage is shared by the entropy minimization presented in chapter 9. It
encourages the class-conditional probabilities $P(y|x)$ to be close to either 1 or 0 at
labeled and unlabeled points. As a consequence of the smoothness assumption, the
probability will tend to be close to 0 or 1 throughout any high-density region, while
class boundaries correspond to intermediate probabilities.

A different way of using entropy or information is the data-dependent regularization developed in chapter 10. As compared to the TSVM, this seems to implement
the low-density separation even more directly: the standard squared-norm regularizer is multiplied by a term reflecting the density close to the decision boundary.

1.3.3   Graph-Based Methods

During the last couple of years, the most active area of research in semi-supervised
learning has been in graph-based methods, which are the topic of part III of this
book. The common denominator of these methods is that the data are represented
by the nodes of a graph, the edges of which are labeled with the pairwise distances
of the incident nodes (and a missing edge corresponds to infinite distance). If the
distance of two points is computed by minimizing the aggregate path distance over
all paths connecting the two points, this can be seen as an approximation of the
geodesic distance of the two points with respect to the manifold of data points.

Thus, graph methods can be argued to build on the manifold assumption.

Most graph methods refer to the graph by utilizing the graph Laplacian. Let $\mathbf{g} = (V, E)$ be a graph with real edge weights given by $w : E \to \mathbb{R}$. Here, the weight $w(e)$ of an edge e indicates the similarity of the incident nodes (and a missing edge corresponds to zero similarity). Now the weighted adjacency matrix (or weight matrix, for short) $\mathbf{W}$ of the graph $\mathbf{g} = (V, E)$ is defined by

weight matrix

$$\mathbf{W}_{ij} := \begin{cases} w(e) & \text{if } e = (i, j) \in E, \\ 0 & \text{if } e = (i, j) \in E. \end{cases} \tag{1.2}$$

graph Laplacian

The diagonal matrix $\mathbf{D}$ defined by $\mathbf{D}_{ii} := \sum_j W_{ij}$ is called the degree matrix of $\mathbf{g}$. Now there are different ways of defining the graph Laplacian, the two most prominent of which are the normalized graph Laplacian, $\mathcal{L}$, and the unnormalized graph Laplacian, L:

$$\begin{aligned} \mathcal{L} &:= \mathbf{I} - \mathbf{D}^{-1/2} \mathbf{W} \mathbf{D}^{-1/2}, \\ L &:= \mathbf{D} - \mathbf{W}. \end{aligned} \tag{1.3}$$

Many graph methods that penalize nonsmoothness along the edges of a weighted graph can in retrospect be seen as different instances of a rather general family of algorithms, as is outlined in chapter 11. Chapter 13 takes a more theoretical point of view, and transfers notions of smoothness from the continuous case onto graphs as the discrete case. From that, it proposes different regularizers based on a graph representation of the data.

Usually the prediction consists of labels for the unlabeled nodes. For this reason, this kind of algorithm is intrinsically transductive, i.e., it returns only the value of the decision function on the unlabeled points and not the decision function itself. However, there has been recent work in order to extend graph-based methods to produce inductive solutions, as discussed in chapter 12.

Information propagation on graphs can also serve to improve a given (possibly strictly supervised) classification, taking unlabeled data into account. Chapter 14 presents a probabilistic method for using directed graphs in this manner.

Often the graph $\mathbf{g}$ is constructed by computing similarities of objects in some other representation, e.g., using a kernel function on Euclidean data points. But sometimes the original data already have the form of a graph. Examples include the linkage pattern of webpages and the interactions of proteins (see chapter 20). In such cases, the directionality of the edges may be important.

1.3.4 Change of Representation

The topic of part IV is algorithms that are not intrinsically semi-supervised, but instead perform two-step learning:

1. Perform an unsupervised step on all data, labeled and unlabeled, but ignoring the available labels. This can, for instance, be a change of representation, or the

construction of a new metric or a new kernel.

2. Ignore the unlabeled data and perform plain supervised learning using the new distance, representation, or kernel.

This can be seen as direct implementation of the semi-supervised smoothness assumption, since the representation is changed in such a way that small distances in high-density regions are conserved.

Note that the graph-based methods (part III) are closely related to the ones presented in this part: the very construction of the graph from the data can be seen as an unsupervised change of representation. Consequently, the first chapter of part IV, chapter 15, discusses spectral transforms of such graphs in order to build kernels. Spectral methods can also be used for nonlinear dimensionality reduction, as extended in chapter 16. Furthermore, in chapter 17, metrics derived from graphs are investigated, for example, those derived from shortest paths.

1.3.5 Semi-Supervised Learning in Practice

Semi-supervised learning will be most useful whenever there are far more unlabeled data than labeled. This is likely to occur if obtaining data points is cheap, but obtaining the labels costs a lot of time, effort, or money. This is the case in many application areas of machine learning, for example:

■ In speech recognition, it costs almost nothing to record huge amounts of speech, but labeling it requires some human to listen to it and type a transcript.

■ Billions of webpages are directly available for automated processing, but to classify them reliably, humans have to read them.

■ Protein sequences are nowadays acquired at industrial speed (by genome sequencing, computational gene finding, and automatic translation), but to resolve a three-dimensional (3D) structure or to determine the functions of a single protein may require years of scientific work.

Webpage classification is introduced in chapter 3 in the context of generative models.

Since unlabeled data carry less information than labeled data, they are required in large amounts in order to increase prediction accuracy significantly. This implies the need for fast and efficient SSL algorithms. Chapters 18 and 19 present two approaches to dealing with huge numbers of points. In chapter 18 methods are developed for speeding up the label propagation methods introduced in chapter 11. In chapter 19 cluster kernels are shown to be an efficient SSL method.

Chapter 19 also presents the first of two approaches to an important bioinformatics application of semi-supervised learning: the classification of protein sequences. While here the predictions are based on the protein sequences themselves, Chapter 20 moves on to a somewhat more complex setting: The information is here assumed to be present in the form of graphs that characterize the interactions of proteins. Several such graphs exist and have to be combined in an appropriate way.

This book part concludes with a very practical chapter: the presentation and evaluation of the benchmarks associated with this book (chapter 21). It is intended to give hints to the practitioner on how to choose suitable methods based on the properties of the problem.

1.3.6   Outlook

The last part of the book, part VI, is devoted to some of the most interesting directions of ongoing research in SSL.

Until now this book has mostly resticted itself to classification. Chapter 23 introduces another approach to SSL that is suited for both classification and regression, and derives algorithms from it. Interestingly it seems not to require the assumptions proposed in chapter 1.

Further, this book mostly presented *algorithms* for SSL. While the assumptions discussed above supply some intuition on when and why SSL works, and chapter 4 investigates when and why it can fail, it would clearly be more satisfactory to have a thorough theoretical understanding of SSL in total. Chapter 22 offers a PAC-style framework that yields error bounds for SSL problems.

In chapter 24 inductive semi-supervised learning and transduction are compared in terms of Vapnik-Chervonenkis (VC) bounds and other theoretical and philosophical concepts.

The book closes with a hypothetical discussion (chapter 25) between three machine learning researchers on the relationship of (and the differences between) semi-supervised learning and transduction.

I   Generative Models

2   A Taxonomy for Semi-Supervised Learning Methods

Matthias Seeger   MATTHIAS.SEEGER@TUEBINGEN.MPG.DE

We propose a simple taxonomy of probabilistic graphical models for the semi-supervised learning problem. We give some broad classes of algorithms for each of the families and point to specific realizations in the literature. Finally, we shed more detailed light on the family of methods using input-dependent regularization (or conditional prior distributions) and show parallels to the co-training paradigm.

2.1   The Semi-Supervised Learning Problem

The *semi-supervised learning (SSL)* problem has recently drawn large attention in the machine learning community, mainly due to its significant importance in practical applications. In this section we define the problem and introduce the notation to be used in the rest of this chapter.

In statistical machine learning, we distinguish between *unsupervised* and *supervised learning*. In the former scenario we are given a sample $\{x_i\}$ of patterns in $\mathcal{X}$ drawn *independently and identically distributed (i.i.d.)* from some unknown data distribution with density $P(x)$. Our goal is to estimate the density or a (known) functional thereof. Supervised learning consists of estimating a functional relationship $x \to y$ between a covariate $x \in \mathcal{X}$ and a class variable[1] $y \in \{1, \ldots, M\}$, with the goal of minimizing a functional of the (joint) data distribution $P(x, y)$ such as the probability of classification error. The marginal data distribution $P(x)$ is referred to as input distribution. Classification can be treated as a special case of estimating the joint density $P(x, y)$, but this is wasteful since x will always be given at prediction time, so there is no need to estimate the input distribution.

The terminology "unsupervised learning" is a bit unfortunate: the term *density*

---

1. We restrict ourselves to classification scenarios in this chapter.

estimation should probably be preferred. Traditionally, many techniques for density estimation propose a latent (unobserved) class variable y and estimate $P(\boldsymbol{x})$ as *mixture distribution* $\sum_{y=1}^{M} P(\boldsymbol{x}|y)P(y)$. Note that y has a fundamentally different role than in classification, in that its existence and range c is a modeling choice rather than observable reality. However, in other density estimation techniques, such as nonlinear dimensionality reduction, the term "unsupervised" does not make sense.

The semi-supervised learning problem belongs to the supervised category, since the goal is to minimize the classification error, and an estimate of $P(\boldsymbol{x})$ is not sought after.[2] The difference from a standard classification setting is that along with a *labeled sample* $D_l = \{(\boldsymbol{x}_i, y_i) \,|\, i = 1, \ldots, n\}$ drawn i.i.d. from $P(\boldsymbol{x}, y)$ we also have access to an additional *unlabeled sample* $D_u = \{\boldsymbol{x}_{n+j} \,|\, j = 1, \ldots, m\}$ from the marginal $P(\boldsymbol{x})$. We are especially interested in cases where $m \gg n$ which may arise in situations where obtaining an unlabeled sample is cheap and easy, while labeling the sample is expensive or difficult. We denote $\boldsymbol{X}_l = (\boldsymbol{x}_1, \ldots, \boldsymbol{x}_n), Y_l = (y_1, \ldots, y_n)$ and $\boldsymbol{X}_u = (\boldsymbol{x}_{n+1}, \ldots, \boldsymbol{x}_{n+m})$. The unobserved labels are denoted $Y_u = (y_{n+1}, \ldots, y_{n+m})$. In a straightforward generalization of SSL (not discussed here) uncertain information about Y_u is available.

There are two obvious baseline methods for SSL. We can treat it as a supervised classification problem by ignoring D_u, or we can treat y as a latent class variable in a mixture estimate of $P(\boldsymbol{x})$ which is fitted using an unsupervised method, then associate latent groups with observed classes using D_l (see section 2.3.1 for more details). One would agree that any valid SSL technique should outperform both baseline methods significantly in a range of practically relevant situations. If this sounds rather vague, note that in general for a *fixed* SSL method it should be easy to construct data distributions for which either of the baseline methods does better.[3] In our view, SSL is much more a practical than a theoretical problem. A useful SSL technique should be configurable to the specifics of the task in a similar way as Bayesian learning, through the choice of prior and model. While some theoretical work has been done for SSL, the bulk of relevant work so far has tackled real-world applications.

---

2. While this statement is probably open to debate, it is in fact agreed upon in statistics. In our opinion, methods should be classified foremost according to the problem they try to solve, *not* by which sources of data they make use of. On the other hand, there are problems in which density estimation is the goal and labeled data are treated as an auxiliary source. However, these fall into a category with very different characteristics and are not in the scope of this chapter. In our opinion, it would be very confusing to lump them together with methods we classify as SSL here. A label like "semi-unsupervised learning" would be more appropriate.

3. This is a "no free lunch" statement for SSL, but in practice it seems to be a more serious problem than in the purely supervised context (where a "no free lunch" statement holds as well). See chapter 4 for some examples.

2.2   Paradigms for Semi-Supervised Learning

Since SSL methods are supervised learning techniques, they can be classified according to the standard taxonomy into *generative* and *diagnostic* paradigms. In this section we present these paradigms and highlight their differences in the case of SSL. We also note that this taxonomy, which originated for purely supervised methods, can be ambiguous when applied to SSL, and we suggest how the borderline can be drawn exactly.

In the figures of this section, we employ a convenient graphical notation frequently used in statistics and machine learning (Lauritzen, 1996; Jordan, 1999). These so-called directed *graphical models* (or independence diagrams) have the following intuitive semantics. Nodes represent random variables. The parents of a node i are the nodes j for which a directed edge $j \rightarrow i$ exists.[4] It is possible to sample the value of a node once the values of all its parents are known. Thus, a graphical model is a simple way of representing the sampling mechanism from a distribution over several variables. As such, the graphical model encodes conditional independency constraints that have to hold for the distribution. In order to sample from the distribution, we start with nodes without parents and work in the directions of the edges. We also make use of *plates* which are rectangular boxes grouping a set of nodes. This means that the group is sampled repeatedly and independently from the same distribution (i.i.d.) conditioned on all nodes which are parents of any plate member. For example, the figure of section 2.2.1 means that we first sample $\boldsymbol{\theta}$ and $\boldsymbol{\pi}$ independently (neither has parents), then draw a sample $\{(x_i, y_i)\}$ i.i.d. conditioned on $\boldsymbol{\theta}$, $\boldsymbol{\pi}$ (which are parents of the plate).

Note that we describe the generative and diagnostic paradigm from an explicitly Bayesian viewpoint. This is somewhat a matter of personal choice here, and certainly one could sketch these classes without ever mentioning concepts like prior distributions. On the other hand, the Bayesian view avoids many unnecessary complications, in that all variables are random, no difference has to be made between functional and probabilistic independence, and so on, so we do not think our presentation lacks clarity or generality because of this choice.

---

4. Directed cycles are not allowed. In other words, it must be impossible to return to a node by moving along edges and respecting their direction.

2.2.1   The Generative Paradigm

We refer to architectures following the *generative paradigm*
as *generative methods.* Within such, we model the class dis-
tributions $P(\boldsymbol{x}|y)$ using model families $\{P(\boldsymbol{x}|y,\boldsymbol{\theta})\}$, further-
more the class priors $P(y)$ by $\pi_y = P(y|\boldsymbol{\pi})$, $\boldsymbol{\pi} = (\pi_y)_y$.
We refer to an architecture of this type as a *joint density
model*, since we are modeling the full joint density $P(\boldsymbol{x},y)$
by $\pi_y P(\boldsymbol{x}|y,\boldsymbol{\theta})$. For any fixed $\hat{\boldsymbol{\theta}},\hat{\boldsymbol{\pi}}$, an estimate of $P(y|\boldsymbol{x})$
can then be computed by Bayes' formula:

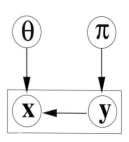

$$P(y|\boldsymbol{x},\hat{\boldsymbol{\theta}},\hat{\boldsymbol{\pi}}) = \frac{\hat{\pi}_y P(\boldsymbol{x}|y,\hat{\boldsymbol{\theta}})}{\sum_{y'=1}^{M}\hat{\pi}_{y'}P(\boldsymbol{x}|y',\hat{\boldsymbol{\theta}})}.$$

This is sometimes referred to as *plug-in estimate.* Alternatively, one can obtain
the Bayesian predictive distribution $P(y|\boldsymbol{x},D_l)$ by averaging $P(y|\boldsymbol{x},\boldsymbol{\theta},\boldsymbol{\pi})$ over the
posterior $P(\boldsymbol{\theta},\boldsymbol{\pi}|D_l)$.[5] Within the generative paradigm, a model for the marginal
$P(\boldsymbol{x})$ emerges naturally as

$$P(\boldsymbol{x}|\boldsymbol{\theta},\boldsymbol{\pi}) = \sum_{y=1}^{M}\pi_y P(\boldsymbol{x}|y,\boldsymbol{\theta}).$$

If labeled and unlabeled data are available, a natural criterion emerges as the *joint
log likelihood* of both D_l and D_u,

$$\sum_{i=1}^{n}\log \pi_{y_i}P(\boldsymbol{x}_i|y_i,\boldsymbol{\theta}) + \sum_{i=n+1}^{n+m}\log\sum_{y=1}^{M}\pi_y P(\boldsymbol{x}_i|y,\boldsymbol{\theta}), \tag{2.1}$$

or alternatively the posterior $P(\boldsymbol{\theta},\boldsymbol{\pi}|D_l,D_u)$.[6] This is essentially an issue of max-
imum likelihood in the presence of missing data (treating y as a latent variable),
which can in principle be attacked by the expectation-maximization (EM) algorithm
(see section 2.3.1) or by direct gradient descent.

Some researchers have been quick in hailing this strategy as an obvious solution
to the SSL problem, but this is not the case, in about the same sense as generative
methods often do not provide good solutions to classification problems. Generative
techniques provide an estimate of $P(\boldsymbol{x})$ along the way, although this is not required
for classification, and in general this proves wasteful given limited data. For ex-

---

5. In a sense, the predictive distribution is a Bayesian's best estimate of the underlying
true data distribution $P(y|\boldsymbol{x})$. It is, however, obtained as posterior expectation, not by
maximizing some criterion.
6. To predict, we average $P(y|\boldsymbol{x},\boldsymbol{\theta},\boldsymbol{\pi})$ over the posterior. If we know that $\boldsymbol{x}$ is drawn from
$P(\boldsymbol{x})$ and independent from D, we should rather employ the posterior $P(\boldsymbol{\theta},\boldsymbol{\pi}|D_l,D_u,\boldsymbol{x})$.
However, in this case the test set usually forms a part of D_u, and the two posteriors are
the same.

ample, maximizing the joint likelihood of a finite sample need not lead to a small classification error, because depending on the model it may be possible to increase the likelihood more by improving the fit of $P(\boldsymbol{x})$ than the fit of $P(y|\boldsymbol{x})$. This is an instance of the general problem of balancing the impact of D_l and D_u on the final predictions, especially in the case $m \gg n$. This issue is discussed in section 2.3.1. Furthermore, in the SSL setting y is a latent variable which has to be summed out on D_u, leading to highly multimodal posteriors, so that likelihood or posterior maximization techniques are plagued by the presence of very many (local) minima.

2.2.2   The Diagnostic Paradigm

In *diagnostic methods*, we model the conditional distribution $P(y|\boldsymbol{x})$ directly using the family $\{P(y|\boldsymbol{x},\boldsymbol{\theta})\}$. To arrive at a complete sampling model for the data, we also have to model $P(\boldsymbol{x})$ by a family $P(\boldsymbol{x}|\boldsymbol{\mu})$; however if we are only interested in updating our belief in $\boldsymbol{\theta}$ or in predicting y on unseen points, this is not necessary, as we will see next. Under this model, $\boldsymbol{\theta}$ and $\boldsymbol{\mu}$ are a priori *independent*, i.e. $P(\boldsymbol{\theta},\boldsymbol{\mu}) = P(\boldsymbol{\theta})P(\boldsymbol{\mu})$.

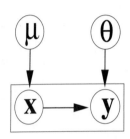

The likelihood factors as

$$P(D_l, D_u|\boldsymbol{\theta},\boldsymbol{\mu}) = P(Y_l|\boldsymbol{X}_l,\boldsymbol{\theta})P(\boldsymbol{X}_l, D_u|\boldsymbol{\mu}),$$

which implies that $P(\boldsymbol{\theta}|D_l, D_u) \propto P(Y_l|\boldsymbol{X}_l,\boldsymbol{\theta})P(\boldsymbol{\theta})$, i.e. $P(\boldsymbol{\theta}|D_l, D_u) = P(\boldsymbol{\theta}|D_l)$, and $\boldsymbol{\theta}$ and $\boldsymbol{\mu}$ are a posteriori *independent*. Furthermore, $P(\boldsymbol{\theta}|D_l, \boldsymbol{\mu}) = P(\boldsymbol{\theta}|D_l)$. This means that neither knowledge of the unlabeled data D_u nor *any* knowledge of $\boldsymbol{\mu}$ changes the posterior belief $P(\boldsymbol{\theta}|D_l)$ of the labeled sample. Therefore, in the standard data generation model for diagnostic methods, unlabeled data D_u cannot be used for Bayesian inference, and modeling the input distribution $P(\boldsymbol{x})$ is not necessary. There are non-Bayesian diagnostic techniques in which we can make use of D_u (see section 2.3.2), but the impact of doing so (as opposed to ignoring D_u) is usually very limited. In order to make significant use of unlabeled data in diagnostic methods, the data generation model discussed above has to be modified as discussed in the following section.

2.2.3   Regularization Depending on the Input Distribution

When learning from a sample D_l of limited size, typically very many associations $\boldsymbol{x} \to y$ are consistent with the data. The idea of *regularization* is to bias our choice of classifier toward "simpler" hypotheses, by adding a regularization functional to the criterion to be minimized which grows with complexity. Here, the notion of simplicity depends on the task and the model setup. For example, for a linear model it is customary to penalize a norm of the weight vector, and for some commonly used regularization functionals this can be shown to be equivalent to placing a zero-mean prior distribution on the weight vector. From now on we will only be interested in regularization by priors and will use the terms interchangeably.

We have seen in section 2.2.2 that with straight diagnostic Bayesian methods for classification, we cannot make use of additional unlabeled data D_u, because $\boldsymbol{\theta}$ (parameterizing $P(y|\boldsymbol{x})$) and $\boldsymbol{\mu}$ (parameterizing $P(\boldsymbol{x})$) are a priori independent. In other words, the model family $\{P(y|\boldsymbol{x}, \boldsymbol{\theta})\}$ is regularized *independently* of the input distribution.

If we allow prior dependencies between $\boldsymbol{\theta}$ and $\boldsymbol{\mu}$, e.g. $P(\boldsymbol{\theta}, \boldsymbol{\mu}) = P(\boldsymbol{\theta}|\boldsymbol{\mu})P(\boldsymbol{\mu})$ and $P(\boldsymbol{\theta}) = \int P(\boldsymbol{\theta}|\boldsymbol{\mu})P(\boldsymbol{\mu}) \, d\boldsymbol{\mu}$ (as shown in the independence diagram to the right), the situation is different. The conditional prior $P(\boldsymbol{\theta}|\boldsymbol{\mu})$ in principle allows information about $\boldsymbol{\mu}$ to be transferred to $\boldsymbol{\theta}$. In general, $\boldsymbol{\theta}$ and D_u will be dependent given the labeled data D_l, therefore unlabeled data can change our posterior belief in $\boldsymbol{\theta}$.

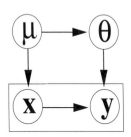

We conclude that to make use of additional unlabeled data within the context of diagnostic Bayesian supervised techniques, we have to allow an a priori dependence between the latent function representing the conditional probability and the input probability itself. In other words, we have to use a *regularization of the latent function which depends on the input distribution*. The potential gain can be demonstrated by the following argument. Note that conditional priors imply a marginal prior $P(\boldsymbol{\theta})$ which is a mixture distribution: $P(\boldsymbol{\theta}) = \int P(\boldsymbol{\theta}|\boldsymbol{\mu})P(\boldsymbol{\mu}) \, d\boldsymbol{\mu}$. By conditioning on the unlabeled data, this is replaced by $P(\boldsymbol{\theta}|D_u) = \int P(\boldsymbol{\theta}|\boldsymbol{\mu})P(\boldsymbol{\mu}|D_u) \, d\boldsymbol{\mu}$ which can have a much smaller entropy than $P(\boldsymbol{\theta})$, implying that the posterior belief $P(\boldsymbol{\theta}|D_l, D_u)$ can be much narrower than $P(\boldsymbol{\theta}|D_l)$. On the other hand, the same argument can be used to demonstrate that using additional unlabeled data D_u can hurt instead of help. Namely, if the priors $P(\boldsymbol{\theta}|\boldsymbol{\mu})$ enforce certain constraints very rigidly, but these happen to be violated in the true distribution $P(\boldsymbol{x}, y)$, the conditional "prior" $P(\boldsymbol{\theta}|D_u)$ will assign much lower probability than $P(\boldsymbol{\theta})$ to models $P(y|\boldsymbol{x}, \boldsymbol{\theta})$ close to the truth, and the posterior $P(\boldsymbol{\theta}|D_l, D_u)$ can be concentrated around suboptimal models. While it is certainly easy to construct artificial situations where additional unlabeled data hurt, it is worrying that such failures do happen quite unexpectedly in practically relevant settings as well. For a more thorough analysis of this problem, see Cozman and Cohen (chapter 4 in this volume).

We note that while the modification to the standard data generation model for diagnostic methods suggested here is straightforward, choosing appropriate conditional priors $P(\boldsymbol{\theta}|\boldsymbol{\mu})$ suitable for a task at hand can be challenging. However, several general techniques for SSL can actually be seen as realizing input-dependent regularization, as is demonstrated in section 2.3.3.

The reader may feel uneasy at this point. If we use a priori dependent $\boldsymbol{\theta}$ and $\boldsymbol{\mu}$, the final predictive distribution *depends* on the prior $P(\boldsymbol{\mu})$ over the input distribution. This forces us to model the input distribution itself, in contrast to the situation for standard diagnostic methods. In this case, will our method still be a diagnostic one? Is it not the case that any method which models $P(\boldsymbol{x})$ in some way must automatically be generative? Diagnostic methods can be much more parsimonious simply because $P(\boldsymbol{x})$ need not be estimated. In order to implement input-dependent regularization, do we have to use a generative model with the drawbacks discussed in section 2.2.1? There is indeed some ambiguity here, but we will try to clarify this point in section 2.2.4. Under this general viewpoint, input-dependent regularization is indeed a diagnostic SSL technique.

In the diagnostic paradigm for purely supervised tasks, $\boldsymbol{\theta}$ and $\boldsymbol{\mu}$ are treated as a priori independent, leading to the fact that no aspects of $P(\boldsymbol{x})$ have to be estimated. While this is convenient, it is not clear whether we should really believe in such independence for a real-world task. For example, suppose that $P(\boldsymbol{\theta})$ enforces smoothness of the relationship $P(y|\boldsymbol{x},\boldsymbol{\theta})$. Is it sensible to enforce smoothness of $\boldsymbol{x} \rightarrow y$ around all $\boldsymbol{x}$, or should we not rather penalize rough behavior only where $P(\boldsymbol{x})$ has significant volume? The former is more conservative and possibly more robust, but also risks ignoring valuable information sources (see section 2.3.3.1 for an example).

2.2.4   The Borderline between the Paradigms

While the borderline between supervised and unsupervised methods is clearly drawn, the distinction between generative and diagnostic techniques can be ambiguous, especially if we apply this taxonomy to SSL. In this section we give two criteria for a clear discrimination: a simple and a more elaborate one. In a sense they are both based on the same issue, namely the *role* that the $P(\boldsymbol{x})$ estimate plays for the prediction.

Recall that we restrict ourselves to methods whose ultimate goal it is to estimate $P(y|\boldsymbol{x})$. Traditionally, generative methods achieve this by modeling the joint distribution $P(y,\boldsymbol{x})$ and fit this model to data by capturing characteristics of the true joint data distribution. An estimate of $P(\boldsymbol{x})$ can always be obtained by marginalizing the joint estimate. In contrast, diagnostic methods concentrate on modeling the conditional distribution $P(y|\boldsymbol{x})$ only, and an estimate of $P(\boldsymbol{x})$ cannot be extracted. However, in the SSL case we do have to model $P(\boldsymbol{x})$ in order to profit from D_u. So are all SSL methods generative? We argue against this viewpoint and try to classify SSL techniques according to the role which the $P(\boldsymbol{x})$ estimate actually plays.

While it is true that any SSL method has to model $P(\boldsymbol{x})$ in some way, in a generative technique we model the class-conditional distributions $P(\boldsymbol{x}|y)$ explicitly, so that the model for $P(\boldsymbol{x})$ is a mixture of those. From these estimates (and the estimates of $P(y)$) we obtain an estimate of $P(y|\boldsymbol{x})$ using the Bayes formula. Characteristics of the predictive estimate (such as the function class in a parametric situation) depend entirely on the class-conditional models. For example, if the latter are Gaussian with the same covariance matrix, the predictive estimates will be based on linear functions. In a nutshell, we specify the $P(\boldsymbol{x}|y)$ using our modeling toolbox, which implies the form of our $P(y|\boldsymbol{x})$ and $P(\boldsymbol{x})$ estimates (the latter is a mixture of the $P(\boldsymbol{x}|y)$). The only way to encode *specific* properties for the latter estimates is to find $P(\boldsymbol{x}|y)$ candidates which are both tractable to work with and imply the desired properties of $P(y|\boldsymbol{x})$ and $P(\boldsymbol{x})$. In contrast to that, in a diagnostic method we model $P(y|\boldsymbol{x})$ directly, and also typically have considerable freedom in modeling $P(\boldsymbol{x})$. In SSL we regularize the $P(y|\boldsymbol{x})$ estimates using information from $P(\boldsymbol{x})$, but we do not have to specify the class-conditional distributions explicitly.[7] While this definition is workable for the SSL methods mentioned here, it may be too restrictive on the generative side. For example, the "many-centers-per-class" model of section 2.3.1 is clearly generative, but works with a mixture model for $P(\boldsymbol{x})$ which has several components for each class y, and $P(\boldsymbol{x}|y)$ is modeled indirectly via $P(\boldsymbol{x}|y) = \sum_k \pi_y \beta_{y,k} P(\boldsymbol{x}|k)$, i.e., as a mixture itself. In the following paragraph we suggest an alternative view which leaves more freedom for generative techiques.

The practical success of SSL has shown that unlabeled data, i.e., knowledge about $P(\boldsymbol{x})$, can be useful for supervised tasks, but it is not necessarily the same *type* of knowledge that would lead to a good estimate of $P(\boldsymbol{x})$ according to common performance criteria for density estimation. In fact, it is actually a few general characteristics of $P(\boldsymbol{x})$ which seem to help classification (see e.g.: section 2.3.3.1). For example, if we convert a purely diagnostic technique such as SVM or logistic regression into an SSL technique by employing a regularizer penalizing $P(y|\boldsymbol{x})$ estimates which violate *certain aspects* of $P(\boldsymbol{x})$ such as the cluster assumption (see section 2.3.3.1), the influence of $P(\boldsymbol{x})$ on the final $P(y|\boldsymbol{x})$ estimate is restricted to just these aspects that we hope are important for better classification. These restrictions are engineered by us because we want to make best use of D_u *in order to predict* $P(y|\boldsymbol{x})$. In contrast, if we perform SSL by maximizing a suitably reweighted version of the joint log likelihood (2.1) of a mixture model (see section 2.3.1), such a restriction to classification-relevant aspects is not given or at least not directly planned. In fact the joint model is designed in much the same way as we would do for density estimation.

For example, consider the framework of conditional priors of section 2.2.3. While it is essential to learn about $P(\boldsymbol{x})$ in SSL, the impact of an oversimple model for $P(\boldsymbol{x})$ on the final prediction is much less severe than in density estimation. This is because a suitable regularization will only depend on certain aspects of $P(\boldsymbol{x})$ (e.g., on the coarse locations of high-density regions under the cluster assumption; see section 2.3.3.1), and our model for the $\boldsymbol{x}$ distribution only has to be able to capture those accurately.

2.3   Examples

In this section we provide examples of SSL methods falling in each of the categories introduced in the previous section. We do not try to provide a comprehensive

---

7. There are, of course, class-conditional distributions which are *implied* by the models of $P(y|\boldsymbol{x})$ and $P(\boldsymbol{x})$ (use the Bayes formula), but importantly we do not have to work with them directly, so that their form is not restricted by tractability requirements.

literature review here (see (Seeger, 2000b) for review of work up to about 2001), but are selective in order to point out characteristics of and differences between the categories. Note that in this context (and also in (Seeger, 2000b)) some methods are classified as "baseline methods." This does not constitute a devaluation, and in fact some of these methods belong to the top performers on some tasks. Furthermore, we think that theoretical analyses of such methods are of great value, not least because many practitioners use them. Our label applies to methods which can be derived fairly straightforwardly from standard unsupervised or supervised methods, and we hope that truly novel proposals are in fact compared against the most closely related baseline methods.

2.3.1   Generative Techniques

Recall from section 2.2.1 that generative techniques use a model family $\{P(\boldsymbol{x}, y | \boldsymbol{\theta}, \boldsymbol{\pi})\}$ in order to model the joint data distribution $P(\boldsymbol{x}, y)$. The simplest idea is to run a mixture density estimation method for $P(\boldsymbol{x})$ on $\boldsymbol{X}_l \cup \boldsymbol{X}_u$, treating y as a latent class variable, then using the labeled sample D_l in order to associate latent classes with actual ones. An obvious problem with this approach is that the labeling provided by the unsupervised method may be inconsistent with D_l, in which case the clustering should be modified to achieve consistency with D_l. Castelli and Cover (Castelli and Cover, 1995) provide a simple analysis of this baseline method under fairly unrealistic identifiability conditions. Namely, they assume that the data distribution is exactly identifiable by the unsupervised method at hand, which employs a mixture model with one component for each class. It is not clear how to achieve this in practice, even if $P(\boldsymbol{x})$ is exactly known.[8] In the large-sample limit, all class distributions can be learned perfectly, but the assignment of classes to label names obviously remains completely open. However, only a few additional labeled points are required in order to learn this assignment. In fact, it is easy to see that the error rate converges to the Bayes error exponentially fast (in the number of labeled examples drawn from $P(\boldsymbol{x}, y)$).

Another baseline method consists of maximizing the joint likelihood of Eq. 2.1. For $m > 0$, the criterion to be minimized is not convex and typically multimodal, so we have to contend ourselves with finding a local maximum. This can be done by direct gradient descent or more conveniently by applying the *expectation-maximization (EM)* algorithm (Dempster et al., 1977). The latter is an iterative procedure which is guaranteed to converge to a local maximum of the likelihood. If all data in Eq. 2.1 were labeled, a local maximum would be found by a single optimization over $\boldsymbol{\theta}$. In fact, if the class-conditional distributions $P(\boldsymbol{x} | y, \boldsymbol{\theta})$ are from

---

8. It is not unrealistic to assume that $P(\boldsymbol{x})$ is exactly known, or that $m \to \infty$. The problem is that they assume that if $P(\boldsymbol{x})$ is viewed as mixture distribution, then the model can fit the class distributions $P(\boldsymbol{x} | y)$ exactly. This is not realistic for real-world problems, especially if the quantities of interest are simply good estimates of $P(y | \boldsymbol{x})$ or a small generalization error of the resulting classifier.

an exponential family, the global maximum can be found analytically. EM works by assigning label distributions $q(y|\boldsymbol{x}_i)$ to all points $\boldsymbol{x}_i$. For a labeled point, the label is represented in that $q(y|\boldsymbol{x}_i) = \delta_{y,y_i}$. If $\boldsymbol{x}_i$ is unlabeled, we use the conditional posterior (for the current $\boldsymbol{\theta}$), i.e. $q(y|\boldsymbol{x}_i) \propto \pi_y P(\boldsymbol{x}_i|y, \boldsymbol{\theta})$. Intuitively, this choice reflects our best current point estimate for the label of $\boldsymbol{x}_i$. The E step in EM consists of computing $q(y|\boldsymbol{x}_i)$ for all points. In the M step, the parameters $\boldsymbol{\theta}$, $\boldsymbol{\pi}$ are updated by maximizing the expected log likelihood under the q distributions:

$$\phi(\boldsymbol{\theta}', \boldsymbol{\pi}') = \sum_{i=1}^{n+m} \sum_{y=1}^{M} q(y|\boldsymbol{x}_i) \log \pi'_y P(\boldsymbol{x}_i|y, \boldsymbol{\theta}').$$

E and M steps are iterated until convergence. It is easy to show that ϕ is a lower bound on the joint log likelihood (2.1) for *any* choice of q on the unlabeled points. The bound becomes an equality if the q are chosen as posteriors and the parameters $\boldsymbol{\theta}$, $\boldsymbol{\pi}$ are not changed. Furthermore, under this choice the gradient of lower bound and joint log likelihood are the same at $\boldsymbol{\theta}$, $\boldsymbol{\pi}$, so that if EM converges we have found a local maximum of Eq. 2.1.

The idea of using EM on a joint generative model to train on labeled and unlabeled data is almost as old as EM itself. Titterington et.al. (Titterington et al., 1985, section 5.7) review early theoretical work on the problem of discriminant analysis in the presence of additional unlabeled data. The most common assumption is that the data have been generated from a mixture of two Gaussians with equal covariance matrices, in which case the Bayes discriminant is linear. They analyze the "plug-in" method from the generative paradigm (see section 2.2.1) in which the parameters of the class distributions are estimated by maximum likelihood. If the two Gaussians are somewhat well separated, the asymptotic gain of using unlabeled samples is very significant. For details, see (O'Neill, 1978; Ganesalingam and McLachlan, 1978, 1979). McLachlan (McLachlan, 1975) gives a practical algorithm for this case which is essentially a "hard" version of EM, i.e. in every E step the unlabeled points are allocated to one of the populations, using the discriminant derived from the mixture parameters of the previous step (note that the general EM algorithm had not been proposed at that time). He proves that for "moderate-sized" training sets from each population and for a pool D_u of points sampled from the mixture, if the algorithm is initialized with the maximum-likelihood (ML) solution based on the labeled data, the solutions computed by the method converge almost surely against the true mixture distribution with $|D_u| = m \to \infty$. These early papers provide some important insight into properties of the semi-supervised problem, but their strict assumptions limit the conclusions that can be drawn for large real-world problems.

The EM algorithm has been applied to text classification by Nigam et.al. (see (Nigam et al., 2000), or chapter 3 in this book). From Eq. 2.1 we see that in the joint log likelihood, labeled and unlabeled data are weighted at the ratio n to m. This "natural" weighting makes sense if the likelihood is taken at face value, i.e. as a correct description of the sampling mechanism for the data, but it is somewhat irrelevant to the problem of SSL where a strong sampling bias is present whose exact size is usually unknown. In other words, unlabeled data are often available in huge quantities simply because they can be obtained much cheaper than labeled data. If we use the natural weighting in the interesting case $m \gg n$, the labeled data D_l are effectively ignored. Nigam et.al. suggest reweighting the terms in Eq. 2.1 by $(1 - \lambda)/n$ and λ/m respectively (the natural weighting is given by $\lambda = m/(m + n)$) and adjusting λ by standard techniques such as cross-validation on D_l.

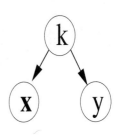

Note that y is treated as the latent class variable as far as the estimation of $P(\boldsymbol{x})$ from D_u is concerned, and we can just as well allow for more mixture components than classes. Namely, we can introduce an additional *separator variable* k such that under the model $\boldsymbol{x}$ and y are independent given k. This means that all the information $\boldsymbol{x}$ contains about its class y is already captured in k. This fact is illustrated in the independence model on the right.

The reweighted joint log-likelihood is

$$\frac{1 - \lambda}{n} \sum_{i=1}^{n} \log \sum_{k} \beta_{y_i,k} \pi_k P(\boldsymbol{x}_i|k, \boldsymbol{\theta}) + \frac{\lambda}{m} \sum_{i=n+1}^{n+m} \log \sum_{k} \pi_k P(\boldsymbol{x}_i|k, \boldsymbol{\theta}),$$

where $\pi_k = P(k|\boldsymbol{\theta})$ and $\beta_{y,k} = P(y|k, \boldsymbol{\theta})$. It is straightforward to maximize this criterion using EM. Miller and Uyar (Miller and Uyar, 1997) present some results using this model together with Gaussian components $P(\boldsymbol{x}|k, \boldsymbol{\theta})$. The "many-centers-per-class" case in (Nigam et al., 2000) is equivalent to this method.

Some drawbacks of this simple generative mixture model approach have already been mentioned in section 2.2.1. First, the weighting λ between the labeled and unlabeled data sources has to be chosen carefully; for example, the natural weighting is usually not appropriate. A selection of λ by cross-validation on D_l is robust in principle, but bound to fail if n is very small. Second, for λ not close to 0 the joint log likelihood has many (local) maxima, and for $\lambda \to 1$ consistency with D_l is less and less enforced. Both problems are adressed in a principal manner by Corduneanu and Jaakkola (Corduneanu and Jaakkola, 2002). Under suitable identifiability conditions[9] on $P(\boldsymbol{x}|y, \boldsymbol{\theta})$ the maximum point for $\lambda = 0$ (labeled data only) is unique, while for $\lambda = 1$ (unlabeled data only) there are many equivalent maximum points at least due to label permutation symmetry. Therefore, as we trace the maximum point for growing λ starting from 0, the path must split at a first critical $\lambda^* > 0$. The authors argue that the maximum point of the log likelihood at this λ^* provides a promising solution to the SSL problem (in this generative setting) in that it still fully incorporates the label information. Also, the path up to λ^* is unique, while it splits for larger λ, and the decision of which one to

---

9. These are not very restrictive; for example, they hold for all (regular) exponential families.

follow is independent of the label information. They show how to employ homotopy continuation (path-following) methods in order to trace the solution path up to λ^* fairly efficiently. By restricting themselves to $\lambda \leq \lambda^*$ they circumvent the many (local) maxima problem, and their choice of $\lambda = \lambda^*$ is well motivated.

Murray and Titterington [1978] (see also (Titterington et al., 1985), ex. 4.3.11) suggest using D_l for each class to obtain kernel-based estimates of the densities $P(\boldsymbol{x}|y)$. They fix these estimates and use EM in order to maximize the joint likelihood of D_l, D_u w.r.t. the mixing coefficients π_t only.[10] This procedure is robust, but does not make a lot of use of the unlabeled data. If D_l is small, the kernel-based estimates of the $P(\boldsymbol{x}|y)$ will be poor, and even if D_u can be used to obtain better values for the mixing coefficients, this is not likely to rescue the final discrimination. Furthermore, the procedure has been suggested for situations where the natural weighting between D_l, D_u is appropriate, which is typically not the case for SSL.

Shahshahani and Landgrebe (Shahshahani and Landgrebe, 1994) provide an analysis aimed toward the general question whether unlabeled data can help in classification, based on methods originating in asymptotic maximum-likelihood theory. Their argumentation is somewhat unclear and has been criticized by various other authors (e.g., (Nigam et al., 2000; Zhang and Oles, 2000)). They do not define model classes and seem to confuse asymptotic and finite-sample terms. After all, their claim seems to be that unlabeled data can reduce the asymptotic variance of an estimator, but they do not worry about the fact that such modifications could actually introduce new bias, especially in the interesting case where $m \gg n$. On the practical side, the algorithm they suggest is the joint EM scheme discussed above.

Another analysis of SSL which also employs Fisher information, is given by Zhang and Oles (Zhang and Oles, 2000). The authors show that for purely diagnostic models, unlabeled data cannot help (this fact has of course been known for a long time; see also section 2.2.2). In the generative setup, they show that D_u can only help. While this is true under their assumptions, it draws on asymptotic concepts and may not be relevant in practical situations. The Fisher information characterizes the minimal *asymptotic* variance of an unbiased estimator only, and the maximum-likelihood estimator is typically only *asymptotically* unbiased. Applying such concepts to the case where D_l is small cannot lead to strong conclusions, and the question of (even asymptotic) bias remains in the case where m grows much faster than n. On the practical side, some empirical evidence is presented on a text categorization task which shows that unlabeled data can lead to instabilities in common transduction algorithms and therefore "hurt" (see comments in section 2.2.3).

---

10. EM w.r.t. the mixing coefficients only always converges to a unique *global* optimum. It is essentially a variant of the *Blahut-Arimoto algorithm* to compute the *rate distortion function* which is important for quantization (see (Cover and Thomas, 1991)).

2.3.2 Diagnostic Techniques

We noted in section 2.2.2 that unlabeled data cannot be used in Bayesian diagnostic methods if $\boldsymbol{\theta}$ and $\boldsymbol{\mu}$ are a priori independent, so in order to make use of D_u we have to employ conditional priors $P(\boldsymbol{\theta}|\boldsymbol{\mu})$. Unlabeled data may still be useful in non-Bayesian settings. An example has been given by Tong and Koller (Tong and Koller, 2000) under the name of *restricted Bayes optimal classification (RBOC)*. Consider a diagnostic method in which the sum of an empirical loss term and a regularization functional is minimized. The empirical loss term is the expectation w.r.t. the labeled sample D_l of a loss function relevant to the problem (e.g., the zero-one loss $L(\boldsymbol{x}, y, h) = \mathrm{I}_{\{y \neq h(\boldsymbol{x})\}}$). The authors suggest incorporating unlabeled data D_u by estimating $P(\boldsymbol{x}, y)$ from $D_l \cup D_u$, then replacing the empirical loss term by the expectation of the loss under this estimate. The regularization term is not changed. We can compare this method directly with input-dependent regularization (see section 2.2.3). In the former, the empirical loss part (the negative log likelihood for a probabilistic model) is modified based on D_u; in the latter it is the regularization term. We would not expect RBOC to produce very different results from the corresponding diagnostic technique, especially if n is rather small (which is the interesting case in practice). This is somewhat confirmed by the weak results in (Tong and Koller, 2000). A very similar idea is proposed in (Chapelle et al., 2001) in order to modify the diagnostic SVM framework.

Anderson (Anderson, 1979) suggested an interesting modification of logistic regression in which unlabeled data can be used. In binary logistic regression, the log odds are modeled as linear function, which gives $P(\boldsymbol{x}|1) = \exp(\boldsymbol{\beta}^T \boldsymbol{x})P(\boldsymbol{x}|2)$ and $P(\boldsymbol{x}) = (\pi_1 \exp(\boldsymbol{\beta}^T \boldsymbol{x}) + 1 - \pi_1)P(\boldsymbol{x}|2)$, where $\pi_1 = P\{t = 1\}$. Anderson now chooses the parameters $\boldsymbol{\beta}$, π_1 and $P(\boldsymbol{x}|2)$ in order to maximize the likelihood of both D_l and D_u, subject to the constraints that $P(\boldsymbol{x}|1)$ and $P(\boldsymbol{x}|2)$ are normalized. For finite $\mathfrak{X}$, this problem can be transformed into an unconstrained optimization w.r.t. the parameters $\boldsymbol{\beta}$, π_1. For a continuous input variable $\boldsymbol{x}$, Anderson advocates using the form of $P(\boldsymbol{x}|2)$ derived for the "finite $\mathfrak{X}$" case, although this is not a smooth function. Unfortunately, it is not clear how to generalize this idea to more realistic models, for example how to "kernelize" it, and the form of $P(\boldsymbol{x}|2)$ is inadequate for many problems with infinite $\mathfrak{X}$.

2.3.3 Input-Dependent Regularization

We discussed in section 2.2.3 that unlabeled data D_u can be useful within a diagnostic technique if $\boldsymbol{\theta}$ and $\boldsymbol{\mu}$ are dependent a priori. In order to implement this idea, we have to specify conditional priors $P(\boldsymbol{\theta}|\boldsymbol{\mu})$ encoding our belief in how characteristics of $\boldsymbol{x} \to y$ depend on knowledge about $P(\boldsymbol{x})$.

2.3.3.1   The Cluster Assumption

It is not hard to construct "malicious" examples of $P(\boldsymbol{x}, y)$ which defy any given dependence assumption on $\boldsymbol{\theta}, \boldsymbol{\mu}$. However, in practice it is often the case that cluster structure in the data for $\boldsymbol{x}$ indeed is mostly consistent with the labeling. It is not very fruitful to speculate about why this is the case, although certainly there is a selection bias toward features (i.e. components in $\boldsymbol{x}$) which are *relevant* w.r.t. the labeling process, which means they should group in the same way (w.r.t. a simple distance) as labelings. The *cluster assumption (CA)* (e.g., (Seeger, 2000b)) provides a general way of exploiting this observation for SSL. It postulates that two points $\boldsymbol{x}'$, $\boldsymbol{x}''$ should have the same label y with high probability if there is a "path" between them in $\mathcal{X}$ which moves through regions of significant density $P(\boldsymbol{x})$ only. In other words, a discrimination function between the classes should be smooth within connected high-density regions of $P(\boldsymbol{x})$. Thus, the CA can be compared directly with *global* smoothness assumptions requiring the discriminant to change smoothly everywhere, independent of $P(\boldsymbol{x})$. While the latter penalize sharp changes also in regions which will be sparsely populated by training and test data, the CA remains indifferent there.

The CA is implemented (to different extent) in a host of methods proposed for SSL. Most prominent are probably *label propagation* methods (Szummer and Jaakkola, 2002b; Belkin and Niyogi, 2003b; Zhu et al., 2003b). The rough idea is to construct a graph with vertices from $\boldsymbol{X}_l \cup \boldsymbol{X}_u$ which contains the test set to be labeled and all of $\boldsymbol{X}_l$. Nearest neighbors are joined by edges with a weight proportional to local correlation strength. We then initialize the nodes corresponding to $\boldsymbol{X}_l$ with the labels Y_l and propagate label distributions over the remaining nodes in the manner of a Markov chain on the graph (Szummer and Jaakkola, 2002b). It is also possible to view the setup as a Gaussian field with the graph and edge weights specifying the inverse covariance matrix (Zhu et al., 2003b). Label propagation techniques implement the CA relative to unsupervised spectral clustering (Belkin and Niyogi, 2003b). The CA has been implemented for kernel machines by way of the cluster kernel (Chapelle et al., 2003). Furthermore, the generative SSL techniques of section 2.3.1 can be seen as implementing the CA relative to a mixture model clustering.

A generalization of the CA has been given by Corduneanu and Jaakkola (see chapter 10 in this book) who show how to obtain a regularizer for the conditional distribution $P(y|\boldsymbol{x})$ from information-theoretic arguments.

2.3.3.2   The Fisher Kernel

The *Fisher kernel* was proposed in (Jaakkola and Haussler, 1999) in order to exploit additional unlabeled data within a kernel-based *support vector machine (SVM)* framework for detecting remote protein homologies. The idea is to fit a generative model $P(\boldsymbol{x}|\boldsymbol{\mu})$ to D_u by maximum likelihood (resulting in $\hat{\boldsymbol{\mu}}$, say). If $\boldsymbol{x}$ are DNA sequences, a hidden Markov model (HMM) can be employed. $P(\boldsymbol{x}|\hat{\boldsymbol{\mu}})$

represents the knowledge extracted from D_u, and the Fisher kernel is a general way of constructing a covariance kernel $K_{\hat{\mu}}$ which depends on this knowledge. We can then fit an SVM or a Gaussian process (GP) classifier to D_u using the kernel $K_{\hat{\mu}}$. Identifying this setup as an instance of input-dependent regularization is easiest in the GP context. Here, $\boldsymbol{\theta}$ is a process representing the discriminant function (we assume $c = 2$ for simplicity), and $P(\boldsymbol{\theta}|\boldsymbol{\mu})$ is a GP distribution with zero-mean function and covariance kernel $K_{\boldsymbol{\mu}}$. In the ML context, $P(\boldsymbol{\mu}|D_u)$ is approximated by the delta distribution $\delta_{\hat{\mu}}$.

Define the Fisher score to be $F_{\hat{\mu}}(\boldsymbol{x}) = \nabla_{\hat{\mu}} \log P(\boldsymbol{x}|\boldsymbol{\mu})$ (the gradient w.r.t. $\boldsymbol{\mu}$ is evaluated at $\hat{\mu}$). The Fisher information matrix is $\boldsymbol{F} = \mathbf{E}_{P(\cdot|\hat{\mu})}\left[F_{\hat{\mu}}(\boldsymbol{x})F_{\hat{\mu}}(\boldsymbol{x})^T\right]$. The naive Fisher kernel is $K_{\hat{\mu}}(\boldsymbol{x}, \boldsymbol{x}') = F_{\hat{\mu}}(\boldsymbol{x})^T \boldsymbol{F}^{-1} F_{\hat{\mu}}(\boldsymbol{x}')$. In a variant, $\boldsymbol{F}$ is replaced by $\alpha\boldsymbol{I}$ for a scale parameter α. Other variants of the Fisher kernel are obtained by using the Fisher score $F_{\hat{\mu}}(\boldsymbol{x})$ as feature vector for $\boldsymbol{x}$ and plugging these into a standard kernel such as the Gaussian radial basis function (RBF) one. The latter "embeddings" seem to be more useful in practice. The Fisher kernel can be motivated from various angles (see (Jaakkola and Haussler, 1999)), for example, as first-order approximation to a sample mutual information between $\boldsymbol{x}$, $\boldsymbol{x}'$ (Seeger, 2002).

2.3.3.3 Co-Training

Co-training was introduced by Blum and Mitchell (Blum and Mitchell, 1998) and is related to earlier work on unsupervised learning (Becker and Hinton, 1992). The idea is to make use of different "views" on the objects to be classified (here we restrict ourselves to binary classification, $c = 2$, and to two views). For example, a webpage can be represented by the text on the page, but also by the text of hyperlinks referring to the page. We can train classifiers separately which are specialized to each of the views, but in this context unlabeled data D_u can be helpful in that, although the true label is missing, it must be the same for all the views. It turns out that co-training can be seen as a special case of Bayesian inference using conditional priors (see section 2.2.3), as is demonstrated below in this section.

Let $\mathcal{X} = \mathcal{X}^{(1)} \times \mathcal{X}^{(2)}$ be a finite or countable input space. If $\boldsymbol{x} = (\boldsymbol{x}^{(1)}, \boldsymbol{x}^{(2)})$, the $\boldsymbol{x}^{(j)}$ are different "views" on $\boldsymbol{x}$. We are also given spaces $\Theta^{(j)}$ of concepts (binary classifiers) $\boldsymbol{\theta}^{(j)}$. Elements $\boldsymbol{\theta} = (\boldsymbol{\theta}^{(1)}, \boldsymbol{\theta}^{(2)}) \in \Theta = \Theta^{(1)} \times \Theta^{(2)}$ are called concepts over $\mathcal{X}$, although we may have $\boldsymbol{\theta}^{(1)}(\boldsymbol{x}^{(1)}) \neq \boldsymbol{\theta}^{(2)}(\boldsymbol{x}^{(2)})$ for some $\boldsymbol{x} = (\boldsymbol{x}^{(1)}, \boldsymbol{x}^{(2)}) \in \mathcal{X}$. Whenever the $\boldsymbol{\theta}^{(j)}$ agree, we write $\boldsymbol{\theta}(\boldsymbol{x}) = \boldsymbol{\theta}^{(1)}(\boldsymbol{x}^{(1)})$. If $A \subset \mathcal{X}$, we say that a concept $\boldsymbol{\theta} = (\boldsymbol{\theta}^{(1)}, \boldsymbol{\theta}^{(2)})$ is *compatible* with A if $\boldsymbol{\theta}^{(1)}(\boldsymbol{x}^{(1)}) = \boldsymbol{\theta}^{(2)}(\boldsymbol{x}^{(2)})$ for all $\boldsymbol{x} = (\boldsymbol{x}^{(1)}, \boldsymbol{x}^{(2)}) \in A$. Denote by $\Theta(A)$ the space of all concepts compatible with A.[11] If $Q(\boldsymbol{x})$ is a distribution over $\mathcal{X}$ with *support* $S = \operatorname{supp} Q(\boldsymbol{x}) = \{\boldsymbol{x}|Q(\boldsymbol{x}) > 0\}$, we say that a concept $\boldsymbol{\theta}$ is *compatible* with the distribution Q if it is compatible

---

11. In order not to run into trivial problems, we assume that $\Theta(A)$ is never empty, which can be achieved by adding the constant concept 1 to both $\Theta^{(j)}$.

with S.

In the co-training setting, there is an unknown input distribution $P(\boldsymbol{x})$. A *target concept* $\boldsymbol{\theta}$ is sampled from some unknown distribution over Θ, and the data distribution is $P(y|\boldsymbol{x}) = I_{\{\theta(\mathbf{x})=y\}}$ if $\boldsymbol{\theta} \in \Theta(\{\boldsymbol{x}\})$, $1/2$ otherwise.[12] However, the central assumption is that the target concept $\boldsymbol{\theta}$ is *compatible* with the input distribution $P(\boldsymbol{x})$. More specifically, the support of the concept distribution must be contained in $\Theta(\mathrm{supp}\,P(\boldsymbol{x}))$. Therefore, unlabeled data D_u can be used by observing that $\Theta(\mathrm{supp}\,P(\boldsymbol{x})) \subset \Theta(D_u \cup \boldsymbol{X}_l)$, so the effective concept space can be shrunk from Θ to $\Theta(D_u \cup \boldsymbol{X}_l)$.

We demonstrate that co-training can be understood as Bayesian inference with conditional priors encoding the compatibility assumption. We model $P(\boldsymbol{x})$ by $\{P(\boldsymbol{x}|\boldsymbol{\mu})\}$ and introduce the variable $S = \mathrm{supp}\,P(\boldsymbol{x}|\boldsymbol{\mu})$ for convenience, then define $P(\boldsymbol{\theta}|\boldsymbol{\mu}) = P(\boldsymbol{\theta}|S)$ as

$$P(\boldsymbol{\theta}|S) = f_S(\boldsymbol{\theta})I_{\{\boldsymbol{\theta} \in \Theta(S)\}}, \ S \subset \mathcal{X},$$

where $f_S(\boldsymbol{\theta}) > 0$, and all $P(\boldsymbol{\theta}|S)$ are properly normalized. For example, if $\Theta(S)$ is finite, we can choose $f_S(\boldsymbol{\theta}) = |\Theta(S)|^{-1}$. The likelihood is given by $P(y|\boldsymbol{x},\boldsymbol{\theta}) = (1/2)(I_{\{\boldsymbol{\theta}^{(1)}(\boldsymbol{x}^{(1)})=y\}} + I_{\{\boldsymbol{\theta}^{(2)}(\boldsymbol{x}^{(2)})=y\}})$ (noiseless case). Since $P(\boldsymbol{\theta}|S) = 0$ for $\boldsymbol{\theta} \notin \Theta(S)$, the conditional prior encodes the compatibility assumption. The posterior belief about $\boldsymbol{\theta}$ is given by

$$P(\boldsymbol{\theta}|D_l, D_u) \propto I_{\{\boldsymbol{\theta}(\boldsymbol{x}_i)=y_i, \ i=1,\dots,n\}} \int P(\boldsymbol{\theta}|S)P(S|\boldsymbol{X}_l, D_u)\,dS,$$

so that $P(\boldsymbol{\theta}|D_l, D_u) \neq 0$ iff $\boldsymbol{\theta}$ is consistent with the labeled data D_l and $\boldsymbol{\theta} \in \Theta(D_u \cup \boldsymbol{X}_l)$. Namely, if $\boldsymbol{\theta} \notin \Theta(D_u \cup \boldsymbol{X}_l)$, then $P(\boldsymbol{\theta}|S) = 0$ for all S which contain $D_u \cup \boldsymbol{X}_l$, and $P(S|D_u, \boldsymbol{X}_l) = 0$ for all other S. On the other hand, if $\boldsymbol{\theta} \in \Theta(D_u \cup \boldsymbol{X}_l)$, then we have $P(\boldsymbol{\theta}|\hat{S}) > 0$ and $P(\hat{S}|D_u, \boldsymbol{X}_l) > 0$ at least for $\hat{S} = D_u \cup \boldsymbol{X}_l$. In the terminology of Blum and Mitchell, $\mathrm{supp}\,P(\boldsymbol{\theta}|D_l, D_u)$ is equal to the "version space" given all the data. The biases for the learning methods on $\Theta^{(j)}$ may be encoded in the potentials $f_S(\boldsymbol{\theta})$.

Once co-training is understood within a Bayesian framework with conditional priors, one can employ standard techniques in order to perform inference. In fact, we showed in (Seeger, 2000a) that the co-training algorithm suggested by Blum and Mitchell can be seen as a variant of (sequential) EM on the probabilistic model sketched above. This viewpoint allows us to generalize co-training along various dimensions, e.g., allowing for noise, smoother prior distributions, using batch rather than online training, uncertain rather than fixed labels on the test points, etc. We refer to (Seeger, 2000a) for details.

---

12. Here, I_E is 1 if E is true, 0 otherwise. The scenario is called *noiseless* because the only source of randomness is the uncertainty in the target function.

2.4   Conclusions

In this chapter we have described a simple taxonomy of methods for semi-supervised learning and given many examples of SSL methods for each of the categories. Advantages and potential pitfalls of each group have been discussed. We have underlined the importance of using conditional priors in diagnostic Bayesian SSL techniques and have given several examples of methods proposed in the literature which fall into this category.

3   Semi-Supervised Text Classification Using EM

Kamal Nigam   KNIGAM@KAMALNIGAM.COM
Andrew McCallum   MCCALLUM@CS.UMASS.EDU
Tom Mitchell   TOM.MITCHELL@CMU.EDU

For several decades, statisticians have advocated using a combination of labeled and unlabeled data to train classifiers by estimating parameters of a generative model through iterative expectation-maximization (EM) techniques. This chapter explores the effectiveness of this approach when applied to the domain of text classification. Text documents are represented here with a bag-of-words model, which leads to a generative classification model based on a mixture of multinomials. This model is an extremely simplistic representation of the complexities of written text. This chapter explains and illustrates three key points about semi-supervised learning for text classification with generative models. First, despite the simplistic representation, some text domains have a high positive correlation between generative model probability and classification accuracy. In these domains, a straightforward application of EM with the naive Bayes text model works well. Second, some text domains do not have this correlation. Here we can adopt a more expressive and appropriate generative model that does have a positive correlation. In these domains, semi-supervised learning again improves classification accuracy. Finally, EM suffers from the problem of local maxima, especially in high-dimension domains such as text classification. We demonstrate that deterministic annealing, a variant of EM, can help overcome the problem of local maxima and increase classification accuracy further when the generative model is appropriate.

3.1   Introduction

The idea of learning classifiers from a combination of labeled and unlabeled data is an old one in the statistics community. At least as early as 1968, it was suggested that labeled and unlabeled data could be combined to build classifiers with likelihood maximization by testing all possible class assignments (Hartley and Rao, 1968). The seminal paper by Day (1969) presents an iterative EM-like approach for parameters of a mixture of two normals with known covariances from unlabeled data alone. Similar iterative algorithms for building maximum-likelihood classifiers from labeled and unlabeled data with an explicit generative model followed, primarily for mixtures of normal distributions (McLachlan, 1975; Titterington, 1976).

Dempster et al. (1977) presented the theory of the EM framework, bringing together and formalizing many of the commonalities of previously suggested iterative techniques for likelihood maximization with missing data. Its applicability to estimating maximum likelihood (or maximum a posteriori) parameters for mixture models from labeled and unlabeled data (Murray and Titterington, 1978) and then using this for classification (Little, 1977) was recognized immediately. Since then, this approach continues to be used and studied (McLachlan and Ganesalingam, 1982; Ganesalingam, 1989; Shahshahani and Landgrebe, 1994). Using likelihood maximization of mixture models for combining labeled and unlabeled data for classification has more recently made its way to the machine learning community (Miller and Uyar, 1996; Nigam et al., 1998; Baluja, 1999).

The theoretical basis for expectation-maximization shows that with sufficiently large amounts of unlabeled data generated by the model class in question, a more probable model can be found than if using just the labeled data alone. If the classification task is to predict the latent variable of the generative model, then with sufficient data a more probable model will also result in a more accurate classifier.

This approach rests on the assumption that the generative model is correct. When the classification task is one of classifying human-authored texts (as we consider here) the true generative model is impossible to parameterize, and instead practitioners tend to use very simple representations. For example, the commonly used naive Bayes classifier represents each authored document as a bag of words, discarding all word-ordering information. The generative model for this classifier asserts that documents are created by a draw from a class-conditional multinomial. As this is an extreme simplification of the authoring process, it is interesting to ask whether such a generative modeling approach to semi-supervised learning is appropriate or beneficial in the domain of text classification.

This chapter demonstrates that generative approaches are appropriate for semi-supervised text classification when the selected generative model probabilities are well correlated with classification accuracy, and when suboptimal local maxima can be mostly avoided. In some cases, the naive Bayes generative model, despite its simplicity, is sufficient. We find that model probability is strongly correlated with classification accuracy, and expectation-maximization techniques yield classifiers with unlabeled data that are significantly more accurate than those built with labeled data alone. In other cases, the naive Bayes generative model is not well correlated with classification accuracy. By adopting a more expressive generative model, accuracy and model probability correlations are restored, and again EM yields good results.

One of the pitfalls of EM is that it only guarantees the discovery of local maxima and not global maxima in model probability space. In domains like text classification, with a very large number of parameters, this effect can be very significant. We show that when model probability and classification are well correlated, the use of deterministic annealing, an alternate modeling estimation process, finds more probable and thus more accurate classifiers.

Nongenerative approaches have also been used for semi-supervised text classification. Joachims (1999) uses transductive support vector machines to build discriminative classifiers for several text classification tasks. Blum and Mitchell (1998) use the co-training setting to build naive Bayes classifiers for webpages, using anchor text and the page itself as two different sources of information about an instance. Zelikovitz and Hirsh (2000) use unlabeled data as background knowledge to augment a nearest-neighbor classifier. Instead of matching a test example directly to its closest labeled example, they instead match a test example to a labeled example by measuring their similarity to a common set of unlabeled examples.

This chapter proceeds as follows. Section 3.2 presents the generative model used for text classification and shows how to perform semi-supervised learning with EM. Section 3.3 shows an example where this approach works well. Section 3.4 presents a more expressive generative model that works when the naive Bayes assumption is not sufficient, and experimental results from a domain that needs it. Section 3.5 presents deterministic annealing and shows that this finds model parameterizations that are much more probable than those found by EM, especially when labeled data are sparse.

3.2   A Generative Model for Text

This section presents a framework for characterizing text documents and shows how to use this to train a classifier from labeled and unlabeled data. The framework defines a probabilistic generative model, and embodies three assumptions about the generative process: (1) the data are produced by a mixture model, (2) there is a one-to-one correspondence between mixture components and classes, and (3) the mixture components are multinomial distributions of individual words. These are the assumptions used by the naive Bayes classifier, a commonly used tool for standard supervised text categorization (Lewis, 1998; McCallum and Nigam, 1998a).

We assume documents are generated by a *mixture of multinomials* model, where each mixture component corresponds to a class. Let there be M classes and a vocabulary of size $|\mathcal{X}|$; each document x_i has $|x_i|$ words in it. How do we create a document using this model? First, we roll a biased M-sided die to determine the class of our document. Then, we pick up the biased $|\mathcal{X}|$-sided die that corresponds to the chosen class. We roll this die $|x_i|$ times, and count how many times each word occurs. These word counts form the generated document.

Formally, every document is generated according to a probability distribution defined by the parameters for the mixture model, denoted θ. The probability distribution consists of a mixture of components $c_j \in [M]$.[1] A document, x_i, is created by first selecting a mixture component according to the mixture weights (or class probabilities), $P(c_j|\theta)$, then using this selected mixture component to generate a document according to its own parameters, with distribution $P(x_i|c_j;\theta)$. Thus, the likelihood of seeing document x_i is a sum of total probability over all mixture components:

$$P(x_i|\theta) = \sum_{j\in[M]} P(c_j|\theta)P(x_i|c_j;\theta). \tag{3.1}$$

Each document has a class label. We assume a one-to-one correspondence between mixture model components and classes, and thus use c_j to indicate the jth mixture component, as well as the jth class. The class label for a particular document x_i is written y_i. If document x_i was generated by mixture component c_j we say $y_i = c_j$.

A document, x_i, is a vector of word counts. We write x_{it} to be the number of times word w_t occurs in document x_i. When a document is to be generated by a particular mixture component a document length, $|x_i| = \sum_{t=1}^{|\mathcal{X}|} x_{it}$, is first chosen independently of the component.[2] Then, the selected mixture component is used to generate a document of the specified length, by drawing from its multinomial distribution.

From this we can expand the second term from (3.1), and express the probability of a document given a mixture component in terms of its constituent features: the document length and the words in the document.[3]

$$P(x_i|c_j;\theta) \propto P(|x_i|) \prod_{w_t\in\mathcal{X}} P(w_t|c_j;\theta)^{x_{it}}. \tag{3.2}$$

This formulation embodies the standard naive Bayes assumption: that the words of a document are conditionally independent of the other words in the same document, given the class label.

Thus the parameters of an individual mixture component define a multinomial distribution over words, i.e. the collection of word probabilities, each written $\theta_{w_t|c_j}$, such that $\theta_{w_t|c_j} \equiv P(w_t|c_j;\theta)$, where $t \in [|\mathcal{X}|]$ and $\sum_t P(w_t|c_j;\theta) = 1$. Since we assume that for all classes, document length is identically distributed, it does not need to be parameterized for classification. The only other parameters

---

1. We use the notation $[M]$ to refer to the set $\{1,\ldots,M\}$.
2. This assumes that document length is independent of class, though length could also be modeled and parameterized on a class-by-class basis.
3. We omit here the multinomial coefficients for notational simplicity. For classification purposes, these coefficients cancel out.

of the model are the mixture weights (class probabilities),$\theta_{c_j} \equiv P(c_j|\theta)$, which indicate the probabilities of selecting the different mixture components. Thus the complete collection of model parameters, θ, defines a set of multinomials and class probabilities: $\theta = \{\theta_{w_t|c_j} : w_t \in \mathcal{X}, c_j \in [M] \; ; \; \theta_{c_j} : c_j \in [M]\}$.

To summarize, the full generative model, given by combining Eqs. 3.1 and 3.2, assigns probability $P(x_i|\theta)$ to generating document x_i as follows:

$$P(x_i|\theta) \propto P(|x_i|) \sum_{j \in [M]} P(c_j|\theta) \prod_{w_t \in \mathcal{X}} P(w_t|c_j;\theta)^{x_{it}} \tag{3.3}$$

where the set of word counts x_{it} is a sufficient statistic for the parameter vector θ in this generative model.

3.2.1 Supervised Text Classification with Generative Models

Learning a naive Bayes text classifier from a set of labeled documents consists of estimating the parameters of the generative model. The estimate of the parameters θ is written $\hat{\theta}$. Naive Bayes uses the maximum a posteriori (MAP) estimate, thus finding $\arg\max_\theta P(\theta|X,Y)$. This is the value of θ that is most probable given the evidence of the training data and a prior.

Our prior distribution is formed with the product of Dirichlet distributions—one for each class multinomial and one for the overall class probabilities. The Dirichlet is the commonly used conjugate prior distribution for multinomial distributions. The form of the Dirichlet is

$$P(\theta_{w_t|c_j}|\alpha) \propto \prod_{w_t \in \mathcal{X}} P(w_t|c_j)^{\alpha_t - 1}. \tag{3.4}$$

where the α_t are constants greater than zero. We set all $\alpha_t = 2$, which corresponds to a prior that favors the uniform distribution. This is identical to Laplace and m-estimate smoothing. A well-presented introduction to Dirichlet distributions is given by Stolcke and Omohundro (1994).

The parameter estimation formulas that result from maximization with the data and our prior are the familiar smoothed ratios of empirical counts. The word probability estimates $\hat{\theta}_{w_t|c_j}$ are

$$\hat{\theta}_{w_t|c_j} \equiv P(w_t|c_j;\hat{\theta}) = \frac{1 + \sum_{x_i \in X} \delta_{ij} x_{it}}{|\mathcal{X}| + \sum_{s=1}^{|\mathcal{X}|} \sum_{x_i \in X} \delta_{ij} x_{is}}, \tag{3.5}$$

where δ_{ij} is given by the class label: 1 when $y_i = c_j$ and 0 otherwise.

The class probabilities, $\hat{\theta}_{c_j}$, are estimated in the same manner, and also involve a ratio of counts with smoothing:

$$\hat{\theta}_{c_j} \equiv \mathrm{P}(c_j|\hat{\theta}) = \frac{1 + \sum_{i=1}^{|X|} \delta_{ij}}{M + |X|}. \tag{3.6}$$

The derivation of these ratios-of-counts formulas comes directly from maximum a posteriori parameter estimation. Finding the θ that maximizes $\mathrm{P}(\theta|X,Y)$ is accomplished by first breaking this expression into two terms by the Bayes rule: $\mathrm{P}(\theta|X,Y) \propto \mathrm{P}(X,Y|\theta)\mathrm{P}(\theta)$. The first term is calculated by the product of all the document likelihoods (from Eq. 3.1). The second term, the prior distribution over parameters, is the product of Dirichlets. The whole expression is maximized by solving the system of partial derivatives of $\log(\mathrm{P}(\theta|X,Y))$, using Lagrange multipliers to enforce the constraint that the word probabilities in a class must sum to one. This maximization yields the ratio of counts seen above.

Given estimates of these parameters calculated from labeled training documents, it is possible to turn the generative model backward and calculate the probability that a particular mixture component generated a given document to perform classification. This follows from an application of the Bayes rule:

$$\begin{aligned}
\mathrm{P}(y_i = c_j|x_i;\hat{\theta}) &= \frac{\mathrm{P}(c_j|\hat{\theta})\mathrm{P}(x_i|c_j;\hat{\theta})}{\mathrm{P}(x_i|\hat{\theta})} \\
&= \frac{\mathrm{P}(c_j|\hat{\theta})\prod_{w_t \in \mathcal{X}} \mathrm{P}(w_t|c_j;\hat{\theta})^{x_{it}}}{\sum_{k=1}^{M} \mathrm{P}(c_k|\hat{\theta})\prod_{w_t \in \mathcal{X}} \mathrm{P}(w_t|c_k;\hat{\theta})^{x_{it}}}. \tag{3.7}
\end{aligned}$$

If the task is to classify a test document x_i into a single class, then the class with the highest posterior probability, $\arg\max_j \mathrm{P}(y_i = c_j|x_i;\hat{\theta})$, is selected.

3.2.2   Semi-Supervised Text Classification with EM

In the semi-supervised setting with labeled and unlabeled data, we would still like to find MAP parameter estimates, as in the supervised setting above. Because there are no labels for the unlabeled data, the closed-form equations from the previous section are not applicable. However, using the EM technique, we can find locally MAP parameter estimates for the generative model.

The EM technique as applied to the case of labeled and unlabeled data with naive Bayes yields a straightforward and appealing algorithm. First, a naive Bayes classifier is built in the standard supervised fashion from the limited amount of labeled training data. Then, we perform classification of the unlabeled data with the naive Bayes model, noting not the most likely class but the probabilities associated with each class. Then, we rebuild a new naive Bayes classifier using all the data—labeled and unlabeled—using the estimated class probabilities as true class labels. This means that the unlabeled documents are treated as several fractional documents according to these estimated class probabilities. We iterate this process of classifying the unlabeled data and rebuilding the naive Bayes model until it converges to a stable classifier and set of labels for the data. This is summarized in algorithm 3.1.

Algorithm 3.1 Basic EM algorithm for semi-supervised learning of a text classifier

- **Inputs:** Collections X_l of labeled documents and X_u of unlabeled documents.

- Build an initial naive Bayes classifier, $\hat{\theta}$, from the labeled documents, X_l, only. Use maximum a posteriori parameter estimation to find $\hat{\theta} = \arg\max_\theta \mathrm{P}(X_l|\theta)\mathrm{P}(\theta)$ (see Eqs. 3.5 and 3.6).

- Loop while classifier parameters improve, as measured by the change in $l(\theta|X, Y)$ (the log probability of the labeled and unlabeled data, and the prior) (see Equation 3.8):

  - **(E step)** Use the current classifier, $\hat{\theta}$, to estimate component membership of each unlabeled document, i.e., the probability that each mixture component (and class) generated each document, $\mathrm{P}(c_j|x_i; \hat{\theta})$ (see Eq. 3.7).

  - **(M step)** Re-estimate the classifier, $\hat{\theta}$, given the estimated component membership of each document. Use maximum a posteriori parameter estimation to find $\hat{\theta} = \arg\max_\theta \mathrm{P}(X, Y|\theta)\mathrm{P}(\theta)$ (see Eqs. 3.5 and 3.6).

- **Output:** A classifier, $\hat{\theta}$, that takes an unlabeled document and predicts a class label.

More formally, learning a classifier is approached as calculating a maximum a posteriori estimate of θ, i.e. $\arg\max_\theta \mathrm{P}(\theta)\mathrm{P}(X, Y|\theta)$, which is equivalent to maximizing the log of the same. Consider the second term of the maximization, the probability of all the observable data. The probability of an individual unlabeled document is a sum of total probability over all the classes, as in Eq. 3.1. For the labeled data, the generating component is already given by label y_i and we do not need to refer to all mixture components—just the one corresponding to the class. Using X_u to refer to the unlabeled examples, and X_l to refer to the examples for which labels are given, the expected log probability of the full data is

$$
\begin{aligned}
l(\theta|X, Y) \;=\; & \log(\mathrm{P}(\theta)) + \sum_{x_i \in X_u} \log \sum_{j \in [M]} \mathrm{P}(c_j|\theta)\mathrm{P}(x_i|c_j; \theta) \\
& + \sum_{x_i \in X_l} \log\left(\mathrm{P}(y_i = c_j|\theta)\mathrm{P}(x_i|y_i = c_j; \theta)\right).
\end{aligned}
\tag{3.8}
$$

(We have dropped the constant terms for convenience.) Notice that this equation contains a log of sums for the unlabeled data, which makes a maximization by partial derivatives computationally intractable. The formalism of EM (Dempster et al., 1977) provides an iterative hill-climbing approach to finding local maxima of model probability in parameter space. The E step of the algorithm estimates the expectations of the missing values (i.e., unlabeled class information) given the latest iteration of the model parameters. The M step maximizes the likelihood of the model parameters using the previously computed expectations of the missing values as if they were the true ones.

In practice, the E step corresponds to performing classification of each unlabeled document using Eq. 3.7. The M step corresponds to calculating a new maximum a posteriori (MAP) estimate for the parameters, $\hat{\theta}$, using Eqs. 3.5 and 3.6 with the current estimates for $P(c_j|x_i; \hat{\theta})$.

Essentially all initializations of the parameters lead to some local maxima with EM. Many instantiations of EM begin by choosing a starting model parameterization randomly. In our case, we can be more selective about the starting point since we have not only unlabeled data but also some labeled data. Our iteration process is initialized with a priming M step, in which only the labeled documents are used to estimate the classifier parameters, $\hat{\theta}$, as in Eqs. 3.5 and 3.6. Then the cycle begins with an E step that uses this classifier to probabilistically label the unlabeled documents for the first time.

The algorithm iterates until it converges to a point where $\hat{\theta}$ does not change from one iteration to the next. Algorithmically, we determine that convergence has occurred by observing a below-threshold change in the log-probability of the parameters (Eq. 3.8), which is the height of the surface on which EM is hill-climbing.

3.2.3   Discussion

The justifications for this approach depend on the assumptions stated in section 3.2, namely, that the data are produced by a mixture model, and that there is a one-to-one correspondence between mixture components and classes. If the generative modeling assumptions were correct, then maximizing model probability would be a good criterion indeed for training a classifier. In this case the Bayes optimal classifier, when the number of training examples approaches infinity, corresponds to the MAP parameter estimates of the model. When these assumptions do not hold—as certainly is the case in real-world textual data—the benefits of unlabeled data are less clear. With only labeled data, the naive Bayes classifier does a good job of classifying text documents (Lewis and Ringuette, 1994; Craven et al., 2000; Yang and Pedersen, 1997; Joachims, 1997; McCallum et al., 1998). This observation is explained in part by the fact that classification estimation is only a function of the sign (in binary classification) of the function estimation (Domingos and Pazzani, 1997; Friedman, 1997). The faulty word independence assumption exacerbates the tendency of naive Bayes to produce extreme (almost 0 or 1) class probability estimates. However, classification accuracy can be quite high even when these estimates are inappropriately extreme.

Semi-supervised learning leans more heavily on the correctness of the modeling assumptions than supervised learning. The next section will show empirically that this method can indeed dramatically improve the accuracy of a document classifier, especially when there are only a few labeled documents.

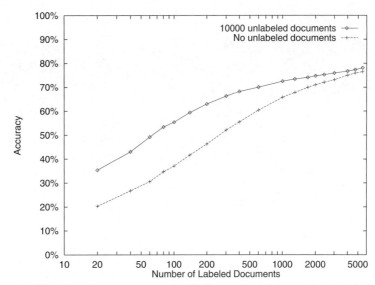

Figure 3.1   Classification accuracy on the 20 Newsgroups data set, both with and without 10,000 unlabeled documents. With small amounts of training data, using EM yields more accurate classifiers. With large amounts of labeled training data, accurate parameter estimates can be obtained without the use of unlabeled data, and classification accuracies of the two methods begin to converge.

3.3   Experimental Results with Basic EM

In this section we demonstrate that semi-supervised learning with labeled and unlabeled data provides text classifiers that are more accurate than those provided by supervised learning using only the labeled data. This is an interesting result as the mixture of multinomials generative model is a dramatic simplification of the true authoring process. However, we demonstrate that for some domains, the optimization criteria of model probability are strongly correlated with classification accuracy.

Experiments in this section use the well-known 20 Newsgroups text classification data set (Mitchell, 1997), consisting of about 20,000 Usenet articles evenly distributed across 20 newsgroups. The task is to classify an article into the newsgroup to which it was posted. For preprocessing, stopwords are removed and word counts of each document are scaled such that each document has constant length, with potentially fractional word counts. As the data have timestamps, a test set is formed from the last 20% of articles from each newsgroup. An unlabeled set is formed by randomly selecting 10,000 articles from those remaining. Labeled training sets are formed by partitioning the remaining documents into nonoverlapping sets. We create up to ten training sets per size of the set, as data are available. When posterior model probability is reported and shown on graphs, some additive and multiplicative constants are dropped, but the relative values are maintained.

Figure 3.1 shows the effect of using EM with unlabeled data on this data set. The

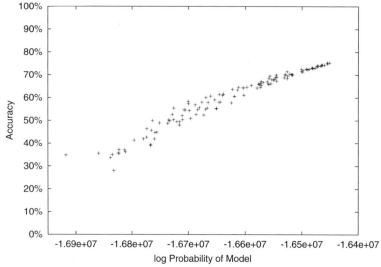

Figure 3.2 A scatterplot showing the correlation between the posterior model probability and the accuracy of a model trained with labeled and unlabeled data. The strong correlation implies that model probability is a good optimization criteria for the 20 Newsgroups data set.

vertical axis indicates average classifier accuracy on test sets, and the horizontal axis indicates the amount of labeled training data on a log scale. We vary the amount of labeled training data, and compare the classification accuracy of traditional naive Bayes (no unlabeled documents) with an EM learner that has access to 10.000 unlabeled documents.

EM performs significantly better than traditional naive Bayes. For example, with 300 labeled documents (15 documents per class), naive Bayes reaches 52% accuracy while EM achieves 66%. This represents a 30% reduction in classification error. Note that EM also performs well even with a very small number of labeled documents; with only 20 documents (a single labeled document per class), naive Bayes obtains 20%, EM 35%. As expected, when there are a lot of labeled data, and the naive Bayes learning curve is close to a plateau, having unlabeled data does not help nearly as much, because there are already enough labeled data to accurately estimate the classifier parameters. With 5500 labeled documents (275 per class), classification accuracy increases from 76% to 78%. Each of these results is statistically significant ($p < 0.05$).[4]

How does EM find more accurate classifiers? It does so by optimizing on posterior model probability, not classification accuracy directly. If our generative model were perfect, then we would expect model probability and accuracy to be correlated and

---

4. When the number of labeled examples is small, we have multiple trials, and use paired t-tests. When the number of labeled examples is large, we have a single trial, and report results instead with a McNemar test. These tests are discussed further by Dietterich (1998).

EM to be helpful. But we know that our simple generative model does not capture many of the properties contained in the text. Our 20 Newsgroups results show that we do not need a perfect model for EM to help text classification. Generative models are representative enough for the purposes of text classification if model probability and accuracy are correlated, allowing EM to indirectly optimize accuracy.

To illustrate this more definitively, let us look again at the 20 Newsgroups experiments, and empirically measure this correlation. Figure 3.2 demonstrates the correlation—each point in the scatterplot is one of the labeled and unlabeled splits from figure 3.1. The labeled data here are used only for setting the EM initialization and are not used during iterations. We plot classification performance as accuracy on the test data and show the posterior model probability.

For this data set, classification accuracy and model probability are in good correspondence. The correlation coefficient between accuracy and model probability is 0.9798, a very strong correlation indeed. We can take this as a post hoc verification that this data set is amenable to using unlabeled data via a generative model approach. The optimization criterion of model probability is applicable here because it is in tandem with accuracy.

3.4   Using a More Expressive Generative Model

The second assumption of the generative model of section 3.2 states that there is a one-to-one correspondence between classes and components in the mixture model. In some text domains, it is clear that such an assumption is a dangerous one. Consider the task of text filtering, where we want to identify a small well-defined class of documents from a very large pool or stream of documents. One example might be a system that watches a network administrator's incoming emails to identify the rare emergency situation that would require paging her on vacation. Modeling the nonemergency emails as the negative class with only one multinomial distribution will result in an unrepresentative model. The negative class contains emails with a variety of subtopics: personal emails, nonemergency requests, spam, and many more.

What would be a more representative model? Instead of modeling a sea of negative examples with a single mixture component, it might be better to model it with many components. In this way, each negative component could, after maximization, capture one clump of the sea of examples. This section takes exactly the approach suggested by this example for text data, and relaxes the assumption of a one-to-one correspondence between mixture components and classes. We replace it with a less restrictive assumption: a *many*-to-one correspondence between mixture components and classes. This allows us to model the subtopic structure of a class.

3.4.1   Multiple Mixture Components per Class

The new generative model must account for a many-to-one correspondence between mixture components and classes. As in the old model, we first pick a class with a biased die roll. Each class has several subtopics; we next pick one of these subtopics, again with a biased die roll. Now that the subtopic is determined, the document's words are generated. We do this by first picking a length (independently of subtopic and class) and then draw the words from the subtopic's multinomial distribution.

Unlike previously, there are now two missing values for each unlabeled document—its class and its subtopic. Even for the labeled data there are missing values; although the class is known, its subtopic is not. Since we do not have access to these missing class and subtopic labels, we must use a technique such as EM to estimate local MAP generative parameters. As in section 3.2.2, EM is instantiated as an iterative algorithm that alternates between estimating the values of missing class and subtopic labels, and calculating the MAP parameters using the estimated labels. After EM converges to high-probability parameter estimates the generative model can be used for text classification by turning it around with the Bayes rule.

The new generative model specifies a separation between mixture components and classes. Instead of using c_j to denote both of these, $c_j \in [N]$ now denotes only the jth mixture component (subtopic). We write $t_a \in [M]$ for the ath class; when component c_j belongs to class t_a, then $q_{aj} = 1$, and otherwise 0. This represents the predetermined, deterministic, many-to-one mapping between mixture components and classes. We indicate the class label and subtopic label of a document by y_i and z_i, respectively. Thus if document x_i was generated by mixture component c_j we say $z_i = c_j$, and if the document belongs to class t_a, then we say $y_i = t_a$.

If all the class and subtopic labels were known for our data set, finding MAP estimates for the generative parameters would be a straightforward application of closed-form equations similar to those for naive Bayes seen in section 3.2.1. The formula for the word probability parameters is identical to Eq. 3.5 for naive Bayes:

$$\hat{\theta}_{w_t|c_j} \equiv \mathrm{P}(w_t|c_j; \hat{\theta}) = \frac{1 + \sum_{x_i \in X} \delta_{ij} x_{it}}{|\mathcal{X}| + \sum_{s=1}^{|\mathcal{X}|} \sum_{x_i \in X} \delta_{ij} x_{is}}. \tag{3.9}$$

The class probabilities are analogous to Eq. 3.6, but using the new notation for classes instead of components:

$$\hat{\theta}_{t_a} \equiv \mathrm{P}(t_a|\hat{\theta}) = \frac{1 + \sum_{i=1}^{|X|} \delta_{ia}}{M + |X|}. \tag{3.10}$$

The subtopic probabilities are similar, except they are estimated only with reference to other documents in that component's class:

$$\hat{\theta}_{c_j|t_a} \equiv \mathrm{P}(c_j|t_a; \hat{\theta}) = \frac{1 + \sum_{i=1}^{|X|} \delta_{ij}\delta_{ia}}{\sum_{j=1}^{N} q_{aj} + \sum_{i=1}^{|X|} \delta_{ia}}. \tag{3.11}$$

At classification time, we must estimate class membership probabilities for an unlabeled document. This is done by first calculating subtopic membership and then summing over subtopics to get overall class probabilities. Subtopic membership is calculated analogously to mixture component membership for naive Bayes, with a small adjustment to account for the presence of two priors (class and subtopic) instead of just one:

$$\mathrm{P}(z_i = c_j|x_i; \hat{\theta}) = \frac{\sum_{a \in [M]} q_{aj} \mathrm{P}(t_a|\hat{\theta})\mathrm{P}(c_j|t_a;\hat{\theta}) \prod_{w_t \in \mathcal{X}} \mathrm{P}(w_t|c_j;\hat{\theta})^{x_{it}}}{\sum_{r \in [N]} \sum_{b \in [M]} q_{br} \mathrm{P}(t_b|\hat{\theta})\mathrm{P}(c_r|t_b;\hat{\theta}) \prod_{w_t \in \mathcal{X}} \mathrm{P}(w_t|c_r;\hat{\theta})^{x_{it}}}. \tag{3.12}$$

Overall class membership is calculated with a sum of probability over all of the class's subtopics:

$$\mathrm{P}(y_i = t_a|x_i; \hat{\theta}) = \sum_{j \in [N]} q_{aj}\mathrm{P}(z_i = c_j|x_i; \hat{\theta}). \tag{3.13}$$

These equations for supervised learning are applicable only when all the training documents have both class and subtopic labels. Without these we use EM. The M step, as with basic EM, builds maximum a posteriori parameter estimates for the multinomials and priors. This is done with Eqs. 3.9, 3.10, and 3.11, using the probabilistic class and subtopic memberships estimated in the previous E step. In the E step, for the unlabeled documents we calculate probabilistically weighted subtopic and class memberships (Eqs. 3.12 and 3.13). For labeled documents, we must estimate subtopic membership. But we know from its given class label that many of the sub-topic memberships must be zero—those subtopics that belong to other classes. Thus we calculate subtopic memberships as for the unlabeled data, but setting the appropriate ones to zero, and normalizing the non-zero ones over only those topics that belong to its class.

If we are given a set of class-labeled data, and a set of unlabeled data, we can now apply EM if there is some specification of the number of subtopics for each class. However, this information is not typically available. As a result we must resort to some techniques for model selection. There are many commonly used approaches to model selection such as cross-validation, Akaike information criterion (AIC), bayesian information criterion (BIC) and others. Since we do have the availability of a limited number of labeled documents, we use cross-validation to select the number of subtopics for classification performance.

Table 3.1   Classification accuracy of binary classifiers on Reuters with traditional naive Bayes (NB1), basic EM (EM1) with labeled and unlabeled data, multiple mixture components using just labeled data (NB*), and multiple mixture components EM with labeled and unlabeled data (EM*). For NB* and EM*, the number of components is selected optimally for each trial, and the median number of components across the trials used for the negative class is shown in parentheses. Note that the multicomponent model is more natural for Reuters, where the negative class consists of many topics. Using both unlabeled data and multiple mixture components per class increases performance over either alone, and over naive Bayes.

Category	NB1	EM1	NB*	EM*
acq	86.9	81.3	88.0 (4)	**93.1** (10)
corn	94.6	93.2	96.0 (10)	**97.2** (40)
crude	94.3	94.9	95.7 (13)	**96.3** (10)
earn	94.9	95.2	**95.9** (5)	95.7 (10)
grain	94.1	93.6	96.2 (3)	**96.9** (20)
interest	91.8	87.6	95.3 (5)	**95.8** (10)
money-fx	93.0	90.4	94.1 (5)	**95.0** (15)
ship	94.9	94.1	**96.3** (3)	95.9 (3)
trade	91.8	90.2	94.3 (5)	**95.0** (20)
wheat	94.0	94.5	96.2 (4)	**97.8** (40)

3.4.2   Experimental Results

Here, we provide empirical evidence that to use unlabeled data with a generative modeling approach, more expressive generative models are sometimes necessary. With the original generative model, classification accuracy and model probability can be negatively correlated, leading to lower classification accuracy when unlabeled data are used. With a more expressive generative model, a moderate positive correlation is achieved, leading to improved classification accuracies.

The Reuters 21578 Distribution 1.0 data set consists of about 13,000 news articles from the Reuters newswire labeled with 90 topic categories. Documents in this data set have multiple class labels, and each category is traditionally evaluated with a binary classifier. Following several other studies (Joachims, 1998; Liere and Tadepalli, 1997) we build binary classifiers for each of the ten most populous classes to identify the topic. We use a stoplist, but do not stem. The vocabulary size for each Reuters trial is selected by optimizing accuracy as measured by leave-one-out cross-validation on the labeled training set. The standard ModApte train/test split is used, which is time-sensitive. Seven thousand of the 9603 documents available for training are left unlabeled. From the remaining, we randomly select up to ten nonoverlapping training sets of just ten positively labeled documents and 40 negatively labeled documents.

The first two columns of results in table 3.1 repeat the experiments of section 3.3

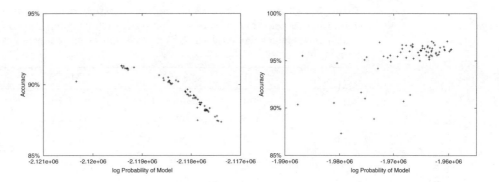

Figure 3.3 Scatterplots showing the relationship between model probability and classification accuracy for the Reuters acq task. On the left, with only one mixture component for the **negative** class, probability and accuracy are inversely proportional, exactly what we would not want. On the right, with ten mixture components for **negative**, there is a moderate positive correlation between model probability and classification accuracy.

with basic EM on the Reuters data set. Here we see that for most categories, classification accuracy decreases with the introduction of unlabeled data. For each of the Reuters categories EM finds a significantly more probable model, given the evidence of the labeled and unlabeled data. But frequently this more probable model corresponds to a lower-accuracy classifier—not what we would hope for.

The first graph in figure 3.3 provides insight into why unlabeled data hurt. With one mixture component per class, the correlation between classification accuracy and model probability is very strong ($r = -0.9906$), but in the wrong direction! Models with higher probability have significantly lower classification accuracy. By examining the solutions found by EM, we find that the most probable clustering of the data has one component with the majority of **negative** documents and the second with most of the **positive documents**, but significantly more **negative** documents. Thus, the classes do not separate with high-probability models.

The documents in this data set often have multiple class labels. With the basic generative model, the **negative** class covers up to 89 distinct categories. Thus, it is unreasonable to expect to capture such a broad base of text with a single mixture component. For this reason, we relax the generative model and model the **positive** class with a single mixture component and the **negative** class with between one and forty mixture components, both with and without unlabeled data.

The second half of table 3.1 shows results of using multiple mixtures per class generative model. Note two different results. First, with labeled data alone (NB*), classification accuracy improves over the single component per class case (NB1). Second, with unlabeled data, the new generative model results (EM*) are generally better than the other results. This increase with unlabeled data, measured over all trials of Reuters, is statistically significant ($p < 0.05$).

With ten mixture components the correlation between accuracy and model probability is quite different. Figure 3.3 on the right shows the correlation between

Table 3.2 Performance of using multiple mixture components when the number of components is selection via cross-validation (EM*CV) compared to the optimal selection (EM*) and straight naive Bayes (NB1). Note that cross-validation usually selects too few components.

Category	NB1	EM*	EM*CV	EM*CV vs NB1
acq	86.9	93.1 (10)	91.1 (5)	+4.2
corn	94.6	97.2 (40)	93.2 (3)	-1.4
crude	94.3	96.3 (10)	95.4 (3)	+1.1
earn	94.9	95.7 (10)	95.2 (1)	+0.3
grain	94.1	96.9 (20)	94.7 (3)	+0.6
interest	91.8	95.8 (10)	92.0 (3)	+0.2
money-fx	93.0	95.0 (15)	92.3 (3)	-0.7
ship	94.9	95.9 (3)	94.4 (3)	-0.5
trade	91.8	95.0 (20)	90.7 (3)	-1.1
wheat	94.0	97.8 (40)	96.3 (6)	+2.3

accuracy and model probability when using ten mixture components to model the **negative** class. Here, there is a moderate correlation between model probability and classification accuracy in the right direction ($r = 0.5474$). For these solutions, one component covers nearly all the **positive** documents and some, but not many, **negatives**. The other ten components are distributed through the remaining **negative** documents. This model is more representative of the data for our classification task because classification accuracy and model probability are correlated. This allows the beneficial use of unlabeled data through the generative model approach.

One obvious question is how to automatically select the best number of mixture components without having access to the test set labels. We use leave-one-out cross-validation. Results from this technique (EM*CV), compared to naive Bayes (NB1) and the best EM (EM*), are shown in table 3.2. Note that cross-validation does not perfectly select the number of components that perform best on the test set. The results consistently show that selection by cross-validation chooses a smaller number of components than is best.

3.4.3 Discussion

There is tension in this model selection process between complexity of the model and data sparsity. With as many subtopics as there are documents, we can perfectly model the training data—each subtopic covers one training document. With still a large number of subtopics, we can accurately model existing data, but generalization performance will be poor. This is because each multinomial will have its many parameters estimated from only a few documents and will suffer from sparse data. With very few subtopics, the opposite problem will arise. We will very accurately estimate the multinomials, but the model will be overly restrictive, and not representative of the true document distribution. Cross-validation should help in selecting a good compromise between these tensions with specific regard to classification performance.

Note that our use of multiple mixture components per class allows us to capture some dependencies between words on the class level. For example, consider a **sports** class consisting of documents about both hockey and baseball. In these documents, the words *ice* and *puck* are likely to co-occur, and the words *bat* and *base* are likely to co-occur. However, these dependencies cannot be captured by a single multinomial distribution over words in the **sports** class. With multiple mixture components per class, one multinomial can cover the hockey subtopic, and another the baseball subtopic. In the hockey subtopic, the word probability for *ice* and *puck* will be significantly higher than they would be for the whole class. This makes their co-occurrence more likely in hockey documents than it would be under a single multinomial assumption.

3.5 Overcoming the Challenges of Local Maxima

In cases where the likelihood in parameter space is well correlated with classification accuracy, our optimization yields good classifiers. However, local maxima significantly hinder our progress. For example, the local maxima we discover with just a few labeled examples in section 3.3 are more than 40 percentage points below the classification accuracy provided when labeled data are plentiful. Thus it is important to consider alternative approaches that can help bridge this gap, especially when labeled data are sparse.

Typically variants of, or alternatives to, EM are created for the purpose of speeding up the rate of convergence (McLachlan and Krishnan, 1997). In the domain of text classification, however, we have seen that convergence is very fast. Thus, we can easily consider alternatives to EM that improve the local maxima situation at the expense of slower convergence. Deterministic annealing makes exactly this tradeoff.

3.5.1 Deterministic Annealing

The intuition behind deterministic annealing is that it begins by maximizing on a very smooth, convex surface that is only remotely related to our true probability surface of interest. Initially we can find the global maximum of this simple surface. Ever so slowly, we change the surface to become both more bumpy, and more close to the true probability surface. If we follow the original maximum as the surface gets more complex, then when the original surface is given, we'll still have a highly probable maximum. In this way, it avoids many of the local maxima that EM would otherwise get caught in.

One can think of our application of EM in the previous sections as an optimization problem where the loss function is the negation of the likelihood function (Eq. 3.8).

The iterations of EM are a hill-climbing algorithm in parameter space that locally minimizes this loss.

Consider the closely related set of loss functions:

$$l(\theta|X,Y) = \sum_{x_i \in X_u} \log \sum_{c_j \in [M]} [\mathrm{P}(c_j|\theta)\mathrm{P}(x_i|c_j;\theta)]^{\beta}$$
$$+ \sum_{x_i \in X_l} \log([\mathrm{P}(y_i = c_j|\theta)\mathrm{P}(x_i|y_i = c_j;\theta)]^{\beta}), \qquad (3.14)$$

where β varies between zero and one. When $\beta = 1$ we have our familiar probability surface of the previous sections, with good correlation to classification accuracy, but with many harmful local maximum. In the limit as β approaches zero, the surface value of the loss function in parameter space becomes convex with just a single global maximum. But, at this extreme, the provided data have no effect on the loss function, so the correlation with classification accuracy is poor. Values between zero and one represent various points in the tradeoff between smoothness of the parameter space and the similarity to the well-correlated probability surface provided by the data.

This insight is the one that drives the approach called deterministic annealing (Rose et al., 1992), first used as a way to construct a hierarchy during unsupervised clustering. It has also been used to estimate the parameters of a mixture of Gaussians from unlabeled data (Ueda and Nakano, 1995) and to construct a text hierarchy from unlabeled data (Hofmann and Puzicha, 1998).

For a fixed value of β, we can find a local maximum given the loss function by iterating the following steps:

- E step: Calculate the expected value of the class assignments,

$$\hat{z}_{ij}^{(k+1)} = E[y_i = c_j|x_i;\hat{\theta}^k] = \frac{[\mathrm{P}(c_j|\hat{\theta}^k)\mathrm{P}(x_i|c_j;\hat{\theta}^k)]^{\beta}}{\sum_{c_r \in [M]} [\mathrm{P}(c_r|\hat{\theta}^k)\mathrm{P}(x_i|c_r;\hat{\theta}^k)]^{\beta}}. \qquad (3.15)$$

- M step: Find the most likely model using the expected class assignments,

$$\hat{\theta}^{(k+1)} = \arg\max_\theta \mathrm{P}(\theta|X;Y;\hat{\mathbf{z}}^{(k+1)}). \qquad (3.16)$$

The M step is identical to that of section 3.2.2, while the E step includes reference to the loss constraint through β.

Formally, β is a Lagrange multiplier when solving for a fixed loss in the likelihood space subject to an optimization criterion of maximum entropy (or minimum relative entropy to the prior distribution). A β near zero corresponds to finding the maximum entropy parameterization for a model with a very large allowable loss.

Consider how model likelihood (Eq. 3.14) is affected by different target losses.

When the target loss is very large, β will be very close to zero; the probability of each model will very nearly be its prior probability as the influence of the data will be negligible. In the limit as β goes to zero, the probability surface will be convex with a single global maximum. For a somewhat smaller loss target, β will be small but not negligible. Here, the probability of the data will have a stronger influence. There will no longer be a single global maximum, but several. When $\beta = 1$ we have our familiar probability surface of the previous chapters, with many local maxima.

These observations suggest an annealing-like process for finding a low-loss model. If we initialize β to be very small, we can easily find the global maximum a posteriori solution with EM, as the surface is convex. When we raise β the probability surface will get slightly more bumpy and complex, as the data likelihood will have a larger impact on the probability of the model. Although more complex, the new maximum will be very close to the old maximum if we have lowered the temperature $(1/\beta)$ only slightly. Thus, when searching for the maximum with EM, we can initialize it with the old maximum and will converge to a good maximum for the new probability surface. In this way, we can gradually raise β, while tracking a highly probable solution. Eventually, when β becomes 1, we will have a good local maximum for our generative model assumptions. Thus, we will have found a high-probability local maximum from labeled and unlabeled data that we can then use for classification.

Note that the computational cost of deterministic annealing is significantly higher than EM. While each iteration takes the same computation, there are many more iterations with deterministic annealing, as the temperature is reduced very slowly. For example, in our experiments, we performed 390 iterations for deterministic annealing, and only seven for EM. When this extra computation can be afforded, the benefit may be more accurate classifiers.

3.5.2   Experimental Results

In this section we see empirically that deterministic annealing finds more probable parameters and more accurate classifiers than EM when labeled training data are sparse.

For the experimental results, we use the News5 data set, a subset of 20 Newsgroups containing the five confusable **comp.*** classes. We fix a single vocabulary for all experiments as the top 4000 words as measured by mutual information over the entire labeled data set. For running the deterministic annealing, we initialize β to 0.02, and at each iteration we increase β by a multiplicative factor of 1.01 until $\beta = 1$. We made little effort to tune these parameters. Since each time we increase β the probability surface changes only slightly, we run only one iteration of EM at each temperature setting. Six hundred random documents per class (3000 total) are treated as unlabeled. A fixed number of labeled examples per class are also randomly selected. The remaining documents are used as a test set.

Figure 3.4 compares classification accuracy achieved with deterministic annealing to that achieved by regular EM. The initial results indicate that the two methods perform essentially the same when labeled data are plentiful, but deterministic an-

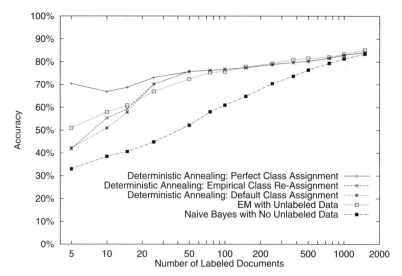

Figure 3.4 The performance of deterministic annealing compared to EM. If class-to-component assignment was done perfectly deterministic annealing would be considerably more accurate than EM when labeled data are sparse. Although the default correspondence is poor, this can be corrected with a small amount of domain knowledge.

nealing actually performs worse when labeled data are sparse. For example, with two labeled examples per class (ten total) EM gives 58% accuracy where deterministic annealing gives only 51%. A close investigation of the confusion matrices shows that there is a significant detrimental effect of incorrect class-to-component correspondence with deterministic annealing when labeled data are sparse. This occurs because, when the temperature is very high, the global maximum will have each multinomial mixture component very close to its prior, and the influence of the labeled data is minimal. Since the priors are the same, each mixture component will be essentially identical. As the temperature lowers and the mixture components become more distinct, one component can easily track the cluster associated with the wrong class, when there are insufficient labeled data to pull it toward the correct class.

In an attempt to remedy this, we alter the class-to-cluster correspondence based on the classification of each labeled example after deterministic annealing is complete. Figure 3.4 shows both the accuracy obtained by empirically selected correspondence, and also the optimal accuracy achieved by perfect correspondence. We see that by empirically setting the correspondence, deterministic annealing improves accuracy only marginally. Where before it got 51%, by changing the correspondence we increase this to 55%, still not better than EM at 58%. However if we could perform perfect class correspondence, accuracy with deterministic annealing would be 67%, considerably higher than EM.

To verify that the higher accuracy of deterministic annealing comes from finding more probable models, figure 3.5 shows a scatterplot of model probability versus

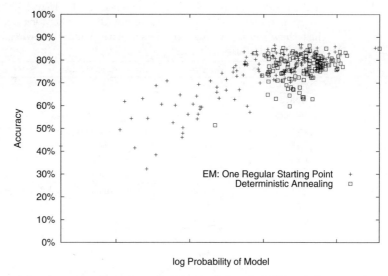

Figure 3.5   A scatterplot comparing the model probabilities and accuracies of EM and deterministic annealing. The results show that deterministic annealing succeeds because it finds models with significantly higher probability.

accuracy for deterministic annealing (with optimal class assignment) and EM. Two results of note stand out. The first is that indeed deterministic annealing finds much more probable models, even with a small amount of labeled data. This accounts for the added accuracy of deterministic annealing. A second note of interest is that models found by deterministic annealing still lie along the same probability-accuracy correlation line. This provides further evidence that model probability and accuracy are strongly correlated for this data set, and that the correlation is not just an artifact of EM.

3.5.3   Discussion

The experimental results show that deterministic annealing indeed could help classification considerably if class-to-component correspondence were solved. Deterministic annealing successfully avoids getting trapped in some poor local maxima and instead finds more probable models. Since these high-probability models are correlated with high-accuracy classifiers, deterministic annealing makes good use of unlabeled data for text classification.

The class-correspondence problem is most severe when there are only limited labeled data. This is because with fewer labeled examples, it is more likely that small perturbations can lead the correspondence astray. However, with just a little bit of human knowledge, the class-correspondence problem can typically be solved trivially. In all but the largest and most confusing classification tasks, it is straightforward to identify a class given its most indicative words, as measured by a metric such as the weighted log-likelihood ratio. For example, the top ten words

Table 3.3 The top ten words per class of the **News5** data set, Usenet groups in the comp hierarchy. The words are sorted by the weighted log-likelihood ratio. Note that from just these ten top words, any person with domain knowledge could correctly correspond clusters and classes.

graphics	os.ms-windows.misc	sys.ibm.pc.hardware	sys.mac.hardware	windows.x
jpeg	windows	scsi	apple	window
image	ei	ide	mac	widget
graphics	win	drive	lc	motif
images	um	controller	duo	xterm
gif	dos	bus	nubus	server
format	ms	dx	fpu	lib
pub	ini	bios	centris	entry
ray	microsoft	drives	quadra	openwindows
tiff	nt	mb	iisi	usr
siggraph	el	card	powerbook	sun

per class of our data set by this metric are shown in table 3.3. From just these ten words, any person with even the slightest bit of domain knowledge would have no problem perfectly assigning classes to components. Thus, it is not unreasonable to require a small amount of human effort to correct the class correspondence after deterministic annealing has finished. This effort can be positioned within the active learning framework. Thus, when labeled training data are sparsest, and a modest investment by a trainer is available to map class labels to cluster components, deterministic annealing will successfully find more probable and more accurate models than traditional EM.

Even when this limited domain knowledge or human effort is not available, it should be possible to estimate the class correspondence automatically. One could perform both EM and deterministic annealing on the data. Since EM solutions generally have the correct class correspondence, this model could be used to fix the correspondence of the deterministic annealing model. That is, one could measure the distance between each EM class multinomial and each deterministic annealing class multinomial (with Kullback-Leibler divergence, for example). Then, this matrix of distances could be used to assign the class labels of the EM multinomials to their closest match to a multinomial in the deterministic annealing model.

3.6   Conclusions and Summary

This chapter has explored the use of generative models for semi-supervised learning with labeled and unlabeled data in domains of text classification. The widely used naive Bayes classifier for supervised learning defines a mixture of multinomials mixture models. In some domains, model likelihood and classification accuracy are strongly correlated, despite the overly simplified generative model. Here, expectation-maximization finds more likely models and improved classification accuracy. In other domains, likelihood and accuracy are not well correlated with the naive Bayes model. Here, we can use a more expressive generative model that allows for multiple mixture components per class. This helps restore a moderate correlation between model likelihood and classification accuracy, and again, EM finds more accurate models. Finally, even with a well-correlated generative model, local maxima are a significant hindrance with EM. Here, the approach of deterministic annealing does provide much higher likelihood models, but often loses the correspondence with the class labels. When class label correspondence is easily corrected, high accuracy models result.

4 Risks of Semi-Supervised Learning: How Unlabeled Data Can Degrade Performance of Generative Classifiers

Fabio Cozman   FGCOZMAN@USP.BR
Ira Cohen   IRA.COHEN@HP.COM

Empirical and theoretical results have often testified favorably to the semi-supervised learning of generative classifiers, as described in other chapters of this book. However, the literature has also brought to light a number of situations where semi-supervised learning fails to produce good generative classifiers. Here some clarification is due. We are not simply concerned with classifiers that produce high classification error — this can also happen in supervised learning. Our concern is this: it is frequently the case that we would be better off just discarding the unlabeled data and employing a supervised method, rather than taking a semi-supervised route. Thus we worry about the embarrassing situation where the addition of unlabeled data degrades the performance of a classifier.

How can this be? Typically we do not expect to be better off by discarding data; how can we understand this aspect of semi-supervised learning? In this chapter we focus on the effect of modeling errors in semi-supervised learning, and show how modeling errors can lead to performance degradation.

4.1 Do Unlabeled Data Improve or Degrade Classification Performance?

Perhaps it would be reasonable to expect an average improvement in classification performance for any increase in the number of samples (labeled or unlabeled): the more data, the better. In fact, existing literature presents empirical findings that attribute positive value to unlabeled data; other chapters present some of these results. O'Neill's statement that "unclassified observations should certainly not be discarded" (O'Neill, 1978) seems to be confirmed by theoretical studies, most notably by Castelli (1994), Castelli and Cover (1995, 1996), and Ratsaby and

Venkatesh (1995).

The gist of these previous theoretical investigations is this. Suppose samples (x_i, y_i) are realizations of random variables X_v and Y_v that are distributed according to distribution $p(X_v, Y_v)$. Suppose one learns a parametric model $p(X_v, Y_v | \theta)$ such that $p(X_v, Y_v | \theta)$ is equal to $p(X_v, Y_v)$ for some value of θ — that is, the "model is

positive results: "correct" model

correct" in the sense that it can exactly represent $p(X_v, Y_v)$.[1] Then one is assured to have an expected reduction in classification error as more and more data are collected (labeled or unlabeled). Moreover, labeled data are exponentially more effective in reducing classification error than unlabeled data. In these optimistic results, unlabeled data can be profitably used whenever available.

However, a more detailed analysis of current empirical results does reveal some

examples of performance degradation

puzzling aspects of unlabeled data. For example, Shahshahani and Landgrebe (1994) report experiments where unlabeled data degraded the performance of naive Bayes classifiers with Gaussian variables. They attribute such cases to deviations from modeling assumptions, such as outliers and "samples of unknown classes" — they even suggest that unlabeled samples should be used with care, and only when the labeled data alone produce a poor classifier. Another representative example is the work by Nigam et al. (2000) on text classification, where classifiers sometimes display performance degradation. They suggest several possible sources of difficulties: numerical problems in the learning algorithm, mismatches between the natural clusters in feature space and the actual labels. Additional examples are easy to find. Baluja (1999) used naive Bayes and tree-augmented naive Bayes (TAN) classifiers (Friedman et al., 1997) to detect faces in images, but there were cases where unlabeled data degraded performance. Bruce (2001) used labeled and unlabeled data to learn Bayesian network classifiers, from naive Bayes classifiers to fully connected networks; the naive Bayes classifiers displayed bad classification performance, and in fact the performance degraded as more unlabeled data were used (more complex networks also displayed performance degradation as unlabeled samples were added). A final example: Grandvalet and Bengio (2004) describe experiments where outliers are added to a Gaussian model, causing generative classifiers to degrade with unlabeled data.

Figure 4.1 shows a number of experiments that corroborate this anecdotal evidence. All of them involve binary classification with categorical variables; in all of them X_v is actually a vector containing several attributes X_{vi}. In all experiments the generative classifiers were learned by maximum likelihood using the expectation-maximization (EM) algorithm (chapters 2, 3). Figure 4.1(a) shows the performance of naive Bayes classifiers learned with increasing amounts of unlabeled data (for several fixed amounts of labeled data), where the data are distributed according to naive Bayes assumptions. That is, the data were generated by randomly generated

---

1. Note that here and in the remainder of the chapter we employ p to denote distributions and densities (for discrete/continuous variables using appropriate measures); we indicate the type of object we deal with whenever it is not clear from the context.

statistical models that comply with the independence assumptions of naive Bayes classifiers. In the naive Bayes model, all attributes X_v are independent of each other given the class Y_v: $p(X_v, Y_v) = p(Y_v) \prod p(X_{vi})$. The result is simple: the more unlabeled data, the better. Figure 4.1(b) shows an entirely different picture. Here a series of naive Bayes classifiers were learned with data distributed according to TAN assumptions: each attribute is directly dependent on the class and on at most another attribute — the attributes form a "tree" of dependencies, hence the name tree-augmented naive Bayes (Friedman et al., 1997). That is, in figure 4.1(b) the "model is incorrect." The graphs in figure 4.1(b) indicate performance degradation with increasing amounts of unlabeled data.

Figure 4.1(c) depicts a more complex scenario. Again a series of naive Bayes classifiers were learned with data distributed according to TAN assumptions, so the "model is incorrect." Note that two of the graphs show a trend of decreasing error (as the number of unlabeled samples increases), while the other graph shows a trend of increasing error. Here unlabeled data improve performance in the presence of a few labeled samples, but unlabeled data degrade performance when added to a larger number of labeled samples. A larger set of experiments with artificial data is described by Cozman and Cohen (2002).

Figure 4.1(d) shows the result of learning naive Bayes classifiers using different combinations of labeled and unlabeled data sets for the adult classification problem (using the training and testing data sets available in the UCI repository [2]). We see that adding unlabeled data can improve classification when the labeled data set is small (30 labeled data), but degrade performance as the labeled data set becomes larger. Thus the properties of this real data set lead to behavior similar to figure 4.1(c).

Finally, figure 4.1(e) and 4.1(f) shows the result of learning naive Bayes and TAN classifiers using data set 8 in the benchmark data (chapter 21). Both show similar trends as those displayed in previous graphs.

4.2   Understanding Unlabeled Data: Asymptotic Bias

We can summarize the previous section as follows. First, there are results that guarantee benefits from unlabeled data when the learned generative classifier is based on a "correct" model. Second, there is strong empirical evidence that unlabeled data may degrade performance of classifiers. Performance degradation may occur whenever the modeling assumptions adopted for a particular classifier do not match the characteristics of the distribution generating the data.[3] This is

---

2. `ftp://ftp.ics.uci.edu/pub/machine-learning-databases/adult`
3. As we show in this and subsequent sections, performance degradation occurs even in the absence of numerical errors or existence of local optima for parameter estimation. In fact our presentation is independent of numerical techniques, so that results are not clouded by the intricacies of numerical analysis.

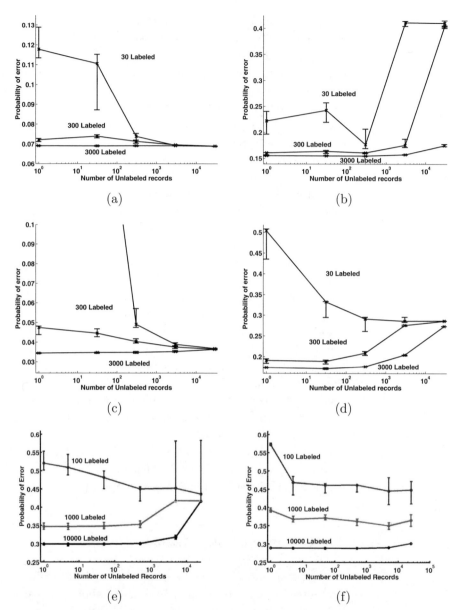

Figure 4.1 (a) Naive Bayes classifiers learned from data distributed according to naive Bayes assumptions with ten attributes; attributes with two to four values. (b) Naive Bayes classifiers learned from data distributed according to TAN assumptions with ten attributes. (c) Naive Bayes classifiers learned from data distributed according to TAN assumptions with 49 attributes. (d) Naive Bayes classifiers generated from the adult database. (e) Naive Bayes classifiers generated from the data set `SecStr`, benchmark data (chapter 21). (f) TAN classifiers generated from the data set `SecStr`, benchmark data (chapter 21). In all graphs, points summarize ten runs of each classifier on testing data (bars cover 30th to 70th percentiles).

troubling because it is usually difficult, if not impossible, to guarantee a priori that a particular statistical model is a "correct" one.

key: asymptotic
bias

The key to understanding the vagaries of semi-supervised learning is to study asymptotic bias. In this section we present an intuitive discussion, leaving more formal analysis to section 4.3. Our arguments here and in the remainder of this chapter focus on generative classifiers learned by maximum-likelihood methods. As most of our arguments are asymptotic, the same rationale will apply to maximum a posteriori and other Bayesian estimators, as their asymptotic behavior is dominated by the likelihood function (DeGroot, 1970).

The gist of the argument is as follows. As we formally show in section 4.3, the asymptotic bias of the maximum-likelihood estimator produced with labeled data *can be different* from the asymptotic bias of the maximum- likelihood estimator produced with unlabeled data, for the same classifier. Suppose then that one learns a classifier with a reasonable amount of labeled data. The resulting classifier may be relatively close to its asymptotic limit, yielding some classification error. Now suppose one takes a much larger amount of unlabeled data, and learns the same classifier with all available data. Now the classifier may be tending to the asymptotic limit *for unlabeled data* — and the performance for this limiting classifier may be worse than the performance for the first "labeled" limiting classifier. The net result is that by adding a large number of unlabeled samples one produces a worse classifier.

However puzzling, this situation can be found even in seemingly innocent situations, and does not require sophisticated modeling errors. We now discuss a simple example where unlabeled data degrade the performance of a generative classifier; this (fictitious) example may help the reader grasp the sometimes unexpected effects of unlabeled data.

classifying baby's
gender

Consider the following classification problem. We are interested in predicting a baby's gender (G = Boy or G = Girl) at the 20th week of pregnancy based on two attributes: whether the mother craved chocolate in the first trimester (Ch = Yes or Ch = No), and whether the mother's weight gain was more or less than 15 lb (W = More or W = Less). Suppose that W and G are independent conditional on Ch; that is, the direct dependencies in the domain are expressed by the graph $G \rightarrow Ch \rightarrow W$, leading to the following decomposition of the joint distribution: $P(G, Ch, W) = P(G)P(Ch|G)P(W|Ch)$. Suppose also that data are distributed according to

$$
\begin{aligned}
P(G = \text{Boy}) &= 0.5, \\
P(Ch = \text{No}|G = \text{Boy}) &= 0.1, \\
P(Ch = \text{No}|G = \text{Girl}) &= 0.8, \\
P(W = \text{Less}|Ch = \text{No}) &= 0.7, \\
P(W = \text{Less}|Ch = \text{Yes}) &= 0.2.
\end{aligned}
$$

Note that from the above distribution we can compute the probabilities of W given

G to get

$$P(W = \text{Less}|G = \text{Boy}) \quad = \quad 0.25,$$
$$P(W = \text{Less}|G = \text{Girl}) \quad = \quad 0.6.$$

To classify the baby's gender given weight gain and chocolate craving, we compute the a posteriori probability of G given W and Ch (which, from the independence stated above, depends only on Ch):

$$P(G = \text{Girl}|Ch = \text{No}) \quad = \quad 0.89,$$
$$P(G = \text{Boy}|Ch = \text{No}) \quad = \quad 0.11,$$
$$P(G = \text{Girl}|Ch = \text{Yes}) \quad = \quad 0.18,$$
$$P(G = \text{Boy}|Ch = \text{Yes}) \quad = \quad 0.82.$$

Bayes rule

From the a posteriori probabilities, the optimal classification rule (the Bayes rule, discussed in the next section) is

$$\text{if } Ch = \text{No, choose } G = \text{Girl;} \qquad \text{if } Ch = \text{Yes, choose } G = \text{Boy.} \qquad (4.1)$$

The Bayes error rate (i.e., the probability of error under the Bayes rule) for this problem can be easily computed and found to be at about 15%.

assuming naive Bayes

Suppose that we incorrectly assume a naive Bayes model for the problem; that is, we assume that dependencies are expressed by the graph $Ch \leftarrow G \rightarrow W$. Thus we incorrectly assume that weight gain is independent of chocolate craving given the gender; thus we incorrectly assume that the factorization of the joint probability distribution can be written as $P(G, Ch, W) = P(G)P(Ch|G)P(W|G)$. Suppose that a friend gave us the "true" values of $P(Ch|G)$, so we do not have to estimate these quantities. We wish to estimate $P(G)$ and $P(W|G)$ using maximum-likelihood techniques.

In the case where only labeled data are available, estimators are obtained by relative frequencies, with zero bias and variance inversely proportional to the size of the database. Thus even a relatively small database will produce excellent estimates of probability values. The estimate for $P(G)$ will most likely be close to 0.5; likewise, estimates of $P(W = \text{Less}|G = \text{Girl})$ will be close to 0.6 and estimates of $P(W = \text{Less}|G = \text{Boy})$ will be close to 0.25. With these estimated parameters and the assumed decomposition of the joint probability distribution, the a posteriori probabilities for G will likely be close to

	$P(G = \text{Girl}|Ch, W)$	$P(G = \text{Boy}|Ch, W)$
$Ch = \text{No}, W = \text{Less}$	0.95	0.05,
$Ch = \text{No}, W = \text{More}$	0.81	0.19,
$Ch = \text{Yes}, W = \text{Less}$	0.35	0.65,
$Ch = \text{Yes}, W = \text{More}$	0.11	0.89.

Suppose we take these estimates and classify incoming observations using the

the "labeled" classifier

maximum a posteriori value of G. Even though the bias from the "true" a posteriori probabilities is not zero, this will *produce the same optimal Bayes rule 4.1*; that is, the "labeled" classifier is likely to yield the minimum classification error.

Now suppose that unlabeled data are available. As more and more unlabeled samples are collected, the ratio between the number of labeled samples and the total number of samples goes to zero. In section 4.3 we show how to compute the asymptotic estimates in this case. The computation, which is performed in closed form for this case, yields the following asymptotic estimates: $P(G = \text{Boy}) = 0.5$, $P(W = \text{Less}|G = \text{Girl}) = 0.78$, $P(W = \text{Less}|G = \text{Boy}) = 0.07$. The a posteriori probabilities for G will therefore tend to

	$P(G = \text{Girl}|Ch, W)$	$P(G = \text{Boy}|Ch, W)$
$Ch = \text{No}, W = \text{Less}$	0.99	0.01,
$Ch = \text{No}, W = \text{More}$	0.55	0.45,
$Ch = \text{Yes}, W = \text{Less}$	0.71	0.29,
$Ch = \text{Yes}, W = \text{More}$	0.05	0.95.

Classification using the maximum a posteriori value of G yields

$$\text{if } \{Ch = \text{No}, W = \text{Less}\}, \text{ choose } G = \text{Girl};$$
$$\text{if } \{Ch = \text{No}, W = \text{More}\}, \text{ choose } G = \text{Girl};$$
$$\text{if } \{Ch = \text{Yes}, W = \text{Less}\}, \text{ choose } G = \text{Girl};$$
$$\text{if } \{Ch = \text{Yes}, W = \text{More}\}, \text{ choose } G = \text{Boy}.$$

the "unlabeled" classifier

Here we see that the prediction has changed from the optimal in the case $\{Ch = \text{Yes}, W = \text{Less}\}$; instead of predicting $\{G = \text{Boy}\}$, we predict $\{G = \text{Girl}\}$. We can easily find the expected error rate to be at 22%, an *increase* of 7% in error.

What happened? The labeled data take us to a particular asymptotic limit, and the unlabeled data take us to a distinct limit. In section 4.3 we will see that this transition is smooth as unlabeled samples are collected. Because the latter limit is worse (from the point of view of classification) than the former, the gradual addition of unlabeled samples degrades performance.

Consider again figure 4.1(a). The graphs there illustrate the situation where the "model is correct": labeled and unlabeled data lead to identical asymptotic estimates. The other graphs in figure 4.1 illustrate situations where the "model is incorrect." In these cases the asymptotic estimates tend to the "unlabeled" classifier as more and more unlabeled data are available — depending on the amount of labeled data, the graphs start above or below this "unlabeled" limit.

4.3 The Asymptotic Analysis of Generative Semi-Supervised Learning

We start by collecting a few assumptions in this section, at the cost of repeating definitions already stated in previous chapters. The goal here is to classify a vector of attributes X_v. Each instantiation x of X_v is a *sample*. There exists a *class variable* Y_v that takes values in a set of *labels*. To simplify the discussion, we assume that Y_v is a binary variable with values -1 and $+1$. We assume 0-1 loss, hence our objective is to minimize the probability of classification errors. If we knew exactly the joint distribution $p(X_v, Y_v)$, the optimal rule would be to select the label with highest posterior probability; this is the *Bayes rule*, and it produces the smallest classification error, referred to as the *Bayes error* (Devroye et al., 1996). A classifier is learned using n independent samples in a database; there are l labeled samples and u labeled samples ($n = l + u$), and without loss of generality we assume that the samples are ordered with labeled ones coming first. We assume that a sample has probability $(1 - \lambda)$ of having its label hidden (the same distribution $p(X_v|Y_v)$ generates the labeled and the unlabeled samples).

parametric model and assumptions

Consider that a generative model is adopted as a representation for the joint distribution $p(X_v, Y_v)$. Suppose that a parametric representation $p(X_v, Y_v|\theta)$ with parameters θ is employed, and a database containing *training* samples is available to produce estimates $\hat{\theta}$. All samples x_i are collected in a database denoted by X, and all samples y_i are collected in a database denoted by Y. We consider "plug-in" classification: compute the optimal rule pretending that $p(Y_v|X_v, \hat{\theta})$ is the correct posterior density of Y_v.

Throughout the chapter we denote the distributions/densities generating the data by $p(\cdot)$ and the statistical models that are employed to learn the distribution by $p(\cdot|\theta)$. Several smoothness and measurability assumptions on these distributions/densities are necessary to proceed with asymptotic analysis and are adopted throghout.[4]

Two principles often used to generate estimates are *maximum likelihood* and *maximization of posterior loss* (DeGroot, 1970); the computation of estimates using these principles generally requires iterative methods, the most popular of which is the EM algorithm (Dempster et al., 1977). Generative models are well suited for semi-supervised learning by maximum likelihood, because the likelihood is directly affected by unlabeled data — as opposed to discriminative models, where the associated likelihood is not affected by unlabeled data (Zhang and Oles, 2000).

likelihood

We take that estimates $\hat{\theta}$ are produced by maximizing the likelihood $L(\theta) = \prod_{i=1}^{l} p(x_i, y_i|\theta) \prod_{j=l+1}^{n} p(x_j|\theta)$. When a sample is unlabeled, its likelihood can be written as a mixture $p(X_v|Y_v = +1, \theta)p(Y_v = +1|\theta) + p(X_v|Y_v = -1, \theta)p(Y_v = -1|\theta)$; we assume that such mixtures are identifiable (Redner and Walker, 1984).

We use the following known result (Berk, 1966; Huber, 1967; White, 1982). Con-

---

4. Distributions must be defined on measurable Euclidean spaces, with measurable Radon-Nikodym densities. The dependence of $p(X_v, Y_v|\theta)$ on θ must be continuous so that second derivatives exist (and first derivatives must be measurable). Likelihoods, their derivatives and second derivatives, must be dominated by integrable functions. Finally, expected values $\mathbf{E}_{p(Z)}[\log p(Z|\theta)]$ must exist for Z equal to X_v, Y_v and (X_v, Y_v). These conditions are listed in detail by Cozman et al. (2003b).

sider a parametric model $p(Z|\theta)$ and a sequence of maximum-likelihood estimates $\hat{\theta}_n$, obtained by maximization of $\sum_{i=1}^{n} \log p(z_i|\theta)$, with an increasing number n of independent samples z_i, all identically distributed according to $p(Z)$. Then $\hat{\theta}_n \to \theta^*$ as $n \to \infty$ for θ in an open neighborhood of θ^*, where θ^* maximizes $\mathbf{E}_{p(Z)}[\log p(Z|\theta)]$. If θ^* is interior to the parameter space, then estimates are asymptotically Gaussian.

central result

Extending the result above to semi-supervised learning we have:

Theorem 4.1 *The limiting value θ^* of maximum-likelihood estimates is*

$$\arg\max_{\theta} \left(\lambda \mathbf{E}_{p(X_v, Y_v)}\left[\log p(X_v, Y_v|\theta)\right] + (1-\lambda)\mathbf{E}_{p(X_v, Y_v)}\left[\log p(X_v|\theta)\right] \right). \quad (4.2)$$

Proof   In semi-supervised learning, the samples are realizations of (X_v, Y_v) with probability λ, and of X_v with probability $(1-\lambda)$. Denote by $\tilde{Y}_v$ a random variable that assumes the same values of Y_v plus the "unlabeled" value 0. We have $p(\tilde{Y}_v \neq 0) = \lambda$. The actually observed samples are realizations of $(X_v, \tilde{Y}_v)$, thus

$$\tilde{p}(X_v, \tilde{Y}_v = y) = (\lambda p(X_v, Y_v = y))^{I_{\{\tilde{Y}_v \neq 0\}}(y)} ((1-\lambda)p(X_v))^{I_{\{\tilde{Y}_v = 0\}}(y)},$$

where $p(X_v)$ is a mixture density. Accordingly, the parametric model adopted for $(X_v, \tilde{Y}_v)$ has the same form:

$$\tilde{p}(X_v, \tilde{Y}_v = y|\theta) = (\lambda p(X_v, Y_v = y|\theta))^{I_{\{\tilde{Y}_v \neq 0\}}(y)} ((1-\lambda)p(X_v|\theta))^{I_{\{\tilde{Y}_v = 0\}}(y)}.$$

The value θ^* that maximizes $\mathbf{E}_{\tilde{p}(X_v, \tilde{Y}_v)}\left[\log \tilde{p}(X_v, \tilde{Y}_v|\theta)\right]$ is

$$\arg\max_{\theta} \mathbf{E}_{\tilde{p}(X_v, \tilde{Y}_v)}\left[I_{\{\tilde{Y}_v \neq 0\}}(\tilde{Y}_v)\left(\log \lambda p(X_v, Y_v|\theta)\right) + I_{\{\tilde{Y}_v = 0\}}(\tilde{Y}_v)\left(\log(1-\lambda)p(X_v|\theta)\right)\right].$$

Hence θ^* maximizes

$$\beta + \mathbf{E}_{\tilde{p}(X_v, \tilde{Y}_v)}\left[I_{\{\tilde{Y}_v \neq 0\}}(\tilde{Y}_v) \log p(X_v, Y_v|\theta)\right] + \mathbf{E}_{\tilde{p}(X_v, \tilde{Y}_v)}\left[I_{\{\tilde{Y}_v = 0\}}(\tilde{Y}_v) \log p(X_v|\theta)\right],$$

where $\beta = \lambda \log \lambda + (1-\lambda)\log(1-\lambda)$. As β does not depend on θ, we must only maximize the last two terms, which are equal to $\lambda \mathbf{E}_{\tilde{p}(X_v, \tilde{Y}_v)}\left[\log p(X_v, Y_v|\theta)|\tilde{Y}_v \neq 0\right] +$ $(1-\lambda)\mathbf{E}_{\tilde{p}(X_v, \tilde{Y}_v)}\left[\log p(X_v|\theta)|\tilde{Y}_v = 0\right]$. As we have $\tilde{p}(X_v, \tilde{Y}_v|\tilde{Y}_v \neq 0) = p(X_v, Y_v)$ and $\tilde{p}(X_v|\tilde{Y}_v = 0) = p(X_v)$, the last expression is equal to $\lambda \mathbf{E}_{p(X_v, Y_v)}\left[\log p(X_v, Y_v|\theta)\right] +$ $(1-\lambda)\mathbf{E}_{p(X_v, Y_v)}\left[\log p(X_v|\theta)\right]$. Thus we obtain expression 4.2.   ∎

Results by White (1982) can also be adapted to the context of semi-supervised learning to prove that generally the variance of estimates decreases with increasing n. The asymptotic variance depends on the inverse of the Fisher information; the Fisher information is typically larger for larger proportions of labeled data (Castelli, 1994; Castelli and Cover, 1995, 1996).

semi-supervised learning as "convex" combination

Expression 4.2 indicates that the objective function in semi-supervised learning can be viewed asymptotically as a "convex" combination of objective functions for supervised learning ($\mathbf{E}[\log p(X_v, Y_v|\theta)]$) and for unsupervised learning ($\mathbf{E}[\log p(X_v|\theta)]$). Denote by θ_λ^* the value of θ that maximizes expression 4.2 for a given λ. Denote by θ_l^* the "labeled" limit θ_1^* and by θ_u^* the "unlabeled" limit θ_0^*.[5] We note that, with a few additional assumptions on the modeling densities, theorem 4.1 and the implicit function theorem can be used to prove that θ_λ^* is a continuous function of λ — that is, the "path" followed by the solution is a continuous one.

We can now present more formal versions of the arguments sketched in section 4.2.

model is correct
Suppose first that the family of distributions $p(X_v, Y_v|\theta)$ contains the distribution $p(X_v, Y_v)$; that is, $p(X_v, Y_v|\theta_\top) = p(X_v, Y_v)$ for some $\theta_\top$, so the "model is correct." When such a condition is satisfied, $\theta_l^* = \theta_u^* = \theta_\top$ given identifiability, and then $\theta_\lambda^* = \theta_\top$, for any $0 < \lambda \le 1$, is a maximum-likelihood estimate. In this case, maximum likelihood is consistent, the asymptotic bias is zero, and classification error converges to the Bayes error. As variance decreases with increasing numbers of labeled and unlabeled data, the addition of both kinds of data eventually reaches the "correct" distribution and the Bayes error.

We now study the scenario that is more relevant to our purposes, where the distribution $p(X_v, Y_v)$ does not belong to the family of distributions $p(X_v, Y_v|\theta)$.

model is incorrect
Denote by $e(\theta)$ the classification error with parameter θ, and suppose $e(\theta_u^*) > e(\theta_l^*)$ (as in the Boy-Girl example and in the other examples presented later). If we observe a large number of labeled samples, the classification error is approximately $e(\theta_l^*)$. If we then collect more samples, most of which are unlabeled, we eventually reach a point where the classification error approaches $e(\theta_u^*)$. So, the net result is that we started with a classification error close to $e(\theta_l^*)$, and by adding a great number of unlabeled samples, classification performance degraded towards $e(\theta_u^*)$. A labeled data set can be dwarfed by a much larger unlabeled data set: the classification error using the whole data set can be larger than the classification error using only labeled data.

summary
To summarize, we have the following conclusions. First, labeled and unlabeled data contribute to a reduction in variance in semi-supervised learning under maximum-likelihood estimation. Second, when the model is "correct," maximum-likelihood methods are asymptotically unbiased both with labeled and unlabeled data. Third, when the model is "incorrect," there may be different asymptotic biases for different values of λ. Asymptotic classification error may also vary with λ — an increase in the number of unlabeled samples may lead to a larger estimation asymptotic bias and to a larger classification error. If the performance obtained with a given set of labeled data is better than the performance with infinitely many unlabeled samples, then at some point the addition of unlabeled data must decrease performance.

---

5. We have to handle a difficulty with the classification error for θ_u^*: given only unlabeled data, there is no information to decide the labels for decision regions, and the classification error is 1/2 (Castelli, 1994). Thus we always reason with $\lambda \to 0$ instead of $\lambda = 0$.

4.4   The Value of Labeled and Unlabeled Data

The previous discussion alluded to the possibility that $e(\theta_u^*) > e(\theta_l^*)$ when the model is "incorrect." To understand a few important details about this phenomenon, consider another example.

Gaussian
example

Suppose we have attributes X_{v1} and X_{v2} from two classes -1 and $+1$. We know that (X_{v1}, X_{v2}) is a Gaussian vector with mean $(0, 3/2)$ conditional on $\{Y_v = -1\}$, and mean $(3/2, 0)$ conditional on $\{Y_v = +1\}$; variances for X_{v1} and for X_{v2} conditional on Y_v are equal to 1. We believe that X_{v1} and X_{v2} are independent given Y_v, but actually X_{v1} and X_{v2} are *dependent* conditional on $\{Y_v = +1\}$: the correlation $\rho = \mathbf{E}\left[(X_{v1} - \mathbf{E}\left[X_{v1}|Y_v = +1\right])(X_{v2} - \mathbf{E}\left[X_{v2}|Y_v = +1\right])|Y_v = +1\right]$ is equal to $4/5$ (X_{v1} and X_{v2} are independent conditional on $\{Y_v = -1\}$). Data are sampled from a distribution such that $\eta = \mathrm{P}(Y_v = -1) = 3/5$, but we do not know this probability. If we knew the value of ρ and η, we would easily compute the optimal classification boundary on the plane $X_{v1} \times X_{v2}$ (this optimal classification boundary is quadratic). By mistakenly assuming that ρ is zero we are generating a naive Bayes classifier that approximates $\mathrm{P}(Y_v|X_{v1}, X_{v2})$.

Under the incorrect assumption that $\rho = 0$, the "optimal" classification boundary is linear: $x_{v2} = x_{v1} + 2\log((1 - \hat{\eta})/\hat{\eta})/3$. With labeled data we can easily obtain $\hat{\eta}$ (a sequence of Bernoulli trials); then $\eta_l^* = 3/5$ and the classification boundary

the "labeled"
classifier

is given by $x_{v2} = x_{v1} - 0.27031$. Note that this (linear) boundary obtained with labeled data and the generative naive Bayes classifier assumption is not the best possible linear boundary minimizing the classification error. We can in fact find the best possible linear boundary of the form $x_{v2} = x_{v1} + \gamma$. The classification error can be written as a function of γ that has positive second derivative; consequently the function has a single minimum that can be found numerically (the minimizing

the best linear
classifier

γ is -0.45786). If we consider the set of lines of the form $x_{v2} = x_{v1} + \gamma$, we see that the farther we go from the best line, the larger the classification error. Figure 4.2 shows the linear boundary obtained with labeled data and the best possible linear boundary. The boundary from labeled data is "above" the best linear boundary.

Now consider the computation of η_u^*, the asymptotic estimate with unlabeled data. By theorem 4.1, we must obtain:

$$\arg\max_{\eta \in [0,1]} \int_{-\infty}^{\infty} \int_{-\infty}^{\infty} g_0(x_{v1}, x_{v2}) \log(\eta g_1(x_{v1}, x_{v2}) + (1 - \eta)g_3(x_{v1}, x_{v2})) dx_{v2} dx_{v1},$$

where

$$
\begin{aligned}
g_0(x_{v1}, x_{v2}) &= (3/5)g_1(x_{v1}, x_{v2}) + (2/5)g_2(x_{v1}, x_{v2}), \\
g_1(x_{v1}, x_{v2}) &= \mathcal{N}([0, 3/2]^T, \mathrm{diag}[1, 1]), \\
g_2(x_{v1}, x_{v2}) &= \mathcal{N}\left([3/2, 0]^T, \begin{bmatrix} 1 & 4/5 \\ 4/5 & 1 \end{bmatrix}\right), \\
g_3(x_{v1}, x_{v2}) &= \mathcal{N}([3/2, 0]^T, \mathrm{diag}[1, 1]).
\end{aligned}
$$

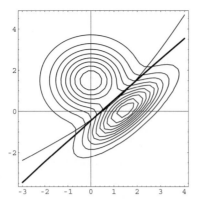 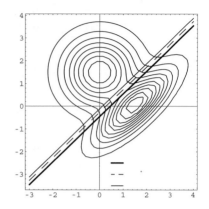

Figure 4.2 Graphs for the Gaussian example. On the left, contour plots of the mixture $p(X_{v1}, X_{v2})$, the optimal classification boundary (quadratic curve), and the best possible classification boundary of the form $x_{v2} = x_{v1} + \gamma$. On the right, the same contour plots, and the best linear boundary (lower line), the linear boundary obtained from labeled data (middle line), and the linear boundary obtained from unlabeled data (upper line).

the "unlabeled" classifier

The second derivative of this double integral is always negative (as can be seen by interchanging differentiation with integration), so the function is concave and there is a single maximum. We can search for the zero of the derivative of the double integral with respect to η. We obtain this value numerically, $\eta_u^* = 0.54495$. Using this estimate, the linear boundary from unlabeled data is $x_{v2} = x_{v1} - 0.12019$. This line is "above" the linear boundary from labeled data, and, given the previous discussion, leads to a larger classification error than the boundary from labeled data. The boundary obtained from unlabeled data is also shown in figure 4.2. The classification error for the best linear boundary is 0.06975, while $e(\eta_l^*) = 0.07356$ and $e(\eta_u^*) = 0.08141$.

This example suggests the following situation. Suppose we collect a large number l of labeled samples from $\mathrm{P}(Y_v, X_{v1}, X_{v2})$, with $\eta = 3/5$ and $\rho = 4/5$. The labeled estimates form a sequence of Bernoulli trials with probability $3/5$, so the estimates quickly approach η_l^* (the variance of $\hat{\eta}$ decreases as $6/(25l)$). If we then add a very large amount of unlabeled data to our data, $\hat{\eta}$ approaches η_u^* and the classification error increases.

changing η and ρ

By changing the values of η and ρ, we can produce other interesting situations. For example, if $\eta = 3/5$ and $\rho = -4/5$, the best linear boundary is $x_{v2} = x_{v1} - 0.37199$, the boundary from labeled data is $x_{v2} = x_{v1} - 0.27031$, and the boundary from unlabeled data is $x_{v2} = x_{v1} - 0.34532$; the latter boundary is "between" the other two — additional unlabeled data lead to improvement in classification performance! As another example, if $\eta = 3/5$ and $\rho = -1/5$, the best linear boundary is $x_{v2} = x_{v1} - 0.29044$, the boundary from labeled data is $x_{v2} = x_{v1} - 0.27031$, and the boundary from unlabeled data is $x_{v2} = x_{v1} - 0.29371$. The best linear boundary is "between" the other two. In this case we attain the best possible linear boundary by mixing labeled and unlabeled data with $\lambda = 0.08075$.

We have so far found that taking larger and larger amounts of unlabeled data changes not only the variance of estimates but also their average behavior. The Gaussian example shows that we cannot always expect labeled data to produce a better classifier than the unlabeled data. Still, one would intuitively expect labeled data to provide more guidance to a learning procedure than unlabeled data. Is there anything that can be said about the (intuitively plausible and empirically visible) more valuable status of labeled data?

"labeled" limit better than the "unlabeled" one?

One informal argument is this. Suppose we have an estimate $\hat{\theta}$. It is typically the case that the smaller the value of the expected Kullback-Leibler divergence between $p(Y_v|X_v)$ and $p(Y_v|X_v, \hat{\theta})$, the smaller the classification error, where the Kullback-Leibler divergence is $EKL(\theta) = \mathbf{E}\left[\log(p(Y_v|X_v)/p(Y_v|X_v, \theta)\right]$ (Garg and Roth, 2001; Cover and Thomas, 1991). Direct minimization of expected Kullback-Leibler divergence yields $EKL(\theta_t^*)$ where $\theta_t^* = \arg\max_\theta \mathbf{E}\left[\log p(Y_v|X_v, \theta)\right]$. Now unlabeled data asymptotically yield $EKL(\theta_u^*)$ where $\theta_u^* = \arg\max_\theta \mathbf{E}\left[\log p(X_v|\theta)\right]$, and labeled data asymptotically yield $EKL(\theta_l^*)$ where $\theta_l^* = \arg\max_\theta \mathbf{E}\left[\log p(Y_v|X_v, \theta)\right] + \mathbf{E}\left[\log p(X_v|\theta)\right]$. Note the following pattern. We are interested in minimizing $\mathbf{E}\left[\log p(Y_v|X_v, \theta)\right]$. While labeled data allow us to minimize a combination of this quantity plus $\mathbf{E}\left[\log p(X_v|\theta)\right]$, unlabeled data only allow us to minimize $\mathbf{E}\left[\log p(X_v|\theta)\right]$. When the "model is incorrect," this last quantity may in fact be far from the "true" $\mathbf{E}\left[\log p(X_v)\right]$, and we may be getting less help from unlabeled data than we might get from labeled data. This informal argument seems to be at the core of the perception that labeled data should be more valuable than unlabeled data when the "model is incorrect." The analysis presented in this chapter adds to this perception the following comment: by trying to (asymptotically) minimize an expected value $\mathbf{E}\left[\log p(X_v)|\theta\right]$ that may even be unrelated to the "true" $\mathbf{E}\left[\log p(X_v)\right]$, we may in fact be *led astray* by the unlabeled data.

4.5 Finite Sample Effects

Asymptotic analysis can provide insight into complex phenomena, but finite sample effects are also important. In practice one may have very little labeled data, and the estimates $\hat{\theta}$ from labeled data may be so poor that the addition of unlabeled data is a positive move. This can be explained as follows. A small number of labeled samples may lead to estimators with high variance, thus likely to yield high classification error (Friedman, 1997). In those circumstances the inclusion of unlabeled data may lead to a substantial decrease in variance and a decrease in classification error, even as the bias is negatively affected by the unlabeled data.

In general, the more parameters one has to estimate, the larger the variance of estimators for the same amount of data. If we have a classifier with a large number of attributes and we have only a few labeled samples, the variance of estimators is likely to be large, and classification performance is likely to be poor — the addition of unlabeled data is then a reasonable action to take. Consider again figure 4.1(c). Here we have a naive Bayes classifier with 49 attributes. If we have a relatively large

many attributes

amount of labeled data, we start close to the "labeled" limit $e(\theta_l^*)$, and then we observe performance degradation as we move toward $e(\theta_u^*)$. However, if we have few labeled samples, we start with very poor performance, and we decrease classification error by moving toward $e(\theta_u^*)$.

text classification

We note that text classification is an important problem where many attributes are often available (often thousands of attributes), and where generative semi-supervised learning has been successful (Nigam et al., 2000).

4.6   Model Search and Robustness

looking for
correct models

In semi-supervised learning we must always consider the possibility that a more accurate statistical model will lead to significant gains from unlabeled data. That is, we should look for the "correct" model whenever possible. In fact, the literature has described situations where a fixed-structure classifier, like the naive Bayes, performs poorly, while model search schemes can lead to excellent classifiers (Bruce, 2001; Cohen et al., 2003, 2004). In particular, Cohen et al. (2004) discuss and compare different model search strategies with labeled and unlabeled data for Bayesian network classifiers. Results show that TAN classifiers, learned with the EM algorithm (Meila, 1999), can sometimes improve classification and eliminate performance degradation with unlabeled data compared to the simpler naive Bayes. In contrast, structure learning algorithms that maximize the likelihood of class and attributes, such as those proposed by Friedman (1998) and van Allen and Greiner (2000), are not likely to find structures yielding good classifiers in a semi-supervised manner, because of their focus on fitting the joint distribution rather than the a posteriori distribution (as also argued by Friedman et al. (1997) for the purely supervised case). The class of independence-based methods for structure learning, also known as constraint-based or test-based methods, is another alternative for attempting to learn the correct model. However, these methods do not easily adapt to the use of unlabeled data. Such a modification of algorithms by Cheng et al. (1997) is presented in Cohen et al. (2004), showing either none or marginal improvement compared to the EM version of TAN, while requiring much greater computational complexity. A third alternative is to perform structure search, attempting to maximize classification accuracy directly. Cohen et al. (2004) proposed using a stochastic structure search algorithm (Markov chain Monte Carlo), accepting or rejecting models based on their classification accuracy (estimated using the labeled training data), while learning the parameters of each model using maximum-likelihood estimation with both labeled and unlabeled data. This strategy yielded very good results for data sets with a moderate number of labeled samples (and a much larger number of unlabeled samples), but did not work well for data sets with a very small number of labeled samples, because of its dependence on estimation of the classification error during the search.

Given the results in this chapter, unlabeled data can also be useful in testing modeling assumptions. If the addition of unlabeled data to an existing pool of

detecting
incorrect models

labeled data degrades performance, then there is clear indication that modeling assumptions are incorrect. In fact one can test whether differences in performance are statistically significant, using results by O'Neill (1978); once one finds that a particular set of modeling assumptions is flawed, a healthy process of model revision may be started. In fact, one might argue that model search/revision should always be an important component in the tool set of semi-supervised learning (Cozman et al., 2003a).

4.7   Conclusion

Given the possibility of performance degradation, it seems that some care must be taken in generative semi-supervised learning. Statements that are intuitively and provably true when models are "correct" may fail (sometimes miserably!) when models are "incorrect." Apparently mild modeling errors may cause unlabeled data to degrade performance, even in the absence of numerical errors, and even in situations where more labeled data would be beneficial. Examples of performance degradation from outliers and other common modeling errors can be easily concocted (Cozman et al., 2003b).

In the absence of modeling errors, labeled data differ from unlabeled data only on the "information they carry about the decisions associated with the decision regions" (Castelli and Cover, 1995). However, as we consider the possibility of modeling errors, labeled data and unlabeled data also differ in the biases they induce on estimates. The analysis in sections 4.2, 4.3, and 4.4 focused on asymptotic bias, a strategy that avoids distractions from finite sample effects and numerical errors. However, we note that finite sample effects may be important in practice, as we discuss in section 4.5.

methodology

At this point it is perhaps useful to add a few comments of methodological character. Given a pool of labeled and unlabeled data, generative semi-supervised learning is an attractive strategy. However, one should always start by learning a *supervised* classifier with the labeled data. This "baseline" classifier can then be compared to other semi-supervised classifiers through cross-validation or similar techniques. Whenever modeling assumptions seem inaccurate, unlabeled data can be used to test modeling assumptions. If time and resources are available, a model search should be conducted, attempting to reach a "correct" model — that is, a model where unlabeled data will be truly beneficial. Techniques discussed in section 4.6 can be employed in this setting. An additional step is to compare the baseline classifier to nongenerative methods. There are many semi-supervised nongenerative classifiers, as discussed in other chapters of this book. There are also a significant number of methods that use labeled and unlabeled data for different purposes — for example, methods where the unlabeled data are used only to conduct dimensionality reduction (chapter 12). However we should warn that a few empirical results in the literature suggest the possibility of performance degradation in nongenerative semi-supervised learning paradigms, such as transductive support vector machine (SVM)

(Zhang and Oles, 2000) and co-training (Ghani, 2002).

active learning

A final methodological comment concerns *active* learning — that is, the option of labeling selected samples among the unlabeled data. This option should be seriously considered whenever possible. It may be that the most profitable use of unlabeled data in a particular problem is exactly as a pool of samples from which some samples can be carefully selected and labeled. In general, we should take the value of a labeled sample to be considerably higher than the value of an unlabeled sample.

5 Probabilistic Semi-Supervised Clustering with Constraints

Sugato Basu   SUGATO@CS.UTEXAS.EDU
Mikhail Bilenko   MBILENKO@CS.UTEXAS.EDU
Arindam Banerjee   ABANERJE@ECE.UTEXAS.EDU
Raymond Mooney   MOONEY@CS.UTEXAS.EDU

In certain clustering tasks it is possible to obtain limited supervision in the form of pairwise constraints, i.e., pairs of instances labeled as belonging to same or different clusters. The resulting problem is known as *semi-supervised clustering*, an instance of semi-supervised learning stemming from a traditional unsupervised learning setting. Several algorithms exist for enhancing clustering quality by using supervision in the form of constraints. These algorithms typically utilize the pairwise constraints to either modify the clustering objective function or to learn the clustering distortion measure. This chapter describes an approach that employs hidden Markov random fields (HMRFs) as a probabilistic generative model for semi-supervised clustering, thereby providing a principled framework for incorporating constraint-based supervision into prototype-based clustering. The HMRF-based model allows the use of a broad range of clustering distortion measures, including Bregman divergences (e.g., squared Euclidean distance, Kullback-Leibler divergence) and directional distance measures (e.g., cosine distance), making it applicable to a number of domains. The model leads to the HMRF-KMEANS algorithm which minimizes an objective function derived from the joint probability of the model, and allows unification of constraint-based and distance-based semi-supervised clustering methods. Additionally, a two-phase active learning algorithm for selecting informative pairwise constraints in a query-driven framework is derived from the HMRF model, facilitating improved clustering performance with relatively small amounts of supervision from the user.

5.1 Introduction

semi-supervised
clustering with
constraints

This chapter focuses on _semi-supervised clustering with constraints_, the problem of partitioning a set of data points into a specified number of clusters when limited supervision is provided in the form of pairwise constraints. While clustering is traditionally considered to be a form of unsupervised learning since no class labels are given, inclusion of pairwise constraints makes it a semi-supervised learning task, where the performance of unsupervised clustering algorithms can be improved using the limited training data.

must-link and
cannot-link
constraints

Pairwise supervision is typically provided as _must-link_ and _cannot-link_ constraints on data points: a _must-link_ constraint indicates that both points in the pair should be placed in the same cluster, while a _cannot-link_ constraint indicates that two points in the pair should belong to different clusters. Alternatively, must-link and cannot-link constraints are sometimes called _equivalence_ and _nonequivalence_ constraints respectively. Typically, the constraints are "soft", that is, clusterings that violate them are undesirable but not prohibited.

In certain applications, supervision in the form of class labels may be unavailable, while pairwise constraints are easily obtained, creating the need for methods that exploit such supervision. For example, complete class labels may be unknown in the context of clustering for speaker identification in a conversation (Bar-Hillel et al., 2003), or clustering GPS data for lane-finding (Wagstaff et al., 2001). In some domains, pairwise constraints occur naturally, e.g., the database of interacting proteins (DIP) data set in biology contains information about proteins co-occurring in processes, which can be viewed as must-link constraints during clustering. Moreover, in an interactive learning setting, a user who is not a domain expert can sometimes provide feedback in the form of must-link and cannot-link constraints more easily than class labels, since providing constraints does not require the user to have significant prior knowledge about the categories in the data set.

constraint-based
and
distance-based
methods

Proposed methods for semi-supervised clustering fall into two general categories that we call _constraint-based_ and _distance-based_. Constraint-based methods use the provided supervision to guide the algorithm toward a data partitioning that avoids violating the constraints (Demiriz et al., 1999; Wagstaff et al., 2001; Basu et al., 2002). In distance-based approaches, an existing clustering algorithm that uses a particular distance function between points is employed; however, the distance function is parameterized and the parameter values are learned to bring must-linked points together and take cannot-linked points further apart (Bilenko and Mooney, 2003; Cohn et al., 2003; Klein et al., 2002; Xing et al., 2003).

This chapter describes an approach to semi-supervised clustering based on hidden Markov random fields (HMRFs) that combines the constraint-based and distance-based approaches in a unified probabilistic model. The probabilistic formulation leads to a clustering objective function derived from the joint probability of observed data points, their cluster assignments, and generative model parameters. This objective function can be optimized using an expectation-maximimzation

(EM)-style clustering algorithm, HMRF-KMEANS, that finds a local minimum of the objective function. HMRF-KMEANS can be used to perform semi-supervised clustering using a broad class of distortion (distance) functions,[1] namely *Bregman divergences* (Banerjee et al., 2005b), which include a wide variety of useful distances, e.g., KL divergence, squared Euclidean distance, I divergence, and Itakuro-Saito distance. In a number of applications, such as text clustering based on a vector-space model, a directional distance measure based on the cosine of the angle between vectors is more appropriate (Baeza-Yates and Ribeiro-Neto, 1999). Clustering algorithms have been developed that utilize distortion measures appropriate for directional data (Dhillon and Modha, 2001; Banerjee et al., 2005a), and the HMRF-KMEANS framework naturally extends them.

A practical aspect of semi-supervised clustering with constraints is how maximally informative constraints can be acquired in a real-life setting, where a limited set of queries can be made to a user in an interactive learning setting (McCallum and Nigam, 1998b). In that case, fewer queries should be posed to the user to obtain constraints that can significantly enhance the clustering accuracy. To this end, a new method for active learning is presented—it selects good pairwise constraints for semi-supervised clustering by asking queries to the user of the form "Are these two examples in same or different classes?" leading to improved clustering performance.

5.2   HMRF Model for Semi-Supervised Clustering

Partitional prototype-based clustering is the underlying unsupervised clustering setting under consideration. In such a setting, a set of data points is partitioned into a prespecified number of clusters, where each cluster has a representative (or "prototype"), so that a well-defined cost function, involving a distortion measure between the points and the cluster representatives, is minimized. A well-known unsupervised clustering algorithm that follows this framework is K-Means (MacQueen, 1967).

problem setting   Our semi-supervised clustering model considers a sample of n data points $X = (x_1, \ldots, x_n)$, each $x_i \in \mathbb{R}^d$ being a d-dimensional vector, with x_{im} representing its mth component. The model relies on a distortion measure d_A used to compute distance between points: $d_A : \mathbb{R}^d \times \mathbb{R}^d \to \mathbb{R}$, where A is the set of distortion measure parameters. Supervision is provided as two sets of pairwise constraints: must-link constraints $C_{ML} = \{(x_i, x_j)\}$ and cannot-link constraints $C_{CL} = \{(x_i, x_j)\}$, where $(x_i, x_j) \in C_{ML}$ implies that x_i and x_j are labeled as belonging to the same cluster, while $(x_i, x_j) \in C_{CL}$ implies that x_i and x_j are labeled as belonging to different clusters. The constraints may be accompanied by associated violation costs W, where w_{ij} represents the cost of violating the constraint between points x_i and x_j if such a constraint exists, that is, either $(x_i, x_j) \in C_{ML}$ or $(x_i, x_j) \in C_{CL}$. The task

---

1. In this chapter, "distance measure" is used synonymously with "distortion measure": both terms refer to the distance function used for clustering.

is to partition the data points X into K disjoint clusters $(X_1, \ldots, X_K)$ so that the total distortion between the points and the corresponding cluster representatives is minimized according to the given distortion measure d_A, while constraint violations are kept to a minimum.

5.2.1   HMRF Model Components

The HMRF probabilistic framework (Zhang et al., 2001) for semi-supervised constrained clustering consists of the following components:

- An *observable* set $X = (x_1, \ldots, x_n)$ corresponding to the given data points X. Note that we overload notation and use X to refer to both the given set of data points and their corresponding random variables.

- An *unobservable* (hidden) set $Y = (y_1, \ldots, y_n)$ corresponding to cluster assignments of points in X. Each hidden variable y_i encodes the cluster label of the point x_i and takes values from the set of cluster indices $(1, \ldots, K)$.

- An *unobservable* (hidden) set of generative model parameters Θ, which consists of distortion measure parameters A and cluster representatives $M = (\mu_1, \ldots, \mu_K)$: $\Theta = \{A, M\}$.

- An *observable* set of constraint variables $C = (c_{12}, c_{13}, \ldots, c_{n-1,n})$. Each c_{ij} is a tertiary variable taking on a value from the set $(-1, 0, 1)$, where $c_{ij} = 1$ indicates that $(x_i, x_j) \in C_{ML}$, $c_{ij} = -1$ indicates that $(x_i, x_j) \in C_{CL}$, and $c_{ij} = 0$ corresponds to pairs (x_i, x_j) that are not constrained.

Since constraints are fully observed and the described model does not attempt to model them generatively, the joint probability of X, Y, and Θ is conditioned on the constraints encoded by C.

HMRF example   Figure 5.1 shows a simple example of an HMRF. X consists of five data points with corresponding variables $(x_1, \ldots, x_5)$ that have cluster labels $Y = (y_1, \ldots, y_5)$, which may each take on values $(1, 2, 3)$ denoting the three clusters. Three pairwise constraints are provided: two must-link constraints (x_1, x_2) and (x_1, x_4), and one cannot-link constraint (x_2, x_3). Corresponding constraint variables are $c_{12} = 1$, $c_{14} = 1$, and $c_{23} = -1$; all other variables in C are set to zero. The task is to partition the five points into three clusters. Figure 5.1 demonstrates one possible clustering configuration which does not violate any constraints. The must-linked points x_1, x_2, and x_4 belong to cluster 1; the point x_3, which is cannot-linked with x_2, is assigned to cluster 2; x_5, which is not involved in any constraints, belongs to cluster 3.

5.2.2   Markov Random Field over Labels

Each hidden random variable $y_i \in Y$ representing the cluster label of $x_i \in X$ is associated with a set of neighbors N_i. The set of neighbors is defined as all points to which x_i is must-linked or cannot-linked: $N_i = \{y_j | (x_i, x_j) \in C_{ML} \text{ or } (x_i, x_j) \in$

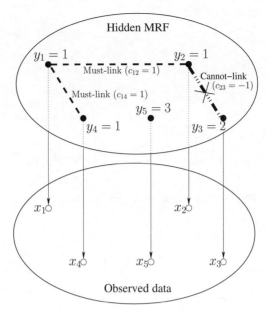

Figure 5.1   A hidden Markov random field.

C_{CL}}. The resulting random field defined over the hidden variables Y is a Markov random field (MRF), where the conditional probability distribution over the hidden variables obeys the Markov property:

Markov field over labels

$$\forall i, \ \mathrm{P}(y_i|Y - \{y_i\}, \Theta, C) = \mathrm{P}(y_i|N_i, \Theta, C). \tag{5.1}$$

Thus the conditional probability of y_i for each x_i, given the model parameters and the set of constraints, depends only on the cluster labels of the observed variables that are must-linked or cannot-linked to x_i. Then, by the Hammersley-Clifford theorem (Hammersley and Clifford, 1971), the prior probability of a particular label configuration Y can be expressed as a Gibbs distribution (Geman and Geman, 1984), so that

$$\mathrm{P}(Y|\Theta, C) = \frac{1}{Z}\exp\left(-v(Y)\right) = \frac{1}{Z}\exp\left(-\sum_{N_i \in N} v_{N_i}(Y)\right), \tag{5.2}$$

where N is the set of all neighborhoods, Z is the partition function (normalizing term), and $v(Y)$ is the overall label configuration potential function, which can be decomposed into a sum of functions $v_{N_i}(Y)$, each denoting the potential for every neighborhood N_i in the label configuration Y. Since the potentials for every neighborhood are based on pairwise constraints in C (and model parameters Θ),

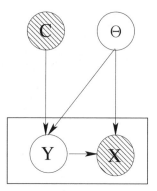

Figure 5.2   Graphical plate model of variable dependence.

the label configuration can be further decomposed as

$$P(Y|\Theta, C) = \frac{1}{Z} \exp\left(-\sum_{i,j} v(i,j)\right), \tag{5.3}$$

constraint
potential function

where each constraint potential function $v(i,j)$ has the following form:

$$v(i,j) = \begin{cases} w_{ij} f_{ML}(i,j) & \text{if } c_{ij} = 1 \text{ and } y_i \neq y_j, \\ w_{ij} f_{CL}(i,j) & \text{if } c_{ij} = -1 \text{ and } y_i = y_j, \\ 0 & \text{otherwise.} \end{cases} \tag{5.4}$$

The penalty functions f_{ML} and f_{CL} encode the lowered probability of observing configurations of Y where constraints encoded by C are violated. To this end, function f_{ML} penalizes violated must-link constraints and function f_{CL} penalizes violated cannot-link constraints. These functions are chosen to correspond with the distortion measure by employing same model parameters Θ, and will be described in detail in section 5.3. Overall, this formulation for observing the label assignment Y results in higher probabilities being assigned to configurations in which cluster assignments do not violate the provided constraints.

5.2.3   Joint Probability in HMRF

The joint probability of X, Y, and Θ, given C, in the described HMRF model can be factorized as follows:

$$P(X, Y, \Theta|C) = P(\Theta|C) \, P(Y|\Theta, C) \, P(X|Y, \Theta, C). \tag{5.5}$$

graphical plate
model

The graphical plate model (Buntine, 1994) of the dependence between the random variables in the HMRF is shown in figure 5.2, where the unshaded nodes represent the hidden variables, the shaded nodes are the observed variables, the directed links show dependencies between the variables, while the lack of an edge between two variables implies conditional independence. The prior probability of Θ is assumed to be independent of C. The probability of observing the label configuration Y depends on the constraints C and current generative model parameters Θ. Observed data points corresponding to variables X are generated using the model parameters Θ based on cluster labels Y, independent of the constraints C. The variables X are assumed to be mutually independent: each x_i is generated individually from a conditional probability distribution $P(x|y, \Theta)$. Then, the conditional probability $P(X|Y, \Theta, C)$ can be written as

$$P(X|Y, \Theta, C) = P(X|Y, \Theta) = \prod_{i=1}^{n} p(x_i|y_i, \Theta), \tag{5.6}$$

where $p(\cdot|y_i, \Theta)$ is the parameterized probability density function for the y_ith cluster, from which x_i is generated. This probability density is related to the clustering distortion measure d_A, as described below in section 5.2.4.

From Eqs. 5.3, 5.5, and 5.6, it follows that maximizing the joint probability on the HMRF is equivalent to maximizing

$$P(X, Y, \Theta|C) = P(\Theta) \left(\frac{1}{Z} \exp \left(- \sum_{c_{ij} \in C} v(i, j) \right) \right) \left(\prod_{i=1}^{n} p(x_i|y_i, \Theta) \right). \tag{5.7}$$

joint probability
factorization

The joint probability in Eq. (5.7) has three factors. The first factor describes a probability distribution over the model parameters preventing them from converging to degenerate values, thereby providing regularization. The second factor is the conditional probability of observing a particular label configuration given the provided constraints, effectively assigning a higher probability to configurations where the cluster assignments do not violate the constraints. Finally, the third factor is the conditional probability of generating the observed data points given the labels and the parameters: if *maximum-likelihood* (ML) estimation was performed on the HMRF, the goal would have been to maximize this term in isolation.

Overall, maximizing the joint HMRF probability in (5.7) is equivalent to jointly maximizing the likelihood of generating data points from the model and the probability of label assignments that respect the constraints, while regularizing the model parameters.

5.2.4   Semi-Supervised Clustering Objective Function on HMRF

Formulation 5.7 suggests a general framework for incorporating constraints into clustering. The choice of the conditional probability $p(x|y, \Theta)$ in a particular instantiation of the framework is directly connected to the choice of the distortion measure appropriate for the clustering task.

generative
probability for X

When considering the conditional probability $p(x_i|y_i, \Theta)$—the probability of generating a data point x_i from the y_ith cluster—our attention is restricted to probability densities from the exponential family, where the expectation parameter corresponding to the y_ith cluster is μ_{y_i}, the mean of the points of that cluster. Using this assumption and the bijection between regular exponential distributions and regular Bregman divergences (Banerjee et al., 2005b), the conditional density for observed data can be represented as

$$p(x_i|y_i, \Theta) = \frac{1}{Z_\Theta} \exp\bigl(-d_A(x_i, \mu_h)\bigr), \tag{5.8}$$

where $d_A(x_i, \mu_{y_i})$ is the Bregman divergence between x_i and μ_{y_i}, corresponding to the exponential density p, and Z_Θ is the normalizer.[2] Different clustering models fall into this exponential form:

- If x_i and μ_{y_i} are vectors in Euclidean space, and d_A is the square of the L_2 distance parameterized by a positive semidefinite weight matrix A ($d_A(x_i, \mu_{y_i}) = \|x_i - \mu_{y_i}\|_A^2$), then the cluster conditional probability is a Gaussian with covariance encoded by A^{-1} (Kearns et al., 1997);

- If x_i and μ_{y_i} are probability distributions and d_A is the KL divergence ($d_A(x_i, \mu_{y_i}) = \sum_{m=1}^d x_{im} \log \frac{x_{im}}{\mu_{y_i m}}$), then the cluster conditional probability is a multinomial distribution (Dhillon and Guan, 2003).

The relation in Eq. 5.8 holds even if d_A is not a Bregman divergence but a directional distance measure like cosine distance. For example, if x_i and μ_{y_i} are vectors of unit length and d_A is one minus the dot-product of the vectors ($d_A(x_i, \mu_{y_i}) = 1 - \frac{\sum_{m=1}^d x_{im}\mu_{y_i m}}{\|x_i\|\|\mu_{y_i}\|}$), then the cluster conditional probability is a von Mises Fisher (vMF) distribution with unit concentration parameter (Banerjee et al., 2005a), which is essentially the spherical analog of a Gaussian. The connection between specific distortion measures studied in this chapter and their corresponding cluster conditional probabilities is discussed in more detail in section 5.3.3.

Putting Eq. 5.8 into 5.7 and taking logarithms gives the following cluster objective function, minimizing which is equivalent to maximizing the joint probability over the HMRF in Eq. 5.7:

$$\mathcal{J}_{\text{obj}} = \sum_{x_i \in X} d_A(x_i, \mu_{y_i}) + \sum_{c_{ij} \in C} v(i, j) - \log \mathrm{P}(\Theta) + \log Z + n \log Z_\Theta. \tag{5.9}$$

Thus, the task is to minimize $\mathcal{J}_{\text{obj}}$ over the hidden variables Y and Θ (note that given Y, the means $M = (\mu_1, \ldots, \mu_K)$ are uniquely determined).

---

2. When $A = I$ (identity matrix), the bijection result (Banerjee et al., 2005b) ensures that the normalizer Z_Θ is 1. In general, there are additional multiplicative terms that depend only on x, and hence can be safely ignored for parameter estimation purposes.

5.3   HMRF-KMeans **Algorithm**

Since the cluster assignments and the generative model parameters are unknown in a clustering setting, minimizing Eq. 5.9 is an "incomplete-data problem". A popular solution technique for such problems is the *expectation-maximization* (EM) algorithm (Dempster et al., 1977). The K-Means algorithm (MacQueen, 1967) is known to be equivalent to the EM algorithm with hard clustering assignments, under certain assumptions (Kearns et al., 1997; Basu et al., 2002; Banerjee et al., 2005b). This section describes a K-Means-type hard partitional clustering algorithm, HMRF-KMeans, that finds a local minimum of the semi-supervised clustering objective function $\mathcal{J}_{\text{obj}}$ in Eq. 5.9.

5.3.1   Normalizing Component Estimation

Before describing the details of the clustering algorithm, it is important to consider the normalizing components: the MRF partition function $\log Z$ and the distortion function normalizer $\log Z_{\Theta}$ in Eq. 5.9. Estimation of the partition function cannot be performed in closed form for most nontrivial dependency structures, and approximate inference methods must be employed for computing it (Wainwright and Jordan, 2003).

normalizer approximation

Estimation of the distortion normalizer $\log Z_{\Theta}$ depends on the distortion measure d_A used by the model. This chapter considers three parameterized distortion measures: parameterized squared Euclidean distance, parameterized cosine distance, and parameterized Kullback-Leibler (KL) divergence. For Euclidean distance, Z_{Θ} can be estimated in closed form, and this estimation is performed while minimizing the clustering objective function $\mathcal{J}_{\text{obj}}$ in Eq. 5.9. For the other distortion measures, estimating the distortion normalizer Z_{Θ} cannot be performed in closed form, and approximate inference must be again used (Banerjee et al., 2005a).

Since approximate inference methods can be very expensive computationally, two simplifying assumptions can be made: the MRF partition function may be considered to be constant in the clustering process, and the distortion normalizer may be assumed constant for all distortion measures that do not provide its closed-form estimate. With these assumptions, the objective function $\mathcal{J}_{\text{obj}}$ in Eq. 5.9 no longer exactly corresponds to a joint probability on an HMRF. However, minimizing this simplified objective has been shown to work well empirically (Bilenko et al., 2004; Basu et al., 2004b). However, if in some applications it is important to preserve the semantics of the underlying joint probability model, then the normalizers Z and Z_{Θ} must be estimated by approximate inference methods.

5.3.2   Parameter Priors

Following the definition of Θ in section 5.2.1, the prior term $\log \mathrm{P}(\Theta)$ in (5.9) and the subsequent equations can be factored as follows:

$$\log \mathrm{P}(\Theta) = \log\big(\mathrm{P}(A)\mathrm{P}(M)\big) = \log \mathrm{P}(A) + P_M,$$

where the distortion parameters A are assumed to be independant of the cluster centroids $M = (\mu_1, \ldots, \mu_K)$, and uniform priors are considered over the cluster centroids (leading to the constant term P_M). For different distortion measures, parameter values may exist that lead to degenerate solutions of the optimization problem. For example, for squared Euclidean distance, the zero matrix $A = \mathbf{0}$ is one such solution. To prevent degenerate solutions, $\mathrm{P}(A)$ is used to regularize the parameter values using a prior distribution.

Rayleigh prior
If the standard Gaussian prior was used on the parameters of the distortion function, it would allow the parameters to take negative values. Since it is desirable to constrain the parameter values to be non-negative, it is more appropriate to use the Rayleigh distribution (Papoulis and Pillai, 2001). Assuming independence of the parameters $a_{ij} \in A$, the prior term based on the Rayleigh distribution is the following:

$$\mathrm{P}(A) = \prod_{a_{ij} \in A} \frac{a_{ij} \exp\left(-\frac{a_{ij}^2}{s^2}\right)}{s^2}, \tag{5.10}$$

where s is the width parameter.

5.3.3   Adaptive Distortion Measures

Selecting an appropriate distortion measure d_A for a clustering task typically involves knowledge about properties of the particular domain and data set. For example, squared Euclidean distance is most appropriate for low-dimensional data with distribution close to Gaussian, while cosine distance best captures distance between data described by vectors in high-dimensional space where differences in angles are important but vector lengths are not.

distortion
measure selection
Distortion measures from two families are considered in this chapter: *Bregman divergences* (Banerjee et al., 2005b), which include parameterized squared Euclidean distance and KL divergence, and distortion measures based on *directional* similarity functions, which include cosine similarity and Pearson's correlation (Mardia and Jupp, 2000). The distortion measure for directional functions is chosen to be the directional similarity measure subtracted from a constant sufficiently large so that the resulting value is non-negative. For both Bregman divergences and cosine distance, there exist efficient K-Means-type iterative relocation algorithms that minimize the corresponding clustering objective (Banerjee et al., 2005a,b), which the HMRF-KMEANS naturally extends to incorporate pairwise supervision.

For many realistic data sets, off-the-shelf distortion measures may fail to capture the correct notion of similarity in a clustering setting. While some unsupervised measures like squared Euclidean distance and Pearson's distance attempt to correct distortion estimates using the global mean and variance of the data set, these measures may still fail to estimate distances accurately if the attributes' true contributions to the distance are not correlated with their variance. Several semi-supervised clustering approaches exist that incorporate adaptive distortion measures, including parameterizations of Jensen-Shannon divergence (Cohn et al., 2003) and squared Euclidean distance (Bar-Hillel et al., 2003; Xing et al., 2003). However, these techniques use only constraints to learn the distortion measure parameters and exclude unlabeled data from the parameter learning step, as well as separate the parameter learning step from the clustering process.

adaptive distortion measure

Going a step further, the HMRF model provides an integrated framework which incorporates *both* learning the distortion measure parameters and constraint-sensitive cluster assignments. In HMRF-KMEANS, the parameters of the distortion measure are learned iteratively as the clustering progresses, utilizing both unlabeled data and pairwise constraints. The parameters are modified to decrease the parameterized distance between violated must-linked constraints and increase it between violated cannot-link constraints, while allowing constraint violations if they accompany a more cohesive clustering.

This section presents three examples of distortion functions and their parameterizations for use with HMRF-KMEANS: squared Euclidean distance, cosine distance, and KL divergence. Through parameterization, each of these functions becomes adaptive in a semi-supervised clustering setting, permitting clusters of varying shapes.

constraint potential function

Once a distortion measure is chosen for a given domain, the functions f_{ML} and f_{CL}, introduced in section 5.2.2 for penalizing must-link and cannot-link constraint violations, respectively, must be defined. These functions typically follow a functional form identical or similar to the corresponding distortion measure, and are chosen as follows:

$$f_{ML}(i,j) = \varphi(i,j), \tag{5.11}$$

$$f_{CL}(i,j) = \varphi^{\max} - \varphi(i,j), \tag{5.12}$$

where $\varphi : X \times X \to \mathbb{R}^+$ is a non-negative function that penalizes constraint violation, and $\varphi^{\max}$ is an upper bound on the maximum value of φ over any pair of points in the data set; examples of such bounds for specific distortion functions are shown below. The function φ is chosen to correlate with the distortion measure, assigning higher penalties to violations of must-link constraints between points that are distant with respect to the current parameter values of the distortion measure. Conversely, penalties for violated cannot-link constraints are higher for points that have low distance between them. With this formulation of the penalty functions, constraint violations lead to changes in the distortion measure parameters that attempt to mend the violations. The φ function for different clustering distortion measures is discussed in the following sections.

Accordingly, the potential function $v(i, j)$ in (5.4) becomes

$$v(i, j) = \begin{cases} w_{ij}\varphi(x_i, x_j) & \text{if } c_{ij} = 1 \text{ and } y_i \neq y_j \\ w_{ij}\left(\varphi^{\max} - \varphi(x_i, x_j)\right) & \text{if } c_{ij} = -1 \text{ and } y_i = y_j \\ 0 & \text{otherwise} \end{cases} , \qquad (5.13)$$

and the objective function for semi-supervised clustering in (5.9) can be expressed as

$$\mathcal{J}_{\text{obj}} = \sum_{x_i \in X} d_A(x_i, \mu(i)) + \sum_{\substack{(x_i, x_j) \in C_{ML} \\ s.t. \ y_i \neq y_j}} w_{ij}\varphi(x_i, x_j)$$

$$+ \sum_{\substack{(x_i, x_j) \in C_{CL} \\ s.t. \ y_i = y_j}} w_{ij}\left(\varphi^{\max} - \varphi(x_i, x_j)\right) - \log \mathrm{P}(A) + n \log Z_\Theta. \qquad (5.14)$$

Note that as discussed in section 5.3.1, the MRF partition function term $\log Z$ has been dropped from the objective function.

5.3.3.1 *Parameterized Squared Euclidean Distance*

Squared Euclidean distance is parameterized using a symmetric positive-definite matrix A as follows:

$$d_{euc_A}(x_i, x_j) = \|x_i - x_j\|_A^2 = (x_i - x_j)^T A(x_i - x_j). \qquad (5.15)$$

This form of the parameterized squared Euclidean distance is equivalent to Mahalanobis distance with an arbitrary positive semidefinite weight matrix A in place of the inverse covariance matrix, and it was previously used for semi-supervised clustering by (Xing et al., 2003) and (Bar-Hillel et al., 2003). Such formulation can also be viewed as a projection of every instance x onto a space spanned by $A^{1/2}$: $x \to A^{1/2}x$.

To use parameterized squared Euclidean distance as the adaptive distortion measure for clustering, the φ function that penalizes constraint violations is defined as $\varphi(x_i, x_j) = d_{euc_A}(x_i, x_j)$. One possible initialization of the upper bound for cannot-link penalties is $\varphi^{\max}_{euc_A} = \sum_{(x_i, x_j) \in C_{CL}} d_{euc_A}(x_i, x_j)$, which guarantees that the penalty is always positive. Using these definitions along with (5.14), the following objective function is obtained for semi-supervised clustering with adaptive squared Euclidean distance:

$$\mathcal{J}_{euc_A} = \sum_{x_i \in X} d_{euc_A}(x_i, \mu(i)) + \sum_{\substack{(x_i, x_j) \in C_{ML} \\ s.t. \ y_i \neq y_j}} w_{ij} d_{euc_A}(x_i, x_j)$$

$$+ \sum_{\substack{(x_i, x_j) \in C_{CL} \\ s.t. \ y_i = y_j}} w_{ij} \left(\varphi_{euc_A}^{\max} - d_{euc_A}(x_i, x_j) \right) - \log \mathrm{P}(A) - n \log \det(A).$$

$$(5.16)$$

Note that as discussed in section 5.3.1, the $\log Z_\Theta$ term is computable in closed-form for a Gaussian distribution with covariance matrix A^{-1}, which is the underlying cluster conditional probability distribution for parameterized squared Euclidean distance. The $\log \det(A)$ term (5.16) corresponds to the $\log Z_\Theta$ term in this case.

5.3.3.2   *Parameterized Cosine Distance*

Cosine distance can be parameterized using a symmetric positive-definite matrix A, which leads to the following distortion measure:

$$d_{\cos_A}(x_i, x_j) = 1 - \frac{x_i^T A x_j}{\|x_i\|_A \|x_j\|_A}. \tag{5.17}$$

Because for realistic high-dimensional domains computing the full matrix A would be computationally expensive, a diagonal matrix is considered in this case, such that $a = diag(A)$ is a vector of positive weights.

To use parameterized squared Euclidean distance as the adaptive distortion measure for clustering, the φ function is defined as $\varphi(x_i, x_j) = d_{\cos_A}(x_i, x_j)$. Using this definition along with Eq. 5.14, and setting $\varphi^{\max} = 1$ as an upper bound on $\varphi(x_i, x_j)$, the following objective function is obtained for semi-supervised clustering with adaptive cosine distance:

$$\mathcal{J}_{\cos_A} = \sum_{x_i \in X} d_{\cos_A}(x_i, \mu(i)) + \sum_{\substack{(x_i, x_j) \in C_{ML} \\ s.t. \ y_i \neq y_j}} w_{ij} d_{\cos_A}(x_i, x_j)$$

$$+ \sum_{\substack{(x_i, x_j) \in C_{CL} \\ s.t. \ y_i = y_j}} w_{ij} \left(1 - d_{\cos_A}(x_i, x_j) \right) - \log \mathrm{P}(A). \tag{5.18}$$

Note that as discussed in section 5.3.1, it is difficult to compute the $\log Z_\Theta$ term in closed form for parameterized cosine distance. So, the simplifying assumption is made that $\log Z_\Theta$ is constant during the clustering process and the normalizer term is dropped from (5.18).

5.3.3.3   *Parameterized KL Divergence*

In certain domains, data are described by probability distributions, e.g., text documents can be represented as probability distributions over words generated by a multinomial model (Pereira et al., 1993). KL divergence is a widely used distance measure for such data: $d_{KL}(x_i, x_j) = \sum_{m=1}^{d} x_{im} \log \frac{x_{im}}{x_{jm}}$, where x_i and x_j are probability distributions over d events: $\sum_{m=1}^{d} x_{im} = \sum_{m=1}^{d} x_{jm} = 1$. In previous work, Cohn et al. (2003) parameterized KL divergence by multiplying the mth component by a weight γ_m: $d'_{KL}(x_i, x_j) = \sum_{m=1}^{d} \gamma_m x_{im} \log \frac{x_{im}}{x_{jm}}$.

I divergence

In our framework, KL distance is parameterized using a diagonal matrix A, where $a = diag(A)$ is a vector of positive weights. This parameterization of KL by A converts it to I divergence, a function that also belongs to the class of Bregman divergences (Banerjee et al., 2005b). I divergence has the form: $d_I(x_i, x_j) = \sum_{m=1}^{d} x_{im} \log \frac{x_{im}}{x_{jm}} - \sum_{m=1}^{d} (x_{im} - x_{jm})$, where x_i and x_j no longer need to be probability distributions but can be any non-negative vectors.[3] The following parameterization of KL is used:

$$d_{I_A}(x_i, x_j) = \sum_{m=1}^{d} a_m x_{im} \log \frac{x_{im}}{x_{jm}} - \sum_{m=1}^{d} a_m (x_{im} - x_{jm}), \qquad (5.19)$$

which can be interpreted as scaling every component of the original probability distribution by a weight contained in the corresponding component of A, and then taking I divergence between the transformed distributions.

For every distortion measure, the clustering framework described in section 5.2.4 requires defining an appropriate constraint potential function that is symmetric, since the constraint pairs are unordered. To meet this requirement, a sum of weighted I divergences from x_i and x_j to the mean vector $\frac{x_i + x_j}{2}$ is used. This parameterized I divergence to the mean, d_{IM_A}, is analogous to Jensen-Shannon divergence (Cover and Thomas, 1991), the symmetric KL divergence to the mean, and is defined as follows:

$$d_{IM_A}(x_i, x_j) = \sum_{m=1}^{d} a_m \left(x_{im} \log \frac{2x_{im}}{x_{im} + x_{jm}} + x_{jm} \log \frac{2x_{jm}}{x_{im} + x_{jm}} \right). \qquad (5.20)$$

To use parameterized squared Euclidean distance as the adaptive distortion measure for clustering, the φ function is defined as $\varphi(x_i, x_j) = d_{IM_A}(x_i, x_j)$. Using this definition along with Eq. 5.14, the following objective function is obtained for semi-supervised clustering with adaptive KL distance:

---

3. For probability distributions, I divergence and KL divergence are equivalent.

$$\mathcal{J}_{I_A} = \sum_{x_i \in X} d_{I_A}(x_i, \mu(i)) + \sum_{\substack{(x_i, x_j) \in C_{ML} \\ s.t. \ y_i \neq y_j}} w_{ij} d_{IM_A}(x_i, x_j)$$

$$+ \sum_{\substack{(x_i, x_j) \in C_{CL} \\ s.t. \ y_i = y_j}} w_{ij} \left(d_{IM_A}^{\max} - d_{IM_A}(x_i, x_j) \right) - \log \mathrm{P}(A). \tag{5.21}$$

The upper bound $d_{IM_A}^{\max}$ can be initialized as $d_{IM_A}^{\max} = \sum_{m=1}^{d} a_m$, which follows from the fact that unweighted Jensen-Shannon divergence is bounded above by 1 (Lin, 1991).

Note that as discussed in section 5.3.1, it is difficult to compute the $\log Z_\Theta$ term in closed form for parameterized KL distance. So, analogously to the parameterized cosine distance case, the simplifying assumption is made that $\log Z_\Theta$ is constant during the clustering process and that term is dropped from Eq. 5.21.

5.3.4   EM Framework

As discussed earlier in this section, $\mathcal{J}_{\mathrm{obj}}$ can be minimized by a K-Means-type iterative algorithm HMRF-KMEANS. The outline of the algorithm is presented in algorithm 5.1. The basic idea of HMRF-KMEANS is as follows: the constraints are used to get a good initialization of the clustering. Then in the E step, given the current cluster representatives, every data point is reassigned to the cluster which minimizes its contribution to $\mathcal{J}_{\mathrm{obj}}$. In the M step, the cluster representatives $M = (\mu_1, \ldots, \mu_K)$ are re-estimated from the cluster assignments to minimize $\mathcal{J}_{\mathrm{obj}}$ for the current assignment. The clustering distortion measure d_A is subsequently updated in the M step to reduce the objective function by modifying the parameters A of the distortion measure.

generalized EM   Note that this corresponds to the generalized EM algorithm (Neal and Hinton, 1998; Dempster et al., 1977), where the objective function is reduced but not necessarily minimized in the M step. Effectively, the E step minimizes $\mathcal{J}_{\mathrm{obj}}$ over cluster assignments Y, the M step (A) minimizes $\mathcal{J}_{\mathrm{obj}}$ over cluster representatives M, and the M step (B) reduces $\mathcal{J}_{\mathrm{obj}}$ over the parameters A of the distortion measure d_A. The E step and the M step are repeated till a specified convergence criterion is reached. The specific details of the E step and M step are discussed in the following sections.

5.3.5   Initialization

Good initial centroids are essential for the success of partitional clustering algorithms such as K-Means. Good centroids are inferred from both the constraints and unlabeled data during initialization. For this, a two-stage initialization process is used.

Algorithm 5.1 HMRF-KMEANS algorithm.

Input: Set of data points $X = (x_1, \ldots, x_n)$, number of clusters K, set of
   constraints C, constraint violation costs W, distortion measure D.
Output: Disjoint K-partitioning $(X_1, \ldots, X_K)$ of X such that objective
   function $\mathcal{J}_{\text{obj}}$ in Eqn. (3.9) is (locally) minimized.
Method:
1. Initialize the K clusters centroids $M^{(0)} = (\mu_1^{(0)}, \ldots, \mu_K^{(0)})$, set t $\leftarrow$ 0
2. Repeat until *convergence*
2a.   **E-step:** Given centroids $M^{(t)}$ and distortion parameters $A^{(t)}$,
      re-assign cluster labels $Y^{(t+1)} = (y_1^{(t+1)}, \ldots, y_n^{(t+1)})$ on X to minimize $\mathcal{J}_{\text{obj}}$.
2b.   **M-step(A):** Given cluster labels $Y^{(t+1)}$ and distortion parameters $A^{(t+1)}$,
      re-calculate centroids $M^{(t+1)} = (\mu_1^{(t+1)}, \ldots, \mu_K^{(t+1)})$ to minimize $\mathcal{J}_{\text{obj}}$.
2c.   **M-step(B):** Given cluster labels $Y^{(t+1)}$ and centroids $M^{(t+1)}$,
      re-estimate parameters $A^{(t+1)}$ of the distortion measure to reduce $\mathcal{J}_{\text{obj}}$.
2d.   t $\leftarrow$ t+1

Neighborhood Inference   At first, the transitive closure of the must-link constraints is taken to get connected components consisting of points connected by must-links. Let there be λ connected components, which are used to create λ neighborhoods. These correspond to the must-link neighborhoods in the MRF over the hidden cluster variables.

Cluster Selection   The λ neighborhood sets produced in the first stage are used to initialize the HMRF-MEANS algorithm. If $\lambda = K$, λ cluster centers are initialized with the centroids of all the λ neighborhood sets. If $\lambda < K$, λ clusters are initialized from the neighborhoods, and the remaining $K - \lambda$ clusters are initialized with points obtained by random perturbations of the global centroid of X. If $\lambda > K$, a weighted variant of farthest-first traversal (Hochbaum and Shmoys, 1985) is applied to the centroids of the λ neighborhoods, where the weight of each centroid is proportional to the size of the corresponding neighborhood. Weighted farthest-first traversal selects neighborhoods that are relatively far apart as well as large in size, and the chosen neighborhoods are set as the K initial cluster centroids for HMRF-KMEANS.

   Overall, this two-stage initialization procedure is able to take into account both unlabeled and labeled data to obtain cluster representatives that provide a good initial partitioning of the data set.

5.3.6   E Step

In the E step, assignments of data points to clusters are updated using the current estimates of the cluster representatives. In the general unsupervised K-Means algorithm, there is no interaction between the cluster labels, and the E step is a simple assignment of every point to the cluster representative that is nearest to it according to the clustering distortion measure. In contrast, the HMRF model incorporates interaction between the cluster labels defined by the random field over the hidden variables. As a result, computing the assignment of data points to cluster representatives to find the global minimum of the objective function, given the cluster centroids, is NP-hard in any nontrivial HMRF model, similar to other graphical models such as MRFs and belief networks (Roth, 1996).

greedy ICM
assignment

There exist several techniques for computing cluster assignments that approximate the optimal solution in this framework, e.g., iterated conditional modes (ICM) (Besag, 1986; Zhang et al., 2001), belief propagation (Pearl, 1988; Segal et al., 2003b), and linear programming relaxation (Kleinberg and Tardos, 1999). ICM is a greedy strategy that sequentially updates the cluster assignment of each point, keeping the assignments for the other points fixed. In many settings it has comparable performance to more expensive global approximation techniques, but is computationally more efficient; it has been compared with several other approaches by Bilenko and Basu (2004), while in more recent work Lange et al. (2005) have described an alternative efficient method based on the mean-field approximation. ICM performs sequential cluster assignment for all the points in random order. Each point x_i is assigned to the cluster representative μ_h that minimizes the point's contribution to the objective function $\mathcal{J}_{obj}(x_i, \mu_h)$:

$$
\mathcal{J}_{\text{obj}}(x_i, \mu_h) = d_A(x_i, \mu_h) + \sum_{\substack{(x_i, x_j) \in C^i_{ML} \\ s.t. \ y_i \neq y_j}} w_{ij} \varphi(x_i, x_j)
$$
$$
+ \sum_{\substack{(x_i, x_j) \in C^i_{CL} \\ s.t. \ y_i = y_j}} w_{ij} \left(\varphi^{\max} - \varphi(x_i, x_j) \right) - \log \mathrm{P}(A), \tag{5.22}
$$

where C^i_{ML} and C^i_{CL} are the subsets of C_{ML} and C_{CL} respectively in which x_i appears in the constraints. The optimal assignment for every point minimizes the distortion between the point and its cluster representative (first term of $\mathcal{J}_{\text{obj}}$) along with incurring a minimal penalty for constraint violations caused by this assignment (second and third terms of $\mathcal{J}_{\text{obj}}$). After all points are assigned, they are randomly reordered, and the assignment process is repeated. This process proceeds until no point changes its cluster assignment between two successive iterations.

Overall, the assignment of points to clusters incorporates pairwise supervision by discouraging constraint violations proportionally to their severity, which guides the algorithm toward a desirable partitioning of the data.

5.3.7 M Step

The M step of the algorithm consists of two parts: centroid re-estimation and distortion measure parameter update.

5.3.7.1   M Step (A): Centroid Re-estimation

In the first part of the M step, the cluster centroids M are re-estimated from points currently assigned to them, to decrease the objective function $\mathcal{J}_{\text{obj}}$ in Eq. 5.9. For Bregman divergences and cosine distance, the cluster representative calculated in the M step of the EM algorithm is equivalent to the expectation value over the points in that cluster, which is equal to their arithmetic mean (Banerjee et al., 2005a,b). Additionally, it has been experimentally demonstrated that for clustering with distribution-based measures, e.g., KL divergence, smoothing cluster representatives by a prior using a deterministic annealing schedule leads to considerable improvements (Dhillon and Guan, 2003). With smoothing controlled by a positive parameter α, each cluster representative μ_h is estimated as follows when d_{I_A} is the distortion measure:

$$\mu_h^{(I_A)} = \frac{1}{1+\alpha}\left(\frac{\sum_{x_i \in X_h} x_i}{|X_h|} + \frac{\alpha}{n}\mathbf{1}\right). \tag{5.23}$$

For directional measures, each cluster representative is the arithmetic mean projected onto unit sphere (Banerjee et al., 2005a). Taking the distortion parameters into account, centroids are estimated as follows when $d_{\cos_A}$ is the distortion measure:

$$\frac{\mu_h^{(\cos_A)}}{\left\|\mu_h^{(\cos_A)}\right\|_A} = \frac{\sum_{x_i \in X_h} x_i}{\left\|\sum_{x_i \in X_h} x_i\right\|_A}. \tag{5.24}$$

5.3.7.2   M Step (B): Update of Distortion Parameters

In the second part of the M step, the parameters of the parameterized distortion measure are updated to decrease the objective function. In general, for parameterized Bregman divergences or directional distances with general parameter priors, it is difficult to attain a closed-form update for the parameters of the distortion measure that can minimize the objective function.[4] Gradient descent provides an alternative avenue for learning the distortion measure parameters.

gradient update   For squared Euclidean distance, a full parameter matrix A is updated during
for full A   gradient descent using the rule: $A = A + \eta\frac{\partial\mathcal{J}_{euc_A}}{\partial A}$ (where η is the learning rate). Using (5.16), $\frac{\partial\mathcal{J}_{euc_A}}{\partial A}$ can be expressed as

---

4. For the specific case of parameterized squared Euclidean distance, a closed-form update of the parameters can be obtained (Bilenko et al., 2004).

$$\frac{\partial \mathfrak{J}_{euc_A}}{\partial A} = \sum_{x_i \in X} \frac{\partial d_{euc_A}(x_i, \mu(i))}{\partial A} + \sum_{\substack{(x_i, x_j) \in C_{ML} \\ s.t. \ y_i \neq y_j}} w_{ij} \frac{\partial d_{euc_A}(x_i, x_j)}{\partial A}$$

$$+ \sum_{\substack{(x_i, x_j) \in C_{CL} \\ s.t. \ y_i = y_j}} w_{ij} \left[\frac{\partial \varphi_{euc_A}^{\max}}{\partial A} - \frac{\partial d_{euc_A}(x_i, x_j)}{\partial A} \right] - \frac{\partial \log \mathrm{P}(A)}{\partial A} - n \frac{\partial \log \det(A)}{\partial A}.$$

$$(5.25)$$

The gradient of the parameterized squared Euclidean distance is given by

$$\frac{\partial d_{euc_A}(x_i, x_j)}{\partial A} = (x_i - x_j)(x_i - x_j)^T.$$

The derivative of the upper bound $\varphi_{euc_A}^{\max}$ is $\frac{\partial \varphi_{euc_A}^{\max}}{\partial A} = \sum_{(x_i, x_j) \in C_{CL}} (x_i - x_j)(x_i - x_j)^T$ if $\varphi_{euc_A}^{\max}$ is computed as described in section 5.3.3.1.[5]

When Rayleigh priors are used on the set of parameters A, the partial derivative of the log-prior with respect to every individual parameter $a_m \in A$, $\frac{\partial \log \mathrm{P}(A)}{\partial a_m}$, is given by

$$\frac{\partial \log \mathrm{P}(A)}{\partial a_m} = \frac{1}{a_m} - \frac{a_m}{s^2}.$$

$$(5.26)$$

The gradient of the distortion normalizer $\log \det(A)$ term is as follows:

$$\frac{\partial \log \det(A)}{\partial A} = 2A^{-1} - diag(A^{-1}).$$

$$(5.27)$$

gradient update for diagonal A

For parameterized cosine distance and KL divergence, a diagonal parameter matrix A is considered, where $a = diag(A)$ is a vector of positive weights. During gradient descent, each weight a_m is individually updated as $a_m = a_m + \eta \frac{\partial \mathfrak{J}_{obj}}{\partial a_m}$ (η is the learning rate). Using (5.14), $\frac{\partial \mathfrak{J}_{obj}}{\partial a_m}$ can be expressed as

$$\frac{\partial \mathfrak{J}_{obj}}{\partial a_m} = \sum_{x_i \in X} \frac{\partial d_A(x_i, \mu(i))}{\partial a_m} + \sum_{\substack{(x_i, x_j) \in C_{ML} \\ s.t. \ y_i \neq y_j}} w_{ij} \frac{\partial \varphi(x_i, x_j)}{\partial a_m}$$

$$+ \sum_{\substack{(x_i, x_j) \in C_{CL} \\ s.t. \ y_i = y_j}} w_{ij} \left[\frac{\partial \varphi^{\max}}{\partial a_m} - \frac{\partial \varphi(x_i, x_j)}{\partial a_m} \right] - \frac{\partial \log \mathrm{P}(A)}{\partial a_m}.$$

$$(5.28)$$

---

5. In practice, one can initialize $\varphi_{euc_A}^{\max}$ with a sufficiently large constant, which would make its derivative zero. Accordingly, an extra condition must be then inserted into the algorithm to guarantee that penalties for violated cannot-link constraints are never negative, in which case the constant must be increased.

Calculation of the gradient $\frac{\partial \mathcal{J}_{\text{obj}}}{\partial a_m}$ for cosine distance and KL divergence, which are parameterized by a diagonal matrix A, needs the gradients of the corresponding distortion measures and constraint potential functions, which are

$$
\begin{aligned}
\frac{\partial d_{\cos_A}(x_i, x_j)}{\partial a_m} &= \frac{x_{im} x_{jm} \|x_i\|_A \|x_j\|_A - x_i^T A x_j \frac{x_{im}^2 \|x_j\|_A^2 + x_{jm}^2 \|x_i\|_A^2}{2\|x_i\|_A \|x_j\|_A}}{\|x_i\|_A^2 \|x_j\|_A^2}, \\
\frac{\partial d_{I_A}(x_i, x_j)}{\partial a_m} &= x_{im} \log \frac{x_{im}}{x_{jm}} - (x_{im} - x_{jm}), \\
\frac{\partial d_{IM_A}(x_i, x_j)}{\partial a_m} &= x_{im} \log \frac{2x_{im}}{x_{im} + x_{jm}} + x_{jm} \log \frac{2x_{jm}}{x_{im} + x_{jm}},
\end{aligned}
\tag{5.29}
$$

while the gradient of the upper bound $\frac{\partial \varphi^{\max}}{\partial a_m}$ is 0 for parameterized cosine and 1 for parameterized KL divergence, as follows from the expressions for these constants in sections 5.3.3.2 and 5.3.3.3.

Overall, the distance learning step results in modifying the distortion measure so that data points in violated must-link constraints are brought closer together, while points in violated cannot-link constraints are pulled apart. This process leads to a transformed data space that facilitates partitioning of the unlabeled data, by attempting to mend the constraint violations as well as reflecting the natural variance in the data. See part IV (chapters 15–17) for several alternative techniques that change the data representation leading to better estimates of similarity between data points.

5.3.8 Convergence of HMRF-KMeans

The HMRF-KMeans algorithm alternates between updating the assignment of points to clusters, and updating the parameters. Since all updates ensure a decrease in the objective function, each iteration of HRMF-KMeans monotonically decreases the objective function. Let us inspect each step in the update to ensure that this is indeed the case.

For analyzing the cluster assignment step, let us consider Eq. 5.14. Each point x_i moves to a new cluster h only if the following component, contributed by the point x_i, is decreased with the move:

$$
d_A(x_i, \mu(i)) + \sum_{\substack{(x_i, x_j) \in C_{ML}^i \\ s.t.\ y_i \neq y_j}} w_{ij} \varphi(x_i, x_j) + \sum_{\substack{(x_i, x_j) \in C_{CL}^i \\ s.t.\ y_i = y_j}} w_{ij} \big(\varphi^{\max} - \varphi(x_i, x_j)\big) - \log \mathrm{P}(A).
$$

Given a set of centroids and distortion parameters, the new cluster assignment of points will decrease $\mathcal{J}_{\text{obj}}$ or keep it unchanged.

For analyzing the centroid re-estimation step, let us consider an equivalent form of Eq. 5.14:

$$\mathfrak{J}_{\text{obj}} = \sum_{h=1}^{K} \sum_{x_i \in X_h} d_A(x_i, \mu_h) + \sum_{\substack{(x_i, x_j) \in C_{ML}^i \\ s.t. \ y_i \neq y_j}} w_{ij} \varphi(x_i, x_j)$$

$$+ \sum_{\substack{(x_i, x_j) \in C_{CL}^i \\ s.t. \ y_i = y_j}} w_{ij} \left(\varphi^{\max} - \varphi(x_i, x_j) \right) - \log \mathrm{P}(A). \tag{5.30}$$

Each cluster centroid μ_h is re-estimated by taking the mean of the points in the partition X_h, which minimizes the component $\sum_{x_i \in X_h} d_A(x_i, \mu_h)$ of $\mathfrak{J}_{\text{obj}}$ in Eq. 5.30 contributed by the partition X_h. The constraint potential and the prior term in the objective function do not take a part in centroid re-estimation, because they are not explicit functions of the centroid. So, given the cluster assignments and the distortion parameters, $\mathfrak{J}_{\text{obj}}$ will decrease or remain the same in this step.

For the parameter estimation step, the gradient-descent update of the parameters in M step (B) decreases $\mathfrak{J}_{\text{obj}}$ or keeps it unchanged. Hence the objective function decreases after every cluster assignment, centroid re-estimation, and parameter re-estimation step. Now, note that the objective function is bounded below by a constant: being the negative log likelihood of a probabilistic model with the normalizer terms, $\mathfrak{J}_{\text{obj}}$ is bounded below by zero. Even without the normalizers, the objective function is bounded below by zero, since the distortion and potential terms are non-negative due to the fact that A is positive definite. Since $\mathfrak{J}_{\text{obj}}$ is bounded below, and HMRF-KMEANS results in a decreasing sequence of objective function values, the value sequence must have a limit. The limit in this case will be a fixed point of $\mathfrak{J}_{\text{obj}}$ since neither updating the assignments nor the parameters can further decrease the value of the objective function. As a result, the HMRF-KMEANS algorithm will converge to a fixed point of the objective. In practice, convergence can be determined if subsequent iterations of HMRF-KMEANS result in insignificant changes in $\mathfrak{J}_{\text{obj}}$.

5.4   Active Learning for Constraint Acquisition

In the semi-supervised setting where training data are not already available, getting constraints on pairs of data points may be expensive. In this section an active learning scheme for the HMRF model is presented, which can improve clustering performance with as few queries as possible. Formally, the scheme has access to a (noiseless) oracle that can assign a must-link or cannot-link label to a given pair (x_i, x_j), and it can pose a constant number of queries to the oracle.[6]

In order to get pairwise constraints that are more informative than random in

---

6. The oracle can also give a *don't-know* response to a query, in which case that response is ignored (pair not considered as a constraint) and that query is not posed again later.

farthest-first
traversal

the HMRF model, an active learning scheme for selecting pairwise constraints using the *farthest-first* traversal scheme is developed. In farthest-first traversal, a starting point is first selected at random. Then, the next point farthest from it is chosen and added to the traversed set. After that, the next point farthest from the traversed set (using the standard notion of distance from a set: $d(x, S) = \min_{x' \in S} d(x, x')$) is selected, and so on. Farthest-first traversal gives an efficient approximation of the *K-center* problem (Hochbaum and Shmoys, 1985), and has also been used to construct hierarchical clusterings with performance guarantees at each level of the hierarchy (Dasgupta, 2002).

good
initialization for
K-MEANS

Basu et al. (2002) observed that initializing K-MEANS with centroids estimated from a set of labeled examples for each cluster gives significant performance improvements. Under certain generative model-based assumptions, one can connect the mixture of Gaussians model to K-Means with squared Euclidean distance (Kearns et al., 1997). A direct calculation using Chernoff bounds shows that if a particular cluster with an underlying Gaussian model is seeded with points drawn independently at random from the corresponding Gaussian distribution, the deviation of the centroid estimates falls exponentially with the number of seeds; hence seeding results in good initial centroids. Since good initial centroids are very critical for the success of greedy algorithms such as K-MEANS, the same principle is followed for the pairwise case: the goal is to get as many points as possible per cluster (proportional to the actual cluster size) by asking pairwise queries, so that HMRF-KMEANS is initialized from a very good set of centroids. The proposed active learning scheme has two phases, EXPLORE and CONSOLIDATE, which are discussed next.

5.4.1 Exploration

The EXPLORE phase explores the given data using farthest-first traversal to get K pairwise disjoint non-null neighborhoods as fast as possible, with each neighborhood belonging to a different cluster in the underlying clustering of the data. Note that even if there is only one point per neighborhood, this neighborhood structure defines a correct skeleton of the underlying clustering. Our algorithm EXPLORE (algorithm 5.2) uses farthest-first traversal for getting a skeleton structure of the neighborhoods, and terminates when it has run out of queries, or when at least one point from all the clusters has been labeled. In the latter case, active learning enters the consolidation phase.

form skeleton of
neighborhoods

5.4.2 Consolidation

The basic idea in CONSOLIDATE (algorithm 5.3) is as follows: since there is at least one labeled point from all the clusters, the proper neighborhood of any unlabeled point x can be determined within a maximum of $(K - 1)$ queries. The queries will be formed by taking a point y from each of the neighborhoods in turn and asking for the label on the pair (x, y) until a must-link is obtained. Either a must-link reply

consolidate
neighborhoods

Algorithm 5.2 EXPLORE

Input: Set of data points $X = (x_1, \ldots, x_n)$, access to an oracle that
answers pairwise queries, number of clusters K, total number
of queries Q.

Output: $\lambda \leq K$ disjoint neighborhoods $N = (N_1, \ldots, N_\lambda)$ corresponding
to the true clustering of X with at least one point per neighborhood.

Method:

1. Initialize: set all neighborhoods N_p to null
2. Pick the first point x at random, add to N_1, $\lambda \leftarrow 1$
3. While queries are allowed and $\lambda < K$

    $x \leftarrow$ point farthest from existing neighborhoods N

    if, by querying, it is found that x is cannot-linked to all
    existing neighborhoods

        $\lambda \leftarrow \lambda + 1$, start a new neighborhood N_λ with x

    else

        add x to the neighborhood with which it is must-linked

---

is obtained in $(K - 1)$ queries, or it can be inferred that the point is must-linked
to the remaining neighborhood. Note that it is practical to sort the neighborhoods
in increasing order of the distance of their centroids from x so that the correct
must-link neighborhood for x is encountered sooner in the querying process.

Algorithm 5.3 CONSOLIDATE

Input: Set of data points $X = (x_1, \ldots, x_n)$, access to an oracle that
answers pairwise queries, number of clusters K, total number
of queries Q, K disjoint neighborhoods corresponding to true
clustering of X with at least one point per neighborhood.

Output: K disjoint neighborhoods corresponding to the true
clustering of X with higher number of points per neighborhood.

Method:

1. Estimate centroids $(\mu_1, \ldots, \mu_K)$ of each of the neighborhoods
2. While queries are allowed
2a.   randomly pick a point x not in the existing neighborhoods
2b.   sort the indices h with increasing distances $\|x - \mu_h\|^2$
2c.   for $h = 1$ to K

      query x with each of the neighborhoods in sorted order
      till a must-link is obtained, add x to that neighborhood

---

When the right number of clusters K is not known to the clustering algorithm,
K is also unknown to the active learning scheme. In this case, only EXPLORE is
used while queries are allowed. EXPLORE will keep discovering new clusters as fast
as it can. When it has obtained all the clusters, it will not have any way of knowing
this. However, from this point onward, for every farthest-first x it draws from the
data set, it will always find a neighborhood that is must-linked to it. Hence, after

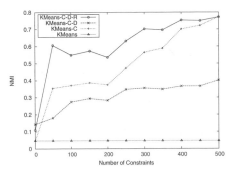
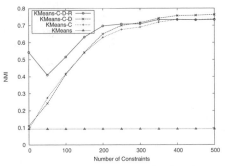

Figure 5.3 Clustering results for $D_{\cos_a}$ on *News-Different-3* data set.

Figure 5.4 Clustering results for D_{I_a} on *News-Different-3* data set.

discovering all of the clusters, EXPLORE will essentially consolidate the clusters too. However, when K is known, it makes sense to invoke CONSOLIDATE since (1) it adds points to clusters at a faster rate than EXPLORE, and (2) it picks random samples following the underlying data distribution, which is advantageous for estimating good centroids (e.g., Chernoff bounds on the centroid estimates exist), while samples obtained using farthest-first traversal may not have such properties.

5.5   Experimental Results

5.5.1   Data Sets

To demonstrate the effectiveness of our semi-supervised clustering framework, we consider three data sets that have the characteristics of being sparse, high-dimensional, and having a small number of points compared to the dimensionality of the space. This is done for two reasons:

- When clustering sparse high-dimensional data, e.g., text documents represented using the vector space model, it is particularly difficult to cluster small data sets, as observed by clustering researchers (Dhillon and Guan, 2003). The purpose of performing experiments on these subsets is to scale down the sizes of the data sets for computational reasons but at the same time not scale down the difficulty of the tasks.

- Clustering small number of sparse high-dimensional data points is a likely scenario in realistic applications. For example, when clustering the search results in a websearch engine like Vivísimo,[7] typically the number of webpages that are being clustered is on the order of hundreds. However the dimensionality of the feature space, corresponding to the number of unique words in all the webpages, is on the order of thousands. Moreover, each webpage is sparse, since it contains only a

---

7. http://www.vivisimo.com

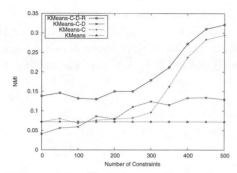

Figure 5.5 Clustering results for $D_{\cos_a}$ on *News-Related-3* data set.

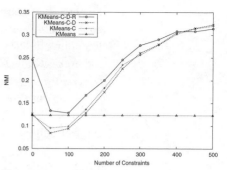

Figure 5.6 Clustering results for D_{I_a} on *News-Related-3* data set.

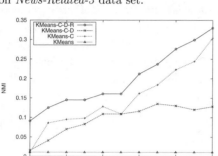

Figure 5.7 Clustering results for $D_{\cos_a}$ on *News-Similar-3* data set.

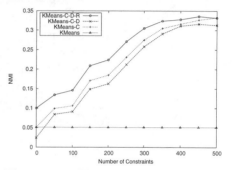

Figure 5.8 Clustering results for D_{I_a} on *News-Similar-3* data set.

small number of all the possible words. On such data sets, clustering algorithms can easily get stuck in local optima: in such cases it has been observed that there is little relocation of documents between clusters for most initializations, which leads to poor clustering quality after convergence of the algorithm (Dhillon and Guan, 2003). Supervision in the form of pairwise constraints is most beneficial in such cases and may significantly improve clustering quality.

We derived three data sets from the *20-Newsgroups* collection.[8] This collection has messages harvested from 20 different Usenet newsgroups, 1000 messages from each newsgroup. From the original data set, a reduced data set was created by taking a random subsample of 100 documents from each of the 20 newsgroups. Three data sets were created by selecting three categories from the reduced collection. *News-Similar-3* consists of three newsgroups on similar topics (`comp.graphics`, `comp.os.ms-windows`, `comp.windows.x`) with significant overlap between clusters due to cross-posting. *News-Related-3* consists of three newsgroups on related topics (`talk.politics.misc`, `talk.politics.guns`, and `talk.politics.mideast`). *News-Different-3* consists of articles posted in three newsgroups that cover different topics (`alt.atheism`, `rec.sport.baseball`, `sci.space`) with well-separated

---

8. `http://www.ai.mit.edu/people/jrennie/20Newsgroups`

clusters. The vector-space model of *News-Similar-3* has 300 points in 1864 dimensions, *News-Related-3* has 300 points in 3225 dimensions, and *News-Different-3* had 300 points in 3251 dimensions. Since the overlap between topics in *News-Similar-3* and *News-Related-3* is significant, they are more challenging data sets than *News-Different-3*.

All the data sets were preprocessed by stopword removal, TF-IDF weighting, removal of very high-frequency and low-frequency words, etc., following the methodology of Dhillon et al. (Dhillon and Modha, 2001).

5.5.2 Clustering Evaluation

We used *normalized mutual information* (NMI) as our clustering evaluation measure. NMI is an external clustering validation metric that estimates the quality of the clustering with respect to a given underlying class labeling of the data: it measures how closely the clustering algorithm could reconstruct the underlying label distribution in the data (Strehl et al., 2000; Dom, 2001). If C is the random variable denoting the cluster assignments of the points and K is the random variable denoting the underlying class labels on the points (Banerjee et al., 2005a), then the NMI measure is defined as

$$NMI = \frac{I(C;K)}{(H(C) + H(K))/2},\tag{5.31}$$

where $I(X;Y) = H(X) - H(X|Y)$ is the mutual information between the random variables X and Y, $H(X)$ is the Shannon entropy of X, and $H(X|Y)$ is the conditional entropy of X given Y (Cover and Thomas, 1991). NMI effectively measures the amount of statistical information shared by the random variables representing the cluster assignments and the user-labeled class assignments of the data points.

5.5.3 Methodology

We generated learning curves using 20 runs of twofold cross-validation for each data set. For studying the effect of constraints in clustering, 50% of the data set is set aside as the test set at any particular fold. The different points along the learning curve correspond to constraints that are given as input to the semi-supervised clustering algorithm. These constraints are obtained from the training set corresponding to the remaining 50% of the data by randomly selecting pairs of points from the training set, and creating must-link or cannot-link constraints depending on whether the underlying classes of the two points are same or different. Unit constraint costs $\mathcal{W}$ and $\overline{\mathcal{W}}$ were used for all constraints, original and inferred, since the data sets did not provide individual weights for the constraints. Based on a few pilot studies, gradient step size η was chosen to have values $\eta = 1.75$ for clustering with $D_{\cos_a}$ and $\eta = 1.0^{-8}$ for clustering with D_{I_a}; weights were restricted to be non-negative. In a realistic setting, these parameters could be tuned using cross-validation with a holdout set. The clustering algorithm was run on the whole data set, but NMI was calculated only on the test set. The learning curve results were averaged over the 20 runs.

5.5.4   Results and Discussion

We compared the proposed HMRF-KMEANS algorithm with two ablations as well as unsupervised K-Means clustering. The following variants were compared for distortion measures $D_{\cos_a}$ and D_{I_a} as representatives for Bregman divergences and directional measures respectively:

- KMEANS-I-C-D is the complete HMRF-KMEANS algorithm that includes use of supervised data in initialization (I) as described in section 5.3.5, incorporates constraints in cluster assignments (C) as described in section 5.3.6, and performs distance learning (D) as described in section 5.3.7;

- KMEANS-I-C is an ablation of HMRF-KMEANS that uses pairwise supervision for initialization and cluster assignments, but does not perform distance learning;

- KMEANS-I is a further ablation that only uses the constraints to initialize cluster representatives;

- KMEANS is the unsupervised K-Means algorithm.

Figures 5.3, 5.5, and 5.7 demonstrate the results for experiments where weighted cosine similarity $D_{\cos_a}$ was used as the distortion measure, while figures 5.4, 5.6, and 5.8 summarize experiments where weighted I divergence D_{I_a} was used.

As the results demonstrate, the full HMRF-KMEANS algorithm outperforms the unsupervised K-Means baseline as well as the ablated versions of HMRF-KMEANS for both $D_{\cos_a}$ and D_{I_a}. Relative performance of KMEANS-I-C and KMEANS-I indicates that using supervision for initializing cluster representatives is highly beneficial, while the constraint-sensitive cluster assignment step does not lead to significant additional improvements for $D_{\cos_a}$. For D_{I_a}, KMEANS-I-C outperforms KMEANS-I on *News-Different-3* (figure 5.4) and *News-Similar-3* (figure 5.8) which indicates that incorporating constraints in the cluster assignment process is useful for these data sets. This result is reversed for *News-Related-3* (figure 5.6), implying that in some cases using constraints in the E step may be unnecessary, which agrees with previous results on other domains (Basu et al., 2002). However, incorporating supervised data in all the three stages of the algorithm in KMEANS-I-C-D, namely initialization, cluster assignment, and distance update, always leads to substantial performance improvement.

As can be seen from results for 0 pairwise constraints in figures 5.3 through 5.8, distance learning is beneficial even in the absence of any pairwise constraints, since it is able to capture the relative importance of the different attributes in the unsupervised data. In the absence of supervised data or when no constraints are violated, distance learning attempts to minimize the objective function by adjusting the weights given the distortion between the unsupervised data points and their corresponding cluster representatives.

In realistic application domains, supervision in the form of constraints would be in most cases provided by human experts, in which case it is important that any semi-supervised clustering algorithm performs well with a small number of constraints. KMEANS-I-C-D starts outperforming its variants and the unsupervised clustering baseline early on in the learning curve, and is therefore a very appropriate algorithm to use in actual semi-supervised data clustering systems.

Overall, our results show that the HMRF-KMEANS algorithm effectively incorporates labeled and unlabeled data in three stages, each of which improves the clustering quality.

5.6   Related Work

The problem of integrating limited supervision in clustering algorithms has been studied by a number of authors in recent work. Early approaches to semi-supervised clustering relied on incorporating penalties for violating constraints into the objective function, leading to algorithms that avoid clusterings in which constraints are not satisfied. COP-KMeans is one such method where constraint violations are explicitly avoided in the assignment step of the K-Means algorithm (Wagstaff et al., 2001; Wagstaff, 2002). Another method, proposed by Demiriz et al. (1999), utilizes genetic algorithms to optimize an objective function that combines cluster compactness and cluster purity and that decreases with constraint violations.

In subsequent work, several approaches have been proposed that consider semi-supervised clustering within a probabilistic framework. Segal et al. (2003b) describe a model for semi-supervised clustering with constraints that combines a binary Markov network derived from pairwise protein interaction data and a naive Bayes Markov network modeling gene expression data. Another probabilistic approach described by Shental et al. (2004) incorporates must-link constraints via modeling them as *chunklets*, sets of points known to belong to the same class, while cannot-link constraints are utilized via potentials in a binary Markov network. HMRFs have previously been used for image segmentation by Zhang et al. (2001), who have also described an EM-based clustering algorithm. More recently, Lange et al. (2005) proposed an approach that incorporates labeled and unlabeled data within an HMRF-like model, while a mean field approximation method for posterior inference is used in the E step of the algorithm. The HMRF framework described in this chapter differs from these approaches in that it explicitly incorporates learning of the distortion measure parameters within the clustering algorithm and facilitates the use of diverse distance measures; however, a number of the proposed methods could be integrated within the HMRF framework.

Spectral clustering methods—algorithms that perform clustering by decomposing the pairwise affinity matrix derived from data—have been increasingly popular recently (Weiss, 1999; Ng et al., 2002), and several semi-supervised approaches have been developed within the spectral clustering framework. Kamvar et al. (2003) have proposed directly injecting the constraints into the affinity matrix before subsequent clustering, while De Bie et al. (2004) reformulated the optimization problem corresponding to spectral clustering by incorporating a separate label constraint matrix. Additionally, spectral clustering methods can be viewed as variants of the graph-cut approaches to clustering (Shi and Malik, 2000), a connection that motivated the *correlation clustering* method proposed by (Bansal et al., 2002), where the constraints correspond to edge labels between vertices representing data points.

Another family of semi-supervised clustering methods has focused on modifying the distance function employed by the clustering algorithm. In early work, Cohn et al. (2003) proposed using a weighted variant of Jensen-Shannon divergence within the EM clustering algorithm, with the weights learned using gradient descent based on constraint violations. Within the family of hierarchical agglomerative clustering algorithms, Klein et al. (2002) proposed modifying the squared Euclidean distance using the shortest-path algorithm. Several researchers have proposed methods for learning the parameters of the weighted Mahalanobis distance, a generalization of Euclidean distance, within the context of semi-supervised clustering. Xing et al. (2003) utilized convex optimization and iterative projections to learn the weight matrix of Mahalanobis distance within K-Means clustering. Another approach focused on parameterized Mahalanobis distance is the relevant component analysis (RCA) algorithm proposed by Bar-Hillel et al. (2003), where convex optimization is also used to learn the weight matrix.

Learning distance metrics within semi-supervised clustering relates to a large set of approaches for transforming the data representation to make it more suitable to a particular learning task. Within this book, part IV (chapters 15–17) describes several advanced techniques for changing the geometry of the data space to obtain better estimates of similarity between data points; integrating these methods with clustering algorithms provides a number of promising avenues for future work.

5.7 Conclusions

In this chapter, a generative probabilistic framework for semi-supervised clustering has been introduced. It relies on hidden random Markov fields (HMRFs) to utilize both unlabeled data and supervision in the form of pairwise constraints during the clustering process. The framework can be used with a number of distortion (distance) measures, including Bregman divergences and directional measures, and it facilitates training the distance parameters to adapt to specific data sets.

An algorithm HMRF-KMeans for performing clustering in this framework has been presented that incorporates pairwise supervision in different stages of the clustering: initialization, cluster assignment, and parameter estimation. Three particular instantiations of the algorithm, based on different distortion measures, have been discussed: squared Euclidean distance, which is common for clustering low-dimensional data, and KL divergence and cosine distance, which are popular for clustering high-dimensional directional data. Finally, a new method has been presented for acquiring supervision from a user in the form of effective pairwise constraints for semi-supervised clustering – such an active learning algorithm would be useful in an interactive query-driven clustering framework.

The HMRF model can be viewed as a unification of constraint-based and distance-based semi-supervised clustering approaches. It can be expanded to a more general setting where every cluster has a corresponding distinct distortion measure (Bilenko et al., 2004), leading to a clustering algorithm that can identify clusters of different shapes. Empirical evaluation of the framework described in this chapter can be found in several previous publications: active learning experiments are discussed in (Basu et al., 2004a), while (Bilenko et al., 2004) and (Basu et al., 2004b) contain results for low-dimensional and high-dimensional data sets respectively, and (Bilenko and Basu, 2004) compares several approximate inference methods for E Step discussed in section 5.3.6.

An important practical issue in using generative models for semi-supervised learning is model selection. For semi-supervised clustering with constraints, the key model selection issue is one of choosing the right number of clusters. One can consider using a traditional model selection criterion suitable for the supervised setting, or perform model selection by cross-validation. An alternative is to perform model-selection using bounds on the test-set error rate such that valuable supervised data are saved for learning. The PAC-MDL bounds (Blum and Langford, 2003) provide such a tool that has been successfully applied to model selection for clustering (Banerjee et al., 2005a), and can be readily extended to the semi-supervised clustering setting. In fact, the semi-supervised clustering setting is more natural since PAC-MDL bounds are applicable for transductive learning. Alternative methods of model selection are a good topic for future research.

II Low-Density Separation

6 Transductive Support Vector Machines

Thorsten Joachims   TJ@CS.CORNELL.EDU

In contrast to learning a general prediction rule, V. Vapnik proposed the transductive learning setting where predictions are made only at a fixed number of known test points. This allows the learning algorithm to exploit the location of the test points, making it a particular type of semi-supervised learning problem. Transductive support vector machines (TSVMs) implement the idea of transductive learning by including test points in the computation of the margin. This chapter will provide some examples for why the margin on the test examples can provide useful prior information for learning, in particular for the problem of text classification. The resulting optimization problems, however, are difficult to solve. The chapter reviews exact and approximate optimization methods and discusses their properties. Finally, the chapter discusses connections to other related semi-supervised learning approaches like co-training and methods based on graph cuts, which can be seen as solving variants of the TSVM optimization problem.

6.1 Introduction

The setting of transductive inference was introduced by Vapnik (e.g. (Vapnik, 1998)). As an example of a transductive learning task, consider the problem of learning from relevance feedback in information retrieval (see (Baeza-Yates and Ribeiro-Neto, 1999)). The user marks some documents returned by a search engine in response to an initial query as relevant or irrelevant. These documents then serve as a training set for a binary text classification problem. The goal is to learn a rule that accurately classifies all remaining documents in the database according to their relevance. Clearly, this problem can be thought of as a supervised learning problem. But it is different from many other (inductive) learning problems in at least two respects.

First, the learning algorithm does not necessarily have to learn a general rule, but it only needs to predict accurately for a finite number of test examples (i.e., the documents in the database). Second, the test examples are known a priori and can be observed by the learning algorithm during training. This allows the learning algorithm to exploit any information that might be contained in the location of the test examples. Transductive learning is therefore a particular case of semi-supervised learning, since it allows the learning algorithm to exploit the unlabeled examples in the test set. The following focuses on this second point, while chapter 24 elaborates on the first point.

transductive learning setting   More formally, the transductive learning setting can be formalized as follows.[1] Given is a set

$$S = \{1, 2, ..., n\} \tag{6.1}$$

that enumerates all n possible examples. In our relevance feedback example from above, there would be one index i for each document in the collection. We assume that each example i is represented by a feature vector $\mathbf{x}_i \in \mathbb{R}^d$. For text documents, this could be a TFIDF vector representation (see e.g. (Joachims, 2002)), where each document is represented by a scaled and normalized histogram of the words it contains. The collection of feature vectors for all examples in S is denoted as

$$X = (\mathbf{x}_1, \mathbf{x}_2, ..., \mathbf{x}_n). \tag{6.2}$$

For the examples in S, labels

$$Y = (\mathbf{y}_1, \mathbf{y}_2, ..., \mathbf{y}_n) \tag{6.3}$$

are generated independently according to a distribution $P(\mathbf{y}_1, ..., \mathbf{y}_n) = \prod_{i=1}^{n} P(\mathbf{y}_i)$. For simplicity, we assume binary labels $\mathbf{y}_i \in \{-1, +1\}$.

As the training set, the learning algorithm can observe the labels of l randomly selected examples $S_{train} \subset S$. The remaining $u = n - l$ examples form the test set $S_{test} = S \setminus S_{train}$.

$$S_{train} = \{l_1, ..., l_l\} \qquad S_{test} = \{u_1, ..., u_u\} \tag{6.4}$$

When training a transductive learning algorithm $\mathcal{L}$, it not only has access to the training vectors X_{train} and the training labels Y_{train},

$$X_{train} = (\mathbf{x}_{l_1}, \mathbf{x}_{l_2}, ..., \mathbf{x}_{l_l}) \qquad Y_{train} = (\mathbf{y}_{l_1}, \mathbf{y}_{l_2}, ..., \mathbf{y}_{l_l}), \tag{6.5}$$

but also to the unlabeled test vectors

$$X_{test} = (\mathbf{x}_{u_1}, \mathbf{x}_{u_2}, ..., \mathbf{x}_{u_l}). \tag{6.6}$$

The transductive learner uses X_{train}, Y_{train}, and X_{test} (but not the labels Y_{test} of

---

1. While several other, more general, definitions of transductive learning exist (Vapnik, 1998; Joachims, 2002; Derbeko et al., 2003), this one was chosen for the sake of simplicity.

the test examples) to produce predictions,

$$Y^*_{test} = (\mathbf{y}^*_{u_1}, \mathbf{y}^*_{u_2}, ..., \mathbf{y}^*_{u_u}), \tag{6.7}$$

for the labels of the test examples. The learner's goal is to minimize the fraction of erroneous predictions,

$$Err_{test}(Y^*_{test}) = \frac{1}{u} \sum_{i \in S_{test}} \delta_{0/1}(\mathbf{y}^*_i, \mathbf{y}_i), \tag{6.8}$$

on the test set. $\delta_{0/1}(a, b)$ is zero if $a = b$, otherwise it is one.

At first glance, the problem of transductive learning may not seem profoundly different from the usual inductive setting. One could learn a classification rule based on the training data and then apply it to the test data afterward. However, a crucial difference is that the inductive strategy would ignore any information potentially conveyed in X_{test}.

What information do we get from studying the test sample X_{test} and how could we use it? The fact that we deal with only a finite set of points means that the hypothesis space $\mathcal{H}$ of a transductive learner is necessarily finite — namely, all vectors $\{-1, +1\}^n$. Following the principle of structural risk minimization (Vapnik, 1998), we can structure $\mathcal{H}$ into a nested structure

structural risk
minimization

$$\mathcal{H}_1 \subset \mathcal{H}_2 \subset \cdots \subset \mathcal{H} = \{-1, +1\}^n. \tag{6.9}$$

The structure should reflect prior knowledge about the learning task. In particular, the structure should be constructed so that, with high probability, the correct labeling of S (or labelings that make few errors) is contained in an element $\mathcal{H}_i$ of small cardinality. This structuring of the hypothesis space $\mathcal{H}$ can be motivated using generalization error bounds from statistical learning theory. In particular, for a learner $\mathcal{L}$ that searches for a hypothesis $(Y^*_{train}, Y^*_{test}) \in \mathcal{H}_i$ with small training error,

$$Err_{test}(Y^*_{train}) = \frac{1}{l} \sum_{i \in S_{train}} \delta_{0/1}(\mathbf{y}^*_i, \mathbf{y}_i), \tag{6.10}$$

it is possible to upper-bound the fraction of test errors $Err_{test}(Y^*_{test})$ (Vapnik, 1998; Derbeko et al., 2003). With probability $1 - \eta$

transductive
generalization
error bound

$$Err_{test}(Y^*_{test}) \leq Err_{train}(Y^*_{train}) + \Omega(l, u, |\mathcal{H}_i|, \eta) \tag{6.11}$$

where the confidence interval $\Omega(l, u, |\mathcal{H}_i|, \eta)$ depends on the number of training examples l, the number of test examples u, and the cardinality $|\mathcal{H}_i|$ of $\mathcal{H}_i$ (see (Vapnik, 1998) for details). The smaller the cardinality $|\mathcal{H}_i|$, the smaller is the confidence interval $\Omega(l, u, |\mathcal{H}_i|, \eta)$ on the deviation between training and test error.

The bound indicates that a good structure ensures accurate prediction of the test labels. And here lies a crucial difference between transductive and inductive learners. Unlike in the inductive setting, we can study the location X_{test} of the test

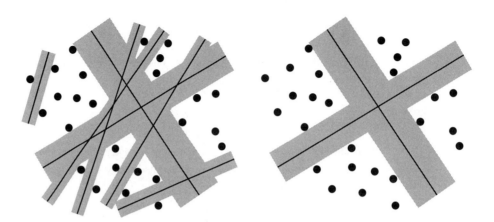

Figure 6.1   The two graphs illustrate the labelings that margin hyperplanes can realize dependent on the margin size. Example points are indicated as dots: the margin of each hyperplane is illustrated by the gray area. The left graph shows the separators $\mathcal{H}_\rho$ for a small margin threshold ρ. The number of possible labelings N_ρ decreases as the margin threshold is increased, as in the graph on the right.

examples when defining the structure. *In particular, in the transductive setting it is possible to encode prior knowledge we might have about the relationship between the geometry of $X = (\mathbf{x}_1, ..., \mathbf{x}_n)$ and $P(\mathbf{y}_1, ..., \mathbf{y}_n)$.* If such a relationship exists, we can build a more appropriate structure and reduce the number of training examples necessary for achieving a desired level of prediction accuracy. This line of reasoning is detailed in chapter 24.

6.2   Transductive Support Vector Machines

train and test set
margin

Transductive support vector machines (TSVMs) assume a particular geometric relationship between $X = (\mathbf{x}_1, ..., \mathbf{x}_n)$ and $P(\mathbf{y}_1, ..., \mathbf{y}_n)$. They build a structure on $\mathcal{H}$ based on the margin of hyperplanes $\{\mathbf{x} : \mathbf{w} \cdot \mathbf{x} + b = 0\}$ on the complete sample $X = (\mathbf{x}_1, \mathbf{x}_2, ..., \mathbf{x}_n)$, including both the training and the test vectors. The margin of a hyperplane on X is the minimum distance to the closest example vectors in X.

$$\min_{i \in [1..n]} \left[\frac{\mathbf{y}_i}{\|\mathbf{w}\|} \left(\mathbf{w} \cdot \mathbf{x}_i + b \right) \right] \tag{6.12}$$

The structure element $\mathcal{H}_\rho$ contains all labelings of X which can be achieved with hyperplane classifiers $h(\mathbf{x}) = sign\{\mathbf{x} \cdot \mathbf{w} + b\}$ that have a margin of at least ρ on X. The dependence of $\mathcal{H}_\rho$ on ρ is illustrated in figure 6.1. Intuitively, building the structure based on the margin gives preference to labelings that follow cluster boundaries over labelings that cut through clusters. Vapnik shows that the size of the margin ρ can be used to control the cardinality of the corresponding set of

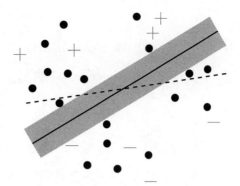

Figure 6.2   For the same data as in figure 6.1, some examples are now labeled. Positive/negative examples are marked as $+/-$. The dashed line is the solution of an inductive SVM, which finds the hyperplane that separates the training data with largest margin, but ignores the test vectors. The solid line shows the hard-margin transductive classification, which is the labeling that has zero training error and the largest margin with respect to both the training and the test vectors. The TSVM solution aligns the labeling with the cluster structure in the training and test vectors.

labelings $\mathcal{H}_\rho$. More formally, the following theorem provides an upper bound on the number of labelings $|\mathcal{H}_\rho|$ that can be achieved with hyperplanes that have a margin of at least ρ.

Theorem 6.1 ((Vapnik, 1998))
For any n vectors $\mathbf{x}_1, ..., \mathbf{x}_n \in \mathbb{R}^d$ that are contained in a ball of diameter R, the number $|\mathcal{H}_\rho|$ of possible binary labelings $\mathbf{y}_1, ..., \mathbf{y}_n \in \{-1, +1\}$ that can be realized with hyperplane classifiers $h(\mathbf{x}) = sign\{\mathbf{x} \cdot \mathbf{w} + b\}$ of margin at least ρ,

$$\forall_{i=1}^n : \frac{\mathbf{y}_i}{\|\mathbf{w}\|} \left[\mathbf{w} \cdot \mathbf{x}_i + b\right] \geq \rho \tag{6.13}$$

is bounded by

$$|\mathcal{H}_\rho| \leq e^{d\left(\ln \frac{n+k}{d} + 1\right)}, \qquad d = \frac{R^2}{\rho^2} + 1. \tag{6.14}$$

Note that the number of labelings $|\mathcal{H}_\rho|$ does not necessarily depend on the number of features d. As suggested by the theorem, TSVMs sort all labelings by their margin ρ on X to build the structure on $\mathcal{H}$. Structural risk minimization argues that a learning algorithm should select the labeling $Y^* \in \mathcal{H}_\rho$ for which training error $Err_{train}(Y^*_{train})$ and cardinality of $\mathcal{H}_\rho$ minimize the generalization error bound (6.11). For the special case of requiring zero training error (i. e. $Err_{train}(Y^*_{train}) = 0$), optimizing the bound means finding the labeling with the largest margin on the complete set of vectors. This leads to the following optimization problem (OP) (Vapnik, 1998).

hard-margin
TSVM

OP1 (Transductive SVM (hard-margin))

$$\text{minimize:} \quad V(\mathbf{y}_{u_1}^*, ..., \mathbf{y}_{u_u}^*, \mathbf{w}, b) = \frac{1}{2}\mathbf{w} \cdot \mathbf{w} \tag{6.15}$$

$$\text{subject to:} \quad \forall_{i=1}^l : \mathbf{y}_{l_i}[\vec{w} \cdot \mathbf{x}_{l_i} + b] \geq 1 \tag{6.16}$$

$$\forall_{j=1}^u : \mathbf{y}_{u_j}^*[\vec{w} \cdot \mathbf{x}_{u_j}^* + b] \geq 1 \tag{6.17}$$

$$\forall_{j=1}^u : \mathbf{y}_{u_j}^* \in \{-1, +1\} \tag{6.18}$$

Solving this problem means finding the labeling $\mathbf{y}_{u_1}^*, ..., \mathbf{y}_{u_k}^*$ of the test data for which the hyperplane that separates both training and test data has maximum margin. Figure 6.2 illustrates this. The figure also shows the solution that an inductive SVM (Cortes and Vapnik, 1995; Vapnik, 1998) computes. An inductive SVM also finds a large-margin hyperplane, but it considers only the training vectors while ignoring all test vectors. In particular, a hard-margin inductive SVM computes the separating hyperplane that has zero training error and the largest margin with respect to the training examples.

To be able to handle nonseparable data, one can introduce slack variables ξ_i (Joachims, 1999) similar to inductive SVMs (Cortes and Vapnik, 1995).

soft-margin
TSVM

OP2 (Transductive SVM (soft-margin))

$$\text{min: } W(\mathbf{y}_{u_1}^*, ..., \mathbf{y}_{u_u}^*, \mathbf{w}, b, \xi_1, ..., \xi_l, \xi_1^*, ..., \xi_u^*) = \frac{1}{2}\mathbf{w} \cdot \mathbf{w} + C\sum_{i=1}^l \xi_i + C^* \sum_{j=1}^u \xi_j^* \tag{6.19}$$

$$\text{s.t.: } \forall_{i=1}^l : \mathbf{y}_{l_i}[\mathbf{w} \cdot \mathbf{x}_{l_i} + b] \geq 1 - \xi_i \tag{6.20}$$

$$\forall_{j=1}^u : \mathbf{y}_{u_j}^*[\mathbf{w} \cdot \mathbf{x}_{u_j}^* + b] \geq 1 - \xi_j^* \tag{6.21}$$

$$\forall_{j=1}^u : \mathbf{y}_{u_j}^* \in \{-1, +1\} \tag{6.22}$$

$$\forall_{i=1}^l : \xi_i \geq 0 \tag{6.23}$$

$$\forall_{j=1}^u : \xi_j^* \geq 0 \tag{6.24}$$

C and C^* are parameters set by the user. They allow trading off margin size against misclassifying training examples or excluding test examples. C^* can be used reduce sensitivity toward outliers (i.e., single examples falsely reducing the margin on the test data).

kernels

Both inductive and transductive SVMs can be extended to include kernels (Boser et al., 1992; Vapnik, 1998). Making use of duality techniques from optimization theory, kernels allow learning nonlinear rules as well as classification rules over nonvectorial data (see e.g. (Schölkopf and Smola, 2002)) without substantially changing the optimization problems.

Note that in both the hard-margin formulation (OP1) and the soft-margin formulation (OP2) of the TSVM, the labels of the test examples enter as integer variables. Due to the constraints in Eqs. 6.18 and 6.22 respectively, both OP1 and OP2 are no longer convex quadratic programs like the analogous optimization problems for inductive SVMs. Before discussing methods for (approximately) solving the TSVM

	nuclear	physics	atom	parsley	basil	salt	and
D1	1						1
D2	1	1	1				1
D3			1				1
D4				1	1		1
D5				1		1	1
D6					1	1	1

Figure 6.3   Example of a text-classification problem with co-occurrence pattern. Rows correspond to documents, columns to words. A table entry of 1 denotes the occurrence of a word in a document.

optimization problems, let's first discuss some intuition about why structuring the hypothesis space based on the margin on the test examples might be reasonable.

6.3   Why Use Margin on the Test Set?

Why should it be reasonable to prefer a labeling with a large margin over a labeling with a smaller margin, even if both have the same training error? Clearly, this question can only be addressed in the context of a particular learning problem. In the following, we will consider text classification as an example. In particular, for topic-based text classification it is known that good classification rules typically have a large margin (Joachims, 2002). The following example gives some intuition for why this is the case.

In the field of information retrieval it is well known that words in natural language occur in co-occurrence patterns (see e.g. (van Rijsbergen, 1977)). Some words are likely to occur together in one document; others are not. For examples, when asking Google about all documents containing the words `pepper` and `salt`, it returns 3,500,000 webpages. When asking for the documents with the words `pepper` and `physics`, we get only 248,000 hits, although `physics` (162,000,000 hits) is a more popular word on the web than `salt` (63,200,000 hits). Many approaches in information retrieval try to exploit this cluster structure of text (see e.g. (Baeza-Yates and Ribeiro-Neto, 1999, chapter 5)). It is this co-occurrence information that TSVMs exploit as prior knowledge about the learning task.

Consider the example in figure 6.3. Imagine document $D1$ was given as a training example for class A and document $D6$ was given as a training example for class B. How should we classify documents $D2$ to $D5$ (the test set)? Even if we did not understand the meaning of the words, we would classify $D2$ and $D3$ into class A, and $D4$ and $D5$ into class B. We would do so even though $D1$ and $D3$ do not share any informative words. The reason we choose this classification of the test data over the others stems from our prior knowledge about the properties of text and common text-classification tasks. Often we want to classify documents by

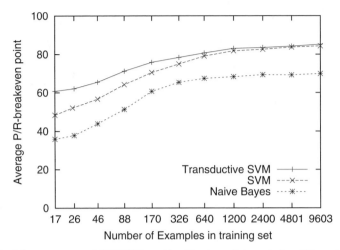

Figure 6.4   Macro-averaged PRBEP on the Reuters data set for different training set sizes and a test set size of 3299.

topic, source, or style. For these types of classification tasks we find stronger co-occurrence patterns within classes than between different classes. In our example we analyzed the co-occurrence information in the test data and found two clusters. These clusters indicate different topics of $\{D1, D2, D3\}$ versus $\{D4, D5, D6\}$, and we choose the cluster separator as our classification. Note again that we got to this classification by studying the location of the test examples, which is not possible for an inductive learner.

The TSVM outputs the same classification as we suggested above, although all 16 labelings of $D2$ to $D5$ can be achieved with linear separators. Assigning $D2$ and $D3$ to class A and $D4$ and $D5$ to class B is the maximum-margin solution (i.e., the solution of OP1). The maximum-margin bias appears to reflect our prior knowledge about text classification well. By measuring margin on the test set, the TSVM exploits co-occurrence patterns that indicate boundaries between topics.

6.4   Experiments and Applications of TSVMs

Structuring the hypothesis space using margin was obviously beneficial in the toy example above. Experiments have confirmed that this also holds in practice.

TSVMs in text classification

Figures 6.4 and 6.5 (from Joachims (1999)) give empirical evidence that TSVMs improve prediction performance on real text-classification tasks, namely the Reuters-21578 text-classification benchmark. The standard "ModApte" training/test split is used, leading to a corpus of 9603 training documents and 3299 test documents. The results are averaged over the ten most frequent topics, while keeping all documents. Each topic leads to a binary classification problem, where documents about the topic are positive examples, and all other documents are neg-

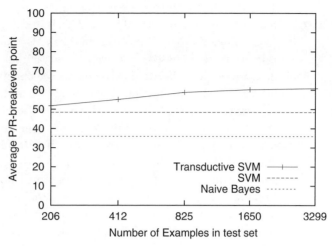

Figure 6.5   Macro-averaged PRBEP on the Reuters data set for 17 training documents and varying test set size for the TSVM.

ative examples. The performance of each binary classifier is measured in terms of the precision/recall breakeven point (PRBEP). The PRBEP is the percentage of positive test examples that are classified correctly, if the classifier is allowed to predict as many test examples as positive as there are true positives in the test set (see e.g. (Joachims, 2002)). The precise setup is described in (Joachims, 1999).

Figures 6.4 and 6.5 show the effect of using TSVM instead of inductive methods. To provide a baseline for comparison, the results of the inductive SVM and a multinomial naive Bayesnaive Bayes classifier are added. The SVM and the TSVM are trained using SVM^{light}, available at `svmlight.joachims.org`. Figure 6.4 shows the effect of varying the size of the training set. The advantage of using the transductive approach is largest for small training sets. For increasing training set size, the performance of the SVM approaches that of the TSVM. This is to be expected, since labeled examples eventually convey the same information about the distribution of the example vectors as the unlabeled data.

The influence of the test set size on the performance of the TSVM is displayed in figure 6.5. The bigger the test set, the larger the performance gap between SVM and TSVM. Adding more test examples beyond 3299 is not likely to increase performance by much, since the graph appears to flatten out. The curves are fairly typical and similar behavior was also observed on other problems. The results for other text classification data sets can be found in (Joachims, 2002).

Similar gains in performance of the TSVM over an inductive SVM were reported by Chapelle et al. (2003). For classifying net news articles they report that the TSVM almost halves the prediction error for small training sets of 16 examples. For an email classification problem, the results of Kockelkorn et al. (2003) also indicate that TSVMs substantially outperform inductive SVMs for small training sets. Small improvements on text classification problems are also reported by Tong and Koller (2001). However, they conclude that the effect of active learning,

TSVMs for image
retrieval

where the algorithm can ask for the labels of particular examples, dominates the improvement seen from the TSVM. This is in contrast to the findings of Wang et al. (2003). They find that incorporating TSVMs into their active learning procedure for image retrieval based on relevance feedback substantially improves performance. For more text-classification experiments see chapter 3.

TSVMs for UCI
benchmarks

Beyond text classification, Bennett and Demiriz (1999) have applied their L_1-norm variant of transductive SVMs to several UCI benchmark problems. They find small but fairly consistent improvements over these tasks. A key difference from most other experiments with transductive learning are the small test sets that were used. Due to efficiency limitations of the mixed-integer programming code they used for training, all test sets contained no more than 70 examples. Their evaluation of regular TSVMs on a subset of these UCI benchmarks shows mixed results (Demiriz and Bennett, 2000). Similar findings on UCI benchmarks are also reported by Joachims (2003), where the differences between inductive SVMs and TSVMs were found to be small.

TSVMs in
bioinformatics

Several applications of TSVMs in bioinformatics have been explored. For example, they have been used to recognize promoter sequences in genes. Kasabov and Pang (2004) report that TSVMs substantially outperform inductive SVMs in their experiments. However, for the problem of predicting the functional properties of proteins, Krogel and Scheffer (2004) find that TSVMs significantly decrease performance compared to inductive SVMs.

TSVMs for
named entity
recognition

Goutte et al. (2002) apply TSVMs to a problem of recognizing entities (e.g., gene names, protein names) in medical text. They find that TSVMs substantially improve performance for medium-sized training sets, and perform at least comparably to an alternative transductive learning method based on Fisher kernels.

Summarizing the results, it appears that TSVMs are particularly well suited for text classification and several other (typically high-dimensional) learning problems. However, on some problems the TSVM performs roughly equivalently to an inductive SVM, or sometimes even worse. This is to be expected, since it is likely that structuring the hypothesis space according to margin size is inappropriate for some applications. Furthermore, it is likely that the difficulty of finding the optimum of the TSVM optimization problem has led to suboptimal results in some cases. We discuss algorithms for solving the TSVM optimization problem next.

6.5   Solving the TSVM Optimization Problem

Both the hard soft-margin TSVM optimization problems can be written as mixed-integer problems with a quadratic objective and linear constraints. Unfortunately, currently no algorithm is known to efficiently find a globally optimal solution.

mixed-integer
programming

Vapnik and colleagues (Vapnik and Sterin, 1977; Wapnik and Tscherwonenkis, 1979) proposed the use of branch-and-bound search to find the global optimium of the TSVM optimization problem. Similarly, Bennett and Demiriz (1999) consider standard mixed-integer programming software like CPLEX to solve a variant of the TSVM optimization problem. To be able to use such software, they replace the term $\mathbf{w} \cdot \mathbf{w} = \|\mathbf{w}\|_2^2$ in the objective with $\|\mathbf{w}\|_1$ so that the objective becomes linear. However, while both approaches produce globally optimal solutions, they can solve only small problems with less than 100 test examples in reasonable time. Unfortunately, figure 6.5 suggests that the biggest benefits of transductive learning occur only for larger test sets.

SVM^{light} The algorithm implemented in SVM^{light} does not necessarily produce a globally optimal solution, but can handle test sets with up to 100,000 examples in reasonable time (Joachims, 1999, 2002). Most of the empirical results in the previous section were produced using this algorithm. The algorithm performs a kind of coordinate-descent local search starting from an initial labeling of the test examples derived from an inductive SVM. The ratio of test examples that are classified as positive (by adjusting the hyperplane threshold b) in this initial labeling is specified by the user or estimated from the ratio of positive to negative examples in the training set. This ratio is maintained throughout the optimization process to avoid degenerate solutions that assign all test examples to the same class.[2] In every step of the local search, the algorithm selects two examples (one positive and one negative) and swaps their labels. The way the examples are selected guarantees a strict improvement of the objective function (i.e., the soft margin) in every such step. In addition, the algorithm starts with a small value of C^* and raises it throughout the optimization process. This means that most ξ^* are non-zero in the initial phase of the search, resulting in a smoother objective function. Toward the end of the search, incrementally increasing the value of C^* toward the desired target value makes the problem closer to the desired objective. A more detailed explanation of the algorithm is given in (Joachims, 2002).

gradient descent   A related block coordinate descent method was proposed by Demiriz and Bennett (2000). The algorithm also alternates between changing the labels of the test examples and recomputing the margin. Differences compared to the SVM^{light} algorithm lie in the selection of the labels to change, the number of labels that are changed in each iteration, and in the heuristics that are aimed to avoid local optima. A similar algorithm for the L_1-norm variant of the TSVM is described by Fung and Mangasarian (2001).

semi-definite relaxation   De Bie and Cristianini (2004a) explore a convex approximation of the TSVM optimization problem (also see chapter 7). They present a relaxation that takes the form of a semi-definite program. While this program can be solved in polynomial time, it becomes too inefficient for test sets with more than 100 examples. However, assuming a low-rank structure of the test labels derived from a spectral decomposition technique, De Bie and Cristianini push the efficieny limit to several thousands of test examples.

---

2. In text classification, assigning all test examples to the same class typically gives larger margins than any other labeling. Clearly, this is an undesirable solution and indicates a problem with the TSVM approach. A method that does not exhibit this problem is presented in Joachims (2003).

6.6   Connection to Related Approaches

graph cuts

The difficulty in solving the TSVM optimization problem has led to much interest in other formulations of transductive learning algorithms. The goal is to exploit the same type of relationship between the geometry of the test examples — or unlabeled examples more generally — and their labels, but that have computationally more convenient properties. Graph partitioning approaches based on st-min-cuts (Blum and Chawla, 2001) and spectral graph partitioning explicitly or implicitly pursued this goal (Belkin and Niyogi, 2002; Chapelle et al., 2003; Joachims, 2003; Zhu et al., 2003b) (see also chapters 11, 12, 13, 14, and 15). For example, the method in (Joachims, 2003) is explicitly derived analogous to a TSVM as a transductive version of the k-nearest neighbor classifier.

ridge regression

Ridge regression is a method closely related to regression SVMs. Chapelle et al. (1999) derive a tranductive variant of ridge regression. Since the class labels do not need to be discrete for regression problems, they show that the solution of the associated optimization problem can be computed efficiently.

co-training

Co-training (Blum and Mitchell, 1998) exploits two redundant representations of a learning problem for semi-supervised learning. A connection to general transductive learning comes from the insight that co-training produces transductive learning problems that have large margin (Joachims, 2003, 2002). In fact, TSVMs and spectral partitioning methods appear to perform well on co-training problems (Joachims, 2003).

confidence estimation

Connecting to concepts of algorithmic randomness, Gammerman et al. (1998), Vovk et al. (1999), and Saunders et al. (1999) presented approaches to estimating the confidence of a prediction based on a transductive setting. A similar goal using a Bayesian approach is pursued by Graepel et al. (2000). Since their primary aim is not a reduced error rate in general, but a measure of confidence for a particular prediction, they consider only test sets with exactly one example.

6.7   Summary and Conclusions

Transductive support vector machines exploit the geometric (cluster) structure in the feature vectors of the test examples, which makes them a particular kind of semi-supervised learning method. In particular, TSVMs find the labeling of the test examples that maximizes margin jointly on the training and the test data. Intuitively, this produces labeling of the test examples so that class boundaries follow cluster boundaries. Empirical findings suggest that TSVMs are particularly well suited for text classification and several other (typically high-dimensional) learning problems, often showing large accuracy gains for small training sets and large test sets. However, on some problems the TSVM performs roughly equivalently to an inductive SVM, or sometimes even worse. Partially, failure on some tasks may be due to the difficulty of finding the optimum of the TSVM optimization problem.

Finding the globally optimal solution is intractable for interestingly sized test sets. Existing algorithms resort to local search or to relaxing the optimization problem. More work is needed on tractable formulations and algorithms for transductive learning, as well as a deeper theoretical and empirical understanding of its potential.

7 Semi-Supervised Learning Using Semi-Definite Programming

Tijl De Bie   TIJL.DEBIE@GMAIL.COM
Nello Cristianini   NELLO@SUPPORT-VECTOR.NET

We discuss the problem of support vector machine (SVM) transduction, which is a combinatorial problem with exponential computational complexity in the number of unlabeled samples. Different approaches to such combinatorial problems exist, among which are exact integer programming approaches (only feasible for very small sample sizes, e.g. (Bennett and Demiriz, 1999)) and local search heuristics starting from a suitably chosen start value such as the approach explained in chapter 6, transductive support vector machines, and introduced in (Joachims, 1999) (scalable to large problem sizes, but sensitive to local optima).

In this chapter, we discuss an alternative approach introduced in (De Bie and Cristianini, 2004a), which is based on a convex relaxation of the optimization problem associated with support vector machine transduction. The result is a semi-definite programming (SDP) problem which can be optimized in polynomial time, the solution of which is an approximation of the optimal labeling as well as a bound on the true optimum of the original transduction objective function. To further decrease the computational complexity, we propose an approximation that allows solving transduction problems of up to 1000 unlabeled samples.

Lastly, we extend the formulation to more general settings of semi-supervised learning, where equivalence and inequivalence constraints are given on labels of some of the samples.

7.1 Relaxing SVM Transduction

In transduction problems, we are provided with a set of labeled data points (training set), as well as a set of unlabeled data points (test set). Our interest is to find suitable labels for the second set, with no immediate ambition to make predictions for yet unseen data points that may become available later on. The way the SVM transduction problems handle this is by finding those test set labels for which, after training an SVM on the combined training and test set, the margin on the full data set is maximal. This involves optimizing over all labelings of the test set an integer programming problem with exponential cost.

Primal   Let us recall the primal soft-margin SVM problem (see e.g. (Cristianini and Shawe-Taylor, 2000) and (Shawe-Taylor and Cristianini, 2004) for an introduction to SVMs and kernel methods):

$$\min_{\xi_i, \mathbf{w}} \quad \frac{1}{2}\mathbf{w}^T\mathbf{w} + C\sum_{i=1}^{l}\xi_i$$
$$\text{s.t.} \quad y_i\mathbf{w}^T\mathbf{x}_i \geq 1 - \xi_i$$
$$\xi_i \geq 0.$$

We omitted the bias term here, as we will do throughout the entire chapter. This is not a problem, as argued in (Poggio et al., 2001). Only the labeled data points are involved in this optimization problem. Then, the transductive SVM can be written

primal transductive SVM formulation

as

$$\min_{\xi_i, \mathbf{w}, Y_u} \quad \frac{1}{2}\mathbf{w}^T\mathbf{w} + C\sum_{i=1}^{n}\xi_i$$
$$\text{s.t.} \quad y_i\mathbf{w}^T\mathbf{x}_i \geq 1 - \xi_i$$
$$\xi_i \geq 0$$
$$Y_u \in \{-1, 1\}^u, \tag{7.1}$$

where we used the notation $Y_u = (y_{l+1}, \ldots y_n)$ for the set of test set labels, a column vector containing the labels for the test points, and $n = l + u$ for the total number of training and test points. It is the combinatorial constraint 7.1 that makes this optimization problem very hard to solve exactly.

Dual   Very often it is more interesting to focus on the dual problem, as it allows us to use the kernel trick for nonlinear classification and for classification of nonvectorial data. The standard soft-margin SVM problem is given by

$$\max_{\boldsymbol{\alpha}_l} \quad 2\boldsymbol{\alpha}_l^T\mathbf{1} - \boldsymbol{\alpha}_l^T(K_l \odot Y_lY_l^T)\boldsymbol{\alpha}_l$$
$$\text{s.t.} \quad C \geq \alpha_i \geq 0,$$

where $\boldsymbol{\alpha}_l = (\alpha_1, \ldots \alpha_l)$ is a column vector of dual variables α_i, and K_l is the kernel matrix for the training set. With $\odot$, the element-wise matrix product is meant. The optimum of this optimization problem is equal to the *inverse* square of the margin (plus an additional cost term in the soft margin formulation). Hence, since we want to maximize the margin, the dual formulation of the transductive SVM

dual transductive SVM formulation

can be written as

$$\min_Y \max_{\boldsymbol{\alpha}} \quad 2\boldsymbol{\alpha}^T \mathbf{1} - \boldsymbol{\alpha}^T (K \odot YY^T) \boldsymbol{\alpha}$$

$$\text{s.t.} \quad C \geq \alpha_i \geq 0$$

$$Y = \begin{pmatrix} Y_l \\ Y_u \end{pmatrix}$$

$$Y_u \in \{-1, 1\}^u.$$

Here, $\boldsymbol{\alpha} = (\alpha_1, \ldots, \alpha_l, \alpha_{l+1}, \ldots \alpha_n)$ is a vector containing the dual variables for both the training and the test set, K is the complete kernel matrix, and Y is the complete label vector. Without loss of generality, we assume that the first l rows and columns of K correspond to training points, the last u to test points. Again, it is the same combinatorial constraint that makes finding an exact solution infeasible for reasonably sized problems.

label matrix Γ

Without affecting the solution, we slightly reformulate the optimization problem by introducing the matrix variable $\Gamma = YY^T$ which we will refer to as the label matrix. The dual formulation then becomes

$$\min_\Gamma \max_{\boldsymbol{\alpha}} \quad 2\boldsymbol{\alpha}^T \mathbf{1} - \boldsymbol{\alpha}^T (K \odot \Gamma) \boldsymbol{\alpha}$$

$$\text{s.t.} \quad C \geq \alpha_i \geq 0$$

$$\Gamma = YY^T = \begin{pmatrix} Y_l Y_l^T & Y_l Y_u^T \\ Y_u Y_l^T & Y_u Y_u^T \end{pmatrix} \tag{7.2}$$

$$Y_u \in \{-1, 1\}^u. \tag{7.3}$$

All constraints are now linear (matrix) inequalities, and the objective is linear in Γ and concave in $\boldsymbol{\alpha}$. However, the problem is still an integer program due to constraint 7.3 and hence the overall problem is not convex.

7.1.1   Relaxation to an SDP Problem

We will write the label matrix Γ as a block matrix using the notation

$$\Gamma = \begin{pmatrix} \Gamma_{ll} & \Gamma_{lu} \\ \Gamma_{ul} & \Gamma_{uu} \end{pmatrix} = \begin{pmatrix} Y_l Y_l^T & Y_l Y_u^T \\ Y_u Y_l^T & Y_u Y_u^T \end{pmatrix}.$$

Symmetry constraints such as $\Gamma_{uu} = \Gamma_{uu}^T$ and $\Gamma_{lu} = \Gamma_{ul}^T$ are understood and we will never mention them explicitly. Now, observe that any matrix of rank 1 with ones on the diagonal can be written as an outer product of a vector with itself where this vector only contains 1 and -1 as its elements. Thus, the following proposition holds:

Proposition 7.1 *We can reformulate the constraints (7.2) and (7.3) by the equiv-*

alent set of constraints:

$$
\begin{aligned}
diag\,(\Gamma) &= \mathbf{1} \\
rank\,(\Gamma) &= 1 \\
\Gamma &= \begin{pmatrix} Y_l Y_l^T & \Gamma_{lu} \\ \Gamma_{ul} & \Gamma_{uu} \end{pmatrix}.
\end{aligned}
$$

These constraints are linear in the parameters, except for the rank constraint, which is clearly nonconvex (indeed, a convex combination of two matrices of rank 1 will generally be of rank 2). To deal with this problem, in this chapter we propose to relax the constraint set by extending the feasible region to a convex set over which optimization can be accomplished in a reasonable computation time. To retain a good performance, it should not be much larger than the nonconvex set specified by the constraints above.

Note that the constraints imply that the matrix Γ is positive semi-definite (PSD). So, we can add $\Gamma \succeq 0$ as an additional constraint without modifying the problem. The relaxation then consists in simply dropping the rank constraint.[1] The resulting relaxed optimization problem is

$$
\begin{aligned}
\min_{\Gamma} \max_{\boldsymbol{\alpha}} \quad & 2\boldsymbol{\alpha}^T \mathbf{1} - \boldsymbol{\alpha}^T (K \odot \Gamma)\boldsymbol{\alpha} \\
\text{s.t.} \quad & C \geq \alpha_i \geq 0 \\
& \mathrm{diag}\,(\Gamma) = \mathbf{1} \\
& \Gamma \succeq 0 \\
& \Gamma = \begin{pmatrix} Y_l Y_l^T & \Gamma_{lu} \\ \Gamma_{ul} & \Gamma_{uu} \end{pmatrix}.
\end{aligned}
$$

Of course, the rank of the resulting optimal matrix Γ will not necessarily be equal to 1 anymore, and its entries not equal to 1 and -1. However, we can see that each entry of Γ will still lie in the interval $[-1, 1]$. Indeed, since all principal submatrices of a PSD matrix have to be PSD as well, every 2×2 principal submatrix has to be PSD, which for a matrix containing ones on its diagonal can only be achieved for off-diagonal elements in $[-1, 1]$. Furthermore:

---

1. Ideally, we should relax the constraints so as to extend the feasible region to just the *convex hull* of the constraints, which is the smallest convex set containing the feasible region of the original problem. For a label matrix YY^T with $Y \in \{-1, 1\}^n$, this convex hull is referred to as the *cut polytope*. However, no efficient description of the cut polytope is known. Hence, one has to resort to convex relaxations of the cut polytope itself, such as the *elliptope*, which is essentially the relaxation used in this chapter. Other relaxations of the cut polytope are known (such as the *metric polytope*), and they can be used alternatively or in addition. Tighter relaxations tend to be computationally more challenging, though, and for brevity we will not consider these here. For more information we refer the reader to (Helmberg, 2000; Anjos, 2001).

Theorem 7.2 *The above optimization problem is convex. More specifically, it is an SDP problem.*

Proof   By introducing the notation

$$f(\Gamma) = \max_{\alpha} \quad 2\alpha^T \mathbf{1} - \alpha^T (K \odot \Gamma)\alpha$$
$$\text{s.t.} \quad C \geq \alpha_i \geq 0,$$

we can rewrite this optimization problem as

$$\min_{\Gamma} \quad f(\Gamma)$$
$$\text{s.t.} \quad \text{diag}(\Gamma) = \mathbf{1}$$
$$\Gamma \succeq 0$$
$$\Gamma = \begin{pmatrix} Y_l Y_l^T & \Gamma_{lu} \\ \Gamma_{ul} & \Gamma_{uu} \end{pmatrix}.$$

Let us first concentrate on $f(\Gamma)$. For a given $\Gamma \succeq 0$, the objective is concave and the constraints are all linear, i.e., we have a convex optimization problem. One can easily verify Slater's constraint qualification (the existence of a strictly feasible point in the constraint set, see e.g. (Anjos, 2001)), showing that strong duality holds. Let us now write the dual optimization problem by using Lagrange multipliers $2\mu \geq 0$ and $2\nu \geq 0$ for the inequality constraints $C \geq \alpha_i$ and $\alpha_i \geq 0$ respectively (the factor 2 in front of μ and ν is used for notational convenience). By invoking strong duality, which states that the dual optimum is equal to the primal optimum, we can now write $f(\Gamma)$ as

$$f(\Gamma) = \min_{\mu,\nu} \max_{\alpha} \quad 2\alpha^T (\mathbf{1} - \mu + \nu) - \alpha^T (K \odot \Gamma)\alpha + 2C\mu^T \mathbf{1}$$
$$\text{s.t.} \quad \mu \geq 0$$
$$\nu \geq 0.$$

We note in passing that the optimal value for $\mathbf{1} - \mu + \nu$ will be orthogonal to the null space of $K \odot \Gamma$, since otherwise the solution could grow to infinity by increasing the component of α along this null space. Now, the maximization with respect to α can be carried out explicitly: the optimum is reached for $\alpha = (K \odot \Gamma)^{\dagger} (\mathbf{1} - \mu + \nu) + \alpha_0$, where α_0 is a term in the null space of $K \odot \Gamma$. Here $\dagger$ is used to denote the Moore-Penrose inverse. Plugging this in gives

$$f(\Gamma) = \min_{\mu,\nu} \quad (\mathbf{1} - \mu + \nu)^T (K \odot \Gamma)^{\dagger} (\mathbf{1} - \mu + \nu) + 2C\mu^T \mathbf{1}$$
$$\text{s.t.} \quad \mu \geq 0$$
$$\nu \geq 0.$$

Note that $\boldsymbol{\alpha}_0$ has vanished. After introducing an additional variable t,

$$
\begin{aligned}
f(\Gamma) = \quad & \min_{\boldsymbol{\mu},\boldsymbol{\nu},t} \quad t \\
& \text{s.t.} \quad \boldsymbol{\mu} \geq 0 \\
& \qquad \boldsymbol{\nu} \geq 0 \\
& \qquad t \geq (\mathbf{1} - \boldsymbol{\mu} + \boldsymbol{\nu})^T (K \odot \Gamma)^\dagger (\mathbf{1} - \boldsymbol{\mu} + \boldsymbol{\nu}) + 2C\boldsymbol{\mu}^T \mathbf{1}.
\end{aligned}
$$

Using the extended Schur complement lemma (see appendix), we can rewrite the latter constraint as

$$
\begin{pmatrix}
K \odot \Gamma & (\mathbf{1} - \boldsymbol{\mu} + \boldsymbol{\nu}) \\
(\mathbf{1} - \boldsymbol{\mu} + \boldsymbol{\nu})^T & t - 2C\boldsymbol{\mu}^T \mathbf{1}
\end{pmatrix} \succeq 0,
$$

which is a PSD constraint on a matrix that is a linear function of the variables. We can thus rewrite the entire optimization problem as a linear optimization problem subject to linear (matrix) inequalities:

$$
\begin{aligned}
\min_{\Gamma,\boldsymbol{\mu},\boldsymbol{\nu},t} \quad & t \\
\text{s.t.} \quad & \boldsymbol{\mu} \geq 0 \\
& \boldsymbol{\nu} \geq 0 \\
& \operatorname{diag}(\Gamma) = \mathbf{1} \\
& \Gamma \succeq 0 \\
& \begin{pmatrix}
K \odot \Gamma & (\mathbf{1} - \boldsymbol{\mu} + \boldsymbol{\nu}) \\
(\mathbf{1} - \boldsymbol{\mu} + \boldsymbol{\nu})^T & t - 2C\boldsymbol{\mu}^T \mathbf{1}
\end{pmatrix} \succeq 0 \\
& \Gamma = \begin{pmatrix}
Y_l Y_l^T & \Gamma_{lu} \\
\Gamma_{ul} & \Gamma_{uu}
\end{pmatrix}.
\end{aligned}
$$

(7.4)

(7.5)

This is a convex optimization problem that is solvable in polynomial time (see e.g. (Nesterov and Nemirovsky, 1994; Vandenberghe and Boyd, 1996)).   ∎

7.1.2   Some Simplifications

We can simplify the problem using the following two propositions:

Proposition 7.3 *The optimal value for* Γ *will be of the form*

$$
\Gamma = \begin{pmatrix}
Y_l Y_l^T & Y_l \gamma_u^T \\
\gamma_u Y_l^T & \Gamma_{uu}
\end{pmatrix}.
$$

Proof From the extended Schur complement lemma it follows that the column space of Γ_{lu} should be orthogonal to the null space of $Y_l Y_l^T$. This can only be if $\Gamma_{lu} = Y_l \gamma_u^T$ for some vector γ_u.   ∎

Proposition 7.4 *The constraint* $\Gamma \succeq 0$ *is equivalent with* $\begin{pmatrix} 1 & \gamma_u^T \\ \gamma_u & \Gamma_{uu} \end{pmatrix} \succeq 0.$

Proof   We use the fact that a principal submatrix of a PSD matrix is PSD as well (Horn and Johnson, 1985). By taking a principal submatrix of Γ containing exactly one row and the corresponding column among the first l, and all of the last u rows and columns, we can see that $\Gamma \succeq 0$ implies $\begin{pmatrix} 1 & \gamma_u^T \\ \gamma_u & \Gamma_{uu} \end{pmatrix} \succeq 0.$ On the other hand,

from $\begin{pmatrix} 1 & \gamma_u^T \\ \gamma_u & \Gamma_{uu} \end{pmatrix} \succeq 0$ we get

$$\begin{pmatrix} Y_l & 0 \\ 0 & \mathbf{I} \end{pmatrix} \begin{pmatrix} 1 & \gamma_u^T \\ \gamma_u & \Gamma_{uu} \end{pmatrix} \begin{pmatrix} Y_l & 0 \\ 0 & \mathbf{I} \end{pmatrix}^T = \begin{pmatrix} Y_l Y_l^T & Y_l \gamma_u^T \\ \gamma_u Y_l^T & \Gamma_{uu} \end{pmatrix} = \Gamma \succeq 0. \qquad \blacksquare$$

Thus, the final formulation of the relaxed SVM transduction problem is given by

$$
\begin{aligned}
\min_{\Gamma_{uu}, \gamma_u, \boldsymbol{\mu}, \boldsymbol{\nu}, t} \quad & t \\
\text{s.t.} \quad & \boldsymbol{\mu} \geq 0 \\
& \boldsymbol{\nu} \geq 0 \\
& \operatorname{diag}(\Gamma_{uu}) = \mathbf{1} \\
& \begin{pmatrix} 1 & \gamma_u^T \\ \gamma_u & \Gamma_{uu} \end{pmatrix} \succeq 0 \\
& \begin{pmatrix} K \odot \begin{pmatrix} Y_l Y_l^T & Y_l \gamma_u^T \\ \gamma_u Y_l^T & \Gamma_{uu} \end{pmatrix} & (\mathbf{1} - \boldsymbol{\mu} + \boldsymbol{\nu}) \\ (\mathbf{1} - \boldsymbol{\mu} + \boldsymbol{\nu})^T & t - 2C\boldsymbol{\mu}^T \mathbf{1} \end{pmatrix} \succeq 0.
\end{aligned}
$$

Here we would like to point out that the equality constraint on the diagonal can also be turned into an inequality constraint without affecting the solution: $\operatorname{diag}(\Gamma_{uu}) \leq \mathbf{1}$. Indeed, if the diagonal were lower than $\mathbf{1}$, we could simply increase it without affecting the constraints or increasing the objective. We will use this fact later in this chapter.

Computational Complexity   The total number of variables is equal to $O(l + u^2)$, the number of linear inequality constraints being $O(l + u)$, and we have an SDP constraint of size $O(l + u)$ and one of size $O(u)$. This implies a worst-case computational complexity of $O\left((l + u^2)^2 (l + u)^{2.5}\right)$ (see (Vandenberghe and Boyd, 1996) for a computational study of SDP problems).

7.1.3   Estimation of the Label Vector

As noted earlier, the optimal value for Γ may have a rank different from 1. So it does not provide us with a direct estimate for the label vector Y_u. However, the previous section gives us a hint of what a suitable estimate for it can be: it is given by simply one of the columns of Γ corresponding to a positively labeled training point. In other words, we propose to take the (thresholded) vector γ_u as an estimate for the optimal test label vector.

Other approaches are possible, such as taking the dominant eigenvector of Γ, or using a randomized approach. For more information on such methods, see (Helmberg, 2000).

7.1.4   A Bound on the Performance of the Transductive SVM

The minimum of a relaxed minimization problem is always smaller than the minimum of the unrelaxed problem. Therefore, our method immediately provides a lower bound on the squared inverse margin (plus a cost term for the soft-margin formulation), and hence an upper bound on the (soft) margin that can be achieved. On the other hand, the (soft) margin of the SVM trained on the training and test set with estimated test labels provides us with a lower bound. If both bounds are close to each other, we can be confident that the global optimum has been found.

7.2   An Approximation for Speedup

In most practical cases, the computational complexity of this relaxation is still too high. In this section we present an approximation technique that will allow for a considerable speedup of the method at the cost of a reasonable performance loss. It is notable that this technique may have wider applicability to speed up convex relaxations of combinatorial problems, such as for the max-cut problem (see e.g. (Helmberg, 2000)).

7.2.1   The Subspace Trick

Let us assume for a moment that we can come up with a d-dimensional subspace of $\mathbb{R}^n$ that contains the optimal label vector Y. We represent this subspace by the columns of the matrix $\mathbf{V} \in \mathbb{R}^{n \times d}$ which form a basis for it. Then the optimal label matrix $\Gamma = YY^T$ can be represented as $\Gamma = \mathbf{V}\mathbf{M}\mathbf{V}^T$, with $\mathbf{M} \in \mathbb{R}^{d \times d}$, a symmetric matrix of rank 1. Our relaxation of the rank constraint on Γ to an SDP constraint then translates in an analogous relaxation on $\mathbf{M}$. The resulting optimization problem can be obtained by simply replacing all occurrences of Γ with $\mathbf{V}\mathbf{M}\mathbf{V}^T$ in Eqs. 7.4 and 7.5 and optimizing over $\mathbf{M}$ instead of over Γ:

$$\min_{\mathbf{M},\boldsymbol{\mu},\boldsymbol{\nu},t} \quad t$$
$$\text{s.t.} \quad \boldsymbol{\mu} \geq 0$$
$$\boldsymbol{\nu} \geq 0$$
$$\mathrm{diag}\left(\mathbf{V}\mathbf{M}\mathbf{V}^T\right) = \mathbf{1}$$
$$\mathbf{M} \succeq 0$$
$$\begin{pmatrix} \overset{*}{K} \odot \left(\mathbf{V}\mathbf{M}\mathbf{V}^T\right) & (\mathbf{1} - \boldsymbol{\mu} + \boldsymbol{\nu}) \\ (\mathbf{1} - \boldsymbol{\mu} + \boldsymbol{\nu})^T & t - 2C\boldsymbol{\mu}^T\mathbf{1} \end{pmatrix} \succeq 0.$$

7.2.2   Finding a Subspace Close to the Label Vector

In practice, it seems impossible to come up with exactly such a subspace $\mathbf{V}$. However, there are several techniques to approximate it, which are based on fast eigenvalue problems (De Bie et al., 2004; Kamvar et al., 2003; Joachims, 2003). Here we choose to use the method proposed in (De Bie et al., 2004), which is based on a spectral relaxation of the normalized graph cut cost function (see e.g. (De Bie et al., 2005) for an introduction to spectral clustering and other eigenvalue problems in pattern recognition). Let us first briefly recapitulate the basic spectral clustering method (without label constraints). Subsequently we will show how it is possible to constrain the result to satisfy the training label information.

The basic spectral clustering problem is solved by the following generalized eigenvalue problem:

$$(\mathrm{diag}\left(K\mathbf{1}\right) - K)\mathbf{v} = \lambda\mathrm{diag}\left(K\mathbf{1}\right)\mathbf{v},$$

and the generalized eigenvectors belonging to the small eigenvalues capture the cluster structure in the data (which means that a label vector corresponding to a good clustering of the data is likely to be close to the space spanned by these generalized eigenvectors).

In order to ensure that the given training label information is respected by this solution, additional constraints should be imposed on $\mathbf{v}$. This can be achieved constructively by making use what we call the label constraint matrix $\mathbf{L}$, defined by

$$\mathbf{L} = \begin{pmatrix} \mathbf{1}_{l+} & \mathbf{1}_{l+} & 0 \\ \mathbf{1}_{l-} & -\mathbf{1}_{l-} & 0 \\ \mathbf{1}_{u} & 0 & \mathbf{I} \end{pmatrix},$$

where $\mathbf{1}_{l+}$ and $\mathbf{1}_{l-}$ are vectors containing as many ones as there are positively and, respectively, negatively, labeled training points, and $\mathbf{1}_u$ contains u ones. Using $\mathbf{L}$, we can constrain $\mathbf{v}$ to respect the training label information by parameterizing it as $\mathbf{v} = \mathbf{L}\mathbf{z}$. Then the generalized eigenvalue problem to be solved is

$$\mathbf{L}'((\mathrm{diag}\,(K\mathbf{1}) - K)\mathbf{L}\mathbf{z} = \lambda\mathbf{L}'\mathrm{diag}\,(K\mathbf{1})\,\mathbf{L}\mathbf{z}, \tag{7.6}$$

and the corresponding constrained solution is $\mathbf{v} = \mathbf{L}\mathbf{z}$. For more details about this method we encourage the reader to consult (De Bie et al., 2004).

A good subspace to which the label vector is likely to be close is then spanned by the vectors $\mathbf{v}_i = \mathbf{L}\mathbf{z}_i$ with $\mathbf{z}_i$ the generalized eigenvectors of (7.6) corresponding to the d smallest eigenvalues*(except for the one equal to zero). Hence, we can construct a good matrix $\mathbf{V}$ by stacking these $\mathbf{v}_i$ next to each other.

We are interested in solutions $\Gamma = \mathbf{V}\mathbf{M}\mathbf{V}^T$ for which oppositely labeled training points x_i and x_j have entries $\Gamma(i,j) = \Gamma(j,i) = -\Gamma(i,i) = -\Gamma(j,j)$ in the label matrix Γ. This could be ensured by imposing additional constraints on our optimization problem. However, it is easy to see that it can be ensured constructively as well, by ignoring the contribution of the constant column in $\mathbf{L}$ to $\mathbf{v}_i$, the ith column of $\mathbf{V}$ (i.e., by equating the first entry of $\mathbf{z}_i$ to 0 before computing $\mathbf{v}_i$ as $\mathbf{v}_i = \mathbf{L}\mathbf{z}_i$.

The constraint on the diagonal $\mathrm{diag}\,(\Gamma) = \mathbf{1}$ will in general be infeasible when using the subspace trick. However, as noted above, we can turn it into an inequality constraint $\mathrm{diag}\,(\Gamma) \le \mathbf{1}$ without fundamentally changing the problem. In fact, if the dimensionality d (i.e., the number of columns) of $\mathbf{V}$ were equal to u, there would be no difference between the optimal solutions obtained with or without the subspace approximation, as then the entire feasible region of Γ is the same. The diagonal would then be equal to $\mathbf{1}$, even if only an inequality constraint is specified.

Computational Complexity   The number of constraints remains roughly the same as in the unapproximated optimization problem. However, we potentially gain a lot in terms of number of free variables, which is now $O(d^2 + n)$. Therefore, for fixed d, the worst-case computational complexity is $O(n^{4.5})$. The actual value for d can be chosen as large as can be handled by the available computational resources.

7.3   General Semi-Supervised Learning Settings

Thus far we have discussed the transductive setting, which is just one of the semi-supervised learning tasks described in chapter 1. We will briefly point out, however, how the technology in this chapter can straightforwardly be extended to deal with more general settings.

7.3.1   Equivalence and Inequivalence Label Constraints

As in (De Bie et al., 2004) and in chapter 5 of this book, we are able to handle more general semi-supervised learning settings (see also (De Bie et al., 2003) and

(Shental et al., 2004) where similar constraints are exploited for doing dimensionality reduction and in computing a Gaussian mixture model respectively). Imagine the situation where we are given *grouplets* of points for which a label vector Y_i is specified. If we allow such grouplets to contain only one data point, we can assume without loss of generality that each point belongs to exactly one grouplet. The label vector Y_i indicates which points within the grouplet are given to be in the same class (an equivalence constraint), namely those with the same entry 1 or -1 in Y_i, and which ones are given to belong to opposite classes (when their entry in Y_i is different, an inequivalence constraint). In between different grouplets no information is given. This means that the overall sign of such a grouplet label vector Y_i is arbitrary.

equivalence and
inequivalence
constraints

Then, using similar techniques as we used above, one can show that the label matrix Γ should be a block matrix, with the diagonal blocks equal to $Y_i Y_i^T$, and the off-diagonal blocks (i, j) equal to $\gamma_{i,j} Y_j Y_i^T$:

$$\Gamma = \begin{pmatrix} Y_1 Y_1^T & \gamma_{1,2} Y_1 Y_2^T & \cdots & \gamma_{1,k} Y_1 Y_k^T \\ \gamma_{2,1} Y_2 Y_1^T & Y_2 Y_2^T & \cdots & \gamma_{2,k} Y_2 Y_k^T \\ \vdots & \vdots & \ddots & \vdots \\ \gamma_{k,1} Y_k Y_1^T & \gamma_{k,2} Y_k Y_2^T & \cdots & Y_k Y_k^T \end{pmatrix}.$$

where $\gamma_{i,j} = \gamma_{j,i}$ are the variables over which we have to optimize. Clearly, the label matrix as in the transduction scenario explained at the beginning of this chapter is a special case thereof. Now we can also see that the sign of the label vectors Y_i is irrelevant: upon changing the sign of Y_i; the optimal solution will simply change accordingly by reversing the signs of $\gamma_{i,j}$ and $\gamma_{j,i}$ for all j.

We want to point out that this method makes it possible to tackle the transductive SVM problem in a hierarchical way. First one can perform a crude clustering of the data points into many small clusters (grouplets) that respect the training data. Then, at a second stage, the semi-supervised SVM approach outlined above can be employed. This may greatly reduce the computational cost of the overall algorithm.

7.3.2   The Subspace Trick

Also here the subspace trick can be applied in a very analogous way. Again we can rely on the method described in (De Bie et al., 2004), which is also able to deal with equivalence and inequivalence constraints.

7.4   Empirical Results

For all implementations we used SeDuMi, a general purpose primal-dual interior point solver (Sturm, 1999) for Matlab. We only used the hard-margin SVM versions, which are obtained from the soft-margin formulations by equating μ to 0. Comparisons with SVM^{light} (Joachims, 1999) are reported, with default parameter settings.

7.4.1   The Basic SDP Relaxation

The kernel used in all experiments in this subection is the radial basis function (RBF) kernel, and the width is set to the average over all data points of the distance to their closest neighbor. Figure 7.1 shows an artificially constructed example of a transduction problem solved by the basic SDP relaxation of the transductive SVM. Only two data points were labeled, one for each of both classes. Clearly, a standard inductive SVM would fail in this extreme case.

Furthermore, the transductive optimum is so far from the inductive optimum that a greedy strategy such as SVM^{light} is bound to get stuck in a local optimum. Indeed, the norm of the SVM weight vector at the optimal labeling found by the SDP relaxation is 5.7, and for the SVM^{light} local optimum it is 7.3. Thus, the labeling found by the SDP relaxation achieves a larger margin.[2] Furthermore, it is notable that the optimum of the relaxed optimization problem is 35.318608 while the (inductive) SVM optimum when using the predicted labels for the unlabeled data points is only slightly larger: 35.318613. This indicates that most likely the optimal labeling has been found, since the optimal labeling of the SVM optimum has to lie between these values (see section 7.1.4).

In figure 7.2 we show another artificial example, where the data seem to consist of five clusters. We labeled six samples, at least one in each of the clusters. Both the SDP relaxation and SVM^{light} clearly succeed in assigning the same label to all data points that are within the same cluster, and consistent with the training label in that cluster. Figure 7.3 shows the same data set with a different labeling of the training points. The transductive optimum found by the SDP relaxation is slightly imbalanced: 38 data points in one class, and 42 in the other. For this reason SVM^{light} seems to classify two data points differently, as, by default, it tries to find a solution with the same proportion of positively versus negatively labeled test points as in the training set. The norm of the SVM weight vector for the optimal labeling as found by the SDP relaxation is equal to 5.92, which is slightly smaller than 5.96, the weight vector norm for the SVM^{light} solution. Hence also here the SDP approach achieves a larger margin.

Again, in both cases the lower bound provided by the optimum of the SDP relaxation supports the conclusion that the optimal labeling has been found. For the first problem, the optimum of the SDP relaxation is 35.338, while the SVM optimum for the predicted labels is 35.341. For the second problem, those optima

---

2. There is a catch in the comparison of both optima: the SDP method does not use an offset parameter b, whereas SVM^{light} does include such an offset. The numbers reported are the weight vector norms when *including* an offset, hence favoring SVM^{light}.

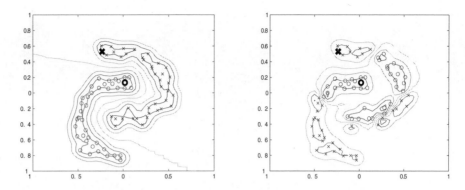

Figure 7.1   The result of the basic SDP relaxation (*left*) and of SVM^{light} (*right*) on an artificially constructed transduction problem. The 'o' and 'x' signs represent the negatively and positively labeled training points. The other data points are labeled by the algorithms. The contour lines are drawn for the SVM as trained on the complete set of data points with labels as determined by the transduction algorithms. The SDP relaxation yields the desired result, while apparently SVM^{light} got stuck in a local optimum.

are 32.3934 and 32.3937 respectively.

7.4.2   The Subspace Approximation

We conducted a few experiments on the constitution data set used in (De Bie and Cristianini, 2004c). This data set contains 780 articles, an equal number in German, French, Italian, and English, that are translations of each other. Furthermore, the articles are organized in so-called Titles. In our experiments, we solved two different problems: one is the classification of English + French texts versus Italian + English texts, and the other is the classification of the largest Title (roughly containing half of all articles) versus the smaller Titles. We tested the SDP relaxation as well as SVM^{light} on both problems for different training set sizes, and plot the results in figure 7.4. The kernel used is the normalized bag of words kernel, and $d = 4$.

Apparently, SVM^{light} outperforms the approximated SDP relaxation on the difficult problem of classifying articles according to the Title they belong to. This is most likely due to the fact that the four-dimensional subspace is too small to capture the fine cluster structure due to the different Titles. Only a subspace dimensionality d larger than four would solve the problem. However, even though the computational cost is polynomial in d, this quickly becomes computationally demanding.

On the other hand, the approximated SDP relaxation outperforms an already good performance of SVM^{light} for the easier problem, indicating that here the spectral transduction method finds a subspace sufficiently close to the correct label vector.

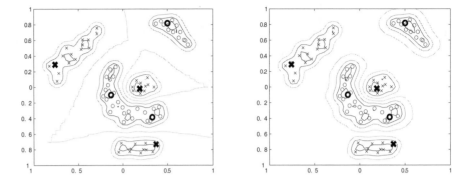

Figure 7.2   The result of the basic SDP relaxation on an artificially constructed transduction problem (*left*), and the result of SVM^{light} (*right*). Here we organized the data
points in a few small clusters. In each of the clusters, one or two samples are labeled (in
total there are six training points). For both methods, the training label determines the
test labels of all data points within the cluster, as is desirable in most applications.

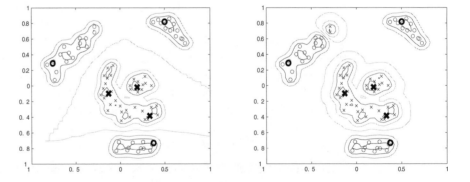

Figure 7.3   SDP transduction (*left*) and SVM^{light} (*right*) are applied to the same data
set as in figure 7.2, now with a different labeling of the training points. If we label the
data points according to the labeled point in the cluster they (visually) belong to, this
transduction problem is slightly unbalanced: one class of 38 points, the other of 42 points.
Since SVM^{light} fixes the fraction of positively and negatively labeled data points to their
fraction in the training set (by default), two data points are split off the cluster left above
to satisfy this constraint.

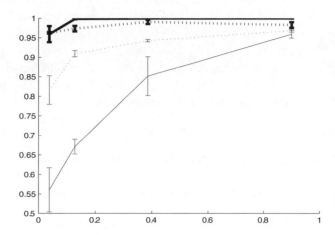

Figure 7.4 The receiver operating characteristics (ROC) score evaluated on the test set, as a function of the size of the training set for both classification problems. The bold lines are for the easy classification problem classifying languages, and the faint lines are for the harder classification problem classifying articles according to their "Title". The performance of the approximated SDP relaxation is shown in solid lines, the SVM^{light} performance in dotted lines. Bars indicate the standard deviation over three randomizations.

7.5 Summary and Outlook

In this chapter we have presented an alternative approach to the transductive SVM as a combinatorial problem. Whereas early approaches to transduction are based on learning a suitable metric (Cristianini et al., 2002b,a), and other methods tackled the problem using exact integer programming approaches (Bennett and Demiriz, 1999) (with very limited scalability) or using a local search heuristic (Joachims, 1999), our approach consists of a relaxation of the combinatorial problem to a convex optimization problem. More specifically, the resulting optimization problem is an SDP, which can be solved in a worst-case polynomial time. The application of SDP and other convex optimization techniques seems a very promising line of current research in machine learning (see e.g. also (Lanckriet et al., 2004b,a)).

While the empirical results for the relaxation are generally better than with SVM^{light}, unfortunately the scalability is still limited. To solve this problem, we introduced an approximation technique of general applicability in relaxations of combinatorial problems. The performance of this approximation strongly depends on the quality of the approximation, and mixed empirical results in comparison with SVM^{light} are reported.

Future work includes investigating whether the problem structure can be exploited to speed up the optimization problem. An important theoretical question that remains unanswered is whether the relaxation allows finding a solution with a margin that is provably within a fixed constant factor of the unrelaxed optimum. As we pointed out, the relaxation does provide us with an interval within which the true optimal solution must lie. However, the size of this interval is not known a priori as is the case for, e.g., the relaxation of the max-cut problem (see e.g. (Helmberg, 2000)). Lastly, it would be interesting to investigate theoretically what the influence is of the subspace approximation on the optimum.

Appendix: The Extended Schur Complement Lemma

We state the Schur complement lemma without proof (see e.g. (Helmberg, 2000)):

Lemma 7.5 (Schur complement lemma) *For symmetric matrices* $\mathbf{A} \succ 0$ *and* $\mathbf{C} \succeq 0$:

$$
\mathbf{C} \succeq \mathbf{B}^T \mathbf{A}^{-1} \mathbf{B} \quad \Leftrightarrow \quad \begin{pmatrix} \mathbf{A} & \mathbf{B} \\ \mathbf{B}^T & \mathbf{C} \end{pmatrix} \succeq 0.
$$

When the matrix $\mathbf{A}$ may be rank deficient, the following extended Schur complement lemma should be used. It is a generalization of the standard Schur complement lemma. We provide it here with a proof:

Extended Schur complement lemma

Lemma 7.6 (Extended Schur complement lemma) *For symmetric matrices* $\mathbf{A} \succeq 0$ *and* $\mathbf{C} \succeq 0$:

$$
\left. \begin{array}{c} \textit{The column space of } \mathbf{B} \perp \textit{ the null space of } \mathbf{A} \\ \mathbf{C} \succeq \mathbf{B}^T \mathbf{A}^\dagger \mathbf{B} \end{array} \right\} \quad \Leftrightarrow \quad \begin{pmatrix} \mathbf{A} & \mathbf{B} \\ \mathbf{B}^T & \mathbf{C} \end{pmatrix} \succeq 0.
$$

Proof We write the singular value decomposition (SVD) of $\mathbf{A}$ as

$$
\mathbf{A} = \begin{pmatrix} \mathbf{V} & \mathbf{V}_0 \end{pmatrix} \begin{pmatrix} \Lambda & 0 \\ 0 & 0 \end{pmatrix} \begin{pmatrix} \mathbf{V} & \mathbf{V}_0 \end{pmatrix}^T = \mathbf{V} \Lambda \mathbf{V}^T,
$$

where $\mathbf{V}_0$ denotes the singular vectors for the null space of $\mathbf{A}$, $\mathbf{V}$ the other singular vectors, and Λ is a diagonal matrix containing the non-zero singular values of $\mathbf{A}$, i.e. $\Lambda \succ 0$. The blocks are assumed to be compatible. Similarly, we write the SVD of $\mathbf{C}$ as

$$
\mathbf{C} = \begin{pmatrix} \mathbf{W} & \mathbf{W}_0 \end{pmatrix} \begin{pmatrix} \Delta & 0 \\ 0 & 0 \end{pmatrix} \begin{pmatrix} \mathbf{W} & \mathbf{W}_0 \end{pmatrix}^T = \mathbf{W} \Delta \mathbf{W}^T.
$$

($\Rightarrow$) If the column space of $\mathbf{B} \perp \mathbf{V}_0$, we can write $\mathbf{B}$ as $\mathbf{B} = \mathbf{V}\mathbf{B_V}$ for some matrix $\mathbf{B_V}$. Then also $\mathbf{B}^T \mathbf{A}^\dagger \mathbf{B} = \mathbf{B_V}^T \Lambda^{-1} \mathbf{B_V}$. So, from $\mathbf{C} \succeq \mathbf{B}^T \mathbf{A}^\dagger \mathbf{B} = \mathbf{B_V}^T \Lambda^{-1} \mathbf{B_V}$ and from $\Lambda \succ 0$ and $\mathbf{C} \succeq 0$, it follows from the Schur complement lemma that

$$\begin{pmatrix} \Lambda & \mathbf{B_V} \\ \mathbf{B_V}^T & \mathbf{C} \end{pmatrix} \succeq 0.$$ Left multiplication of both sides of this inequality with $\begin{pmatrix} \mathbf{V} & 0 \\ 0 & \mathbf{I} \end{pmatrix}$ and on the right with its transpose, yields $\begin{pmatrix} \mathbf{A} & \mathbf{B} \\ \mathbf{B}^T & \mathbf{C} \end{pmatrix} \succeq 0.$

($\Leftarrow$) We will prove the orthogonality of the column space of $\mathbf{B}$ with the null space of $\mathbf{A}$ by contradiction. So, assume that the column space of $\mathbf{B}$ is not orthogonal to the null space $\mathbf{V}_0$ of $\mathbf{A}$. Then, there exists a vector v_0 in the span of $\mathbf{V}_0$ for which $\mathbf{B}^T v_0 = b \neq 0$. Now, we have that $\begin{pmatrix} \mathbf{A} & \mathbf{B} \\ \mathbf{B}^T & \mathbf{C} \end{pmatrix} = \begin{pmatrix} \mathbf{V}\Lambda\mathbf{V} & \mathbf{B} \\ \mathbf{B}^T & \mathbf{C} \end{pmatrix} \succeq 0.$ Thus, for any vector w, multiplying this matrix with $\begin{pmatrix} v_0 \\ w \end{pmatrix}$ on the right and on the left with its transpose must result in a non-negative number: $2b^T w + w^T \mathbf{C} w \geq 0$. However, plugging in $w = -\mathbf{C}^\dagger b - \mathbf{W}_0 \mathbf{W}_0^T b$ yields $2b^T w + w^T \mathbf{C} w = -2b^T \mathbf{W}_0 \mathbf{W}_0^T b - b^T \mathbf{C}^\dagger b < 0$, and thus we reached a contradiction. So we have established that the column space of $\mathbf{B}$ is orthogonal to the span of $\mathbf{V}_0$.

This means that we can write $\mathbf{B}$ as $\mathbf{B} = \mathbf{V}\mathbf{B_V}$ for some particular $\mathbf{B_V}$, and

$$\begin{pmatrix} \mathbf{A} & \mathbf{B} \\ \mathbf{B}^T & \mathbf{C} \end{pmatrix} = \begin{pmatrix} \mathbf{V}\Lambda\mathbf{V}^T & \mathbf{V}\mathbf{B_V} \\ \mathbf{B_V}^T\mathbf{V}^T & \mathbf{C} \end{pmatrix} = \begin{pmatrix} \mathbf{V} & 0 \\ 0 & \mathbf{I} \end{pmatrix} \begin{pmatrix} \Lambda & \mathbf{B_V} \\ \mathbf{B_V}^T & \mathbf{C} \end{pmatrix} \begin{pmatrix} \mathbf{V} & 0 \\ 0 & \mathbf{I} \end{pmatrix}^T,$$

so that:

$$\begin{pmatrix} \mathbf{A} & \mathbf{B} \\ \mathbf{B}^T & \mathbf{C} \end{pmatrix} \succeq 0 \Rightarrow \begin{pmatrix} \Lambda & \mathbf{B_V} \\ \mathbf{B_V}^T & \mathbf{C} \end{pmatrix} \succeq 0.$$

Since $\Lambda \succ 0$ and $\mathbf{C} \succeq 0$ we can invoke the Schur complement lemma, which gives $\mathbf{C} \succeq \mathbf{B_V}^T\Lambda^{-1}\mathbf{B_V} \succeq 0$. However from the orthonormality of singular vectors $\mathbf{V}^T\mathbf{V} = \mathbf{I}$, and thus $\mathbf{B_V}^T\Lambda^{-1}\mathbf{B_V} = \mathbf{B_V}^T\mathbf{V}^T\mathbf{V}\Lambda^{-1}\mathbf{V}^T\mathbf{V}\mathbf{B_V} = \mathbf{B}^T\mathbf{A}^\dagger\mathbf{B}$, meaning that $\mathbf{B}^T\mathbf{A}^\dagger\mathbf{B} \succeq 0$. $\blacksquare$

8   Gaussian Processes and the Null-Category Noise Model

Neil D. Lawrence   NEIL@DCS.SHEF.AC.UK

Michael I. Jordan   JORDAN@CS.BERKELEY.EDU

Gaussian process classifiers (GPCs) aim to predict the posterior probability of the class label y_i given a covariate vector x_i. Under the standard assumptions generally invoked by GPC practitioners, this posterior probability is unaffected by unlabeled data points, providing no role for unlabeled data. This is in marked contrast to margin-based methods such as the support vector machine (SVM); for these methods the unlabeled data can influence the location of the decision boundary, causing it to pass through regions of low data density (see chapter 6). In this chapter we present an augmentation of the standard probabilistic classification model which incorporates a *null-category*. Given a suitable probabilistic model for the model category, we obtain a probabilistic counterpart of the margin. By combining this noise model with a GPC we obtain a classification methodology that is simultaneously discriminative, semi-supervised, and Bayesian. Our approach incorporates the cluster assumption without explicitly modeling the data density and without requiring specialized kernels.

8.1   Introduction

In this chapter we consider a Bayesian formulation of the classification problem and propose a solution to the semi-supervised learning problem within the Bayesian framework.

Bayesian methods are naturally used in the formulation of *generative* approaches to classification problems. Generative approaches explicitly model the class-conditional densities $p(x_i | y_i = 1)$ and $p(x_i | y_i = -1)$, combining these densities with the class prior probabilities $p(y_i = 1)$ and $p(y_i = -1)$ and using the Bayes theorem to form posterior probabilities:

$$p\left(y_i = 1 | x_i\right) = \frac{p\left(x_i | y_i = 1\right) p\left(y_i = 1\right)}{\sum_{y_i} p\left(x_i | y_i\right) p\left(y_i\right)}.$$

In the semi-supervised setting in which a label y_i is not observed, the corresponding contribution to the likelihood is obtained by marginalizing over y_i. This yields a mixture density for x_i, a contribution to the likelihood that is handled readily within the Bayesian formulation as a standard missing-data problem. Thus semi-supervised learning is easily accommodated within a generative Bayesian framework.

discriminative
classification

Generative methods have well-known limitations in terms of prediction performance, however, and most of the recent literature on classification has been devoted to the development of *discriminative* approaches. Many of the well-known examples of discriminative classifiers are non-Bayesian, including the support vector machine (SVM), kernelized logistic regression (KLR), and AdaBoost (Shawe-Taylor and Cristianini, 2004). It is, however, also possible to develop discriminative classifiers within a Bayesian framework; in particular, Gaussian process classifiers are discriminative classifiers that share with SVM and KLR the use of a kernel function to form nonlinear discriminant boundaries in the input space (O'Hagan, 1992).

Bayesian approaches to discriminative classification focus on modeling the posterior probability $p\left(y_i | x_i\right)$. Naively, it would seem that semi-supervised learning is simply not accommodated within any such approach—marginalizing over y_i yields a constant contribution to the likelihood, thus providing no information regarding the parameters. Non-Bayesian approaches can skirt this difficulty. In particular, statistical inference for a non-Bayesian classifier involves the specification of a "loss function" (e.g., a margin-based loss function) in addition to the specification of the model, and, as shown by several of the other chapters in this book, loss functions can be concocted to capture information coming from unlabeled data points. A related point is that non-Bayesian approaches need not model the posterior probability, and this provides additional flexibility in the design of the loss function. Bayesian approaches, on the other hand, start with the posterior probability and this appears to tie the hands of the designer, making it difficult, if not impossible, to develop discriminative, semi-supervised Bayesian learners.

graphical model
representation

In this chapter we show that it is in fact possible to solve the semi-supervised learning problem within a discriminative, Bayesian framework. To motivate the basic idea, let us first be more precise regarding the naive intuition referred to above by making use of graphical model representations of Bayesian classifiers. Consider first the graphical model representation of a generative classifier, shown in the left panel of figure 8.1. In this diagram θ parameterizes the class-conditional densities. (We have omitted a node representing the class prior probabilities.) The rectangle, or "plate," captures replication. In particular, the diagram captures an assumption that the data $\{y_i\}$ are independent and identically distributed, conditional on $\{x_i\}$ and θ. Finally, shading represents conditioning; thus the graphical model in figure 8.1 captures the standard supervised learning setting in which the labels $\{y_i\}$ are fully observed.

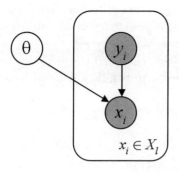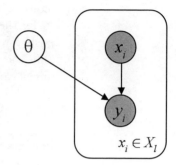

Figure 8.1 (*Left*) The graphical representation of a generative model. (*Right*) The graphical representation of a discriminative model.

The right panel of figure 8.1 presents a graphical representation of a discriminative classifier. In this case θ parameterizes the posterior probability (the meaning of θ is different in the two diagrams). Again the figure captures the standard supervised learning setting.

Let us now consider the semi-supervised learning problem. In semi-supervised learning the data X are split into a subset that is labeled, X_l, and a subset that is unlabeled, X_u. This is captured in the graphical model representations shown in figure 8.2. Consider the model shown in the left panel for the generative case. Using the d-separation criterion for assessing conditional independence in graphical models (Pearl, 1988), we see that the parameter θ and the class label y_j are *dependent*, by virtue of the fact that their common descendant x_j is observed (shaded in the graph). This graphical motif is often referred to as a "v-structure." When two nodes point to a common descendant they are (necessarily) independent only when the descendant is *unobserved*. This holds true both when y_j is observed and when it is not. Thus both labeled and unlabeled data points will affect the Bayesian posterior distribution for θ.

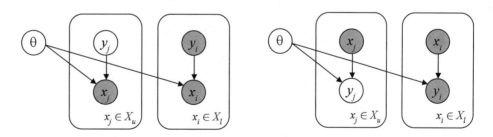

Figure 8.2 Graphical models for semi-supervised data in the generative framework (*left*) and the discriminative framework (*right*).

Contrast this with the situation in the discriminative model (right panel of figure 8.2). In this case the d-separation criterion shows that θ is *independent* of x_j for the unlabeled data. The observed value of x_j will not have an effect on the posterior distribution of θ when y_j is unobserved.

In the remaining sections of this chapter we will show how the discriminative model can be augmented to allow it to handle unlabeled data.

8.1.1 Augmenting the Model

In figure 8.2 (right panel) we saw how, in the discriminative approach, an unlabeled data point fails to influence the posterior for θ and thus the position of the decision boundary. This is because the unlabeled points and the parameters become d-separated (independent from one another) when the label y_j is unobserved. To restore the dependence we need to augment the model. This can be done by introducing an additional variable z_i that is a child of y_j and is always observed. As shown in figure 8.3 this breaks the d-separation of x_j and θ and allows probabilistic dependence to flow between these variables—even when y_j is unobserved.

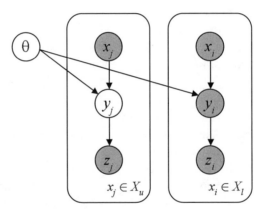

Figure 8.3 The augmented discriminative model. Even when y_j is unobserved x_j is no longer d-separated from θ because they have a common descendant which is observed. Note that for labeled examples the parameters are d-separated from the indicator variable z_j by the observation of y_j.

observability
indicator

As a simple (and naive) example of such an augmented model, let z_j be an indicator variable that identifies whether or not the data point is labeled; i.e., z_j is taken to be 0 if the ith point is labeled and 1 if the point is unlabeled. Certainly z_j is itself always observed. Now by allowing the probability of a point being labeled to depend on its label y_i — i.e., by a particular specification of the model probability $p(z_i|y_i)$ — we can reintroduce the dependence of the parameters on the unlabeled data.

Of course this simple device does not solve the semi-supervised learning problem. Indeed, if we have no reason to believe that the probability of a data point being unlabeled is different in the two classes; i.e., if $p\left(z_j = 1 | y_j = 1\right) = p\left(z_j = 1 | y_j = -1\right)$, then we have $p\left(z_j\right) = p\left(z_j | y_j\right)$ and z_j is effectively decoupled from y_j, once again d-separating θ from x_j.

On the other hand, there is no need to restrict ourselves to binary indicator variables; we can be more clever about the augmentation. The remainder of the chapter develops the specific augmentation that we propose. As will be seen, our proposal is similar in spirit to the transductive SVM (see chapter 6); we want to place the decision boundary in a region of low data density. The assumption that the interclass regions have lower data density is known as the *cluster assumption* (see chapter 1). We will show how an augmented model can capture the spirit of the cluster assumption—but without implementing an explicit density model.

8.2 The Noise Model

Our approach is based on the notion of a *null-category*, a class for which we never observe any data. The null-category can be viewed as a probabilistic interpretation of the "margin" in the SVM.[1]

To simplify our discussion of the null-category noise model, we first introduce a latent process variable f_i. This variable will allow us to discuss the noise model independently of the "process model." The latent variable allows the probability of class membership to decompose as

$$p\left(y_i | x_i\right) = \int p\left(y_i | f_i\right) p\left(f_i | x_i\right) df_i,$$

where we refer to $p\left(y_i | f_i\right)$ as the *noise model* and $p\left(f_i | x_i\right)$ as the *process model*.

8.2.1 Ordered Categorical Models

The *null-category noise model* derives from the general class of *ordered categorical models* (Agresti, 2002). In the specific context of binary classification we will consider an ordered categorical model containing three categories:

$$p\left(y_i | f_i\right) = \begin{cases} \phi\left(-\left(f_i + \frac{a}{2}\right)\right) & \text{for} \quad y_i = -1 \\ \phi\left(f_i + \frac{a}{2}\right) - \phi\left(f_i - \frac{a}{2}\right) & \text{for} \quad y_i = 0 \\ \phi\left(f_i - \frac{a}{2}\right) & \text{for} \quad y_i = 1 \end{cases},$$

where $\phi\left(x\right) = \int_{-\infty}^{x} \mathcal{N}\left(z | 0, 1\right) dz$ is the cumulative Gaussian distribution function and a is a parameter giving the width of category $y_i = 0$ (see figure 8.4).

---

1. We are not the first to consider a probabilistic interpretation of the SVM loss function. Sollich (1999, 2000) treats the margin in terms of a "not sure" class, but this interpretation suffers from problems of normalization.

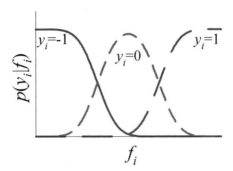

Figure 8.4   The ordered categorical noise model. The plot shows $p\left(y_i|f_i\right)$ for different values of y_i. Here we have assumed three categories.

We can also express this model in an equivalent and simpler form by replacing the cumulative Gaussian distribution by a Heaviside step function,

$$
H(x) = \begin{cases} 0 & \text{if} \quad x < 0 \\ 1 & \text{if} \quad x > 0 \end{cases},
$$

and adding independent Gaussian noise to the process model:

$$
p\left(y_i|f_i\right) = \begin{cases} H\left(-\left(f_i + \frac{1}{2}\right)\right) & \text{for} \quad y_i = -1 \\ H\left(f_i + \frac{1}{2}\right) - H\left(f_i - \frac{1}{2}\right) & \text{for} \quad y_i = 0 \\ H\left(f_i - \frac{1}{2}\right) & \text{for} \quad y_i = 1 \end{cases},
$$

where we have standardized the width parameter to 1, by assuming that the overall scale is also handled by the process model.

8.2.2   The Null-Category Noise Model

As stated previously, to induce a statistical dependence between the unlabeled data point, x_i, and the parameters, θ, we can augment the model with an additional variable z_i which indicates whether the label is missing. For the null-category noise model we also impose the constraint that

$$
p\left(z_i = 1|y_i = 0\right) = 0; \tag{8.1}
$$

in other words, a data point cannot be from the category $y_i = 0$ and be unlabeled. We then parameterize the probabilities of missing labels for the other classes as $p\left(z_i = 1|y_i = 1\right) = \gamma_+$ and $p\left(z_i = 1|y_i = -1\right) = \gamma_-$.

For points where the label is present the latent process is updated as usual (because z_i is d-separated from θ by y_i). When the data point's label is missing, the posterior process is updated using the likelihood

$$p\left(z_i = 1 | f_i\right) = \sum_{y_i} p\left(y_i | f_i\right) p\left(z_i = 1 | y_i\right).$$

effective
likelihood
function

By marginalizing across y_i when the label is missing and otherwise using the standard likelihood, we recover the "effective likelihood function" for a single data point, $L\left(f_i\right)$. It takes one of three forms:

$$L\left(f_i\right) = \begin{cases} H\left(-\left(f_i + \frac{1}{2}\right)\right) & \text{for} \quad y_i = -1,\, z_i = 0 \\ \gamma_- H\left(-\left(f_i + \frac{1}{2}\right)\right) + \gamma_+ H\left(f_i - \frac{1}{2}\right) & \text{for} \quad z_i = 1 \\ H\left(f_i - \frac{1}{2}\right) & \text{for} \quad y_i = 1,\, z_i = 0 \end{cases}.$$

The constraint imposed by (8.1) implies that an unlabeled data point never comes from the class $y_i = 0$. Since $y_i = 0$ lies between the labeled classes this is equivalent to a hard assumption that no data come from the region around the decision boundary. We can also soften this hard assumption, if so desired, by injection of noise into the process model. If we also assume that our labeled data only come from the classes $y_i = 1$ and $y_i = -1$ we will never obtain any evidence for data with $y_i = 0$; for this reason we refer to this category as the *null-category* and the overall model as a *null-category noise model* (NCNM).

8.3   Process Model and Effect of the Null-Category

The noise model we have described can be used within a range of optimization frameworks. Indeed, viewing the noise model as a probabilistic interpretation of the SVM's margin, if we specify

$$f_i = w^{\mathrm{T}} x_i,$$

prescribe a Gaussian prior distribution for w,

$$p\left(w\right) = \mathcal{N}\left(w | \mathbf{0}, \mathbf{I}\right),$$

and let z have a multivariate Gaussian distribution with mean m and covariance Σ,

$$\mathcal{N}\left(z | m, \Sigma\right) = \frac{1}{\left(2\pi\right)^{\frac{d}{2}} |\Sigma|^{\frac{1}{2}}} \exp\left(-\frac{1}{2}\left(z - m\right)^{\mathrm{T}} \Sigma^{-1}\left(z - m\right)\right),$$

SVM as MAP
solution

then the maximum a posteriori (MAP) solution for w is given by the linear SVM algorithm. Naturally f_i can then be "kernelized" and the MAP solution for the model becomes equivalent to the nonlinear SVM. However, in this domain the meaning of a prior distribution over w is not entirely clear, and it is generally more convenient to consider a process prior over f_i. As is well known, the process prior which leads to the SVM as a MAP solution is the Gaussian process prior (for two useful reviews of Gaussian processes see O'Hagan (1992); Williams (1998)). Under the Gaussian process prior the values $\{f_i\}$ are jointly distributed as a zero-mean Gaussian distribution with covariance given by the kernel matrix K.

8.3.1   Gaussian Processes

In the remainder of this chapter we will consider the use of a Gaussian process prior over f_i. The algorithms we consider update the process posterior in a sequential manner, incorporating a single data point at a time. It is therefore sufficient to consider a univariate distribution over f_i given x_i, of the form

$$p\left(f_i | x_i\right) = \mathcal{N}\left(f_i | \mu\left(x_i\right), \varsigma\left(x_i\right)\right),$$

effect on
posterior

where the mean $\mu\left(x_i\right)$ and the variance $\varsigma\left(x_i\right)$ are functions of the covariate x_i. A natural consideration in this setting is the effect of our likelihood function on the distribution over f_i when incorporating a new data point. As we have already mentioned, if we observe y_i, then the parameters are d-separated from z_i. In this case the effect of the likelihood on the posterior process will be similar to that incurred in binary classification, in that the posterior will be a convolution of the step function and a Gaussian distribution. However, when the data point's label is missing the effect will depend on the mean and variance of $p\left(f_i | x_i\right)$. If this Gaussian has little mass in the null-category region (i.e., the region between the classes), the posterior will be similar to the prior. However, if the Gaussian has significant mass in the null-category region, the outcome may be loosely described in two ways:

1. If $p\left(f_i | x_i\right)$ "spans the likelihood," figure 8.5 (left), then the mass of the posterior can be apportioned to either side of the null-category region, leading to a bimodal posterior. The variance of the posterior will be greater than the variance of the prior, a consequence of the fact that the effective likelihood function is not log-concave (as can be easily verified).

2. If $p\left(f_i | x_i\right)$ is "rectified by the likelihood," figure 8.5 (right), then the mass of the posterior will be pushed into one side of the null-category and the variance of the posterior will be smaller than the variance of the prior.

Note that for all situations in which a portion of the mass of the prior distribution falls within the null-category region it is pushed out to one side or both sides. The intuition behind the two situations is that in case 1, it is not clear what label the data point has, but it is clear that it shouldn't be where it currently is (in the null-category). The result is that the process variance increases. In case 2 the data point is being assigned a label and the decision boundary is pushed to one side of the point so that it is classified according to the assigned label.

In figure 8.6, we demonstrate the effect of the null-category. We sampled a vector $\left(f_i\right)_{i=1}^{500}$ from a Gaussian process with an radial basis function (RBF) kernel. The covariates $\left(x_i\right)_{i=1}^{500}$ were sampled uniformly from the two-dimensional unit square.

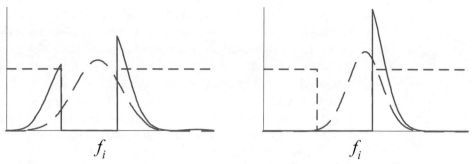

Figure 8.5 Two situations of interest. Diagrams show the prior distribution over f_i (long dashes), the effective likelihood function from the noise model when $z_i = 1$ (short dashes), and a schematic of the resulting posterior over f_i (solid line). (*Left*) The posterior is bimodal and has a larger variance than the prior. (*Right*) The posterior has one dominant mode and a lower variance than the prior. In both cases the process is pushed away from the null-category.

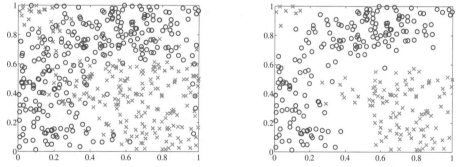

Figure 8.6 Samples from a standard Gaussian process classifier with a probit noise model (*left*) and a Gaussian process with the null-category noise model (*right*). The covariate vectors were originally sampled uniformly from the unit square. The null-category noise model has the effect of reducing the data density in the region of the decision boundary.

In the left panel, points were assigned to the class of $y_i = 1$ with probability $\phi(f_i)$ and were otherwise assigned a class of $y_i = -1$. In the right panel they were assigned the class $y_i = 1$ with probability $\phi\left(f_i - \frac{1}{2}\right)$ and the class $y_i = -1$ with probability $\phi\left(-f_i - \frac{1}{2}\right)$; all other points were assumed to have come from the null category and were removed. Note that this rejection of points has the effect of reducing the data density near the decision boundary.

8.4 Posterior Inference and Prediction

Broadly speaking, the effects discussed above are independent of the process model: the effective likelihood will always force the latent function away from the null-category. To implement our model, however, we must choose a specific process model and inference method. The nature of the noise model means that it is unlikely that we will find a nontrivial process model for which inference (in terms of marginalizing f_i) will be tractable. We therefore turn to approximations which are inspired by "assumed density filtering" (ADF) methods; see, e.g., Csató (2002). The idea in ADF is to approximate the (generally non-Gaussian) posterior with a Gaussian by matching the moments between the approximation and the true posterior. ADF has also been extended to allow each approximation to be revisited and improved as the posterior distribution evolves (Minka, 2001).

One further complication is that the "effective likelihood" associated with the null-category noise model is not log-concave. The implication of this is that the variance of the posterior process can increase when a point is included. This situation is depicted in figure 8.5 (left); the posterior depicted in this plot has a larger variance than the prior distribution. This increase in variance is difficult to accommodate within the ADF approximation framework and in our implementation it was ignored.

learning the hyperparameters
One important advantage of the Gaussian process framework is that it is amenable to an empirical Bayesian treatment—the hyperparameters in the covariance function can be learned by optimizing the marginal likelihood. In practice, however, if the process variance is maximized in an unconstrained manner the effective width of the null-category can be driven to zero, yielding a model that is equivalent to a standard binary classification noise model. The process variance controls the scale of the function. If the process variance is allowed to grow in an unconstrained manner the effective width of the null-category region becomes zero, removing any effect from unlabeled data points. To prevent this from happening we regularize by imposing an L1 penalty on the process variances (this is equivalent to placing an exponential prior on those parameters). The L1 penalty prefers smaller process variances thereby increasing the effective width of the null-category region. The model therefore prefers a large null-category region. This is analogous to maximizing the margin in a support vector machine.

8.4.1   Prediction with the NCNM

Once the parameters of the process model have been learned, we wish to make predictions about a new test-point x_* via the marginal distribution $p(y_*|x_*)$. For the NCNM an issue arises here: this distribution will have a non-zero probability of $y_* = 0$, a label that does not exist in either our labeled or unlabeled data. This is where the role of z_* becomes essential. The new point also has $z_* = 1$ so in reality the probability that a data point is from the positive class is given by

$$p(y_*|x_*, z_* = 1) \propto p(z_* = 1|y_*)\, p(y_*|x_*). \tag{8.2}$$

The constraint that $p(z_* = 1|y_* = 0) = 0$ causes the predictions to be correctly normalized. So for the distribution to be correctly normalized for a test data point we must assume that we have observed $z_* = 1$.

An interesting consequence is that observing x_* will have an effect on the process model. This is contrary to the standard Gaussian process setup (see, e.g., Williams (1998)) in which the predictive distribution depends only on the labeled training data and the location of the test point x_*. In the NCNM the entire process model $p(f_*|x_*)$ should be updated after the observation of x_*. This is not a particular disadvantage of the NCNM; it is an inevitable consequence of any method that allows unlabeled data to affect the location of the decision boundary—a consequence the probabilistic framework makes explicit. In practice, however, we may disregard such considerations and make (possibly suboptimal) predictions of the class labels according to (8.2) without updating the location of the decision boundary.

8.5   Results

Sparse representations of the training data are essential for speeding up the process of learning. We made use of the informative vector machine (IVM) approach in which the data are sparsified via a sequential greedy method in which points are placed in an active set according to information-theoretic criteria. This approach provides an approximation to a full Gaussian process classifier which is competitive with the SVM in terms of speed and accuracy. The IVM also enables efficient learning of kernel hyperparameters, and we made use of this feature in all of our experiments.

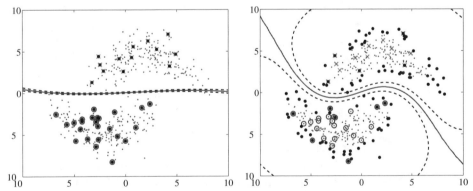

Figure 8.7   Results from the toy problem. There are 400 points, which have probability 0.1 of receiving a label. Labeled data points are shown as circles and crosses. Data points in the active set are shown as large dots. All other data points are shown as small dots. (*Left*) Learning on the labeled data with the IVM algorithm. All labeled points are used in the active set. (*Right*) Learning on the labeled and unlabeled data with the NCNM. There are 100 points in the active set. In both plots decision boundaries are shown as a solid line; dotted lines represent contours within 0.5 of the decision boundary (for the NCNM this is the edge of the null-category).

In all our experiments we used a kernel of the form

$$k_{nm} = \theta_2 \exp\left(-\theta_1 \left(\mathbf{x}_n - \mathbf{x}_m\right)^{\mathrm{T}} \left(\mathbf{x}_n - \mathbf{x}_m\right)\right) + \theta_3 \delta_{nm},$$

where δ_{nm} is the Kronecker delta function. The parameters of the kernel were learned by performing type II maximum likelihood over the active set. Since active set selection causes the marginalized likelihood to fluctuate it cannot be used to monitor convergence; we therefore simply iterated fifteen times between active set selection and kernel parameter optimization. The parameters of the noise model, $\{\gamma_+, \gamma_-\}$, can also be optimized, but note that if we constrain $\gamma_+ = \gamma_- = \gamma$, then the likelihood is maximized by setting γ to the proportion of the training set that is unlabeled.

We first considered an illustrative toy problem to demonstrate the capabilities of our model. We generated two-dimensional data in which two class-conditional densities interlock. There were 400 points in the original data set. Each point was assigned a label with probability 0.1; leading to 37 labeled points. First a standard IVM classifier was trained on the labeled data only (figure 8.7, left). We then used the null-category approach to train a classifier that incorporates the unlabeled data. As shown in figure 8.7 (right), the resulting decision boundary finds a region of low data density and more accurately reflects the underlying data distribution.

8.5.1   USPS Digits

We next considered the null-category noise model for learning of the USPS hand-written digit data set. This data set is fully labeled, but we can ignore a proportion of the labels and treat the data set as a semi-supervised task. In the experiments that followed we used an RBF kernel with a linear component. We ran each experiment ten times, randomly selecting the data points that were labeled. The fraction of labeled points, r, was varied between 0.01 and 0.25. Each digit was treated as a separate "one against the others" binary classification class. We also summarized these binary classification tasks with an overall error rate by allocating each test data point to the class with the highest probability. In the first of our experiments, we attempted to learn the parameters of the kernel by maximizing the IVM's approximation to the marginal likelihood. The results are summarized in table 8.1.

As can be seen in the table, good classification results are obtained for values of r above 0.1, but poor results are obtained for values of r below 0.1. This appears troublesome at first sight, given that many semi-supervised learning algorithms give reasonable performance even when the proportion of unlabeled data is as low as 0.1. It must be borne in mind, however, that the algorithm presented here faces the additional burden of learning the kernel hyperparameters. Most other approaches do not have this capability and therefore results are typically reported for a given, tuned set of kernel parameters. To make a more direct comparison we also undertook experiments in which the kernel hyperparameters were fixed to the values found by an IVM trained on the fully labeled data set. These results are summarized in

Table 8.1 Table of results for semi-supervised learning on the USPS digit data.

r	0	1	2	3	4	
0.010	18 ± 0.0	8.0 ± 6.5	9.9 ± 0.0	8.3 ± 0.0	10 ± 0.0	
0.025	11 ± 8.8	0.98 ± 0.1	9.9 ± 0.0	6.5 ± 2.4	10 ± 0.0	
0.050	1.7 ± 0.2	1.0 ± 0.1	3.7 ± 0.4	5.4 ± 2.7	7.4 ± 3.5	
0.10	1.7 ± 0.1	0.95 ± 0.1	3.2 ± 0.2	3.2 ± 0.3	3.3 ± 0.3	
0.25	1.6 ± 0.2	0.97 ± 0.1	2.5 ± 0.2	2.9 ± 0.2	2.8 ± 0.1	
r	5	6	7	8	9	Overall
0.010	8.0 ± 0.0	8.5 ± 0.0	7.3 ± 0.0	8.3 ± 0.0	8.8 ± 0.0	83 ± 7.3
0.025	8.0 ± 0.0	8.5 ± 0.0	7.3 ± 0.0	8.3 ± 0.0	8.8 ± 0.0	64 ± 5.0
0.05	7.1 ± 1.9	1.7 ± 0.2	7.3 ± 0.0	7.4 ± 1.9	7.6 ± 2.7	33 ± 7.2
0.1	3.0 ± 0.3	1.5 ± 0.1	1.3 ± 0.1	3.4 ± 0.2	2.0 ± 0.3	7.7 ± 0.2
0.25	2.4 ± 0.2	1.3 ± 0.2	1.2 ± 0.1	2.6 ± 0.3	1.6 ± 0.2	6.4 ± 0.2

For these results the model learned the kernel parameters. We give the results for the individual binary classification tasks and the overall error computed from the combined classifiers. Each result is summarized by the mean and standard deviation of the percent classification error across ten runs with different random seeds.

table 8.2. As expected these results are much better in the range where $r < 0.1$. With the exception of the digit 2 at $r = 0.01$ a sensible decision boundary was learned for at least one of the runs even when $r = 0.01$.

8.6 Discussion

We have presented a Bayesian approach to the semi-supervised learning problem. While Bayesian approaches to semi-supervised learning are well known and easy to formulate in the generative setting, they appear to be more difficult to formulate in the discriminative setting—an unfortunate state of affairs given the superior performance attainable with discriminative methods. Indeed, we are aware of no previous work on classification algorithms that is simultaneously discriminative, semi-supervised, and Bayesian. The approach presented in the previous paper shows that this gap in the literature is not due to a fundamental limitation. Indeed, discriminative, semi-supervised, Bayesian algorithms exist, and can be developed via a relatively straightforward augmentation involving a "null-category." Drawing its inspiration from the role of the margin in the support vector machine, our null-category noise model provides a probabilistic implementation of the assumption that discriminant boundaries should pass through regions of low data density. We achieve this within a fully discriminative framework that does not require modeling of class-conditional densities.

Our approach provides a practical approach to performing kernel-based, semi-

Table 8.2   Table of results for semi-supervised learning on the USPS digit data.

r	0	1	2	3	4
0.010	3.2 ± 5.2	13 ± 14	9.9 ± 0.0	3.1 ± 0.2	8.3 ± 2.6
0.025	1.5 ± 0.2	1.5 ± 0.9	5.2 ± 2.0	2.9 ± 0.2	4.4 ± 2.1
0.050	1.5 ± 0.2	1.2 ± 0.2	3.4 ± 0.4	2.9 ± 0.1	3.3 ± 0.2
0.10	1.5 ± 0.1	1.2 ± 0.1	2.8 ± 0.2	2.8 ± 0.2	3.0 ± 0.2
0.25	1.4 ± 0.2	1.3 ± 0.2	2.4 ± 0.2	2.6 ± 0.2	2.8 ± 0.2
r	5	6	7	8	9	Overall
0.010	7.5 ± 1.0	7.7 ± 8.5	12 ± 17	7.5 ± 1.2	35 ± 23	42 ± 10
0.025	5.0 ± 1.3	1.6 ± 0.2	1.9 ± 1.9	4.3 ± 0.5	9.9 ± 8.5	14 ± 6.1
0.050	3.6 ± 0.6	1.5 ± 0.1	1.3 ± 0.1	4.1 ± 0.4	2.6 ± 1.3	8.4 ± 0.7
0.10	2.8 ± 0.2	1.3 ± 0.1	1.3 ± 0.1	3.5 ± 0.3	2.0 ± 0.2	7.2 ± 0.5
0.25	2.3 ± 0.2	1.2 ± 0.1	1.2 ± 0.1	2.7 ± 0.2	1.6 ± 0.2	6.1 ± 0.4

For these results the model was given the kernel parameters learned by the IVM on the standard fully labeled data. We give the results for the individual binary classification tasks and the overall error computed from the combined classifiers.

supervised learning without requiring the design of specialized kernels.

Code for recreating our experiments is available from `http://www.dcs.shef.ac.uk/~neil/ncnm`.

9 Entropy Regularization

Yves Grandvalet   YVES.GRANDVALET@UTC.FR
Yoshua Bengio   BENGIOY@IRO.UMONTREAL.CA

The problem of semi-supervised induction consists in learning a decision rule from labeled and unlabeled data. This task can be undertaken by discriminative methods, provided that learning criteria are adapted consequently. In this chapter, we motivate the use of entropy regularization as a means to benefit from unlabeled data in the framework of maximum a posteriori estimation. The learning criterion is derived from clearly stated assumptions and can be applied to any smoothly parameterized model of posterior probabilities. The regularization scheme favors low-density separation, without any modeling of the density of input features. The contribution of unlabeled data to the learning criterion induces local optima, but this problem can be alleviated by deterministic annealing. For well-behaved models of posterior probabilities, deterministic annealing expectation-maximization (EM) provides a decomposition of the learning problem in a series of concave subproblems. Other approaches to the semi-supervised problem are shown to be close relatives or limiting cases of entropy regularization. A series of experiments illustrates the good behavior of the algorithm in terms of performance and robustness with respect to the violation of the postulated low-density separation assumption. The minimum entropy solution benefits from unlabeled data and is able to challenge mixture models and manifold learning in a number of situations.

9.1 Introduction

semi-supervised induction

This chapter addresses semi-supervised induction, which refers to the learning of a decision rule, on the entire input domain $\mathcal{X}$, from labeled and unlabeled data. The objective is identical to the one of supervised classification: generalize from examples. The problem differs in the respect that the supervisor's responses are missing for some training examples. This characteristic is shared with transduction, which has, however, a different goal, that is, of predicting labels on a set of predefined patterns.

In the probabilistic framework, semi-supervised induction is a missing data problem, which can be addressed by generative methods such as mixture models thanks to the EM algorithm and extensions thereof (McLachlan, 1992). Generative models apply to the joint density of patterns x and class y. They have appealing features, but they also have major drawbacks. First, the modeling effort is much more demanding than for discriminative methods, since the model of $p(x, y)$ is necessarily more complex than the model of $P(y|x)$. Being more precise, the generative model is also more likely to be misspecified. Second, the fitness measure is not discriminative, so that better models are not necessarily better predictors of class labels. These issues are addressed in chapters 2 and 4.

These difficulties have led to proposals where unlabeled data are processed by supervised classification algorithms. Here, we describe an estimation principle applicable to any probabilistic classifier, aiming at making the most of unlabeled data when they should be beneficial to the learning process, that is, when classes are well apart. The method enables control of the contribution of unlabeled examples, thus providing robustness with respect to the violation of the postulated low-density separation assumption.

Section 9.2 motivates the estimation criterion. It is followed by the description of the optimization algorithms in section 9.3. The connections with some other principles or algorithms are then detailed in section 9.4. Finally, the experiments of section 9.5 offer a test bed to evaluate the behavior of entropy regularization, with comparisons to generative models and manifold learning.

9.2   Derivation of the Criterion

In this section, we first show that unlabeled data do not contribute to the maximum-likelihood estimation of discriminative models. The belief that "unlabeled data should be informative" should then be encoded as a prior to modify the estimation process. We argue that assuming high entropy for $P(y|x)$ is a sensible encoding of this belief, and finally we describe the learning criterion derived from this assumption.

9.2.1   Likelihood

The maximum-likelihood principle is one of the main estimation techniques in supervised learning, which is closely related to the more recent margin maximization techniques such as boosting and support vector machines (SVMs) (Friedman et al., 2000). We start here by looking at the contribution of unlabeled examples to the (conditional) likelihood.

The learning set is denoted $\mathcal{L}_n = \{(x_1, y_1), \ldots, (x_l, y_l), x_{l+1}, \ldots, x_n\}$, where the l first examples are labeled, and the $u = n - l$ last ones are unlabeled. We missing value   assume that labels are missing at random, that is, the missingness mechanism
mechanism

is independent from the missing class information. Let h be the random variable encoding missingness: $h = 1$ if y is hidden and $h = 0$ if y is observed. The missing at random assumption reads

$$P(h|x, y) = P(h|x) . \tag{9.1}$$

This assumption excludes cases where missingness may indicate a preference for a particular class (this can happen, for example, in opinion polls where the "refuse to answer" option may hide an inclination toward a shameful answer). Assuming independent examples, the conditional log likelihood is then

$$L(\theta; \mathcal{L}_n) = \sum_{i=1}^{l} \ln P(y_i|x_i; \theta) + \sum_{i=1}^{n} \ln P(h_i|x_i). \tag{9.2}$$

Maximizing (9.2) with respect to θ can be performed by dropping the second term of the right-hand side. It corresponds to maximizing the complete likelihood when no assumption whatsoever is made on $p(x)$ (McLachlan, 1992). As unlabeled data are not processed by the model of posterior probabilities, they do not convey information regarding $P(y|x)$. In the maximum a posteriori (MAP) framework, unlabeled data are useless regarding discrimination when the priors on $p(x)$ and $P(y|x)$ factorize and are not tied (see chapter 2): observing x does not inform about y, unless the modeler assumes so. Benefiting from unlabeled data requires assumptions of some sort on the relationship between x and y. In the MAP framework, this will be encoded by a prior distribution. As there is no such thing as a universally relevant prior, we should look for an induction bias allowing the processing of unlabeled data when the latter are known to convey information.

9.2.2   When Are Unlabeled Examples Informative?

Theory provides little support for the numerous experimental evidence showing that unlabeled examples can help the learning process. Learning theory is mostly developed at the two extremes of the statistical paradigm: in parametric statistics where examples are known to be generated from a known class of distribution, and in the distribution-free structural risk minimization (SRM) or probably approximately correct (PAC) frameworks. Semi-supervised induction does not fit the distribution-free frameworks: no positive statement can be made without distributional assumptions, as for some distributions $p(x, y)$, unlabeled data are noninformative while supervised learning is an easy task. In this regard, generalizing from labeled and unlabeled data may differ from transductive inference.

In parametric statistics, theory has shown the benefit of unlabeled examples, either for specific distributions (O'Neill, 1978), or for mixtures of the form $p(x) = \pi p(x|y = 1) + (1 - \pi)p(x|y = 2)$, where the estimation problem is essentially reduced to the one of estimating the mixture parameter π (Castelli and Cover, 1996). These studies conclude that the (asymptotic) information content of unlabeled examples

missing at random

information content of unlabeled examples

decreases as classes overlap.[1] Hence, in the absence of general results, postulating that classes are well apart, separated by a low-density area, is sensible when one expects to take advantage of unlabeled examples.

9.2.3   A Measure of Class Overlap

There are many possible measures of class overlap. We chose Shannon's conditional entropy, which is invariant to the parameterization of the model, but the framework developed below could be applied to other measures of class overlap, such as Renyi entropies. Note, however, that the algorithms detailed in section 9.3.1 are specific to this choice. Obviously, the conditional entropy may only be related to the usefulness of unlabeled data where labeling is indeed ambiguous. Hence, the measure of class overlap should be conditioned on missingness:

conditional entropy

$$H(y|x, h = 1) = -\mathbf{E}_{xy}\left[\ln P(y|x, h = 1)\right] \tag{9.3}$$

$$= -\int \sum_{m=1}^{M} \ln P(y = m|x, h = 1)p(x, y = m|h = 1)\ dx\ .$$

In the MAP framework, assumptions are encoded by means of a prior on the model parameters. Stating that we expect a high conditional entropy does not uniquely define the form of the prior distribution, but the latter can be derived by resorting to the maximum entropy principle.[2]

The maximum entropy prior verifying $\mathbf{E}_\theta\left[H(y|x, h = 1)\right] = c$, where the constant c quantifies how small the entropy should be on average, takes the form

$$p(\theta) \propto \exp\left(-\lambda H(y|x, h = 1))\right)\ , \tag{9.4}$$

where λ is the positive Lagrange multiplier corresponding to the constant c.

Computing $H(y|x, h = 1)$ requires a model of $p(x, y|h = 1)$, whereas the choice of supervised classification is motivated by the possibility of limiting modeling to conditional probabilities. We circumvent the need of additional modeling by applying the plug-in principle, which consists in replacing the expectation with respect to $(x|h = 1)$ by the sample average. This substitution, which can be interpreted as "modeling" $p(x|h = 1)$ by its empirical distribution, yields

plug-in principle

$$H_{\text{emp}}(y|x, h = 1; \mathcal{L}_n) = -\frac{1}{u}\sum_{i=l+1}^{n}\sum_{m=1}^{M} P(m|x_i, t_i = \mathbf{1})\ln P(m|x_i, t_i = \mathbf{1})\ . \tag{9.5}$$

---

1. This statement, given explicitly by O'Neill (1978), is also formalized, though not stressed, by Castelli and Cover (1996), where the Fisher information for unlabeled examples at the estimate $\hat{\pi}$ is clearly a measure of the overlap between class-conditional densities: $I_u(\hat{\pi}) = \int \frac{(p(x|y=1) - p(x|y=2))^2}{\hat{\pi}p(x|y=1) + (1-\hat{\pi})p(x|y=2)}\ dx$.
2. Here, maximum entropy refers to the construction principle which enables derivation of distributions from constraints, not to the content of priors regarding entropy.

The missing at random assumption (9.1) yields $P(y|x, h = 1) = P(y|x)$, hence

$$H_{\text{emp}}(y|x, h = 1; \mathcal{L}_n) = -\frac{1}{u} \sum_{i=l+1}^{n} \sum_{m=1}^{M} P(m|x_i) \ln P(m|x_i) \ . \tag{9.6}$$

This empirical functional is plugged in (9.4) to define an empirical prior on parameters θ, that is, a prior whose form is partly defined from data (Berger, 1985).

9.2.4 Entropy Regularization

The MAP estimate is defined as the maximizer of the posterior distribution, that is, the maximizer of

$$
\begin{aligned}
C(\theta, \lambda; \mathcal{L}_n) &= L(\theta; \mathcal{L}_n) - \lambda H_{\text{emp}}(y|x, h = 1; \mathcal{L}_n) \\
&= \sum_{i=1}^{l} \ln P(y_i|x_i; \theta) + \lambda \sum_{i=l+1}^{n} \sum_{m=1}^{M} P(m|x_i; \theta) \ln P(m|x_i; \theta) \ , \tag{9.7}
\end{aligned}
$$

where the constant terms in the log likelihood (9.2) and log prior (9.4) have been dropped.

While $L(\theta; \mathcal{L}_n)$ is only sensitive to labeled data, $H_{\text{emp}}(y|x, h = 1; \mathcal{L}_n)$ is only affected by the value of $P(m|x; \theta)$ on unlabeled data. Since these two components of the learning criterion are concave in $P(m|x; \theta)$, their weighted difference is usually not concave, except for $\lambda = 0$. Hence, the optimization surface is expected to possess local maxima, which are likely to be more numerous as u and λ grow. Semi-supervised induction is halfway between classification and clustering; hence, the progressive loss of concavity in the shift from supervised to unsupervised learning is not surprising, as most clustering optimization problems are nonconvex (Rose et al., 1990).

The empirical approximation H_{emp} (9.5) of H (9.3) breaks down for wiggly functions $P(m|\cdot)$ with abrupt changes between data points (where $p(x)$ is bounded from below). As a result, it is important to constrain $P(m|\cdot)$ in order to enforce the closeness of the two functionals. In the following experimental section, we imposed such a constraint on $P(m|\cdot)$ by adding a smoothness penalty to the criterion C (9.7). Note that this penalty also provides a means to control the capacity of the classifier.

9.3 Optimization Algorithms

9.3.1 Deterministic Annealing EM and IRLS

In its application to semi-supervised learning, the EM algorithm is generally used to maximize the joint likelihood from labeled and unlabeled data. This iterative algorithm increases the likelihood at each step and converges toward a stationary point of the likelihood surface.

The criterion $C(\theta, \lambda; \mathcal{L}_n)$ (9.7) departs from the conditional likelihood by its entropy term. It is in fact formulated as each intermediate optimization subproblem solved in the deterministic annealing EM algorithm. This scheme was originally proposed to alleviate the difficulties raised by local maxima in joint likelihood for some clustering problems (Rose et al., 1990; Yuille et al., 1994). It consists in optimizing the likelihood subject to a constraint on the level of randomness, measured by the entropy of the model of $P(y|x)$. The Lagrangian formulation of this optimization problem is precisely (9.7), where $T = 1 - \lambda$ is the analogue of a temperature. Deterministic annealing is the cooling process defining the continuous path of solutions indexed by the temperature. Following this path is expected to lead to a final solution with lower free energy, that is, higher likelihood.

deterministic annealing

If the optimization criteria are identical, the goals, and the hyperparameters used are different. On the one hand, in deterministic annealing EM, one aims at reaching the global maximum (or at least a good local optimum) of the joint likelihood. For this purpose, one starts from a concave function ($T \to \infty$) and the temperature is gradually lowered down to $T = 1$, in order to reach a state with high likelihood. On the other hand, the goal of entropy regularization is to alter the maximum-likelihood solution, by biasing it toward low entropy. One starts from a possibly concave conditional likelihood ($\lambda = 0$, i.e., $T = 1$) and the temperature is gradually lowered until it reaches some predetermined value $1 - \lambda_0 = T_0 \geq 0$, to return a good local maximum of $C(\theta, \lambda_0; \mathcal{L}_n)$.

Despite these differences, the analogy with deterministic annealing EM is useful because it provides an optimization algorithm for maximizing $C(\theta, \lambda; \mathcal{L}_n)$ (9.7). Deterministic annealing EM (Yuille et al., 1994) is a simple generalization of the standard EM algorithm. Starting from the solution obtained at the highest temperature, the path of solution is computed by gradually increasing λ. For each trial value of λ, the corresponding solution is computed by a two-step iterative procedure, where the expected log likelihood is maximized at the M step, and where soft (expected) assignments are imputed at the E step for unlabeled data. The only difference with standard EM takes place at the E step, where the expected value of labels is computed using the Gibbs distribution

deterministic annealing EM

$$g_m(x_i; \theta) = \frac{P(m|x_i; \theta)^{\frac{1}{1-\lambda}}}{\sum_{\ell=1}^{M} P(\ell|x_i; \theta)^{\frac{1}{1-\lambda}}} \quad,$$

which distributes the probability mass according to the current estimated posterior $P(m|\cdot)$ (for labeled examples, the assignment is clamped at the original label $g_m(x_i; \theta) = \delta_{my_i}$). For $0 < \lambda \leq 1$, the Gibbs distribution is more peaked than the estimated posterior. One recovers EM for $\lambda = 0$, and the hard assignments of classification EM (CEM) (Celeux and Govaert, 1992) correspond to $\lambda = 1$.

The M step then consists in maximizing the expected log likelihood with respect to θ,

$$\theta^{s+1} = \arg\max_\theta \sum_{i=1}^{n} \sum_{m=1}^{M} g_m(x_i; \theta^s) \ln P(m|x_i; \theta) \ , \tag{9.8}$$

where the expectation is taken with respect to the distribution $(g_1(\cdot; \theta^s), \ldots, g_M(\cdot; \theta^s))$, and θ^s is the current estimate of θ.

The optimization problem (9.8) is concave in $P(m|x; \theta)$ and also in θ for logistic regression models. Hence it can be solved by a second-order optimization algorithm, such as the Newton-Raphson algorithm, which is often referred to as iteratively reweighted least squares, or IRLS in statistical textbooks (Friedman et al., 2000).

IRLS

We omit the detailed derivation of IRLS, and provide only the update equation for θ in the standard logistic regression model for binary classification problems. [3] The model of posterior distribution is defined as

$$P(1|x; \theta) = \frac{1}{1 + e^{-(\mathbf{w}^\top x + b)}} \ , \tag{9.9}$$

where $\theta = (\mathbf{w}, b)$. In the binary classification problem, the M-step (9.8) reduces to

$$\theta^{s+1} = \arg\max_\theta \sum_{i=1}^{n} g_1(x_i; \theta^s) \ln P(1|x_i; \theta) + (1 - g_1(x_i; \theta^s)) \ln(1 - P(1|x_i; \theta)) \ ,$$

where

$$g_1(x_i; \theta) = \frac{P(1|x_i; \theta)^{\frac{1}{1-\lambda}}}{P(1|x_i; \theta)^{\frac{1}{1-\lambda}} + (1 - P(1|x_i; \theta))^{\frac{1}{1-\lambda}}}$$

for unlabeled data and $g_1(x_i; \theta) = \delta_{1y_i}$ for labeled examples. Let $\mathbf{p}_\theta$ and $\mathbf{g}$ denote the vector of $P(1|x_i; \theta)$ and $g_1(x_i; \theta^s)$ values respectively, $\mathbf{X}$ the $(n \times (d+1))$ matrix of x_i values concatenated with the vector $\mathbf{1}$, and $\mathbf{W}_\theta$ the $(n \times n)$ diagonal matrix with ith diagonal entry $P(1|x_i; \theta)(1 - P(1|x_i; \theta))$. The Newton-Raphson update is

$$\theta \leftarrow \theta + \left(\mathbf{X}^\top \mathbf{W}_\theta \mathbf{X}\right)^{-1} \mathbf{X}^\top (\mathbf{g} - \mathbf{p}_\theta) \ . \tag{9.10}$$

Each Newton-Raphson update can be interpreted as solving a weighted least squares problem, and the scheme is iteratively reweighted by updating $\mathbf{p}_\theta$ (and hence $\mathbf{W}_\theta$) and applying (9.10) until convergence.

9.3.2   Conjugate Gradient

Depending on how $P(y|x)$ is modeled, the M step (9.8) may not be concave, and other gradient-based optimization algorithms should be used. Even in the case

---

3. The generalization to kernelized logistic regression is straightforward, and the generalization to more than two classes results in similar expressions, but they would require numerous extra notations.

where a logistic regression model is used, conjugate gradient may turn out being computationally more efficient than the IRLS procedure. Indeed, even if each M step of the deterministic annealing EM algorithm consists in solving a convex problem, this problem is nonquadratic. IRLS solves exactly each quadratic subproblem, a strategy which becomes computationally expensive for high-dimensional data or kernelized logistic regression. The approximate solution provided by a few steps of conjugate gradient may turn out to be more efficient, especially since the solution θ^{s+1} returned at the sth M step is not required to be accurate.

Depending on whether memory is an issue or not, conjugate gradient updates may use the optimal steps computed from the Hessian, or approximations returned by a line search. These alternatives have experimentally been shown to be much more efficient than IRLS on large problems (Komarek and Moore, 2003).

Finally, when EM does not provide a useful decomposition of the learning task, one can directly address the minimization of the learning criterion (9.7) with conjugate gradient, or other gradient-based algorithms. Here also, it is useful to define an annealing scheme, where λ is gradually increased from 0 to 1, in order to avoid poor local maxima of the optimization surface.

9.4   Related Methods

9.4.1   Minimum Entropy in Pattern Recognition

Minimum entropy regularizers have been used in other contexts to encode learnability priors (Brand, 1999). In a sense, H_{emp} can be seen as a poor man's way to generalize this approach to continuous input spaces. This empirical functional was also used as a criterion to learn scale parameters in the context of transductive manifold learning (Zhu et al., 2003b). During learning, discrepancies between H (9.3) and H_{emp} (9.5) are prevented to avoid hard unstable solutions by smoothing the estimate of posterior probabilities.

9.4.2   Input-Dependent and Information Regularization

Input-dependent regularization, introduced by Seeger (2000b) and detailed in chapter 2, aims at incorporating some knowledge about the density $p(x)$ in the modeling of $P(y|x)$. In the framework of Bayesian inference, this knowledge is encoded by structural dependencies in the prior distributions.

Information regularization, introduced by Szummer and Jaakkola (2002a) and extended as detailed in chapter 10, is another approach where the density $p(x)$ is assumed to be known, and where the mutual information between variables x and y is penalized within predefined small neighborhoods. As the mutual information $I(x;y)$ is related to the conditional entropy by $I(x;y) = H(y) - H(y|x)$, low entropy and low mutual information are nearly opposite quantities. However, penalizing mutual information locally, subject to the class constraints provided by labeled examples, highly penalizes the variations of $P(y|x)$ in the high-density regions. Hence, like entropy regularization, information regularization favors solution where label switching is restricted to low density areas between disagreeing labels.

Entropy regularization differs from these schemes in that it is expressed only in terms of $P(y|x)$ and does not involve a model of $p(x)$. However, we stress that for unlabeled data, the MAP minimum entropy estimation is consistent with the maximum (complete)-likelihood approach when $p(x)$ is small near the decision surface. Indeed, whereas the complete likelihood maximizes $\ln p(x)$ on unlabeled data, the regularizer minimizes the conditional entropy on the same points. Hence, the two criteria agree provided the class assignments are confident in high-density regions, or conversely, when label switching occurs in a low-density area.

9.4.3   Self-Training

Self-training is an iterative process, where a learner imputes the labels of examples which have been classified with confidence in the previous step. This idea, which predates EM, was independently proposed by several authors (see chapter 1). Amini and Gallinari (2002) analyzed this technique and have shown that it is equivalent to a version of the classification EM algorithm (Celeux and Govaert, 1992), which minimizes the likelihood deprived of the entropy of the partition.

In the context of conditional likelihood estimation from labeled and unlabeled examples, self-training minimizes C (9.7) with $\lambda = 1$. The optimization process itself is identical to the generalized EM described in section 9.3.1 with hard assignments (Grandvalet, 2002; Jin and Ghahramani, 2003).

Minimum entropy regularization is expected to have two benefits. First, the influence of unlabeled examples can be controlled, in the spirit of EM-λ (Nigam et al., 2000) Second, the deterministic annealing process, by which λ is slowly increased, is expected to help the optimization process to avoid poor local minima of the criterion. This scheme bears some similarity to the increase of the C^* parameter in the transductive SVM algorithm of Joachims (1999).

9.4.4   Maximal Margin Separators

Maximal margin separators are theoretically well-founded models which have shown great success in supervised classification. For linearly separable data, they have been shown to be a limiting case of probabilistic hyperplane separators (Tong and Koller, 2000).

In the framework of transductive learning, Vapnik (1998) proposed broadening the margin definition to unlabeled examples, by taking the smallest Euclidean distance between any (labeled and unlabeled) training point to the classification boundary. The following theorem, whose proof is given in the appendix, generalizes theorem 5, corollary 6 of Tong and Koller (2000) to the margin defined in transductive learning[4] when using the proposed minimum entropy criterion.

Theorem 9.1 *Consider the two-class linear classification problem with linearly separable labeled examples, where the classifier is obtained by optimizing $P(1|x; (\mathbf{w}, b)) = 1/(1 + e^{-(\mathbf{w}^\top x + b)})$ with the semi-supervised minimum entropy criterion (9.7), under the constraint that $\|\mathbf{w}\| \leq B$. The margin of that linear classifier converges toward the maximum possible margin among all such linear classifiers, as the bound B goes to infinity.*

Hence, the minimum entropy solution can approach semi-supervised SVM (Vapnik, 1998; Bennett and Demiriz, 1999). We, however, recall that the MAP criterion is not concave in $P(m|x; \theta)$, so that the convergence toward the global maximum cannot be guaranteed with the algorithms presented in section 9.3. This problem is shared by all inductive semi-supervised algorithms dealing with a large number of unlabeled data in reasonable time, such as mixture models or the transductive SVM of Joachims (1999). Explicitly or implicitly, inductive semi-supervised algorithms impute labels which are somehow consistent with the decision rule returned by the learning algorithm. The enumeration of all possible configurations is only avoided thanks to a heuristic process, such as deterministic annealing, which may fail.

Most graph-based transduction algorithms avoid this enumeration problem because their labeling process is not required to comply with a parameterized decision rule. This clear computational advantage has, however, its counterpart: label propagation is performed via a user-defined similarity measure. The selection of a discriminant similarity measure is thus left to the user, or to an outer loop, in which case the overall optimization process is not convex anymore. The experimental section below illustrates that the choice of discriminant similarity measures is difficult in high-dimensional spaces, and when a priori similar patterns should be discriminated.

9.5   Experiments

9.5.1   Artificial Data

In this section, we chose a simple experimental setup in order to avoid artifacts stemming from optimization problems. This setting enables checking to what extent supervised learning can be improved by unlabeled examples, and when minimum entropy can compete with generative methods which are traditionally advocated in this framework. The minimum entropy criterion is applied to the logistic regression model. It is compared to logistic regression fitted by maximum likelihood (ignoring unlabeled data) and logistic regression with all labels known.

---

4. That is, the margin on an unlabeled example is defined as the absolute value of the margin on a labeled example at the same location.

The former shows what has been gained by handling unlabeled data, and the latter provides the "crystal ball" ultimate performance obtained by guessing correctly all labels. All hyperparameters (weight-decay for all logistic regression models plus the λ parameter (9.7) for minimum entropy) are tuned by tenfold cross-validation.

These discriminative methods are compared to generative models. Throughout all experiments, a two-components Gaussian mixture model was fitted by the EM algorithm (two means and one common covariance matrix estimated by maximum likelihood on labeled and unlabeled examples (McLachlan, 1992)). The problem of local maxima in the likelihood surface is artificially avoided by initializing EM with the parameters of the true distribution when the latter is truly a two-component Gaussian mixture, or with maximum likelihood parameters on the (fully labeled) test sample when the distribution departs from the model. This initialization advantages EM, which is guaranteed to pick, among all local maxima of the likelihood, the one which is in the basin of attraction of the optimal value. In particular, this initialization prevents interferences that may result from the "pseudolabels" given to unlabeled examples at the first E step. The "label switching" problem (badly labeled clusters) is prevented at this stage.

Correct Joint Density Model   In the first series of experiments, we consider two-class problems in a 50-dimensional input space. Each class is generated with equal probability from a normal distribution. Class 1 is normal with mean $(a\, a \ldots a)$ and unit covariance matrix. Class 2 is normal with mean $-(a\, a \ldots a)$ and unit covariance matrix. Parameter a tunes the Bayes error which varies from 1 % to 20 % (1 %, 2.5 %, 5 %, 10 %, 20 %). The learning sets comprise l labeled examples, $(l = 50, 100, 200)$ and u unlabeled examples, $(u = l \times (1, 3, 10, 30, 100))$. Overall, 75 different setups are evaluated, and for each one, ten different training samples are generated. Generalization performances are estimated on a test set of size $10,000$.

This first benchmark provides a comparison for the algorithms in a situation where unlabeled data are known to convey information. Besides the favorable initialization of the EM algorithm to the optimal parameters, the generative models benefit from the *correctness* of the model: data were generated according to the model, that is, two Gaussian subpopulations with identical covariances. The logistic regression model is only *compatible* with the joint distribution, which is a weaker fulfillment than correctness.

As there is no modeling bias, differences in error rates are only due to differences in estimation efficiency. The overall error rates (averaged over all settings) are in favor of minimum entropy logistic regression (14.1 ± 0.3 %). EM (15.7 ± 0.3 %) does worse on average than logistic regression (14.9 ± 0.3 %). For reference, the average Bayes error rate is 7.7 % and logistic regression reaches 10.4 ± 0.1 % when all examples are labeled.

Figure 9.1 provides more informative summaries than these raw numbers. The first plot represents the error rates (averaged over l) versus the Bayes error rate and the u/l ratio. The second plot represents the same performances on a common scale along the abscissa, by showing the relative improvement of using unlabeled

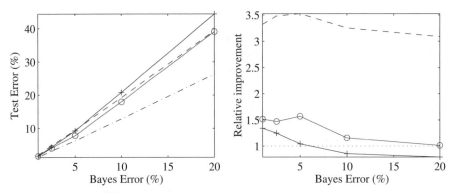

Figure 9.1 (*Left*): Test error of minimum entropy logistic regression (○) and mixture models (+) versus Bayes error rate for $u/l = 10$. The errors of logistic regression (dashed), and logistic regression with all labels known (dash-dotted) are shown for reference. (*Right*): Relative improvement to logistic regression versus Bayes error rate.

examples when compared to logistic regression ignoring unlabeled examples. The relative improvement is defined here as the ratio of the gap between test error and Bayes error for the considered method to the same gap for logistic regression. This plot shows that, as asymptotic theory suggests (O'Neill, 1978; Castelli and Cover, 1996), unlabeled examples are more beneficial when the Bayes error is low. This observation supports the relevance of the minimum entropy assumption.

Figure 9.2 illustrates the consequence of the demanding parametrization of generative models. Mixture models are outperformed by the simple logistic regression model when the sample size is low, since their number of parameters grows quadratically (versus linearly) with the number of input features. This graph also shows that the minimum entropy model takes quick advantage of unlabeled data when classes are well separated. With $u = 3l$, the model considerably improves upon the one discarding unlabeled data. At this stage, the generative models do not perform well, as the number of available examples is low compared to the number of parameters in the model. However, for very large sample sizes, with 100 times more unlabeled examples than labeled examples, the generative method eventually becomes more accurate than the discriminative one.

These results are reminiscent of those of Efron (1975), in the respect that the generative method is asymptotically slighly more efficient than the discriminative one, mainly because logistic regression makes little use of examples far from the decision surface. In the same respect, our observations differ from the comparison of Ng and Jordan (2001), which shows that naive Bayes can be competitive in terms of test error for small training sample sizes. This may be explained by the more general generative model used here, which does not assume feature independance.

Misspecified Joint Density Model In a second series of experiments, the setup is slightly modified by letting the class-conditional densities be corrupted by

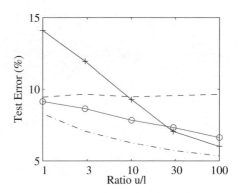

Figure 9.2   Test error versus u/l ratio for 5 % Bayes error ($a = 0.23$). Test errors of minimum entropy logistic regression ($\circ$) and mixture models ($+$). The errors of logistic regression (dashed), and logistic regression with all labels known (dash-dotted) are shown for reference.

outliers. For each class, the examples are generated from a mixture of two Gaussians centered on the same mean: a unit variance component gathers 98 % of examples, while the remaining 2 % are generated from a large variance component, where each variable has a standard deviation of 10. The mixture model used by EM is now slightly misspecified since the whole distribution is still modeled by a simple two-components Gaussian mixture. The results, displayed in the left-hand-side of figure 9.3, should be compared with figure 9.2. The generative model dramatically suffers from the misspecification and behaves worse than logistic regression for all sample sizes. The unlabeled examples have first a beneficial effect on test error, then have a detrimental effect when they overwhelm the number of labeled examples. On the other hand, the discriminative models behave smoothly as in the previous case, and the minimum entropy criterion performance steadily improves with the addition of unlabeled examples.

The last series of experiments illustrate the robustness with respect to the cluster assumption, by which the decision boundary should be placed in low-density regions. The samples are drawn from a distribution such that unlabeled data do not convey information, and where a low-density $p(x)$ does not indicate class separation. This distribution is modeled by two Gaussian clusters, as in the first series of experiments, but labeling is now independent from clustering: example x_i belongs to class 1 if $x_{i2} > x_{i1}$ and belongs to class 2 otherwise; the Bayes decision boundary now separates each cluster in its middle. The mixture model is unchanged. It is now far from the model used to generate data. The right-hand side plot of figure 9.3 shows that the favorable initialization of EM does not prevent the model from being fooled by unlabeled data: its test error steadily increases with the amount of unlabeled data. Conversely, the discriminative models behave well, and the minimum entropy algorithm is not distracted by the two clusters; its performance is nearly identical to the one of training with labeled data only (cross-

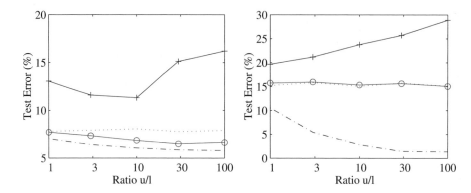

Figure 9.3 Test error versus u/l ratio for $a = 0.23$. Average test errors for minimum entropy logistic regression ($\circ$) and mixture models ($+$). The test error rates of logistic regression (dotted), and logistic regression with all labels known (dash-dotted) are shown for reference. (*Left*): Experiment with outliers. (*Right*): Experiment with uninformative unlabeled data.

Table 9.1 Error rates (%) of minimum entropy (ME) versus consistency method (CM), for $a = 0.23$, $l = 50$, and (a) pure Gaussian clusters, (b) Gaussian clusters corrupted by outliers, and (c) class boundary separating one Gaussian cluster

n_u	50	150	500	1500
a) ME	10.8 ± 1.5	9.8 ± 1.9	8.8 ± 2.0	8.3 ± 2.6
a) CM	21.4 ± 7.2	25.5 ± 8.1	29.6 ± 9.0	26.8 ± 7.2
b) ME	8.5 ± 0.9	8.3 ± 1.5	7.5 ± 1.5	6.6 ± 1.5
b) CM	22.0 ± 6.7	25.6 ± 7.4	29.8 ± 9.7	27.7 ± 6.8
c) ME	8.7 ± 0.8	8.3 ± 1.1	7.2 ± 1.0	7.2 ± 1.7
c) CM	51.6 ± 7.9	50.5 ± 4.0	49.3 ± 2.6	50.2 ± 2.2

validation provides λ values close to zero), which can be regarded as the ultimate achievable performance in this situation.

Comparison with Manifold Transduction Although this chapter focuses on inductive classification, we also provide comparisons with a transduction algorithm relying on the manifold assumption. The consistency method (Zhou et al., 2004) is a very simple label propagation algorithm with only two tuning parameters. As suggested by Zhou et al. (2004), we set $\alpha = 0.99$ and the scale parameter σ^2 was optimized on test results. The results are reported in table 9.1. The experiments are limited due to the memory requirements of the consistency method in our naive implementation.

The results are extremely poor for the consistency method, whose error is way

| Anger | Fear | Disgust | Joy | Sadness | Surprise | Neutral |

Figure 9.4   Examples from the facial expression recognition database.

above minimum entropy, and which does not show any sign of improvement as the sample of unlabeled data grows. In particular, when classes do not correspond to clusters, the consistency method performs random class assignments.

In fact, the experimental setup, which was designed for the comparison of global classifiers, is not favorable to manifold methods, since the input data are truly 50-dimensional. In this situation, finding a discriminant similarity measure may require numerous degrees of freedom, and the consistency method provides only one tuning parameter: the scale parameter σ^2. Hence, these results illustrate that manifold learning requires more tuning efforts for truly high-dimensional data, and some recent techniques may respond to this need (Sindhwani et al., 2005).

9.5.2   Facial Expression Recognition

We now consider an image recognition problem, consisting in recognizing seven (balanced) classes corresponding to the universal emotions (anger, fear, disgust, joy, sadness, surprise, and neutral). The patterns are gray level images of frontal faces, with standardized positions, as displayed in figure 9.4. The data set comprises 375 such pictures made of 140×100 pixels (Abboud et al., 2003; Kanade et al., 2000)

We tested kernelized logistic regression (Gaussian kernel), its minimum entropy version, nearest neighbor, and the consistency method. We repeatedly (10 times) sampled 1/10 of the data set for providing the labeled part, and the remainder for testing. Although (α, σ^2) were chosen to minimize the test error, the consistency method performed poorly with 63.8 ± 1.3 % test error (compared to 86 % error for random assignments). Nearest neighbor gets similar results with 63.1 ± 1.3 % test error, and kernelized logistic regression (ignoring unlabeled examples) improved to reach 53.6 ± 1.3 %. Minimum entropy kernelized logistic regression regression achieves 52.0 ± 1.9 % error (compared to about 20 % errors for human on this database). The scale parameter chosen for kernelized logistic regression (by tenfold cross-validation) amount to using a global classifier.

The failure of local methods may be explained by the fact that the database contains several pictures of each person, with different facial expressions. Hence, local methods are likely to pick the same identity instead of the same expression, while global methods are able to learn the discriminating directions.

9.6   Conclusion

Although discriminative methods do not benefit from unlabeled data in the maximum-likelihoood framework, *maximum a posteriori* estimation enables addressing the semi-supervised induction problem. The information content of unlabeled data decreases with class overlap, which can be measured by the conditional entropy of labels given patterns. Hence, the minimum entropy prior encodes a premise of semi-supervised induction, that is, the belief that unlabeled data may be useful. The postulate is optimistic in some problems where unlabeled data do not convey information regarding labels, but the strength of the prior is controlled by a tuning parameter, so that the contribution of unlabeled examples to the estimate may vanish.

Minimum entropy regularization is related to self-training in general and to transductive SVMs in particular. It promotes classifiers with high confidence on the unlabeled examples. A deterministic annealing process smoothly drives the decision boundary away from unlabeled examples, favoring low-density separation.

The regularizer can be applied to local and global models of posterior probabilities. As a result, it can improve over local models when they suffer from the curse of dimensionality. Minimum entropy regularization may also be a serious contender for generative methods. It compares favorably to these mixture models in three situations: for small sample sizes, where the generative model cannot completely benefit from the knowledge of the correct joint model; when the joint distribution is (even slightly) misspecified; when the unlabeled examples turn out to be noninformative regarding class probabilities.

Finally, the algorithms presented in this chapter can be applied to a generalized version of the semi-supervised induction problem, where the examples may be labeled by any subset of labels, representing the set of plausible classes. This kind of information is sometimes a more faithful description of the true state of knowledge when labeling is performed by an expert.

Appendix: Proof of Theorem 9.1

Theorem 9.1 *Consider the two-class linear classification problem with linearly separable labeled examples, where the classifier is obtained by optimizing $P(1|x;(\mathbf{w},b)) = 1/(1 + e^{-(\mathbf{w}^\top x + b)})$ with the semi-supervised minimum entropy criterion (9.7), under the constraint that $||\mathbf{w}|| \leq B$. The margin of that linear classifier converges toward the maximum possible margin among all such linear classifiers, as the bound B goes to infinity.*

Proof Consider the logistic regression model $P(1|x;\theta)$ parameterized by $\theta = (\mathbf{w},b)$. Let $z_i \in \{-1,+1\}$ be a binary variable defined as follows: if x_i is a positive labeled example, $z_i = +1$; if x_i is a negative labeled example, $z_i = -1$; if x_i is an unlabeled example, $z_i = \text{sign}(P(1|x;\theta) - 1/2)$. The *margin* for the ith labeled or unlabeled example is defined as $m_i(\theta) = z_i(\mathbf{w}^\top x_i + b)$.

The criterion C (9.7) can be written as a function of $m_i = m_i(\theta)$ as follows:

$$C(\theta) = -\sum_{i=1}^{l} \ln(1 + e^{-m_i}) - \lambda \sum_{i=l+1}^{n} \left(\ln(1 + e^{-m_i}) + \frac{m_i e^{-m_i}}{1 + e^{-m_i}} \right) , \qquad (9.11)$$

where the indices $[1, l]$ and $[l + 1, n]$ correspond to labeled and unlabeled data, respectively.

On the one hand, for all θ such that there exists an example with non-negative margin, the cost (9.11) is trivially upper-bounded by $-\ln(2)$ if the example is labeled and $-\lambda \ln(2)$ otherwise. On the other hand, by the linear separability assumption, there exists $\theta = (\mathbf{w}, b)$ with, say, $\|\mathbf{w}\| = 1$ such that $m_i > 0$. Consider now the cost obtained with the admissible solution $B\theta$ as $B \to +\infty$. In this limit, since $m_i(B\theta) = Bm_i(\theta)$, all the terms of the finite sum (9.11) converge to zero, so that the value of the cost converges to its maximum value ($\lim_{B \to +\infty} C(B\theta) = 0$). Hence, in the limit of $B \to +\infty$ all margins of the maximizer of C are positive.

We now show that the maximizer of C achieves the largest minimal margin. The cost (9.11) is simplified by using the following equivalence relations when $B \to +\infty$:

$$\ln(1 + e^{-Bm_i}) \quad \sim \quad e^{-Bm_i}$$
$$\frac{Bm_i e^{-Bm_i}}{1 + e^{-Bm_i}} \quad \sim \quad Bm_i e^{-Bm_i} ,$$

which yields

$$C(B\theta) = -\sum_{i=1}^{l} e^{-Bm_i} + o(e^{-Bm_i}) - \lambda \sum_{i=l+1}^{n} Bm_i e^{-Bm_i} + o(Bm_i e^{-Bm_i}) .$$

Let us write $m^* > 0$ the minimum margin among the labeled examples and $m_* > 0$ the minimum margin among the unlabeled examples, N^* the number of minimum margin labeled examples (with $m_i = m^*$), and N_* the number of minimum margin unlabeled examples (with $m_i = m_*$). As $e^{-Bm_i} = o(e^{-Bm^*})$ when $m_i > m^*$, we obtain

$$C(B\theta) = -N^* e^{-Bm^*} + o(e^{-Bm^*}) - \lambda N_* Bm_* e^{-Bm_*} + o(Bm_* e^{-Bm_*}) .$$

Now we note that if $m^* < m_*$, then $Bm_* e^{-Bm_*} = o(e^{-Bm^*})$, and that if $m^* \geq m_*$ then $e^{-Bm^*} = o(Bm_* e^{-Bm_*})$. Hence, depending on whether $m^* < m_*$ or $m^* \geq m_*$ we either obtain

$$C(B\theta) = -N^* e^{-Bm^*} + o(e^{-Bm^*}) \qquad (9.12)$$

or

$$C(B\theta) = -\lambda N_* Bm_* e^{-Bm_*} + o(Bm_* e^{-Bm^*}) . \qquad (9.13)$$

Now, consider two different values of θ, θ_1 and θ_2, giving rise to minimum margins

M_1 and M_2 respectively, with $M_1 > M_2$. The solution $B\theta_1$ will be prefered to $B\theta_2$ if $C(B\theta_1)/C(B\theta_2) < 1$. From (9.12) and (9.13), we see that it does not matter whether M_i is among the labels or the unlabeled, but only whether $M_1 > M_2$ or $M_2 > M_1$. In all cases $C(B\theta_1)/C(B\theta_2) \to 0$ when $M_1 > M_2$. This allows the conclusion that as $B \to \infty$, the global maximum of $C(B\theta)$ over θ tends to a maximum margin solution, where the minimum margin M (over both labeled and unlabeled examples) is maximized.   ∎

10   Data-Dependent Regularization

Adrian Corduneanu   ADRIANC@MIT.EDU

Tommi Jaakkola   TOMMI@CSAIL.MIT.EDU

Information regularization is a principle for assigning labels to unlabeled data points in a semi-supervised setting. The broader principle is based on finding labels that minimize the information induced between examples and labels relative to a topology over the examples; any label variation within a small local region of examples ties together the identities of examples and their labels. Such variation should be minimized unless supported directly or indirectly by the available labeled examples. The principle can be cast in terms of Tikhonov style regularization for maximizing likelihood of labeled examples with an information-theoretic regularization penalty. We consider two ways of representing the topology over examples, either based on complete knowledge of the marginal density, or by grouping together examples whose labels should be related. We discuss the learning algorithms and sample complexity issues that result from each representation.

10.1   Introduction

A substantial number of algorithms and methods exist for solving supervised learning problems with little or no assumptions about the distribution generating the samples. Semi-supervised learning methods, in contrast, have to rely on assumptions about the problem so as to relate the available unlabeled data to possible class decisions. The most common such assumption is the cluster assumption (see chapter 1, or (Seeger, 2000b)) that, loosely speaking, prefers class decisions that cut between rather than through clusters of unlabeled points. The effect of the assumption is that it can significantly reduce the set of possible (reasonable) decisions that need to be considered in response to a few labeled examples. The same effect can also be achieved through representational constraints (e.g., (Blum and Mitchell, 1998)).

The definition of what constitutes a cluster and how the cluster assumption is formalized varies from one method to another. For example, clusters may be defined in terms of a weighted graph so that class decisions correspond to a graph partition (Szummer and Jaakkola, 2001; Blum and Chawla, 2001; Blum et al., 2004). In a regularization setting, the graph may be used to introduce a smoothness penalty on the discriminant function so as to limit how the discriminant function can change within graph neighborhoods (e.g., see chapter 12). Alternatively, we may define a model for each cluster via generative mixture models, and associate a single class decision (distribution over classes) with each mixture component (e.g., see chapter 3).

The strength of the bias from unlabeled data can be directly controlled via the regularization parameter or by weighting likelihoods corresponding to labeled and unlabeled data. The choice of the weight may have a substantial effect on the resulting classifier, however (e.g., (Corduneanu and Jaakkola, 2002)).

regularization approach

We approach here the semi-supervised learning problem as a regularization problem , consistent with the broader cluster assumption, but define the regularization penalty by appealing to information theory. The key idea is to express the penalty as a bit cost of deviating decisions from those consistent with some assumed structure over the unlabeled examples. In our case the structure corresponds to a collection of overlapping sets or regions that play a role similar to clusters; decisions are biased to be the same within each set and their specification is tied to the marginal distribution over the examples. In practice, the sets can be derived from weighted graph neighborhoods for discrete objects or from ϵ-balls covering the unlabeled points.

information regularization

We begin by introducing the overall *information regularization* principle. The structure of the remaining sections is modeled after figure 10.1, successively elaborating the principle under variations in the example space, type of unlabeled data that is available, and which modeling assumptions we are willing to make.

Consider a typical semi-supervised learning problem with a few labeled examples $((x_1, y_1), \ldots, (x_l, y_l))$ and a large number of unlabeled examples $(x_{l+1}, \ldots, x_n)$ or the marginal distribution $p(x)$. We assume that the labels are discrete taking values in $\mathcal{Y} = \{1, \ldots, M\}$ for some finite M. The goal is to estimate the conditional distributions $Q(y|x)$ associated with each available example x (labeled or unlabeled).

We will introduce the information regularization approach here from two alternative perspectives: smoothness and communication. By smoothness we mean constraining how $Q(y|x)$ is allowed to vary from one point to another. The smoothness preference is expressed as a regularization penalty over different choices of $Q(\cdot|x)$, $x \in \mathcal{X}$. The communication perspective, on the other hand, characterizes the regularization penalty in terms of the cost of encoding labels for all the points using $Q(y|x)$ relative to a basic coding scheme.

unlabeled bias as regions

In either case the key role is played by a collection of regions, denoted by $\mathcal{R}$. Each region $R \in \mathcal{R}$ represents a set of a priori equivalent examples. In other words, in the absence of any other information, we would prefer to associate the same distribution of labels with all $x \in R$. Figure 10.2 illustrates two possible overlapping regions. We will use these regions to exemplify the basic ideas.

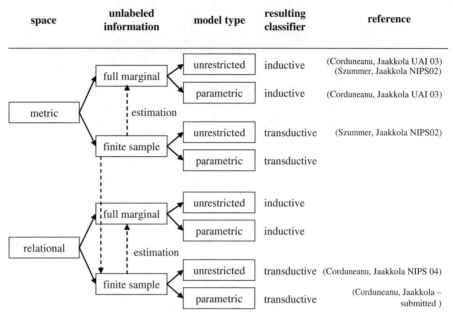

space	unlabeled information	model type	resulting classifier	reference
metric	full marginal	unrestricted	inductive	(Corduneanu, Jaakkola UAI 03) (Szummer, Jaakkola NIPS02)
		parametric	inductive	(Corduneanu, Jaakkola UAI 03)
	finite sample	unrestricted	transductive	(Szummer, Jaakkola NIPS02)
		parametric	transductive	
relational	full marginal	unrestricted	inductive	
		parametric	inductive	
	finite sample	unrestricted	transductive	(Corduneanu, Jaakkola NIPS 04)
		parametric	transductive	(Corduneanu, Jaakkola – submitted)

Figure 10.1 Outline of information regularization methods under different assumptions about the space, data, and model. Dotted arrows indicate that one setting can be cast as another through a simple transformation (estimation, or relations derived from metric)

10.1.1   Regions and Smoothness

Consider the six unlabeled examples in region R in figure 10.2. We assume that each point has the same probability of being a member of the region so that $P(x|R) = 1/6$. The membership probabilities provide an additional degree of freedom for specifying smoothness constraints. Given the region R and the membership probabilities $P(x|R)$, $x \in R$, we would like to introduce a penalty for any variation in the conditionals $Q(y|x)$ across the examples in the region. A natural choice for this penalty is the Kullback-Leibler (KL) divergence between each conditional $Q(y|x)$ and the best common choice $Q(y|R)$:

$$I_R(x;y) = \min_{Q(\cdot|R)} \sum_{x \in R} P(x|R) \sum_{y \in \mathcal{Y}} Q(y|x) \log \frac{Q(y|x)}{Q(y|R)}, \tag{10.1}$$

$$= \sum_{x \in R} P(x|R) \sum_{y \in \mathcal{Y}} Q(y|x) \log \frac{Q(y|x)}{Q(y|R)}, \tag{10.2}$$

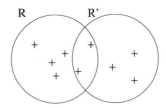

Figure 10.2 Example regions.

mutual
information

where $Q(y|R) = \sum_{x \in R} P(x|R)Q(y|x)$.[1] Note that we can interpret the result as the mutual information between x and y within the region so long as the joint distribution $Q(x,y)$ is defined as $Q(y|x)P(x|R)$. The mutual information involves no prior penalty on what the common distribution should be; $I_R(x,y)$ is zero if all the points in the region are labeled $y = 1$ or all of them have entirely uncertain conditionals $Q(y|x) = 1/M$.

Suppose now that some of the six examples in region R have been labeled. We will formulate the resulting estimation task as a regularization problem with the mutual information serving as a regularization penalty. To this end, let Q refer collectively to the parameters $Q(\cdot|x), x \in R$. Define $J(Q) = I_R(x;y)$ (which we will extend shortly to multiple regions) so that the penalized maximum-likelihood criterion is given by

$$\sum_{i=1}^{l} \log Q(y_i|x_i) - \lambda J(Q),$$

where λ is a regularization parameter that balances the fit to the available labeled points and the smoothness bias expressed by $J(Q)$. If only one of the six points is labeled, all the points in the region will be labeled with the observed label. This is because the value of the regularizer is independent of the common choice within the region but biases any differences within the region. In case of two distinctly labeled points, the remaining points would be labeled such that the conditionals $Q(y|x)$ assign all their weight equally to the two observed labels while excluding all others. The conditionals associated with the labeled points would be drawn toward their respective labels, also excluding other than observed label values.

Multiple Regions In the single-region case the labels for unlabeled points are pulled equally toward the optimized common distribution without further distinguishing between the points. The notion of locality arises from multiple regions, such as $\mathcal{R} = \{R, R'\}$ in the figure. In this setting, the overall regularization

---

1. $I_R(x;y)$ is exactly the general Jensen-Shannon divergence between $Q(\cdot|x)$ for all $x \in R$, weighted by $P(x|R)$

penalty must be a (weighted) average of the individual region penalties:

$$J(Q) = \sum_{R \in \mathcal{R}} \gamma(R) \, I_R(x; y),$$

where $\gamma(R)$ represents the weight of region R, where the choice of $\gamma(R)$ is a modeling decision. $\gamma(R)$ expresses a priori belief in the relative importance of the regions, thus it is not necessarily related to $\mathrm{P}(R) = \int_R p(x)dx$, the probability of region R derived from the generative distribution of the data.

In figure 10.2 there are three sets of equivalent points that are not further distinguished in this regularizer. They are $R \setminus R'$, $R \cap R'$, and $R' \setminus R$. We call atomic regions these sets that are not further partitioned by other regions *atomic regions*. By introducing more regions, we partition the space into smaller atomic regions and thus can make finer distinctions between the conditional distributions associated with the points; within each atomic region, the conditional distributions can differ only if some of the points are explicitly labeled.

A sequence of overlapping regions can mediate influence between the conditionals associated with more "remote" points, those that do not appear in a common region. For example, labeling any point in $R \setminus R'$ will also set all the labels in $R' \setminus R$ via the intersection. Note, however, that labeling the points in the intersection would not completely remove this influence; the Markov properties associated with the regions pertain to the conditional distributions, not labels directly.

The choice of the regions, region weights $\gamma(R)$, and the membership probabilities $P(x|R)$ will change the regularizer. While these provide additional degrees of freedom that have to be set (or learned), there are nevertheless simple ways of specifying them directly based on the problem. For example, suppose we are given weighted graph a weighted undirected graph with vertex set V, edge set E, and edge weights $w(u, v)$ representation associated with any $(u, v) \in E$. Then we can simply associate the regions with edges, specify equal membership probabilities for vertices in each edge, and set $\gamma(R)$ equal to the weight of the corresponding edge in the graph. The resulting regularizer is analogous to the graph-based regularizers for discriminant functions except that it is cast in terms of conditional probabilities.

10.1.2   Communication Principle

The information regularization objective can be also derived from a communication principle. Suppose we have the same collection of regions $\mathcal{R}$, region weights $\gamma(R)$, membership probabilities $P(x|R)$, and the conditionals $\{Q(y|x)\}$ associated with the points. The regularizer is defined as the bit rate of communicating labels for points according to the following communication game. In this scheme, the regions, points, and labels are sampled as follows. First, we select a region $R \in \mathcal{R}$ with probability (proportional to) $\gamma(R)$, then a point within the region according to the membership probabilities $P(x|R)$, and finally the label y from $Q(y|x)$. The label is then communicated to the receiver using a coding scheme tailored to the region, i.e., on the basis of $Q(y|R)$. The receiver is assumed to have prior access to x, R, and the region-specific coding scheme. Under these assumptions, the amount of information that must be sent to the receiver to accurately reconstruct the samples on average is

$$J(Q) = \sum_{R \in \mathcal{R}} \gamma(R) I_R(x\,;\,y),$$

which is the regularizer previously defined. Equivalently, we can rewrite the regularizer as

$$J(Q) = I(x\,;\,y) - I(R\,;\,y).$$

Therefore the communication principle aims to minimize any information x has to communicate about y beyond what has already been communicated by the region from which x was drawn. This information is minimal when the label within each region does not depend on which x we sampled.

10.2 Information Regularization on Metric Spaces

We adapt here the information regularization principle to the setting where $\mathcal{X}$ is a metric space and assume that its metric is correlated with the labeling of points. In other words, points that are close according to the metric are likely to have the same label. For example, if $\mathcal{X}$ is a real vector space the metric could be the Euclidean distance between the points, possibly weighted by feature relevance. Using a metric to introduce a bias in semi-supervised learning is quite common, and many existing algorithms require an explicit or implicit metric.

10.2.1 Full Knowledge of the Marginal

We begin by considering the ideal situation in which we have access to unlimited unlabeled data, which, together with the metric, amounts to knowing the marginal density $p(x)$. In this case the information regularizer will relate the structure of $p(x)$ to the possible labelings of points. While we develop the ideas in the context of knowing the marginal, the resulting algorithms apply also to finite sample cases, by replacing $p(x)$ with an empirical estimate.

10.2.1.1 *The Information Regularizer*

In order to construct the regularizer we need to specify how the regions cover the metric space along with the weights $\gamma(R)$ associated with the regions. The cover $\mathcal{R}$ should provide connected and significantly overlapping regions. This is necessary since labeling one point can only affect another if they can be connected through a overlap   path of overlapping regions.

In covering the space we have to balance the size of the regions with their overlap. We derive here the form of the regularizer in the limit of vanishing but highly overlapping regions. Under mild constraints about how the limit is taken, the resulting regularizer is the same. The limiting form has the additional benefit that it no longer requires us to engineer a particular covering of the space.

We choose the regions such that as their size approaches 0, the overlap between neighbors approaches 100% (this is required for smoothness). In the limit, therefore, each point belongs to infinitely many regions, resulting in an infinite sum of local regularizers. An appropriate choice of λ, the regularization parameter, is needed to rescale the regularizer to take into account this increase.

avoid systematic
bias

In choosing the cover $\mathcal{R}$ care must be taken not to introduce systematic biases into the regularizer. Assuming that $\mathcal{X}$ has vector space structure, we can cover it with a homogeneous set of overlapping regions of identical shape: regions centered at the axis-parallel lattice points spaced at distance l'. In what follows the regions are going to be axis-parallel cubes of length l, where l is much larger than l'. Because $\mathcal{R}$ covers $\mathcal{X}$ uniformly, we can weight the regions based on the marginal density, i.e., $\gamma(R) = \mathrm{P}(R)$ up to a multiplicative constant.

Assuming that l and l' are such that l/l' is an integer, each (nonlattice) point belongs to $(l/l')^d$ cubic regions, where d is the dimension of the vector space. Let $\mathcal{R}'$ be the *partitioning* of $\mathcal{R}$ into atomic lattice cubes of length l'. Each region in $\mathcal{R}$ is partitioned into $(l/l')^d$ disjoint atomic cubes from $\mathcal{R}'$, and each atomic cube is contained in $(l/l')^d$ overlapping regions from $\mathcal{R}$. We may now rewrite the global regularizer as a sum over the partition $\mathcal{R}'$:

$$J(p) = \lim_{l \to 0} \sum_{R \in \mathcal{R}} \mathrm{P}(R) I_R(x; y) = \lim_{l \to 0} \sum_{R' \in \mathcal{R}'} \mathrm{P}(R') \sum_{R \supseteq R'} I_R(x; y) =$$

$$(l/l')^d \lim_{l' \to 0} \sum_{R' \in \mathcal{R}'} \mathrm{P}(R') I_R(x; y) = \lim_{l \to 0} (l/l')^d \cdot \int_{\mathcal{X}} p(x) \frac{dI_R(x; y)}{dx} dx.$$

Note that the factor in front of the integral can be factored into the regularization parameter λ as a multiplicative constant.

Infinitesimal Mutual Information   We derive the local mutual information as the diameter of R approaches 0. If x_0 is the expectation of x over R, mutual information takes the following asymptotic form:

$$I_R(x; y) = \frac{1}{2} \mathbf{tr} \left(\mathbf{Var}_R [x] F(x_0) \right) + \mathcal{O} \left(\mathrm{diam}(R)^3 \right),$$

where $F(x) = \mathbf{E}_{Q(y|x)} \left[\nabla_x \log Q(y|x) \cdot \nabla_x \log Q(y|x)^\top \right]$ is the Fisher information and $\mathbf{Var}_R [x]$ is the covariance of $p_R(x)$ (for a proof of this result see (Corduneanu and Jaakkola, 2003)). Note that since the covariance is $\mathcal{O} \left(\mathrm{diam}(R)^2 \right)$, $I_R(x; y) \to 0$ as $\mathrm{diam}(R) \to 0$. Therefore $\lim_{\mathrm{diam}(R) \to 0} I_R(x; y)/\mathrm{diam}(R)^2$ is well defined, and this is the infinitesimal quantity that we will integrate to obtain $J(p)^2$:

$$J(p) = \int_{\mathcal{X}} p(x)\mathbf{tr}\left(F(x)\lim_{\text{diam}(R)\to 0}\frac{\mathbf{Var}_R[x]}{\text{diam}(R)^2}\right)dx$$

Given this form of the regularizer we can argue that regions in the shape of a cube are indeed appropriate. We start from the principle that the regularizer should not introduce any systematic directional bias in penalizing changes in the label. If the diameter of a region R is small enough, $p_R(x)$ is almost uniform, and $p(y = 1|x)$ can be approximated well by $\mathbf{v} \cdot x + c$, where $\mathbf{v}$ is the direction of highest variation. In this setting we have the following result (Corduneanu and Jaakkola, 2003):

Theorem 10.1 *Let R be such that* $\text{diam}(R) = 1$. *The local information regularizer is independent of $\mathbf{v}/\|\mathbf{v}\|$ if and only if $\mathbf{Var}_R[\cdot]$ is a multiple of the identity.*

Proof We have $F(x_0) = \mathbf{v}\mathbf{v}^\top$. The relevant quantity that should be independent of $\mathbf{v}/\|\mathbf{v}\|$ is therefore $\mathbf{v}^\top\mathbf{Var}_R[\cdot]\mathbf{v}$. Let $v = \Phi_i/\|\Phi_i\|$, where Φ_i is an eigenvector of $\mathbf{Var}_R[\cdot]$ of eigenvalue ϕ_i. Then $\mathbf{v}^\top\mathbf{Var}_R[\cdot]\mathbf{v} = \phi_i$ should not depend on the eigenvector. If follows that $\mathbf{Var}_R[\cdot]$ has equal eigenvalues, thus $\mathbf{Var}_R[\cdot] = \phi\mathbf{I}$. The converse is trivial. ∎

It follows that in order to remove any directional bias, $\mathbf{Var}_R[x] \approx \text{diam}(R)^2 \cdot \mathbf{I}$, as is the case if R is a cube or a sphere. We thus reach our final form of the information regularizer for metric space when the marginal is fully known:

$$J(p) = \int_{\mathcal{X}} p(x)\mathbf{tr}\left(F(x)\right)dx \tag{10.3}$$

Note that the dependence of $\mathcal{R}$ is only implicit.

10.2.1.2   *Classification Algorithm*

We would like to estimate a label confidence $Q(\cdot|x)$ (that is, a *soft* label in $[0, 1]^M$) for every $x \in \mathcal{X}$ given the knowledge of $p(x)$, and a labeled sample $\{(x_i, y_i)\}_{i=1\ldots l}$. The information regularization principle requires us to maximize the regularized log likelihood:

$$\max_{\{Q(y|x)\,;\,x\in\mathcal{X},y\in\mathcal{Y}\}}\sum_{i=1}^{l}\log Q(y_i|x_i) - \lambda\int_{\mathcal{X}}p(x)\mathbf{tr}\left(F(x)\right)dx, \tag{10.4}$$

where $F(x) = \mathbf{E}_{Q(y|x)}\left[\nabla_x\log Q(y|x)\cdot\nabla_x\log Q(y|x)^\top\right]$, and the maximization is subject to $0 \le Q(y|x) \le 1$ and $\sum_{y\in\mathcal{Y}}Q(y|x) = 1$.

---

2. To be consistent with the derivation of $J(p)$, we should normalize $I_R(x; y)$ by $\text{diam}(R)^d$, but unless $d = 2$ the regularizer would be either 0 or ∞. We can afford to choose the convenient normalization without compromising the principle because we are free to choose λ

It is interesting that the above optimization defines a labeling even in a completely unrestricted nonparametric setting (save for differentiability constraints on $Q(\cdot|x)$. In this situation labels of distinct data points are related only through the information regularizer. We show that if we fix the values of the labels at the observed labeled samples, $Q(y_i|x_i) = P_0(y_i|x_i)$, for all $i = 1 \ldots l$, the regularizer extends $Q(y|x)$ to unobserved x's uniquely. In what follows, we restrict the analysis to binary classification ($\mathcal{Y} = \{-1, 1\}$).

We cast the optimization as solving a differential equation that characterizes the optimal conditional. The conditional that minimizes the regularizer $\int p(x)\mathbf{tr}\,(F(x))$ is a differentiable function (except maybe at the labeled samples, where it is only continuous) that satisfies the Euler-Lagrange condition (Corduneanu and Jaakkola, 2003):

$$\nabla_x \log p(x) \nabla_x Q(1|x)^\top + \mathbf{tr}\,\left(\nabla^2_{xx} Q(1|x)\right) + \frac{1}{2}\frac{Q(1|x) - Q(-1|x)}{Q(1|x)Q(-1|x)}\,\|\nabla_x Q(1|x)\|^2 = 0.$$

This differential equation defines a unique solution given the natural boundary conditions $p(x) = 0$ and $\nabla_x Q(y|x) = 0$ at infinity, as well as the labels $P_0(y_i|x_i)$ at labeled samples.

In order to optimize (10.4) one could solve the differential equation for various values $\{P_0(y_i|x_i)\}_{i=1\ldots l}$, then optimize with respect to $P_0(y_i|x_i)$. Unfortunately, solving the differential equation numerically involves discretizing $\mathcal{X}$, which is impractical for all but low-dimensional spaces. That is why the nonparametric but inductive (find a label for each point in $\mathcal{X}$) information regularization is of more theoretical than practical interest.

Nevertheless, if $\mathcal{X}$ is the one-dimensional real line the differential equation can be solved analytically (Corduneanu and Jaakkola, 2003). We present the solution here to illustrate the type of biases imposed by the information regularizer. When $\mathcal{X}$ is one-dimensional, the labeled samples $x_1, x_2, \ldots, x_l$ split the real line into disjoint intervals; thus if $P_0(y|x_i)$ are given, the differential equation can be solved independently on each interval determined by the samples. The solution only depends on the labels of the endpoints, and is given by the following:

$$Q(1|x) = \frac{1}{1 + \tan^2\left(-c\int \frac{1}{p(x)}\right)},$$

where c and the additive constant in $\int 1/p$ can be determined from the values of the conditional at the endpoints. These two parameters need not be the same on different intervals.

Figure 10.3 shows the influence of various $p(x)$ on $Q(1|x)$ through information regularization under the boundary conditions $P(y = 1|x = 0) = 0.9$ and $P(y = 1|x = 1) = 0.1$. The property of preferring changes in the label in regions of low data density is evident. Note that the optimal $P(y|x)$ will always be between its values at the boundary; otherwise for some $x_1 \neq x_2$ we would have $P(y|x_1) = P(y|x_2)$, and because the cumulative variation is minimized, necessarily $P(y|x) = P(y|x_1)$

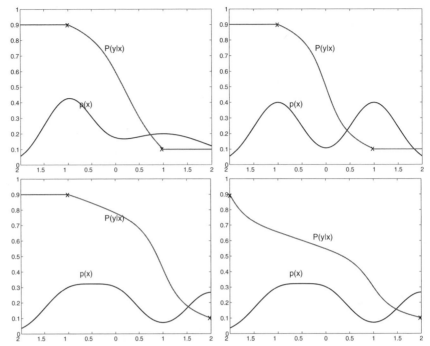

Figure 10.3 Nonparametric conditionals that minimize the information regularizer for various one-dimensional data densities while the label at boundary labeled points is fixed

for every $x \in [x_1, x_2]$.

10.2.1.3   Learning Theoretical Properties

We extend the analysis of information regularization on metric spaces given the full knowledge of the marginal with a learning theoretical framework. The aim is to show that the information regularizer captures the learning complexity, in the sense that bounding it makes the labels learnable without any additional assumptions about $\{Q(y|x)\}_{x \in \mathcal{X}, y \in \mathcal{Y}}$. Because the setting is nonparametric, and the only link that relates labels of distinct points is the information regularizer, $\{Q(y|x)\}_{x \in \mathcal{X}, y \in \mathcal{Y}}$ would not be learnable without placing a constraint on the information regularizer. While the learning framework is general, due to technical constraints [3] we derive an explicit sample-size bound only for binary classification when $\mathcal{X}$ is one-dimensional.

We need to formalize the concepts, the concept class (from which to learn them), and a measure of achievement consistent with (10.4). The key is then to show that the task is learnable in terms of the complexity of the concept class.

Standard probably approximately correct (PAC)-learning of indicator functions

---

3. Only in one dimension do the labeled points give rise to segments that can be optimized independently.

p-concept
learning

of class membership will not suffice for our purpose. Indeed, conditionals with very small information regularizer can still have very complex decision boundaries, of infinite Vapnik-Chervonenkis dimension. Instead, we rely on the *p-concept* Kearns and Schapire (1994) model of learning full conditional densities: concepts are functions $Q(y|x) : \mathcal{X} \to [0, 1]$. Then the concept class is that of conditionals with bounded information regularizer:

$$\mathcal{I}_\gamma(p) = \left\{ Q : \int_\mathcal{X} p(x) \sum_{y \in \mathcal{Y}} Q(y|x) \left\| \nabla_x \log Q(y|x) \right\|^2 dx \leq \gamma \right\}.$$

We measure the quality of learning by a loss function $L_Q : \mathcal{X} \times \mathcal{Y} \to [0, \infty)$. This can be the log loss $- \log Q(y|x)$ associated with maximizing likelihood, or the square loss $(Q(y|x) - 1)^2$. The goal is to estimate from a labeled sample a concept Q_{opt} from $\mathcal{I}_\gamma(p)$ that minimizes the expected loss $\mathbf{E}_{p(x)P(y|x)}[L_Q]$, where $P(y|x)$ is the true conditional.

One cannot devise an algorithm that optimizes the expected loss directly, because this quantity depends on the unknown $P(y|x)$. We make the standard approximation of estimating Q_{opt} by minimizing instead the empirical estimate of the expected loss from the labeled sample:

$$\hat{Q} = \arg \min_{Q \in \mathcal{I}_\gamma(p)} \hat{\mathbf{E}}[L_Q] = \arg \min_Q \frac{1}{l} \sum_{i=1}^{l} L_Q(x_i, y_i).$$

If the loss function is the log loss, finding $\hat{Q}$ is equivalent to maximizing the information regularization objective (10.4) for a specific value of λ. However, we will present the learning bound for the square loss, as it is bounded and easier to work with. A similar result holds for the log-loss by using the equivalence results between the log loss and square loss presented in (Abe et al., 2001).

The question is how different $\hat{Q}$ (estimated from the sample) and Q_{opt} (estimated from the true conditional) can be due to this approximation. Learning theoretical results provide guarantees that given enough labeled samples the minimization of $\hat{\mathbf{E}}[L_Q]$ and $\mathbf{E}_{p(x)P(y|x)}[L_Q]$ are equivalent. We say the task is learnable if with high probability in the sample the empirical loss converges to the true loss uniformly for all concepts as $l \to \infty$. This guarantees that $\mathbf{E}\left[L_{\hat{Q}}\right]$ approximates $\mathbf{E}\left[L_{Q_{opt}}\right]$ well. Formally,

$$P\{\exists Q \in \mathcal{I}_\gamma(p) : |\hat{\mathbf{E}}[L_Q] - \mathbf{E}[L_Q]| > \epsilon\} \leq \delta, \tag{10.5}$$

where the probability is with respect to all samples of size l. The inequality should hold for l polynomially large in $1/\epsilon, 1/\delta, 1/\gamma$.

We have the following sample complexity bound on the square loss, derived in (Corduneanu and Jaakkola, 2003):

Theorem 10.2 *Let $\epsilon, \delta > 0$. Then*

$$\mathrm{P}\{\exists Q \in \mathcal{I}_\gamma(p) : |\hat{\mathbf{E}}\,[L_Q] - \mathbf{E}\,[L_Q]\,| > \epsilon\} < \delta,$$

where the probability is over samples of size l greater than

$$\mathcal{O}\left(\frac{1}{\epsilon^4}\left(\log\frac{1}{\epsilon}\right)\left[\log\frac{1}{\delta} + c_p(m_p^{-1}(\epsilon^2)) + \frac{\gamma}{(m_p^{-1}(\epsilon^2))^2}\right]\right).$$

Here $m_p(\alpha) = \mathrm{P}\{x : p(x) \leq \alpha\}$, and $c_p(\alpha)$ is the number of disconnected sets in $\{x : p(x) > \alpha\}$.

The quantities $m_p(\cdot)$ and $c_p(\cdot)$ characterize how difficult the classification is due to the structure of $p(x)$. Learning is more difficult when significant probability mass lies in regions of small $p(x)$ because in such regions the variation of $Q(y|x)$ is less constrained. Also, the larger $c_p(\cdot)$ is, the labels of more "clusters" need to be learned from labeled data. The two measures of complexity are well behaved for the useful densities. Densities of bounded support, Laplace and Gaussian, as well as mixtures of these, have $m_p(\alpha) < u\alpha$, where u is some constant. Mixtures of single-mode densities have $c_p(\alpha)$ bounded by the number of mixtures.

10.2.2   Finite Unlabeled Sample

We discuss here classification by information regularization when $\mathcal{X}$ is endowed with a metric but the true marginal $p(x)$ is unknown save for a large unlabeled sample $(x_{l+1}, \ldots, x_n)$. In practice we might already have a domain-specific model (class) of how the labels are generated and we show how to apply information regularization if the labels must come from a parametric family $Q(y|x, \theta)$.

Although it is possible to approach this scenario directly by partitioning the space into regions as in (Szummer and Jaakkola, 2002a), here we reduce the task to the situation in which the full marginal is known by replacing the full marginal with an empirical estimate obtained from the unlabeled sample.

logistic regression   We illustrate this method on logistic regression, in which we restrict the conditional to linear decision boundaries with the following parametric form: $Q(y|x; \theta) = \sigma(y\theta^\top x)$, where $y \in \{-1, 1\}$ and $\sigma(x) = 1/(1 + \exp(-x))$. The Fisher information is therefore $F(x; \theta) = \sigma(\theta^\top x)\sigma(-\theta^\top x)\theta\theta^\top$ and according to Eq. 10.3 the information regularizer takes the form

$$\|\theta\|^2 \int \hat{p}(x)\sigma(\theta^\top x)\sigma(-\theta^\top x)dx.$$

Here $\hat{p}(x)$ is the empirical estimate of the true marginal. We compare two ways of estimating $p(x)$, the empirical approximation $\frac{1}{n}\sum_{j=1}^n \delta(x - x_j')$, as well as a Gaussian kernel density estimator. The empirical approximation leads to optimizing the following criterion:

$$\max_{\theta} \sum_{i=1}^{l} \log \sigma(y_i \theta^\top x_i) - \|\theta\|^2 \frac{\lambda}{n} \sum_{j=1}^{n} \sigma(\theta^\top x_j)\sigma(-\theta^\top x_j).$$

It is instructive to contrast this information regularization objective with the criterion optimized by *transductive support vector machines (SVMs)*, as in chapter 6. Changing the SVM loss function to logistic loss, transductive SVM/logistic regression optimizes

$$\max_{\theta, y_{l+1}, \ldots, y_n} \sum_{i=1}^{n} \log \sigma(y_i \theta^\top x_i) - \frac{\lambda}{2} \|\theta\|^2$$

over all labelings of unlabeled data. In contrast, our algorithm contains the unlabeled information in the regularizer.

The presented information regularization criterion can be easily optimized by gradient-ascent or Newton-type algorithms. Note that the term $\sigma(\theta^\top x)\sigma(-\theta^\top x) = Q(1|x)Q(-1|x)$ focuses on the decision boundary. Therefore, compared to the standard logistic regression regularizer $\|\theta\|^2$, we penalize more decision boundaries crossing regions of high data density. Also, the term makes the regularizer nonconvex, making optimization potentially more difficult. This level of complexity is, however, unavoidable by any semi-supervised algorithm for logistic regression, because the structure of the problem introduces locally optimal decision boundaries.

If unlabeled data are limited, we may prefer a kernel estimate $\hat{p}(x) = \frac{1}{n} \sum_{j=1}^{n} K(x, x'_j)$ to the empirical approximation, provided the regularization integral remains tractable. In logistic regression, if the kernels are Gaussian we can make the integral tractable by approximating $\sigma(\theta^\top x)\sigma(-\theta^\top x)$ with a degenerate Gaussian. Either from the Laplace approximation, or the Taylor expansion $\log(1 + e^x) \approx \log 2 + x/2 + x^2/8$, we derive the following approximation, as in (Corduneanu and Jaakkola, 2003):

$$\sigma(\theta^\top x)\sigma(-\theta^\top x) \approx \frac{1}{4} \exp\left(-\frac{1}{4}(\theta^\top x)^2\right).$$

With this approximation computing the integral of the regularizer over the kernel centered μ of variance $\tau \mathbf{I}$ becomes integration of a Gaussian:

$$\frac{1}{4} \exp\left(-\frac{1}{4}(\theta^\top x)^2\right) \mathcal{N}(x; \mu, \tau \mathbf{I}) =$$
$$\frac{1}{4} \sqrt{\frac{\det \Sigma_\theta}{\det \tau \mathbf{I}}} \exp\left(-\frac{\mu^\top (\tau \mathbf{I} - \Sigma_\theta) \mu}{2\tau^2}\right) \mathcal{N}\left(x; \frac{\Sigma_\theta \mu}{\tau}, \Sigma_\theta\right),$$

where $\Sigma_\theta = \left(\frac{1}{\tau}\mathbf{I} + \frac{1}{2}\theta\theta^\top\right)^{-1} = \tau \left[\mathbf{I} - \frac{1}{2}\theta\theta^\top / \left(\frac{1}{\tau} + \frac{1}{2}\|\theta\|^2\right)\right].$

After integration only the multiplicative factor remains:

$$\frac{1}{4}\left(1 + \frac{\tau}{2}\|\theta\|^2\right)^{-\frac{1}{2}} \exp\left(-\frac{1}{4}\frac{(\theta^\top \mu)^2}{1 + \frac{\tau}{2}\|\theta\|^2}\right).$$

Therefore, if we place a Gaussian kernel of variance $\tau\mathbf{I}$ at each sample x_j we obtain the following approximation to the information regularization penalty:

$$\frac{\|\theta\|^2}{\sqrt{1+\frac{\tau}{2}\|\theta\|^2}}\frac{1}{4n}\sum_{j=1}^{n}\exp\left(-\frac{1}{4}\frac{(\theta^\top x_j)^2}{1+\frac{\tau}{2}\|\theta\|^2}\right).$$

This regularizer can be also optimized by gradient ascent or Newton's method.

10.2.2.1 *Logistic Regression Experiments*

We demonstrate the logistic information regularization algorithm as derived in the previous section on synthetic classification tasks. The data are generated from two bivariate Gaussian densities of equal covariance, a model in which the linear decision boundary can be Bayes optimal. However, the small number of labeled samples is not enough to accurately estimate the model, and we show that information regularization with unlabeled data can significantly improve error rates.

We compare a few criteria: logistic regression trained only on labeled data and regularized with the standard $\|\theta\|^2$; logistic regression regularized with the information regularizer derived from the empirical estimate to $p(x)$; and logistic regression with the information regularizer derived from a Gaussian kernel estimate of $p(x)$.

We have optimized the regularized likelihood $L(\theta)$ both with gradient ascent $\theta \leftarrow \theta + \alpha\nabla_\theta L(\theta)$, and with Newton's method (iterative reweighted least squares) $\theta \leftarrow \theta - \alpha\nabla_{\theta\theta}^2 L(\theta)^{-1}\nabla_\theta L(\theta)$ with similar results. Newton's method converges with fewer iterations, but computing the Hessian becomes prohibitive if data are high-dimensional, and convergence depends on stronger assumptions that those for gradient ascent. Gradient ascent is safer but slower.

We ran 100 experiments with data drawn from the same model and averaged the error rates to obtain statistically significant results. In figure 10.4 (Corduneanu and Jaakkola, 2003) we have obtained the error rates on 5 labeled and 100 unlabeled samples. On each data set we initialized the iteration randomly multiple times. We set the kernel width τ of the Gaussian kernel approximation to the regularizer by standard cross-validation for density estimation. Nevertheless, on such a large number of unlabeled samples the information regularizers derived from kernel and empirical estimates perform indistinguishably. They both outperform the standard supervised regularization significantly.

10.3   Information Regularization and Relational Data

In a large number of classification domains we do not have a natural metric relevant to the classification task (correlating $Q(y|x)$ and $Q(y|x')$ for $x \neq x'$). In the absence of a metric, biases about labelings are often naturally expressed in relational form. For example, consider the task of categorization of webpages in the presence of

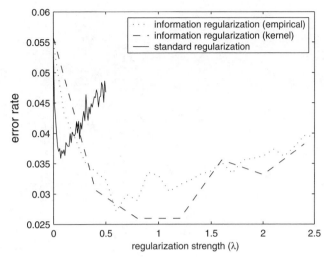

Figure 10.4 Average error rates of logistic regression with and without information regularization on 100 random selections of 5 labeled and 100 unlabeled samples from bivariate Gaussian classes.

information about their link structure. It is natural to believe that pages that are linked in the same manner (common parents and common children) are biased to have similar topics even before we see any information about their content. Similarly, all other things being equal, pages that share common words are likely to have similar topics. In classifying gene function, genes whose protein products interact are more likely to participate in the same process with similar function; or in retrieving science publications, co-cited articles, or articles published in the same journal, are likely to have similar relevance assessments.

relational classification
Relational classification is not new – it has been studied extensively from a Bayesian network perspective, as in (Taskar et al., 2002). Nevertheless, information regularization can exploit the relational structure with minimal assumptions about the distribution of data, even in a nonparametric, purely transductive context.

Let us begin by representing the relational constraints as a collection of regions (sets) $\mathcal{R}$, derived from observed examples $(x_1, x_2, \ldots, x_n)$, where we expect the labels to be similar within each region. The regions here differ from the continuous case in that they are discrete subsets of indices $\{1, 2, \ldots, n\}$ in the training set. It is useful to depict the region cover as a bipartite graph with points on one side and regions on the other, as in figure 10.5. Note that regions can also be derived from a metric if such a metric exists. For example, we could define regions centered at each observed data point of a certain radius. For this reason every algorithm discussed in this section is also applicable to finite sample metric settings.

We consider a generative process over the finite sample $(x_1, x_2, \ldots, x_n)$ by selecting a region R from $\mathcal{R}$ with probability $\gamma(R)$, and then an observed point x_i

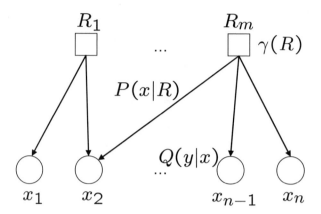

Figure 10.5   Covering of the observed samples with a set of relational regions represented as a bipartite graph. The lower nodes are the observed data points, and the upper nodes are the regions.

from R according to the membership [4] probability $P(i|R)$. The probabilities $\gamma(R)$ and $P(x|R)$ are task specific and must be selected such that $\sum_{R \in \mathcal{R}} \gamma(R)P(i|R) = P(x_i)$, the probability of sampling x_i from $(x_1, \ldots, x_n)$. If the true marginal is known, then we can replace $P(x_i)$ with its true value; otherwise, a reasonable empirical estimate is $P(x_i) = 1/n$ for all $i = 1 \ldots n$. If there is no reason to prefer one region over another, $\gamma(R)$ could be uniform on $\mathcal{R}$; the constraint $P(x_i) = 1/n$ cannot be typically simultaneously enforced, however.

In this context the goal of classification is purely transductive: given the labels of the labeled training set, the classifier assigns labels to the unlabeled training set in a manner consistent with the relational biases $\mathcal{R}$. Nothing is inferred about unobserved $x \in \mathcal{X}$.

10.3.1   Nonparametric Classification

Without constraining the family of label distributions $Q(y|x)$, the objective that must be optimized according to the information regularization principle is

$$\max_{\{Q(y|x_i)\}_{i=1\ldots n}} \frac{1}{l} \sum_{i=1}^{l} \log Q(y_i|x_i) - \lambda J(Q; \mathcal{R}),$$

---

4. In the finite sample case we use the index of the example interchangeably with the example itself.

where the information regularizer is given by

$$J(Q; \mathcal{R}) = \sum_{R \in \mathcal{R}} \gamma(R) I_R(x; y) = \sum_{R \in \mathcal{R}} \gamma(R) \sum_{j \in R} \sum_{y \in \mathcal{Y}} \mathrm{P}(j|R) Q(y|x_j) \log \frac{Q(y|x_j)}{Q(y|R)},$$

where $Q(y|R) = \sum_{j \in R} \mathrm{P}(j|R) Q(y|x_j)$ is the overall probability of y within the region.

As opposed to the continuous version of information regularization, the above objective depends on a finite set of parameters $\{Q(y|x_i)\}_{i=1...n}$; thus optimization is efficient. Moreover, in the nonparametric setting the objective is convex due to the convexity of mutual information (Cover and Thomas, 1991). The following lemma from (Corduneanu and Jaakkola, 2004) formalizes the result:

Lemma 10.3 *The relational regularization objective for $\lambda > 0$ is a strictly convex function of the conditionals $\{Q(y|x_i)\}$ provided that (1) each point $i \in \{1, \ldots, n\}$ belongs to at least one region containing at least two points, and (2) the membership probabilities $\mathrm{P}(i|R)$ and $\gamma(R)$ are all non-zero.*

10.3.1.1 *Distributed Propagation Algorithm*

As in (Corduneanu and Jaakkola, 2004) we derive a local propagation algorithm for minimizing the relational regularization objective that is both easy to implement and provably convergent. The algorithm can be seen as a variant of the Blahut-Arimoto algorithm in rate-distortion theory (Blahut, 1972). We begin by rewriting each mutual information term $I_R(x; y)$ in the criterion

$$
\begin{aligned}
I_R(x; y) &= \sum_{j \in R} \sum_{y \in \mathcal{Y}} \mathrm{P}(j|R) Q(y|x_j) \log \frac{Q(y|x_j)}{Q(y|R)} \\
&= \min_{Q_R(\cdot)} \sum_{j \in R} \sum_{y \in \mathcal{Y}} \mathrm{P}(j|R) Q(y|x_j) \log \frac{Q(y|x_j)}{Q_R(y)},
\end{aligned}
$$

where the variational distribution $Q_R(y)$ can be chosen independently from $Q(y|x_j)$ but the unique minimum is attained when $Q_R(y) = Q(y|R) = \sum_{j \in R} \mathrm{P}(j|R) Q(y|x_j)$. We can extend the regularizer over both $\{Q(y|x_i)\}$ and $\{Q_R(y)\}$ by defining

$$J(Q, Q_R; \mathcal{R}) = \sum_{R \in \mathcal{R}} \gamma(R) \sum_{j \in R} \sum_{y \in \mathcal{Y}} \mathrm{P}(j|R) Q(y|x_j) \log \frac{Q(y|x_j)}{Q_R(y)}$$

so that $J(Q; \mathcal{R}) = \min_{\{Q_R(\cdot), R \in \mathcal{R}\}} J(Q, Q_R; \mathcal{R})$ recovers the original regularizer.

local propagation algorithm

The local propagation algorithm follows from optimizing each $Q(y|x_i)$ based on fixed $\{Q_R(y)\}$ and subsequently finding each $Q_R(y)$ given fixed $\{Q(y|x_i)\}$. We omit the straightforward derivation and provide only the resulting algorithm: for all points x_i, $i = (l+1) \ldots n$ (not labeled), and for all regions $R \in \mathcal{R}$ we perform the following complementary averaging updates

$$Q(y|x_i) \quad \leftarrow \quad \frac{1}{Z_{x_i}} \exp\Big(\sum_{R:j\in R} \mathrm{P}(R|j) \log Q_R(y) \Big) \tag{10.6}$$

$$Q_R(y) \quad \leftarrow \quad \sum_{j\in R} \mathrm{P}(x_j|R) Q(y|x_j), \tag{10.7}$$

where Z_{x_j} is a normalization constant, and $P(R|j) \propto P(j|R)\gamma(R)$. In other words, $Q(y|x_i)$ is obtained by taking a weighted geometric average of the distributions associated with the regions, whereas $Q_R(y)$ is (as before) a weighted arithmetic average of the conditionals within each region.

Updating $Q(y|x_i)$ for each labeled point x_i, $i = 1 \ldots l$ involves minimizing

$$\frac{1}{l} \log Q(y_i|x_i) - \frac{\lambda}{n} H(Q(\cdot|x_i)) - \lambda \sum_{y\in\mathcal{Y}} Q(y|x_i) \Big(\sum_{R:j\in R} \gamma(R)\mathrm{P}(j|R) \log Q_R(y) \Big),$$

where $H(Q(\cdot|x_i))$ is the Shannon entropy of the conditional. While the objective is strictly convex, the solution cannot be written in closed form and has to be found iteratively (e.g., via Newton-Raphson or simple bracketing when the labels are binary). A much simpler update $Q(y|x_i) = \delta(y, y_i)$, where y_i is the observed label for x_i, may suffice in practice. This update results from taking the limit of small λ and approximates the iterative solution.

Thus the transduction information regularization algorithm in the nonparametric setting consists of the following steps:

1. Associate with each region $R \in \mathcal{R}$ a label probability distribution $Q_R(y)$.

2. Initialize $\{Q(y|x_i)\}_{i=1\ldots n}$ and $\{Q_R(y)\}_{R\in\mathcal{R}}$. The initialization values are irrelevant because the objective is convex and admits a unique minimum.

3. Iterate (10.6) and (10.7) alternatively until convergence. For labeled points a slightly different update than (10.6) must be used to account for the observation.

10.3.1.2 *Learning Theoretical Properties*

As in the metric case, we seek to show that the information regularizer is an adequate measure of complexity, in the sense that learning a labeling consistent with a cap on the regularizer requires fewer labeled samples. We consider only the simpler setting where the labels are hard and binary, $Q(y|x_i) \in \{0,1\}$, and show that bounding the information regularizer significantly reduces the number of possible labelings. Assuming that the points in a region have uniform weights $P(j|R)$, let $N(\gamma)$ be the number of labelings of $\{x_1, x_2, \ldots, x_n\}$ consistent with

$$J(Q, \mathcal{R}) < \gamma.$$

According to (Corduneanu and Jaakkola, 2004) we have the following result:

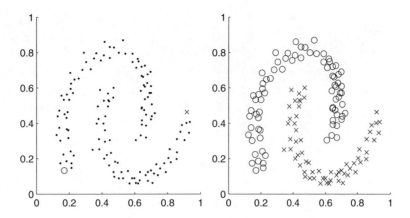

Figure 10.6   Clusters correctly separated by information regularization given one label from each class.

Theorem 10.4 $\log_2 N(\gamma) \leq C(\gamma) + \gamma \cdot n \cdot t(\mathcal{R})/\min_R \gamma(R)$, *where* $C(\gamma) \to 1$ *as* $\gamma \to 0$, *and* $t(\mathcal{R})$ *is a property of* $\mathcal{R}$ *that does not depend on the cardinality of* $\mathcal{R}$.

Therefore when γ is small, $N(\gamma)$ is exponentially smaller than 2^n, and

$$\lim_{\gamma \to 0} N(\gamma) = 2.$$

10.3.1.3   Experiments

To begin with we illustrate the performance of transductive information regularization on two two-dimensional generated binary classification tasks (Corduneanu and Jaakkola, 2004). In this setting we convert the tasks to relational classification by deriving regions of observed points contained in spheres centered at each data point and of a certain radius.

On the classic semi-supervised data set in figure 10.6 the method correctly propagates the labels to the clusters starting from a single labeled point in each class. In the example in figure 10.7 we demonstrate that information regularization can be used as a post-processing to supervised classification and improve error rates by taking advantage of the topology of the space. All points are a priori labeled by a linear classifier that is nonoptimal and places a decision boundary through the negative and positive clusters. Information regularization is able to correct the mislabeling of the clusters. Both results are quite robust in the choice of the radius of the regions as long as all regions remain connected with each other.

Next we test the algorithm on a web document classification task, the WebKB data set of (Blum and Mitchell, 1998). The data consist of 1051 pages collected from the websites of four universities. This particular subset of WebKB is a binary classification task into "course" and "non-course" pages. 22% of the documents are positive ("course"). The data set is interesting because apart from the documents' contents we have information about the link structure of the documents. The two

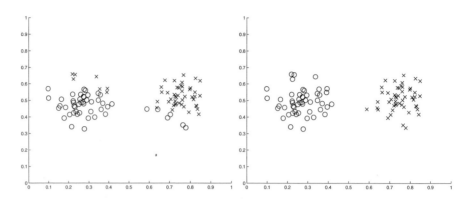

Figure 10.7 Ability of information regularization to correct the output of a prior classifier (*left*: before; *right*: after)

sources of information can illustrate the capability of information regularization of combining heterogeneous unlabeled representations.

Both "text" and "link" features used here are a bag-of-words representation of documents. To obtain "link" features we collect text that appears under all links that link to that page from other pages, and produce its bag-of-words representation. We employ no stemming, or stopword processing, but restrict the vocabulary to 2000 text words and 500 link words. The experimental setup consists of 100 random selections of three positive-labeled, nine negative-labeled, and the rest unlabeled. The test set includes all unlabeled documents. We report a naive Bayes baseline based on the model that features of different words are independent given the document class. The naive Bayes algorithm can be run on text features, link features, or combine the two feature sets by assuming independence. We also quote the performance of the semi-supervised method obtained by combining naive Bayes with the expectation-maximization (EM) algorithm as in chapter 3.

We measure the performance of the algorithms by the F-score equal to $2pr/(p+r)$, where p and r are the precision and recall. A high F-score indicates that the precision and recall are high and also close to each other. To compare algorithms independently of the probability threshold that decides between positive and negative samples, the results reported are the best F-scores for all possible settings of the threshold.

The key issue in applying information regularization is the selection of sound relational biases (i.e., $\mathcal{R}$). For document classification we obtained the best results by grouping all documents that share a certain word into the same region; thus each region is in fact a word, and there are as many regions as the size of the vocabulary. Regions are weighted equally, as well as the words belonging to the same region. The choice of λ is also task dependent. Here cross-validation selected an optimal value $\lambda = 90$. When running information regularization with both text and link features we combined the coverings with a weight of 0.5.

All results are reported in table 10.1. We observe that information regularization

Table 10.1   Webpage classification comparison between naive Bayes and information regularization and semi-supervised naive Bayes + EM on text, link, and joint features

	naive Bayes	inforeg	naive Bayes + EM
text	82.85	85.10	93.69
link	65.64	82.85	67.18
both	83.33	86.15	91.01

performs better than naive Bayes on all types of features, that combining text and link features improves performance of the regularization method, and that on link features the method performs better than the semi-supervised naive Bayes + EM.

10.3.2   Parametric Classification

We briefly discuss extensions to the transductive information regularization algorithm with relational biases when the conditional takes a parametric form (unpublished work). The extended framework subsumes standard estimation principles such as supervised maximum likelihood, EM from incomplete data, as well as information regularization presented above. One of the key modifications is to associate with each region R a parametric model $Q_R(x, y|\theta_R)$ instead of the standard average label $Q_R(y)$ as introduced in the above transductive algorithm. With this change the meaning of the regions shifts to represent groups of data points that are modeled in a similar way (same parametric family), where the parametric family may change from region to region. This revision increases the expressive power of information regularization significantly while remaining tractable. Preliminary results are encouraging.

10.4   Discussion

We have presented the broader information regularization framework, a principle for assigning labels to unlabeled data in a semi-supervised setting. The principle seeks to minimize the information induced between examples and labels relative to a topology over the examples. In other words, we minimize spurious information content not forced by the observed labels.

The information regularization principle manifests itself in different forms depending on assumptions about the space of examples – metric or relational. We demonstrated the resulting algorithms both under the idealized setting where the marginal is known, as well as when only a finite unlabeled sample is available. Transductive nonparametric classification results in an efficient algorithm that is provably convergent to a unique optimum.

We can also constrain the conditional probabilities to take a particular parametric form. This extension can be generalized considerably, leading to a unifying framework.

III   Graph-Based Methods

11 Label Propagation and Quadratic Criterion

Yoshua Bengio   BENGIOY@IRO.UMONTREAL.CA
Olivier Delalleau   DELALLEA@IRO.UMONTREAL.CA
Nicolas Le Roux   NICOLAS.LE.ROUX@UMONTREAL.CA

Various graph-based algorithms for semi-supervised learning have been proposed in the recent literature. They rely on the idea of building a graph whose nodes are data points (labeled and unlabeled) and edges represent similarities between points. Known labels are used to propagate information through the graph in order to label all nodes. In this chapter, we show how these different algorithms can be cast into a common framework where one minimizes a quadratic cost criterion whose closed-form solution is found by solving a linear system of size n (total number of data points). The cost criterion naturally leads to an extension of such algorithms to the inductive setting, where one obtains test samples one at a time: the derived induction formula can be evaluated in $O(n)$ time, which is much more efficient than solving again exactly the linear system (which in general costs $O(kn^2)$ time for a sparse graph where each data point has k neighbors). We also use this inductive formula to show that when the similarity between points satisfies a locality property, then the algorithms are plagued by the curse of dimensionality, with respect to the dimensionality of an underlying manifold.

11.1 Introduction

Many semi-supervised learning algorithms rely on the geometry of the data induced by both labeled and unlabeled examples to improve on supervised methods that use only the labeled data. This geometry can be naturally represented by an empirical graph $\mathbf{g} = (V, E)$ where nodes $V = \{1, \ldots, n\}$ represent the training data and edges E represent similarities between them (cf. section 1.3.3). These similarities are given

weight matrix   by a weight matrix $\mathbf{W}$: $\mathbf{W}_{ij}$ is non-zero iff x_i and x_j are "neighbors", i.e., the edge (i, j) is in E (weighted by $\mathbf{W}_{ij}$). The weight matrix $\mathbf{W}$ can be, for instance, the k-nearest neighbor matrix: $\mathbf{W}_{ij} = 1$ iff x_i is among the k-nearest neighbors of x_j

or vice versa (and is 0 otherwise). Another typical weight matrix is given by the Gaussian kernel of width σ:

$$\mathbf{W}_{ij} = e^{-\frac{\|x_i - x_j\|^2}{2\sigma^2}}. \tag{11.1}$$

In general, we assume $\mathbf{W}_{ij}$ is given by a symmetric positive function W_X (possibly dependent on the data set $X = (x_1, \ldots, x_n)$) by $\mathbf{W}_{ij} = W_X(x_i, x_j) \geq 0$. This functional view will be useful in the inductive setting (section 11.4).

This chapter is organized as follows. In section 11.2 we present algorithms based on the idea of using the graph structure to spread labels from labeled examples to the whole data set (Szummer and Jaakkola, 2002b; Zhu and Ghahramani, 2002; Zhou et al., 2004; Zhu et al., 2003b). An alternative approach originating from smoothness considerations yields algorithms based on graph regularization, which naturally leads to a regularization term based on the graph Laplacian (Belkin and Niyogi, 2003b; Joachims, 2003; Zhou et al., 2004; Zhu et al., 2003b; Belkin et al., 2004b; Delalleau et al., 2005). This approach, detailed in section 11.3, is then shown to be tightly linked to the previous label propagation algorithms. In sections 11.4 and 11.5 we present two extensions of these algorithms: first, a simple way to turn a number of them, originally designed for the transductive setting, into induction algorithms, then a method to better balance classes using prior information about the classes' distribution. Section 11.6 finally explores theoretical limitations of these methods which, being based mostly on the local geometry of the data in small neighborhoods, are subject to the curse of dimensionality when the intrinsic dimension of the underlying distribution (the dimensionality of the manifold near which it concentrates) increases, when this manifold is far from being flat.

11.2   Label Propagation on a Similarity Graph

11.2.1   Iterative Algorithms

label propagation   Given the graph g, a simple idea for semi-supervised learning is to *propagate labels* on the graph. Starting with nodes $1, 2, \ldots, l$ labeled[1] with their known label (1 or -1) and nodes $l + 1, \ldots, n$ labeled with 0, each node starts to propagate its label to its neighbors, and the process is repeated until convergence.

An algorithm of this kind has been proposed by Zhu and Ghahramani (2002), and is described in algorithm 11.1. Estimated labels on both labeled and unlabeled data are denoted by $\hat{Y} = (\hat{Y}_l, \hat{Y}_u)$, where $\hat{Y}_l$ may be allowed to differ from the given

---

1. If there are $M > 2$ classes, one can label each node i with an M-dimensional vector (one-hot for labeled samples, i.e., with 0 everywhere except a 1 at index y_i = class of x_i), and use the same algorithms in a one-versus-rest fashion. We consider here the classification case, but extension to regression is straightforward since labels are treated as real values.

Algorithm 11.1 Label propagation (Zhu and Ghahramani, 2002)

Compute affinity matrix $\mathbf{W}$ from (11.1)
Compute the diagonal degree matrix $\mathbf{D}$ by $\mathbf{D}_{ii} \leftarrow \sum_j W_{ij}$
Initialize $\hat{Y}^{(0)} \leftarrow (y_1, \ldots, y_l, 0, 0, \ldots, 0)$
Iterate
   1. $\hat{Y}^{(t+1)} \leftarrow \mathbf{D}^{-1}\mathbf{W}\hat{Y}^{(t)}$
   2. $\hat{Y}_l^{(t+1)} \leftarrow Y_l$
until convergence to $\hat{Y}^{(\infty)}$
Label point x_i by the sign of $\hat{y}_i^{(\infty)}$

---

labels $Y_l = (y_1, \ldots, y_l)$. In this particular algorithm, $\hat{Y}_l$ is constrained to be equal to Y_l. We propose in algorithm 11.2 below a slightly different label propagation scheme (originally inspired from the Jacobi iterative method for linear systems), similar to the previous algorithm except that

- we advocate forcing $\mathbf{W}_{ii} = 0$, which often works better;
- we allow $\hat{Y}_l \neq Y_l$ (which may be useful, e.g., when classes overlap); and
- we use an additional regularization term ϵ for better numerical stability.

Algorithm 11.2 Label propagation (inspired from Jacobi iteration algorithm)

Compute an affinity matrix $\mathbf{W}$ such that $\mathbf{W}_{ii} = 0$
Compute the diagonal degree matrix $\mathbf{D}$ by $\mathbf{D}_{ii} \leftarrow \sum_j W_{ij}$
Choose a parameter $\alpha \in (0, 1)$ and a small $\epsilon > 0$
$\mu \leftarrow \frac{\alpha}{1-\alpha} \in (0, +\infty)$
Compute the diagonal matrix $\mathbf{A}$ by $\mathbf{A}_{ii} \leftarrow I_{[l]}(i) + \mu\mathbf{D}_{ii} + \mu\epsilon$
Initialize $\hat{Y}^{(0)} \leftarrow (y_1, \ldots, y_l, 0, 0, \ldots, 0)$
Iterate $\hat{Y}^{(t+1)} \leftarrow \mathbf{A}^{-1}(\mu\mathbf{W}\hat{Y}^{(t)} + \hat{Y}^{(0)})$ until convergence to $\hat{Y}^{(\infty)}$
Label point x_i by the sign of $\hat{y}_i^{(\infty)}$

The iteration step of algorithm 11.2 can be rewritten for a labeled example $(i \leq l)$

$$\hat{y}_i^{(t+1)} \leftarrow \frac{\sum_j \mathbf{W}_{ij}\hat{y}_j^{(t)} + \frac{1}{\mu}y_i}{\sum_j \mathbf{W}_{ij} + \frac{1}{\mu} + \epsilon} \tag{11.2}$$

and for an unlabeled example $(l + 1 \leq i \leq n)$

$$\hat{y}_i^{(t+1)} \leftarrow \frac{\sum_j \mathbf{W}_{ij}\hat{y}_j^{(t)}}{\sum_j \mathbf{W}_{ij} + \epsilon}. \tag{11.3}$$

These two equations can be seen as a weighted average of the neighbors' current labels, where for labeled examples we also add the initial label (whose weight is inversely proportional to the parameter μ). The ϵ parameter is a regularization term to prevent numerical problems when the denominator becomes too small. The convergence of this algorithm follows from the convergence of the Jacobi iteration method for a specific linear system, and will be discussed in section 11.3.3.

Another similar label propagation algorithm was given by Zhou et al. (2004): at each step a node i receives a contribution from its neighbors j (weighted by the normalized weight of the edge (i, j)), and an additional small contribution given by its initial value. This process is detailed in algorithm 11.3 below (the name "label spreading" was inspired from the terminology used by Zhou et al. (2004)). Compared to algorithm 11.2, it corresponds to the minimization of a slightly different cost criterion, maybe not as intuitive: this will be studied later in sections 11.3.2 and 11.3.3.

Algorithm 11.3 Label spreading (Zhou et al., 2004)

Compute the affinity matrix $\mathbf{W}$ from (11.1) for $i \neq j$ (and $\mathbf{W}_{ii} \leftarrow 0$)
Compute the diagonal degree matrix $\mathbf{D}$ by $\mathbf{D}_{ii} \leftarrow \sum_j W_{ij}$
Compute the normalized graph Laplacian $\mathcal{L} \leftarrow \mathbf{D}^{-1/2}\mathbf{W}\mathbf{D}^{-1/2}$
Initialize $\hat{Y}^{(0)} \leftarrow (y_1, \ldots, y_l, 0, 0, \ldots, 0)$
Choose a parameter $\alpha \in [0, 1)$
Iterate $\hat{Y}^{(t+1)} \leftarrow \alpha\mathcal{L}\hat{Y}^{(t)} + (1 - \alpha)\hat{Y}^{(0)}$ until convergence to $\hat{Y}^{(\infty)}$
Label point x_i by the sign of $\hat{y}_i^{(\infty)}$

The proof of convergence of algorithm 11.3 is simple (Zhou et al., 2004). The iteration equation being $\hat{Y}^{(t+1)} \leftarrow \alpha\mathcal{L}\hat{Y}^{(t)} + (1 - \alpha)\hat{Y}^{(0)}$, we have

$$\hat{Y}^{(t+1)} = (\alpha\mathcal{L})^t\hat{Y}^{(0)} + (1 - \alpha)\sum_{i=0}^{t}(\alpha\mathcal{L})^i\hat{Y}^{(0)}.$$

The matrix $\mathcal{L}$ being similar to $\mathbf{P} = \mathbf{D}^{-1}\mathbf{W} = \mathbf{D}^{-1/2}\mathcal{L}\mathbf{D}^{1/2}$, it has the same eigenvalues. Since $\mathbf{P}$ is a stochastic matrix by construction, its eigenvalues are in $[-1, 1]$, and consequently the eigenvalues of $\alpha\mathcal{L}$ are in $(-1, 1)$ (remember $\alpha < 1$). It follows that when $t \rightarrow \infty$, $(\alpha\mathcal{L})^t \rightarrow 0$ and

$$\sum_{i=0}^{t}(\alpha\mathcal{L})^i \rightarrow (\mathbf{I} - \alpha\mathcal{L})^{-1}$$

so that

$$\hat{Y}^{(t)} \rightarrow \hat{Y}^{(\infty)} = (1 - \alpha)(\mathbf{I} - \alpha\mathcal{L})^{-1}\hat{Y}^{(0)}. \tag{11.4}$$

The convergence rate of these three algorithms depends on specific properties of the graph such as the eigenvalues of its Laplacian. In general, we can expect it to be at worst on the order of $O(kn^2)$, where k is the number of neighbors of a point in the graph. In the case of a dense weight matrix, the computational time is thus cubic in n.

11.2.2 Markov Random Walks

transition
probabilities

A different algorithm based on label propagation on the similarity graph was proposed earlier by Szummer and Jaakkola (2002b). They consider Markov random walks on the graph with transition probabilities from i to j,

$$p_{ij} = \frac{\mathbf{W}_{ij}}{\sum_k \mathbf{W}_{ik}}, \tag{11.5}$$

in order to estimate probabilities of class labels. Here, $\mathbf{W}_{ij}$ is given by a Gaussian kernel for neighbors and 0 for non-neighbors, and $\mathbf{W}_{ii} = 1$ (but one could also use $\mathbf{W}_{ii} = 0$). Each data point x_i is associated with a probability $P(y = 1|i)$ of being of class 1. Given a point x_k, we can compute the probability $P^{(t)}(y_{start} = 1|k)$ that we started from a point of class $y_{start} = 1$ given that we arrived to x_k after t steps of random walk by

$$P^{(t)}(y_{start} = 1|k) = \sum_{i=1}^{n} P(y = 1|i) P_{0|t}(i|k),$$

where $P_{0|t}(i|k)$ is the probability that we started from x_i given that we arrived at k after t steps of random walk (this probability can be computed from the p_{ij}). x_k is then classified to 1 if $P^{(t)}(y_{start} = 1|k) > 0.5$, and to -1 otherwise. The authors propose two methods to estimate the class probabilities $P(y = 1|i)$. One is based on an iterative expectation-maximization (EM) algorithm, the other on maximizing a margin-based criterion, which leads to a closed-form solution (Szummer and Jaakkola, 2002b).

It turns out that this algorithm's performance depends crucially on the hyperparameter t (the length of the random walk). This parameter has to be chosen by cross-validation (if enough data are available) or heuristically (it corresponds intuitively to the amount of propagation we allow in the graph, i.e., to the scale of the clusters we are interested in). An alternative way of using random walks on the graph is to assign to point x_i a label depending on the probability of arriving at a positively labeled example when performing a random walk *starting from x_i and until a labeled example is found* (Zhu and Ghahramani, 2002; Zhu et al., 2003b). The length of the random walk is not constrained anymore to a fixed value t. In the following, we will show that this probability, denoted by $P(y_{end} = 1|i)$, is equal (up to a shift and scaling) to the label obtained with algorithm 11.1 (this is similar to the proof by Zhu and Ghahramani (2002)).

When x_i is a labeled example, $P(y_{end} = 1|i) = \delta_{y_i 1}$, and when it is unlabeled we have the relation

$$P(y_{end} = 1|i) = \sum_{j=1}^{n} P(y_{end} = 1|j) p_{ij}, \tag{11.6}$$

with the p_{ij} computed as in (11.5). Let us consider the matrix $\mathbf{P} = \mathbf{D}^{-1}\mathbf{W}$, i.e., such that $\mathbf{P}_{ij} = p_{ij}$. We will denote $\hat{z}_i = P(y_{end} = 1|i)$ and $\hat{Z} = (\hat{Z}_l, \hat{Z}_u)$

the corresponding vector split into its labeled and unlabeled parts. Similarly, the matrices $\mathbf{D}$ and $\mathbf{W}$ can be split into four parts:

$$\mathbf{D} = \begin{pmatrix} \mathbf{D}_{ll} & 0 \\ 0 & \mathbf{D}_{uu} \end{pmatrix}$$

$$\mathbf{W} = \begin{pmatrix} \mathbf{W}_{ll} & \mathbf{W}_{lu} \\ \mathbf{W}_{ul} & \mathbf{W}_{uu} \end{pmatrix}.$$

Equation (11.6) can then be written

$$\hat{Z}_u = \left(\mathbf{D}_{uu}^{-1} \mathbf{W}_{ul} \mid \mathbf{D}_{uu}^{-1} \mathbf{W}_{uu} \right) \begin{pmatrix} \hat{Z}_l \\ \hat{Z}_u \end{pmatrix}$$

$$= \mathbf{D}_{uu}^{-1} \left(\mathbf{W}_{ul} \hat{Z}_l + \mathbf{W}_{uu} \hat{Z}_u \right),$$

which leads to the linear system

$$L_{uu} \hat{Z}_u = \mathbf{W}_{ul} \hat{Z}_l, \tag{11.7}$$

where $L = \mathbf{D} - \mathbf{W}$ is the un-normalized graph Laplacian. Since $\hat{Z}_l$ is known ($\hat{z}_i = 1$ if $y_i = 1$, and 0 otherwise), this linear system can be solved in order to find the probabilities $\hat{Z}_u$ on unlabeled examples. Note that if $(\hat{Z}_u, \hat{Z}_l)$ is a solution of (11.7), then $(\hat{Y}_u, \hat{Y}_l)$ is also a solution, with

$$\hat{Y}_u = 2\hat{Z}_u - (1, 1, \ldots, 1)^\top$$
$$\hat{Y}_l = 2\hat{Z}_l - (1, 1, \ldots, 1)^\top = Y_l.$$

This allows us to rewrite the linear system (11.7) in terms of the vector of original labels Y_l as follows:

$$L_{uu} \hat{Y}_u = \mathbf{W}_{ul} \hat{Y}_l \tag{11.8}$$

with the sign of each element y_i of $\hat{Y}_u$ giving the estimated label of x_i (which is equivalent to comparing $\hat{z}_i$ to a 0.5 threshold).

The solution of this random walk algorithm is thus given in closed form by a linear system, which turns out to be equivalent to iterative algorithm 11.1 (or equivalently, algorithm 11.2 when $\mu \to 0$ and $\epsilon = 0$), as we will see in section 11.3.4.

11.3   Quadratic Cost Criterion

In this section, we investigate semi-supervised learning by minimization of a cost function derived from the graph $\mathbf{g}$. Such methods will be shown to be equivalent to label propagation algorithms presented in the previous section.

11.3.1 Regularization on Graphs

The problem of semi-supervised learning on the graph **g** consists in finding a labeling of the graph that is consistent with both the initial (incomplete) labeling and the geometry of the data induced by the graph structure (edges and weights **W**). Given a labeling $\hat{Y} = (\hat{Y}_l, \hat{Y}_u)$, consistency with the initial labeling can be measured, e.g., by

$$\sum_{i=1}^{l}(\hat{y}_i - y_i)^2 = \|\hat{Y}_l - Y_l\|^2. \tag{11.9}$$

smoothness assumption

On the other hand, consistency with the geometry of the data, which follows from the smoothness (or manifold) assumption discussed in section 1.2, motivates a penalty term of the form

$$\begin{aligned}
\frac{1}{2}\sum_{i,j=1}^{n}\mathbf{W}_{ij}(\hat{y}_i - \hat{y}_j)^2 &= \frac{1}{2}\left(2\sum_{i=1}^{n}\hat{y}_i^2\sum_{j=1}^{n}\mathbf{W}_{ij} - 2\sum_{i,j=1}^{n}\mathbf{W}_{ij}\hat{y}_i\hat{y}_j\right) \\
&= \hat{Y}^\top(\mathbf{D} - \mathbf{W})\hat{Y} \\
&= \hat{Y}^\top L\hat{Y}
\end{aligned} \tag{11.10}$$

graph Laplacian

with $L = \mathbf{D} - \mathbf{W}$ the un-normalized graph Laplacian. This means we penalize rapid changes in $\hat{Y}$ between points that are close (as given by the similarity matrix **W**).

Various algorithms have been proposed based on such considerations. Zhu et al. (2003b) force the labels on the labeled data ($\hat{Y}_l = Y_l$), then minimize (11.10) over $\hat{Y}_u$. However, if there is noise in the available labels, it may be beneficial to allow the algorithm to relabel the labeled data (this could also help generalization in a noise-free setting where, for instance, a positive sample had been drawn from a region of space mainly filled with negative samples). This observation leads to a more general cost criterion involving a tradeoff between (11.9) and (11.10) (Belkin et al., 2004b; Delalleau et al., 2005). A small regularization term can also be added in order to prevent degenerate situations, for instance, when the graph **g** has a connected component with no labeled sample. We thus obtain the following general labeling cost[2]:

$$C(\hat{Y}) = \|\hat{Y}_l - Y_l\|^2 + \mu\hat{Y}^\top L\hat{Y} + \mu\epsilon\|\hat{Y}\|^2. \tag{11.11}$$

spectral clustering

Joachims (2003) obtained the same kind of cost criterion from the perspective of spectral clustering. The unsupervised minimization of $\hat{Y}^\top L\hat{Y}$ (under the constraints $\hat{Y}^\top\mathbf{1} = 0$ and $\|\hat{Y}\|^2 = n$) is a relaxation of the NP-hard problem of minimizing the normalized cut of the graph **g**, i.e. splitting **g** into two subsets $\mathbf{g}^+ = (V^+, E^+)$ and

---

2. Belkin et al. (2004b) first center the vector Y_l and also constrain $\hat{Y}$ to be centered: these restrictions are needed to obtain theoretical bounds on the generalization error, and will not be discussed in this chapter.

$g^- = (V^-, E^-)$ such as to minimize

$$\frac{\sum_{i \in V^+, j \in V^-} W_{ij}}{|V^+||V^-|},$$

where the normalization by $|V^+||V^-|$ favors balanced splits. Based on this approach, Joachims (2003) introduced an additional cost which corresponds to our part $\|\hat{Y}_l - Y_l\|^2$ of the cost (11.11), in order to turn this unsupervised minimization into a semi-supervised transductive algorithm (called spectral graph transducer). Note, however, that although very similar, the solution obtained differs from the straightforward minimization of (11.11) since

■ the labels are not necessarily +1 and −1, but depend on the ratio of the number of positive examples over the number of negative examples (this follows from the normalized cut optimization);

■ the constraint $\|\hat{Y}\|^2 = n$ used in the unsupervised setting remains, thus leading to an eigenvalue problem instead of the direct quadratic minimization that will be studied in the next section;

■ the eigenspectrum of the graph Laplacian is normalized by replacing the ordered Laplacian eigenvalues by a monotonically increasing function, in order to focus on the ranking among the smallest cuts and abstract, for example, from different magnitudes of edge weights.

graph Laplacian   Belkin and Niyogi (2003b) also proposed a semi-supervised algorithm based on the same idea of graph regularization, but using a regularization criterion different from the quadratic penalty term (11.10). It consists in taking advantage of properties of the graph Laplacian L, which can be seen as an operator on functions defined on nodes of the graph g. The graph Laplacian is closely related to the Laplacian on the manifold, whose eigenfunctions provide a basis for the Hilbert space of $\mathcal{L}^2$ functions on the manifold (Rosenberg, 1997). Eigenvalues of the eigenfunctions provide a measure of their smoothness on the manifold (low eigenvalues correspond to smoother functions, with the eigenvalue 0 being associated with the constant function). Projecting any function in $\mathcal{L}^2$ on the first p eigenfunctions (sorted by order of increasing eigenvalue) is thus a way of smoothing it on the manifold. The same principle can be applied to our graph setting, thus leading to algorithm 11.4 (Belkin and Niyogi, 2003b) below. It consists in computing the first p eigenvectors of the graph Laplacian (each eigenvector can be seen as the corresponding eigenfunction applied on training points), then finding the linear combination of these eigenvectors that best predicts the labels (in the mean-squared sense). The idea is to obtain a smooth function (in the sense that it is a linear combination of the p smoothest eigenfunctions of the Laplacian operator on the manifold) that fits the labeled data. This algorithm does not explicitly correspond to the minimization of a nonparametric quadratic criterion such as (11.11) and thus is not covered by the connection shown in section 11.3.3 with label propagation algorithms, but one must keep in mind that it is based

---

Algorithm 11.4 Laplacian regularization (Belkin and Niyogi, 2003b)

Compute the affinity matrix $\mathbf{W}$ (with $\mathbf{W}_{ii} = 0$)

Compute the diagonal degree matrix $\mathbf{D}$ by $\mathbf{D}_{ii} \leftarrow \sum_j W_{ij}$

Compute the un-normalized graph Laplacian $L = \mathbf{D} - \mathbf{W}$

Compute the p eigenvectors $\mathbf{e}_1, \ldots, \mathbf{e}_p$ corresponding to the p smallest eigenvalues of L

Minimize over $a_1, \ldots, a_p$ the quadratic criterion $\sum_{i=1}^{l} \left(y_i - \sum_{j=1}^{p} a_j \mathbf{e}_{j,i} \right)^2$

Label point x_i $(1 \leq i \leq n)$ by the sign of $\sum_{j=1}^{p} a_j \mathbf{e}_{j,i}$

---

on similar graph regularization considerations and offers competitive classification performance.

11.3.2   Optimization Framework

In order to minimize the quadratic criterion (11.11), we can compute its derivative with respect to $\hat{Y}$. We will denote by $\mathbf{S}$ the diagonal matrix $(n \times n)$ given by $\mathbf{S}_{ii} = I_{[l]}(i)$, so that the first part of the cost can be rewritten $\|\mathbf{S}\hat{Y} - \mathbf{S}Y\|^2$. The derivative of the criterion is then

$$\frac{1}{2} \frac{\partial C(\hat{Y})}{\partial \hat{Y}} = \mathbf{S}(\hat{Y} - Y) + \mu L \hat{Y} + \mu \epsilon \hat{Y}$$
$$= (\mathbf{S} + \mu L + \mu \epsilon \mathbf{I}) \hat{Y} - \mathbf{S}Y.$$

The second derivative is

$$\frac{1}{2} \frac{\partial^2 C(\hat{Y})}{\partial \hat{Y} \partial \hat{Y}^\top} = \mathbf{S} + \mu L + \mu \epsilon \mathbf{I},$$

which is a positive definite matrix when $\epsilon > 0$ (L is positive semi-definite as shown by (11.10)). This ensures the cost is minimized when the derivative is set to 0, i.e.,

$$\hat{Y} = (\mathbf{S} + \mu L + \mu \epsilon \mathbf{I})^{-1} \mathbf{S}Y. \tag{11.12}$$

This shows how the new labels can be obtained by a simple matrix inversion. It is interesting to note that this matrix does not depend on the original labels, but only on the graph Laplacian L; the way labels are "propagated" to the rest of the graph is entirely determined by the graph structure.

An alternative (and very similar) criterion was proposed by Zhou et al. (2004), and can be written

$$C'(\hat{Y}) \;\;=\;\; \|\hat{Y} - \mathbf{S}Y\|^2 + \frac{\mu}{2} \sum_{i,j} \mathbf{W}_{ij} \left(\frac{\hat{y}_i}{\sqrt{\mathbf{D}_{ii}}} - \frac{\hat{y}_j}{\sqrt{\mathbf{D}_{jj}}} \right)^2 \tag{11.13}$$

$$= \;\; \|\hat{Y}_l - Y_l\|^2 + \|\hat{Y}_u\|^2 + \mu \hat{Y}^\top (\mathbf{I} - \mathcal{L}) \hat{Y}$$

$$= \;\; \|\hat{Y}_l - Y_l\|^2 + \|\hat{Y}_u\|^2 + \mu \hat{Y}^\top \mathbf{D}^{-1/2} (\mathbf{D} - \mathbf{W}) \mathbf{D}^{-1/2} \hat{Y}$$

$$= \;\; \|\hat{Y}_l - Y_l\|^2 + \|\hat{Y}_u\|^2 + \mu (\mathbf{D}^{-1/2}\hat{Y})^\top L (\mathbf{D}^{-1/2}\hat{Y}).$$

This criterion C' has two main differences with C (11.11):

- the term $\|\hat{Y} - \mathbf{S}Y\|^2 = \|\hat{Y}_l - Y_l\|^2 + \|\hat{Y}_u\|^2$ not only tries to fit the given labels but also to pull to 0 labels of unlabeled samples (this is a similar but stronger regularization compared to the term $\mu\epsilon\|\hat{Y}\|^2$ in the cost C), and

- labels are normalized by the square root of the degree matrix elements $\mathbf{D}_{ii}$ when computing their similarity. This normalization may not be intuitive, but is necessary for the equivalence with the label propagation algorithm 11.3, as seen below.

11.3.3   Links with Label Propagation

The optimization algorithms presented above turn out to be equivalent to the label propagation methods from section 11.2. Let us first study the optimization of the cost $C(\hat{Y})$ from (11.11). The optimum $\hat{Y}$ is given by (11.12), but another way to obtain this solution, besides matrix inversion, is to solve the linear system using one of the many standard methods available. We focus here on the simple

Jacobi iteration   Jacobi iteration method (Saad, 1996), which consists in solving for each component iteratively. Given the system

$$\mathbf{M}x = b \tag{11.14}$$

the approximate solution at step $t + 1$ is

$$x_i^{(t+1)} = \frac{1}{\mathbf{M}_{ii}} \left(b - \sum_{j \neq i} \mathbf{M}_{ij} x_j^{(t)} \right). \tag{11.15}$$

Applying this formula with $x := \hat{Y}$, $b := \mathbf{S}Y$ and $\mathbf{M} := \mathbf{S} + \mu L + \mu\epsilon\mathbf{I}$, we obtain

$$\hat{y}_i^{(t+1)} = \frac{1}{I_{[l]}(i) + \mu \sum_{j \neq i} \mathbf{W}_{ij} + \mu\epsilon} \left(I_{[l]}(i) y_i + \mu \sum_{j \neq i} \mathbf{W}_{ij} \hat{y}_j^{(t)} \right),$$

i.e. exactly the update equations (11.2) and (11.3) used in algorithm 11.2. Convergence of this iterative algorithm is guaranteed by the following theorem (Saad, 1996): if the matrix $\mathbf{M}$ is strictly diagonally dominant, the Jacobi iteration (11.15) converges to the solution of the linear system (11.14). A matrix $\mathbf{M}$ is strictly diagonally dominant iff $|\mathbf{M}_{ii}| > \sum_{j \neq i} |\mathbf{M}_{ij}|$, which is clearly the case for the matrix

$\mathbf{S} + \mu L + \mu\epsilon\mathbf{I}$ (remember $L = \mathbf{D} - \mathbf{W}$ with $\mathbf{D}_{ii} = \sum_{i \neq j} \mathbf{W}_{ij}$, and all $\mathbf{W}_{ij} \geq 0$). Note that this condition also guarantees the convergence of the Gauss-Seidel iteration, which is the same as the Jacobi iteration except that updated coordinates $x_i^{(t+1)}$ are used in the computation of $x_j^{(t+1)}$ for $j > i$. This means we can apply Eqs. 11.2 and 11.3 with $\hat{Y}^{(t+1)}$ and $\hat{Y}^{(t)}$ sharing the same storage.

To show the equivalence between algorithm 11.3 and the minimization of C' given in (11.13), we compute its derivative with respect to $\hat{Y}$:

$$\frac{1}{2} \frac{\partial C'(\hat{Y})}{\partial \hat{Y}} = \hat{Y} - \mathbf{S}Y + \mu\left(\hat{Y} - \mathcal{L}\hat{Y}\right)$$

and is zero iff

$$\hat{Y} = ((1 + \mu)\mathbf{I} - \mu\mathcal{L})^{-1}\,\mathbf{S}Y,$$

which is the same equation as (11.4) with $\mu = \alpha/(1 - \alpha)$, up to a positive factor (which has no effect on the classification since we use only the sign).

11.3.4 Limit Case and Analogies

It is interesting to study the limit case when $\mu \to 0$. In this section we will set $\epsilon = 0$ to simplify notations, but one should keep in mind that it is usually better to use a small positive value for regularization. When $\mu \to 0$, the cost (11.11) is dominated by $\|\hat{Y}_l - Y_l\|^2$. Intuitively, this corresponds to

1. forcing $\hat{Y}_l = Y_l$, then
2. minimizing $\hat{Y}^\top L\hat{Y}$.

Writing $\hat{Y} = (Y_l, \hat{Y}_u)$ (i.e. $\hat{Y}_l = Y_l$) and

$$L = \begin{pmatrix} L_{ll} & L_{lu} \\ L_{ul} & L_{uu} \end{pmatrix}$$

the minimization of $\hat{Y}^\top L\hat{Y}$ with respect to $\hat{Y}_u$ leads to

$$L_{ul}Y_l + L_{uu}\hat{Y}_u = 0 \Rightarrow \hat{Y}_u = -L_{uu}^{-1}L_{ul}Y_l. \tag{11.16}$$

If we consider now Eq. 11.12 where $\hat{Y}_l$ is not constrained anymore, when $\epsilon = 0$ and $\mu \to 0$, using the continuity of the inverse matrix application at $\mathbf{I}$, we obtain that

$$\hat{Y}_l \to Y_l \quad and$$
$$\hat{Y}_u = -L_{uu}^{-1}L_{ul}\hat{Y}_l,$$

which, as expected, gives us the same solution as (11.16).

Analogy with Markov Random Walks In section 11.2.2, we presented an algorithm of label propagation based on Markov random walks on the graph, leading to the linear system (11.8). It is immediately seen that this system is exactly the same as the one obtained in (11.16). The equivalence of the solutions discussed in the previous section between the linear system and iterative algorithms thus shows that the random walk algorithm described in section 11.2.2 is equivalent to the iterative algorithm 11.2 when $\mu \to 0$, i.e., when we keep the original labels instead of iteratively updating them by (11.2).

Analogy with Electric Networks   Zhu et al. (2003b) also link this solution to heat kernels and give an electric network interpretation taken from Doyle and Snell (1984), which we now present. This analogy is interesting as it gives a physical interpretation to the optimization and label propagation framework studied in this chapter. Let us consider an electric network built from the graph **g** by adding resistors with conductance $\mathbf{W}_{ij}$ between nodes i and j (the conductance is the inverse of the resistance). The positive labeled nodes are connected to a positive voltage source $(+1V)$, the negative ones to a negative source $(-1V)$, and we want to compute the voltage on the *unlabeled* nodes (i.e., their label). Denoting the intensity between i and j by I_{ij}, and the voltage by $V_{ij} = \hat{y}_j - \hat{y}_i$, we use Ohm's law,

$$I_{ij} = \mathbf{W}_{ij} V_{ij},\tag{11.17}$$

and Kirchoff's law on an unlabeled node $i > l$:

$$\sum_j I_{ij} = 0.\tag{11.18}$$

Kirchoff's law states that the sum of currents flowing out from i (such that $I_{ij} > 0$) is equal to the sum of currents flowing into i ($I_{ij} < 0$). Here, it is only useful to apply it to unlabeled nodes as the labeled ones are connected to a voltage source, and thus receive some unknown (and uninteresting) current. Using (11.17), we can rewrite (11.18),

$$\begin{aligned}
0 &= \sum_j \mathbf{W}_{ij}(\hat{y}_j - \hat{y}_i) \\
&= \sum_j \mathbf{W}_{ij}\hat{y}_j - \hat{y}_i \sum_j \mathbf{W}_{ij} \\
&= (\mathbf{W}\hat{Y} - \mathbf{D}\hat{Y})_i \\
&= -(L\hat{Y})_i,
\end{aligned}$$

and since this is true for all $i > l$, it is equivalent in matrix notations to

$$L_{ul}Y_l + L_{uu}\hat{Y}_u = 0,$$

which is exactly (11.16). Thus the solution of the limit case (when labeled examples are forced to keep their given label) is given by the voltage in an electric network where labeled nodes are connected to voltage sources and resistors correspond to weights in the graph **g**.

11.4   From Transduction to Induction

inductive setting

The previous algorithms all follow the transduction setting presented in section 1.2.4. However, it could happen that one needs an inductive algorithm, for instance, in a situation where new test examples are presented one at a time and solving the linear system turns out to be too expensive. In such a case, the cost criterion (11.11) naturally leads to an induction formula that can be computed in $O(n)$ time. Assuming that labels $\hat{y}_1, \ldots, \hat{y}_n$ have already been computed by one of the algorithms above, and we want the label $\hat{y}$ of a new point x: we can minimize $C(\hat{y}_1, \ldots, \hat{y}_n, \hat{y})$ only with respect to this new label $\hat{y}$, i.e. minimize

$$\text{constant} + \mu \left(\sum_j W_X(x, x_j)(\hat{y} - \hat{y}_j)^2 + \epsilon \hat{y}^2 \right),$$

where W_X is the (possibly data-dependent) function that generated the matrix $\mathbf{W}$ on $X = (x_1, \ldots, x_n)$. Setting to zero the derivative with respect to $\hat{y}$ directly yields

$$\hat{y} = \frac{\sum_j W_X(x, x_j)\hat{y}_j}{\sum_j W_X(x, x_j) + \epsilon}, \tag{11.19}$$

a simple inductive formula whose computational requirements scale linearly with the number of samples already seen.

Parzen windows

It is interesting to note that, if W_X is the k-nearest neighbor function, (11.19) reduces to k-nearest neighbor classification. Similarly, if W_X is the Gaussian kernel (11.1), it is equivalent to the formula for Parzen windows or Nadaraya-Watson nonparametric regression (Nadaraya, 1964; Watson, 1964). However, we use in this formula the *learned* predictions on the labeled and unlabeled examples *as if they were observed training values*, instead of relying only on labeled data.

11.5   Incorporating Class Prior Knowledge

From the beginning of the chapter, we have assumed that the class label is given by the sign of $\hat{y}$. Such a rule works well when classes are well separated and balanced. However, if this is not the case (which is likely to happen with real-world data sets), the classification resulting from the label propagation algorithms studied in this chapter may not reflect the prior class distribution.

A way to solve this problem is to perform *class mass normalization* (Zhu et al., 2003b), i.e. to rescale classes so that their respective weights over unlabeled examples match the prior class distribution (estimated from labeled examples). Until now, we had been using a scalar label $\hat{y}_i \in [-1, 1]$, which is handy in the binary case. In this section, for the sake of clarity, we will use an M-dimensional vector (M being the number of classes), with each element $\hat{y}_{i,k}$ between 0 and 1 giving a score (or weight) for class k (see also footnote 1 at the beginning of this chapter). For instance, in the binary case, a scalar $\hat{y}_i \in [-1, 1]$ would be represented by the vector $\left(\frac{1}{2}(1 + \hat{y}_i), \frac{1}{2}(1 - \hat{y}_i)\right)^{\top}$, where the second element would be the score for class -1.

Class mass normalization works as follows. Let us denote by p_k the prior probability of class k obtained from the *labeled* examples, i.e.,

$$p_k = \frac{1}{l} \sum_{i=1}^{l} y_{i,k}.$$

The *mass* of class k as given by our algorithm will be the average of *estimated* weights of class k over unlabeled examples, i.e.,

$$m_k = \frac{1}{u} \sum_{i=l+1}^{n} \hat{y}_{i,k}.$$

Class mass normalization consists in scaling each class k by the factor

$$w_k = \frac{p_k}{m_k},$$

i.e. to classify x_i in the class given by $\mathrm{argmax}_k \ w_k \hat{y}_{i,k}$ (instead of the simpler decision function $\mathrm{argmax}_k \ \hat{y}_{i,k}$, equivalent to $\mathrm{sign}(\hat{y}_i)$ in the scalar binary case studied in the previous sections). The goal is to make the scaled masses match the prior class distribution, i.e. after normalization we have that for all k

$$\frac{w_k m_k}{\sum_{j=1}^{M} w_j m_j} = p_k.$$

In general, such a scaling gives a better classification performance *when there are enough labeled data* to accurately estimate the class distribution, and *when the unlabeled data come from the same distribution*. Note also that if there is an m such that each class mass is $m_k = m p_k$, i.e., the masses already reflect the prior class distribution, then the class mass normalization step has no effect, as $w_k = m^{-1}$ for all k.

11.6   Curse of Dimensionality for Semi-Supervised Learning

A large number of the semi-supervised learning algorithms proposed in recent years and discussed in this book are essentially nonparametric local learning algorithms, relying on a neighborhood graph to approximate manifolds near which the data density is assumed to concentrate. It means that the out-of-sample or transductive prediction at x depends mostly on the unlabeled examples very near x and on the labeled examples that are close in the sense of this graph. In this section, we present theoretical arguments that suggest that such methods are unlikely to scale well (in terms of generalization performance) when the intrinsic dimension of these manifolds becomes large (curse of dimensionality), if these manifolds are sufficiently curved (or the functions to learn vary enough).

11.6.1   The Smoothness Prior, Manifold Assumption, and Nonparametric Semi-Supervised Learning

smoothness and
cluster
assumptions

As introduced in section 1.2, the *smoothness assumption* (or its semi-supervised variant) about the underlying target function $y(\cdot)$ (such that $y(x_i) = y_i$) is at the core of most of the algorithms studied in this book, along with the *cluster assumption* (or its variant, the *low-density separation assumption*). The former implies that if x_1 is near x_2, then y_1 is expected to be near y_2, and the latter implies that the data density is low near the decision surface. The smoothness assumption is intimately linked to a definition of what it means for x_1 to be near x_2, and that can be embodied in a similarity function on input space, $W_X(\cdot, \cdot)$, which is at the core of the graph-based algorithms reviewed in this chapter, transductive support vector machines (SVMs) (where W_X is seen as a kernel), and semi-supervised Gaussian processes (where W_X is seen as the covariance of a prior over functions), both in part II of this book, as well as the algorithms based on a first unsupervised step to learn a better representation (part IV).

The central claim of this section is that in order to obtain good results with algorithms that rely solely on the smoothness assumption and on the cluster assumption (or the low-density separation assumption), an acceptable decision surface (in the sense that its error is at an acceptable level) must be "smooth" enough. This can happen if the data for each class lie near a low-dimensional manifold (i.e., the manifold assumption), and these manifolds are smooth enough, i.e., do not have high curvature where it matters, i.e., where a wrong characterization of the manifold would yield to large error rate. This claim is intimately linked to the well-known *curse of dimensionality*, so we start the section by reviewing results on generalization error for classical nonparametric learning algorithms as dimension increases. We present theoretical arguments that suggest notions of *locality* of the learning algorithm that make it sensitive to the dimension of the manifold near which data lie. These arguments are not trivial extensions of the arguments for classical nonparametric algorithms, because the semi-supervised algorithms such as those studied in this book involve expansion coefficients (e.g., the $\hat{y}_j$ in equation (11.19)) that are nonlocal, i.e., the coefficient associated with the jth example x_j may depend on inputs x_i that are far from x_j, in the sense of the similarity function or kernel $W_X(x_i, x_j)$. For instance, a labeled point x_i far from an unlabeled point x_j (i.e. $W_X(x_i, x_j)$ is small) may still influence the estimated label of x_j if there exists a path in the neighborhood graph $\mathbf{g}$ that connects x_i to x_j (going through unlabeled examples).

nonlocal learning

In the last section (11.6.5), we will try to argue that it is possible to build *nonlocal* learning algorithms, while not using very specific priors about the task to be learned. This goes against common folklore that when there are not enough training examples in a given region, one cannot generalize properly in that region. This would suggest that difficult learning problems such as those encountered in artificial intelligence (e.g., vision, language, robotics, etc.) would benefit from the development of a larger array of such nonlocal learning algorithms.

In order to discuss the curse of dimensionality for semi-supervised learning, we introduce a particular notion of locality. It applies to learning algorithms that can be labeled as *kernel machines*, i.e., shown to explicitly or implicitly learn a predictor function of the form

kernel machine

$$f(x) = b + \sum_{i=1}^{n} \alpha_i k_X(x, x_i),$$ (11.20)

where i runs over all the examples (labeled and unlabeled), and $k_X(\cdot, \cdot)$ is a symmetric function (kernel) that is either chosen a priori or using the whole data set X (and does not need to be positive semi-definite). The learning algorithm is then allowed to choose the scalars b and α_i.

Most of the decision functions learned by the algorithms discussed in this chapter can be written as in (11.20). In particular, the label propagation algorithm 11.2 leads to the induction formula (11.19) corresponding to

$$
\begin{aligned}
b &= 0 \\
\alpha_i &= \hat{y}_i \\
k_X(x, x_i) &= \frac{W_X(x, x_i)}{\epsilon + \sum_j W_X(x, x_j)}.
\end{aligned}
$$ (11.21)

The Laplacian regularization algorithm (algorithm 11.4) from Belkin and Niyogi (2003b), which first learns about the shape of the manifold with an embedding based on the principal eigenfunctions of the Laplacian of the neighborhood, also falls into

Nyström formula

this category. As shown by Bengio et al. (2004a), the principal eigenfunctions can be estimated by the Nyström formula:

$$f_k(x) = \frac{\sqrt{n}}{\lambda_k} \sum_{i=1}^{n} v_{k,i} k_X(x, x_i),$$ (11.22)

where (λ_k, v_k) is the kth principal (eigenvalue, eigenvector) pair of the Gram matrix K obtained by $K_{ij} = k_X(x_i, x_j)$, and where $k_X(\cdot, \cdot)$ is a data-dependent equivalent kernel derived from the Laplacian of the neighborhood graph g. Since the resulting decision function is a linear combination of these eigenfunctions, we obtain again a kernel machine (11.20).

In the following, we say that a kernel function $k_X(\cdot, \cdot)$ is *local* if for all $x \in X$, there exists a neighborhood $\mathcal{N}(x) \subset X$ such that

$$f(x) \simeq b + \sum_{x_i \in \mathcal{N}(x)} \alpha_i k_X(x, x_i).$$ (11.23)

Intuitively, this means that only the near neighbors of x have a significant contribution to $f(x)$. For instance, if k_X is the Gaussian kernel, $\mathcal{N}(x)$ is defined as the points in X that are close to x with respect to σ (the width of the kernel). If (11.23) is an equality, we say that k_X is *strictly local*. An example is when W_X is the k-nearest neighbor kernel in algorithm 11.2. k_X obtained by (11.21) is then also the k-nearest neighbor kernel, and we have $\mathcal{N}(x) = \mathcal{N}_k(x)$ the set of the k nearest neighbors of

x, so that

$$f(x) = \sum_{x_i \in \mathcal{N}_k(x)} \frac{\hat{y}_i}{k}.$$

Similarly, we say that k_X is *local-derivative* if there exists another kernel $\tilde{k}_X$ such that for all $x \in X$, there exists a neighborhood $\mathcal{N}(x) \subset X$ such that

$$\frac{\partial f}{\partial x}(x) \simeq \sum_{x_i \in \mathcal{N}(x)} \alpha_i(x - x_i)\tilde{k}_X(x, x_i). \tag{11.24}$$

Intuitively, this means that the derivative of f at point x is a vector contained mostly in the span of the vectors $x - x_i$ with x_i a near neighbor of x. For instance, with the Gaussian kernel, we have $k_X(x, x_i) = e^{-\|x - x_i\|^2/2\sigma^2}$ and

$$\frac{\partial k_X(x, x_i)}{\partial x} = -\frac{x - x_i}{\sigma^2} \exp\left(-\frac{\|x - x_i\|^2}{2\sigma^2}\right)$$

so that

$$f(x) \simeq b + \sum_{x_i \in \mathcal{N}(x)} \alpha_i(x - x_i)\left(-\frac{1}{\sigma^2}\exp\left(-\frac{\|x - x_i\|^2}{2\sigma^2}\right)\right).$$

Because here $\tilde{k}_X$ is proportional to a Gaussian kernel with width σ, the neighborhood $\mathcal{N}(x)$ is also defined as the points in X which are close to x with respect to σ. Again, we say that k_X is *strictly local-derivative* when (11.24) is an equality (for instance, when k_X is a thresholded Gaussian kernel, i.e. $k_X(x, x_i) = 0$ when $\|x - x_i\| > \delta$).

11.6.2 Curse of Dimensionality for Classical Nonparametric Learning

curse of
dimensionality

The term *curse of dimensionality* has been coined by Bellman (1961) in the context of control problems, but it has been used rightfully to describe the poor generalization performance of local nonparametric estimators as the dimensionality increases. We define *bias* as the square of the expected difference between the estimator and the true target function, and we refer generically to *variance* as the variance of the estimator, in both cases the expectations being taken with respect to the training set as a random variable. It is well known that classical nonparametric estimators must trade bias and variance of the estimator through a smoothness hyperparameter, e.g., kernel bandwidth σ for the Nadarya-Watson estimator (Gaussian kernel). As σ increases, bias increases and the predictor

bias-variance
dilemma

becomes less local, but variance decreases, hence the *bias-variance dilemma* (Geman et al., 1992) is also about the *locality* of the estimator.

A nice property of classical nonparametric estimators is that one can prove their convergence to the target function as $n \to \infty$, i.e., these are consistent estimators. One obtains consistency by appropriately varying the hyperparameter that controls the locality of the estimator as n increases. Basically, the kernel should be allowed to become more and more local, so that bias goes to zero, but the "effective number of examples" involved in the estimator at x,

$$\frac{1}{\sum_{i=1}^{n} k_X(x, x_i)^2},$$

(equal to k for the k-nearest neighbor estimator, with $k_X(x, x_i) = 1/k$ for x_i a neighbor of x) should increase as n increases, so that variance is also driven to 0. For example, one obtains this condition with $\lim_{n \to \infty} k = \infty$ and $\lim_{n \to \infty} \frac{k}{n} = 0$ for the k-nearest neighbor. Clearly the first condition is sufficient for variance to go to 0 and the second for the bias to go to 0 (since k/n is proportional to the volume around x containing the k-nearest neighbors). Similarly, for the Nadarya-Watson estimator with bandwidth σ, consistency is obtained if $\lim_{n \to \infty} \sigma = 0$ and $\lim_{n \to \infty} n\sigma = \infty$ (in addition to regularity conditions on the kernel). See the book by Härdle et al. (2004) for a recent and easily accessible exposition (with web version). The bias is due to smoothing the target function over the volume covered by the effective neighbors. As the intrinsic dimensionality of the data increases (the number of dimensions that they actually span locally), bias increases. Since that volume increases exponentially with dimension, the effect of the bias quickly becomes very severe. To see this, consider the classical example of the $[0, 1]^d$ hypercube in $\mathbb{R}^d$ with uniformly distributed data in the hypercube. To hold a fraction p of the data in a subcube of it, that subcube must have sides of length $p^{1/d}$. As $d \to \infty$, $p^{1/d} \to 1$, i.e., we are averaging over distances that cover almost the whole span of the data, just to keep variance constant (by keeping the effective number of neighbors constant).

For a wide class of kernel estimators with kernel bandwidth σ, the expected generalization error (bias plus variance, ignoring the noise) can be written as follows (Härdle et al., 2004):

$$\text{expected error} = \frac{C_1}{n\sigma^d} + C_2\sigma^4,$$

with C_1 and C_2 not depending on n nor d. Hence an optimal bandwidth is chosen proportional to $n^{-1/(4+d)}$, and the resulting generalization error converges in $n^{-4/(4+d)}$, which becomes very slow for large d. Consider for example the increase in number of examples required to get the same level of error, in one dimension versus d dimensions. If n_1 is the number of examples required to get a level of error e, to get the same level of error in d dimensions requires on the order of $n_1^{(4+d)/5}$ examples, i.e. the *required number of examples is exponential in d*. However, if the data distribution is concentrated on a lower-dimensional manifold, it is the *manifold dimension* that matters. Indeed, for data on a smooth lower-dimensional manifold, the only dimension that, for instance, a k-nearest neighbor classifier sees is the dimension of the manifold, since it only uses the Euclidean distances between the near neighbors, and if they lie on such a manifold then the local Euclidean distances approach the local geodesic distances on the manifold (Tenenbaum et al., 2000). The curse of dimensionality on a manifold (acting with respect to the dimensionality

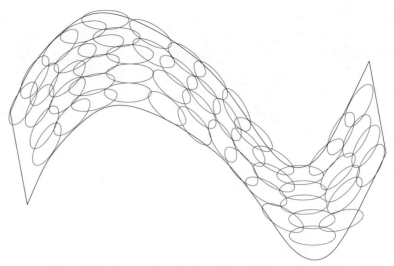

Figure 11.1 Geometric illustration of the effect of the curse of dimensionality on manifolds: the effect depends on the dimension on the manifold, as long as the data are lying strictly on the manifold. In addition to dimensionality, the lack of smoothness (e.g. curvature) of the manifold also has an important influence on the difficulty of generalizing outside of the immediate neighborhood of a training example.

of the manifold) is illustrated in figure 11.1.

11.6.3   Manifold Geometry: The Curse of Dimensionality for Local Nonparametric Manifold Learning

Let us first consider how semi-supervised learning algorithms could learn about the shape of the manifolds near which the data concentrate, and how either a high-dimensional manifold or a highly curved manifold could prevent this when the algorithms are local, in the *local-derivative* sense discussed above. As a prototypical example, let us consider the algorithm proposed by Belkin and Niyogi (2003b) (algorithm 11.4). The embedding coordinates are given by the eigenfunctions f_k from (11.22).

The first derivative of f_k with respect to x represents the *tangent vector* of the kth embedding coordinate. Indeed, it is the direction of variation of x that gives rise locally to the maximal increase in the kth coordinate. Hence the set of manifold tangent vectors $\{\frac{\partial f_1(x)}{\partial x}, \frac{\partial f_2(x)}{\partial x}, \ldots, \frac{\partial f_d(x)}{\partial x}\}$ spans the estimated *tangent plane* of the manifold.

By the local-derivative property (strict or not), each of the tangent vectors at x is constrained to be exactly or approximately in the span of the difference vectors $x - x_i$, where x_i is a neighbor of x. Hence *the tangent plane is constrained to be a subspace of the span of the vectors $x - x_i$, with x_i neighbors of x*. This is illustrated in figure 11.2. In addition to the algorithm of Belkin and Niyogi (2003b), a number

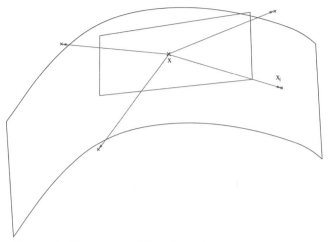

Figure 11.2   Geometric illustration of the effect of the local derivative property shared by semi-supervised graph-based algorithms and spectral manifold learning algorithms. The tangent plane at x is implicitly estimated, and is constrained to be in the span of the vectors $(x_i - x)$, with x_i near neighbors of x. When the number of neighbors is small the estimation of the manifold shape has high variance, but when it is large, the estimation would have high bias unless the true manifold is very flat.

of nonparametric manifold learning algorithms can be shown (e.g. see (Bengio et al., 2005)) to have the local derivative property (or the strictly local derivative property): locally linear embedding (LLE), Isomap, and spectral clustering with Gaussian or nearest neighbor kernels.

Hence the local-derivative property gives a strong locality constraint to the tangent plane, in particular when the set of neighbors is small. If the number of neighbors is not large in comparison with the manifold dimension, then the locally estimated shape of the manifold will have *high variance*, i.e., we will have a poor estimator of the manifold structure. If the manifold is approximately flat in a large region, then we could simply increase the number of neighbors. However, if the manifold has high curvature, then we cannot increase the number of neighbors without significantly increasing bias in the estimation of the manifold shape. Bias will restrict us to small regions, and the number of such regions could grow exponentially with the dimension of the manifold (figure 11.1).

A good estimation of the manifold structure – in particular in the region near the decision surface – is crucial for all the graph-based semi-supervised learning algorithms studied in this chapter. It is thanks to a good estimation of the regions in data space where there is high density that we can "propagate labels" in the right places and obtain an improvement with respect to ordinary supervised learning on the labeled examples. The problems due to high curvature and high dimensionality of the manifold are therefore important to consider when applying these graph-based semi-supervised learning algorithms.

11.6.4   Curse of Dimensionality for Local Nonparametric Semi-Supervised Learning

In this section we focus on algorithms of the type described in part III of the book (graph-based algorithms), using the notation and the induction formula presented in this chapter (on label propagation and a quadratic criterion unifying many of these algorithms).

We consider here that the ultimate objective is to learn a decision surface, i.e., we have a classification problem, and therefore the region of interest in terms of theoretical analysis is mostly the region near the decision surface. For example, if we do not characterize the manifold structure of the underlying distribution in a region far from the decision surface, it is not important, as long as we get it right near the decision surface. Whereas in the previous section we built an argument based on capturing the shape of the manifold associated with each class, here we focus directly on the discriminant function and on learning the shape of the decision surface.

An intuitive view of label propagation suggests that a region of the manifold around a labeled (e.g. positive) example will be entirely labeled positively, as the example spreads its influence by propagation on the graph representing the underlying manifold. Thus, the number of regions with constant label should be on the same order as (or less than) the number of labeled examples. This is easy to see in the case of a sparse weight matrix $\mathbf{W}$, i.e. when the affinity function is *strictly local*. We define a region with constant label as a connected subset of the graph **g** where all nodes x_i have the same estimated label (sign of $\hat{y}_i$), and such that no other node can be added while keeping these properties. The following proposition then holds (note that it is also true, but trivial, when $\mathbf{W}$ defines a fully connected graph, i.e. $\mathcal{N}(x) = X$ for all x).

Proposition 11.1 *After running a label propagation algorithm minimizing a cost of the form (11.11), the number of regions with constant estimated label is less than (or equal to) the number of labeled examples.*

Proof By contradiction, if this proposition is false, then there exists a region with constant estimated label that does not contain any labeled example. Without loss of generality, consider the case of a positive constant label, with $x_{l+1}, \ldots, x_{l+q}$ the q samples in this region. The part of the cost (11.11) depending on their labels is

$$
\begin{aligned}
C(\hat{y}_{l+1}, \ldots, \hat{y}_{l+q}) = \quad & \frac{\mu}{2} \sum_{i,j=l+1}^{l+q} \mathbf{W}_{ij}(\hat{y}_i - \hat{y}_j)^2 \\
+ \quad & \mu \sum_{i=l+1}^{l+q} \left(\sum_{j \notin \{l+1,\ldots,l+q\}} \mathbf{W}_{ij}(\hat{y}_i - \hat{y}_j)^2 \right) \\
+ \quad & \mu\epsilon \sum_{i=l+1}^{l+q} \hat{y}_i^2 .
\end{aligned}
$$

The second term is stricly positive, and because the region we consider is maximal (by definition) all samples x_j outside of the region such that $\mathbf{W}_{ij} > 0$ verify $\hat{y}_j < 0$ (for x_i a sample in the region). Since all $\hat{y}_i$ are strictly positive for $i \in \{l+1, \ldots, l+q\}$, this means this second term can be strictly decreased by setting all $\hat{y}_i$ to 0 for $i \in \{l+1, \ldots, l+q\}$. This also sets the first and third terms to zero (i.e. their minimum), showing that the set of labels $\hat{y}_i$ are not optimal, which is in contradiction with their definition as the labels that minimize C.   ■

This means that if the class distributions are such that there are many distinct regions with constant labels (either separated by low-density regions or regions with samples from the other class), we will need at least the same number of labeled samples as there are such regions (assuming we are using a strictly local kernel such as the k-nearest neighbor kernel, or a thresholded Gaussian kernel). But this number could *grow exponentially with the dimension of the manifold(s) on which the data lie,* for instance in the case of a labeling function varying highly along each dimension, *even if the label variations are "simple" in a nonlocal sense,* e.g. if they alternate in a regular fashion.

When the affinity matrix $\mathbf{W}$ is not sparse (e.g., Gaussian kernel), obtaining such a result is less obvious. However, for local kernels, there often exists a sparse approximation of $\mathbf{W}$ (for instance, in the case of a Gaussian kernel, one can set to 0 entries below a given threshold or that do not correspond to a k-nearest neighbor relationship). Thus we conjecture that the same kind of result holds for such dense weight matrices obtained from a local kernel.

Another indication that highly varying functions are fundamentally hard to learn with graph-based semi-supervised learning algorithms is given by the following theorem (Bengio et al., 2006a):

Theorem 11.2 *Suppose that the learning problem is such that in order to achieve a given error level for samples from a distribution P with a Gaussian kernel machine (11.20), then f must change sign at least $2k$ times along some straight line (i.e., in the case of a classifier, the decision surface must be crossed at least $2k$ times by that straight line). Then the kernel machine must have at least k examples (labeled or unlabeled).*

The theorem is proven for the case where k_X is the Gaussian kernel, but we conjecture that the same result applies to other local kernels, such as the normalized Gaussian or the k-nearest neighbor kernels implicitly used in graph-based semi-supervised learning algorithms. It is coherent with proposition 11.1 since both tell us that we need at least k examples to represent k "variations" in the underlying target classifier, whether along a straight line or as the number of regions of differing class on a manifold.

11.6.5 Outlook: Nonlocal Semi-Supervised Learning

What conclusions should we draw from the previous results? They should help to better circumscribe where the current local semi-supervised learning algorithms are likely to be most effective, and they should also help to suggest directions of research into nonlocal learning algorithms, either using nonlocal kernels or similarity functions, or using altogether other principles of generalization.

When applying a local semi-supervised learning algorithm to a new task, one should consider the plausibility of the hypothesis of a low-dimensional manifold near which the distribution concentrates. For some problems this could be very reasonable a priori (e.g., printed digit images varying mostly due to a few geometric and optical effects). For others, however, one would expect tens or hundreds of degrees of freedom (e.g., many artificial intelligence problems, such as natural language processing or recognition of complex composite objects).

Concerning new directions of research suggested by these results, several possible approaches can already be mentioned:

- Semi-supervised algorithms that are not based on the neighborhood graph, such as the one presented in chapter 9, in which a discriminant training criterion for supervised learning is adapted to semi-supervised learning by taking advantage of the *cluster hypothesis*, more precisely, the *low-density separation hypothesis* (see section 1.2).

- Algorithms based on the neighborhood graph but in which the kernel or similarity function (a) is nonisotropic or (b) is adapted based on the data (with the spread in different directions being adapted). In that case the predictor will be neither local nor local-derivative. More generally, the structure of the similarity function at x should be inferred based not just on the training data in the close neighborhood of x. For an example of such nonlocal learning in the unsupervised setting, see (Bengio and Monperrus, 2005; Bengio et al., 2006b).

- Other data-dependent kernels could be investigated, but one should check whether the adaptation allows nonlocal learning, i.e., that information at x could be used to usefully alter the prediction at a point x' far from x.

- More generally, algorithms that *learn a similarity function* $Sim(x, y)$ in a nonlocal way (i.e., taking advantage of examples far from x and y) should be good candidates to consider to defeat the curse of dimensionality.

11.7 Discussion

This chapter shows how different graph-based semi-supervised learning algorithms can be cast into a common framework of label propagation and quadratic criterion optimization. They benefit from both points of view: the iterative label propagation methods can provide simple efficient approximate solutions, while the analysis of the quadratic criterion helps to understand what these algorithms really do. The solution can also be linked to physical phenomena such as voltage in an electric network built from the graph, which provides other ways to reason about this problem. In addition, the optimization framework leads to a natural extension of the inductive setting that is closely related to other classical nonparametric learning algorithms such as k-nearest neighbor or Parzen windows. Induction will be studied in more depth in the next chapter, and the induction formula (11.19) will turn out to be the basis for a subset approximation algorithm presented in chapter 18. Finally, we have shown that the local semi-supervised learning algorithms are likely to be limited to learning smooth functions for data living near low-dimensional manifolds. Our approach of locality properties suggests a way to check whether new semi-supervised learning algorithms have a chance to scale to higher-dimensional tasks or learning less smooth functions, and motivates further investigation in nonlocal learning algorithms.

Acknowledgments

The authors would like to thank the editors and anonymous reviewers for their helpful comments and suggestions. This chapter has also greatly benefited from advice from Mikhail Belkin, Dengyong Zhou, and Xiaojin Zhu, whose papers first motivated this research (Belkin and Niyogi, 2003b; Zhou et al., 2004; Zhu et al., 2003b). The authors also thank the following funding organizations for their financial support: Canada Research Chair, NSERC, and MITACS.

12   The Geometric Basis of Semi-Supervised Learning

Vikas Sindhwani   VIKASS@CS.UCHICAGO.EDU
Misha Belkin   MBELKIN@CSE.OHIO-STATE.EDU
Partha Niyogi   NIYOGI@CS.UCHICAGO.EDU

In this chapter, we present an algorithmic framework for semi-supervised inference based on geometric properties of probability distributions. Our approach brings together Laplacian-based spectral techniques, regularization with kernel methods, and algorithms for manifold learning. This framework provides a natural semi-supervised extension for kernel methods and resolves the problem of out-of-sample inference in graph-based transduction. We discuss an interpretation in terms of a family of globally defined data-dependent kernels and also address unsupervised learning (clustering and data representation) within the same framework. Our algorithms effectively exploit both manifold and cluster assumptions to demonstrate state-of-the-art performance on various classification tasks. This chapter also reviews other recent work on out-of-sample extension for transductive graph-based methods.

12.1   Introduction

We start by providing some intuitions for the geometric basis of semi-supervised learning. These intuitions are demonstrated in pictures (figures 12.1, 12.2 and 12.3).

Consider first the two labeled points (marked "+" and "−") in the left panel of figure 12.1. Our intuition may suggest that a simple linear separator such as the one shown in figure 12.1 is an optimal choice for a classifier. Indeed, considerable effort in learning theory has been invested into deriving optimality properties for such a classification boundary.

The right panel, however, shows that the two labeled points are in fact located on two concentric circles of unlabeled data. Looking at the right panel, it becomes clear that the circular boundary is more natural given unlabeled data.

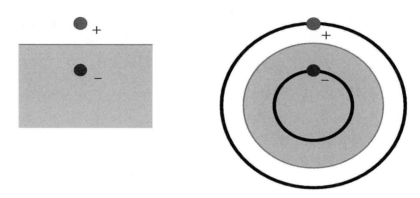

Figure 12.1   Circle.

Figure 12.2   Curve.

Consider now the left panel in figure 12.2. In the absence of unlabeled data the black dot (marked "?") is likely to be classified as blue (marked "−"). The unlabeled data, however, makes classifying it as red (marked "+") seem much more reasonable.

A third example is shown in figure 12.3. In the left panel, the unlabeled point may be classified as blue (−) to agree with its nearest neighbor. However, unlabeled data shown as gray clusters in the right panel change our belief.

These examples show how the geometry of unlabeled data may radically change our intuition about classifier boundaries. We seek to translate these intuitions into a framework for learning from labeled and unlabeled examples.

Recall now the standard setting of learning from examples. Given a pattern space $\mathcal{X}$, there is a probability distribution $\mathcal{P}$ on $\mathcal{X} \times \mathbb{R}$ according to which examples are generated for function learning. Labeled examples are (x, y) pairs drawn according to $\mathcal{P}$. Unlabeled examples are simply $x \in \mathcal{X}$ sampled according to the marginal distribution $\mathcal{P}_{\mathcal{X}}$ of $\mathcal{P}$.

As we have seen, the knowledge of the marginal $\mathcal{P}_X$ can be exploited for better function learning (e.g., in classification or regression tasks). On the other hand, if there is no identifiable relation between $\mathcal{P}_X$ and the conditional $\mathcal{P}(y|x)$, the knowledge of $\mathcal{P}_X$ is unlikely to be of use.

Two possible connections between $\mathcal{P}_X$ and $\mathcal{P}(y|x)$ can be stated as the following important assumptions (also see the tutorial introduction in chapter 1 for related discussion):

geometry of
unlabeled data

Figure 12.3   Blobs.

assumptions for
semi-supervised
learning

1. *Manifold assumption:* Suppose that the marginal probability distribution underlying the data is supported on a low-dimensional manifold. Then the family of conditional distributions $P(y|x)$ is smooth, as a function of x, with respect to the underlying structure of the manifold.

2. *Cluster assumption:* The probability distribution $\mathcal{P}$ is such that points in the same "cluster" are likely to have the same label.

We see that the data shown in figures 12.1 and 12.2 satisfy the manifold assumption.

The picture in figure 12.3 is meant to show Gaussian clusters. The concentric circles in figure 12.1 can also be thought of as "clusters," although such clusters are highly non-Gaussian and have an interesting geometric structure. One may conjecture that many clusters in real-world data sets have such non-Gaussian structures. This is evidenced, for example, by the frequent superiority of spectral clustering over more traditional methods such as k-means.

In many natural situations, it is clear that the data are supported on a low-dimensional manifold. This is often the case when points are generated by some physical process. For example, in speech production the articulatory organs can be modeled as a collection of tubes. The space of speech sounds is therefore a low-dimensional manifold parameterized by lengths and widths of the tubes. Photographs of an object from various angles form a three dimensional submanifold of the image space. In other cases, such as in text retrieval tasks, it may be less clear whether a low-dimensional manifold is present. However, even then, and also for almost any imaginable source of meaningful high-dimensional data, the space of possible configurations occupies only a tiny portion of the total volume available. One therefore suspects that a nonlinear low-dimensional manifold may yield a useful approximation to this structure.

To proceed with our discussion, we will make a specific assumption about the connection between the marginal and the conditional distributions. We will assume

smoothness with
respect to
marginal
distribution

that if two points $x_1, x_2 \in \mathcal{X}$ are *close* in the *intrinsic* geometry of $\mathcal{P}_{\mathcal{X}}$, then the conditional distributions $\mathcal{P}(y|x_1)$ and $\mathcal{P}(y|x_2)$ are similar. In other words, the conditional probability distribution $\mathcal{P}(y|x)$ varies smoothly along the geodesics in the intrinsic geometry of $\mathcal{P}_{\mathcal{X}}$. A more formal statement for this smoothness property is that $\int \|\nabla \mathcal{P}(y|x)\|^2 d\mu_{\mathcal{X}}$ is small, where μ is the probability distribution over the manifold. That last quantity can be rewritten as $\langle \mathcal{L}\mathcal{P}(y|x), \mathcal{P}(y|x) \rangle$, where $\mathcal{L}$ is the weighted Laplacian associated to probability measure μ. We will elaborate on these objects later in the chapter.

We will introduce a new framework for data-dependent regularization that exploits the geometry of the probability distribution. It is important to note that the resulting algorithms will take into account both manifold and cluster assumptions. While this framework allows us to approach the full range of learning problems from unsupervised to supervised, we focus on the problem of semi-supervised learning. This chapter gathers material from Belkin et al. (2004c, 2005); Sindhwani (2004); Sindhwani et al. (2005).

12.2   Incorporating Geometry in Regularization

We will now assume that the marginal distribution $\mathcal{P}_{\mathcal{X}}$ is supported on a low-dimensional manifold $\mathcal{M}$ embedded in $\mathbb{R}^N$. We will be interested in constructing spaces of functions which are attuned to the geometric structure of $\mathcal{P}_{\mathcal{X}}$. More specifically we will want to control the gradient of the functions of interest with respect to the measure $\mathcal{P}_{\mathcal{X}}$: $\int_{\mathcal{M}} \|\nabla_{\mathcal{M}} f\|^2 d\mathcal{P}_{\mathcal{X}}$. Here the gradient is taken with respect to the underlying Riemannian manifold $\mathcal{M}$ and the integral is weighted by the measure on that manifold.

If the manifold $\mathcal{M}$ has no boundary or if the probability distribution $\mathcal{P}_{\mathcal{X}}$ vanishes

Laplace-Beltrami
operator

at the boundary, it can be shown that

$$\int_{\mathcal{M}} \|\nabla_{\mathcal{M}} f\|^2 d\mathcal{P}_{\mathcal{X}} = \int_{\mathcal{M}} f \mathcal{L}_{\mathcal{P}_{\mathcal{X}}}(f) d\mathcal{P}_{\mathcal{X}} = \langle f, \mathcal{L}_{\mathcal{P}_{\mathcal{X}}}(f) \rangle_{L^2(\mathcal{P}_{\mathcal{X}})},$$

where $\nabla_{\mathcal{M}}$ is the gradient on $\mathcal{M}$ and $\mathcal{L}_{\mathcal{P}_{\mathcal{X}}}$ is the weighted Laplace-Beltrami operator associated to measure $\mathcal{P}_{\mathcal{X}}$. This operator is key to penalizing functions according to the intrinsic geometry of the probability distribution $\mathcal{P}_{\mathcal{X}}$.

We utilize these geometric intuitions to extend an established framework for function learning. A number of popular algorithms such as support vector machines (SVMs), ridge regression, splines, and radial basis functions may be broadly interpreted as regularization algorithms with different empirical cost functions and complexity measures in an appropriately chosen reproducing kernel Hilbert space (RKHS) (Poggio and Girosi, 1990; Vapnik, 1998; Schölkopf and Smola, 2002).

Recall that for a Mercer kernel $K : \mathcal{X} \times \mathcal{X} \to \mathbb{R}$, there is an associated RKHS $\mathcal{H}_K$ of functions $\mathcal{X} \to \mathbb{R}$ with the corresponding norm $\| \ \|_K$. Given a set of labeled examples (x_i, y_i), $i = 1, \ldots, l$ the standard framework estimates an unknown function by learning in RKHS   minimizing

$$f^* = \operatorname*{argmin}_{f \in \mathcal{H}_K} \frac{1}{l} \sum_{i=1}^{l} V(x_i, y_i, f) + \gamma \|f\|_K^2, \tag{12.1}$$

where V is some loss function, such as squared loss $(y_i - f(x_i))^2$ for regularized least squares (RLS) or the soft margin loss function $\max[0, 1 - y_i f(x_i)]$ for SVM. Penalizing the RKHS norm imposes smoothness conditions on possible solutions. The classical representer theorem states that the solution to this minimization problem exists in $\mathcal{H}_K$ and can be written as

representer
theorem

$$f^*(x) = \sum_{i=1}^{l} \alpha_i K(x_i, x). \tag{12.2}$$

Therefore, the problem is reduced to optimizing over the finite dimensional space of coefficients α_i, which is the algorithmic basis for SVM, RLS, and other regression and classification schemes.

We first consider the case when the marginal distribution is already known.

12.2.1   Marginal Distribution $\mathcal{P}_{\mathcal{X}}$ Is Known

Our goal is to extend the kernel framework by incorporating additional information about the geometric structure of the marginal $\mathcal{P}_{\mathcal{X}}$. We would like to ensure that the solution is smooth with respect to both the ambient space and the marginal distribution $\mathcal{P}_{\mathcal{X}}$. To achieve that, we introduce an additional regularizer :

manifold
regularization
given the
marginal
distribution

$$f^* = \operatorname*{argmin}_{f \in \mathcal{H}_K} \frac{1}{l} \sum_{i=1}^{l} V(x_i, y_i, f) + \gamma_A \|f\|_K^2 + \gamma_I \|f\|_I^2, \tag{12.3}$$

where $\|f\|_I^2$ is an appropriate penalty term that should reflect the intrinsic structure of $\mathcal{P}_{\mathcal{X}}$, e.g., $\langle f, \mathcal{L}_{\mathcal{P}_{\mathcal{X}}}(f) \rangle_{L^2(\mathcal{P}_{\mathcal{X}})}$.

Here γ_A controls the complexity of the function in the *ambient* space while γ_I controls the complexity of the function in the *intrinsic* geometry of $\mathcal{P}_{\mathcal{X}}$. One can derive an explicit functional form for the solution f^* as shown in the following theorem under some fairly general conditions (Belkin et al., 2004c):

Theorem 12.1 *Assume that the intrinsic regularization term is given by*

$$\|f\|_I^2 = \int_{\mathcal{X}} f D f \, d\mathcal{P}_{\mathcal{X}},$$

where D is a bounded operator from the RKHS associated to K to $L^2(\mathcal{P}_{\mathcal{X}})$. Then the solution f^* to the optimization problem in (12.3) above exists and admits the

representer
theorem given
the marginal

following representation:

$$f^*(x) = \sum_{i=1}^{l} \alpha_i K(x_i, x) + \int_{\mathcal{X}} \alpha(y) K(x, y) \, d\mathcal{P}_{\mathcal{X}}(y). \tag{12.4}$$

We note that the Laplace operator as well as any differentiable operator will satisfy the boundedness condition, assuming that the kernel is sufficiently differentiable.

The representer theorem above allows us to express the solution f^* directly in terms of the labeled data, the (ambient) kernel K, and the marginal $\mathcal{P}_{\mathcal{X}}$. If $\mathcal{P}_{\mathcal{X}}$ is unknown, we see that the solution may be expressed in terms of an empirical estimate of $\mathcal{P}_X$. Depending on the nature of this estimate, different approximations to the solution may be developed. In the next section, we consider a particular approximation scheme that leads to a simple algorithmic framework for learning from labeled and unlabeled data.

12.2.2 Marginal Distribution $\mathcal{P}_{\mathcal{X}}$ Unknown

In most applications of interest in machine learning the marginal $\mathcal{P}_{\mathcal{X}}$ is not known. Therefore we must attempt to get empirical estimates of $\mathcal{P}_{\mathcal{X}}$ and $\| \; \|_I$. Note that in order to get such empirical estimates it is sufficient to have *unlabeled* examples.

As discussed before, the natural penalty on a Riemannian manifold is the Laplace operator. The optimization problem then becomes

$$f^* = \underset{f \in \mathcal{H}_K}{\operatorname{argmin}} \frac{1}{l} \sum_{i=1}^{l} V(x_i, y_i, f) + \gamma_A \|f\|_K^2 + \gamma_I \int_{\mathcal{M}} \langle \nabla_{\mathcal{M}} f, \nabla_{\mathcal{M}} f \rangle.$$

It can be shown that the Laplace-Beltrami operator on a manifold can be approximated by graph Laplacian using the appropriate adjacency matrix (see (Belkin, 2003; Lafon, 2004) for more details).

Thus, given a set of l labeled examples $\{(x_i, y_i)\}_{i=1}^{l}$ and a set of u unlabeled examples $\{x_j\}_{j=l+1}^{j=l+u}$, we consider the following optimization problem :

manifold regularization given unlabeled data

$$f^* = \underset{f \in \mathcal{H}_K}{\operatorname{argmin}} \frac{1}{l} \sum_{i=1}^{l} V(x_i, y_i, f) + \gamma_A \|f\|_K^2 + \frac{\gamma_I}{(u+l)^2} \sum_{i,j=1}^{l+u} (f(x_i) - f(x_j))^2 W_{ij}$$

$$= \underset{f \in \mathcal{H}_K}{\operatorname{argmin}} \frac{1}{l} \sum_{i=1}^{l} V(x_i, y_i, f) + \gamma_A \|f\|_K^2 + \frac{\gamma_I}{(u+l)^2} \mathbf{f}^T L \mathbf{f}, \qquad (12.5)$$

graph Laplacian

where W_{ij} are edge weights in the data adjacency graph, $\mathbf{f} = [f(x_1), \ldots, f(x_{l+u})]^T$, and L is the graph Laplacian given by $L = D - W$. Here, the diagonal matrix D is given by $D_{ii} = \sum_{j=1}^{l+u} W_{ij}$. The normalizing coefficient $\frac{1}{(u+l)^2}$ is the natural scale factor for the empirical estimate of the Laplace operator (on a sparse adjacency graph, one may normalize by $\sum_{i,j=1}^{l+u} W_{ij}$ instead). The following version of the representer theorem shows that the minimizer has an expansion in terms of both labeled and unlabeled examples and is a key to our algorithms.

representer
theorem given
unlabeled data

Theorem 12.2 *The minimizer of optimization problem (12.5) admits an expansion*

$$f^*(x) = \sum_{i=1}^{l+u} \alpha_i K(x_i, x) \tag{12.6}$$

in terms of the labeled and unlabeled examples.

The proof is a variation of a standard orthogonality argument (Schölkopf and Smola, 2002).

Remark *Several natural choices of $\| \ \|_I$ exist. Some examples are:*

1. Iterated Laplacians $\mathcal{L}^k$. Differential operators $\mathcal{L}^k$ and their linear combinations provide a natural family of smoothness penalties.

2. Heat semigroup $e^{-\mathcal{L}t}$ is a family of smoothing operators corresponding to the process of diffusion (Brownian motion) on the manifold. For corresponding operators on graphs, see (Kondor and Lafferty, 2002). One can take $\|f\|_I^2 = \int_{\mathcal{M}} f \, e^{\mathcal{L}t}(f)$. We note that for small values of t the corresponding Green's function (the heat kernel of $\mathcal{M}$) can be approximated by a sharp Gaussian in the ambient space.

3. Squared norm of the Hessian (cf. (Donoho and Grimes, 2003)). While the Hessian $\mathbf{H}(f)$ (the matrix of second derivatives of f) generally depends on the coordinate system, it can be shown that the Frobenius norm (the sum of squared eigenvalues) of $\mathbf{H}$ is the same in any geodesic coordinate system and hence is invariantly defined for a Riemannian manifold $\mathcal{M}$. Using the Frobenius norm of $\mathbf{H}$ as a regularizer presents an intriguing generalization of thin-plate splines. We also note that $\mathcal{L}(f) = \text{tr}(\mathbf{H}(f))$.

Remark *Note that K restricted to $\mathcal{M}$ (denoted by $K_{\mathcal{M}}$) is also a kernel defined on $\mathcal{M}$ with an associated RKHS $\mathcal{H}_{\mathcal{M}}$ of functions $\mathcal{M} \to \mathbb{R}$. While this might suggest $\|f\|_I = \|f_{\mathcal{M}}\|_{K_{\mathcal{M}}}$ ($f_{\mathcal{M}}$ is f restricted to $\mathcal{M}$) as a reasonable choice for $\|f\|_I$, it turns out, that for the minimizer f^* of the corresponding optimization problem, we get $\|f^*\|_I = \|f^*\|_K$, yielding the same solution as standard regularization, although with a different γ. This observation follows from the restriction properties of RKHS (Belkin et al., 2004c). Therefore it is impossible to have an out-of-sample extension without two different measures of smoothness. On the other hand, a different ambient kernel restricted to $\mathcal{M}$ can potentially serve as the intrinsic regularization term. For example, a sharp Gaussian kernel can be used as an approximation to the heat kernel on $\mathcal{M}$.*

The representer theorem allows us to convert the optimization problem in (12.5) into a finite dimensional problem of estimating the $(l + u)$ coefficients α^* for the expansion above. A family of algorithms can now be developed with different choices of loss functions, ambient kernels, graph regularizers, and optimization strategies.

12.3 Algorithms

12.3.1 Semi-Supervised Classification

We now present solutions to the optimization problem posed in (12.5). To fix notation, we assume we have l labeled examples $\{(x_i, y_i)\}_{i=1}^{l}$ and u unlabeled examples $\{x_j\}_{j=l+1}^{j=l+u}$. We use K interchangeably to denote the kernel function or the Gram matrix.

Laplacian Regularized Least Squares (LapRLS) The Laplacian regularized least squares algorithm solves (12.5) with the squared loss function: $V(x_i, y_i, f) = [y_i - f(x_i)]^2$. Since the solution is of the form given by (12.6), the objective function can be reduced to a convex differentiable function of the $(l + u)$-dimensional expansion coefficient vector $\alpha = [\alpha_1, \ldots, \alpha_{l+u}]^T$ whose minimizer is given by

Laplacian RLS

$$\alpha^* = (JK + \gamma_A lI + \frac{\gamma_I l}{(u+l)^2} LK)^{-1} Y. \tag{12.7}$$

Here, K is the $(l + u) \times (l + u)$ Gram matrix over labeled and unlabeled points; Y is an $(l + u)$ dimensional label vector given by $Y = [y_1, \ldots, y_l, 0, \ldots, 0]$; and J is an $(l + u) \times (l + u)$ diagonal matrix given by $J = diag(1, \ldots, 1, 0, \ldots, 0)$ with the first l diagonal entries as 1 and the rest 0.

Note that when $\gamma_I = 0$, (12.7) gives zero coefficients over unlabeled data. The coefficients over labeled data are exactly those for standard RLS.

Laplacian Support Vector Machines (LapSVM) Laplacian SVMs solve the optimization problem in (12.5) with the soft-margin loss function defined as $V(x_i, y_i, f) = \max [0, 1 - y_i f(x_i)], y_i \in \{-1, +1\}$. Introducing slack variables and using standard Lagrange multiplier techniques used for deriving SVMs (Vapnik, 1998), we first arrive at the following quadratic program in l dual variables β :

$$\beta^\star = \max_{\beta \in \mathbb{R}^l} \sum_{i=1}^{l} \beta_i - \frac{1}{2} \beta^T Q \beta \tag{12.8}$$

subject to the contraints : $\sum_{i=1}^{l} y_i \beta_i = 0, \ \ 0 \leq \beta_i \leq \frac{1}{l} \ \ , i = 1, \ldots l$, where

$$Q = YJK(2\gamma_A I + 2\frac{\gamma_I}{(u+l)^2} LK)^{-1} J^T Y. \tag{12.9}$$

Here, Y is the diagonal matrix $Y_{ii} = y_i$, K is the Gram matrix over both the labeled and the unlabeled data; L is the data adjacency graph Laplacian; J is an $l \times (l + u)$ matrix given by $J_{ij} = 1$ if $i = j$, x_i is a labeled example, and $J_{ij} = 0$ otherwise. To obtain the optimal expansion coefficient vector $\alpha^* \in \mathbb{R}^{(l+u)}$, one has to solve the

Laplacian SVM   following linear system after solving the quadratic program above :

Table 12.1

	Laplacian SVM/RLS
Input:	l labeled examples $\{(x_i, y_i)\}_{i=1}^{l}$, u unlabeled examples $\{x_j\}_{j=l+1}^{l+u}$
Output:	Estimated function $f : \mathbb{R}^n \to \mathbb{R}$
Step 1	▶ Construct data adjacency graph with $(l + u)$ nodes using, e.g., k-nearest neighbors. Choose edge weights W_{ij}, e.g., binary weights or heat kernel weights $W_{ij} = e^{-\|x_i - x_j\|^2/4t}$.
Step 2	▶ Choose a kernel function $K(x, y)$. Compute the Gram matrix $K_{ij} = K(x_i, x_j)$.
Step 3	▶ Compute graph Laplacian matrix : $L = D - W$ where D is a diagonal matrix given by $D_{ii} = \sum_{j=1}^{l+u} W_{ij}$.
Step 4	▶ Choose γ_A and γ_I.
Step 5	▶ Compute α^* using (12.7) for squared loss (Laplacian RLS) or using Eqs. 12.9 and 12.10 together with the SVM QP solver for soft margin loss (Laplacian SVM).
Step 6	▶ Output function $f^*(x) = \sum_{i=1}^{l+u} \alpha_i^* K(x_i, x)$.
	Equivalently, after step 4 construct the kernel function $\tilde{K}(x, y)$ given by Eq. 12.15, and use it in standard SVM/RLS (or with other suitable kernel methods).

$$\alpha^* = (2\gamma_A I + 2\frac{\gamma_I}{(u+l)^2}LK)^{-1}J^T Y \beta^\star. \tag{12.10}$$

One can note that when $\gamma_I = 0$, the SVM QP and Eqs. 12.9 and 12.10, give zero expansion coefficients over the unlabeled data. The expansion coefficients over the labeled data and the Q matrix are as in standard SVM, in this case. Laplacian SVMs can be easily implemented using standard SVM software and packages for solving linear systems.

In section 12.4, we will discuss a data-dependent kernel defined using unlabeled examples (Sindhwani et al., 2005), with which standard supervised SVM/RLS implement Laplacian SVM/RLS. In table 12.1, we outline these algorithms.

The choice of the regularization parameters γ_A, γ_I is a subject of future research. If there are enough labeled data, they can be be based on cross-validation or performance on a held-out test set. In figure 12.4 we provide an intuition toward the role of these parameters on a toy two-moons data set. When $\gamma_I = 0$, Laplacian SVM recovers standard supervised SVM boundaries. As γ_I is increased, the effect of unlabeled data increases and the classification boundaries are appropriately adjusted.

In figure 12.5 we plot the learning curves for Laplacian SVM/RLS on a two-class

effect of increasing γ_I

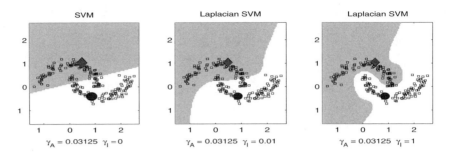

Figure 12.4 Two moons data set: Laplacian SVM with increasing intrinsic regularization.

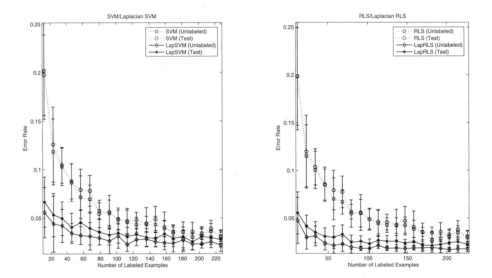

Figure 12.5 Image classification: Laplacian SVM/RLS performance with respect to number of labeled examples on unlabeled and test data.

image recognition problem. In many such real-world application settings, one may expect significant benefit from utilizing unlabeled data and high-quality out-of-sample extensions with these algorithms. For further empirical results see (Belkin et al., 2004c; Sindhwani et al., 2005) and elsewhere in this book.

12.3.2   Unsupervised Learning and Data Representation

Regularized Spectral Clustering The unsupervised case can be viewed as a special case of semi-supervised learning where one is given a collection of unlabeled data points $x_1, \ldots, x_u$ and no labeled examples. Our basic algorithmic framework embodied in the optimization problem in (12.3) has three terms: (i) fit to labeled data, (ii) extrinsic regularization, and (iii) intrinsic regularization. Since no labeled data are available, the first term does not arise anymore. Therefore we are left with the following optimization problem:

$$\min_{f \in \mathcal{H}_K} \gamma_A \|f\|_K^2 + \gamma_I \|f\|_I^2. \tag{12.11}$$

Of course, only the ratio $\frac{\gamma_A}{\gamma_I}$ matters. As before, $\|f\|_I^2$ can be approximated using the unlabeled data. Choosing $\|f\|_I^2 = \int_{\mathcal{M}} \langle \nabla_{\mathcal{M}} f, \nabla_{\mathcal{M}} f \rangle$ and approximating it by the empirical Laplacian, we are left with the following optimization problem :

Clustering

$$f^* = \underset{\substack{\sum_i f(x_i)=0;\ \sum_i f(x_i)^2=1 \\ f \in \mathcal{H}_K}}{\operatorname{argmin}} \gamma \|f\|_K^2 + \sum_{i \sim j} (f(x_i) - f(x_j))^2. \tag{12.12}$$

Note that without the additional constraints (cf. (Belkin et al., 2004b)) the above problem gives degenerate solutions.

As in the semi-supervised case, a version of the empirical representer theorem holds showing that the solution to (12.12) admits a representation of the form

$$f^* = \sum_{i=1}^u \alpha_i K(x_i, \cdot).$$

By substituting back in (12.12), we come up with the following optimization problem:

$$\alpha = \underset{\substack{\mathbf{1}^T K\alpha=0 \\ \alpha^T K^2\alpha=1}}{\operatorname{argmin}} \gamma \|f\|_K^2 + \sum_{i \sim j} (f(x_i) - f(x_j))^2,$$

where $\mathbf{1}$ is the vector of all ones and $\alpha = (\alpha_1, \ldots, \alpha_u)$ and K is the corresponding Gram matrix.

Letting P be the projection onto the subspace of $\mathbb{R}^u$ orthogonal to $K\mathbf{1}$, one obtains the solution for the constrained quadratic problem, which is given by the generalized eigenvalue problem.

eigenvalue problem

$$P(\gamma K + KLK)P\mathbf{v} = \lambda P K^2 P\mathbf{v}. \tag{12.13}$$

The final solution is given by $\alpha = P\mathbf{v}$, where $\mathbf{v}$ is the eigenvector corresponding to the smallest eigenvalue.

effect of increasing γ

The method sketched above is a framework for regularized spectral clustering. The regularization parameter γ controls the smoothness of the resulting function in the ambient space. We also obtain a natural out-of-sample extension for clustering points not in the original data set. Figure 12.5 shows this method on a toy two-moons clustering problem. Unlike recent work (Bengio et al., 2004b; Brand, 2003) on out-of-sample extensions, our method is based on a Representer theorem for RKHS.

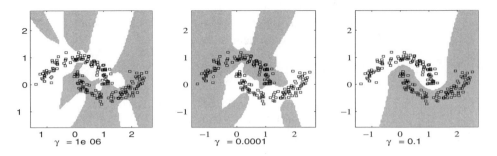

Figure 12.6   Two moons data set: regularized clustering

Regularized Laplacian Eigenmaps   One can take multiple eigenvectors of the
system in (12.13) and represent a point x in $\mathbb{R}^m$ as

dimensionality
reduction

$$
x \mapsto \left[\sum_{i=1}^{u} \alpha_i^1 K(x_i, x), \dots, \sum_{i=1}^{u} \alpha_i^m K(x_i, x) \right],
$$

where $(\alpha_1^j \dots \alpha_u^j)$ is the jth eigenvector.

This leads to a new method for dimensionality reduction and data representation
that provides a natural out-of-sample extension of Laplacian eigenmaps (Belkin,
2003). The new representation of the data in $\mathbb{R}^m$ is optimal in the sense that it best
preserves its local structure (as estimated by the graph) in the original ambient
space.

12.3.3   Fully Supervised Learning

The fully supervised case represents the other end of the spectrum of learning. Since
standard supervised algorithms (SVM and RLS) are special cases of manifold regularization, our framework is also able to deal with a labeled data set containing no
unlabeled examples. Additionally, manifold regularization can augment supervised
learning with intrinsic regularization, possibly in a class-dependent manner, which
suggests the following learning problem:

$$
f^* = \underset{f \in \mathcal{H}_K}{\arg\min} \frac{1}{l} \sum_{i=1}^{l} V(x_i, y_i, f) \,+\, \gamma_A \|f\|_K^2 \,+\, \gamma_I^+ \mathbf{f}_+^T L_+ \mathbf{f}_+ \,+\, \gamma_I^- \mathbf{f}_-^T L_- \mathbf{f}_-. \quad (12.14)
$$

supervised
manifold
regularization

Here we introduce two intrinsic regularization parameters γ_I^+, γ_I^- and regularize
separately for the two classes : $\mathbf{f}_+$, $\mathbf{f}_-$ are the vectors of evaluations of the function
f, and L_+, L_- are the graph Laplacians, on positive and negative examples
respectively. The solution to the above problem for RLS and SVM can be obtained
by replacing $\gamma_I L$ by the block-diagonal matrix $\begin{pmatrix} \gamma_I^+ L_+ & 0 \\ 0 & \gamma_I^- L_- \end{pmatrix}$ in the Laplacian
SVM and Laplacian RLS algorithms.

12.4   Data-Dependent Kernels for Semi-Supervised Learning

warping an
RKHS

By including an intrinsic regularization term $\|f\|_I$ in addition to the prior measure of complexity $\|f\|_K$ of a function f in the RKHS $\mathcal{H}_K$, the algorithmic framework presented above reflects how unlabeled data may alter our complexity beliefs. This data-dependent modification of the norm can be viewed as an attempt to appropriately warp an RKHS to conform to the geometry of the marginal distribution (for a discussion, see (Sindhwani et al., 2005)). This is made precise in the following discussion. The set of functions in $\mathcal{H}_K$ has an associated inner product $\langle f, g \rangle_{\mathcal{H}_K}$ for $f, g \in \mathcal{H}_K$. Given unlabeled data, the space of functions $\tilde{\mathcal{H}}_{\tilde{K}}$ containing functions in $\mathcal{H}_K$ but with the following modified inner product

$$\langle f, g \rangle_{\tilde{\mathcal{H}}_{\tilde{K}}} = \langle f, g \rangle_{\mathcal{H}} + \frac{\gamma_I}{\gamma_A} \mathbf{f}^T L \mathbf{g}$$

kernels for
semi-supervised
learning

can be shown to be an RKHS with an associated kernel $\tilde{K}$. The regularization term $\gamma_A \|f\|_{\tilde{H}_{\tilde{K}}}$ in this RKHS provides the same complexity penalty as the joint intrinsic and ambient regularization terms in $\mathcal{H}_K$. Thus, once the kernel $\tilde{K}$ is available, one can employ the standard machinery of kernel methods designed for supervised learning for semi-supervised inference. The form of the new kernel $\tilde{K}$ can be derived in terms of the kernel function K using reproducing properties of an RKHS and orthogonality arguments (see (Sindhwani, 2004; Sindhwani et al., 2005) for a derivation) and is given by

$$\tilde{K}(x, z) = K(x, z) - \mathbf{k}_x^T (I + \frac{\gamma_I}{\gamma_A} L K)^{-1} L \mathbf{k}_z, \tag{12.15}$$

where $\mathbf{k}_x$ (and similarly $\mathbf{k}_z$) denotes the vector $[K(x_1, x), \ldots, K(x_{l+u}, x)]^T$. The standard representer theorem can be now be invoked to show that the minimizer of optimization problem (12.5) admits the following expansion in terms of labeled examples only:

$$f^*(x) = \sum_{i=1}^{l} \alpha_i \tilde{K}(x_i, x). \tag{12.16}$$

other algorithms

With the new kernel $\tilde{K}$, this representer theorem reduces the minimization problem (12.5) to that of estimating the l expansion coefficients α^*. In addition to recovering the algorithms in section 12.3, this kernel can also be used to implement, e.g., semi-supervised extensions of support vector regression, one-class SVM, and Gaussian processes (see (Sindhwani et al., 2006)).

To develop an intuition toward how the intrinsic norm warps the structure of an RKHS, consider the pictures shown in figure 12.4. A practitioner of kernel methods would approach the two-circles problem posed in figure 12.1 by choosing a kernel function $K(x, y)$, and then taking a particular linear combination of this kernel

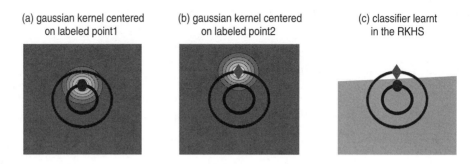

Figure 12.7   Learning in an RKHS.

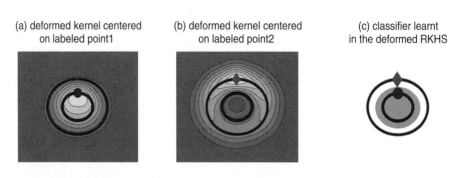

Figure 12.8   Warping an RKHS.

warping
interpretation in
pictures

centered at the two labeled points in order to construct a classifier. Figure 12.7 (a,b) shows this attempt with the popular Gaussian kernel. The resulting linear decision surface, shown in figure 12.7 (c), is clearly inadequate for this problem.

In figure 12.8 (a,b) we see level sets for the deformed kernel $\tilde{K}$ centered on the two labeled points in the two-circles problem.

The kernel deforms along the circle under the influence of the unlabeled data. Using this kernel, instead of $K(x, y)$, produces a satisfactory class boundary with just two labeled points, as shown in figure 12.8 (c).

The procedure described above is a general nonparametric approach for constructing data-dependent kernels for semi-supervised learning. This approach differs from prior constructions that have largely focussed on data-dependent methods for parameter selection to choose a kernel from some parametric family, or by defining a kernel matrix on the data points alone (transductive setting).

12.5   Linear Methods for Large-Scale Semi-Supervised Learning

To turn semi-supervised learning into a technology, one needs to address issues of scalability of algorithms and applicability to large data sets. The algorithms we have described deal with dense matrices of size $n \times n$ and have $O(n^3)$ training complexity with naive implementations. The expansion over labeled or unlabeled examples is in general not sparse, even for Laplacian SVMs. One can possibly employ, for example, various reduced set methods, low-rank kernel approximations, or sparse greedy methods (see (Schölkopf and Smola, 2002) for a discussion of general implementation issues in kernel methods) for efficient implementation of these algorithms.

linear manifold regularization

Due to their potential for dealing with massive data sets and widespread applicability, linear semi-supervised methods generate special interest. The algorithms described above can easily be specialized for constructing linear classifiers by choosing the linear kernel $K(x, y) = x^T y$. However, if the data-dimensionality d is much smaller than the number of examples or the data are highly sparse, one can much more efficiently solve the primal problem directly, once the graph regularizer is constructed. We can learn a weight vector $w \in \mathbb{R}^d$ defining the linear classifier $f(x) = \text{sign}(w^T x)$ as follows:

$$w^\star = \underset{w \in \mathbb{R}^d}{\text{argmin}} \frac{1}{l} \sum_{i=1}^{l} V(x_i, y_i, w^T x_i) + \gamma_A \|w\|^2 + \frac{\gamma_I}{(u+l)^2} w^T X^T L X w. \quad (12.17)$$

Here, X is the $(l + u) \times d$ data matrix.

linear Laplacian RLS

For linear Laplacian RLS, taking V to be the squared loss and setting the gradient of the objective function to 0, we immediately obtain a linear system that can be solved to obtain the desired weight vector:

$$(X_l^T X_l + \gamma_A l I + \frac{\gamma_I l}{(l+u)^2} X^T L X) w = X_l^T Y. \quad (12.18)$$

Here X_l is the submatrix of X corresponding to labeled examples and Y is the vector of labels. This is a $d \times d$ system which can be easily solved when d is small. When d is large but feature vectors are highly sparse, we can employ conjugate gradient (CG) methods to solve this system. CG techniques are Krylov methods that involve repeated multiplication of a candidate solution z by A for solving a linear system $Ax = b$. The matrix A need not be explicitly constructed so long as the matrix vector product Az can be computed. In the case of linear Laplacian RLS, we can construct the matrix-vector product fast due to the sparsity of X and L.[1]

---

1. Fast matrix-vector products can also be formed for dense graph regularizers given by a power series in the (sparse) graph Laplacian

For linear Laplacian SVMs, we can rewrite problem 12.17 as

$$w^* = \operatorname*{argmin}_{w \ in \mathbb{R}^d} \gamma_A w^T T T^T w + \frac{1}{l} \sum_{i=1}^{l} \max \left[0, 1 - y_i(w^T x_i)\right]$$

linear Laplacian
SVM

in terms of the Cholesky factorization TT^T of the positive definite matrix $(\gamma_A I + \frac{\gamma_I}{(l+u)^2} X^T L X)$. Changing variables by $\tilde{w} = T^T w$ and $\tilde{x} = T^{-1} x$, we can convert the above problem into a standard SVM running only on the labeled examples that are preprocessed with T^{-1}. When d is small, the preprocessing matrix can be computed cheaply. The reparameterized SVM then runs only on a small number of labeled examples and returns a weight vector $\tilde{w}^*$. We obtain the solution of the original problem by setting $w^* = \left(T^T\right)^{-1} \tilde{w}^*$. We note in passing that the inner product in the preprocessed space is given by $\tilde{x}^T \tilde{z} = x^T (TT^T)^{-1} z$. An application of the Woodbury formula to compute the inverse $(TT^T)^{-1}$ followed by appropriate manipulations gives a simple "feature-space" derivation of the data-dependent kernel in section 12.4. For high-dimensional sparse data sets, we can use the large-scale training algorithm in (Keerthi and DeCoste, 2005) for L_2-SVM. At the core of this algorithm are RLS iterations implemented using conjugate gradient techniques. In conjunction with linear Laplacian RLS for large sparse data sets, this algorithm can also be extended for large-scale semi-supervised learning.

12.6   Connections to Other Algorithms and Related Work

The broad connections of our approach to graph-based learning techniques and kernel methods are summarized in table 12.2 through a comparison of objectives. When $\gamma_I = 0$, our algorithms ignore unlabeled data and perform standard regularization, e.g in SVMs and RLS. By optimizing over an RKHS of functions defined everywhere in the ambient space, we get out-of-sample extension for graph regularization, when $\gamma_A \to 0, \gamma_I > 0$. In the absence of labeled examples, we perform a regularized version of spectral clustering that is often viewed as a relaxation of the discrete graph min-cut problem. We can also obtain useful data representations within the same framework by regularized Laplacian eigenmaps.

The conceptual framework of our work is close, in spirit, to the *measure-based regularization* approach of (Bousquet et al., 2004). The authors consider a gradient-based regularizer that encourages smoothness with respect to the data density. While Bousquet et al. (2004) use the gradient $\nabla f(x)$ in the ambient space, we use the gradient over a submanifold $\nabla_{\mathcal{M}} f$. In a situation where the data truly lie on or near a submanifold $\mathcal{M}$, the difference between these two penalizers can be significant since smoothness in the normal direction to the data manifold is irrelevant to classification or regression.

The intuition of incorporating a graph-based regularizer in the design of semi-supervised variants of inductive algorithms has also been explored in (Yu et al., 2004; Krishnapuram et al., 2004; Kegl and Wang, 2004). In (Yu et al., 2004), a

Table 12.2   Objective functions for comparison (in the third column for unsupervised algorithms, additional constraints are added to avoid trivial or unbalanced solutions). In addition to these learning problems, the framework also provides the regularized Laplacian eigenmaps algorithm for dimensionality reduction and data representation.

Supervised	Partially Supervised	Clustering
Kernel-based Classifiers	*Graph Regularization*	*Graph Min-cut*
$\operatorname{argmin}_{f \in \mathcal{H}_K}$ $\frac{1}{l}\sum_{i=1}^{l} V(y_i, f(x_i))$ $+\gamma\|f\|_K^2$	$\operatorname{argmin}_{\mathbf{f} \in \mathbb{R}^{(l+u)}}$ $\frac{1}{l}\sum_{i=1}^{l} V(y_i, \mathbf{f_i}) + \gamma\mathbf{f}^T L\mathbf{f}$	$\operatorname{argmin}_{\mathbf{f} \in \{-1,+1\}^u}$ $\frac{1}{4}\sum_{i,j=1}^{u} W_{ij}(\mathbf{f}_i - \mathbf{f}_j)^2$
	Out-of-sample Extn.	*Spectral Clustering*
	$\operatorname{argmin}_{f \in \mathcal{H}_K}$ $\frac{1}{l}\sum_{i=1}^{l} V(y_i, \mathbf{f_i}) + \gamma\mathbf{f}^T L\mathbf{f}$	$\operatorname{argmin}_{\mathbf{f} \in \mathbb{R}^u} \frac{1}{2}\mathbf{f}^T L\mathbf{f}$
	Manifold Regularization	*Out-of-sample Extn.*
	$\operatorname{argmin}_{f \in \mathcal{H}_K}$	$\operatorname{argmin}_{f \in \mathcal{H}_K} \frac{1}{2}\mathbf{f}^T L\mathbf{f}$
	$\frac{1}{l}\sum_{i=1}^{l} V(y_i, f(x_i))+$	*Reg. Spectral Clust.*
	$\gamma_A\|f\|_K^2 + \frac{\gamma_I}{(l+u)^2}\mathbf{f}^T L\mathbf{f}$	$\operatorname{argmin}_{f \in \mathcal{H}_K}$ $\frac{1}{2}\mathbf{f}^T L\mathbf{f} + \gamma\|f\|_K^2$

least-squares algorithm is proposed that provides an out-of-sample extension for graph transduction in the span of a fixed set of basis functions $\{\phi_i : \mathcal{X} \mapsto \mathbb{R}\}_{i=1}^s$. Thus, the optimization problem in Eq. 12.5 is solved over this span for the squared loss leading to a linear system such as Eq. 12.18 (set $X_{ij} = \phi_j(x_i)$ and $\gamma_A = 0$) whose size is given by the number of basis functions s. For a small set of basis functions, this system can be solved more efficiently. Yu et al. (2004) also discuss data representation within this framework.

In (Krishnapuram et al., 2004), the authors impose a prior derived from the graph Laplacian, over parameters of a multinomial logistic regression model. For an r-class problem, the class probabilities are modeled as

$$P(y^{(j)} = 1|x) = \frac{e^{w^{(i)T}x}}{\sum_{i=1}^{r} e^{w^{(i)T}x}} \qquad 1 \le j \le r,$$

where $y^{(j)}$ is an indicator variable for class j and $w^{(i)} \in \mathbb{R}^d$ is the weight vector for class i. The prior on weight vector $w^{(i)}$ is given by

$$P(w^{(i)}) \propto \exp\left\{\frac{-w^{(i)T}\left(\gamma_I^{(i)} X^T L X + D^{(i)}\right) w^{(i)T}}{2}\right\},$$

where $D^{(i)}$ is a parameterized diagonal matrix providing extra regularization similar to the ambient penalty term in manifold regularization. Bayesian inference is performed to learn the maximum a posteriori (MAP) estimate of the model parameters with an expectation-maximization algorithm.

In (Kegl and Wang, 2004), an extension of the Adaboost algorithm is proposed (also discussed elsewhere in this book) that implements similar intuitions within the framework of boosting techniques. In (Altun et al., 2005), a generalization of the problem in Eq. 12.5 is presented for semi-supervised learning of structured variables.

By introducing approximations to avoid graph recomputation, methods for out-of-sample extension have also been suggested without explicitly operating in an ambiently defined function or model space. In (Delalleau et al., 2005) an induction formula is derived by assuming that the addition of a test point to the graph does not change the transductive solution over the unlabeled data. In other words, if $\mathbf{f} = [f_1 \ldots f_{l+u} \; f_t]$ denotes a function defined on the augmented graph, with f_t as its value on the node corresponding to the test point, then minimizing the objective function for graph regularization (with L as the regularizer) keeping the values on the original nodes fixed, one can obtain a Parzen windows expression for f_t:

$$f_t = \frac{\sum_i W_{ti} f_i}{\sum_i W_{ti}},$$

where W denotes the adjacency matrix as before. In (Zhu et al., 2003c), a test point is classified according to its nearest neighbor on the graph, whose classification is available after transductive inference. In (Chapelle et al., 2003), graph kernels are constructed by modifying the spectrum of the Gram matrix of a kernel evaluated over labeled and unlabeled examples. Unseen test points are approximated in the span of the labeled and unlabeled data, and this approximation is used to extend the graph kernel.

The regularized Laplacian eigenmap algorithms presented in section 12.3.2 have also been simultaneously and independently developed by Vert and Yamanishi (2004) in the context of extending a partially known graph. The graph inference problem is posed as follows: Suppose a graph $G = (V, E)$ with vertices V and edges E is observed and is known to be a subgraph of an unknown graph $G' = (V', E')$ with $V \subset V'$ and $E \subset E'$. Given the vertices $V' - V$, infer the edges $E' - E$. If the vertices v are elements of some set $\mathcal{V}$ on which a kernel function $K : \mathcal{V} \times \mathcal{V}$ is defined, then one can infer the graph in two steps: Find a map $\psi : \mathcal{V} \mapsto \mathbb{R}^m$ and induce a nearest-neighbor graph on the embedded points. To find the map ψ in the RKHS corresponding to K, one can set up an optimization problem (similar to that in regularized classification), involving a graph Laplacian-based "data fit" term that measures how well ψ preserves the local structure of the observed graph and the RKHS regularizer that provides ambient smoothness. This is also the objective function of regularized Laplacian eigenmaps, and involes solving the generalized eigenvalue problem (12.13) for multiple eigenvectors.

12.7   Future Directions

We have discussed a general framework for incorporating geometric structures in the design of learning algorithms. Our framework may be extended to include additional domain structure, e.g., in the form of invariances and structured outputs. Many directions are being pursued toward improving the scalability and efficiency of our algorithms, while developing extensions to handle unlabeled data in, e.g., support vector regression, one-class SVMs, and Gaussian processes. We plan to pursue applications of these methods to a variety of real-world learning tasks, and investigate issues concerning generalization analysis and model selection.

13 Discrete Regularization

Dengyong Zhou   DENGYONG.ZHOU@TUEBINGEN.MPG.DE
Bernhard Schölkopf   BERNHARD.SCHOELKOPF@TUEBINGEN.MPG.DE

Many real-world machine learning problems are situated on finite discrete sets, including dimensionality reduction, clustering, and transductive inference. A variety of approaches for learning from finite sets has been proposed from different motivations and for different problems. In most of those approaches, a finite set is modeled as a graph, in which the edges encode pairwise relationships among the objects in the set. Consequently many concepts and methods from graph theory are applied, in particular, graph Laplacians.

In this chapter we present a systemic framework for learning from a finite set represented as a graph. We develop discrete analogues of a number of differential operators, and then construct a discrete analogue of classical regularization theory based on those discrete differential operators. The graph Laplacian-based approaches are special cases of this general discrete regularization framework. More importantly, new approaches based on other different differential operators are derived as well.

13.1 Introduction

Many real-world machine learning problems can be described as follows: given a set of objects $X = \{x_1, x_2, \ldots, x_l, x_{l+1}, \ldots, x_n\}$ from a domain $\mathcal{X}$ (e.g., $\mathbb{R}^d$) in which the first l objects are labeled as $y_1, \ldots, y_l \in \mathcal{Y} = \{1, -1\}$, the goal is to predict the labels of remaining unlabeled objects indexed from $l + 1$ to n. If the objects to classify are totally unrelated to each other, we cannot make any prediction statistically better than random guessing. Typically we may assume that there exist pairwise relationships among data. For example, given a finite set of vectorial data, the pairwise relationships among data points may be described by a kernel (Schölkopf and Smola, 2002). A data set endowed with pairwise relationships can be naturally *weighted graph* modeled as a weighted graph. The vertices of the graph represent the objects, and the weighted edges encode the pairwise relationships. If the pairwise relationships

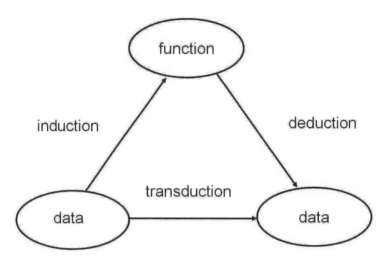

Figure 13.1   The relations among induction, deduction, and transduction.

are symmetric, the graph is undirected; otherwise, the graph is directed. A typical example for directed graphs is the World Wide Web (WWW), in which hyperlinks between webpages may be thought of as directed edges.

Any supervised learning algorithm can be applied to the above inference problem, e.g., by training a classifier $f : \mathcal{X} \rightarrow \mathcal{Y}$ with the set of pairs $\{(x_1, y_1), \ldots, (x_l, y_l)\}$, and then using the trained classifier f to predict the labels of the unlabeled objects. Following this approach, one will have estimated a classification function defined on the whole domain $\mathcal{X}$ before predicting the labels of the unlabeled objects. According to (Vapnik, 1998) (see also chapter 24), estimating a classification function defined on the whole domain $\mathcal{X}$ is more complex than the original problem which only requires predicting the labels of the given unlabeled objects, and a better approach is to directly predict the labels of the given unlabeled objects. Therefore here we consider estimating a discrete classification function which is defined on the given objects X only. Such an estimation problem is called *transductive inference* (Vapnik, 1998). In psychology, transductive reasoning means linking particular to particular with no consideration of the general principles. It is generally used by young children. In contrast, deductive reasoning, which is used by adults and older children, means the ability to come to a specific conclusion based on a general premise (cf. figure 13.1).

It is well known that many meaningful inductive methods such as support vector machines (SVMs) can be derived from a regularization framework, which minimizes an empirical loss plus a regularization term. Inspired by this work, we define discrete analogues of a number of differential operators, and then construct a discrete analogue of classical regularization theory (Tikhonov and Arsenin, 1977; Wahba, 1990) using the discrete operators. Much existing work, including spectral clustering, transductive inference, and dimensionality reduction can be understood

transductive
inference

discrete
regularization
theory

in this framework. More importantly, a family of new approaches is derived.

13.2   Discrete Analysis

In this section, we first introduce some basic notions on graph theory, and then propose a family of discrete differential operators, which constitute the basis of the discrete regularization framework presented in the next section.

13.2.1   Preliminaries

weighted graph

A graph $G = (V, E)$ consists of a finite set V, together with a subset $E \subseteq V \times V$. The elements of V are the *vertices* of the graph, and the elements of E are the *edges* of the graph. We say that an edge e is *incident* on vertex v if e starts from v. A *self-loop* is an edge which starts and ends at the same vertex. A *path* is a sequence of vertices $(v_1, v_2, \ldots, v_m)$ such that $[v_{i-1}, v_i]$ is an edge for all $1 < i \leq m$. A graph is *connected* when there is a path between any two vertices. A graph is *undirected* when the set of edges is *symmetric*, i.e., for each edge $[u, v] \in E$ we also have $[v, u] \in E$. In the following, the graphs are always assumed to be connected, undirected, and have no self-loops or multiple edges; for an example, see figure 13.2.

A graph is *weighted* when it is associated with a function $w : E \to \mathbb{R}_+$ which is symmetric, i.e. $w([u, v]) = w([v, u])$, for all $[u, v] \in E$. The *degree* function $d : V \to \mathbb{R}_+$ is defined to be

$$d(v) := \sum_{u \sim v} w([u, v]),$$

Hilbert spaces

where $u \sim v$ denote the set of the vertices *adjacent with* v, i.e. $[u, v] \in E$. Let $\mathcal{H}(V)$ denote the Hilbert space of real-valued functions endowed with the usual inner product

$$\langle f, g \rangle_{\mathcal{H}(V)} := \sum_{v \in V} f(v) g(v),$$

for all $f, g \in \mathcal{H}(V)$. Similarly define $\mathcal{H}(E)$. In what follows, we will omit the subscript of inner products if we do not think it is necessary. Note that function $h \in \mathcal{H}(E)$ have not to be symmetric. In other words, we do not require $h([u, v]) = h([v, u])$.

13.2.2   Gradient and Divergence Operators

We define the discrete gradient and divergence operators, which can be thought of as discrete analogues of their counterparts in the continuous case.

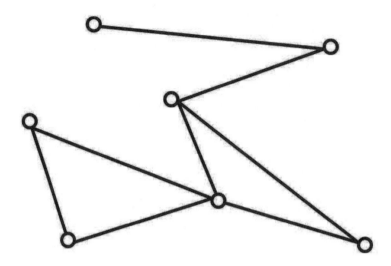

Figure 13.2   An undirected graph.

Definition 13.1 *The graph gradient is an operator* $\nabla : \mathcal{H}(V) \to \mathcal{H}(E)$ *defined by*

$$(\nabla f)([u,v]) := \sqrt{\frac{w([u,v])}{d(v)}} f(v) - \sqrt{\frac{w([u,v])}{d(u)}} f(u), \ \text{for all } [u,v] \in E. \quad (13.1)$$

graph gradient

The gradient measures the variation of a function on each edge. Clearly,

$$(\nabla f)([u,v]) = -(\nabla f)([v,u]), \quad (13.2)$$

i.e., ∇f is skew-symmetric.

Remark 13.2 *An obvious problem is why we define a graph gradient as Eq 13.1. In the uniform 2-dimensional lattice case, a natural discrete gradient is defined by*

$$(\nabla f)([i, i+1]) = f(i+1) - f(i),$$

where i denotes the index of a node of the lattice. Unlike the lattice case, the problem that we have to deal with here is the irregularity of a general graph. Intuitively, in our definition, before computing the variation of a function between two adjacent vertices, we break the function value at each vertex among its adjacent edges, and the value assigned to each edge is proportional to the edge weight. Mathematically, such a definition can make us finally recover the well-known graph Laplacian in a way parallel to continuous case (see section 13.2.3).

We may also define the graph gradient at each vertex. Given a function $f \in \mathcal{H}(V)$ and a vertex v, the gradient of f at v is defined by $\nabla f(v) := \{(\nabla f)([v,u]) | [v,u] \in E\}$. We also often denote $\nabla f(v)$ by $\nabla_v f$. Then the norm of the graph gradient ∇f at vertex v is defined by

discrete
p-Dirichlet form

$$\|\nabla_v f\| := \left(\sum_{u \sim v} (\nabla f)^2 ([u,v]) \right)^{\frac{1}{2}},$$

and the *p-Dirichlet form* of the function f is defined by

$$S_p(f) := \frac{1}{2} \sum_{v \in V} \|\nabla_v f\|^p.$$

Intuitively, the norm of the graph gradient measures the roughness of a function around a vertex, and the p-Dirichlet form the roughness of a function over the graph. In addition, we define $\|\nabla f([v,u])\| := \|\nabla_v f\|$. Note that $\|\nabla f\|$ has been defined in the space $\mathcal{H}(E)$ as $\|\nabla f\| = \langle \nabla f, \nabla f \rangle_{\mathcal{H}(E)}^{1/2}$.

Definition 13.3 *The graph divergence is an operator* div : $\mathcal{H}(E) \to \mathcal{H}(V)$ *which satisfies*

graph divergence

$$\langle \nabla f, h \rangle_{\mathcal{H}(E)} = \langle f, -\operatorname{div} h \rangle_{\mathcal{H}(V)}, \text{ for all } f \in \mathcal{H}(V), h \in \mathcal{H}(E). \tag{13.3}$$

In other words, $-\operatorname{div}$ is defined to be the adjoint of the graph gradient. Equation (13.3) can be thought of as a discrete analogue of the Stokes theorem.[1] Note that the inner products in the left and right sides of (13.3) are respectively in the spaces $\mathcal{H}(E)$ and $\mathcal{H}(V)$.

Proposition 13.4 *The graph divergence can be computed as*

$$(\operatorname{div} h)(v) = \sum_{u \sim v} \sqrt{\frac{w([u,v])}{d(v)}} \left(h([v,u]) - h([u,v]) \right), \tag{13.4}$$

---

1. Given a compact Riemannian manifold (M,g) with a function $f \in C^\infty(M)$ and a vector field $X \in \mathcal{X}(M)$, it follows from the Stokes theorem that $\int_M \langle \nabla f, X \rangle = -\int_M (\operatorname{div} X) f$.

Proof

$$
\begin{aligned}
\langle \nabla f, h \rangle &= \sum_{[u,v] \in E} \nabla f([u,v]) h([u,v]) \\
&= \sum_{[u,v] \in E} \left(\sqrt{\frac{w([u,v])}{d(v)}} f(v) - \sqrt{\frac{w([u,v])}{d(u)}} f(u) \right) h([u,v]) \\
&= \sum_{[u,v] \in E} \sqrt{\frac{w([u,v])}{d(v)}} f(v) h([u,v]) - \sum_{[u,v] \in E} \sqrt{\frac{w([u,v])}{d(u)}} f(u) h([u,v]) \\
&= \sum_{r \in V} \sum_{u \sim r} \sqrt{\frac{w([u,r])}{d(r)}} f(r) h([u,r]) - \sum_{r \in V} \sum_{v \sim r} \sqrt{\frac{w([r,v])}{d(r)}} f(r) h([r,v]) \\
&= \sum_{r \in V} f(r) \left(\sum_{u \sim r} \sqrt{\frac{w([u,r])}{d(r)}} h([u,r]) - \sum_{v \sim r} \sqrt{\frac{w([r,v])}{d(r)}} h([r,v]) \right) \\
&= \sum_{r \in V} f(r) \sum_{u \sim r} \sqrt{\frac{w([u,r])}{d(r)}} \Big(h([u,r]) - h([r,u]) \Big).
\end{aligned}
$$

The last equality implies (13.4).   ∎

net flow

Intuitively, the divergence measures the net outflow of function h at each vertex. Note that if h is symmetric, then $(\mathrm{div}\, h)(v) = 0$ for all $v \in V$.

13.2.3   Laplace Operator

In this section, we define the graph Laplacian, which can be thought of as discrete analogue of the Laplace-Beltrami operator on Riemannian manifolds.

Definition 13.5 *The graph Laplacian is an operator* $\Delta : \mathcal{H}(V) \to \mathcal{H}(V)$ *defined by* [2]

$$
\Delta f := -\frac{1}{2} \mathrm{div}(\nabla f). \tag{13.5}
$$

graph Laplacian

Substituting (13.1) and (13.4) into (13.5), we have

$$
\begin{aligned}
(\Delta f)(v) &= \frac{1}{2} \sum_{u \sim v} \sqrt{\frac{w([u,v])}{d(v)}} \Big((\nabla f)([u,v]) - (\nabla f)([v,u]) \Big) \\
&= \sum_{u \sim v} \sqrt{\frac{w([u,v])}{d(v)}} \left(\sqrt{\frac{w([u,v])}{d(v)}} f(v) - \sqrt{\frac{w([u,v])}{d(u)}} f(u) \right) \\
&= f(v) - \sum_{u \sim v} \frac{w([u,v])}{\sqrt{d(u)d(v)}} f(u). \tag{13.6}
\end{aligned}
$$

---

2. The Laplace-Beltrami operator $\Delta : C^\infty(M) \to C^\infty(M)$ is defined to be $\Delta f = -\mathrm{div}(\nabla f)$. The additional factor $1/2$ in (13.5) is due to each edge being counted twice.

self-adjoint

positive definite

The graph Laplacian is a linear operator because both the gradient and divergence operators are linear. Furthermore, the graph Laplacian is self-adjoint,

$$\langle \Delta f, g \rangle = \frac{1}{2}\langle -\operatorname{div}(\nabla f), g \rangle = \frac{1}{2}\langle \nabla f, \nabla g \rangle = \frac{1}{2}\langle f, -\operatorname{div}(\nabla g) \rangle = \langle f, \Delta g \rangle,$$

and positive semi-definite:

$$\langle \Delta f, f \rangle = \frac{1}{2}\langle -\operatorname{div}(\nabla f), f \rangle = \frac{1}{2}\langle \nabla f, \nabla f \rangle = \mathcal{S}_2(f) \geq 0. \tag{13.7}$$

It immediately follows from (13.7) that

Theorem 13.6 $2\Delta f = D_f \mathcal{S}_2$.

Remark 13.7 *Equation (13.6) shows that our graph Laplacian defined by (13.5) is identical to the Laplace matrix in (Chung, 1997) defined to be $\Delta = D^{-1/2}(D - W)D^{-1/2}$, where D is a diagonal matrix with $D(v, v) = d(v)$, and W a matrix*

Laplace matrix

with $W(u, v) = w([u, v])$ if $[u, v]$ is an edge and $W(u, v) = 0$ otherwise. It is worth mentioning that the matrix $L = D - W$ is often referred to as the combinatorial (or unnormalized) graph Laplacian, or simply the graph Laplacian. Obviously, this Laplacian can also be derived in a similar way. Specifically, define a graph gradient by

$$(\nabla f)([u, v]) := \sqrt{w([u, v])}(f(v) - f(u)), \; \text{ for all } [u, v] \in E,$$

and then the rest proceeds as the above.

Remark 13.8 *For the connection between graph Laplacians (including the Laplacian we presented here) and the usual Laplacian in continuous case, we refer the*

convergence

reader to (von Luxburg et al., 2005; Hein et al., 2005; Bousquet et al., 2004). The main point is that, if we assume the vertices of a graph are identically and independently sampled from some unknown but fixed distribution, when the sampling size goes to infinity, the combinatorial graph Laplacian does not converge to the usual Laplacian unless the distribution is uniform.

13.2.4   Curvature Operator

In this section, we define the graph curvature which can be regarded as a discrete analogue of the mean curvature in continuous case.

Definition 13.9 *The graph curvature is an operator $\kappa : \mathcal{H}(V) \to \mathcal{H}(V)$ defined by*

$$\kappa f := -\frac{1}{2}\operatorname{div}\left(\frac{\nabla f}{\|\nabla f\|}\right). \tag{13.8}$$

graph curvature

Substituting (13.1) and (13.4) into (13.8), we obtain

$$
\begin{aligned}
(\kappa f)(v) &= \sum_{u \sim v} \sqrt{\frac{w([u,v])}{d(v)}} \left(\frac{\nabla f}{\|\nabla f\|}([u,v]) - \frac{\nabla f}{\|\nabla f\|}([v,u]) \right) \\
&= \sum_{u \sim v} \frac{w([u,v])}{\sqrt{d(v)}} \left[\frac{1}{\|\nabla_u f\|} \left(\frac{f(v)}{\sqrt{d(v)}} - \frac{f(u)}{\sqrt{d(u)}} \right) - \frac{1}{\|\nabla_v f\|} \left(\frac{f(u)}{\sqrt{d(u)}} - \frac{f(v)}{\sqrt{d(v)}} \right) \right] \\
&= \frac{1}{2} \sum_{u \sim v} \frac{w([u,v])}{\sqrt{d(v)}} \left(\frac{1}{\|\nabla_u f\|} + \frac{1}{\|\nabla_v f\|} \right) \left(\frac{f(v)}{\sqrt{d(v)}} - \frac{f(u)}{\sqrt{d(u)}} \right). \quad (13.9)
\end{aligned}
$$

Unlike the graph Laplacian (13.5), the graph curvature is a nonlinear operator.

As in theorem 13.6, we have

Theorem 13.10 $\kappa f = D_f \mathcal{S}_1$.

Proof

$$
\begin{aligned}
(D_f \mathcal{S}_1)(v) &= \sum_{u \sim v} \left[\frac{w([u,v])}{\|\nabla_u f\|} \left(\frac{f(v)}{d(v)} - \frac{f(u)}{\sqrt{d(u)d(v)}} \right) + \frac{w([u,v])}{\|\nabla_v f\|} \left(\frac{f(v)}{d(v)} - \frac{f(u)}{\sqrt{d(u)d(v)}} \right) \right] \\
&= \sum_{u \sim v} w([u,v]) \left(\frac{1}{\|\nabla_u f\|} + \frac{1}{\|\nabla_v f\|} \right) \left(\frac{f(v)}{d(v)} - \frac{f(u)}{\sqrt{d(u)d(v)}} \right) \\
&= \sum_{u \sim v} \frac{w([u,v])}{\sqrt{d(v)}} \left(\frac{1}{\|\nabla_u f\|} + \frac{1}{\|\nabla_v f\|} \right) \left(\frac{f(v)}{\sqrt{d(v)}} - \frac{f(u)}{\sqrt{d(u)}} \right).
\end{aligned}
$$

Comparing the last equality with (13.9) completes the proof.   ∎

13.2.5 p-**Laplace Operator**

In this section, we generalize the graph Laplacian and curvature to an operator, which can be thought of as the discrete analogue of the p-Laplacian in continuous case (Hardt and Lin, 1987; Heinonen et al., 1993).

Definition 13.11 *The graph p-Laplacian is an operator* $\Delta_p : \mathcal{H}(V) \to \mathcal{H}(V)$ *defined by*

$$
\Delta_p f := -\frac{1}{2} \operatorname{div}(\|\nabla f\|^{p-2} \nabla f). \quad (13.10)
$$

graph
p-Laplacian

Clearly, $\Delta_1 = \kappa$, and $\Delta_2 = \Delta$. Substituting (13.1) and (13.4) into (13.10), we obtain

$$
(\Delta_p f)(v) = \frac{1}{2} \sum_{u \sim v} \frac{w([u,v])}{\sqrt{d(v)}} (\|\nabla_u f\|^{p-2} + \|\nabla_v f\|^{p-2}) \left(\frac{f(v)}{\sqrt{d(v)}} - \frac{f(u)}{\sqrt{d(u)}} \right), \quad (13.11)
$$

which generalizes (13.6) and (13.9).

As before, it can be shown that

Theorem 13.12 $p\Delta_p f = D_f \mathcal{S}_p$.

Remark 13.13 *There is much literature on the p-Laplacian in continuous case. We refer the reader to (Heinonen et al., 1993) for a comprehensive study. There is also some work on the discrete analogue of the p-Laplacian, e.g., see (Yamasaki, 1986), where it is defined as*

$$\Delta_p f(v) = \frac{1}{g_p(v)} \sum_{u \sim v} w^{p-1}([u,v])|f(u) - f(v)|^{p-1} \operatorname{sign}(f(u) - f(v)),$$

where $g_p(v) = \sum_{u \sim v} w^{p-1}([u,v])$ and $p \in [2, \infty[$. Note that $p = 1$ is not allowed.

13.3   Discrete Regularization

discrete
regularization

Given a graph $G = (V, E)$ and a label set $\mathcal{Y} = \{1, -1\}$, the vertices v in a subset $S \subset V$ are labeled as $y(v) \in \mathcal{Y}$. Our goal is to label the remaining unlabeled vertices, i.e., the vertices in the complement of S. Assume a classification function $f \in \mathcal{H}(V)$, which assigns a label sign $f(v)$ to each vertex $v \in V$. Obviously, a good classification function should vary as slowly as possible between closely related vertices while changing the initial label assignment as little as possible.

Define a function $y \in \mathcal{H}(V)$ with $y(v) = 1$ or -1 if vertex v is labeled as positive or negative respectively, and 0 if it is unlabeled. Thus we may consider the optimization problem

$$f^* = \underset{f \in \mathcal{H}(V)}{\operatorname{argmin}} \{ \mathcal{S}_p(f) + \mu \| f - y \|^2 \}, \tag{13.12}$$

where $\mu \in]0, \infty[$ is a parameter specifying the tradeoff between the two competing terms. It is not hard to see that the objective function is strictly convex, and hence by standard arguments in convex analysis the optimization problem has a unique solution.

13.3.1   Regularization with $p = 2$

When $p = 2$, the following equation can derived from theorem 13.6.

Theorem 13.14 *The solution of (13.12) satisfies that*

$$\Delta f^* + \mu(f^* - y) = 0.$$

heat diffusion

The equation in the theorem can be thought of as discrete analogue of the *Euler-Lagrange equation*. It is easy to see that we can obtain a closed-form solution $f^* = \mu(\Delta + \mu I)^{-1} y$, where I denotes the identity operator. Define the function $c : E \to \mathbb{R}_+$ by

$$c([u,v]) = \frac{1}{1+\mu} \frac{w([u,v])}{\sqrt{d(u)d(v)}}, \text{ if } u \neq v; \text{ and } c([v,v]) = \frac{\mu}{1+\mu}. \tag{13.13}$$

We can show that the iteration

$$f^{(t+1)}(v) = \sum_{u \sim v} c([u,v]) f^{(t)}(v) + c([v,v]) y(v), \text{ for all } v \in V, \qquad (13.14)$$

where t indicates the iteration step, converges to a closed-form solution (Zhou et al., 2004). Moreover, the iterative result is independent of the setting of the initial value. The iteration can be intuitively thought of as a sort of information diffusion. At every step, each node receives the values from its neighbors, which are weighted by the normalized pairwise relationships. At the same time, they also retain some fraction of their values. The relative amount by which these updates occur is specified by the coefficients defined in (13.13). In what follows, this iteration approach will be generalized to arbitrary p.

Remark 13.15 *It is easy to see that the regularizer of $p = 2$ can be rewritten into*

$$\frac{1}{2} \sum_{u,v} w([u,v]) \left(\frac{f(u)}{\sqrt{d(u)}} - \frac{f(v)}{\sqrt{d(v)}} \right)^2, \qquad (13.15)$$

unnormalized regularizer

which we earlier suggested for transductive inference (Zhou et al., 2004). A closely related one is

$$\frac{1}{2} \sum_{u,v} w([u,v]) (f(u) - f(v))^2, \qquad (13.16)$$

which appeared in (Joachims, 2003; Belkin et al., 2004a; Zhu et al., 2003b). From the point of view of spectral clustering, (13.15) can be derived from the normalized cut (Shi and Malik, 2000), and corresponds to the (normalized) graph Laplacian (13.5); and (13.16) is derived from the ratio cut (Hagen and Kahng, 1992), and corresponds to the combinatorial graph Laplacian (see also remark 13.7). On many real-world experiments, a remarkable difference between these two regularizers is that the transductive approaches based on (13.16) (Joachims, 2003; Zhu et al., 2003b) strongly depend on the prior knowledge of proportion among different classes while the approach based on (13.15) (Zhou et al., 2004) can work well without such prior knowledge. For more details, we refer the reader to chapter 21 (Analysis of Benchmarks) and chapter 11 (Label Propagation and Quadratic Criterion).

locally linear embedding regularizer

Remark 13.16 *One can construct many other similar regularizers. For instance, one might consider (Roweis and Saul, 2000)*

$$\frac{1}{2} \sum_{u,v} \left(f(v) - \sum_{u \sim v} p([u,v]) f(u) \right)^2, \qquad (13.17)$$

where the function $p: E \to \mathbb{R}_+$ is defined to be $p([u,v]) = w([u,v])/d(u)$. Note that p is not symmetric. This regularizer measures the difference of function f at vertex v, and the average of f on the neighbors of v.

13.3.2   Regularization with $p = 1$

When $p = 1$, it follows from theorem 13.10 that

Theorem 13.17 *The solution of (13.12) satisfies that*

$$\kappa f^* + 2\mu(f^* - y) = 0.$$

As we have mentioned before, the curvature κ is a nonlinear operator, and we are not aware of any closed-form solution for this equation. However, we can construct an iterative algorithm to obtain the solution. Substituting (13.9) into the equation in the theorem, we have

$$\sum_{u \sim v} \frac{w([u,v])}{\sqrt{d(v)}} \left(\frac{1}{\|\nabla_u f^*\|} + \frac{1}{\|\nabla_v f^*\|} \right) \left(\frac{f^*(v)}{\sqrt{d(v)}} - \frac{f^*(u)}{\sqrt{d(u)}} \right) + 2\mu(f^*(v) - y(v)) = 0. \tag{13.18}$$

Define the function $m : E \to \mathbb{R}_+$ by

$$m([u,v]) = w([u,v]) \left(\frac{1}{\|\nabla_u f^*\|} + \frac{1}{\|\nabla_v f^*\|} \right). \tag{13.19}$$

Then

$$\sum_{u \sim v} \frac{m([u,v])}{\sqrt{d(v)}} \left(\frac{f^*(v)}{\sqrt{d(v)}} - \frac{f^*(u)}{\sqrt{d(u)}} \right) + 2\mu(f^*(v) - y(v)) = 0,$$

which can be transformed into

$$\left(\sum_{u \sim v} \frac{m([u,v])}{d(v)} + 2\mu \right) f^*(v) = \sum_{u \sim v} \frac{m([u,v])}{\sqrt{d(u)d(v)}} f^*(u) + 2\mu y(v).$$

curvature flow   Define the function $c : E \to \mathbb{R}_+$ by

$$c([u,v]) = \frac{\dfrac{m([u,v])}{\sqrt{d(u)d(v)}}}{\displaystyle\sum_{u \sim v} \frac{m([u,v])}{d(v)} + 2\mu}, \quad \text{if } u \neq v, \tag{13.20}$$

and

$$c([v,v]) = \frac{2\mu}{\displaystyle\sum_{u \sim v} \frac{m([u,v])}{d(v)} + 2\mu}. \tag{13.21}$$

Then

$$f^*(v) = \sum_{u \sim v} c([u,v]) f^*(v) + c([v,v]) y(v). \tag{13.22}$$

Thus we can use the iteration

$$f^{(t+1)}(v) = \sum_{u \sim v} c^{(t)}([u, v]) f^{(t)}(v) + c^{(t)}([v, v]) y(v), \text{ for all } v \in V \qquad (13.23)$$

to obtain the solution, in which the coefficients $c^{(t)}$ are updated according to (13.20) and (13.19). It can be shown that this iterative result is independent of the setting of the initial value. Compared with the iterative algorithm (13.14) in the case of $p = 2$, the coefficients in the present method are adaptively updated at each iteration, in addition to the function being updated.

13.3.3   Regularization with Arbitrary p

For arbitrary p, it follows from theorem 13.12 that

Theorem 13.18 *The solution of (13.12) satisfies that*

$$p \Delta_p f^* + 2\mu(f^* - y) = 0.$$

general diffusion   We can construct a similar iterative algorithm to obtain the solution. Specifically,

$$f^{(t+1)}(v) = \sum_{u \sim v} c^{(t)}([u, v]) f^{(t)}(v) + c^{(t)}([v, v]) y(v), \text{ for all } v \in V, \qquad (13.24)$$

where

$$c^{(t)}([u, v]) = \frac{\dfrac{m^{(t)}([u, v])}{\sqrt{d(u)d(v)}}}{\displaystyle\sum_{u \sim v} \dfrac{m^{(t)}([u, v])}{d(v)} + \dfrac{2\mu}{p}}, \text{ if } u \neq v, \qquad (13.25)$$

and

$$c^{(t)}([v, v]) = \frac{\dfrac{2\mu}{p}}{\displaystyle\sum_{u \sim v} \dfrac{m^{(t)}([u, v])}{d(v)} + \dfrac{2\mu}{p}}, \qquad (13.26)$$

and

$$m^{(t)}([u, v]) = \frac{w([u, v])}{p} (\|\nabla_u f^{(t)}\|^{p-2} + \|\nabla_v f^{(t)}\|^{p-2}). \qquad (13.27)$$

It is easy to see that the iterative algorithms in sections 13.3.1 and 13.3.2 are the special cases of this general one with $p = 2$ and $p = 1$ respectively. Moreover, it is interesting to note that $p = 2$ is a critical point.

13.4   Conclusion

In this chapter, we proposed the discrete analogues of a family of differential operators, and the discrete analogue of classical regularization theory based on those discrete differential operators. A family of transductive inference algorithms corresponding to different discrete differential operators was naturally derived from the discrete regularization framework.

There are many possible extensions to this work. One may consider defining discrete high-order differential operators, and then building a regularization framework that can penalize high-order derivatives. One may also develop a parallel framework on directed graphs (Zhou et al., 2005b), which model many real-world data structures, such as the World Wide Web. Finally, it is of interest to explore the properties of the graph p-Laplacian as the nonlinear extension of the usual graph Laplacian, since the latter has been intensively studied, and has many nice properties (Chung, 1997).

14 Semi-Supervised Learning with Conditional Harmonic Mixing

Christopher J. C. Burges   CHRIS.BURGES@MICROSOFT.COM

John C. Platt   JPLATT@MICROSOFT.COM

Recently graph-based algorithms, in which nodes represent data points and links encode similarities, have become popular for semi-supervised learning. In this chapter we introduce a general probabilistic formulation called conditional harmonic mixing (CHM), in which the links are directed, a conditional probability matrix is associated with each link, and where the numbers of classes can vary from node to node. The posterior class probability at each node is updated by minimizing the Kullback-Leibler (KL) divergence between its distribution and that predicted by its neighbors. We show that for arbitrary graphs, as long as each unlabeled point is reachable from at least one training point, a solution always exists, is unique, and can be found by solving a sparse linear system iteratively. This result holds even if the graph contains loops, or if the conditional probability matrices are not consistent. We show how, given a classifier for a task, CHM can learn its transition probabilities. Using the Reuters database, we show that CHM improves the accuracy of the best available classifier, for small training set sizes.

14.1   Introduction

Graphical models provide a powerful framework for approaching machine learning problems. Two common examples are probabilistic graphical models (Jordan, 1999) and semi-supervised learning on graphs (see chapter 11 and (Zhu and Ghahramani, 2002; Zhu et al., 2003b; Zhou et al., 2004)) and which we refer to here as Laplacian SSL. Graphs have been used as a general representation of preference relations in ranking problems (Dekel et al., 2004) and play a role in various approaches to dimensional reduction (Burges, 2005). In this chapter, we propose a new graph-based approach to semi-supervised learning called conditional harmonic mixing (CHM).

conditional harmonic mixing

Probabilistic graphical models such as Bayes nets write a probability distribution as a product of conditionals, which live on the nodes; the arcs encode conditional independence assumptions. Laplacian semi-supervised learning (SSL) is more closely related to random walks on networks (Doyle and Snell, 1984): each arc encodes the similarity between the nodes at its endpoints, and the goal is to use neighborhood structure to guide the choice of classification (or regression, clustering, or ranking) function. For Laplacian SSL models, the probabilistic interpretation is somewhat indirect (Zhu et al., 2003b); for probabilistic graphical models, it is central. In CHM we propose an intermediate model, where both a probabilistic interpretation and Laplacian SSL are central. In CHM, no attempt is made to model an overall joint density; we are only interested, ultimately, in the class-conditional posteriors. Although it is assumed that there exists some underlying joint, the model itself is viewed as an approximation; in particular, the conditional probabilities may be approximations, and as a result, inconsistent (i.e., no joint may exist for which they are the conditionals). This results in some striking differences between CHM and well-known probabilistic graphical models such as Bayes nets: for example, in CHM, the process of learning the posteriors, given the conditionals, converges to a global optimum via a straightforward iterative optimization procedure, whatever the structure of the graph (in particular, even if there are loops), provided only that there exists a path to each unlabeled point from at least one labeled point. In this regard, CHM is similar to dependency networks (Heckerman et al., 2001). In CHM, as in Laplacian SSL, each node corresponds to a random variable, but unlike the original Laplacian SSL, the arcs are directed , and each arc carries a matrix which models a conditional probability.[1] The matrices can even be rectangular, which corresponds to the posteriors at different nodes corresponding to different numbers of classes for that random variable. We will also investigate learning the conditional probability matrices themselves from data. In this chapter we will consider CHM models for classification, but the same ideas could be extended for regression, clustering, ranking, etc.

directed graphs

14.1.1 Conditional Harmonic Mixing: Motivation

CHM is a highly redundant model, in that for a "perfect" CHM model of a given problem, the posterior for a given node can be computed from the posterior at any adjacent node, together with the conditional probability matrix on the arc joining them. However this is an idealization: CHM handles this by asking that the posterior at a given node be that distribution such that the number of bits needed to describe the distributions predicted at that node, by the adjacent nodes, is minimized. This is accomplished by minimizing a Kullback-Leibler (KL) divergence (see below). Building on an idea proposed in Zhu et al. (2003b), CHM can also be used to improve the accuracy of another, given base classifier.

Kullback-Leibler divergence

1. Recently, Zhou et al. (2005b) have extended Laplacian SSL to the case of directed arcs.

In the graphical approaches to semi-supervised learning of Zhu and Ghahramani (2002); Zhu et al. (2003b), and Zhou et al. (2004) (see also chapter 11), the underlying intuition is that the function should vary smoothly across the graph, so that closely clustered points tend to be assigned similar function values (the "clustering assumption"). This leads to the use of undirected arcs in the graph, since the graph is used essentially to model the density. However, there is a second intuition that we wish to add, and that is of the propagation of information. Consider the graph shown in figure 14.1, left panel (in this chapter, filled (unfilled) circles represent labeled (unlabeled) points), where both arcs have the same weight. In the harmonic solutions of Zhu and Ghahramani (2002); Zhu et al. (2003b), and Zhou et al. (2004), the state of node 2 is the weighted average of its neighbors. However, in this particular graph, it seems strange to have node 2 care about the state of node 3, since from the information propagation point of view, all of the label information propagates out from node 1, and all label information about node 3 has already passed through node 2. By making the arcs directed, as in the right panel, this problem can be addressed with no loss of generality, since an undirected arc between nodes A and B can be simulated by adding arcs A→B and B→A.

Figure 14.1   Directional arcs for information flow.

A second reason for using directed arcs is that the relations between points can themselves be asymmetric (even if both are unlabeled). For example, in k-nearest neighbor, if point A is the nearest neighbor of point B, point B need not be that of point A. Such asymmetric relations can be captured with directed arcs.

harmonic
solutions

CHM shares with Laplacian SSL the desirable property that its solutions are harmonic, and unique, and can be computed iteratively and efficiently. It shares with Bayesian graphical models the desirable property that it is a probabilistic model from the ground up. We end this section with a simple but useful observation, but first we must introduce some notation. Suppose nodes i and j $(i, j \in \{1, \ldots, N\})$ are connected by a directed arc from i to j (throughout, we will index nodes by i, j, k and vector indices by a, b). We will represent the posterior at any node k as the vector $P(X_k = M_a) \equiv P_k$ (so that P_k is a vector indexed by a), and the conditional on the arc as $P(X_j|X_i, G) \equiv P_{ji}$ (so that P_{ji} is a matrix indexed by the class index at node j and the class index at node i). Then the computation of i's prediction of the posterior at j is just the matrix vector multiply $P_{ji}P_i \doteq \sum_b (P_{ji})_{ab}(P_i)_b$. Note that all conditional matrices are also conditioned on the training data, the graph structure, and other factors, which we denote collectively by G. We emphasize that the number of classes at different nodes can differ, in which case the conditional matrices joining them will be rectangular. Note also that the P_{ji} are column stochastic matrices. Similarly we will call any vector whose components are a non-negative partition of unity a stochastic vector. Then we have the following observation.

Proposition 14.1 *Given any two stochastic vectors P_i and P_j, there always exists a conditional probability matrix P_{ij} such that $P_i = P_{ij}P_j$.*

This follows trivially from the choice $(P_{ij})_{ab} = (P_i)_a \quad \forall b$, and just corresponds to the special case that the probability vectors P_i and P_j are independent. This shows that CHM is able, in principle, to model any set of posteriors on the nodes, and that some form of regularization will therefore be needed if we expect, for example, to learn nontrivial matrices P_{ij} given a set of posteriors P_i. We will impose this regularization by partitioning the N_a arcs in the graph into a small number n of equivalence classes, where $n \ll N_a$, such that arcs in a given equivalence class are to have the same P_{ij}. In this chapter, we will use nearest-neighbor relations to determine the equivalence classes.

14.1.2   Related Work

transductive
learning

harmonic
function

Gaussian process

Zhu and Ghahramani (2002); Zhu et al. (2003b), and Zhou et al. (2004) introduce Laplacian SSL for transductive learning using graphs (see also chapter 11). Each link is given a scalar weight that measures the similarity between the data points attached to the nodes at that link's endpoints, and each node has a scalar value. The objective function is a weighted sum of squared differences in function values between pairs of nodes, with positive weights; minimizing this encourages the modeled function to vary slowly across nodes. The solution is a harmonic function (Doyle and Snell, 1984) in which each function value is the weighted sum of neighboring values. The function is thresholded to make the classification decision. In contrast to Laplacian SSL, at the solution, for nondiagonal conditional probability matrices, the CHM conditional harmonic property generates extra additive terms in the function on the nodes, which are not present in the Gaussian field solution (which is homogeneous in the function values). The two methods coincide only when the random variables at all nodes correspond to just two classes, when the conditional probability matrices in CHM are 2×2 unit matrices, where all the weights in the Gaussian random field are unity, and where all nodes are joined by directed arcs in both directions. Finally, one concrete practical difference is that CHM can handle one-sided classification problems, where training data from only one class are available, by using conditional posterior matrices other than unit matrices. In this case, the objective function in (Zhu et al., 2003b) is minimized by attaching the same label to all the unlabeled data. However, either method can handle one-sided classification problems by leveraging results from an existing one-sided classifier; we will explore this method below.

Zhu et al. (2003c) embed the label propagation work in a probabilistic framework by showing that the model can be viewed in terms of Gaussian processes. However, to establish the connection, extra assumptions and approximations are required: the inverse covariance matrix must be regularized; an extra set of unobserved random variables, which give rise to the labels via a sigmoid conditional, are introduced; and the posteriors must be approximated (the authors use the Laplace approximation). CHM, by contrast, is inherently a probabilistic model.

Directed graph models for semi-supervised learning were also considered in (Zhou et al., 2005b). However, in that work, the kinds of graphs considered were specific to a weblike application, with nodes split into hubs and authorities, and with the fundamental assumption that the similarity of two nodes in the graph is defined by their colinkage (either from parents or children). Again, the aim of the model is to require that the modeled function vary slowly across "similar" nodes, so the notion of information propagation described above does not play a direct role; the model is also not a probabilistic one. More recently, semi-supervised learning on directed graphs was also studied from a more general point of view in (Zhou et al., 2005a).

Bayes nets

Finally we emphasize the main differences between CHM and probabilistic graphical models such as Bayes nets and Markov random fields (MRFs). Belief nets and MRFs use the graph structure to encode conditional independence assumptions about the random variables in the model, whereas CHM uses the (redundant) graph structure to model both the flow of information from the training data, and the smoothness assumptions on the functions being modeled. Evaluating belief nets (for example, using belief propagation) in the presence of loops in the graph gets complicated quickly, whereas, as we shall see, CHM converges under general conditions, even in the presence of loops. However, both approaches share the fact that they are probabilistic models.

14.2 Conditional Harmonic Mixing

The structure of the CHM graph will depend on the problem at hand; however, all graphs share the weak constraint that for every[2] test node i, there must exist a path in the graph joining i with a training node. We will refer to such nodes as *label-connected*, and to the graph as a whole as label-connected if every test node in the graph is label-connected. A neighbor of a given node i is defined to be any node which is adjacent to node i, where "adjacent" means that there exists an arc from j to i.

We use the following notation: we assume that the random variable at node i has M_i states (or classes), and that the arc from node i to node j carries an $M_j \times M_i$ conditional probability matrix P_{ji}. We adopt the convention that P_{ji} is the $M_j \times M_i$ matrix of all zeros if there is no arc from node i to node j. We denote the posterior at node i by the vector $P_i \in \mathbb{R}^{M_i}$ for unlabeled nodes, and by $Q_i \in \mathbb{R}^{M_i}$ for labeled

---

2. For readability we use the indices i, j to denote the nodes themselves, since these quantities appear frequently as subscripts. We use the terms "test node" and "unlabeled node" interchangeably.

nodes. Denote the set of labeled nodes by $\mathcal{L}$, with $l \doteq |\mathcal{L}|$, and the set of unlabeled nodes by $\mathcal{U}$, with $u \doteq |\mathcal{U}|$, let $\mathcal{M}(i)$ ($\mathcal{N}(i)$) denote the set of indices of labeled (unlabeled) nodes adjacent to node i, and define $\mathcal{I} = \mathcal{M} \cup \mathcal{N}$ with $n(i) \doteq \|\mathcal{I}(i)\|$. Finally, for node i, let $p(i)$ be the number of incoming arcs from adjacent test nodes, and let $q(i)$ be the number of incoming arcs from adjacent train nodes.

14.2.1 The CHM Update Rule

A given node in the graph receives an estimate of its posterior from each of its neighbors. These estimates may not agree. Suppose that the hypothesized distribution at node i is Q_i, and let the estimates from its $n(i)$ neighbors be P_j, $j \in$

Kullback-Leibler divergence

$\mathcal{I}(i)$, so that $P_j = P_{jk} P_k$ for each $k \in \mathcal{I}(i)$. Given Q_i, the number of bits required to describe the distributions P_j is $\sum_j \{H(P_j) + D(P_j | Q_i)\}$, where H is the entropy and D the KL divergence. Since we wish to use Q_i to describe the combined distributions P_j as closely as possible, we require that this number of bits be minimized. For fixed P_j, this is accomplished by setting $(Q_i)_a = (1/n(i)) \sum_{j=1}^{n(i)} (P_j)_a$. A function on a

harmonic function

graph is called harmonic (Doyle and Snell, 1984; Zhu et al., 2003b) if at each internal node the value of the function is the (possibly weighted) mean of the values at its neighboring points (an internal node, as opposed to a boundary node, is one whose function value is not fixed; below we will just use the terms "unlabeled node" and "labeled node" for internal and boundary nodes). Assuming that a solution exists, then at the solution, the posterior at a given node is the weighted mean of the posteriors of its neighbors, where the weights are conditional probability matrices; hence the name "conditional harmonic mixing."

14.3   Learning in CHM Models

14.3.1   A Simple Model

It is useful to examine a simple model to fix ideas and to demonstrate a simple convergence proof. Consider the three-point graph shown in figure 14.2, with one labeled and two unlabeled nodes, and where to simplify the exposition we take the number of classes at each node to be C.

The consistency conditions arising from the above update rule are

$$\begin{pmatrix} -1 & \frac{1}{2}P_{12} & \frac{1}{2}P_{13} \\ \frac{1}{2}P_{21} & -1 & \frac{1}{2}P_{23} \end{pmatrix} \begin{pmatrix} P_1 \\ P_2 \\ P_3 \end{pmatrix} = 0, \tag{14.1}$$

where $P_3 = (1, 0, 0, \dots)$ and where the ones in the matrices represent unit matrices. We wish to prove four properties of these equations, for any choice of conditional probability matrices P_{23}, P_{21}, P_{12}, and P_{13}: first, that a solution always exists; second, that it is unique; third, that it results in stochastic vectors for the solution

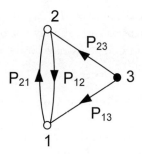

Figure 14.2   A simple three-point CHM graph.

P_2 and P_3; and fourth, that Jacobi iterates will converge to it (by solving with Jacobi iterates, we will be able to take advantage of the sparseness of larger problems, as we will see below). Rearranging, we have

$$\begin{pmatrix} 1 & -\frac{1}{2}P_{12} \\ -\frac{1}{2}P_{21} & 1 \end{pmatrix}\begin{pmatrix} P_1 \\ P_2 \end{pmatrix} = \frac{1}{2}\begin{pmatrix} P_{13}P_3 \\ P_{23}P_3 \end{pmatrix}. \tag{14.2}$$

The equations will always take this general form, where the matrix on the left is square (but not necessarily symmetric) and of side Cu, and where the left-hand side depends only on the unlabeled points (whose posteriors we wish to find) and the right, only on the labeled points. Define

$$b \doteq \frac{1}{2}\begin{pmatrix} P_{13}P_3 \\ P_{23}P_3 \end{pmatrix}, \quad M \doteq \begin{pmatrix} 1 & 0 \\ 0 & 1 \end{pmatrix}, \quad N \doteq \begin{pmatrix} 0 & \frac{1}{2}P_{12} \\ \frac{1}{2}P_{21} & 0 \end{pmatrix} \tag{14.3}$$

and consider the following iterative algorithm for finding the solution, where $x^{(0)}$ is arbitrary:

$$Mx^{(k+1)} = Nx^{(k)} + b. \tag{14.4}$$

With the above definitions, this is a Jacobi iteration (Golub and Van Loan, 1996, p. 510), and we have:

Theorem 14.2 (Golub and Van Loan (1996, Theorem 10.1.1)) *Suppose* $b \in \mathbb{R}^d$ *and* $\Delta \doteq M - N \in \mathbb{R}^{d\times d}$ *is nonsingular. If M is nonsingular and the spectral radius of $M^{-1}N$ satisfies the inequality $\rho(M^{-1}N) < 1$, then the iterates $x^{(k)}$ defined by (14.4) converge to $x = \Delta^{-1}b$ for any starting vector x.*

stochastic vectors and matrices

Since N here is one-half times a column-stochastic matrix, its eigenvalues have absolute value at most $\frac{1}{2}$, so $\rho(M^{-1}N) < 1$. Hence for this graph, a solution always exists and is unique. If we start with stochastic vectors everywhere (chosen arbitrarily on the unlabeled nodes), then they will remain stochastic since each Jacobi iterate maintains this property, and the solution will be stochastic.[3] Note

3. In fact this is true even if the initial vectors on the unlabeled nodes are chosen

also that the matrix $M - N$ is diagonally dominant, and so has an inverse. However, for the general case, N may not be proportional to a column stochastic matrix, and furthermore $M - N$ may not be diagonally dominant; we will need a more general argument.

14.3.2   A General Convergence Proof

At the CHM solution, for each node i, we have the consistency conditions

$$P_i - \frac{1}{p(i) + q(i)} \left(\sum_{j \in \mathcal{N}(i)} P_{ij} P_j \right) = \frac{1}{p(i) + q(i)} \left(\sum_{j \in \mathcal{M}(i)} P_{ij} Q_j \right), \qquad (14.5)$$

where the right-hand side is defined to be zero if $\mathcal{M}(i) = \emptyset$. Let $p = \sum_{i \in \mathcal{U}} M_i$, and define a block matrix $A \in \mathbb{R}^{p \times p}$ with ones along the diagonal and whose off-diagonal elements, which are either zero matrices or are the matrices $\frac{1}{p(i)+q(i)} P_{ij}$, are chosen so that (14.5) can be written as

$$AP = Q, \qquad (14.6)$$

where P, $Q \in \mathbb{R}^p$. Note that the right-hand side of (14.6) is determined by the training data, that all conditional probability matrices associated with unlabeled-unlabeled arcs are in A, and that all conditional probability matrices associated with labeled-unlabeled arcs are in Q. Thus (14.5) corresponds to the ith row of (14.6) and encapsulates M_i equations. Define the kth Jacobi iterate by

Jacobi iterations

$$P_i^{(k)} = \frac{1}{p(i) + q(i)} \left(\sum_{j \in \mathcal{N}(i)} P_{ij} P_j^{(k-1)} \right) + \frac{1}{p(i) + q(i)} \left(\sum_{j \in \mathcal{M}(i)} P_{ij} Q_j \right). \quad (14.7)$$

Referring to theorem 14.2, we see that in this case, $A \doteq M - N$ where $M = \mathbf{I}$ and $N_{ij} \doteq \frac{1}{p(i)+q(i)} P_{ij}$ (recall that we define P_{ij} to be the matrix of all zeros, if there is no arc from node j to node i), and b is the second term on the right-hand side of (14.7). Then the kth Jacobi iterate takes the form $MP^{(k)} = NP^{(k-1)} + b$. We can now state:

Theorem 14.3 *Consider a label-connected CHM graph with l labeled nodes. Assume that the vectors at the labeled nodes are fixed and stochastic. Then a solution to the corresponding CHM equations, (14.6), always exists and is unique. Furthermore, at the solution, the vector $P_i^* \in \mathbb{R}^{M_i}$ at the ith unlabeled node is stochastic for all i, and the Jacobi iterates on the graph will always converge to the same solution, regardless of the initial values given to the P_i.*

We present the proof in the proof-style advocated by Lamport (1993).

---

arbitrarily, by theorem 14.2, since the solution is unique.

Proof

1. **Assume: the CHM graph is label-connected.**

2. $\rho(N) < 1$.

   2.1. **Proof** Consider the eigenvalue equation:

$$N\boldsymbol{\mu} = \lambda\boldsymbol{\mu}. \tag{14.8}$$

Just as we view N as a block matrix whose ith, jth element is the matrix $\frac{1}{p(i)+q(i)}P_{ij}$, similarly view $\boldsymbol{\mu}$ as a vector whose ith element is a vector of dimension M_i. Then let $\boldsymbol{\mu}_i$ be that component of $\boldsymbol{\mu}$ whose L_1 norm is largest (or any such component if there are more than one) and consider the corresponding rows of (14.8), which encapsulates the M_i equations

$$\frac{1}{p(i)+q(i)}\left(\sum_{j\in N(i)} P_{ij}\boldsymbol{\mu}_j\right) = \lambda\boldsymbol{\mu}_i. \tag{14.9}$$

   2.1.1 **Assume:** $q(i) > 0$ and $i : \|\boldsymbol{\mu}_i\|_1 \geq \|\boldsymbol{\mu}_j\|_1 \ \forall j$.

      2.1.1.1 Since P_{ij} is column stochastic, it has unit L_1 norm. Thus

$$
\begin{aligned}
\left\|\sum_{j\in N(i)} P_{ij}\boldsymbol{\mu}_j\right\|_1 &\leq \sum_{j\in N(i)} \left\|P_{ij}\boldsymbol{\mu}_j\right\|_1 \\
&\leq \sum_{j\in N(i)} \left\|P_{ij}\right\|_1 \left\|\boldsymbol{\mu}_j\right\|_1 \\
&= \sum_{j\in N(i)} \left\|\boldsymbol{\mu}_j\right\|_1 \\
&\leq p(i)\|\boldsymbol{\mu}_i\|_1.
\end{aligned}
$$

where $\|\cdot\|_1$ denotes the L_1 norm, and where the second line follows from an inequality satisfied by all p norms (Golub and Van Loan, 1996). Since by assumption $q(i) \geq 1$, taking the L_1 norm of both sides of (14.9) gives $|\lambda| < 1$.

   2.1.2 **Assume:** $q(i) = 0$ and $i : \|\boldsymbol{\mu}_i\|_1 \geq \|\boldsymbol{\mu}_j\|_1 \ \forall j$.

      2.1.2.1 The argument of 2.1.1.1, but with $q(i) = 0$, gives $|\lambda| \leq 1$, and if $|\lambda| = 1$, then each $\boldsymbol{\mu}_j$ appearing in the sum must have L_1 norm equal to $\|\boldsymbol{\mu}_i\|_1$, since for $|\lambda| = 1$,

$$
\begin{aligned}
\|\boldsymbol{\mu}_i\|_1 &= \frac{1}{p(i)} \left\| \sum_{j \in N(i)} P_{ij} \boldsymbol{\mu}_j \right\|_1 \\
&\leq \frac{1}{p(i)} \sum_{j \in N(i)} \|P_{ij} \boldsymbol{\mu}_j\|_1 \\
&\leq \frac{1}{p(i)} \sum_{j \in N(i)} \|\boldsymbol{\mu}_j\|_1 \; \leq \; \|\boldsymbol{\mu}_i\|_1
\end{aligned}
$$

where the last step follows from the assumption that $\boldsymbol{\mu}_i$ has largest L_1 norm. Thus for each $j \in N(i)$, we can repeat the above argument with $\boldsymbol{\mu}_j$ on the right-hand side of (14.9), and the argument can then be recursively repeated for each $k \in N(j)$, until (14.9) has been constructed for every node for which a path exists to node i. However since the graph is label-connected, that set of nodes will include a test node which is adjacent to a train node. The previous argument, which assumed that $q > 0$, then shows that $|\lambda| < 1$. Thus, in general for any label-connected CHM graph, $|\lambda| < 1$, and so $\rho(N) < 1$.

3. A is nonsingular.

   3.1 **Proof** Since $\rho(N) < 1$, the eigenvalues of N all lie strictly within the unit circle centered on the origin in the complex plane $\mathbb{C}$. Since $N = \mathbf{1} - A$ (cf. (14.6)), if $\boldsymbol{e}$ is an eigenvector of A with eigenvalue λ, then it is an eigenvector of N with eigenvalue $1 - \lambda$, and so since $1 - \lambda$ lies strictly within the unit circle centered on the origin in $\mathbb{C}$, λ itself lies strictly within the unit circle centered on the point $\{1, 0\} \in \mathbb{C}$, so $\lambda \neq 0$. Hence none of A's eigenvalues vanish, and A is nonsingular.

4. A solution to the CHM equations exists and is unique.

   4.1 **Proof** Since A is nonsingular, $AP = Q$ has unique solution $P = A^{-1}Q$.

5. At the solution, the random vector $P_i \in \mathbb{R}^{M_i}$ at each unlabeled node is stochastic, regardless of its initial value.

   5.1 **Proof** For all unlabeled nodes, choose $P_i^{(0)}$ to be that stochastic vector whose first component is 1 and whose remaining components vanish. Then from (14.7), by construction $P_i^{(k)}$ is stochastic for all k. Hence from theorem 14.2 and steps 2 and 3 above, the Jacobi iterates will converge to a unique solution, and at that solution the P_i will be stochastic for all $i \in \mathcal{N}$. Finally, by theorem 14.2, the same (unique) solution will be found regardless of the initial values of the P_i.

   ∎

We emphasize the following points:

conditional
probability
matrices

1. The theorem makes no assumptions on the conditional probability matrices,

beyond the requirement that they be column stochastic. In particular, it does not assume that the conditional probability matrices on the graph are consistent, that is, that there exists a joint probability from which all conditionals (or even any subset of them) could be derived by performing appropriate marginalizations. The CHM algorithm can therefore be applied using measured estimates of the conditional probability matrices, for which no precise joint exists.

2. In general A is not symmetric (and need not be row- or column-diagonally dominant).

3. No structure is imposed on the graph beyond its being label-connected. In particular, the graph can contain loops.

4. The numbers of classes at each node can differ, in which case the conditional probability matrices will be rectangular.

5. The model handles probabilistic class labels, that is, the Q_i can be arbitrary stochastic vectors.

Gauss-Seidel
iterations

6. To improve convergence, Gauss-Seidel iterations should be used, instead of Jacobi iterations. For Gauss-Seidel iterations, the error tends to zero like $\rho(M^{-1}N)^k$ (Golub and Van Loan, 1996, p. 514).

14.4 Incorporating Prior Knowledge

Suppose that we are given the outputs of a given classifier on the data set. The classifier was trained on the available labeled examples, but the amount of training data is limited and we wish to use SSL to improve the results. We can adopt an idea proposed in (Zhu et al., 2003b), and for each node in the graph, attach an additional, labeled node, whose label is the posterior predicted for that data point. In fact CHM allows us to combine several classifiers in this way. This mechanism has the additional advantage of regularizing the CHM smoothing: the model can apply more, or less, weight to the original classifier outputs, by adjusting the conditionals on the arcs. Furthermore, for graphs that fall into several components, some of which are not label-connected, this method results in sensible predictions for the disconnected subgraphs; the CHM relaxation can be performed even for subgraphs containing no labeled data, since the base classifier still makes predictions for those

lifting

nodes. In the context of CHM, for brevity we call this procedure of leveraging a base classifier over a graph "lifting". We will explore this approach empirically below.

14.5 Learning the Conditionals

We are still faced with the problem of finding the conditional matrices P_{ij}. Here we propose one method for solving this, which we explore empirically below. Consider again the simple CHM model shown in figure 14.2, and to simplify the exposition, assume that the number of classes at each node is two, and in addition require that $P_l \doteq P_{13} = P_{23}$ and that $P_u \doteq P_{12} = P_{21}$ (l, u denoting labeled, unlabeled respectively). We can parameterize the matrices as

$$P_l = \begin{pmatrix} 1\text{-}v_1 & v_2 \\ v_1 & 1\text{-}v_2 \end{pmatrix}, \quad P_u = \begin{pmatrix} 1\text{-}v_3 & v_4 \\ v_3 & 1\text{-}v_4 \end{pmatrix}, \tag{14.10}$$

where $0 \le v_i \le 1 \ \forall i$. Now suppose that *the posteriors on every node in figure 14.2 are given*, and denote components by, e.g., $[P_{1a}, P_{1b}]$. In that case, (14.1) may be rewritten as

$$\begin{bmatrix} -P_{3a} & P_{3b} & -P_{2a} & P_{2b} \\ P_{3a} & -P_{3b} & P_{2a} & -P_{2b} \\ -P_{3a} & P_{3b} & -P_{1a} & P_{1b} \\ P_{3a} & -P_{3b} & P_{1a} & -P_{1b} \end{bmatrix} \begin{bmatrix} v_1 \\ v_2 \\ v_3 \\ v_4 \end{bmatrix} = \begin{bmatrix} 2P_{1a} - P_{2a} - P_{3a} \\ 2P_{1b} - P_{2b} - P_{3b} \\ 2P_{2a} - P_{1a} - P_{3a} \\ 2P_{2b} - P_{1b} - P_{3b} \end{bmatrix}, \tag{14.11}$$

which we summarize as $A\mathbf{v} = \mathbf{z}$. The matrix A in general need not be square, and if it is, it may be singular (as it is in this example), and even if it is nonsingular, computing $\mathbf{v}$ by inverting A is not guaranteed to give components v_i that lie in the interval $[0, 1]$. Thus instead we solve the quadratic programming problem:

$$\arg\min_{\mathbf{v}} \|A\mathbf{v} - \mathbf{z}\|^2 \quad \text{subject to} \ \ 0 \le v_i \le 1 \ \forall i. \tag{14.12}$$

The posteriors P_i can simply be the outputs of a given classifier on the problem, if the classifier outputs are well-calibrated probabilities, or thresholded vectors (whose elements are 0 or 1) for arbitrary classifiers. To summarize: given some estimate of the posteriors on every node, the conditional probability matrices on the arcs can be learned by solving a quadratic programming problem.

14.6 Model Averaging

If sufficient labeled data are available, then a validation set can be used to determine the optimal graph architecture (i.e., to which neighbors each point should connect). However, often labeled data are scarce, and in fact semi-supervised learning is really aimed at this case - that is, when labeled data are very scarce, but unlabeled data are plentiful. Thus in general for SSL methods it is highly desirable to find a way around having to use validation sets to choose either the model or its parameters. In this chapter we will use model averaging: that is, for a given graph, given a classifier, use CHM to lift its results; then do this for a variety of graphs, and simply average the posteriors assigned by CHM to each node, across all graphs. This, in combination with learning the conditionals, makes CHM a largely parameter-free approach (once a general algorithm for constructing the graphs has been chosen), although training using many graphs may be more computationally expensive than using a validation set to choose one.

14.7 Experiments

We applied CHM to the problem of text categorization, and to five of the benchmark classification tasks provided with this book.

14.7.1 Reuters-I Data Set

We applied CHM to the problem of the categorization of news articles in the Reuters-I data set (Lewis, 1997), with the ModApte split of 9603 training files and 3744 testing files. Each news article is assigned zero or more labels. Each label is considered to be an independent classification. We train and test on the ten most common labels in the data set, which generates ten separate binary classification problems.

one-sided, two-sided classification

We ran two kinds of classification experiments: one-sided (where only positive labeled examples are given), and two-sided (where labeled examples of both classes are given). The one-sided task is interesting because for some applications, it is much easier to obtain labeled data of one class than of the other, and few algorithms can handle training data that contain no examples of one of the classes. For the one-sided problem we investigated using CHM to lift the Rocchio (inductive) classifier outputs, since of the methods we considered, only the Rocchio algorithm (Rocchio, 1971) was appropriate for the one-sided task.

Rocchio algorithm

For the two-sided problem, we tested two inductive algorithms and one transductive algorithm. The two inductive algorithms were a linear support vector machine (SMV) (Dumais et al., 1998; Drucker et al., 1999) and a mixture of multinomial conditional models (Nigam et al., 2000). For the mixture model, one multinomial model is used to model positive examples, while one or more multinomial models are used to model negative examples. Expectation-maximization (EM) is used to fit the mixture model to the negative examples. Hyperparameters (C for the linear SVM and the number of negative multinomials) are set by optimizing the microaveraged F1 score for the labels for Reuters classes 11–15 on the train/test split. These hyperparameters are then used for all ten classes. We also tested the method of Nigam et al. for transduction using the multinomial mixture model (Nigam et al., 2000). In that transductive method, EM is used, not only to learn the negative mixture but also to infer the labels of the unlabeled data. Nigam et al. (2000) introduce another hyperparameter, which is the fractional weight to assign to each unlabeled case. This weight is also tuned by optimizing the microaveraged F1 score for classes 11–15.

multinomial models

For all experiments, we assume that the prior for the task is known. For the lifting arcs (i.e. those arcs joining the extra nodes carrying the classifier posteriors with the unlabeled nodes), we used unit conditional probability matrices, and we mapped the base classifier outputs to $\{0, 1\}$, both for the computation of the learned matrices, and for the CHM computation itself. We did this because the outputs of the base classifiers were far from well-calibrated probabilities (or from quantities that could be mapped to well-calibrated probabilities) as to be expected for very small training sets.

For the two-sided case, of the three algorithms used, the SVMs were found to give the highest overall accuracy, and so we investigated lifting the SVM outputs with CHM. All of these algorithms make a hard decision about whether a test point is in, or out of, a class. For all algorithms, we choose the threshold for this decision point to reproduce the true number of positives on the entire test set (the "known prior" assumption).

Note that the validation set was not used to tune the CHM model; it was used only to tune the baseline two-sided classifiers. The motivation for this is that we wish to see if CHM can be used to improve the accuracy of a given (black box) classifier, using only very limited training data.

Preprocessing, Graph Construction, and Training Data   Each document is preprocessed into a bag of words: that is, only the frequencies with which words appear in a document are used as features; the position of a word in a document is ignored. All words within the text, title, and body of the document are used, except words within the author or dateline, which are excluded. Words within an 11-word stopword list are also excluded. Every word is stemmed using the Porter stemmer (Porter, 1980), and the number of occurrences for each stem is computed for each document ("term frequency," or TF). The vector of TF values is then fed to the multinomial classifiers (which can only accept TF vectors). For all other classifiers and for constructing the CHM graph, we used TF-IDF features. Here, IDF (inverse document frequency) (Sparck-Jones, 1972) is the log of the ratio of the total number of documents to the number of documents in which a stemmed word appears. This log is multiplied by the term frequency to yield a TF-IDF feature. The TF-IDF vector for a document is then normalized to lie on the unit sphere.

bag-of-words, TF, TF-IDF

For CHM, each graph is constructed using a simple nearest-neighbor algorithm: an arc is added from node i to node j if node i is the kth nearest neighbor of node j, for all $k \leq K$, where $K \in \{1, 3, 5, 7, 9, 11, 15, 20, 25, 30, 40, 50\}$, provided node j is not itself a labeled node. The conditional probability matrices for all arcs for a given k are shared; this imposes a form of regularization on the parameters, and embodies the idea that k alone should determine the type of link joining the two nodes. Note that this results in a directed graph which in general has no undirected equivalent (that is, a pair of unlabeled nodes can have an arc going one way but not the other, and labeled nodes only have outgoing arcs). The CHM posteriors at each unlabeled node were then averaged over all twelve graphs to arrive at the prediction. We tested two CHM algorithms: first, using unit conditional probability matrices, and second, using learned matrices.

nearest neighbor

For the one-sided task, we used labeled sets of size 1, 2, 5, 10, 20, 50, and 100, for each category. For the two-sided task, we used ten times as much labeled data for each experiment (i.e. labeled sets of size 10, 20, 50, 100, 200, 500 and 1000) to further explore dependence on training set size. The two-sided training sets are shared among all classes: we ensure that at least one positive example for each of the ten classes is present in all seven of the training sets.

Results   The results are collected below. For the one-sided task, we plot F1 versus training set size, for Rocchio, Rocchio plus CHM with unit matrices, and Rocchio plus CHM for learned matrices in figure 14.3. It is interesting that, although on this task using unit conditional probability matrices gives better mean results, the learned matrices have lower variance: the results for learned matrices rarely drop below the Rocchio baseline. Results for the two-sided task are collected in tables 14.1 through 14.7, where we show results for all classifiers and for all categories, as well as the microaveraged results.

Table 14.1   F1 for top ten categories + microaverage F1, for training set size = 10

Category	Multinomial Mixture	Nigam	SVM	SVM/CHM Unit	SVM/CHM Learned
1	0.411	0.411	0.446	0.472	0.457
2	0.477	0.477	0.520	**0.603**	**0.592**
3	0.308	0.308	**0.463**	**0.520**	**0.509**
4	0.428	0.428	0.507	**0.628**	**0.538**
5	0.246	0.246	**0.466**	**0.515**	**0.482**
6	**0.249**	**0.249**	0.151	0.111	0.128
7	0.099	0.099	**0.474**	**0.478**	**0.507**
8	0.223	0.223	**0.454**	**0.504**	**0.472**
9	0.347	0.347	0.242	0.274	0.253
10	0.110	0.110	**0.233**	**0.271**	**0.233**
Microaverage	0.374	0.374	0.446	**0.491**	**0.475**

The tables give F1 on the unlabeled subsets only. To determine statistical significance, we treat F1 score as proportions (similar to (Yang and Liu, 1999)). To be conservative with our confidence intervals, we treat the number of samples in the significance test to be the denominator of the F1 score: the number of false positives plus half the number of errors. Thus, we apply a one-way unbalanced analysis of variance (ANOVA) to predict correctness of the sample, given a factor which is the algorithm used. For those experiments where a main effect is found by ANOVA to be greater than 99% significant, a post hoc test comparing all pairs of algorithms is performed (using the Tukey-Kramer correction for repeated tests). In the tables, we boldface the results that are found by the post hoc test to be better than all of the nonboldface algorithms (at a 99% confidence threshold).

For almost all experiments, the SVM gave higher F1 than the multinomial mixture or the algorithm of Nigam et al. CHM gives better results than all other methods, at a 99% confidence threshold, for the case of ten labeled points, and microaveraged over all data sets.

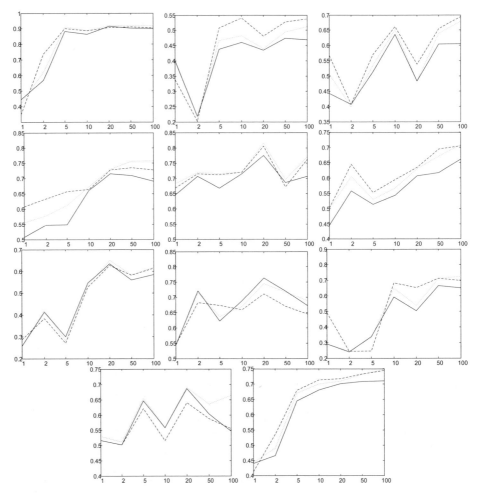

Figure 14.3 Results for the Rocchio classifiers (solid), Rocchio lifted with CHM, unit conditional matrices (dashed), and Rocchio lifted with learned conditional matrices (dotted). The y-axis is F1, the x-axis, training set size. Graphs are arranged left to right in order of increasing category. Most graphs have the y-axis range chosen to be 0.35 for comparison. The last graph (bottom right) is the microaveraged results over all ten categories.

Table 14.2 F1 for top ten categories + microaverage F1, for training set size = 20

Category	Multinomial Mixture	Nigam	SVM	SVM/CHM Unit	SVM/CHM Learned
1	0.851	0.869	**0.903**	**0.899**	**0.908**
2	0.663	**0.797**	0.704	0.723	0.735
3	0.302	**0.401**	**0.453**	**0.516**	**0.497**
4	0.555	0.571	0.572	0.653	0.609
5	0.385	0.170	**0.477**	**0.563**	**0.527**
6	**0.285**	0.153	0.148	0.103	0.126
7	0.138	0.132	**0.488**	**0.484**	**0.507**
8	0.227	0.344	**0.507**	**0.521**	**0.525**
9	**0.407**	0.063	0.228	0.270	0.249
10	0.148	0.284	0.275	0.305	0.280
Microaverage	0.614	0.639	**0.678**	**0.694**	**0.696**

Table 14.3 F1 for top ten categories + microaverage F1, for training set size = 50

Category	Multinomial Mixture	Nigam	SVM	SVM/CHM Unit	SVM/CHM Learned
1	0.906	0.917	0.935	0.914	0.923
2	0.655	**0.711**	**0.735**	**0.741**	**0.749**
3	0.438	0.410	**0.579**	**0.681**	**0.633**
4	0.493	0.512	0.585	0.661	0.626
5	0.268	0.405	**0.666**	**0.697**	**0.708**
6	0.341	0.374	**0.514**	**0.545**	**0.535**
7	0.436	0.404	0.356	0.423	0.379
8	0.394	0.298	0.468	0.532	0.493
9	0.133	**0.274**	0.256	0.288	0.270
10	0.350	0.312	0.444	0.444	0.444
Microaverage	0.652	0.677	**0.734**	**0.748**	**0.744**

Table 14.4   F1 for top ten categories + microaverage F1, for training set size = 100

Category	Multinomial Mixture	Nigam	SVM	SVM/CHM Unit	SVM/CHM Learned
1	**0.917**	0.840	**0.939**	0.912	0.921
2	0.770	**0.863**	0.798	0.777	0.791
3	0.397	**0.596**	0.535	0.599	0.559
4	0.637	0.576	0.668	0.674	0.681
5	0.494	0.606	**0.728**	0.772	0.773
6	0.350	0.333	**0.522**	0.573	0.542
7	0.485	0.471	0.571	0.579	0.573
8	0.466	0.384	**0.680**	0.658	0.673
9	0.313	0.335	**0.489**	0.641	0.595
10	0.333	0.231	0.410	0.410	0.410
Microaverage	0.712	0.715	**0.778**	0.776	0.778

Table 14.5   F1 for top ten categories + microaverage F1, for training set size = 200

Category	Multinomial Mixture	Nigam	SVM	SVM/CHM Unit	SVM/CHM Learned
1	0.921	0.925	**0.950**	0.916	0.923
2	0.799	0.777	0.829	0.817	0.826
3	0.576	0.542	0.587	0.591	0.583
4	0.586	0.628	**0.729**	0.737	0.734
5	0.618	0.533	**0.754**	0.782	0.788
6	0.496	0.463	**0.696**	0.723	0.715
7	0.574	0.493	0.642	0.552	0.595
8	0.361	0.429	**0.721**	0.721	0.729
9	0.406	0.371	0.519	0.693	0.580
10	0.275	0.352	0.421	0.421	0.421
Microaverage	0.747	0.736	**0.813**	0.801	0.804

Table 14.6 F1 for top ten categories + microaverage F1, for training set size = 500

Category	Multinomial Mixture	Nigam	SVM	SVM/CHM Unit	SVM/CHM Learned
1	0.935	0.935	**0.957**	0.920	0.930
2	0.781	0.781	**0.869**	**0.835**	**0.847**
3	0.594	0.594	**0.691**	**0.687**	**0.683**
4	0.714	0.714	**0.816**	**0.814**	**0.820**
5	0.696	0.696	**0.806**	**0.821**	**0.824**
6	0.486	0.486	**0.704**	**0.723**	**0.716**
7	0.600	0.600	0.681	0.657	0.679
8	0.565	0.565	**0.827**	**0.775**	**0.801**
9	0.693	0.693	0.704	0.715	0.726
10	0.439	0.439	0.618	0.583	0.610
Microaverage	0.781	0.781	**0.856**	**0.831**	**0.840**

Table 14.7 F1 for top ten categories + microaverage F1, for training set size = 1000

Category	Multinomial Mixture	Nigam	SVM	SVM/CHM Unit	SVM/CHM Learned
1	0.938	0.940	0.949	0.926	0.933
2	0.843	0.854	0.888	0.854	0.863
3	0.666	0.626	0.702	0.701	0.693
4	0.691	0.638	**0.859**	**0.827**	**0.833**
5	0.803	0.793	0.828	0.807	0.818
6	0.569	0.565	**0.724**	**0.716**	**0.720**
7	0.682	0.611	0.691	0.679	0.693
8	0.627	0.540	**0.841**	**0.762**	**0.802**
9	0.721	0.760	0.806	0.775	0.783
10	0.398	0.385	**0.738**	**0.719**	**0.724**
Microaverage	0.816	0.807	**0.869**	**0.844**	**0.852**

14.7.2   Benchmark Data Sets

We also applied CHM to five of the benchmark classification data sets provided with this book, namely data sets 1, 2, 4, 5, and 7. Each data set contains 1500 points, with either 10 or 100 labeled points, and comes with a 12-fold validation split: all results quoted here are microaveraged over the twelve splits. An SVM was used as the base classifier in these experiments. Given the limited amount of training data, we chose to use a linear SVM with a very high C parameter (C=1000), which was effectively a hard-margin classifier.

Preprocessing, Graph Construction, and Training Data   For each fold of each data set, we trained a linear SVM with several different preprocessing alternatives:

- Raw data — no preprocessing
- Scaling — after subtracting off the mean, scaling each feature so that they all have unit variance
- Norming — after subtracting off the mean for each feature, scaling each data point so that they all have unit L_2 norm
- Sphering — applying PCA to the raw data, and using the latent coordinates as input
- Chopping — as in sphering, but only choosing the top d latent dimensions, where d is chosen to cover 90% of the variance of the data

One of these alternatives was chosen for each fold, by minimizing a generalization bound of the resulting SVM. For each fold, we compute

$$\arg\min_i R_i^2 ||\mathbf{w}_i^2||, \tag{14.13}$$

where $\mathbf{w}_i$ is the primal weight vector from the SVM on preprocessing alternative i, and R_i is the radius of the smallest ball that contains the data (after the ith preprocessing alternative). We approximate this radius by finding the distance of the data point that is farther from the mean over the whole data set. This choosing process usually picks one preprocessing method for all folds of a data set, often choosing "norming." However, some data sets (such as data set 4), alternate between "norming" and "sphering."

We investigated a different graph construction mechanism from that used for the Reuters data. We call the algorithm "flood fill". The flood fill method was found to give similar results to the basic nearest-neighbor method, but resulted in smaller graphs, leading to faster experiments (a typical run, for a given data set, for both training set sizes, and for all 12 splits of the validation set, took approximately 50 minutes on a 3GHz machine). The Flood Fill method works as follows: choose some fixed positive integer n. Add n directed arcs from each labeled node to its nearest n unlabeled neighbors; all such arcs are assigned flavor = 1. Call the set of nodes reached in this way N_1 (where N_1 does not include the training nodes). For each node in N_1, do the same, allowing arcs to land on unlabeled nodes in N_1; assign all arcs generated in this way flavor $= 2$. At the ith iteration, arcs are allowed to fall on unlabeled nodes in N_i, but not on nodes N_j, $j < i$. The process repeats until either all nodes are reached, or until no further arcs can be added (note that graphs with disconnected pieces are allowed here). Here we smoothed (using model averaging) using values for n of 5, 9, 15, 25, and 50. The flood fill algorithm can create disconnected subgraphs, and since it is not clear how best to combine outputs of graphs with different connectedness, we simply thresholded the value at each node after each smoothing step, before taking the average.

Results We present the results in tables 14.8 through 14.11. We chose two normalizations: the "normed/sphered/chopped" normalization, using the above bound; or just using the "normed" normalization everywhere, combined with a soft-margin linear SVM classifier (C=10). As in the Reuters experiments, the prior for each data set is assumed known. The tables give accuracies on the unlabeled subsets only. We applied a two-way ANOVA to assess the statistical significance of these results, where the two factors are the fold number and the algorithm number, and the prediction of the ANOVA is the correctness of a sample. For those experiments where a main effect is found by ANOVA to be greater than a 99% significance level, a post hoc test comparing all pairs of algorithms is performed (using the Tukey-Kramer correction for repeated tests). Using a 99% ($p < 0.01$) significance level for the post hoc comparisons, we find the results shown in the tables, where again statistical significance is indicated with bold versus normal typeface; the results can be summarized as follows:

- In no case is there a statistically significant difference between the learned conditional matrices, and the unit matrices, for CHM.
- CHM beats the SVM for all conditions for data sets 1 and 2.
- For the case of data set 4, with normed-only preprocessing, and $l = 100$, SVM beats CHM.
- There is no statistically significant difference between results for data set 5.
- For data set 7, SVM beats CHM for $l = 10$, and CHM beats SVM for $l = 100$.

Discussion This work demonstrates that CHM can be used to improve the performance of the best available classifier, on several data sets, when labeled data are limited. However, the improvement is not uniform; for some data sets we observed that adding more smoothing (arcs) improved accuracy, while for others increased smoothing caused accuracy to drop. A method to accurately predict the required amount of smoothing for a given problem would boost the CHM accuracies significantly. We attempted to overcome this behavior by model averaging, that is, averaging over different graphs, but this is a crude way to address the problem. Also in this chapter we only discussed two simple heuristics for constructing the graphs;

Table 14.8   Accuracy for labeled sets of size 10, using normed/sphered/chopped preprocessing

Data Set (10)	SVM	SVM/CHM, Unit	SVM/CHM, Learned
1	0.803	**0.860**	**0.859**
2	0.751	**0.779**	**0.776**
4	0.543	0.530	0.530
5	0.605	0.613	0.612
7	**0.589**	0.567	0.566

Table 14.9   Accuracy for labeled sets of size 100, using normed/sphered/chopped preprocessing

Data Set (100)	SVM	SVM/CHM, Unit	SVM/CHM, Learned
1	0.922	**0.966**	**0.966**
2	0.788	**0.816**	**0.813**
4	0.705	0.699	0.702
5	0.747	0.755	0.756
7	0.725	**0.755**	**0.755**

Table 14.10   Accuracy for labeled sets of size 10, using normed preprocessing only

Data Set (10)	SVM	SVM/CHM, Unit	SVM/CHM, Learned
1	0.803	**0.860**	**0.859**
2	0.760	**0.799**	**0.795**
4	0.541	0.525	0.527
5	0.605	0.613	0.612
7	**0.589**	0.567	0.566

Table 14.11   Accuracy for labeled sets of size 100, using normed preprocessing only

Data Set (100)	SVM	SVM/CHM, Unit	SVM/CHM, Learned
1	0.922	**0.966**	**0.966**
2	0.870	**0.939**	**0.935**
4	**0.692**	0.600	0.613
5	0.747	0.755	0.756
7	0.725	**0.755**	**0.755**

it would be useful to explore more sophisticated methods, for example, methods that compute a local metric (see, for example, (Xing et al., 2003)). Other techniques for choosing the conditionals, for example using leave-one-out on the labeled set, or using a subgraph that is close to the labeled data, may also be fruitful to explore.

14.8   Conclusions

We have presented conditional harmonic mixing (CHM), a graphical model that can be used for semi-supervised learning. CHM combines and improves upon earlier work in semi-supervised learning in several ways. First, unlike Bayes networks, CHM can model and learn using conditional probability distributions that do not have a consistent joint. This freedom allows us to learn and infer using simple linear algebra. Second, unlike Laplacian SSL, CHM can model asymmetric influences between random variables. Indeed, our random variables can have different cardinalities: CHM is not limited to simply modeling harmonic functions. Finally, CHM can use a purely inductive algorithm to provide prior knowledge to the semi-supervised learning, which leads to superior performance on one-sided and two-sided empirical benchmarks. As the experiments show, one key open question for research is how to construct graphs that can take full advantage of semi-supervised learning with CHM: for a given data set, for some choice of graphs the improvement is significant, while for other choices of graph for the same data set, applying CHM can even reduce accuracy. This was addressed in the present work by simply using model averaging over graphs; it seems likely that better methods are possible.

Acknowledgments

We thank David Heckerman and Chris Meek for useful discussions.

IV Change of Representation

15   Graph Kernels by Spectral Transforms

Xiaojin Zhu   ZHUXJ@CS.CMU.EDU
Jaz Kandola   JKANDOLA@GATSBY.UCL.AC.UK
John Lafferty   LAFFERTY@CS.CMU.EDU
Zoubin Ghahramani   ZOUBIN@ENG.CAM.AC.UK

Many graph-based semi-supervised learning methods can be viewed as imposing smoothness conditions on the target function with respect to a graph representing the data points to be labeled. The smoothness properties of the functions are encoded in terms of Mercer kernels over the graph. The central quantity in such regularization is the spectral decomposition of the graph Laplacian, a matrix derived from the graph's edge weights. The eigenvectors with small eigenvalues are smooth, and ideally represent large cluster structures within the data. The eigenvectors having large eigenvalues are rugged, and considered noise.

Different weightings of the eigenvectors of the graph Laplacian lead to different measures of smoothness. Such weightings can be viewed as *spectral transforms*, that is, as transformations of the standard eigenspectrum that lead to different regularizers over the graph. Familiar kernels, such as the diffusion kernel resulting by solving a discrete heat equation on the graph, can be seen as simple parametric spectral transforms.

The question naturally arises whether one can obtain effective spectral transforms automatically. In this chapter we develop an approach to searching over a nonparametric family of spectral transforms by using convex optimization to maximize kernel alignment to the labeled data. Order constraints are imposed to encode a preference for smoothness with respect to the graph structure. This results in a flexible family of kernels that is more data-driven than the standard parametric spectral transforms. Our approach relies on a quadratically constrained quadratic program (QCQP), and is computationally practical for large data sets.

15.1   The Graph Laplacian

We are given a labeled data set of input-output pairs $(X_l, Y_l) = \{(x_1, y_1), \ldots, (x_l, y_l)\}$ and an unlabeled data set $X_u = \{x_{l+1}, \ldots, x_n\}$. We form a graph $\mathbf{g} = (V, E)$ where the vertices V are $x_1, \ldots, x_n$, and the edges E are represented by an $n \times n$ matrix W. Entry W_{ij} is the edge weight between nodes i, j, with $W_{ij} = 0$ if i, j are not connected. The entries of W have to be non-negative and symmetric, but it is not necessary for W itself to be positive semi-definite. Let D be the diagonal degree matrix with $D_{ii} = \sum_j W_{ij}$ being the total weight on edges con-

graph Laplacian nected to node i. The *combinatorial graph Laplacian* is defined as $L = D - W$, which is also called the unnormalized Laplacian. The *normalized graph Laplacian* is $\mathcal{L} = D^{-1/2}LD^{-1/2} = \mathbf{I} - D^{-1/2}WD^{-1/2}$.

In graph-based semi-supervised learning the Laplacian L (or $\mathcal{L}$) is a central object. Let us denote the eigenvalues of L by $\lambda_1 \leq \ldots \leq \lambda_n$, and the complete orthonormal set of eigenvectors by $\phi_1 \ldots \phi_n$. Therefore the spectral decomposition

spectral of the Laplacian is given as $L = \sum_{i=1}^{n} \lambda_i \phi_i \phi_i^\top$. We refer readers to (Chung, 1997)
decomposition for a discussion of the mathematical aspects of this decomposition, but briefly summarize two relevant properties:

Theorem 15.1 *The Laplacian L is positive semi-definite, i.e., $\lambda_i \geq 0$.*

Indeed, it is not hard to show that for any function $f : [n] \to \mathbb{R}$,

$$f^\top L f = \frac{1}{2} \sum_{i,j} W_{ij} \left(f(i) - f(j) \right)^2 \geq 0, \tag{15.1}$$

where the inequality holds because W has non-negative entries.

smoothness of f Eq. (15.1) measures the *smoothness* of f on the graph.[1] Roughly speaking, f is smooth if $f(i) \approx f(j)$ for those pairs with large W_{ij}. This is sometimes informally expressed by saying that f varies slowly over the graph, or that f follows the data manifold. In particular, the smoothness of an eigenvector is

$$\phi_i^\top L \phi_i = \lambda_i. \tag{15.2}$$

Thus, eigenvectors with smaller eigenvalues are smoother. Since $\{\phi_i\}$ forms a basis on $\mathbb{R}^n$, we can always write any function f as

$$f = \sum_{i=1}^{n} \alpha_i \phi_i \, , \alpha_i \in \mathbb{R} \tag{15.3}$$

and Eq. 15.1 which measures the smoothness of f can be re-expressed as

$$f^\top L f = \sum_{i=1}^{n} \alpha_i^2 \lambda_i. \tag{15.4}$$

---

1. Note that a smaller value means smoother f.

For semi-supervised learning a smooth function f is part of what we seek, because this is the prior knowledge encoded by the graph—but we also require that the function f fits the labels Y_l on the inputs X_l.

Theorem 15.2 *The graph* **g** *has k connected components if and only if $\lambda_i = 0$ for $i = 1, 2, \ldots, k$.*

The corresponding eigenvectors $\phi_1, \ldots, \phi_k$ of L are constant on the nodes within the corresponding connected component, and zero elsewhere. Note λ_1 is always 0 for any graph (Chung, 1997). We will make use of this property later.

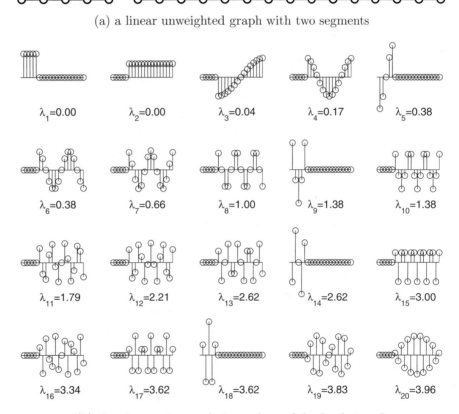

(a) a linear unweighted graph with two segments

(b) the eigenvectors and eigenvalues of the Laplacian L

Figure 15.1   A simple graph and its Laplacian spectral decomposition. Note the eigenvectors become rougher with larger eigenvalues.

As an example, figure 15.1(a) shows an unweighted graph ($W_{ij} = 1$ if there is an edge) consisting of two linear segments. The spectral decomposition of its Laplacian L is shown in (b). Note that the eigenvectors do indeed look smoother for small λ_i, and that the graph has two connected components.

15.2   Kernels by Spectral Transforms

Kernel methods are increasingly being used for classification because of their conceptual simplicity, theoretical properties, and good performance on many tasks. It is attractive to create kernels specifically for semi-supervised learning. We restrict ourselves to transduction, i.e., the unlabeled data X_u are also the test data. As a result we only need to consider kernel matrices $K \in \mathbb{R}^{n \times n}$ on nodes $1, \ldots, n$ in the graph.

In particular, we want K to respect the smoothness preferences encoded in a graph. That is, as a regularizer the kernel should penalize functions that are not smooth over the graph. To establish a link to the graph, we consider K having the form

$$K = \sum_{i=1}^{n} \mu_i \phi_i \phi_i^\top, \tag{15.5}$$

where ϕ are the eigenvectors of the graph Laplacian L, and $\mu_i \geq 0$ are the eigenvalues of K. Since K is the non-negative sum of outer products, it is positive semi-definite, i.e., a kernel matrix.

The matrix K defines a reproducing kernel Hilbert space (RKHS) with norm

$$\|f\|_K^2 = \langle f, f \rangle_K = \sum_{i=1}^{n} \frac{\alpha_i^2}{\mu_i} \tag{15.6}$$

for a function $f = \sum_{i=1}^{n} \alpha_i \phi_i$. Note if some $\mu_i = 0$ the corresponding dimension is not present in the RKHS, and we might define $\frac{1}{0} = 0$ here.

In many learning algorithms, regularization is expressed as an increasing function of $\|f\|_K$. From a semi-supervised learning point of view, we want f to be penalized if it is not smooth with respect to the graph. Comparing the smoothness of f in Eq. 15.4 with Eq. 15.6, we find this can be achieved by making μ_i small if the Laplacian eigenvalue λ_i is large, and vice versa.

Indeed, Chapelle et al. (2003) and Smola and Kondor (2003) both suggest a general principle for creating a semi-supervised kernel K from the graph Laplacian. Define a *spectral transformation* function $r : \mathbb{R}_+ \to \mathbb{R}_+$ that is non-negative and decreasing. Set the kernel spectrum by $\mu_i = r(\lambda_i)$ to obtain the kernel

spectral transformation

$$K = \sum_{i=1}^{n} r(\lambda_i) \phi_i \phi_i^\top. \tag{15.7}$$

Note that r essentially reverses the order of the eigenvalues, so that smooth ϕ_i's have larger eigenvalues in K. Since r is decreasing, a greater penalty is incurred if a function is not smooth.

The transform r is often chosen from a parametric family, resulting in some familiar kernels. For example Chapelle et al. (2003) and Smola and Kondor (2003) list the following transformations on $\mathcal{L}$:

- regularized Laplacian: $r(\lambda) = \frac{1}{\lambda + \epsilon}$
- diffusion kernel: $r(\lambda) = \exp\left(-\frac{\sigma^2}{2}\lambda\right)$
- one-step random walk: $r(\lambda) = (\alpha - \lambda)$ with $\alpha \geq 2$
- p-step random walk: $r(\lambda) = (\alpha - \lambda)^p$ with $\alpha \geq 2$
- inverse cosine: $r(\lambda) = \cos(\lambda\pi/4)$
- step function: $r(\lambda) = 1$ if $\lambda \leq \lambda_{\mathrm{cut}}$

Each has its own special interpretation. The regularized Laplacian is also known as the Gaussian field kernel (Zhu et al., 2003c). Of course there are many other natural choices for r. Although the general principle of Eq. 15.7 is appealing, it does not address the question of which parametric family to use. Moreover, the hyperparameters (e.g., σ or ϵ above) in a particular parametric family may not suit the task at hand, resulting in overly constrained kernels.

Is there an optimal spectral transformation? The following sections address this question. The short answer is yes, in a certain sense. We select a spectral transformation that optimizes kernel alignment to the labeled data, while imposing an ordering constraint but otherwise not assuming any parametric form. Kernel alignment is a surrogate for classification accuracy, and, importantly, leads to a convex optimization problem.

15.3   Kernel Alignment

The empirical kernel alignment (Cristianini et al., 2002a; Lanckriet et al., 2004a) assesses the fitness of a kernel to training labels. The alignment has a number of convenient properties: it can be efficiently computed before any training of the kernel machine takes place, and based only on training data information. The empirical alignment can also be shown to be sharply concentrated around its expected value, allowing it to be estimated from finite samples. A connection between high alignment and good generalization performance has been established in (Cristianini et al., 2002a).

Frobenius product

As we will compare matrices, we introduce here the Frobenius product $\langle .,. \rangle_F$ between two square matrices M and N of the same size:

$$\langle M, N \rangle_F = \sum_{ij} m_{ij} n_{ij} = \mathrm{Tr}(MN).$$

The *empirical kernel alignment* compares the $l \times l$ kernel matrix K_{tr} on the labeled training set $x_1, \ldots, x_l$, and a target matrix T derived from the labels $y_1, \ldots, y_l$. One such target matrix is $T_{ij} = 1$ if $y_i = y_j$, and -1 otherwise. Note for binary $\{+1, -1\}$ training labels $Y_l = (y_1 \ldots y_l)^\top$ this is simply the rank one matrix $T = Y_l Y_l^\top$. The empirical kernel alignment is defined as follows.

Definition 15.3 (empirical kernel alignment) *Let K_{tr} be the kernel matrix*

empirical kernel
alignment

restricted to the training points, and T the target matrix on training data. We define the empirical kernel alignment as

$$\hat{A}(K_{tr}, T) = \frac{\langle K_{tr}, T \rangle_F}{\sqrt{\langle K_{tr}, K_{tr} \rangle_F \langle T, T \rangle_F}}. \tag{15.8}$$

The empirical alignment is essentially the cosine between the matrices K_{tr} and T. The range of the alignment is $[0, 1]$. The larger its value the closer is the kernel to the target. This quantity is maximized when $K_{tr} \propto T$.

15.4 Optimizing Alignment Using QCQP for Semi-Supervised Learning

Having introduced the alignment quantity, now let us consider the problem of semi-supervised kernel construction using a principled nonparametric approach. In short, we will learn the spectral transformation $\{\mu_i \equiv r(\lambda_i)\}$ (15.7) by optimizing the resulting kernel alignment, with certain restrictions. Notice we no longer assume a parametric function $r()$; instead we work with the transformed eigenvalues μ_i's directly.

When the kernel matrix is defined as $K = \sum_{i=1}^{n} \mu_i \phi_i \phi_i^{\top}$ and the target T given, the kernel alignment between the labeled submatrix K_{tr} and T is a convex function in μ_i's. Nonetheless, in general we have to make sure K is a valid kernel matrix, i.e., it is positive semi-definite. This is a semi-definite program (SDP), which has high computational complexity (Boyd and Vandenberghe, 2004). We thus restrict $\mu_i \geq 0, \forall i$. This guarantees K to be positive semi-definite, and reduces the optimization problem into a *quadratically constrained quadratic program* (QCQP),

quadratically
constrained
quadratic
programs

which is computationally more efficient. In a QCQP both the objective function and the constraints are quadratic, as illustrated below:

$$\text{minimize} \qquad \frac{1}{2} x^{\top} P_0 x + q_0^{\top} x + r_0 \tag{15.9}$$

$$\text{subject to} \qquad \frac{1}{2} x^{\top} P_i x + q_i^{\top} x + r_i \leq 0 \quad i = 1 \cdots m \tag{15.10}$$

$$Ax = b, \tag{15.11}$$

where $P_i \in \mathcal{S}_+^n$, $i = 0, \ldots, m$, where $\mathcal{S}_+^n$ defines the set of square symmetric positive semi-definite matrices. In a QCQP, we minimize a convex quadratic function over a feasible region that is the intersection of ellipsoids. The number of iterations required to reach the solution is comparable to the number required for linear programs, making the approach feasible for large data sets.

Previous work using kernel alignment did not take into account that the "building blocks" $K_i = \phi_i \phi_i^{\top}$ were derived from the graph Laplacian with the goal of semi-supervised learning. As such, the μ_i's can take arbitrary non-negative values and there is no preference to penalize components that do not vary smoothly over the graph. This shall be rectified by requiring smoother eigenvectors to receive larger coefficients, as shown in the next section.

15.5   Semi-Supervised Kernels with Order Constraints

order constraints

We would like to maintain a decreasing order on the spectral transformation μ_i to reflect the prior knowledge encoded in the graph, that smooth functions are preferred. This motivates the set of *order constraints*:

$$\mu_i \geq \mu_{i+1}, \quad i = 1 \cdots n - 1. \tag{15.12}$$

And we can specify the desired semi-supervised kernel as follows:

order-constrained kernel

Definition 15.4 *(order-constrained kernel) An* order-constrained *semi-supervised kernel K is the solution to the following convex optimization problem:*

$$max_K \qquad \hat{A}(K_{tr}, T) \tag{15.13}$$
$$subject \; to \qquad K = \sum_{i=1}^{n} \mu_i K_i \tag{15.14}$$
$$\mu_i \geq 0 \tag{15.15}$$
$$\mathrm{Tr}(K) = 1 \tag{15.16}$$
$$\mu_i \geq \mu_{i+1}, \quad i = 1 \cdots n - 1, \tag{15.17}$$

where T is the training target matrix, $K_i = \phi_i \phi_i^\top$ and ϕ_i's are the eigenvectors of the graph Laplacian.

This formulation is an extension of the original kernel alignment of Lanckriet et al. (2004a), with the addition of order constraints, and with special components K_i's from the graph Laplacian. Since $\mu_i \geq 0$ and K_i's are outer products, K will automatically be positive semi-definite and hence a valid kernel matrix. The trace constraint is needed to fix the scale invariance of kernel alignment. It is important to notice the order constraints are convex and as such, definition 15.4 is a convex optimization problem.

convex optimization

The problem is equivalent to

$$\mathrm{max}_K \qquad \langle K_{tr}, T \rangle_F \tag{15.18}$$
$$subject \; to \qquad \langle K_{tr}, K_{tr} \rangle_F \leq 1 \tag{15.19}$$
$$K = \sum_{i=1}^{n} \mu_i K_i \tag{15.20}$$
$$\mu_i \geq 0 \tag{15.21}$$
$$\mu_i \geq \mu_{i+1}, \quad i = 1 \cdots n - 1, \tag{15.22}$$

where the trace constraint is replaced by (15.19) (up to a constant factor). Let $\mathrm{vec}(A)$ be the column vectorization of a matrix A. Defining

$$M = \begin{bmatrix} \mathrm{vec}(K_{1,tr}) \cdots \mathrm{vec}(K_{m,tr}) \end{bmatrix} \tag{15.23}$$

it is not hard to show that the problem can then be expressed as

$$\max_{\mu} \qquad \text{vec}(T)^\top M \mu \qquad (15.24)$$

$$\text{subject to} \qquad \|M\mu\| \leq 1 \qquad (15.25)$$

$$\mu_i \geq 0 \qquad (15.26)$$

$$\mu_i \geq \mu_{i+1}, \quad i = 1 \cdots n - 1. \qquad (15.27)$$

The objective function is linear in μ, and there is a simple cone constraint, making it a QCQP.

We can further improve the kernel. Consider a graph that has a single connected component, i.e., any node can reach any other node via one or more edges. Such graphs are common in practice. By the basic property of the Laplacian we know $\lambda_1 = 0$, and the corresponding eigenvector ϕ_i is a constant. Therefore $K_1 = \phi_i \phi_i^\top$ is a constant matrix. Such a constant matrix acts as a bias term in the graph kernel, as in (15.7). We should not constrain μ_1 as in definition 15.4, but allow the bias of the kernel to vary freely. This motivates the following definition:

bias term

improved
order-constrained
kernel

Definition 15.5 *(improved order-constrained kernel) An* improved order-constrained *semi-supervised kernel K is the solution to the same problem in definition 15.4, but the order constraints (15.17) apply only to nonconstant eigenvectors:*

$$\mu_i \geq \mu_{i+1}, \quad i = 1 \cdots n - 1, \text{ and } \phi_i \text{ not constant.} \qquad (15.28)$$

It should be pointed out that the improved order-constrained kernel is identical to the order-constrained kernel when the graph has disjoint components. This is because the first k eigenvectors are piecewise constant over the components, but not constant overall, when the graph has $k > 1$ connected components. We in fact would like to emphasize these eigenvectors because they might correspond to natural clusters in data. Thus we will still enforce the order constraints on them. The definition in (15.28) is meant to target μ_1 in *connected* graphs only. As discussed above, in this situation μ_1 is the bias term of the kernel. The only "improvement" in the improved order-constrained kernel is that we do not constrain such bias terms. As the experiments show later, this improves the quality of the kernels markedly.

In practice we do not need all n eigenvectors of the graph Laplacian, or equivalently all n K_i's. The first $m < n$ eigenvectors with the smallest eigenvalues work well empirically. Also note we could have used the fact that K_i's are from orthogonal eigenvectors ϕ_i to further simplify the expression. However, we leave it as is, making it easier to incorporate other kernel components if necessary.

maximal-
alignment
kernel

It is illustrative to compare and contrast the order-constrained semi-supervised kernels to other related kernels. We call the original kernel alignment solution in (Lanckriet et al., 2004a) a *maximal-alignment* kernel. It is the solution to definition 15.4 without the order constraints (15.17). Because it does not have the additional constraints, it maximizes kernel alignment among all spectral transformations. The hyperparameters σ and ϵ of the diffusion kernel and Gaussian field kernel (described in section 15.2) can be learned by maximizing the alignment score

different
information usage

also, although the optimization problem is not necessarily convex. These kernels use different information from the original Laplacian eigenvalues λ_i. The maximal-alignment kernels ignore λ_i altogether. The order-constrained semi-supervised kernels only use the *order* of λ_i and ignore their actual values. The diffusion and Gaussian field kernels use the actual values. In terms of the degrees of freedom in choosing the spectral transformation μ_i's, the maximal-alignment kernels are completely free. The diffusion and Gaussian field kernels are restrictive since they have an implicit parametric form and only one free parameter. The order-constrained semi-supervised kernels incorporate desirable features from both approaches.

15.6   Experimental Results

We evaluate kernels on seven data sets. The data sets and the corresponding graphs are summarized in table 15.1. *baseball-hockey, pc-mac* and *religion-atheism* are binary document categorization tasks taken from the 20-newsgroups data set. The distance measure is the cosine similarity between tf.idf vectors. *one-two, odd-even*, and *ten digits* are handwritten digits recognition tasks originally from the Cedar Buffalo binary digits database. *one-two* is digits "1" versus "2"; *odd-even* is the artificial task of classifying odd "1, 3, 5, 7, 9" versus even "0, 2, 4, 6, 8" digits, such that each class has several well-defined internal clusters; *ten digits* is 10-way classification; *isolet* is isolated spoken English alphabet recognition from the UCI repository. For these data sets we use Euclidean distance on raw features. We use 10-nearest-neighbor (10NN) unweighted graphs on all data sets except isolet which is 100NN. For all data sets, we use the smallest $m = 200$ eigenvalue and eigenvector pairs from the graph Laplacian. These values are set arbitrarily without optimizing and do not create an unfair advantage to the order-constrained kernels. For each data set we test on five different labeled set sizes. For a given labeled set size, we perform 30 random trials in which a labeled set is randomly sampled from the whole data set. All classes must be present in the labeled set. The rest is used as an unlabeled (test) set in that trial.

We compare a total of eight different types of kernels. Five are semi-supervised kernels: *improved order-constrained* kernels, *order-constrained* kernels, *Gaussian field* kernels (section 15.2), *diffusion* kernels (section 15.2), and *maximal-alignment* kernels (section 15.5). Three are standard supervised kernels, which do not use unlabeled data in kernel construction: *linear* kernels, *quadratic* kernels, and *radial basis function (RBF)* kernels.

We compute the spectral transformation for improved order-constrained kernels, order-constrained kernels, and maximal-alignment kernels by solving the QCQP using the standard solver SeDuMi/YALMIP (see (Sturm, 1999) and (Löfberg, 2004)). The hyperparameters in the Gaussian field kernels and diffusion kernels are learned with the *fminbnd()* function in Matlab to maximize kernel alignment. The bandwidth of the RBF kernels are learned using fivefold cross-validation on labeled set accuracy. Here and below we use cross-validation – it is done independent

Table 15.1   Summary of data sets

data set	instances	classes	graph
baseball-hockey	1993	2	cosine similarity 10NN unweighted
pc-mac	1943	2	cosine similarity 10NN unweighted
religion-atheism	1427	2	cosine similarity 10NN unweighted
one-two	2200	2	Euclidean 10NN unweighted
odd-even	4000	2	Euclidean 10NN unweighted
ten digits	4000	10	Euclidean 10NN unweighted
isolet	7797	26	Euclidean 100NN unweighted

of and after kernel alignment methods, to optimize a quantity not related to the proposed kernels.

We apply the eight kernels to the same support vector machine (SVM) in order to compute the accuracy on unlabeled data. For each task and kernel combination, we choose the bound on SVM slack variables C with fivefold cross-validation on labeled set accuracy. For multiclass classification we perform one-against-all and pick the class with the largest margin.

Table 15.2   Baseball vs. hockey

Training set size	semi-supervised kernels					standard kernels		
	Improved Order	Order	Gaussian Field	Diffusion	Max-align	RBF $\sigma = 200$	Linear	Quadratic
10	**95.7**±8.9	**93.9**±12.0	63.1±15.8	65.8±22.8	**93.2**±6.8	53.6±5.5	68.1±7.6	68.1±7.6
	0.90 (2)	0.69 (1)	0.35	0.44	0.95 (1)	0.11	0.29	0.23
30	**98.0**±0.2	**97.3**±2.1	91.8±9.3	59.1±17.9	96.6±2.2	69.3±11.2	78.5±8.5	77.8±10.6
	0.91 (9)	0.67 (9)	0.25	0.39	0.93 (6)	0.03	0.17	0.11
50	**97.9**±0.5	**97.8**±0.6	96.7±0.6	93.7±6.8	**97.0**±1.1	77.7±8.3	84.1±7.8	75.6±14.2
	0.89 (29)	0.63 (29)	0.22	0.36	0.90 (27)	0.02	0.15	0.09
70	**97.9**±0.3	**97.9**±0.3	96.8±0.6	**97.5**±1.4	97.2±0.8	83.9±7.2	87.5±6.5	76.1±14.9
	0.90 (68)	0.64 (64)	0.22	0.37	0.90 (46)	0.01	0.13	0.07
90	**98.0**±0.5	**98.0**±0.2	97.0±0.4	97.8±0.2	97.6±0.3	88.5±5.1	89.3±4.4	73.3±16.8
	0.89 (103)	0.63 (101)	0.21	0.36	0.89 (90)	0.01	0.12	0.06

Tables 15.2 through 15.8 list the results. There are two rows for each cell: the upper row is the average *test (unlabeled) set accuracy* with one standard deviation; the lower row is the average *training (labeled) set kernel alignment*, and in parenthesis the average *run time in seconds* for QCQP on a 2.4GHz Linux computer. Each number is averaged over 30 random trials. To assess the statistical significance of the results, we perform paired t-test on test accuracy. We highlight the best accuracy in each row, and those that cannot be distinguished from the best with paired t-test at significance level 0.05.

We find that:

- The five semi-supervised kernels tend to outperform the three standard supervised

Table 15.3   PC vs. MAC

Training set size	semi-supervised kernels					standard kernels		
	Improved Order	Order	Gaussian Field	Diffusion	Max-align	RBF $\sigma = 100$	Linear	Quadratic
10	**87.0**±5.0	**84.9**±7.2	56.4±6.2	57.8±11.5	71.1±9.7	51.6±3.4	63.0±5.1	62.3±4.2
	0.71 (1)	0.57 (1)	0.32	0.35	0.90 (1)	0.11	0.30	0.25
30	**90.3**±1.3	**89.6**±2.3	76.4±6.1	79.6±11.2	85.4±3.9	62.6±9.6	71.8±5.5	71.2±5.3
	0.68 (8)	0.49 (8)	0.19	0.23	0.74 (6)	0.03	0.18	0.13
50	**91.3**±0.9	90.5±1.7	81.1±4.6	87.5±2.8	88.4±2.1	67.8±9.0	77.6±4.8	75.7±5.4
	0.64 (31)	0.46 (31)	0.16	0.20	0.68 (25)	0.02	0.14	0.10
70	**91.5**±0.6	90.8±1.3	84.6±2.1	90.5±1.2	89.6±1.6	74.7±7.4	80.2±4.6	74.3±8.7
	0.63 (70)	0.46 (56)	0.14	0.19	0.66 (59)	0.01	0.12	0.08
90	**91.5**±0.6	**91.3**±1.3	86.3±2.3	**91.3**±1.1	90.3±1.0	79.0±6.4	82.5±4.2	79.1±7.3
	0.63 (108)	0.45 (98)	0.13	0.18	0.65 (84)	0.01	0.11	0.08

Table 15.4   Religion vs. atheism

Training set size	semi-supervised kernels					standard kernels		
	Improved Order	Order	Gaussian Field	Diffusion	Max-align	RBF $\sigma = 130$	Linear	Quadratic
10	**72.8**±11.2	70.9±10.9	55.2±5.8	60.9±10.7	60.7±7.5	55.8±5.8	60.1±7.0	61.2±4.8
	0.50 (1)	0.42 (1)	0.31	0.31	0.85 (1)	0.13	0.30	0.26
30	**84.2**±2.4	83.0±2.9	71.2±6.3	80.3±5.1	74.4±5.4	63.4±6.5	63.7±8.3	70.1±6.3
	0.38 (8)	0.31 (6)	0.20	0.22	0.60 (7)	0.05	0.18	0.15
50	**84.5**±2.3	83.5±2.5	80.4±4.1	83.5±2.7	77.4±6.1	69.3±6.5	69.4±7.0	70.7±8.5
	0.31 (28)	0.26 (23)	0.17	0.20	0.48 (27)	0.04	0.15	0.11
70	**85.7**±1.4	85.3±1.6	83.0±2.9	**85.4**±1.8	82.3±3.0	73.1±5.8	75.7±6.0	71.0±10.0
	0.29 (55)	0.25 (42)	0.16	0.19	0.43 (51)	0.03	0.13	0.10
90	**86.6**±1.3	**86.4**±1.5	84.5±2.1	**86.2**±1.6	82.8±2.6	77.7±5.1	74.6±7.6	70.0±11.5
	0.27 (86)	0.24 (92)	0.15	0.18	0.40 (85)	0.02	0.12	0.09

Table 15.5   One vs. two

Training set size	semi-supervised kernels					standard kernels		
	Improved Order	Order	Gaussian Field	Diffusion	Max-align	RBF $\sigma = 1000$	Linear	Quadratic
10	**96.2**±2.7	90.6±14.0	58.2±17.6	59.4±18.9	85.4±11.5	78.7±14.3	85.1±5.7	85.7±4.8
	0.87 (2)	0.66 (1)	0.43	0.53	0.95 (1)	0.38	0.26	0.30
20	**96.4**±2.8	**93.9**±8.7	87.0±16.0	83.2±19.8	94.5±1.6	90.4±4.6	86.0±9.4	90.9±3.7
	0.87 (3)	0.64 (4)	0.38	0.50	0.90 (3)	0.33	0.22	0.25
30	**98.2**±2.1	97.2±2.5	**98.1**±2.2	**98.1**±2.7	96.4±2.1	93.6±3.1	89.6±5.9	92.9±2.8
	0.84 (8)	0.61 (7)	0.35	0.47	0.86 (6)	0.30	0.17	0.24
40	98.3±1.9	96.5±2.4	98.9±1.8	**99.1**±1.4	96.3±2.3	94.0±2.7	91.6±6.3	94.9±2.0
	0.84 (13)	0.61 (15)	0.36	0.48	0.86 (11)	0.29	0.18	0.21
50	98.4±1.9	95.6±9.0	99.4±0.5	**99.6**±0.3	96.6±2.3	96.1±2.4	93.0±3.6	95.8±2.3
	0.83 (31)	0.60 (37)	0.35	0.46	0.84 (25)	0.28	0.17	0.20

Table 15.6   Odd vs. even

Training set size	semi-supervised kernels					standard kernels		
	Improved Order	Order	Gaussian Field	Diffusion	Max-align	RBF $\sigma = 1500$	Linear	Quadratic
10	**69.6**±6.5	**68.8**±6.1	65.5±8.9	68.4±8.5	55.7±4.4	65.0±7.0	63.1±6.9	65.4±6.5
	0.45 (1)	0.41 (1)	0.32	0.34	0.86 (1)	0.23	0.25	0.27
30	**82.4**±4.1	**82.0**±4.0	79.6±4.1	**83.0**±4.2	67.2±5.0	77.7±3.5	72.4±6.1	76.5±5.1
	0.32 (6)	0.28 (6)	0.21	0.23	0.56 (6)	0.10	0.11	0.16
50	87.6±3.5	87.5±3.4	85.9±3.8	**89.1**±2.7	76.0±5.3	81.8±2.7	74.4±9.2	81.3±3.1
	0.29 (24)	0.26 (25)	0.19	0.21	0.45 (26)	0.07	0.09	0.12
70	89.2±2.6	89.0±2.7	89.0±1.9	**90.3**±2.8	80.9±4.4	84.4±2.0	73.6±10.0	83.8±2.8
	0.27 (65)	0.24 (50)	0.17	0.20	0.39 (51)	0.06	0.07	0.12
90	**91.5**±1.5	**91.4**±1.6	90.5±1.4	**91.9**±1.7	85.4±3.1	86.1±1.8	66.1±14.8	85.5±1.6
	0.26 (94)	0.23 (97)	0.16	0.19	0.36 (88)	0.05	0.07	0.11

Table 15.7   Ten digits (10 classes)

Training set size	semi-supervised kernels					standard kernels		
	Improved Order	Order	Gaussian Field	Diffusion	Max-align	RBF $\sigma = 2000$	Linear	Quadratic
50	**76.6**±4.3	71.5±5.0	41.4±6.8	49.8±6.3	70.3±5.2	57.0±4.0	50.2±9.0	66.3±3.7
	0.47 (26)	0.21 (26)	0.15	0.16	0.51 (25)	-0.62	-0.50	-0.25
100	**84.8**±2.6	83.4±2.6	63.7±3.5	72.5±3.3	80.7±2.6	69.4±1.9	56.0±7.8	77.2±2.3
	0.47 (124)	0.17 (98)	0.12	0.13	0.49 (100)	-0.64	-0.52	-0.29
150	**86.5**±1.7	**86.4**±1.3	75.1±3.0	80.4±2.1	84.5±1.9	75.2±1.4	56.2±7.2	81.4±2.2
	0.48 (310)	0.18 (255)	0.11	0.13	0.50 (244)	-0.66	-0.53	-0.31
200	**88.1**±1.3	**88.0**±1.3	80.4±2.5	84.4±1.6	86.0±1.5	78.3±1.3	60.8±7.3	84.3±1.7
	0.47 (708)	0.16 (477)	0.10	0.11	0.49 (523)	-0.65	-0.54	-0.33
250	**89.1**±1.1	**89.3**±1.0	84.6±1.4	87.2±1.3	87.2±1.3	80.4±1.4	61.3±7.6	85.7±1.3
	0.47 (942)	0.16 (873)	0.10	0.11	0.49 (706)	-0.65	-0.54	-0.33

Table 15.8   Isolet (26 classes)

Training set size	semi-supervised kernels					standard kernels		
	Improved Order	Order	Gaussian Field	Diffusion	Max-align	RBF $\sigma = 30$	Linear	Quadratic
50	**56.0**±3.5	42.0±5.2	41.2±2.9	29.0±2.7	50.1±3.7	28.7±2.0	30.0±2.7	23.7±2.4
	0.27 (26)	0.13 (25)	0.03	0.11	0.31 (24)	-0.89	-0.80	-0.65
100	**64.6**±2.1	59.0±3.6	58.5±2.9	47.4±2.7	63.2±1.9	46.3±2.4	46.6±2.7	42.0±2.9
	0.26 (105)	0.10 (127)	-0.02	0.08	0.29 (102)	-0.90	-0.82	-0.69
150	67.6±2.6	65.2±3.0	65.4±2.6	57.2±2.7	**67.9**±2.5	57.6±1.5	57.3±1.8	53.8±2.2
	0.26 (249)	0.09 (280)	-0.05	0.07	0.27 (221)	-0.90	-0.83	-0.70
200	71.0±1.8	70.9±2.3	70.6±1.9	64.8±2.1	**72.3**±1.7	63.9±1.6	64.2±2.0	60.5±1.6
	0.26 (441)	0.08 (570)	-0.07	0.06	0.27 (423)	-0.91	-0.83	-0.72
250	71.8±2.3	73.6±1.5	73.7±1.2	69.8±1.5	**74.2**±1.5	68.8±1.5	69.5±1.7	66.2±1.4
	0.26 (709)	0.08 (836)	-0.07	0.06	0.27 (665)	-0.91	-0.84	-0.72

kernels. It shows that with properly constructed graphs, unlabeled data can help classification.

▪ The order-constrained kernel is often quite good, but the improved order-constrained kernel is even better. All the graphs on these data sets happen to be connected. Recall this is when the improved order-constrained kernel differs from the order-constrained kernel by not constraining the bias term. Obviously a flexible bias term is important for classification accuracy.

▪ Figure 15.2 shows the spectral transformation μ_i of the five semi-supervised kernels for different tasks. These are the average of the 30 trials with the largest labeled set size in each task. The x-axis is in increasing order of λ_i (the original eigenvalues of the Laplacian). The mean (thick lines) and ± 1 standard deviation (dotted lines) of only the top 50 μ_i's are plotted for clarity. The μ_i values are scaled vertically for easy comparison among kernels. As expected the maximal-alignment kernels' spectral transformation is zigzagged, diffusion's and Gaussian field's are very smooth, while (improved) order-constrained kernels are in between.

▪ The order-constrained kernels (green) have large μ_1 because of the order constraint on the constant eigenvector. Again this seems to be disadvantageous — the spectral transformation tries to balance it out by increasing the value of other μ_i's, so that the bias term K_1's relative influence is smaller. On the other hand, the improved order-constrained kernels (black) allow μ_1 to be small. As a result the rest μ_i's decay fast, which is desirable.

In summary, the improved order-constrained kernel is consistently the best among all kernels.

15.7   Conclusion

We have proposed and evaluated a novel approach for semi-supervised kernel construction using convex optimization. The method incorporates order constraints, and the resulting convex optimization problem can be solved efficiently using a QCQP. In this work the base kernels were derived from the graph Laplacian, and no parametric form for the spectral transformation was imposed, making the approach more general than previous approaches. Experiments show that the method is both computationally feasible and results in improvements in classification performance when used with support vector machines.

There are several future directions:

▪ In both order-constrained kernels and improved order-constrained kernels, we are learning a large number of parameters $\mu_1, \ldots, \mu_n$ based on l labeled examples. Usually $l \ll n$, which suggests the danger of overfitting. However, we have to consider two mitigating factors: the first is that we in practice only learn the top $m < n$ parameters and set the rest at zero; the second is that the μ's are order-constrained, which reduces the effective complexity. One interesting question

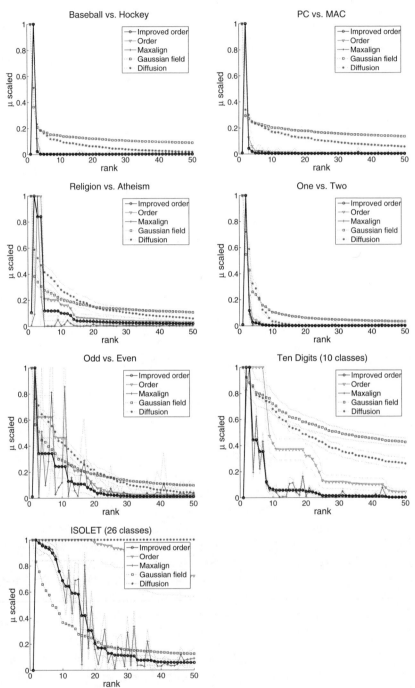

Figure 15.2   Comparison of spectral transformation for the five semi-supervised kernels.

for future research is an estimate of the effective number of parameters in these methods.

- The QCQP problem may be transformed into a standard quadratic program (QP), which may result in further improvements in computational efficiency.

- The alignment is one example of a cost function that can be optimized. With a fixed kernel, margin-based upper bounds on misclassification probability can be derived. As such, other cost functions that directly optimize quantities such as the margin can also be used. This approach has been considered in the work of Chapelle and Vapnik (2000) where the so-called span bound was introduced and optimized using gradient descent; and in (Lanckriet et al., 2004a; Bousquet and Herrmann, 2002) where optimization of tighter Rademacher complexity bounds has been proposed.

Acknowledgment

We thank Olivier Chapelle and the anonymous reviewers for their comments and suggestions.

16 Spectral Methods for Dimensionality Reduction

Lawrence K. Saul   LSAUL@CIS.UPENN.EDU
Kilian Q. Weinberger   KILIANW@SEAS.UPENN.EDU
Fei Sha   FEISHA@CIS.UPENN.EDU
Jihun Ham   JHHAM@SEAS.UPENN.EDU
Daniel D. Lee   DDLEE@SEAS.UPENN.EDU

How can we search for low-dimensional structure in high-dimensional data? If the data are mainly confined to a low-dimensional subspace, then simple linear methods can be used to discover the subspace and estimate its dimensionality. More generally, though, if the data lie on (or near) a low-dimensional submanifold, then its structure may be highly nonlinear, and linear methods are bound to fail.

Spectral methods have recently emerged as a powerful tool for nonlinear dimensionality reduction and manifold learning. These methods are able to reveal low-dimensional structure in high-dimensional data from the top or bottom eigenvectors of specially constructed matrices. To analyze data that lie on a low-dimensional submanifold, the matrices are constructed from sparse weighted graphs whose vertices represent input patterns and whose edges indicate neighborhood relations. The main computations for manifold learning are based on tractable, polynomial-time optimizations, such as shortest-path problems, least-squares fits, semi-definite programming, and matrix diagonalization. This chapter provides an overview of unsupervised learning algorithms that can be viewed as spectral methods for linear and nonlinear dimensionality reduction.

16.1 Introduction

dimensionality reduction

The problem of dimensionality reduction—extracting low-dimensional structure from high-dimensional data—arises often in machine learning and statistical pattern recognition. High-dimensional data take many different forms: from digital image libraries to gene expression microarrays, from neuronal population activities to financial time series. By formulating the problem of dimensionality reduction in a general setting, however, we can analyze many different types of data in the same underlying mathematical framework.

We therefore consider the following problem. Given a high-dimensional data set $X = (x_1, \ldots, x_n)$ of input patterns where $x_i \in \mathbb{R}^d$, how can we compute n corresponding output patterns $\psi_i \in \mathbb{R}^m$ that provide a faithful low-dimensional representation of the original data set with $m \ll d$? By "faithful," we mean generally that nearby inputs are mapped to nearby outputs, while faraway inputs are mapped to faraway outputs; we will be more precise in what follows. Ideally, an unsupervised learning algorithm should also estimate the value of m that is required for a faithful low-dimensional representation. Without loss of generality, we assume everywhere in this chapter that the inputs are centered on the origin, with $\sum_i x_i = 0 \in \mathbb{R}^d$.

inputs $x_i \in \mathbb{R}^d$

outputs $\psi_i \in \mathbb{R}^m$

This chapter provides a survey of so-called spectral methods for dimensionality reduction, where the low-dimensional representations are derived from the top or bottom eigenvectors of specially constructed matrices. The aim is not to be exhaustive, but to describe the simplest forms of a few representative algorithms using terminology and notation consistent with the other chapters in this book. At best, we can only hope to provide a snapshot of the rapidly growing literature on this subject. An excellent and somewhat more detailed survey of many of these algorithms is given by Burges (2005). In the interests of both brevity and clarity, the examples of nonlinear dimensionality reduction in this chapter were chosen specifically for their pedagogical value; more interesting applications to data sets of images, speech, and text can be found in the original papers describing each method.

spectral methods

The chapter is organized as follows. In section 16.2, we review the classical methods of principal component analysis (PCA) and metric multidimensional scaling (MDS). The outputs returned by these methods are related to the input patterns by a simple linear transformation. The remainder of the chapter focuses on the more interesting problem of nonlinear dimensionality reduction. In section 16.3, we describe several graph-based methods that can be used to analyze high-dimensional data that have been sampled from a low-dimensional submanifold. All of these graph-based methods share a similar structure—computing nearest neighbors of the input patterns, constructing a weighted graph based on these neighborhood relations, deriving a matrix from this weighted graph, and producing an embedding from the top or bottom eigenvectors of this matrix. Notwithstanding this shared structure, however, these algorithms are based on rather different geometric intuitions and intermediate computations. In section 16.4, we describe kernel-based methods for nonlinear dimensionality reduction and show how to interpret graph-based methods in this framework. Finally, in section 16.5, we conclude by contrasting the properties of different spectral methods and highlighting various ongoing lines of research. We also point out connections to related work on semi-supervised learning, as described by other authors in this book.

16.2   Linear Methods

Principal components analysis and metric multidimensional scaling are simple spectral methods for linear dimensionality reduction. As we shall see in later sections, however, the basic geometric intuitions behind PCA and metric MDS also play an important role in many algorithms for nonlinear dimensionality reduction.

16.2.1   Principal Components Analysis

PCA is based on computing the low-dimensional representation of a high-dimensional data set that most faithfully preserves its covariance structure (up to rotation). In PCA, the input patterns $x_i \in \mathbb{R}^d$ are projected into the m-dimensional subspace that minimizes the reconstruction error,

minimum
reconstruction
error

$$\mathcal{E}_{\text{PCA}} = \sum_i \left\| x_i - \sum_{\alpha=1}^{m} (x_i \cdot e_\alpha)\, e_\alpha \right\|^2, \tag{16.1}$$

where the vectors $\{e_\alpha\}_{\alpha=1}^m$ define a partial orthonormal basis of the input space. From (16.1), one can easily show that the subspace with minimum reconstruction error is also the subspace with maximum variance. The basis vectors of this subspace are given by the top m eigenvectors of the $d \times d$ covariance matrix,

covariance
matrix

$$C = \frac{1}{n} \sum_i x_i x_i^\top, \tag{16.2}$$

assuming that the input patterns x_i are centered on the origin. The outputs of PCA are simply the coordinates of the input patterns in this subspace, using the directions specified by these eigenvectors as the principal axes. Identifying e_α as the αth top eigenvector of the covariance matrix, the output $\psi_i \in \mathbb{R}^m$ for the input pattern $x_i \in \mathbb{R}^d$ has elements $\psi_{i\alpha} = x_i \cdot e_\alpha$. The eigenvalues of the covariance matrix in Eq. 16.2 measure the projected variance of the high-dimensional data set along the principal axes. Thus, the number of significant eigenvalues measures the dimensionality of the subspace that contains most of the data's variance, and a prominent gap in the eigenvalue spectrum indicates that the data are mainly confined to a lower-dimensional subspace. Figure 16.1 shows the results of PCA applied to a toy data set in which the inputs lie within a thin slab of three-dimensional space. Here, a simple linear projection reveals the data's low-dimensional (essentially planar) structure. More details on PCA can be found in (Jolliffe, 1986). We shall see in section 16.3.2 that the idea of reducing dimensionality by maximizing variance is also useful for nonlinear dimensionality reduction.

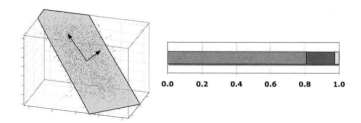

Figure 16.1   Results of PCA applied to $n = 1600$ input patterns in $d = 3$ dimensions that lie within a thin slab. The top two eigenvectors of the covariance matrix, denoted by black arrows, indicate the $m = 2$ dimensional subspace of maximum variance. The eigenvalues of the covariance matrix are shown normalized by their sum: each eigenvalue is indicated by a colored bar whose length reflects its partial contribution to the overall trace of the covariance matrix. There are two dominant eigenvalues, indicating that the data are very nearly confined to a plane.

16.2.2   Metric Multidimensional Scaling

Metric MDS is based on computing the low-dimensional representation of a high-dimensional data set that most faithfully preserves the inner products between different input patterns. The outputs $\psi_i \in \mathbb{R}^m$ of metric MDS are chosen to minimize:

$$\mathcal{E}_{\mathrm{MDS}} = \sum_{ij} (x_i \cdot x_j - \psi_i \cdot \psi_j)^2. \tag{16.3}$$

The minimum error solution is obtained from the spectral decomposition of the Gram matrix of inner products,

Gram matrix

$$G_{ij} = x_i \cdot x_j. \tag{16.4}$$

Denoting the top m eigenvectors of this Gram matrix by $\{v_\alpha\}_{\alpha=1}^m$ and their respective eigenvalues by $\{\lambda_\alpha\}_{\alpha=1}^m$, the outputs of MDS are given by $\psi_{i\alpha} = \sqrt{\lambda_\alpha}v_{\alpha i}$.

distance preservation

Though MDS is designed to preserve inner products, it is often motivated by the idea of preserving pairwise distances. Let $S_{ij} = \|x_i - x_j\|^2$ denote the matrix of squared pairwise distances between input patterns. Often the input to MDS is specified in this form. Assuming that the inputs are centered on the origin, a Gram matrix consistent with these squared distances can be derived from the transformation $G = -\frac{1}{2}(I - uu^\top)S(I - uu^\top)$, where I is the $n \times n$ identity matrix and $u = \frac{1}{\sqrt{n}}(1, 1, \ldots, 1)^\top$ is the uniform vector of unit length. More details on MDS can be found in (Cox and Cox, 1994).

Though based on a somewhat different geometric intuition, metric MDS yields the same outputs $\psi_i \in \mathbb{R}^m$ as PCA—essentially a rotation of the inputs followed by a projection into the subspace with the highest variance. (The outputs of both algorithms are invariant to global rotations of the input patterns.) The Gram matrix of metric MDS has the same rank and eigenvalues up to a constant factor as the covariance matrix of PCA. In particular, letting X denote the $d \times n$ matrix of input patterns, then $C = n^{-1}XX^\top$ and $G = X^\top X$, and the equivalence follows from singular value decomposition. In both matrices, a large gap between the mth and $(m + 1)$th eigenvalues indicates that the high-dimensional input patterns lie to a good approximation in a lower-dimensional subspace of dimensionality m. As we shall see in sections 16.3.1 and 16.4.1, useful nonlinear generalizations of metric MDS are obtained by substituting generalized pairwise distances and inner products in place of Euclidean measurements.

16.3   Graph-Based Methods

Linear methods such as PCA and metric MDS generate faithful low-dimensional representations when the high-dimensional input patterns are mainly confined to a low-dimensional subspace. If the input patterns are distributed more or less throughout this subspace, the eigenvalue spectra from these methods also reveal the data set's intrinsic dimensionality—that is to say, the number of underlying modes of variability. A more interesting case arises, however, when the input patterns lie on or near a low-dimensional submanifold of the input space. In this case, the structure of the data set may be highly nonlinear, and linear methods are bound to fail.

Graph-based methods have recently emerged as a powerful tool for analyzing high-dimensional data that have been sampled from a low-dimensional submanifold. These methods begin by constructing a sparse graph in which the nodes represent input patterns and the edges represent neighborhood relations. The resulting graph (assuming, for simplicity, that it is connected) can be viewed as a discretized approximation of the submanifold sampled by the input patterns. From these graphs, one can then construct matrices whose spectral decompositions reveal the low-dimensional structure of the submanifold (and sometimes even the dimensionality itself). Though capable of revealing highly nonlinear structure, graph-based methods for manifold learning are based on highly tractable (i.e., polynomial-time) optimizations such as shortest-path problems, least-squares fits, semidefinite programming, and matrix diagonalization. In what follows, we review four broadly representative graph-based algorithms for manifold learning: Isomap (Tenenbaum et al., 2000), maximum variance unfolding (Weinberger and Saul, 2004; Sun et al., 2006), locally linear embedding (Roweis and Saul, 2000; Saul and Roweis, 2003), and Laplacian eigenmaps (Belkin and Niyogi, 2003a).

16.3.1   Isomap

Isomap is based on computing the low-dimensional representation of a high-dimensional data set that most faithfully preserves the pairwise distances between input patterns *as measured along the submanifold from which they were sampled.* The algorithm can be understood as a variant of MDS in which estimates of geodesic

geodesic
distances

distances along the submanifold are substituted for standard Euclidean distances. Figure 16.2 illustrates the difference between these two types of distances for input patterns sampled from a Swiss roll.

The algorithm has three steps. The first step is to compute the k-nearest neighbors of each input pattern and to construct a graph whose vertices represent input patterns and whose (undirected) edges connect k-nearest neighbors. The edges are then assigned weights based on the Euclidean distance between nearest neighbors. The second step is to compute the pairwise distances Δ_{ij} between all nodes (i,j) along shortest paths through the graph. This can be done using Djikstra's algorithm which scales as $O(n^2 \log n + n^2 k)$. Finally, in the third step, the pairwise distances Δ_{ij} from Djikstra's algorithm are fed as input to MDS, as described in section 16.2.2, yielding low-dimensional outputs $\psi_i \in \mathbb{R}^m$ for which $\|\psi_i - \psi_j\|^2 \approx \Delta_{ij}^2$. The value of m required for a faithful low-dimensional representation can be estimated by the number of significant eigenvalues in the Gram matrix constructed by MDS.

When it succeeds, Isomap yields a low-dimensional representation in which the Euclidean distances between outputs match the geodesic distances between input patterns on the submanifold from which they were sampled. Moreover, there are formal guarantees of convergence (Tenenbaum et al., 2000; Donoho and Grimes, 2002) when the input patterns are sampled from a submanifold that is isometric to a convex subset of Euclidean space—that is, if the data set has no "holes." This condition will be discussed further in section 16.5.

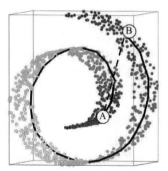 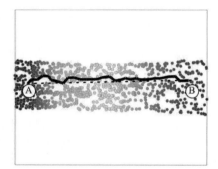

Figure 16.2 *(Left)* Comparison of Euclidean and geodesic distance between two input patterns A and B sampled from a Swiss roll. Euclidean distance is measured along the straight line in input space from A to B; geodesic distance is estimated by the shortest path (in bold) that only directly connects $k = 12$ nearest neighbors. *(Right)* The low-dimensional representation computed by Isomap for $n = 1024$ inputs sampled from a Swiss roll. The Euclidean distances between outputs match the geodesic distances between inputs.

16.3.2   Maximum Variance Unfolding

Maximum variance unfolding (Weinberger and Saul, 2004; Sun et al., 2006) is based on computing the low-dimensional representation of a high-dimensional data set that most faithfully preserves the distances and angles between *nearby* input patterns. Like Isomap, it appeals to the notion of isometry and constructs a Gram matrix whose top eigenvectors yield a low-dimensional representation of the data set; unlike Isomap, however, it does not involve the estimation of geodesic distances. Instead, the algorithm attempts to "unfold" a data set by pulling the input patterns apart as far as possible subject to distance constraints that ensure that the final transformation from input patterns to outputs looks *locally* like a rotation plus translation. To picture such a transformation from $d = 3$ to $m = 2$ dimensions, one can imagine a flag being unfurled by pulling on its four corners (but not so hard as to introduce any tears).

The first step of the algorithm is to compute the k-nearest neighbors of each input pattern. A neighborhood-indicator matrix is defined as $\eta_{ij} = 1$ if and only if the input patterns x_i and x_j are k-nearest neighbors or if there exists another input pattern of which both are k-nearest neighbors; otherwise $\eta_{ij} = 0$. The constraints to preserve distances and angles between k-nearest neighbors can be written as

$$\|\psi_i - \psi_j\|^2 = \|x_i - x_j\|^2 \tag{16.5}$$

for all (i, j) such that $\eta_{ij} = 1$. To eliminate a translational degree of freedom in the low-dimensional representation, the outputs are also constrained to be centered on the origin:

$$\sum_i \psi_i = 0 \in \mathbb{R}^m. \tag{16.6}$$

Finally, the algorithm attempts to "unfold" the input patterns by maximizing the variance of the outputs,

$$\mathrm{var}(\psi) = \sum_i \|\psi_i\|^2, \tag{16.7}$$

while preserving local distances and angles, as in (16.5). Figure 16.3 illustrates the connection between maximizing variance and reducing dimensionality.

The above optimization can be reformulated as an instance of semi-definite programming (Vandenberghe and Boyd, 1996). A semi-definite program is a linear program with the additional constraint that a matrix whose elements are linear semi-definite programming in the optimization variables must be positive semi-definite. Let $K_{ij} = \psi_i \cdot \psi_j$ denote the Gram matrix of the outputs. The constraints in Eqs. 16.5–16.7 can be written entirely in terms of the elements of this matrix. Maximizing the variance of the outputs subject to these constraints turns out to be a useful surrogate for minimizing the rank of the Gram matrix (which is computationally less tractable). The Gram matrix K of the "unfolded" input patterns is obtained by solving the semi-definite program:

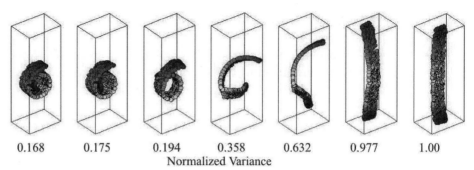

| 0.168 | 0.175 | 0.194 | 0.358 | 0.632 | 0.977 | 1.00 |

Normalized Variance

Figure 16.3 Input patterns sampled from a Swiss roll are "unfolded" by maximizing their variance subject to constraints that preserve local distances and angles. The middle snapshots show various feasible (but nonoptimal) intermediate solutions of the optimization described in section 16.3.2.

Maximize trace(K) subject to:

1) $K \succeq 0$

2) $\Sigma_{ij} K_{ij} = 0$

3) $K_{ii} - 2K_{ij} + K_{jj} = \|\|x_i - x_j\|\|^2$ **for all (i, j) such that $\eta_{ij} = 1$**

The first constraint indicates that the matrix K is required to be positive semi-definite. As in MDS and Isomap, the outputs are derived from the eigenvalues and eigenvectors of this Gram matrix, and the dimensionality of the underlying submanifold (i.e., the value of m) is suggested by the number of significant eigenvalues.

16.3.3 Locally Linear Embedding (LLE)

LLE is based on computing the low-dimensional representation of a high-dimensional data set that most faithfully preserves the local linear structure of nearby input patterns (Roweis and Saul, 2000). The algorithm differs significantly from Isomap and maximum variance unfolding in that its outputs are derived from the bottom eigenvectors of a sparse matrix, as opposed to the top eigenvectors of a (dense) Gram matrix.

The algorithm has three steps. The first step, as usual, is to compute the k-nearest neighbors of each high-dimensional input pattern x_i. In LLE, however, one constructs a *directed* graph whose edges indicate nearest-neighbor relations (which may or may not be symmetric). The second step of the algorithm assigns weights W_{ij} to the edges in this graph. Here, LLE appeals to the intuition that each input pattern and its k-nearest neighbors can be viewed as samples from a small linear "patch" on a low-dimensional submanifold. Weights W_{ij} are computed by reconstructing each input pattern x_i from its k-nearest neighbors. Specifically, they are chosen to minimize the reconstruction error:

local linear
reconstructions

$$\mathcal{E}_W = \sum_i \left\|\left| x_i - \sum_j W_{ij} x_j \right\|\right|^2 . \tag{16.8}$$

The minimization is performed subject to two constraints: (i) $W_{ij} = 0$ if x_j is not among the k-nearest neighbors of x_i; (ii) $\sum_j W_{ij} = 1$ for all i. (A regularizer can also be added to the reconstruction error if its minimum is not otherwise well defined.) The weights thus constitute a sparse matrix W that encodes local geometric properties of the data set by specifying the relation of each input pattern x_i to its k-nearest neighbors.

In the third step, LLE derives outputs $\psi_i \in \mathbb{R}^m$ that respect (as faithfully as possible) these same relations to their k-nearest neighbors. Specifically, the outputs are chosen to minimize the cost function:

$$\mathcal{E}_\psi = \sum_i \left\| \psi_i - \sum_j W_{ij}\psi_j \right\|^2 . \tag{16.9}$$

sparse eigenvalue problem

The minimization is performed subject to two constraints that prevent degenerate solutions: (i) the outputs are centered, $\sum_i \psi_i = 0 \in \mathbb{R}^m$, and (ii) the outputs have unit covariance matrix. The d-dimensional embedding that minimizes (16.9) subject to these constraints is obtained by computing the bottom $m+1$ eigenvectors of the matrix $(I-W)^\top(I-W)$. The bottom (constant) eigenvector is discarded, and the remaining m eigenvectors (each of size n) then yield the low-dimensional outputs $\psi_i \in \mathcal{R}^m$. Unlike the top eigenvalues of the Gram matrices in Isomap and maximum variance unfolding, the bottom eigenvalues of the matrix $(I-W)^\top(I-W)$ in LLE do not have a telltale gap that indicates the dimensionality of the underlying manifold. Thus the LLE algorithm has two free parameters: the number of nearest neighbors k and the target dimensionality m.

Figure 16.4 illustrates one particular intuition behind LLE. The leftmost panel shows $n = 2000$ inputs sampled from a Swiss roll, while the rightmost panel shows the two-dimensional representation discovered by LLE, obtained by minimizing Eq. 16.9 subject to centering and orthogonality constraints. The middle panels show the results of minimizing Eq. 16.9 *without centering and orthogonality constraints*, but with $\ell < n$ randomly chosen outputs constrained to be equal to their corresponding inputs. Note that in these middle panels, the outputs have the same dimensionality as the inputs. Thus, the goal of the optimization in the middle panels is not dimensionality reduction; rather, it is locally linear reconstruction of the entire data set from a small subsample. For sufficiently large ℓ, this alternative optimization is well posed, and minimizing Eq. 16.9 over the remaining $n - \ell$ outputs is done by solving a simple least-squares problem. For $\ell = n$, the outputs of this optimization are equal to the original inputs; for smaller ℓ, they resemble the inputs, but with slight errors due to the linear nature of the reconstructions; finally, as ℓ is decreased further, the outputs provide an increasingly linearized representation of the original data set. LLE (shown in the rightmost panel) can be viewed as a limit of this procedure as $\ell \to 0$, with none of the outputs clamped to the inputs, but with other constraints imposed to ensure that the optimization is well defined.

Figure 16.4   Intuition behind LLE. *(Left)* $n = 2000$ input patterns sampled from a Swiss roll. *(Middle)* Results of minimizing of (16.9) with $k = 20$ nearest neighbors and $\ell = 25$, $\ell = 15$, and $\ell = 10$ randomly chosen outputs (indicated by black landmarks) clamped to the locations of their corresponding inputs. *(Right)* Two-dimensional representation obtained by minimizing Eq. 16.9 with no outputs clamped to inputs, but subject to the centering and orthogonality constraints of LLE.

16.3.4   Laplacian Eigenmaps

Laplacian eigenmaps are based on computing the low-dimensional representation of a high-dimensional data set that most faithfully preserves proximity relations, mapping nearby input patterns to nearby outputs. The algorithm has a similar structure as LLE. First, one computes the k-nearest neighbors of each high-dimensional input pattern x_i and constructs the symmetric undirected graph whose n nodes represent input patterns and whose edges indicate neighborhood relations (in either direction). Second, one assigns positive weights W_{ij} to the edges of this graph; typically, the values of the weights are either chosen to be constant, say $W_{ij} = 1/k$, or exponentially decaying, as $W_{ij} = \exp(-\|x_i - x_j\|^2 / \sigma^2)$ where σ^2 is a scale parameter. Let $\mathbf{D}$ denote the diagonal matrix with elements $D_{ii} = \sum_j W_{ij}$. In the third step of the algorithm, one obtains the outputs $\psi_i \in \mathbb{R}^m$ by minimizing the cost function:

$$\mathcal{E}_{\mathcal{L}} = \sum_{ij} \frac{W_{ij} \|\psi_i - \psi_j\|^2}{\sqrt{D_{ii} D_{jj}}}. \tag{16.10}$$

proximity-
preserving
embedding

This cost function encourages nearby input patterns to be mapped to nearby outputs, with "nearness" measured by the weight matrix $\mathbf{W}$. As in LLE, the minimization is performed subject to constraints that the outputs are centered and have unit covariance. The minimum of Eq. 16.10 is computed from the bottom $m+1$ eigenvectors of the matrix $\mathcal{L} = I - \mathbf{D}^{-\frac{1}{2}} \mathbf{W} \mathbf{D}^{-\frac{1}{2}}$. The matrix $\mathcal{L}$ is a symmetrized, normalized form of the graph Laplacian, given by $\mathbf{D} - \mathbf{W}$. As in LLE, the bottom (constant) eigenvector is discarded, and the remaining m eigenvectors (each of size n) yield the low-dimensional outputs $\psi_i \in \mathcal{R}^m$. Again, the optimization is a sparse eigenvalue problem that scales relatively well to large data sets.

16.4   Kernel Methods

Suppose we are given a real-valued function $k : \mathbb{R}^d \times \mathbb{R}^d \to \mathbb{R}$ with the property that there exists a map $\Phi : \mathbb{R}^d \to \mathcal{H}$ into a dot product "feature" space $\mathcal{H}$ such that for all $x, x' \in \mathbb{R}^d$, we have $\Phi(x) \cdot \Phi(x') = k(x, x')$. The kernel function $k(x, x')$ can be viewed as a nonlinear similarity measure. Examples of kernel functions that satisfy the above criteria include the polynomial kernels $k(x, x') = (1 + x \cdot x')^p$ for positive integers p and the Gaussian kernels $k(x, x') = \exp(-\|x - x'\|^2/\sigma^2)$. Many linear methods in statistical learning can be generalized to nonlinear settings by employing the so-called kernel trick — namely, substituting these generalized dot products in feature space for Euclidean dot products in the space of input patterns (Schölkopf and Smola, 2002). In section 16.4.1, we review the nonlinear generalization of PCA (Schölkopf et al., 1998) obtained in this way, and in section 16.4.2, we discuss the relation between kernel PCA and the manifold learning algorithms of section 16.3. Our treatment closely follows that of Ham et al. (2004).

16.4.1   Kernel PCA

Given input patterns $(x_1, \ldots, x_n)$ where $x_i \in \mathbb{R}^d$, kernel PCA computes the principal components of the feature vectors $(\Phi(x_1), \ldots, \Phi(x_n))$, where $\Phi(x_i) \in \mathcal{H}$. Since in general $\mathcal{H}$ may be infinite-dimensional, we cannot explicitly construct the covariance matrix in feature space; instead we must reformulate the problem so that it can be solved in terms of the kernel function $k(x, x')$. Assuming that the data have zero mean in the feature space $\mathcal{H}$, its covariance matrix is given by

$$\mathbf{C} = \frac{1}{n} \sum_{i=1}^{n} \Phi(x_i)\Phi(x_i)^\top. \tag{16.11}$$

To find the top eigenvectors of $\mathbf{C}$, we can exploit the duality of PCA and MDS mentioned earlier in section 16.2.2. Observe that all solutions to $\mathbf{C}\mathbf{e} = \nu\mathbf{e}$ with $\nu \neq 0$ must lie in the span of $(\Phi(x_1), \ldots, \Phi(x_n))$. Expanding the αth eigenvector as $e_\alpha = \sum_i v_{\alpha i} \Phi(x_i)$ and substituting this expansion into the eigenvalue equation, we obtain a dual eigenvalue problem for the coefficients $v_{\alpha i}$, given by $K v_\alpha = \lambda_\alpha v_\alpha$, where $\lambda_\alpha = n\nu_\alpha$ and $K_{ij} = k(x_i, x_j)$ is the so-called kernel matrix—that is, the Gram matrix in feature space. We can thus interpret kernel PCA as a nonlinear version of MDS that results from substituting generalized dot products in feature space for Euclidean dot products in input space (Williams, 2001). Following the prescription for MDS in section 16.2.2, we compute the top m eigenvalues and eigenvectors of the kernel matrix. The low-dimensional outputs $\psi_i \in \mathbb{R}^m$ of kernel PCA (or equivalently, kernel MDS) are then given by $\psi_{i\alpha} = \sqrt{\lambda_\alpha} v_{\alpha i}$.

One modification to the above procedure often arises in practice. In (16.11), we have assumed that the feature vectors in $\mathcal{H}$ have zero mean. In general, we cannot assume this, and therefore we need to subtract the mean $(1/n) \sum_i \Phi(x_i)$ from each feature vector before computing the covariance matrix in (16.11). This leads to a

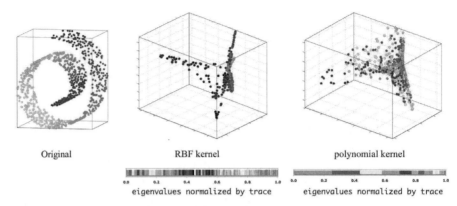

Figure 16.5 Results of kernel PCA with Gaussian and polynomial kernels applied to $n = 1024$ input patterns sampled from a Swiss roll. These kernels do not lead to low-dimensional representations that unfold the Swiss roll.

slightly different eigenvalue problem, where we diagonalize $K' = (I - uu^\top)K(I - uu^\top)$ rather than K, where $u = \frac{1}{\sqrt{n}}(1, \ldots, 1)^\top$.

Kernel PCA is often used for nonlinear dimensionality reduction with polynomial or Gaussian kernels. It is important to realize, however, that these generic kernels are not particularly well suited to manifold learning, as described in section 16.3. Figure 16.5 shows the results of kernel PCA with polynomial ($p = 4$) and Gaussian kernels applied to $n = 1024$ input patterns sampled from a Swiss roll. In neither case do the top two eigenvectors of the kernel matrix yield a faithful low-dimensional representation of the original input patterns, nor do the eigenvalue spectra suggest that the input patterns were sampled from a two-dimensional submanifold.

16.4.2   Graph-Based Kernels

All of the algorithms in section 16.3 can be viewed as instances of kernel PCA, with kernel matrices that are derived from sparse weighted graphs rather than a predefined kernel function (Ham et al., 2004). Often these kernels are described as "data-dependent" kernels, because they are derived from graphs that encode the neighborhood relations of the input patterns in the training set. These kernel matrices may also be useful for other tasks in machine learning besides dimensionality reduction, such as classification and nonlinear regression (Belkin et al., 2004b). In this section, we discuss how to interpret the matrices of graph-based spectral methods as kernel matrices.

The Isomap algorithm in section 16.3.1 computes a low-dimensional embedding by computing shortest paths through a graph and processing the resulting distances by MDS. The Gram matrix constructed by MDS from these geodesic distances can be viewed as a kernel matrix. For finite data sets, however, this matrix is not guaranteed to be positive semi-definite. It should therefore be projected onto the cone of positive semi-definite matrices before it is used as a kernel matrix in other settings.

Maximum variance unfolding in section 16.3.2 is based on learning a Gram matrix by semi-definite programming. The resulting Gram matrix can be viewed as a kernel matrix. In fact, this line of work was partly inspired by earlier work that used semi-definite programming to learn a kernel matrix for classification in support vector machines (Lanckriet et al., 2004a).

The algorithms in sections 16.3.3 and 16.3.4 do not explicitly construct a Gram matrix, but the matrices that they diagonalize can be related to operators on graphs and interpreted as "inverse" kernel matrices. For example, the discrete graph Laplacian arises in the description of diffusion on graphs and can be related to Green's functions and heat kernels in this way (Kondor and Lafferty, 2002; Coifman et al., 2005). In particular, recall that in Laplacian eigenmaps, low-dimensional representations are derived from the bottom (nonconstant) eigenvectors of the graph Laplacian L. These bottom eigenvectors are equal to the top eigenvectors of the pseudoinverse of the Laplacian, $L^\dagger$, which can thus be viewed as a (centered) kernel matrix for kernel PCA. Moreover, viewing the elements $L_{ij}^\dagger$ as inner products, the squared distances defined by $L_{ii}^\dagger + L_{jj}^\dagger - L_{ij}^\dagger - L_{ji}^\dagger$ are in fact proportional to the round-trip commute times of the continuous-time Markov chain with transition rate matrix L. The commute times are non-negative, symmetric, and satisfy the triangle inequality; thus, Laplacian eigenmaps can alternately be viewed as MDS on the metric induced by these graph commute times. (A slight difference is that the outputs of Laplacian eigenmaps are normalized to have unit covariance, whereas in MDS the scale of each dimension would be determined by the corresponding eigenvalue of $L^\dagger$.)

The matrix diagonalized by LLE can also be interpreted as an operator on graphs, whose pseudoinverse corresponds to a kernel matrix. The operator does not generate a simple diffusive process, but in certain cases, it acts similarly to the square of the graph Laplacian (Ham et al., 2004).

The above analysis provides some insight into the differences between Isomap, maximum variance unfolding, Laplacian eigenmaps, and LLE. The metrics induced by Isomap and maximum variance unfolding are related to geodesic and local distances, respectively, on the submanifold from which the input patterns are sampled. On the other hand, the metric induced by the graph Laplacian is related to the commute times of Markov chains; these times involve all the connecting paths between two nodes on a graph, not just the shortest one. The kernel matrix induced by LLE is roughly analogous to the square of the kernel matrix induced by the graph Laplacian. In many applications, the kernel matrices in Isomap and maximum variance unfolding have telltale gaps in their eigenvalue spectra that indicate the dimensionality of the underlying submanifold from which the data were sampled. On the other hand, those from Laplacian eigenmaps and LLE do not reflect the geometry of the submanifold in this way.

16.5   Discussion

Each of the spectral methods for nonlinear dimensionality reduction has its own advantages and disadvantages. Some of the differences between the algorithms have been studied in formal theoretical frameworks, while others have simply emerged over time from empirical studies. We conclude by briefly contrasting the statistical, geometrical, and computational properties of different spectral methods and describing how these differences often play out in practice.

theoretical guarantees

Most theoretical work has focused on the behavior of these methods in the limit $n \to \infty$ of large sample size. In this limit, if the input patterns are sampled from a submanifold of $\mathbb{R}^d$ that is isometric to a convex subset of Euclidean space—that is, if the data set contains no "holes"—then the Isomap algorithm from section 16.3.1 will recover this subset up to a rigid motion (Tenenbaum et al., 2000). Many image manifolds generated by translations, rotations, and articulations can be shown to fit into this framework (Donoho and Grimes, 2002). A variant of LLE known as Hessian LLE has also been developed with even broader guarantees (Donoho and Grimes, 2003). Hessian LLE asymptotically recovers the low-dimensional parameterization (up to rigid motion) of any high-dimensional data set whose underlying submanifold is isometric to an open, connected subset of Euclidean space; unlike Isomap, the subset is not required to be convex.

The asymptotic convergence of maximum variance unfolding has not been studied in a formal setting. Unlike Isomap, however, the solutions from maximum variance unfolding in section 16.3.2 are guaranteed to preserve distances between nearest

manifolds with "holes"

neighbors for any finite set of n input patterns. Maximum variance unfolding also behaves differently than Isomap on data sets whose underlying submanifold is isometric to a connected but not convex subset of Euclidean space. Figure 16.6 contrasts the behavior of Isomap and maximum variance unfolding on two data sets with this property.

computation

Of the algorithms described in section 16.3, LLE and Laplacian eigenmaps scale best to moderately large data sets ($n < 10,000$), provided that one uses special-purpose eigensolvers that are optimized for sparse matrices. The internal iterations of these eigensolvers rely mainly on matrix-vector multiplications which can be done in $O(n)$. The computation time in Isomap tends to be dominated by the calculation of shortest paths. The most computationally intensive algorithm is maximum variance unfolding, due to the expense of solving semi-definite programs (Vandenberghe and Boyd, 1996) over $n \times n$ matrices.

For significantly larger data sets, all of the above algorithms present serious challenges: the bottom eigenvalues of LLE and Laplacian eigenmaps can be tightly spaced, making it difficult to resolve the bottom eigenvectors, and the computational bottlenecks of Isomap and maximum variance unfolding tend to be prohibitive. Accelerated versions of Isomap and maximum variance unfolding have been developed by first embedding a small subset of "landmark" input patterns, then using various approximations to derive the rest of the embedding from the

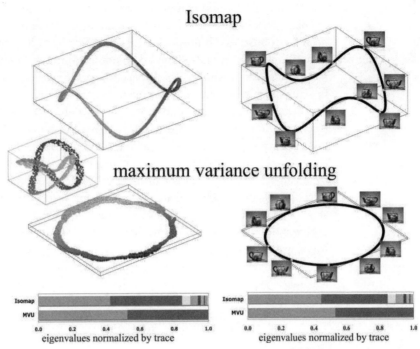

Figure 16.6 Results of Isomap and maximum variance unfolding on two data sets whose underlying submanifolds are not isometric to convex subsets of Euclidean space. *(Left)* 1617 input patterns sampled from a trefoil knot. *(Right)* $n = 400$ images of a teapot rotated through 360 degrees. The embeddings are shown, as well as the eigenvalues of the Gram matrices, normalized by their trace. The algorithms estimate the dimensionality of the underlying submanifold by the number of appreciable eigenvalues. Isomap is foiled in this case by nonconvexity.

landmarks. The landmark version of Isomap (de Silva and Tenenbaum, 2003) is based on the Nyström approximation and scales very well to large data sets (Platt, 2004); millions of input patterns can be processed in minutes on a PC (though the algorithm makes the same assumption as Isomap that the data set contains no "holes"). The landmark version of maximum variance unfolding (Weinberger et al., 2005) is based on a factorized approximation of the Gram matrix, derived from local linear reconstructions of the input patterns (as in LLE). It solves a much smaller SDP than the original algorithm and can handle larger data sets (currently, up to $n = 20,000$), though it is still much slower than the landmark version of Isomap. Note that all the algorithms rely as a first step on computing nearest neighbors, which naively scales as $O(n^2)$, but faster algorithms are possible based on specialized data structures (Friedman et al., 1977; Gray and Moore, 2001; Beygelzimer et al., 2004).

related work   Research on spectral methods for dimensionality reduction continues at a rapid pace. Other algorithms closely related to the ones covered here include Hessian LLE (Donoho and Grimes, 2003), c-Isomap (de Silva and Tenenbaum, 2003), local tangent space alignment (Zhang and Zha, 2004), geodesic null-space analysis (Brand, 2004), and conformal eigenmaps (Sha and Saul, 2005). Motivation for ongoing work includes the handling of manifolds with more complex geometries, the need for robustness to noise and outliers, and the ability to scale to large data sets.

In this chapter, we have focused on nonlinear dimensionality reduction, a problem in unsupervised learning. Graph-based spectral methods also play an important role in semi-supervised learning. For example, the eigenvectors of the normalized graph Laplacian provide an orthonormal basis—ordered by smoothness—for all functions (including decision boundaries and regressions) defined over the neighborhood graph of input patterns; see chapter 12 by Sindhwani, Belkin, and Niyogi. Likewise, as discussed in chapter 15 by Zhu and co-workers, the kernel matrices learned by unsupervised algorithms can be transformed by discriminative training for the purpose of semi-supervised learning. Finally, in chapter 17, Sajama and Orlitsky show how shortest-path calculations and multidimensional scaling can be used to derive more appropriate feature spaces in a semi-supervised setting. In all these ways, graph-based spectral methods are emerging to address the very broad class of problems that lie between the extremes of purely supervised and unsupervised learning.

17 Modifying Distances

Sajama   SSAJAMA@IENG9.UCSD.EDU

Alon Orlitsky   ALON@UCSD.EDU

Learning algorithms use a notion of similarity between data points to make inferences. Semi-supervised algorithms assume that two points are similar to each other if they are connected by a high-density region of the unlabeled data. Apart from semi-supervised learning, such density-based distance metrics also have applications in clustering and nonlinear interpolation. In this chapter, we discuss density-based metrics induced by Riemannian manifold structures. We present asymptotically consistent methods to estimate and compute these metrics and present upper and lower bounds on their estimation and computation errors. Finally, we discuss how these metrics can be used for semi-supervised learning and present experimental results.

17.1 Introduction

When data are in $\mathbb{R}^d$, the standard similarity measure used by learning algorithms is the Euclidean distance. Semi-supervised learning algorithms rely on the intuition that two data points are similar to each other if they are connected by a high-density region. For example, based on this intuition, in the case of the two-dimensional data sample shown in figure 17.1, point 2 is closer to point 3 than to point 1. In this chapter we consider measuring this density-based notion of similarity directly in the form of a distance metric between all pairs of points and then using this resulting metric in standard learning algorithms to perform semi-supervised classification.

To see how a density-based distance (DBD) metric can be defined, let us take a closer look at the two-strips example in figure 17.2. Since there is a path between points 2 and 3 that lies in a high density region (for example, P3), we assume them to be similar or "closer." Conversely, since none of the paths between points 1 and 2 (P1, P2, etc.) can avoid the low-density regions, they are 'farther' according to the density-based notion of distance.

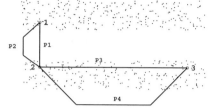

Figure 17.1 According to the semi-supervised smoothness assumption point 2 has greater similarity (is closer) to point 3 than to point 1.

Figure 17.2 This notion of similarity can be written in terms of property of paths between the points.

This observation leads us to consider modifying the standard Euclidean definition of the length of paths and to use the shortest-path length as the density-based distance metric. To make this definition work, those paths that leave the high-density regions should be assigned longer length than those that do not. Note that path length is defined as the sum of lengths of infinitesimally small path segments. One way to define a density-based path length would be to assign different lengths to path segments based on the data density at their location.

Hence, we use a modified definition of the path length Γ of a path γ in $\mathfrak{X}$ which depends on the data density $p(\mathbf{x})$ and a suitably chosen *weighting* function $q : \mathbb{R}^+ \to \mathbb{R}^+$ via the relation

density-based path length

$$\Gamma(\gamma; p) \doteq \int_{t=0}^{LE(\gamma)} q(p(\gamma(t)))|\gamma'(t)|_2 dt,$$

where $|.|_2$ is the L_2 norm on $\mathbb{R}^d$. We can assume, without loss of generality, that all paths are parameterized to have unit speed according to the standard Euclidean metric on $\mathbb{R}^d$ and hence that $LE(\gamma) =$ Euclidean length of curve γ and $|\gamma'(t)|_2 = 1$.

density-based distance

The DBD between two points $\mathbf{x}'$ and $\mathbf{x}''$ is defined to be

$$d(\mathbf{x}', \mathbf{x}''; p) = \inf_{\gamma} \{\Gamma(\gamma; p)\}, \tag{17.1}$$

where γ varies over the set of all paths from $\mathbf{x}'$ to $\mathbf{x}''$.

This DBD metric can be thought of as being induced by a corresponding Riemannian manifold structure. To specify a Riemannian manifold structure on $\mathbb{R}^d$ we need to specify the inner product on the space of tangent vectors at each point in $\mathbb{R}^d$. For $\mathbb{R}^d$ the tangent space at each point is just a copy of $\mathbb{R}^d$ itself. Hence the Riemannian structure at each point is determined by specifying the inner product between the d orthonormal unit vectors which span $\mathbb{R}^d$, i.e., $< \mathbf{e}_i, \mathbf{e}_j > \quad \forall\, i,j = 1, \ldots, d$.

$$< \mathbf{e}_i, \mathbf{e}_j > = q^2(p(\mathbf{x})) \times \begin{cases} 1 & \text{if } i = j \\ 0 & \text{otherwise} \end{cases} \tag{17.2}$$

Semi-supervised learning using density-based Riemannian metrics has been considered by Lebanon (2003); Vincent and Bengio (2003); Bousquet et al. (2004); Sajama and Orlitsky (2005). In particular, Vincent and Bengio (2003) proposed using $q(y) = \frac{1}{y^\alpha}$, $\exp(-\alpha y)$ and $\alpha - \log y$, where α is a parameter that controls the path-segment length in high-density regions relative to the length in low-density regions. Bousquet et al. (2004) proposed $q(y) = \frac{1}{\chi(y)}$ where χ is a strictly increasing function. In this chapter, following (Sajama and Orlitsky, 2005), we will assume that $q(y) : [0, \infty) \longrightarrow (0, \infty)$ is any monotonically decreasing, non-zero function that is constant ($=1$ without loss of generality) for small y. The assumption that q is decreasing ensures that paths in high-density regions have smaller length and $q > 0$ ensures that paths are not assigned zero length. Assuming that $q(y)$ does not change rapidly for small y it is necessary to have uniform bounds on approximation errors when using graph-based lengths to approximate path lengths. This is because the concentration of sample points in the regions with sufficiently low density (low-concentration regions change with sample size) is likely to be small. Hence, using graph edges in these regions to approximate paths will lead to large approximation errors, unless q is relatively slowly changing in these regions.

choosing the weighting function, q

Notice that all of these definitions of the Riemannian metric are nonparametric and hence the space of possible metrics is as large as the space of probability functions that we allow. A different approach was proposed by Lebanon (2003) who suggested picking a Riemannian metric from a parametric set of metrics based on an objective function which gives higher value to those metrics which reduce path lengths for paths passing through high-density regions.

There has also been work on density-based distances that cannot be cast into the Riemannian manifold framework (Fischer et al., 2004; Chapelle and Zien, 2005). These methods consider a fully connected graph constructed on the points, where the edges are weighted by the Euclidean distance between the two points (or a given dissimilarity, if the points do not belong to a Euclidean space). In (Fischer et al., 2004), the length of a path is defined to be the maximum edge weight on the path and the effective density-based distance between any two points is defined to be the smallest path length among all paths connecting the two points. Using these distances, they show a robust and computationally feasible method for clustering elongated high-density regions. In (Chapelle and Zien, 2005), this definition of distance is modified ("softened") in order to avoid connection of otherwise separate clusters by single outliers. They demonstrate how this kernel could be used in transductive support vector machines (SVMs) for semi-supervised learning and present experimental results which show improvement over the standard implementation of transductive SVMs.

estimation and computation errors

Errors in the knowledge of the DBD metric can arise from two sources, viz., estimation and computation. Estimation error arises because the underlying data density is not known a priori and the path-length values need to be estimated from the finite data sample $\{\mathbf{x}_1, \ldots, \mathbf{x}_n\}$ according to the density. Even in the case when the data density is known, computing the Riemannian distance involves the variational problem of minimizing the Riemannian length over all paths between two points. Computation error arises since this minimization cannot be done perfectly when computational resources are limited.

This computation problem has been extensively studied (Sethian, 1999) and finds applications in computational geometry, fluid mechanics, computer vision, and materials science. These methods involve building a grid in $\mathbb{R}^d$ whose size is exponential in d. This is inconvenient for the learning scenario where the data dimension is usually high. It is therefore necessary to consider grids based on data points, in which case the computational complexity grows at a rate polynomial in sample size n. Heuristics for computing the minimum Riemannian distance using graphs constructed on data samples have been suggested by Vincent and Bengio (2003); Bousquet et al. (2004), and Sajama and Orlitsky (2005).

In the sections that follow, we present asymptotically consistent methods to estimate and compute these metrics and show bounds on the estimation and computation errors of these metrics (Sajama and Orlitsky, 2005). We also discuss the various ways in which density-based metrics could be used for semi-supervised learning and present experimental results.

17.2 Estimating DBD Metrics

In this section we consider the error in our knowledge of DBD metrics that comes from the fact that we have a limited data sample, i.e., a set of d-dimensional data points $\{\mathbf{x}_1, \ldots, \mathbf{x}_n\}$ drawn i.i.d. from a probability density function $p(\mathbf{x})$. In other words, we are interested in the estimation of the path length function

$$\Gamma(\gamma; p) \doteq \int_{t=0}^{LE(\gamma)} q(p(\mathbf{x}))|\gamma'(t)|_2 dt$$

(see section 17.1) for any given path γ. Note that for a fixed path γ, $\Gamma(\gamma; p)$ is a functional of the density $p(\mathbf{x})$. Several different ways of analyzing estimators of functionals of data density have been studied in the statistics literature. For bounding the error in estimating the DBD metric we borrow from the proof techniques used by Stone (1980), and Goldstein and Messer (1992).

To characterize the estimators of the path lengths and hence the DBD metric, we use the definitions of upper and lower bounds on rate of convergence of estimators proposed by Stone (1980). Let $\mathcal{W}$ denote the set to which p is known to belong.

Definition 17.1 *A convergence rate r is* achievable *if there is a sequence $\{\hat{\Gamma}_n(\gamma)\}$ of estimators such that*

$$\lim_{c \to \infty} \limsup_{n} \sup_{p \in \mathcal{W}} P_p(|\hat{\Gamma}_n(\gamma) - \Gamma(\gamma; p)| > cn^{-r}) = 0.$$

Definition 17.2 *A rate $r > 0$ is an* upper bound *to the rate of convergence if for* *every sequence* $\hat{\Gamma}_n(\gamma)$ *of estimators of* $\Gamma(\gamma; p)$,

$$\liminf_n \sup_{p \in \mathcal{W}} P_p(|\hat{\Gamma}_n(\gamma) - \Gamma(\gamma; p)| > cn^{-r}) > 0 \qquad \forall c > 0 \tag{17.3}$$

and

$$\lim_{c \to 0} \liminf_n \sup_{p \in \mathcal{W}} P_p(|\hat{\Gamma}_n(\gamma) - \Gamma(\gamma; p)| > cn^{-r}) = 1. \tag{17.4}$$

For statements in probability about random variables T_n, Q_n, whose distributions may depend on $p(\mathbf{x})$, we will use the notation $T_n = O(Q_n)$ when $\lim_{c \to \infty} \limsup_n \sup_{f \in \mathcal{W}_s} P(|T_n| > c|Q_n|) = 0$.

17.2.1   Achievability

We are trying to understand the limits on rate at which the estimation error can converge to zero as sample size n increases. Lower bounds on the achievable rate of convergence can be shown by considering particular estimators and analyzing their performance. This is the basic idea which leads to the first theorem in this section where we consider the plug-in estimators, $\hat{\Gamma}_n$, for the path length Γ, i.e.,

$$\hat{\Gamma}_n(\gamma) = \Gamma(\gamma; \hat{p}_n).$$

This estimator is obtained by plugging in the kernel density estimator $\hat{p}_n$ for data density in place of actual density $p(\mathbf{x})$ into the expression for path length Γ. The kernel density estimator is given by

$$\hat{p}_n(\mathbf{x}) = \frac{1}{n\, h_n^d} \sum_{i=1}^{n} \mathcal{K}\left(\frac{\mathbf{x} - \mathbf{x}_i}{h_n}\right),$$

where h_n is the *width* parameter of the kernel which is chosen to be a function of sample size n and $\mathcal{K}(\mathbf{x})$ is a d-dimensional kernel function. To bound how far this plug-in estimator is from the true path length, we consider the "gradient" of the path length functional with respect to variations in density $p(\mathbf{x})$. We can then use the results on bias and variance of the kernel density estimators to derive a lower bound on the rate of convergence of the estimation error.

To define an estimator for the DBD metric between two points in the support of $p(\mathbf{x})$, we could take the shortest estimated path length among all possible paths between the points. However, this is a large space of paths that contains redundant paths like those that loop over themselves, etc. In order to prove a lower bound on the rate of convergence of the DBD metric, we consider a smaller set of paths, Sp, that nevertheless contains the shortest Riemannian paths between all pairs of points in the support of $p(\mathbf{x})$. Let the maximum Euclidean distance between two points in the support of $p(\mathbf{x})$ be L. Define

$$Sp = \left\{\gamma\, \hat{\Gamma}_n(\gamma) \le L + c\right\},$$

where c is any strictly positive constant.

To see why it is sufficient to look within the set Sp, note that the straight line joining any two such points has length less than L according to this density-based Riemannian metric (because we have defined the weighting function q to be less than or equal to 1). Hence, the shortest Riemannian path between any two points will have length less than or equal to L. By the proof of theorem 17.5, for sufficiently large n, all paths of length $\Gamma \le L$ will have estimated path length $\hat{\Gamma} \le L + c$. Hence for sufficiently large n, Sp will almost surely contain the shortest Riemannian paths between all pairs of points in the support of $p(\mathbf{x})$.

Given the estimator $\hat{\Gamma}_n$ for the lengths of paths, and the set of paths to consider, Sp, we define the estimator $\hat{d}_n(\mathbf{x}', \mathbf{x}'')$ of the DBD metric $d(\mathbf{x}', \mathbf{x}''; p(\mathbf{x}))$ to be

$$\hat{d}_n(\mathbf{x}', \mathbf{x}'') = \inf_{\gamma \in Sp} \{\hat{\Gamma}_n(\gamma)\}.$$

assumptions for the weighting function, q

For proving these bounds, the function q that controls the path length is assumed to have the following properties:

[A1] q is a monotonically decreasing function

[A2] $\inf_y q(y) > 0$

[A3] q has bounded first and second derivatives

assumptions for the density, $p(\mathbf{x})$

One feature of the kernel density estimator is that, when the true data density can be assumed to be smooth (have a certain number of derivatives), its bias can be reduced by choosing an appropriate kernel. Let us denote by $\mathcal{W}_s$, the set of functions which have s or more continuous derivatives. We assume that $p(\mathbf{x})$ has the following properties:

1. $p(\mathbf{x}) \in \mathcal{W}_s$

2. $p(\mathbf{x})$ has bounded support

3. $\exists\ C_1$ such that $\|\nabla p(\mathbf{x})\| \le C_1 \quad \forall \mathbf{x}$

The smoothness parameter s measures the complexity of the class of underlying distributions. Given that $p(\mathbf{x})$ belongs to $\mathcal{W}_s$, we base the density estimate on the d-dimensional kernel $\mathcal{K}(\mathbf{x}) = \Pi_{j=1}^d k(x_j)$. Here k is a one-dimensional kernel with the following properties:

$$k(x) = k(-x), \qquad \int k(x)dx = 1, \qquad \sup_{-\infty < x < \infty} |k(x)| \le A < \infty,$$
$$\int x^m k(x)dx = 0,\ m = 1, \ldots, s-1 \qquad \text{and} \qquad 0 \ne \int x^s k(x)dx < \infty.$$

We use the following two lemmas about well-known (cf. (Nadaraya, 1989)) properties of the kernel density estimators.

Lemma 17.3 (bias of the kernel density estimator) *Let* $\boldsymbol{\mu} = (\mu_1, \ldots, \mu_d)$ *be a d-dimensional vector with* $\mu_i \ge 0$, *and let* $\mathbf{u} = (u_1, \ldots, u_d$ *denote a vector in* $\mathbb{R}^d$. *Let* $|\boldsymbol{\mu}| = \sum_{j=1}^d \mu_j$, $\boldsymbol{\mu}! = \mu_1! \ldots \mu_d!$, $\mathbf{u}^\mu = u_1^{\mu_1} \ldots u_d^{\mu_d}$ *and* $D^{\boldsymbol{\mu}} = \frac{\partial^{\mu_1}}{\partial u_1^{\mu_1}} \ldots \frac{\partial^{\mu_d}}{\partial u_d^{\mu_d}}$.

Then, $\forall \mathbf{x}$, the bias

$$\mathbf{E}_p\left[\hat{p}_n(\mathbf{x})\right] - p(\mathbf{x}) = sh_n^s \int_{\mathbf{u}\in\mathbb{R}^d} F(\mathbf{u},\mathbf{x})\mathcal{K}(\mathbf{u})du_1...du_d,$$

where

$$F(\mathbf{u},\mathbf{x}) = \sum_{|\boldsymbol{\mu}|=s} \frac{\mathbf{u}^{\boldsymbol{\mu}}}{\boldsymbol{\mu}!} \int_{T=0}^{1} (1-T)^{s-1} D^{\boldsymbol{\mu}} p(\mathbf{x}+T\mathbf{u})dT.$$

Lemma 17.4 (variance of the kernel density estimator) $\forall\mathbf{x}$, $\forall\epsilon \geq 0$, *for $n \geq N(\epsilon)$ (where $N(\epsilon)$ is sufficiently large), the variance*

$$\mathbf{E}_p\left[(\hat{p}_n(\mathbf{x}) - \mathbf{E}_p\left[\hat{p}_n(\mathbf{x})\right])^2\right] \leq \frac{(1+\epsilon)p(\mathbf{x})}{nh_n^d} \int_{\mathbf{u}\in\mathbb{R}^d} \mathcal{K}^2(\mathbf{u})d\mathbf{u}.$$

Theorem 17.5 (achievability) *Uniformly over all pairs of points $\mathbf{x}'$ and $\mathbf{x}'' \in$ the support of $p(\mathbf{x})$, the plug-in estimator $\hat{d}_n(\mathbf{x}',\mathbf{x}'')$ that uses the kernel density estimator $\hat{p}_n$, achieves the rate of convergence $r = \frac{s}{2s+d}$ where the width of the kernel density estimators $h_n = \frac{c}{n^{\frac{1}{2s+d}}}$, where c is a constant.*

Proof We begin by defining the derivative T of the functional $\Gamma(\gamma;p)$ with respect to changes $\delta p(\mathbf{x})$ in $p(\mathbf{x})$ to be

$$T(\delta p; p) \doteq \int_{t=0}^{LE(\gamma)} q'(p(\gamma(t)))\delta p(\gamma(t))|\gamma'(t)|_2 dt.$$

Hence, we can write

$$|\Gamma(\gamma;\hat{p}_n) - \Gamma(\gamma;p) - T(\hat{p}_n-p;p)| = \left| \int_{t=0}^{LE(\gamma)} [q(\hat{p}_n) - q(p) - (\hat{p}_n - p)q'(p)] |\gamma'(t)|_2 dt \right|,$$

where p and $\hat{p}_n$ are evaluated at $\gamma(t)$. By a proof similar to the intermediate value theorem, we know that $q(y + \delta y) - q(y) - \delta y q'(y) = \frac{q''(\beta)}{2!}\delta y^2$ for some β in the domain of q. Hence, for some constant C,

$$|\Gamma(\gamma;\hat{p}_n) - \Gamma(\gamma;p) - T(\hat{p}_n - p;p)| \leq C \int_{t=0}^{LE(\gamma)} \{\hat{p}_n(\gamma(t)) - p(\gamma(t))\}^2|\gamma'(t)|_2 dt.$$

Therefore,

$$|\Gamma(\gamma;\hat{p}_n) - \Gamma(\gamma;p)| \leq |T(\hat{p}_n - \mathbf{E}_p\left[\hat{p}_n\right];p)| + |T(\mathbf{E}_p\left[\hat{p}_n\right] - p;p)|$$
$$+ \left| C \int_{t=0}^{LE(\gamma)} \{\hat{p}_n(\gamma(t)) - p(\gamma(t))\}^2|\gamma'(t)|_2 dt \right|.$$

We now bound each of these three terms in turn. The variance of the first term is bounded as follows:

$$\mathbf{E}_p\left[\left(\int_t q'(p(\gamma(t)))\left\{\hat{p}_n - \mathbf{E}_p\left[\hat{p}_n\right]\right\}|\gamma'(t)|_2 dt\right)^2\right]$$

$$\leq L\left(\max_\beta q'(\beta)\right)^2 \mathbf{E}_p\left[\int_t \{\hat{p}_n - \mathbf{E}_p\left[\hat{p}_n\right]\}^2 |\gamma'(t)|_2 dt\right]$$

$$= L\left(\max_\beta q'(\beta)\right)^2 \int_t \mathbf{E}_p\left[(\hat{p}_n - \mathbf{E}_p\left[\hat{p}_n\right])^2\right] |\gamma'(t)|_2 dt$$

$$\leq \frac{(1+\epsilon_1)L^2}{nh_n^d}\left(\max_\beta q'(\beta)\right)^2\left(\max_{\mathbf{x}} p(\mathbf{x})\right)\int_{\mathbb{R}^d}\mathcal{K}^2(\mathbf{u})d\mathbf{u}.$$

The first inequality follows from the Cauchy-Schwarz inequality, and the second equality follows from Fubini's theorem. The third inequality is true for sufficiently large n by lemma 17.4. The constant L is the maximum Euclidean length of the paths that we are considering and hence also upper-bounds the length of these paths according to the density-based Riemannian metric. Since the variance of $T(\hat{p}_n - E\hat{p}_n; p)$ is bounded as above for sufficiently large n, we can conclude that

$$T(\hat{p}_n - \mathbf{E}_p\left[\hat{p}_n\right]; p) = O\left(\frac{1}{(nh_n^d)^{1/2}}\right).$$

The second term $T(\mathbf{E}_p\left[\hat{p}_n\right] - p; p)$ can be bounded in terms of the partial derivatives of $p(\mathbf{x})$ —

$$T(\mathbf{E}_p\left[\hat{p}_n\right] - p; p) = \int_t q'(p(\gamma(t)))(\mathbf{E}_p\left[\hat{p}_n\right] - p)|\gamma'(t)|_2 dt$$

$$\leq (\max q'(\beta))h_n^s\int_t\left[\int_{\mathbf{u}}\left\{\sum_{|\boldsymbol{\mu}|=s}\frac{\mathbf{u}^{\boldsymbol{\mu}}}{\boldsymbol{\mu}!}\{D^{\boldsymbol{\mu}}p(\gamma(t)) + \epsilon_2\}\right\}\mathcal{K}(\mathbf{u})d\mathbf{u}\right]|\gamma'(t)|_2 dt$$

$$= O(h_n^s).$$

Here, we have used lemma 17.3 and the inequality follows from uniform continuity of $D^{\boldsymbol{\mu}}p$ and holds for sufficiently large n.

The third term, $\frac{1}{2}\left(\max_\beta |q''(\beta)|\right)\int_t\{\hat{p}_n(\gamma(t)) - p(\gamma(t))\}^2|\gamma'(t)|_2 dt$, can be bounded by bounding the expectation of $\int_t\{\hat{p}_n(\gamma(t)) - p(\gamma(t))\}^2|\gamma'(t)|_2 dt$ and then using Markov's inequality.

$$\mathbf{E}_p\left[\int_t\{\hat{p}_n(\gamma(t)) - p(\gamma(t))\}^2|\gamma'(t)|_2 dt\right]$$

$$= \int_t \mathbf{E}_p\left[(\hat{p}_n - f)^2\right]|\gamma'(t)|_2 dt$$

$$= \int_t(\mathbf{E}_p\left[\hat{p}_n\right] - p)^2|\gamma'(t)|_2 dt + \int_{t=0}^{LE(\gamma)}\mathbf{E}_p\left[(\hat{p}_n - \mathbf{E}_p\left[\hat{p}_n\right])^2\right]|\gamma'(t)|_2 dt$$

Using lemma 17.3, we can conclude that

$$\int_t (\mathbf{E}_p[\hat{p}_n] - p)^2 p|\gamma'(t)|_2 dt = O(h_n^{2s}).$$

It follows from lemma 17.4 that

$$\int_t \mathbf{E}_p\left[(\hat{p}_n - \mathbf{E}_p[\hat{p}_n])^2\right]|\gamma'(t)|_2 dt = O(\frac{1}{nh_n^d}).$$

Collecting the three terms and assuming that $h_n = \frac{c}{n^{\frac{1}{2s+d}}}$, we conclude

$$|\Gamma(\gamma; \hat{p}_n) - \Gamma(\gamma; p)| = O(\frac{1}{(nh_n^d)^{1/2}} + h_n^s + \frac{1}{nh_n^d} + h_n^{2s}) = O(\frac{1}{n^{\frac{s}{2s+d}}}).$$

$\blacksquare$

17.2.2   Upper Bound

An upper bound on the rate of convergence is a reflection of the inherent difficulty of our estimation problem, since it states that you cannot do better than this limit no matter what estimator you may come up with in the future. In the second theorem in this section, we show an upper bound by showing the existence of a density function $p_0(\mathbf{x})$ and a sequence of densities $\{p_n(\mathbf{x}), n \in \mathbb{N}\}$ with two opposing properties that hold at the same time. The first property is that $p_n(\mathbf{x})$ and $p_0(\mathbf{x})$ are close enough that they cannot be distinguished from one another on the basis of n samples and the second is that $p_n(\mathbf{x})$ and $p_0(\mathbf{x})$ are far enough away from one another that the DBD metric between two fixed points according to the two densities goes to zero slower than the rate given by the upper bound.

Theorem 17.6 (upper bound) *No estimator of the DBD metric can converge at a rate faster than $r = \frac{1}{2}$.*

Proof   To prove this result, we show that there is a density function $p(\mathbf{x})$ and a shortest path between two points γ for which $\hat{\Gamma}(\gamma)$ cannot converge to $\Gamma(\gamma; p)$ faster than the rate r, irrespective of which estimator is used to obtain $\hat{\Gamma}(\gamma)$. The technique, termed "the classification argument," was used by Stone (1980).

Consider a density function $p_0(\mathbf{x})$ with the property that the set $\{\mathbf{x} : p_0(\mathbf{x}) > \alpha\}$ contains an open ball in $\mathbb{R}^d$ over which $p_0(\mathbf{x})$ is constant. Let γ be any line segment contained in this open ball, let $\mathbf{x}_m$ be any point in the relative interior of γ, and let $\mathbf{x}_0$ be any point in the ball which does not lie on the path γ. Since $p_0(\mathbf{x})$ is constant over the ball, any line segment including γ is the shortest path between its two endpoints. Let ψ be a non-negative, infinitely differentiable C^∞ function with compact support (for an example called "the blimp" see Strichartz (1995)). Define

$$w_n(\mathbf{x}) \doteq \delta N n^{-\frac{1}{2}}\{\psi(\mathbf{x} - \mathbf{x}_m) - b_n\psi(\mathbf{x} - \mathbf{x}_0)\}.$$

Here, b_n is chosen such that $\int w_n p_0 d\mathbf{x} = 0$. We define a sequence of densities

$p_n = p_0(1 + w_n)$. From the assumption [Ag1] that q is a monotonically decreasing function and from the definition of p_n, it follows that the straight line γ is the shortest path between its endpoints under the Riemannian metric specified by $p_n \ \forall \ n$. Since b_n is a constant, it remains bounded as $n \longrightarrow \infty$.

Now by the classification argument of Stone (1980) (details are given below), to prove our result it is sufficient to show the following two inequalities:

$$\limsup_n \ n \, \mathbf{E}_{p_0} \left[w_n^2(X) \right] < \infty, \tag{17.5}$$

$$\frac{\Gamma(\gamma; p_n) - \Gamma(\gamma; p_0)}{2} \geq C \delta N \left(n^{-\frac{1}{2}} \right), \tag{17.6}$$

where C is some positive constant.

$$n\mathbf{E}_{p_0} \left[w_n^2(X) \right] = \frac{n\delta^2 N^2}{n} \int p_0(\mathbf{x}) \left\{ \psi(\mathbf{y}) - b_n \psi(\mathbf{y} + (\mathbf{x}_p - \mathbf{x}_0)) \right\}^2 d\mathbf{x} < \infty$$

For sufficiently large n, we have $\Gamma(\gamma; p_n) - \Gamma(\gamma; p_0) = T(p_n - p_0; p_0) + O(\int_{t=0}^{LE(\gamma)} (p_n - p_0)^2 |\gamma'(t)|_2 dt) \geq (\delta N n^{-\frac{1}{2}})$, since $\int_{t=0}^{LE(\gamma)} (p_n - p_0)^2 |\gamma'(t)|_2 dt = O(n^{-1})$.

Now, we show that using Eqs. 17.5 and 17.6, we can prove the two conditions (Eqs. 17.3 and 17.4) needed to show that $1/2$ is an upper bound on the rate of convergence. Note that this part of the proof follows closely the proof in (Stone, 1980) and we are restating it here in detail for completeness. Let μ_n and ν_n denote the joint distribution of the i.i.d. random variables $\mathbf{X}_1, \ldots, \mathbf{X}_n$ under density functions p_0 and p_n respectively. Let L_n denote the Radon-Nikodym derivative $d\nu_n/d\mu_n$ and set $l_n = \log_e L_n$.

$$l_n = \sum_{i=1}^n \log(1 + w_n(\mathbf{X}_i))$$

Using the Taylor expansion $\log(1 + z) = z - \frac{z^2}{2} + \frac{z^3}{3} - + \ldots$ and the fact that $|w_n(\mathbf{x})| \leq 0.5$ for n sufficiently large,

$$\left| l_n - \sum_{i=1}^n w_n(\mathbf{X}_i) \right| \leq \sum_{i=1}^n w_n^2(\mathbf{X}_i) \Rightarrow |l_n| \leq \left| \sum_{i=1}^n w_n(\mathbf{X}_i) \right| + \sum_{i=1}^n w_n^2(\mathbf{X}_i).$$

Now, since we choose b_n such that $\mathbf{E}_{p_0} \left[w_n(\mathbf{X}) \right] = 0$,

$$\mathbf{E}_{p_0} \left[(\sum_{i=1}^n w_n(\mathbf{X}_i))^2 \right] = n\mathbf{E}_{p_0} \left[w_n^2(\mathbf{X}) \right].$$

By Schwarz's inequality

$$\left(\mathbf{E}_{p_0} \left[\sum_{i=1}^{n} w_n(\mathbf{X}_i) \right] \right)^2 \le \mathbf{E}_{p_0} \left[\left(\sum_{i=1}^{n} w_n(\mathbf{X}_i) \right)^2 \right] = \left(n \mathbf{E}_{p_0} \left[w_n^2(\mathbf{X}) \right] \right)^{\frac{1}{2}}.$$

Hence $\mathbf{E}_{p_0} [|l_n|] \le \left(n \mathbf{E}_{p_0} \left[w_n^2(\mathbf{X}) \right] \right)^{\frac{1}{2}} + n \mathbf{E}_{p_0} \left[w_n^2(\mathbf{X}) \right]$. This combined with Eq. 17.5 yields

$$\limsup_n \mathbf{E}_{p_0} [|l_n|] < \infty \qquad \text{and} \qquad \lim_{\delta \longrightarrow 0} \limsup_n \mathbf{E}_{p_0} [|l_n|] = 0 \tag{17.7}$$

Hence, there is a finite, positive M such that $\limsup_n \mathbf{E}_{p_0} [|\log L_n|] < M$. Choose $\epsilon > 0$ such that if $L_n > (1 - \epsilon)/\epsilon$ or $L_n < \epsilon/(1 + \epsilon)$, then $|\log L_n| \ge 2M$. By the Markov inequality,

$$\liminf_n \mu_n \left(\frac{\epsilon}{1 - \epsilon} \le L_n \le \frac{1 - \epsilon}{\epsilon} \right) > \frac{1}{2}.$$

Let n be sufficiently large so that

$$\mu_n \left(\frac{\epsilon}{1 - \epsilon} \le L_n \le \frac{1 - \epsilon}{\epsilon} \right) > \frac{1}{2}.$$

Put prior probabilities $1/2$ each on p_0 and p_n. Then

$$P\{p = p_n | \mathbf{X}_1, \ldots, \mathbf{X}_n\} = \frac{L_n/2}{L_n/2 + 1/2} = \frac{L_n}{L + n + 1}$$

and hence

$$\begin{aligned}
P\{\epsilon \le P\{p = p_n | \mathbf{X}_1, \ldots, \mathbf{X}_n\} \le 1 - \epsilon\} \\
= P\left\{\epsilon \le \frac{L_n}{L + n + 1} \le 1 - \epsilon\right\} = P\left\{\frac{\epsilon}{1 - \epsilon} \le L_n \le \frac{1 - \epsilon}{\epsilon}\right\} \\
\ge \frac{1}{2} \mu_n \left(\frac{\epsilon}{1 - \epsilon} \le L_n \le \frac{1 - \epsilon}{\epsilon} \right) \ge \frac{1}{4}.
\end{aligned}$$

Therefore any method of deciding between p_0 and p_n based on $\mathbf{X}_1, \ldots, \mathbf{X}_n$ must have overall error probability at least $\epsilon/4$. Apply this result to the classifier $\bar{p}_n$ defined by

$$\bar{p}_n = \begin{cases} p_0 & \text{if } \hat{\Gamma}_n(\gamma) \le \frac{\Gamma(\gamma; p_0) + \Gamma(\gamma; p_n)}{2}, \\ 0 & \text{otherwise.} \end{cases}$$

It follows that

$$\begin{aligned}
\frac{1}{2} P_{p_0} \left(|\hat{\Gamma}_n(\gamma) - \Gamma(\gamma; p_0)| \ge \frac{\Gamma(\gamma; p_n) - \Gamma(\gamma; p_0)}{2} \right) \\
+ \frac{1}{2} P_{p_0} \left\{ |\hat{\Gamma}_n(\gamma) - \Gamma(\gamma; p_n)| \ge \frac{\Gamma(\gamma; p_n) - \Gamma(\gamma; p_0)}{2} \right\} \ge \frac{\epsilon}{4},
\end{aligned}$$

consequently,

$$\sup_{p \in \mathcal{W}_s} P_p \left\{ |\hat{\Gamma}_n(\gamma) - \Gamma(\gamma; p)| \geq \frac{\Gamma(\gamma; p_n) - \Gamma(\gamma; p_0)}{2} \right\} \geq \frac{\epsilon}{4},$$

and hence

$$\liminf_n \sup_{p \in \mathcal{W}_s} P_p \left\{ |\hat{\Gamma}_n(\gamma) - \Gamma(\gamma; p)| \geq \frac{\Gamma(\gamma; p_n) - \Gamma(\gamma; p_0)}{2} \right\} > 0.$$

This along with Eq. 17.6 proves the first requirement (Eq. 17.3) for 1/2 to be an upper bound on the rate of convergence .

To prove the second part of the upper-bound definition, we choose a positive integer $i_o \geq 2$ and put prior probability i_o^{-1} on each of the i_o points:

$$p_{ni} = p_0 + \frac{i-1}{i_o - 1}(p_n - p_0).$$

Now, $\exists \delta > 0$ such that for sufficiently large n, any method of classifying $p \in \{p_{n1}, \ldots, p_{ni_o}\}$ based on $\mathbf{X}_1, \ldots, \mathbf{X}_n$ must have overall probability of error $1 - 2/i_o$. This is because

$$P\{p = p_{ni} | \mathbf{X}_1, \ldots, \mathbf{X}_n\} = \frac{1 + \left(\frac{i-1}{i_o-1}\right)(L_n - 1)}{\left(\frac{L_n+1}{2}\right) i_o}$$

and the optimum classifier to choose between p_{ni} is

$$\bar{p}_n = \begin{cases} p_0 & \text{if } L_n < 1 \\ p_n & \text{otherwise} \end{cases},$$

which produces an error whenever one of $p_{n2}, \ldots, p_{n(i_o-1)}$ is chosen in the random draw among the p_{ni}.

Note that

$$(p_{ni} + p_{n(i+1)}) - (p_{n(i-1)} + p_{n(i)}) = \left(p_0 + \frac{1}{2(i_o - 1)}(p_n - p_0)\right).$$

So, considering the classifier

$$\hat{p} = \left\{ p_{ni} \quad \text{if } |\hat{\Gamma}_n - \Gamma(\gamma; p_{ni})| \leq \frac{|\Gamma(\gamma; p_n) - \Gamma(\gamma; p_0)|}{2(i_o - 1)} \right\},$$

we get

$$\sum_i \frac{1}{i_o} P_{p_{ni}} \left\{ |\hat{\Gamma}_n - \Gamma(\gamma; p_{ni})| \geq \frac{|\Gamma(\gamma; p_n) - \Gamma(\gamma; p_0)|}{2(i_o - 1)} \right\} \geq 1 - \frac{2}{i_o}.$$

Consequently,

$$\sup_p P_p \left\{ |\hat{\Gamma}_n - \Gamma(\gamma; p)| \geq \frac{|\Gamma(\gamma; p_n) - \Gamma(\gamma; p_0)|}{2(i_o - 1)} \right\} \geq 1 - \frac{2}{i_o}$$

$$\lim_{i_o \longrightarrow \infty} \liminf_{n} \sup_{p \in \mathcal{W}_s} P_p \left\{ |\hat{\Gamma}_n - \Gamma(\gamma; p)| \geq \frac{|\Gamma(\gamma; p_n) - \Gamma(\gamma; p_0)|}{2(i_o - 1)} \right\} = 1.$$

This along with Eq. 17.6 proves the second requirement (Eq. 17.4) for $1/2$ to be an upper bound on the rate of convergence .

∎

17.3   Computing DBD Metrics

In section 17.2, we analyzed the effect of using an estimate of the density function in place of the density function itself. However, even if the density were known, computing the Riemannian metric between two points is not an easy task. This is a variational minimization problem since the distance is defined as the infimum of path lengths over all paths joining the points (Eq. 17.1). Isomap (Tenenbaum et al., 2000; Bernstein et al., 2000) uses paths along a neighborhood graph to approximate paths along a manifold embedded in $\mathbb{R}^d$. Vincent and Bengio (2003); Bousquet et al. (2004), and Chapelle and Zien (2005) propose graph-based methods to compute density-based metrics for use in semi-supervised learning. However, these heuristics for approximating DBD metrics are not guaranteed to lead to a consistent distance measure, i.e., they do not guarantee convergence of the graph shortest-path length to the Riemannian metric with increasing sample size. In this section we present upper and lower bounds on the rate at which approximation error can converge to zero when a particular graph construction is used for computing the Riemannian metric.

17.3.1   Achievability

We show that the rate $1/2d$ is achievable, i.e., we present a graph construction method which produces graphs such that with high probability the difference between the shortest distance along the graph and the DBD metric is smaller than $c/n^{1/2d}$, for some constant c and for large enough n. In the proof, we use some techniques from Tenenbaum et al. (2000) and Bernstein et al. (2000).

We first describe the method for constructing the graph and assigning weights to the graph edges. In addition to the three assumptions made about the weighting function q in section 17.2, we assume that

[A4] $q(y) = 1 \quad \forall\, y \leq \alpha.$

Note that this is not overly restrictive since we can choose α to be small. As discussed in section 17.1, it is necessary to assume that $q(y)$ does not change rapidly for small y in order to have uniform bounds on approximation errors when using graph-based lengths to approximate path lengths. Let $C_p(\alpha) \doteq \{\mathbf{x} : \hat{p}(\mathbf{x}) \geq \alpha\}$ and let $C_p(\alpha; \epsilon) \doteq \bigcup_{\mathbf{x} \in C_p(\alpha)} B(\mathbf{x}, \epsilon)$ where $B(\mathbf{x}, \epsilon)$ is a d-dimensional ball of radius ϵ centered at $\mathbf{x}$.

A point $\mathbf{x} \in \mathbb{R}^d$ is *high density* if $\mathbf{x} \in C_p(\alpha; \epsilon)$. A maximal connected set of high-density points is a *high-density component*. Since the density $p(\mathbf{x})$ has bounded support and integrates to one, it can be shown that there will be only finitely many high-density components and hence $C_p(\alpha; \epsilon)$ will be partitioned into finitely many high-density components $R_1, \ldots, R_k$. Note that these are high-density components with respect to the estimated distribution $\hat{p}(\mathbf{x})$ and not the "true" distribution $p(\mathbf{x})$. $C_p(\alpha; \epsilon)$ is being defined as a way to mollify the difficult properties of $C_p(\alpha)$ which can have complex boundaries (e.g., dendrils defined in (Blum and Chawla, 2001)) and can have an infinite number of disjoint, maximally connected components.

graph
construction

The graph $\mathbf{g}$ is defined as follows. Its vertices are the observed data points $\mathbf{x}_1, \ldots, \mathbf{x}_n$. Two nodes $\mathbf{x}_i, \mathbf{x}_j$ are connected if at least one of the following holds:

1. The Euclidean distance between two nodes is at most ϵ. The weight of such an edge is $w(\mathbf{x}_i, \mathbf{x}_j) = q(p((\mathbf{x}_i + \mathbf{x}_j)/2))|\mathbf{x}_i - \mathbf{x}_j|_2$.

2. At most one of the nodes is high-density, they are at least ϵ apart, and the straight line joining the two nodes leaves $C_p(\alpha; \epsilon)$. The weight of such an edge is $w(\mathbf{x}_i, \mathbf{x}_j) = |\mathbf{x}_i - \mathbf{x}_j|_2$.

We use three distance metrics between data points $\mathbf{x}$ and $\mathbf{y}$, namely, the DBD metric

$$d_M(\mathbf{x}, \mathbf{y}) \doteq d(\mathbf{x}, \mathbf{y}; \hat{p}_n) = \inf_{\gamma} \{\Gamma(\gamma; \hat{p}_n)\},$$

the graph distance

$$d_{\mathbf{g}}(\mathbf{x}, \mathbf{y}) \doteq \min_P \left(w(\mathbf{x}_0, \mathbf{x}_1) + \ldots + w(\mathbf{x}_{m-1}, \mathbf{x}_m) \right),$$

and an intermediate distance

$$d_S(\mathbf{x}, \mathbf{y}) \doteq \min_P \left(d_M(\mathbf{x}_0, \mathbf{x}_1) + \ldots + d_M(\mathbf{x}_{m-1}, \mathbf{x}_m) \right),$$

where $P = (\mathbf{x}_0, \ldots, \mathbf{x}_m)$ varies over all paths along the edges of $\mathbf{g}$ connecting $\mathbf{x} = \mathbf{x}_0$ to $\mathbf{y} = \mathbf{x}_m$.

To lower-bound the rate of convergence of the shortest path along graph $\mathbf{g}$ to the DBD metric, we bound the difference between the graph distance and DBD metric in theorem 17.10. For this purpose we show the DBD metric and the intermediate distance are close to each other in lemma 17.7. Lemmas 17.8 and 17.9 state that the graph and intermediate distances are close.

Lemma 17.7 (difference between DBD metric and intermediate distance)
If
$\forall \mathbf{x} \in C_p(\alpha; 2\epsilon) \; \exists \text{ some data point } \mathbf{x}_i \text{ for which } d_M(\mathbf{x}, \mathbf{x}_i) \leq \delta \text{ and if } 4\delta < \epsilon, \text{ then } \forall$
pairs of data points $\mathbf{x}$ *and* $\mathbf{y}$,

$$d_M(\mathbf{x}, \mathbf{y}) \leq d_S(\mathbf{x}, \mathbf{y}) \leq \left(1 + \frac{6\delta}{\epsilon} + \frac{8\delta^2}{\epsilon^2} \right) d_M(\mathbf{x}, \mathbf{y}).$$

Proof The first inequality $d_M(\mathbf{x}, \mathbf{y}) \leq d_S(\mathbf{x}, \mathbf{y})$ is true by the definition of d_M and d_S. Let γ be any piecewise-smooth path connecting $\mathbf{x}$ to $\mathbf{y}$ with length l. If we are able to find a path from $\mathbf{x}$ to $\mathbf{y}$ along edges of $\mathbf{g}$ whose length $d_M(\mathbf{x}_0, \mathbf{x}_1) + \ldots + d_M(\mathbf{x}_{m-1}, \mathbf{x}_m)$ is less than $\left(1 + \frac{6\delta}{\epsilon} + \frac{8\delta^2}{\epsilon^2}\right) d_M(\mathbf{x}, \mathbf{y})$, then the right-hand inequality would follow by taking infimum over γ.

Note that it is sufficient to consider only those γ for which contiguous segments outside $C_p(\alpha; \epsilon)$ are straight lines. This is because, given any γ without this property, we can define a path γ' such that the length of γ' is less than the length of γ by just replacing wiggly segments of γ outside $C_p(\alpha; \epsilon)$ by straight lines (recall that the density-based Riemannian metric has been defined to be constant Euclidean in the region outside $C_p(\alpha)$). We consider different cases based on the regions the path γ passes through.

Case (a) : *γ is wholly contained in one of the subregions R_k of $C_p(\alpha)$.*
We use an argument similar to the one used in Isomap (Tenenbaum et al., 2000; Bernstein et al., 2000). If $l \leq \epsilon - 2\delta$, then $\mathbf{x}, \mathbf{y}$ are connected by an edge which we can use as the path through the graph. If $l > \epsilon - 2\delta$, we write $l = l_0 + (l_1 + l_1 + \ldots + l_1) + l_0$, where $l_1 = \epsilon - 2\delta$ and $(\epsilon - 2\delta)/2 \leq l_0 \leq \epsilon - 2\delta$. Now, cut up the arc γ into pieces in accordance with this decomposition giving a sequence of points $r_0 = \mathbf{x}, r_1, \ldots, r_p = \mathbf{y}$, where each point r_i lies within a distance δ of a sample point $\mathbf{x}_i$. Using this construction, we can write

$$d_M(\mathbf{x}_i, \mathbf{x}_{i+1}) \leq d_M(\mathbf{x}_i, r_i) + d_M(r_i, r_{i+1}) + d_M(r_{i+1}, \mathbf{x}_{i+1}) \leq \frac{l_1 \epsilon}{\epsilon - 2\delta}.$$

Similarly,

$$d_M(\mathbf{x}, \mathbf{x}_1) \leq l_0 \frac{\epsilon}{\epsilon - 2\delta} \quad \& \quad d_M(\mathbf{x}_{p-1}, \mathbf{y}) \leq l_0 \frac{\epsilon}{\epsilon - 2\delta}.$$

Since $l_0 \frac{\epsilon}{\epsilon - 2\delta} \leq \epsilon$, we find that each edge has manifold length $\leq \epsilon$ and hence belongs to $\mathbf{g}$. Hence,

$$d_S(\mathbf{x}, \mathbf{y}) \leq l \frac{\epsilon}{\epsilon - 2\delta} < l \left(1 + \frac{4\delta}{\epsilon}\right).$$

Case (b) : *All segments of γ that lie outside $C_p(\alpha; \epsilon)$ have length $\geq \epsilon - 2\delta$.*
We consider the case when both the initial and final points, $\mathbf{x}$ and $\mathbf{y}$ lie in $C_p(\alpha; \epsilon)$. The case when one or both of the endpoints lie outside can be similarly handled. We divide the path γ into $2k + 1$ sections, where k is the number of times γ goes outside $C_p(\alpha; \epsilon)$ i.e., — $\mathbf{x} \ldots r_{o1} \ldots r_{m1} \ldots r_{o2} \ldots r_{m2} \ldots r_{ok} \ldots r_{mk} \ldots \mathbf{y}$ where the sections $r_{oi} - -r_{mi}$ lie outside $C_p(\alpha)$. The d_S and d_M lengths of the interior segments are related exactly as in case (a) and hence we can write

$$d_S(\mathbf{x}, \mathbf{y}) \leq \frac{\epsilon}{\epsilon - 2\delta} \left\{d_M(\mathbf{x}, r_{o1}) + d_M(r_{m1}, r_{o2}) + \ldots + d_M(r_{mk}, \mathbf{y})\right\}$$

$$+ \left\{2\delta + d_M(r_{o1}, r_{m1})\right\} + \ldots + \left\{2\delta + d_M(r_{ok}, r_{mk})\right\}.$$

Since each outside segment has a minimum length $\epsilon - 2\delta$, $d_M(\mathbf{x}, \mathbf{y}) \geq (\epsilon - 2\delta)k$.

Hence $2\delta k \leq 2\delta/(\epsilon - 2\delta)d_M(\mathbf{x}, \mathbf{y})$ and

$$d_S(\mathbf{x}, \mathbf{y}) \leq \left(1 + \frac{6\delta}{\epsilon} + \frac{8\delta^2}{\epsilon^2}\right)d_M(\mathbf{x}, \mathbf{y}).$$

∎

Lemma 17.8 (difference between intermediate and graph distances - 1)
For all pairs of data points $\mathbf{x}_i, \mathbf{x}_j$ *connected by an edge in* g *with* $|\mathbf{x}_i - \mathbf{x}_j|_2 \leq \epsilon$,

$$(1 - \lambda_1)d_{\mathbf{g}}(\mathbf{x}_i, \mathbf{x}_j) \leq d_S(\mathbf{x}_i, \mathbf{x}_j) \leq (1 + \lambda_1)d_{\mathbf{g}}(\mathbf{x}_i, \mathbf{x}_j),$$

where

$$\lambda_1 = 2\frac{\max|\nabla_{\mathbf{x}} q(p(\mathbf{x}))|_2\epsilon}{\min_{\mathbf{x}} q(p(\mathbf{x}))}.$$

Proof Let $\epsilon_2 = d_M(\mathbf{x}_i, \mathbf{x}_j)/2$
and let $B(\text{line}(\mathbf{x}_i, \mathbf{x}_j), \epsilon_2) = \bigcup_{\mathbf{x} \in \text{line}(\mathbf{x}_i, \mathbf{x}_j)} B(\mathbf{x}, \epsilon_2)$.

$$R_{\min} = \min_{\mathbf{x} \in B(\text{line}(\mathbf{x}_i, \mathbf{x}_j), \epsilon_2)} q(p(\mathbf{x}))) \qquad R_{\max} = \min_{\mathbf{x} \in \text{line}(\mathbf{x}_i, \mathbf{x}_j)} q(p(\mathbf{x}))$$

Now,

$$R_{\min}|\mathbf{x}_i - \mathbf{x}_j|_2 \leq d_M(\mathbf{x}_i, \mathbf{x}_j) \leq R_{\max}|\mathbf{x}_i - \mathbf{x}_j|_2 \quad \text{and} \quad d_{\mathbf{g}}(\mathbf{x}_i, \mathbf{x}_j) = |\mathbf{x}_i - \mathbf{x}_j|_2 q\left(p\left(\frac{\mathbf{x}_i + \mathbf{x}_j}{2}\right)\right)$$

Using the fact that the gradient of q is bounded, we can write

$$R_{\max} \leq (1 + \lambda_1)q\left(p\left(\frac{\mathbf{x}_i + \mathbf{x}_j}{2}\right)\right) \qquad \forall \lambda_1 > 2\frac{\max|\nabla_{\mathbf{x}} q(p(\mathbf{x}))|_2\epsilon}{\min_{\mathbf{x}} q(p(\mathbf{x}))}.$$

Hence,

$$(1 - \lambda_1)d_{\mathbf{g}}(\mathbf{x}_i, \mathbf{x}_j) \leq d_M(\mathbf{x}_i, \mathbf{x}_j) \leq (1 + \lambda_1)d_{\mathbf{g}}(\mathbf{x}_i, \mathbf{x}_j).$$

∎

Lemma 17.9 (difference between intermediate and graph distances - 2)
For all pairs of data points $\mathbf{x}_i, \mathbf{x}_j$ *connected by an edge in* g *with* $|\mathbf{x}_i - \mathbf{x}_j|_2 > \epsilon$,

$$(1 - \lambda_2)d_{\mathbf{g}}(\mathbf{x}_i, \mathbf{x}_j) \leq d_S(\mathbf{x}_i, \mathbf{x}_j) \leq (1 + \lambda_2)d_{\mathbf{g}}(\mathbf{x}_i, \mathbf{x}_j),$$

where

$$\lambda_2 = \frac{2\delta^2 \max|\nabla q(p(\mathbf{x}))|_2}{\epsilon}.$$

Proof Since $q \leq 1$, $d_M(\mathbf{x}_i, \mathbf{x}_j) \leq |\mathbf{x}_i - \mathbf{x}_j|_2$. Among the exterior edges, we only need to consider those between nodes which are within δ of the boundary of $C_p(\alpha)$ or outside $C_p(\alpha)$. This is because of the way we approximate paths which leave

$C_p(\alpha)$ in theorem 17.7.

$$R_{\min} \geq 1 - \max_{\mathbf{x}} |\nabla q(p(\mathbf{x}))|_2 \delta$$

Since for exterior edges $d_{\mathbf{g}}(\mathbf{x}_i, \mathbf{x}_j) = |\mathbf{x}_i - \mathbf{x}_j|_2$, we can write

$$d_M(\mathbf{x}_i, \mathbf{x}_j) \geq 2\delta \left(1 - \max |\nabla q(p(\mathbf{x}))|_2 \delta\right) + |\mathbf{x}_i - \mathbf{x}_j|_2 - 2\delta$$

$$\geq |\mathbf{x}_i - \mathbf{x}_j|_2 \left(1 - \frac{2\delta^2 \max |\nabla q(p(\mathbf{x}))|_2}{|\mathbf{x}_i - \mathbf{x}_j|_2}\right)$$

$$\geq d_{\mathbf{g}}(\mathbf{x}_i, \mathbf{x}_j) \left(1 - \frac{2\delta^2 \max |\nabla q(p(\mathbf{x}))|_2}{\epsilon}\right).$$

Hence,

$$(1 - \lambda_2) d_{\mathbf{g}}(\mathbf{x}_i, \mathbf{x}_j) \leq d_M(\mathbf{x}_i, \mathbf{x}_j) \leq d_{\mathbf{g}}(\mathbf{x}_i, \mathbf{x}_j) \qquad \forall \lambda_2 \geq \frac{2\delta^2 \max |\nabla q(p(\mathbf{x}))|_2}{\epsilon}.$$

∎

Theorem 17.10 (lower bound on the computing error) $\forall \zeta < 1/2d$, *a computing error (uniform over all pairs of points* $\mathbf{x}$, $\mathbf{y}$*) of*

$$(1 - \lambda) d_M(\mathbf{x}, \mathbf{y}) \leq d_{\mathbf{g}}(\mathbf{x}, \mathbf{y}) \leq (1 + \lambda) d_M(\mathbf{x}, \mathbf{y})$$

with $\lambda = cn^{-\zeta}$ *can be achieved with probability* $\geq \delta'$ *for a sufficiently large data sample* $n \geq N(\delta')$ *(c is a constant).*

Proof We show that the shortest path along the graph is within λ of the DBD metric, by considering two cases based on the properties of the shortest path. We define a new graph $\mathbf{g}_2$ on the data points which contains only a subset of the edges in $\mathbf{g}$. $\mathbf{g}_2$ contains all edges in $\mathbf{g}$ where $|\mathbf{x}_i - \mathbf{x}_j|_2 \leq \epsilon$. In addition, it contains edges in $\mathbf{g}$ that leave $C_p(\alpha; \epsilon)$ and whose endpoints, $\mathbf{x}_i$ and $\mathbf{x}_j$, lie within δ of the boundary of $C_p(\alpha; \epsilon)$. Note that $\mathbf{g}_2$ is sufficient to approximate all shortest paths between data points. However, it is difficult to compute/generate and hence we define a more dense graph $\mathbf{g}$ with the property that the extra edges are most likely not going to be used in the shortest path unless they form a good approximation to the shortest path along $\mathbf{g}_2$.

Case (a) : *The shortest path along* $\mathbf{g}$ *lies entirely within the subset* $\mathbf{g}_2$.
Using the theorem from Giné and Guillou (2002), we can conclude that the choice in section 17.2 of kernel width, $h_n = \frac{1}{n^{\frac{1}{2s+d}}}$ and other properties assumed about $p(\mathbf{x})$ ensure that almost surely,

$$\max_{\mathbf{x}} |p_n(\mathbf{x}) - p(\mathbf{x})| = O\left(\sqrt{\left(\frac{(2s + d) \log(n)}{n^{\frac{2s}{2s+d}}}\right)}\right).$$

This means that for sufficiently large n, $\forall$ points $\mathbf{y}$ in $C_p(\alpha; 2\epsilon)$ have the property that $p(\mathbf{y}) \geq \alpha - \alpha_1$ for arbitrarily small α_1. Using this fact and the δ-sampling condition (Tenenbaum et al., 2000; Bernstein et al., 2000), we know that the requirement for lemma 17.7 is satisfied when $n = \Omega\left(\left(\frac{1}{\delta}\right)^d \log \frac{1}{\delta}\right)$. This condition is satisfied with a choice of $\zeta < 1/2d$ and letting $\delta = c_1 n^{-2\zeta}$ and $\epsilon = c_2 n^{-\zeta}$) ($c_1$ and c_2 are constants). Let $\lambda_3 = max(\lambda_1, \lambda_2)$, where λ_1 and λ_2 are defined in lemmas 17.8 and 17.9 respectively. Hence we can use lemmas 17.7, 17.8, and 17.9 to conclude that

$$(1 - 2\lambda_3)d_M(\mathbf{x}, \mathbf{y}) \leq d_{\mathbf{g}}(\mathbf{x}, \mathbf{y}) \leq (1 + 2\lambda_3)\left(1 + \frac{6\delta}{\epsilon} + \frac{8\delta^2}{\epsilon^2}\right)d_M(\mathbf{x}, \mathbf{y}),$$

which implies that

$$(1 - \lambda_4)d_M(\mathbf{x}, \mathbf{y}) \leq d_{\mathbf{g}}(\mathbf{x}, \mathbf{y}) \leq (1 + \lambda_4)d_M(\mathbf{x}, \mathbf{y}),$$

where

$$\lambda_4 = O(\epsilon + \frac{\delta}{\epsilon}) = O(n^{-\zeta}).$$

Case (b) : *The shortest path, P, along $\mathbf{g}$ uses some edges that are not part of $\mathbf{g}_2$.* Consider any edge E connecting $\mathbf{x}_l$ and $\mathbf{x}_m$ in the shortest path along $\mathbf{g}$ that is not in $\mathbf{g}_2$. We will show that there is a path through $\mathbf{g}_2$ that can closely approximate this edge E and hence this shortest path. We consider the case when only one section near the endpoint $\mathbf{x}_m$ is more than δ in $C_p(\alpha; \epsilon)$. The case when more sections of E are in $C_p(\alpha; \epsilon)$ can be similarly handled. Consider the boundary point r_b where the straight line starting at $\mathbf{x}_m$ toward $\mathbf{x}_l$ first touches the edge of $C_p(\alpha; \epsilon)$. By the δ-sampling condition, there is a data point $\mathbf{x}_k$ within δ of r_b. Consider the path consisting of the edge $\mathbf{x}_l$–$\mathbf{x}_k$ and the shortest path, P_2, between $\mathbf{x}_k$ and $\mathbf{x}_m$ through those edges of $\mathbf{g}$ that connect nodes within ϵ of one another. Let $d'_{\mathbf{g}2}$ be the length of a path that follows P except when it comes to edges not in $\mathbf{g}_2$ in which case it follows paths P_2 constructed to pass through $\mathbf{g}_2$. Let $d_{\mathbf{g}2}$ be the length of the shortest path along graph $\mathbf{g}_2$. From proof of case (a), we know that

$$(1 - \lambda_4)d_M(\mathbf{x}, \mathbf{y}) \leq d_{\mathbf{g}2}(\mathbf{x}, \mathbf{y}) \leq (1 + \lambda_4)d_M(\mathbf{x}, \mathbf{y}),$$

$$d_{\mathbf{g}}(\mathbf{x}, \mathbf{y}) \leq d'_{\mathbf{g}2}(\mathbf{x}, \mathbf{y}) \leq (1 + \lambda_4)d_{\mathbf{g}}(\mathbf{x}, \mathbf{y}), \text{and}$$

$$d_{\mathbf{g}}(\mathbf{x}, \mathbf{y}) \leq d_{\mathbf{g}2}(\mathbf{x}, \mathbf{y}) \leq d'_{\mathbf{g}2}(\mathbf{x}, \mathbf{y}).$$

Hence,

$$(1 - 2\lambda_4)d_M(\mathbf{x}, \mathbf{y}) \leq d_{\mathbf{g}}(\mathbf{x}, \mathbf{y}) \leq (1 + \lambda_4)d_M(\mathbf{x}, \mathbf{y}).$$

∎

17.3.2   Upper bound

In theorem 17.10, we showed that we can construct a neighborhood-based graph on the data sample which can be used to approximately compute DBD metrics with a rate of convergence of $1/n^{1/2d}$. This is a very slow rate of convergence, especially when data dimension, d, is high. The natural question that follows this analysis is whether this dependence of the rate on the data dimension is because of the curse of dimensionality or whether it is merely because of the way the graph was constructed and analyzed. Theorem 17.11 shows that dimension does limit how much we can reduce the approximation error, regardless of the particular graph construction method we use, so long as we choose to use a neighborhood-based graph. This result is true even when data lie along a manifold, but are noisy and hence do not lie perfectly on the manifold, i.e., the curse of dimensionality cannot be overcome in the case of approximation error when using neighborhood-based graphs, even when the intrinsic dimension of data is small. For this reason, this result provides a lower bound on the approximation error of the ISOMAP algorithm (Tenenbaum et al., 2000) as well.

Theorem 17.11 (upper bound on the computing error) *The computing error, when using an ϵ-neighborhood-based graph on the data sample, cannot converge to zero faster than $\frac{1}{n^{\frac{1}{d-1}}}$ with probability $\geq \delta'$ for sufficiently large data sample $n \geq N(\delta')$.*

Proof This result is shown using an example for which the approximation error when using the graph converges at rate $1/n^{\frac{1}{d-1}}$. Consider the case when data density is uniform over any convex set. (Note that all continuous density functions can be approximated by a constant function in a small enough neighborhood.) In this case the graph construction method described at the beginning of this section reduces to an ϵ-neighborhood graph (with high probability). Consider any two points $\mathbf{x}'$, $\mathbf{x}''$ in the interior of the support of the density. The shortest path between $\mathbf{x}'$ and $\mathbf{x}''$ is the straight line joining them. Consider a d-dimensional cuboid which circumscribes a cylinder of radius $\delta/2$ around this line. If none of the points in the data sample lie in this cuboid, the approximation error in measuring the length of this line along the graph edges will be at least of order δ. The probability of this happening, $(1 - c\delta^{d-1})^n$, can be lower-bounded by a constant if δ is chosen to be of order $1/n^{\frac{1}{d-1}}$. ∎

17.4   Semi-Supervised Learning Using Density-Based Metrics

Given a density-based distance metric, any of the nearest neighbor-based methods (k-nearest neighbors, weighted k-nearest neighbors with various weights) can be used for classification in a semi-supervised learning scenario. Let y_i be the label of $\mathbf{x}_i$ and let classifier be $sign(h(\mathbf{x}_i))$. Let l_M denote the Lipschitz constant according to the manifold specified by $q(p(\mathbf{x}))$. In this manifold, the lengths scale locally as $q(p(\mathbf{x}))$; hence it can be verified that for any function h on $\mathbb{R}^d$

$$|l_M h|_2 = \sup_{\mathbf{x}} \frac{1}{q(p(\mathbf{x}))} |\bigtriangledown_{\mathbf{x}} h|_2.$$

a large-margin classifier that is equivalent to 1NN using DBD metric

von Luxburg and Bousquet (2004) have shown that the 1-nearest neighbor (1NN) classifier corresponds to a large-margin classifier. In the case of the DBD metric, 1NN is equivalent to (using the modified Lipschitz constant according to the density-based manifold), the optimization problem

$$\arg\min_{h} \sup_{\mathbf{x}} \left[\frac{1}{q(p(\mathbf{x}))} |\bigtriangledown_{\mathbf{x}} h|_2 \right] \text{ under constraints } y_i h(\mathbf{x}_i) \geq 1.$$

As $p(\mathbf{x})$ increases, $\frac{1}{q(p(\mathbf{x}))}$ also increases and hence this optimization problem corresponds to penalizing the gradient of the classifier function h in high-density regions and allowing h to change in the low-density regions. This agrees with the intuition that data points in the same high-density region are likely to have similar labels. Please see (Bousquet et al., 2004) for a discussion on regularization appropriate for semi-supervised learning and its relationship to modifying geometry based on the data density.

In this section, we present experimental results on data from the UCI machine learning repository, summarized in table 17.1. The three methods we compare are standard 1NN, DBD metric-based 1NN, and the randomized min-cut method (Blum et al., 2004). The randomized min-cut method involves averaging over results obtained from several min-cuts and it is suggested by Blum et al. (2004) that those min-cuts which lead to a very unbalanced classification are to be rejected. However, there is no clear way to choose this cutoff ratio. For the results presented here we choose the cutoff to be slightly smaller than the "true" ratio between the classes in the data set. For the DBD-based 1NN implementation, we chose the function q to fall exponentially with increase in density beyond α, which in turn was chosen to be smaller than the estimated density at all sample points.

Table 17.1   Description of data sets for the classification problem

DATA SET	DATA DIMENSION	DATA SET SIZE	CLASS RATIO
ADULT	6	1000	0.30
ABALONE - 9 VS. 13	7	892	0.29
ABALONE - 5 VS. 9	7	804	0.17
DIGITS - 1 VS. 2	256	2200	1.00

We performed experiments for labeled set size varying between 2 and 20 and the accuracy results are shown in figure 17.3. We observed that DBD-based 1NN performed better than or similar to the standard 1NN algorithm for all data sets

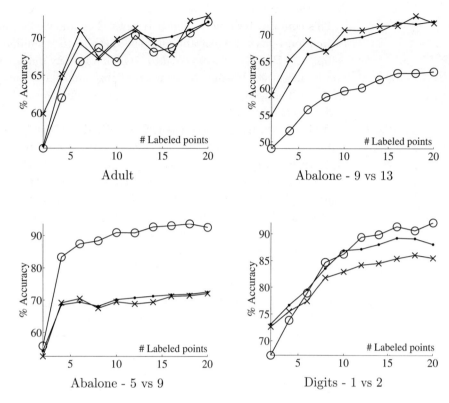

Figure 17.3 Classification results comparing 1NN (.), DBD-based 1NN (x) and randomized min-cut (o) algorithms.

with small dimension. We conjecture that the reason DBD-based 1NN performed worse than 1NN for the digits example is because of difficulty in density estimation in very high dimensions. The DBD-based 1NN algorithm performed better than the other two when the number of labeled examples was very small, except in the case of the digits example. One interesting result was that of the two abalone data examples, in which the randomized min-cut algorithm performed much better than both NN algorithms in one case and much worse in the other.

17.5   Conclusions and Future Work

We have shown that density-based distance metrics which satisfy certain properties can be estimated consistently using an estimator obtained by plugging in the kernel density estimate of the data distribution. In terms of s, a smoothness parameter that corresponds to how many times data density is known to be differentiable and d, the data dimension, we have shown that the rate of convergence of such an estimator is $\frac{s}{2s+d}$. We have also shown that no estimator can converge at a rate faster than $\frac{1}{2}$.

This contains both good and bad news. The knowledge that we have consistent estimation is useful when applying the method to voluminous data (for example, webpages). However, we expect d to be high for many machine learning applications and we might not be able to assume that the smoothness parameter, s, is very high. Hence, when using the plug-in estimator, the convergence rate can be very slow for high-dimensional data.

We have shown a graph construction method that can be used for consistent computation of DBD metrics and shown that with high probability, the approximation error when using this graph goes to zero faster than $1/n^{1/2d}$ with high probability. We have also shown that the shortest distance along a nearest neighborhood-based graph on the data cannot converge to true distance faster than $1/n^{1/(d-1)}$ with high probability. We presented semi-supervised classification results that demonstrate that using DBD metrics can sometimes improve performance over using simple Euclidean distance, when data density can be estimated with reasonable reliability.

While we have been able to give a theoretical understanding of DBD metrics, further experimental investigation of their use for semi-supervised learning in needed to make them a practically viable choice. While several papers have considered DBD metrics, the only papers that present experimental results with real world data use the 1NN algorithm (Lebanon, 2003; Sajama and Orlitsky, 2005). Experiments using these metrics with other classification algorithms, using parametric density estimation in place of the kernel density estimator, and studying alternative graph construction and weighting methods for more accurate and efficient computation will be of practical value.

Acknowledgements

We thank Sanjoy Dasgupta and Thomas John for several helpful discussions. Thanks also to anonymous reviewers for several comments used in revising and improving this paper. In particular, we thank an anonymous reviewer for pointing out an error in the analysis of the estimation error rate in an earlier version.

V Semi-Supervised Learning in Practice

18   Large-Scale Algorithms

Olivier Delalleau   DELALLEA@IRO.UMONTREAL.CA
Yoshua Bengio   BENGIOY@IRO.UMONTREAL.CA
Nicolas Le Roux   NICOLAS.LE.ROUX@UMONTREAL.CA

In chapter 11, it is shown how a number of graph-based semi-supervised learning algorithms can be seen as the minimization of a specific cost function, leading to a linear system with n equations and unknowns (with n the total number of labeled and unlabeled examples). Solving such a linear system will in general require on the order of $O(kn^2)$ time and $O(kn)$ memory (for a sparse graph where each data point has k neighbors), which can be prohibitive on large data sets (especially if $k = n$, i.e., the graph is dense). We present in this chapter a subset selection method that can be used to reduce the original system to one of size $m \ll n$. The idea is to solve for the labels of a subset $S \subset X$ of only m points, while still retaining information from the rest of the data by approximating their label with a linear combination of the labels in S (using the induction formula presented in chapter 11). This leads to an algorithm whose computational requirements scale as $O(m^2 n)$ and memory requirements as $O(m^2)$, thus allowing one to take advantage of significantly bigger unlabeled data sets than with the original algorithms.

18.1   Introduction

The graph-based semi-supervised algorithms presented in chapter 11 do not scale well to very large data sets. In this chapter, we propose an approximation method that significantly reduces the computational and memory requirements of such algorithms. Notations will be the same as in chapter 11, i.e.:

- $Y = (Y_l, Y_u)$ is the set of "original" labels on labeled and unlabeled points (here, Y_u is filled with 0),
- $\hat{Y} = (\hat{Y}_l, \hat{Y}_u)$ is the set of estimated labels on labeled and unlabeled points,
- $\hat{y}$ is the function to learn, which assigns a label to each point of the input space,

- $\hat{y}(x_i) = \hat{y}_i$ is the value of the function $\hat{y}$ on training points (labeled and unlabeled).

In chapter 11, we defined a quadratic cost (Eq. 11.11):

$$C(\hat{Y}) = \|\hat{Y}_l - Y_l\|^2 + \mu \hat{Y}^\top L \hat{Y} + \mu\epsilon\|\hat{Y}\|^2. \tag{18.1}$$

Minimizing this cost gives rise to the following linear system in $\hat{Y}$ with regularization hyperparameters μ and ϵ:

$$(\mathbf{S} + \mu L + \mu\epsilon\mathbf{I})\,\hat{Y} = \mathbf{S}Y, \tag{18.2}$$

where $\mathbf{S}$ is the $(n \times n)$ diagonal matrix defined by $\mathbf{S}_{ii} = \delta_{i \leq l}$, and $L = \mathbf{D} - \mathbf{W}$ is the un-normalized graph Laplacian. This linear system can be solved to obtain the value of $\hat{y}_i$ on the training points x_i. We can extend the formula to obtain the value of $\hat{y}$ on every point x in the input space as shown in section 11.4:

$$\hat{y} = \frac{\sum_j W_X(x, x_j)\hat{y}_j}{\sum_j W_X(x, x_j) + \epsilon}. \tag{18.3}$$

where W_X is the symmetric data-dependent edge weighting function (e.g., a Gaussian kernel) such that $\mathbf{W}_{ij} = W_X(x_i, x_j)$. However, in case of very large training sets, solving the linear system (18.2) may be computationally prohibitive, even using iterative techniques such as those described in section 11.2. In this chapter we consider how to approximate the cost using only a subset of the examples. Even though this will not yield an exact solution to the original problem, it will make the computation time much more reasonable.

18.2   Cost Approximations

18.2.1   Estimating the Cost from a Subset

reduced
parametrization
of solution

A simple way to reduce the $O(kn^2)$ computational requirement and $O(kn)$ memory requirement for training the non-parametric semi-supervised algorithms of chapter 11 is to force the solutions to be expressed in terms of a *subset of the examples*. This idea has already been exploited successfully in a different form for other kernel algorithms, e.g., for Gaussian processes (Williams and Seeger, 2001) or spectral embedding algorithms (Ouimet and Bengio, 2005).

Here we will take advantage of the induction formula (Eq. 18.3) to simplify the linear system to $m \ll n$ equations and variables, where m is the size of a subset of examples that will form a basis for expressing all the other function values. Let $S \subset \{1, \ldots, n\}$ be a subset, with $|S| = m$ and $S \supset \{1, \ldots, l\}$ (i.e., we take all labeled examples in the subset). Define $R = \{1, \ldots, n\} \backslash S$ (the rest of the data). In the following, vector and matrices will be split into their S and R parts, e.g.

$\hat{Y} = (\hat{Y}_S, \hat{Y}_R)$ and

$$L = \begin{pmatrix} L_{SS} & L_{SR} \\ L_{RS} & L_{RR} \end{pmatrix}.$$

The idea is to force $\hat{y}_i \in \hat{Y}_R$ to be expressed as a linear combination of the $\hat{y}_j \in \hat{Y}_S$ following (18.3):

$$\forall i \in R, \ \hat{y}_i = \frac{\sum_{j \in S} \mathbf{W}_{ij} \hat{y}_j}{\sum_{j \in S} \mathbf{W}_{ij} + \epsilon} \tag{18.4}$$

or in matrix notation

$$\hat{Y}_R = \overline{\mathbf{W}}_{RS} \hat{Y}_S \tag{18.5}$$

with $\overline{\mathbf{W}}_{RS}$ the matrix of size $((n - m) \times m)$ with entries $\mathbf{W}_{ij}/(\epsilon + \sum_{k \in S} \mathbf{W}_{ik})$, for $i \in R$ and $j \in S$. We will then split the cost (18.1) in terms that involve only the subset S or the rest R, or both of them. To do so, we must first split the diagonal matrix $\mathbf{D}$ (whose elements are row sums of $\mathbf{W}$) into $\mathbf{D} = \mathbf{D}^S + \mathbf{D}^R$, with $\mathbf{D}^S$ and $\mathbf{D}^R$ the $(n \times n)$ diagonal matrices whose elements are sums over S and R respectively, i.e.,

$$\begin{aligned} \mathbf{D}^S_{ii} &= \sum_{j \in S} \mathbf{W}_{ij} \\ \mathbf{D}^R_{ii} &= \sum_{j \in R} \mathbf{W}_{ij}. \end{aligned}$$

The unnormalized Laplacian $L = \mathbf{D} - \mathbf{W}$ can then be written

$$L = \begin{pmatrix} \mathbf{D}^S_{SS} + \mathbf{D}^R_{SS} - \mathbf{W}_{SS} & -\mathbf{W}_{SR} \\ -\mathbf{W}_{RS} & \mathbf{D}^S_{RR} + \mathbf{D}^R_{RR} - \mathbf{W}_{RR} \end{pmatrix}. \tag{18.6}$$

Using (18.6), the cost (18.1) can now be expanded as follows:

$$\begin{aligned} C(\hat{Y}) &= \mu \hat{Y}^\top L \hat{Y} + \mu \epsilon \|\hat{Y}\|^2 + \|\hat{Y}_l - Y_l\|^2 \\ &= \underbrace{\mu \hat{Y}_S^\top \left(\mathbf{D}^S_{SS} - \mathbf{W}_{SS} \right) \hat{Y}_S + \mu \epsilon \|\hat{Y}_S\|^2}_{C_{SS}} + \underbrace{\mu \hat{Y}_R^\top \left(\mathbf{D}^R_{RR} - \mathbf{W}_{RR} \right) \hat{Y}_R + \mu \epsilon \|\hat{Y}_R\|^2}_{C_{RR}} \\ &\quad + \underbrace{\mu \left(\hat{Y}_S^\top \mathbf{D}^R_{SS} \hat{Y}_S + \hat{Y}_R^\top \mathbf{D}^S_{RR} \hat{Y}_R - \hat{Y}_R^\top \mathbf{W}_{RS} \hat{Y}_S - \hat{Y}_S^\top \mathbf{W}_{SR} \hat{Y}_R \right)}_{C_{RS}} \\ &\quad + \underbrace{\|\hat{Y}_l - Y_l\|^2}_{C_L}. \end{aligned}$$

18.2.2   Resolution

Using the approximation $\hat{Y}_R = \overline{\mathbf{W}}_{RS}\hat{Y}_S$ (18.5), the gradient of the different parts of the above cost with respect to $\hat{Y}_S$ is then

$$\frac{\partial C_{SS}}{\partial \hat{Y}_S} = \left[2\mu\left(\mathbf{D}_{SS}^S - \mathbf{W}_{SS} + \epsilon\mathbf{I}\right)\right]\hat{Y}_S$$

$$\frac{\partial C_{RR}}{\partial \hat{Y}_S} = \left[2\mu\overline{\mathbf{W}}_{RS}^\top\left(\mathbf{D}_{RR}^R - \mathbf{W}_{RR} + \epsilon\mathbf{I}\right)\overline{\mathbf{W}}_{RS}\right]\hat{Y}_S$$

$$\frac{\partial C_{RS}}{\partial \hat{Y}_S} = \left[2\mu\left(\mathbf{D}_{SS}^R + \overline{\mathbf{W}}_{RS}^\top\mathbf{D}_{RR}^S\overline{\mathbf{W}}_{RS} - \overline{\mathbf{W}}_{RS}^\top\mathbf{W}_{RS} - \mathbf{W}_{SR}\overline{\mathbf{W}}_{RS}\right)\right]\hat{Y}_S$$

$$= \left[2\mu\left(\mathbf{D}_{SS}^R - \mathbf{W}_{SR}\overline{\mathbf{W}}_{RS}\right)\right]\hat{Y}_S \tag{18.7}$$

$$\frac{\partial C_L}{\partial \hat{Y}_S} = 2\mathbf{S}_{SS}(\hat{Y}_S - Y),$$

where to obtain (18.7) we have used the equality $\mathbf{D}_{RR}^S\overline{\mathbf{W}}_{RS} = \mathbf{W}_{RS}$, which follows from the definition of $\overline{\mathbf{W}}_{RS}$.

Recall the original linear system in $\hat{Y}$ was $(\mathbf{S} + \mu L + \mu\epsilon\mathbf{I})\hat{Y} = \mathbf{S}Y$ (18.2). Here it is replaced by a new system in $\hat{Y}_S$, written $\mathbf{A}\hat{Y}_S = \mathbf{S}_{SS}Y_S$ with

$$\mathbf{A} = \quad \mu\left(\mathbf{D}_{SS}^S - \mathbf{W}_{SS} + \epsilon\mathbf{I} + \mathbf{D}_{SS}^R - \mathbf{W}_{SR}\overline{\mathbf{W}}_{RS}\right)$$
$$+ \quad \mu\overline{\mathbf{W}}_{RS}^\top\left(\mathbf{D}_{RR}^R - \mathbf{W}_{RR} + \epsilon\mathbf{I}\right)\overline{\mathbf{W}}_{RS}$$
$$+ \quad \mathbf{S}_{SS}.$$

Since the system's size has been reduced from n to $|S| = m$, it can be solved much faster, even if $\mathbf{A}$ is not guaranteed[1] to be sparse anymore (we assume $m \ll n$).

Unfortunately, in order to obtain the matrix $\mathbf{A}$, we need to compute $\mathbf{D}_{RR}^R$, which costs $O(n^2)$ in time, as well as products of matrices that cost $O(mn^2)$ if $\mathbf{W}$ is not sparse. A simple way to get rid of the quadratic complexity in n is to ignore C_{RR} in the total cost. If we remember that C_{RR} can be written

simplified cost function

$$C_{RR} = \mu\left(\frac{1}{2}\sum_{i,j \in R}\mathbf{W}_{ij}(\hat{y}_i - \hat{y}_j)^2 + \epsilon\|\hat{Y}_R\|^2\right),$$

this corresponds to ignoring the smoothness assumption between points in R, as well as the regularization term on R. Even if it may look like a bad idea, it turns out it usually preserves (and even improves) the performance of the semi-supervised classifier, for various reasons:

▪ Assuming the subset S is chosen to correctly "fill" the space, smoothness between points in S and points in R (encouraged by the part C_{RS} of the cost) also enforces smoothness between points in R only.

---

1. In practice, if $\mathbf{W}$ is sparse, $\mathbf{A}$ is also likely to be sparse, even if additional assumptions on $\mathbf{W}$ are needed if one wants to prove it.

- When reducing to a subset, the loss in capacity (we can choose m values instead of n when working with the full set) suggests we should weaken regularization, and the smoothness constraints are a form of regularization; thus dropping some of them is a way to achieve this goal.

- For some points $i \in R$, the approximation (18.4)

$$\hat{y}_i = \frac{\sum_{j \in S} \mathbf{W}_{ij} \hat{y}_j}{\sum_{j \in S} \mathbf{W}_{ij} + \epsilon}$$

may be poor (e.g. for a point far from all points in S, i.e. $\sum_{j \in S} \mathbf{W}_{ij}$ very small); thus smoothness constraints between points in R could be noisy and detrimental to the optimization process (this is not a big issue when considering smoothness between a point x_i in R and a point x_j in S as the smoothness penalty is weighted by $\mathbf{W}_{ij}$, which will be small if x_i is far from all points in S).

Given the above considerations, ignoring the part C_{RR} leads to the new system

$$\left(\mathbf{S}_{SS} + \mu \left(\mathbf{D}_{SS} - \mathbf{W}_{SS} - \mathbf{W}_{SR}\overline{\mathbf{W}}_{RS} + \epsilon \mathbf{I}\right)\right)\hat{Y}_S = \mathbf{S}_{SS}\mathbf{Y}_S$$

which in general can be solved in $O(m^3)$ time (less if the system matrix is sparse).

18.3   Subset Selection

18.3.1   Random Selection

In general, training using only a subset of $m \ll n$ samples will not perform as well as using the whole data set. Carefully choosing the subset S can help in limiting this loss in performance. Even if random selection is certainly the easiest way to choose the points in S, it has two main drawbacks:

- It may not pick points in some regions of the space, resulting in the approximation (18.4) being very poor in these regions.

- It may pick uninteresting points: the region near the decision surface is the one where we are more likely to make mistakes by assigning the wrong label. Therefore, we would like to have as many points as possible in S being in that region, while we do not need points which are far away from that surface.

As a result, it is worthwhile considering more elaborate subset selection schemes, such as the one presented in the next section.

18.3.2   Smart Data Sampling

There could be many ways of choosing which points to take in the subset. The algorithm described below is one solution, based on the previous considerations about the random selection weaknesses. The first step of the algorithm will be to select points somewhat uniformly in order to get a first estimate of the decision surface, while the second step will consist in the choice of points near that estimated surface.

18.3.2.1   *First Step*

Equation 18.4,

$$\hat{y}_i = \frac{\sum_{j \in S} \mathbf{W}_{ij} \hat{y}_j}{\sum_{j \in S} \mathbf{W}_{ij} + \epsilon},$$

suggests that the value of $\hat{y}_i$ is well approximated when there is a point in S near x_i (two points x_i and x_j are nearby if $\mathbf{W}_{ij}$ is high). The idea will therefore be to

covering the manifold cover the manifold where the data lie as well as possible, that is to say ensure that every point in R is near a point (or a set of points) in S. There is another issue we should be taking care of: as we discard the part C_{RR} of the cost, we must now be careful not to modify the structure of the manifold. If there are some parts of the manifold without any point of S, then the smoothness of $\hat{y}$ will not be enforced at such parts (and the labels will be poorly estimated).

This suggests starting with $S = \{1, \dots, l\}$ and $R = \{l+1, \dots, n\}$, then adding samples x_i by iteratively choosing the point farthest from the current subset, i.e. the one that minimizes $\sum_{j \in S} \mathbf{W}_{ij}$. The idea behind this method is that it is useless to have two points near each other in S, as this will not give extra information while increasing the cost. However, one can note that this method may tend to select outliers, which are far from all other points (and especially those from S).

avoiding outliers A way to avoid this is to consider the quantity $\sum_{j \in R \setminus \{i\}} \mathbf{W}_{ij}$ for a given x_i. If x_i is such an outlier, this quantity will be very low (as all $\mathbf{W}_{ij}$ are small). Thus, if it is smaller than a given threshold δ, we do not take x_i in the subset. The cost of this additional check is of $O((m+o)n)$ where o is the number of outliers: assuming there are only a few of them (less than m), it scales as $O(mn)$.

18.3.2.2   *Second Step*

Once this first subset is selected, it can be refined by training the algorithm presented in section 11.3.2 on the subset S, in order to get an approximation of the $\hat{y}_i$ for $i \in S$, and by using the induction formula 18.4 to get an approximation of the

discarding uninformative samples $\hat{y}_j$ for $j \in R$. Samples in S which are far away from the estimated decision surface can then be discarded, as they will be correctly classified no matter whether they belong to S or not, and they are unlikely to give any information on the shape of the decision surface. These discarded samples are then replaced by other samples that are near the decision surface, in order to be able to estimate it more accurately.

The distance from a point x_i to the decision surface is estimated by the confidence we have in its estimated label $\hat{y}_i$. In the binary classification case considered here (with targets -1 and 1), this confidence is given by $|\hat{y}_i|$, while in a multiclass setting it would be the absolute value of the difference between the predicted scores of the

two highest-scoring classes. One should be careful when removing samples, though:
we must make sure we do not leave "empty" regions. This can be done by ensuring
that $\sum_{j\in S} \mathbf{W}_{ij}$ stays above some threshold for all $i \in R$ after a point has been
removed.

Overall, the cost of this selection phase is on the order of $O(mn + m^3)$. It is
summarized in algorithm 18.1.

Algorithm 18.1 Subset selection

Choose a small threshold δ (e.g. $\delta \leftarrow 10^{-10}$)
Choose a small regularization parameter ϵ (e.g. $\epsilon \leftarrow 10^{-11}$)
(1) Greedy selection
$S \leftarrow \{1,\ldots,l\}$ {The subset we are going to build contains the labeled points}
$R \leftarrow \{l+1,\ldots,n\}$ {The rest of the unlabeled points}
while $|S| < m$ **do**
  Find $i \in R$ s.t. $\sum_{j\in R\setminus\{i\}} \mathbf{W}_{ij} \geq \delta$ and $\sum_{j\in S} \mathbf{W}_{ij}$ is minimum
  $S \leftarrow S \cup \{i\}$
  $R \leftarrow R \setminus \{i\}$
end while
(2) Decision surface improvement
Compute an approximate of $\hat{y}_i$ with $i \in S$ by applying the standard semi-
supervised minimization of section 11.3.2 with the data set S
Compute an approximate of $\hat{y}_j$ with $j \in R$ by (18.4)
$S_H \leftarrow$ the points in S with highest confidence (see section 18.3.2.2)
$R_L \leftarrow$ the points in R with lowest confidence
for all $i \in S_H$ **do**
  if $\min_{j\in R} \sum_{k\in S\setminus\{i\}} \mathbf{W}_{jk} \geq \delta$ **then**
    {i can be safely removed from S without leaving empty regions}
    $k^* \leftarrow \arg\min_{k\in R_L} \sum_{j\in S} \mathbf{W}_{jk}$ {Find point with low confidence farthest from
    S}
    Replace i by k^* in S (and k^* by i in R)
  end if
end for

18.3.3   Computational Issues

We are now in position to present the overall computational requirements for the
different algorithms proposed in this chapter. As before, the subset size m is taken
to be much smaller than the total number of points n, and the weight matrix
$\mathbf{W}$ may either be dense or sparse (with k non-zero entries in each row or column).
Table 18.1 summarizes time and memory requirements for the following algorithms:

Table 18.1   Comparative computational requirements of *NoSub*, *RandSub*, and *Smart-Sub* (n = number of labeled and unlabeled training data, m = subset size with $m \ll n$, k = number of neighbors for each point in $\mathbf{W}$ when $\mathbf{W}$ is sparse)

	Time	Memory
NoSub (sparse $\mathbf{W}$)	$O(kn^2)$	$O(kn)$
NoSub (dense $\mathbf{W}$)	$O(n^3)$	$O(n^2)$
RandSub	$O(m^2 n)$	$O(m^2)$
SmartSub	$O(m^2 n)$	$O(m^2)$

■ *NoSub*: the original transductive algorithm (using the whole data set) that consists in solving the system (18.2), as presented in chapter 11 (algorithm 11.2),

■ *RandSub*: the approximation algorithm discussed in section 18.2.2, with the subset S being randomly chosen (section 18.3.1),

■ *SmartSub*: the same approximation algorithm as *RandSub*, but with S being chosen as in section 18.3.2.

The table shows that the approximation method described in this chapter is particularly useful when $\mathbf{W}$ is dense or n is very large. This is confirmed by empirical experimentation in figure 18.1, which compares the training times (on the benchmark data set `SecStr` described in chapter 21 of this book) of *NoSub* with a dense kernel, *NoSub* with a sparse kernel, and *SmartSub* with a dense kernel. With a dense kernel, *NoSub* becomes quickly impractical because of the need to store (and solve) a linear system of size $n = l + u$, with $l = 100$ and $u \in [2000, 50,000]$. With a sparse kernel (and the iterative version presented in algorithm 11.2) it scales much better, but still exhibits a quadratic dependency in n. On the other hand, *SmartSub* can handle much more unlabeled data as its training time scales only linearly in n. We have not presented a sparse version of *SmartSub* since our current code cannot take advantage of a sparse weighting function. However, this could be useful to obtain further improvement, especially in terms of memory usage (working with full $m \times m$ matrices can become problematic when $m \geq 10,000$).

18.4   Discussion

This chapter follows up on chapter 11 to allow large-scale applications of semi-supervised learning algorithms presented previously. The idea is to express the cost to be minimized as a function of only a subset of the unknown labels, in order to reduce the number of free variables: this can be obtained thanks to the induction formula introduced in chapter 11. The form of this formula suggests it is only accurate when the points in the subset cover the whole manifold on which the data lie. This explains why choosing the subset randomly can lead to poor results, while

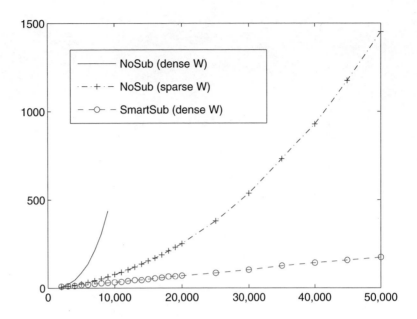

Figure 18.1   Training time (in seconds) w.r.t. the amount of unlabeled samples on benchmark data set `SecStr` (cf. chapter 21). W_X is a Gaussian kernel (combined with an approximate 100-nearest-neighbor kernel in the sparse case). There are $l = 100$ labeled samples, and *SmartSub* selects $m = 500$ unlabeled samples in the subset approximation scheme. Note how the dependence of *SmartSub* in the total number of unlabeled samples $u \in [2000, 50{,}000]$ is only linear. *NoSub* with dense **W** fails for $u \geq 10{,}000$ because of memory shortage. Experiments were performed on a 3.2GHz P4 CPU with 2Gb of RAM.

it is possible to design a simple heuristic algorithm (such as algorithm 18.1) giving much better classification performance. Better selection algorithms (e.g., explicitly optimizing the cost we are interested in) are the subject of future research.

One must note that the idea of expressing the cost from a subset of the data is not equivalent to training a standard algorithm on the subset only, before extending to the rest of the data with the induction formula. Here, the rest of the data are explicitly used in the part of the cost enforcing the smoothness between points in the subset and points in the rest (part C_{RS} of the cost), which helps to obtain a smoother labeling function, usually giving better generalization.

19 Semi-Supervised Protein Classification Using Cluster Kernels

Jason Weston   JASONW@NEC-LABS.COM
Christina Leslie   CLESLIE@CS.COLUMBIA.EDU
Eugene Ie   EIE@CS.COLUMBIA.EDU
William Stafford Noble   NOBLE@GS.WASHINGTON.EDU

In this chapter we describe an experimental study of large-scale semi-supervised learning for the problem of protein classification. The protein classification problem, a central problem in computational biology, is to predict the structural class of a protein given its amino acid sequence. Such a classification helps biologists to understand the function of a protein. Building an accurate protein classification system, as in many tasks, depends critically upon choosing a good representation of the input sequences of amino acids. Early work using string kernels with support vector machines (SVMs) for protein classification achieved state-of-the-art classification performance. However, such representations are based only on labeled data—examples with known three-dimensional (3D) structures, organized into structural classes—while in practice, unlabeled data are far more plentiful.

This chapter compares different approaches that extend these earlier results to take advantage of unlabeled data. In particular, special cases of cluster kernels are described that are scalable to hundreds of thousands of unlabeled points and provide state-of-the-art performance.

19.1 Introduction

The 3D structure that a protein assumes after folding largely determines its function in the cell. However, it is far easier to determine experimentally the primary sequence (the string of amino acids) that make up a protein than it is to discover its 3D structure. Through evolution, structure is more conserved than sequence, so that detecting even very subtle sequence similarities, or remote homology, is

protein remote
homology
detection

important for predicting structure, which can help infer function. Computational techniques have proven very successful at aiding biologists in this task.

The major methods for homology detection can be split into three basic groups: pairwise sequence comparison algorithms (Altschul et al., 1990; Smith and Waterman, 1981), generative models for protein families (Krogh et al., 1994; Park et al., 1998), and discriminative classifiers (Jaakkola et al., 2000; Leslie et al., 2003; Liao and Noble, 2002). Popular sequence comparison methods such as BLAST and Smith-Waterman are based on alignment scores. Generative models such as profile hidden Markov models (HMMs) model positive examples of a protein family, but these models can be trained iteratively using both positively labeled and unlabeled examples by pulling in close homologs and adding them to the positive set. A compromise between these methods is PSI-BLAST (Altschul et al., 1997), which uses BLAST to iteratively build a probabilistic profile of a query sequence and obtain a more sensitive sequence comparison score.

Finally, classifiers such as support vector machines (SVMs) use both positive and negative examples and provide state-of-the-art performance when used with appropriate distance metrics (i.e., appropriate kernels) (Jaakkola et al., 2000; Leslie et al., 2003; Liao and Noble, 2002; Saigo et al., 2004). To be more specific, to solve this task as a classification problem, the input is the string of amino acids: the string is typically hundreds of "characters" in length, and the characters themselves have an alphabet of size 20. Posed as a binary classification problem, a classifier can answer the question: "Does the given protein (amino acid sequence) belong to structural class X or not?" and should be trained with positive and negative examples of this class.

Building an accurate system, as in most machine learning tasks, depends critically upon choosing a good representation of the input sequences of amino acids. The first hurdle is that the inputs are not vectors of fixed dimension, and so to use standard methods like SVMs one must define a similarity on sequences. This is possible by using string kernels, whereby one embeds the strings into a vector space and then performs inner products in this space. This issue is discussed in section 19.2. A study of the performance of these methods compared to more classical techniques is also detailed there.

In practice, however, relatively little labeled data are available—approximately 30,000 proteins with known 3D structure, some belonging to families and superfamilies with only a handful of labeled members—whereas there are close to one million sequenced proteins, providing abundant unlabeled data. The basic method in the literature (Jaakkola et al., 2000; Leslie et al., 2003) to take advantage of this extra data is to use an auxiliary method (such as PSI-BLAST) in order to add predicted homologs of the positive training examples to the training set before training the classifier. New semi-supervised learning techniques should be able to make better use of these unlabeled data.

semi-supervised learning

Some of the recent work in semi-supervised learning has focused on changing the representation given to a classifier by taking into account the structure described by the unlabeled data (Chapelle et al., 2003; Szummer and Jaakkola, 2002b). These

cluster kernels

efforts can be viewed as cases of *cluster kernels*, which learn similarity metrics based on the cluster assumption: when two points are in the same "cluster" (or are connected by a path of high density) in the original metric they should have a small distance to each other in the new metric. This review describes an experimental comparison of cluster kernels and some other competing methods on the protein classification problem. In particular, two simple and scalable cluster kernel methods will be described that were developed explicitly for this problem. The *neighborhood kernel* (Weston et al., 2003a) uses averaging over a neighborhood of sequences defined by a local sequence similarity measure, and the *bagged kernel* (Weston et al., 2003a) uses bagged clustering of the full sequence data set to modify the base kernel. Finally, we compare these two methods to a problem-specific solution, the profile kernel of Kuang et al. (2004). In this kernel, each sequence is represented by a profile estimated from a large unlabeled database (using PSI-BLAST, for example); the profile kernel uses a substring-based feature map, but is defined on sequence profiles rather than the sequences themselves.

In both the semi-supervised and transductive settings, these last three techniques all provide greatly improved classification performance when used with mismatch string kernels, and the techniques achieve equal or superior results to all previously presented cluster kernel methods that we tried. Moreover, they are far more computationally efficient than these competing methods. The profile kernel provides perhaps the best scalability, whereas the neighborhood and bagged kernels provide similar performance and good scaling ability, while providing more general applicability.

The chapter is organized as follows. We begin with an overview of sequence representations for supervised classifiers in section 19.2, followed in section 19.3 by a review of existing cluster kernel methods for incorporating unlabeled data into the kernel representation. In sections 19.3.2, 19.3.3, and 19.3.4, we describe the profile, neighborhood, and bagged mismatch kernels. Finally, detailed experiments comparing these techniques are given in section 19.4.

19.2 Representations and Kernels for Protein Sequences

Proteins can be represented as variable-length sequences, typically several hundred characters long, from the alphabet of 20 amino acids. In order to use learning algorithms that require vector inputs, we must first find a suitable feature vector representation, mapping sequence x into a vector space by $x \mapsto \Phi(x)$. Kernel methods such as SVMs only need to compute inner products, called kernels, $k(x, y) = \langle \Phi(x), \Phi(y) \rangle$, for training and testing. We thus can accomplish the above mapping using a kernel for sequence data.

Biologically motivated sequence comparison scores, like Smith-Waterman or BLAST, provide an appealing representation of sequence data. The Smith-Waterman (SW) algorithm (Smith and Waterman, 1981) uses dynamic programming to compute the optimal local gapped alignment score between two sequences, while BLAST (Altschul et al., 1990) approximates SW by computing a heuristic alignment score. Both methods return empirically estimated E-values[1] indicating the confidence of the score. These alignment-based scores do not define a positive definite kernel; however, one can use a feature representation based on the empirical kernel map

empirical kernel map

$$\Phi(x) = (d(x_1, x), \ldots, d(x_l, x)),$$

where $d(x, y)$ is the pairwise score (or E-value) between x and y, and x_i for $i = 1, \ldots, l$ are the training sequences. Using SW E-values in this fashion — the SVM-pairwise method (Liao and Noble, 2002)— gives strong classification performance. Note, however, that SVM-pairwise is slow, both because computing each SW score is $O(|x|^2)$ and because computing each empirically mapped kernel value is $O(l)$.

Another appealing idea is to derive the feature representation from a generative model for a protein family. In the Fisher kernel method (Jaakkola et al., 2000), one first builds a profile HMM for the positive training sequences, defining a log-likelihood function $\log P(x|\theta)$ for any protein sequence x. Then the gradient vector $\nabla_\theta \log P(x|\theta)|_{\theta=\theta_0}$, where θ_0 is the maximum-likelihood estimate for model parameters, defines an explicit vector of features, called Fisher scores, for x. This representation gives excellent classification results, but the Fisher scores must be computed by an $O(|x|^2)$ forward-backward algorithm, making the kernel tractable but slow.

Fisher kernel

It is possible to construct useful kernels directly without explicitly depending on generative models by using string kernels. For example, the mismatch kernel (Leslie et al., 2003) is defined by a histogram-like feature map that uses mismatches to capture inexact string matching. The feature space is indexed by all possible p-length subsequences $\alpha = a_1, a_2, \ldots, a_p$, where each a_i is a character in the alphabet $\mathcal{A}$ of amino acids. The feature map is defined on p-gram α by $\Phi(\alpha) = (\phi_\beta(\alpha))_{\mathcal{A}^p}$, where $\phi_\beta(\alpha) = 1$ if α is within m mismatches of β, and 0 otherwise. The feature map is extended additively to longer sequences: $\Phi(x) = \sum_{p\text{-grams}\alpha \in x} \Phi(\alpha)$. The mismatch kernel can be computed efficiently using a trie data structure: the complexity of calculating $k(x, y)$ is $O(c_k(|x| + |y|))$, where $c_k = p^{m+1}|\mathcal{A}|^m$. For typical kernel parameters $p = 5$ and $m = 1$ (Leslie et al., 2003), the mismatch kernel is fast, scalable, and yields impressive performance.

p-gram string kernels

string kernels

Other direct string kernel methods include pair HMM and convolution kernels (Watkins, 1999; Haussler, 1999; Lodhi et al., 2002), which are quite general but also have complexity $O(|x||y|)$; more recent and related string alignment kernels (Saigo et al., 2004), also with complexity $O(|x||y|)$; and exact-matching string kernels built with suffix trees and suffix links, with complexity $O(|x| + |y|)$ (Vishwanathan and

---

1. The E-value is the expected number of times that an alignment score as good or better than the observed score is expected to appear by chance in a random sequence database of the given size.

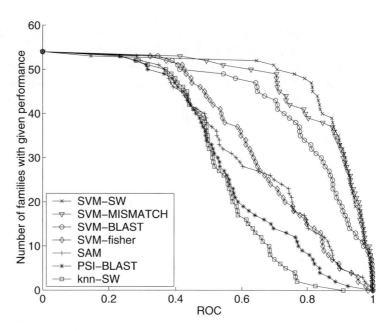

Figure 19.1 Comparison of protein representations and classifiers *without* use of unlabeled data. The graph plots the total number of families for which a given method exceeds a ROC score threshold. The SVM-based methods use the following kernels: Smith-Waterman empirical kernel map (SW), mismatch kernel with $p = 5$ and $m = 1$ (mismatch), BLAST empirical kernel map (BLAST), and a Fisher kernel built from a profile HMM (Fisher). The three non-SVM methods include a hidden Markov model (SAM), the PSI-BLAST algorithm, and the kernel k-nearest neighbor algorithm (k=3) using a Smith-Waterman empirical kernel map.

Smola, 2002). Inexact string matching models similar to the mismatch kernel but with complexity $O(c_k(|x| + |y|))$, with c_k independent of alphabet size, have also been presented (Leslie and Kuang, 2003). The motif kernel (Ben-Hur and Brutlag, 2003) uses features that are built from a fixed database of motifs; computing these features is linear in the length of the sequence. Finally, almost all these kernels can be constructed using the rational kernel framework of Cortes et al. (2002). We concentrate on the mismatch kernel representation for the current work.

In figure 19.1, we summarize the results from Liao and Noble (2002) and Leslie et al. (2003) by comparing SVM performance with these representations and other homology detection methods on a problem *that does not include the use of unlabeled data*. These and subsequent experiments are based upon the structural classification of proteins (SCOP) (Murzin et al., 1995). This is a widely used database of protein structures, in which proteins are organized hierarchically into classes, folds, superfamilies, and families. SCOP contains only proteins for which the 3D structure is available; hence, related proteins can be placed into a single superfamily even when their amino acid sequences have diverged evolutionarily. The SCOP database has been used in a large number of published studies of protein homology detection and fold classification algorithms. Here, we use a benchmark data set of Liao and Noble (2002), which consists of 54 two-class remote homology detection problems. The positive test set is a target protein family to be detected, and the positive training set contains sequences that are only remotely related to the target. The negative training and test sets are proteins from two disjoint sets of folds, and contain no proteins from the target fold. All methods are evaluated by using receiver operating characteristic (ROC) scores. More details concerning the experimental setup can be found at `http://www1.cs.columbia.edu/compbio/svm-pairwise`.

The results indicate that, without unlabeled data, SVM methods using a number of representations perform very strongly. They are superior to both HMMs (SAM-T98 (Park et al., 1998)) and pairwise scoring functions like PSI-BLAST. We believe that the SVM Fisher kernel computed here performs poorly because the underlying HMMs lack sufficient training data. (For a method comparison in the more standard setting, where domain homologs from an unlabeled database are added to the training set, see Leslie et al. (2003); there, SVM-Fisher is competitive with the mismatch kernel.) Note, however, that the performance of k-nearest neighbors (k-NN) with a good representation (the SW representation) performs poorly, so choice of classifier is also important.

It seems clear that string kernel methods with SVMs are a powerful approach, but in a real-world setting, classifiers have access to unlabeled data. We now discuss how to incorporate such data into the representation given to SVMs via the use of cluster kernels.

19.3 Semi-Supervised Kernels for Protein Sequences

cluster
assumption

In semi-supervised learning, one tries to improve a classifier trained on labeled data by exploiting a relatively large set of unlabeled data. The most common assumption one makes in this setting is called the "cluster assumption," namely that *the class does not change in regions of high density.* Equivalently, one assumes that the true decision boundary lies in regions of low density.

19.3.1 Existing Cluster Kernels

We will focus on classifiers that re-represent the given data to reflect structure revealed by unlabeled data. The main idea is to change the distance metric so that the relative distance between two points is smaller if the points are in the same cluster. If one is using kernels, rather than explicit feature vectors, one can modify the kernel representation by constructing a cluster kernel.

random walk and
spectral
clustering kernels

Previous work of Chapelle et al. (2003) presented a general framework for producing cluster kernels by modifying the eigenspectrum of the kernel matrix. Two of the main methods presented are the *random walk kernel* and the *spectral clustering kernel*, which we will briefly summarize below. See chapter 15 for more details on these and other spectral cluster kernels.

The random walk kernel is a normalized and symmetrized version of a transition matrix corresponding to a t-step random walk. As described in Szummer and Jaakkola (2002b), one can define a random walk representation by viewing a radial basis function (RBF) kernel as a transition matrix of a random walk on a graph with vertices x_i. One then uses the eigendecomposition of the normalized transition matrix to compute the t-step random walk kernel. The spectral clustering kernel is a simple use of the representation derived from spectral clustering (Ng et al., 2002) using the first k eigenvectors of a normalized affinity matrix.

A serious problem with these methods is that one must diagonalize a matrix of size n, where n is the number of labeled and unlabeled data, giving a complexity $O(n^3)$. Other methods of implementing the cluster assumption such as transductive SVMs (Joachims, 1999), described in chapter 6, also suffer from computational efficiency issues. A second drawback is that these kernels are better suited to a *transductive* setting (where one is given both the unlabeled and test points in advance) rather than a semi-supervising setting. In sections 19.3.2 and 19.3.3, we will describe two simple methods to implement the cluster assumption that do not suffer from these issues.

19.3.2   The Neighborhood Kernel

fast cluster kernels

In this section and the next, we introduce two fast and general cluster kernels that leverage unlabeled data to improve a base kernel representation. Unlike other cluster kernel approaches, these kernels make use of two complementary (dis)similarity measures: a base kernel representation which implicitly makes use of features useful for discrimination between classes, and a distance measure that describes how close examples are to each other. In our application to protein classification, we use the mismatch string kernel as the base kernel and standard sequence comparison metrics (such as BLAST or PSI-BLAST E-values) as the distance measure. We note that string kernels have proved to be powerful representations for SVM classification (Leslie et al., 2003) but do not give sensitive pairwise similarity scores like the BLAST family methods; thus the two sequence similarity measures play distinct roles in the kernel definition.

neighborhood kernel

For the neighborhood kernel, we use a standard sequence dissimilarity measure like BLAST or PSI-BLAST to define a neighborhood for each input sequence. The neighborhood $\mathrm{Nbd}(x)$ of sequence x is the set of sequences x' with similarity score to x below a fixed E-value threshold, together with x itself. Now given a fixed original feature representation, we represent x by the average of the feature vectors for members of its neighborhood: $\Phi_{nbd}(x) = \frac{1}{|\mathrm{Nbd}(x)|} \sum_{x' \in \mathrm{Nbd}(x)} \Phi_{orig}(x')$. The neighborhood kernel is then defined by

$$k_{nbd}(x, y) = \frac{\sum_{x' \in \mathrm{Nbd}(x), y' \in \mathrm{Nbd}(y)} k_{orig}(x', y')}{|\mathrm{Nbd}(x)||\mathrm{Nbd}(y)|}.$$

We will see in the experimental results that this simple neighborhood-averaging

Before neighborhood averaging   After neighborhood averaging

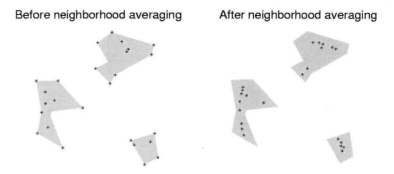

Figure 19.2 Neighborhood averaging for a toy data set. Feature representations for a toy data set before (*left*) and after (*right*) the neighborhood averaging operation. The shaded region is the union of the convex hulls of the neighborhood point sets for the original data.

technique, used in a semi-supervised setting with the mismatch kernel, dramatically improves classification performance.

In general, computing each neighborhood kernel value is quadratic in neighborhood size, as is clear from the kernel expression given above. However, in the special case where we use the mismatch kernel as base kernel, we can modify the mismatch kernel algorithm by presenting each neighborhood set as a concatenation of the neighbor sequences (keeping track of where the ends of sequences are located); using a trie data structure, the kernel computation is linear in sequence length, giving a complexity of $O(p^{m+1}|\mathcal{A}|^m(\sum x' + \sum y'))$ (that is, linear in neighborhood size) to compute $k_{nbd}(x, y)$, where $|\mathcal{A}|$ is the size of the alphabet of amino acids (Leslie et al., 2003).

To see how the neighborhood approach fits with the cluster assumption, consider a set of points in feature space that form a "cluster" or dense region of the data set, and consider the region R formed by the union of the convex hulls of the neighborhood point sets. If the dissimilarity measure is a true distance, then the neighborhood averaged vector $\Phi_{nbd}(x)$ stays inside the convex hull of the vectors in its neighborhood, and all the neighborhood vectors stay within region R. In general, the cluster contracts inside R under the averaging operation. Thus, under the new representation, different clusters can become better separated from each other.

Figure 19.2 gives an illustration of this phenomenon for a toy data set, showing the contraction of clusters within region R after neighborhood averaging.

19.3.3 The Bagged Cluster Kernel

A number of existing clustering techniques are much more efficient than the methods mentioned in section 19.3. For example, the classical k-means algorithm is $O(rknd)$, where n is the number of data points, d is their dimensionality, and r is the number bagged kernel

of iterations required. Empirically, this running time grows sublinearly with k, n, and d. Therefore, in practice, it is computationally efficient to run k-means multiple times, which can be useful because it can converge to local minima. We therefore consider the following method:

1. Run k-means N times, giving $j = 1, \ldots, N$ cluster assignments $c_j(x_i)$ for each i.

2. Build a bagged-clustering representation based upon the fraction of times that x and x' are in the same cluster:

$$k_{bag}(x, x') = \frac{\sum_j [c_j(x) = c_j(x')]}{N}. \tag{19.1}$$

3. Take the product between the original and bagged kernel:

$$k(x, x') = k_{orig}(x, x') \cdot k_{bag}(x, x').$$

Because k-means gives different solutions on each run, step 1 will give different results; for other clustering algorithms one could subsample the data instead. Step 2 is a valid kernel because it is the inner product in an Nk-dimensional space $\Phi(x) = \langle [c_j(x) = q] : j = 1, \ldots, N, q = 1, \ldots, k \rangle$, and products of kernels as in step 3 are also valid kernels. The intuition behind the approach is that the original kernel is rescaled by the "probability" that two points are in the same cluster, hence encoding the cluster assumption. To estimate the kernel on a test sequence x in a semi-supervised setting, one can assign x to the nearest cluster in each of the bagged runs to compute $k_{bag}(x, x_i)$.[2] We apply the bagged kernel method with k_{orig} as the mismatch kernel and k_{bag} built by running k-means on the distances induced by PSI-BLAST.

19.3.4   The Profile Kernel

Recently, Kuang et al. (2004) introduced a semi-supervised profile-based string kernel for protein sequences. The profile kernel is a function that measures the similarity of two protein sequence profiles based on their representation in a high-dimensional vector space indexed by all p-mers (p-length subsequences of amino acids). Each sequence is represented by a profile estimated from a large sequence database (for example, using PSI-BLAST), and each length-p segment of the profile is used to define the local mutation neighborhood and a corresponding contribution to the feature vector in a p-mer feature space. Unlike the Fisher kernel approach— where a single probabilistic model is used to define feature vectors for sequence

---

2. Of course it would also be possible to consider an additive rather than multiplicative combination of kernels, i.e. $k(x_i, x_j) = (1-\lambda)k_{orig}(x_i, x_j) + \lambda k_{bag}(x_i, x_j)$, $0 \leq \lambda \leq 1$. Thus, for $\lambda = 0$ we retain the original distance metric and for larger values of λ we incorporate more and more cluster information. Although we expect this might work better for the right choice of λ in the general case it also has the drawback of introducing yet another hyperparameter.

examples—in the profile kernel, every example is represented by a probabilistic model in the form of a profile, and the kernel is defined on profile examples.

Specifically, for a sequence x and its sequence profile $P(x)$ (e.g. PSI-BLAST profile), the *positional mutation neighborhood* is defined by the corresponding block of the profile $P(x)$:

profile kernel

$$M_{(p,\sigma)}(P(x[j+1:j+p])) = \{\beta = b_1 b_2 \ldots b_p : -\sum_{i=1}^{p} \log P_{j+i}(b_i) < \sigma\}.$$

Note that the emission probabilities, $P_{j+i}(b), i = 1 \ldots p$, come from the profile $P(x)$—for notational simplicity, we do not explicitly indicate the dependence on x. Typically, the profiles are estimated from close homologs found in a large sequence database; however, these estimates may be too restrictive for our purposes. Therefore, we smooth the estimates using background frequencies, $q(b), b \in \mathcal{A}$, of amino acids in the training data set via

$$\tilde{P}_i(b) = \frac{P_i(b) + tq(b)}{1+t}, i = 1 \ldots |x|,$$

where t is a smoothing parameter. We use the smoothed emission probabilities $\tilde{P}_i(b)$ in place of $P_i(b)$ in defining the mutation neighborhoods.

We now define the profile feature mapping as

$$\Phi^{\text{Profile}}_{(p,\sigma)}(P(x)) = \sum_{j=0\ldots|x|-p} (\phi_\beta(P(x[j+1:j+p])))_{\beta\in\mathcal{A}^p}, \tag{19.2}$$

where the coordinate $\phi_\beta(P(x[j+1:j+p])) = 1$ if β belongs to the mutation neighborhood $M_{(p,\sigma)}(P(x[j+1:j+p]))$, and otherwise the coordinate is 0. Note that the profile kernel between two protein sequences is simply defined by the inner product of feature vectors:

$$k^{\text{Profile}}_{(p,\sigma)}(P(x), P(y)) = \langle \Phi^{\text{Profile}}_{(p,\sigma)}(P(x)), \Phi^{\text{Profile}}_{(p,\sigma)}(P(y)) \rangle. \tag{19.3}$$

The use of profile-based string kernels is an example of semi-supervised learning since unlabeled data in the form of a large sequence database are used in the discrimination problem. Moreover, profile kernel values can be efficiently computed in time that scales linearly with input sequence length. The profile kernel is similar to the neighborhood kernel, in that it performs a local smoothing, but takes into account more a priori information about the problem at hand. This problem-specific solution, however, also makes the method more difficult to generalize to other applications.

19.4   Experiments

We measure the recognition performance of cluster kernel methods by testing their ability to classify protein domains into superfamilies in the structural classification of proteins (Murzin et al., 1995). SCOP is a human-curated database of known 3D structures of protein domains. The database is organized hierarchically into classes, folds, superfamilies, and families. For the purposes of this experiment, two domains that come from the same superfamily are assumed to be homologous, and two domains from different folds are assumed to be unrelated. For pairs of proteins in the same fold but different superfamilies, their relationship is uncertain, and so these pairs are not used in evaluating the algorithm. This labeling scheme has been used in several previous studies of remote homology detection algorithms (Jaakkola et al., 2000; Liao and Noble, 2002). We use the same 54 target families and the same test and training set splits as in the remote homology experiments in Liao and Noble (2002). The sequences are 7329 SCOP domains obtained from version 1.59 of the database after purging with `astral.stanford.edu` (Brenner et al., 2000) so that no pair of sequences share more than 95% identity. Compared to Liao and Noble (2002), we reduce the number of available labeled training patterns by roughly a third. Data set sequences that were neither in the training nor test sets for experiments from Liao and Noble (2002) are included as unlabeled data.

All methods are evaluated using ROC analysis (Hanley and McNeil, 1982). An ROC curve plots the rate of true positives as a function of the rate of false positives at varying decision thresholds. The ROC score is the area under this curve. A perfect classifier, which places all positive examples above all negative examples, receives an ROC score of 1, and a random classifier receives a score of approximately 0.5. In addition to the ROC score, we compute the ROC_{50} score, which is the ROC score computed only up to the first 50 false positives (Gribskov and Robinson, 1996). This score focuses on the top of the ranking, which in some applications is the most important. More details concerning the experimental setup can be found at `http://www1.cs.columbia.edu/compbio/svm-pairwise`.

In all experiments, we use an SVM classifier with a small soft-margin parameter, set as $K_{ii} \leftarrow K_{ii} + \gamma$, where γ is 0.02ρ times the median diagonal kernel entry, and ρ is the fraction of training set sequences that have the same label as the ith sequence. The SVM computations are performed using the freely available Spider Matlab machine learning package available at `http://www.kyb.tuebingen.mpg.de/bs/people/spider`. More information concerning the experiments, including data and source code scripts, can be found at `http://www.kyb.tuebingen.mpg.de/bs/people/weston/semiprot`.

We split our experiments into three settings: semi-supervised setting, transductive setting, and large-scale experiments. The first two sets of experiments are smaller so that we can compare with existing methods that are intractable for larger data sets. The transductive setting is included for methods that do not easily generalize to the semi-supervised case.

19.4.1   Semi-Supervised Setting

Our first experiment shows that the neighborhood mismatch kernel makes better use of unlabeled data than the baseline method of "pulling in homologs" prior to

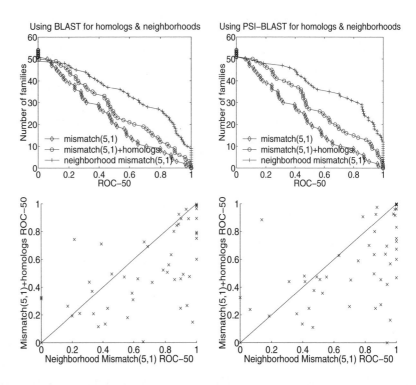

Figure 19.3 **Comparison of protein representations and classifiers using un-labeled data.** The mismatch kernel is used to represent proteins, with close homologs being pulled in from the unlabeled set with BLAST (*left*) or PSI-BLAST (*right*). Building a neighborhood with the neighborhood mismatch kernel in both cases improves over the baseline of pulling in homologs. *Note:* We also pull in homologs during the SVM training for the neighborhood kernel.

training the SVM classifier, that is, simply finding close homologs of the positive training examples in the unlabeled set and adding them to the positive training set for the SVM. Homologs come from the unlabeled set (not the test set), and "neighbors" for the neighborhood kernel come from the training plus unlabeled data. We compare the methods using the mismatch kernel representation with $p = 5$ and $m = 1$, as used in Leslie et al. (2003). Homologs are chosen via BLAST or PSI-BLAST as having a pairwise E-value less than 0.05 (the default parameter setting (Altschul et al., 1990)) with any of the positive training samples. The neighborhood mismatch kernel uses the same threshold to choose neighborhoods. For the neighborhood kernel, we normalize before and after the averaging operation via $K_{ij} \leftarrow K_{ij}/\sqrt{K_{ii}K_{jj}}$. The results are given in figure 19.3 and table 19.1.

Figure 19.3 plots the number of families achieving a given ROC_{50} score. Thus, a strongly performing method produces a curve close to the top right of the plot. A signed rank test shows that the neighborhood mismatch kernel yields significant improvement over adding homologs (*p*-value 3.9e-05). Note that the PSI-BLAST scores in these experiments are built using the whole database of 7329 sequences

Table 19.1   Mean ROC_{50} and ROC scores over 54 target families for *semi-supervised* experiments, using BLAST and PSI-BLAST for adding homologs and defining the neighborhood kernel

	BLAST		PSI-BLAST	
	ROC_{50}	ROC	ROC_{50}	ROC
mismatch kernel	0.416	0.870	0.416	0.870
mismatch kernel + homologs	0.480	0.900	0.550	0.910
neighborhood mismatch kernel	0.639	0.922	0.699	0.923

(that is, test sequences in a given experiment are also available to the PSI-BLAST algorithm), so these results are slightly optimistic. However, the comparison of methods in a truly inductive setting using BLAST shows the same improvement of the neighborhood mismatch kernel over adding homologs (*p*-value 8.4e-05).

The improvement from the neighborhood kernel does not come from the BLAST and PSI-BLAST representations alone: the mean ROC_{50} score for these representations using an empirical map (see the transductive setting for a description) are 0.368 and 0.533 respectively without pulling in homologs, and 0.448 and 0.595 with pulled-in homologs. Moreover, simply adding the BLAST and mismatch kernels together (using an empirical map) without using homologs yields a mean ROC_{50} of 0.3943, so it is also not because the methods give independent information about the targets which can be easily combined.

19.4.2   Transductive Setting

In the following experiments, we consider a *transductive* setting, in which the test points are given to the methods in advance as unlabeled data, giving slightly improved results over the last section. Although this setting is unrealistic for a real protein classification system, it enables comparison with random walk and spectral clustering kernels, which do not easily work in another setting. In figure 19.4 (left), we again show the mismatch kernel compared with pulling in homologs and the neighborhood kernel. This time we also compare with the bagged mismatch kernel using bagged k-means with $k = 100$ and $N = 100$ runs, which gave the best results. We observed an improvement over the baseline for several values of k; the result for $k = 400$ is also given in table 19.2. We then compare these methods to using random walk and spectral clustering kernels. Both methods do not work well for the mismatch kernel (see online supplement), perhaps because the feature vectors are so orthogonal. However, for a PSI-BLAST representation via empirical kernel map, the random walk outperforms pulling in homologs. We take the empirical map with $\Phi(x) = (\exp(-\lambda d(x_1, x)), \ldots, \exp(-\lambda(d(x_l, x))))$, where $d(x, y)$ are PSI-BLAST E-values and $\lambda = \frac{1}{1000}$, which improves over a linear map. We report results for the best parameter choices, $t = 2$ for the random walk and $k = 200$ for spectral clustering. We found the latter quite brittle with respect to the parameter choice; results for other parameters can be found on the supplemental website. For pulling in close homologs, we take the empirical kernel map only for points in

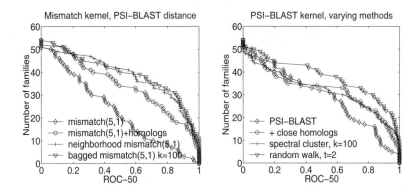

Figure 19.4 Comparison of protein representations and classifiers using unlabeled data in a *transductive* setting. Neighborhood and bagged mismatch kernels outperform pulling in close homologs (*left*) and equal or outperform previous semi-supervised methods (*right*). *Note:* We also pull in homologs during the SVM training for the neighborhood and bagged kernels.

Table 19.2 Mean ROC_{50} and ROC scores over 54 target families for *transductive* experiments

	ROC_{50}	ROC
mismatch kernel	0.416	0.875
mismatch kernel + homologs	0.625	0.924
neighborhood mismatch kernel	0.704	0.917
bagged mismatch kernel ($k = 100$)	0.719	0.943
bagged mismatch kernel ($k = 400$)	0.671	0.935
PSI-BLAST kernel	0.533	0.866
PSI-BLAST+homologs kernel	0.585	0.873
spectral clustering kernel	0.581	0.861
random walk kernel	0.691	0.915
transductive SVM	0.637	0.874

the training set and the chosen close homologs. Finally, we also run transductive SVMs. The results are given in table 19.2 and figure 19.4 (right). A signed rank test (with adjusted *p*-value cutoff of 0.05) finds no significant difference between the neighborhood kernel, the bagged kernel ($k = 100$), and the random walk kernel in this transductive setting. Thus the new techniques are comparable with random walk, but are feasible to calculate on full-scale problems.

19.4.3   Large-Scale Experiments

Semi-supervised and transductive methods are most interesting and potentially give greatest benefit in the realistic setting where a large amount of unlabeled data is used. We therefore test the cluster kernel methods in large-scale experiments, using 101,602 Swiss-Prot protein sequences as additional unlabeled data. For simplicity, we first give results for both the neighborhood and bagged kernels in the transductive setting, that is, in the case where test sequences are available as additional unlabeled examples in all the experiments. Then, for a clean comparison against the profile kernel, we test the neighborhood kernel and the profile kernel in a semi-supervised setting, where the Swiss-Prot database alone is used as the source of unlabeled data.

For the large-scale neighborhood mismatch kernel experiments, we first compute the entire SCOP plus Swiss-Prot kernel ($108,931$ x $108,931$) matrix with mismatch kernel parameters $p = 5$ and $m = 1$. We then apply the neighborhood averaging operation to produce the 7329 x 7329 kernel matrix for SCOP sequences needed for SVM training. We normalize the kernel matrix before and after the neighborhood averaging operation. Results in table 19.3 clearly show that the inclusion of a large amount of additional unlabeled data from Swiss-Prot significantly improves classification performance. Moreover, the neighborhood kernel again outperforms the baseline method of adding homologs of the positive training sequences to the training set.

For the large-scale bagged mismatch kernel experiments, the fact that many of the sequences in the Swiss-Prot database are multidomain protein sequences complicates the clustering step: since the PSI-BLAST E-values used as the dissimilarity metric are based on local alignment, a multidomain sequence can be similar to many unrelated single-domain sequences, and hence the clustering algorithm may fail to converge. As an approximate remedy, we only use Swiss-Prot protein sequences with maximal length of 250 for the large-scale k-means clustering, reasoning that most multidomain sequences would be eliminated by this length constraint. We randomly sample 30,000 protein sequences from the set of Swiss-Prot with length 250 or less to use as unlabeled data for clustering. Since the method mainly depends on the quality of the clusters containing the labeled points, we terminate the k-means clustering algorithm once there are no more changes in the label assignment for the SCOP sequences. It is worth noting that a small amount of two-domain sequences may have length below our cutoff, but we observe that the k-means clustering algorithm still behaves relatively stably. We use the same mismatch kernel parameters for the bagged kernel as the ones we use for the small-scale bagged kernel experiments. A comparison of results is shown in table 19.3. Again, bagged kernel performance significantly improves when a large amount of unlabeled data is provided to the clustering algorithm. Finally, we also compare with the semi-supervised profile kernel approach. The profile kernel representation depends on estimating sequence profiles for each input sequence using a large sequence database, and therefore we only present results in the large-scale setting. The profile kernel performs very well. Note that adding homologs (the baseline approach to semi-supervised learning) can be used in conjunction with any of the cluster kernel methods. We found that this combination of approaches improved the results in all cases.

Finally, in order to make a clean comparison of the stronger of the cluster kernels, the neighborhood kernel, with the profile kernel, we ran a separate experiment, where we use a semi-supervised training setup: the Swiss-Prot database alone is used as the source of unlabeled data for estimating PSI-BLAST profiles and

Table 19.3   Mean ROC_{50} and ROC scores over 54 target families for *large-scale transductive* experiments. *Note:* We include homologs from the unlabeled set and the test set (SCOP + Swiss-Prot) for the training of all the SVMs, apart from the profile kernel, which does not use any homologs.

	Without Swiss-Prot		With Swiss-Prot	
	ROC_{50}	ROC	ROC_{50}	ROC
mismatch kernel + homologs	0.625	0.924	0.706	0.945
bagged mismatch kernel ($k = 100$)	0.719	0.943	0.803	0.953
bagged mismatch kernel ($k = 400$)	0.671	0.935	0.775	0.955
neighborhood mismatch kernel	0.704	0.917	0.871	0.971
profile kernel	-	-	0.84	0.98
profile kernel + homologs	-	-	0.916	0.989

Table 19.4   Mean ROC_{50} and ROC scores over 54 target families for *large-scale semisupervised* experiments. *Note:* We do not include homologs from the unlabeled set (Swiss-Prot) for the training of the SVMs in these experiments.

	ROC_{50}	ROC
neighborhood mismatch kernel	0.810	0.955
profile kernel	0.842	0.980

defining sequence neighborhoods; SCOP sequences are not used for profile learning or for neighborhood averaging. For the cleanest comparison, we do not add SCOP homologs to the positive training set before training the SVMs. Mean ROC_{50} and ROC results are given in table 19.4, and a comparison of ROC_{50} results over all experiments is given in figure 19.5. Results from the cluster kernel and profile kernel methods are similar (20 wins, 25 losses, 9 ties for the cluster kernel); a signed rank test with a p-value threshold of 0.05 finds no significant difference in performance between the two methods.

19.5   Discussion

Two of the most important issues in protein classification are representation of sequences and handling unlabeled data. Two developments in recent kernel methods research, string kernels and cluster kernels, address these issues separately. We have described two kernels—the *neighborhood mismatch kernel* and the *bagged mismatch kernel*—that combine both approaches and yield state-of-the-art performance in protein classification. The former is the best way we found in this problem to incorporate local structure; the latter gave good performance by using global structure information.

Practical use of semi-supervised protein classification techniques requires computational efficiency. Many cluster kernels require diagonalization of the full labeled plus unlabeled data kernel matrix. The neighborhood and bagged kernel approaches, used with an efficient string kernel, are fast and scalable cluster kernels for sequence

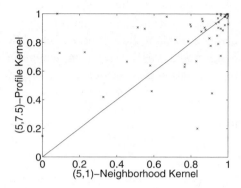

Figure 19.5   Comparison of neighborhood kernel and profile kernel ROC$_{50}$ performance for *large-scale semi-supervised* experiments. No homologs were added to the training set for the purpose of training the SVMs.

data and do not require diagonalization of the kernel matrix as in other cluster kernel methods.

Moreover, these techniques can be applied to any problem with a meaningful local similarity measure or distance function. A potential direction for improvement in the neighborhood kernel would be to extract only those segments of "neighboring" sequences that correspond to the local alignment-based E-value score; when we use entire multidomain Swiss-Prot sequences as neighbors of a single-domain SCOP sequence, these neighbor sequences may include long regions that are unrelated to the SCOP domain, and hence we introduce noise in the neighborhood averaging operation.

While we have motivated these kernels by earlier work on cluster kernels and the cluster assumption, one can also view the neighborhood and bagged kernels as using unlabeled data locally (from nearby sequences or the local cluster) for smoothing the kernel representation. Related work using probabilistic models instead of unlabeled data for smoothing includes the recently introduced Bhattacharyya kernel (Jebara et al., 2004), which assigns a probability distribution to each example and defines a kernel on these distributions.

We also compared to the profile-based string kernels of Kuang et al. (2004), which are also based on a semi-supervised learning paradigm. These string kernels are also scalable and achieve very high classification accuracy; in our experiments, the neighborhood kernel performs similarly to the profile kernel. However, the profile kernel method requires producing a profile for each query sequence, which is necessarily tied to alignment. In contrast, the cluster kernels that we present here are more general, in that any dissimilarity measure can be used for neighborhood averaging or bagging and any base kernel chosen for the initial representation. Moreover, for the bagged kernel any clustering algorithm, not just k-means, can be employed. These kernels may therefore be applicable to a wider range of problems. For example, one could use expression coherence in a set of microarray experiments as a measure of functional similarity of genes combined with a base kernel to define cluster kernels for functional gene classification. One could also hope to further improve performance for the protein classification task by using a more powerful base kernel than the mismatch kernel (for example, the string alignment kernel of Saigo et al. (2004)), though the computational expense of the improved base kernel representation may become a concern.

All the experiments described in this chapter compare methods using a binary classification approach, which is a setup that seems to be established for kernel-based approaches. However, common methods like BLAST and PSI-BLAST address the full multiclass problem directly, and the binary framework seems to favor SVM methods and ignores the additional benefit from methods that address the multiclass task. However, some of our recent work (Ie et al., 2005) does address this issue by applying the profile kernel-based SVM to the multiclass fold recognition task. The results, which are beyond the scope of this chapter to describe in detail, indicate that semi-supervised SVMs are significantly better than PSI-BLAST when applied to the multiclass problem as well.

Future work should extend these results by combining cluster kernels with learning methods that address other additional challenges of protein classification: further analysis of the full multiclass problem, which potentially involves thousands of classes; dealing with very small classes with few homologs; incorporating hierarchical labels and knowledge of relationships between classes; and dealing with missing classes, for which no labeled examples exist.

Supplementary data and source code are available at `www.kyb.tuebingen.mpg.de/bs/people/weston/semiprot`. The Spider Matlab package is available at `www.kyb.tuebingen.mpg.de/bs/people/spider`.

20 Prediction of Protein Function from Networks

Hyunjung Shin   SHIN@TUEBINGEN.MPG.DE

Koji Tsuda   KOJI.TSUDA@TUEBINGEN.MPG.DE

In computational biology, it is common to represent domain knowledge using graphs. Frequently there exist multiple graphs for the same set of nodes, representing information from different sources, and no single graph is sufficient to predict class labels of unlabeled nodes reliably. One way to enhance reliability is to integrate multiple graphs, since individual graphs are partly independent and partly complementary to each other for prediction. In this chapter, we describe an algorithm to assign weights to multiple graphs within graph-based semi-supervised learning. Both predicting class labels and searching for weights for combining multiple graphs are formulated into one convex optimization problem. The graph-combining method is applied to functional class prediction of yeast proteins. When compared with individual graphs, the combined graph with optimized weights performs significantly better than any single graph. When compared with the semi-definite programming-based support vector machine (SDP/SVM), it shows comparable accuracy in a remarkably short time. Compared with a combined graph with equal-valued weights, our method could select important graphs without loss of accuracy, which implies the desirable property of *integration with selectivity*.

20.1 Introduction

graph representation in biological networks

In computational biology, many types of genomic data are frequently represented using graphs. The nodes correspond to genes or proteins, and the edges correspond to biological relationships between them. Some of the proteins have known function classes through biological experiments while those of the others are unknown because of the demanding experimental cost and effort. It is valuable to predict the unknown function of proteins in order to guide experiments and help to understand

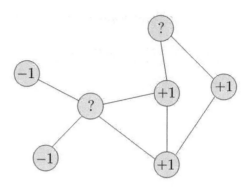

Figure 20.1   Functional class prediction on a protein network: Focusing on a particular functional class, the function prediction problem boils down to two-class classification. An annotated protein is labeled either by +1 or −1. The positive label indicates that the protein belongs to the class. Edges represent associations between proteins. The task is to predict the class of the unlabeled proteins marked as ?.

the complex mechanisms of the cell (Alberts et al., 1998). The function prediction problem can be depicted on an undirected graph (see figure 20.1). Focusing on a particular functional class, the task boils down to a two-class classification problem. A protein whose class label is known is annotated +1 if it belongs to the class, −1 otherwise. The protein whose class label is to be predicted is unannotated (i.e., "?" in the figure). Once a graph is defined, the problem can be dealt with within the framework of graph-based semi-supervised learning thanks to recent progress by (Zhou et al., 2004; Belkin and Niyogi, 2003b; Zhu et al., 2003b; Chapelle et al., 2003). See also part III in this book. The class label of an unannotated protein is inferred from those of adjacent nodes, proportionally being affected by weights of the edges. See section 20.2 for details.

multiple data sources, Graph fusion

Typically, multiple graphs are available to represent the same set of proteins in terms of various source of information. For instance, an edge set can represent physical interactions of the proteins (Schwikowski et al., 2000; Uetz et al., 2000; von Mering et al., 2002), gene regulatory relationships (Lee et al., 2002; Ihmels et al., 2002; Segal et al., 2003a), closeness in a metabolic pathway (Kanehisa et al., 2004), similarities between protein sequences (Yona et al., 1999), etc. (see figure 20.2). Each source contains partially independent and partially complementary information about the task at hand. However, no single information source is sufficient to identify protein functions reliably. One way to enhance reliability is to integrate multiple sources. In computational biology, a number of methods have been proposed to classify proteins based on networks such as majority vote (Schwikowski et al., 2000; Hishigaki et al., 2001), graph-based methods (Vazquez et al., 2003), Bayesian methods (Deng et al., 2003), discriminative learning methods (Vert and Kanehisa, 2003; Lanckriet et al., 2004c), and probabilistic integration by log-likelihood scores (Lee et al., 2004). See also (Tsuda and Noble, 2004) and references therein.

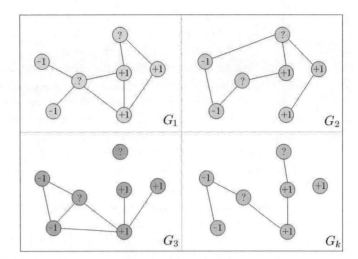

Figure 20.2   Multiple graphs: A set of graphs is given, each of which depicts a different aspect of the proteins. Since different graphs contain partly independent and partly complementary pieces of information, one can enhance the total information by combining these graphs.

a kernel method combining multiple data sources— SDP/SVM

Among those approaches, the semi-definite programming-based SVM method (SDP/SVM) has been particularly successful (Lanckriet et al., 2004c,b). In SDP/SVM, each of the data sources (e.g., vectors, trees, and networks) is represented by a *kernel matrix*. Then a linear combination of such kernel matrices becomes a linear matrix inequality (LMI) which forms the constraints of semi-definite programming (Nesterov and Nemirovsky, 1994; Vandenberghe and Boyd, 1996; Boyd and Vandenberghe, 2004). Since it has been reduced to SDP, finding the weights for combining multiple kernel matrices becomes a convex optimization problem. Practically, the SDP/SVM method has led to good empirical results. However, when trying to apply SDP/SVM to large problems, the computational cost can become prohibitive. The reasons can be categorized into three viewpoints.

Practical difficulties of graph-based kernel methods

First, it is not easy to define a kernel on graphs that plays the role of a similarity metric. For example, Lanckriet et al. (2004b) used the diffusion kernel, which has the time complexity of $O(n^3)$ where n is the number of data. The second obstacle is the density of the kernel matrices. In general, it is difficult to make kernel methods faster than $O(n^3)$ without rather radical approximations (e.g., low rank approximation) (Schölkopf and Smola, 2002). One may attempt to sparsify the kernel matrix by setting small values to zero, but, typically, a kernel matrix artificially sparsified is no longer positive definite. Finally, solving SDP/SVM is also computationally inefficient. In theory, the method has the time complexity of $O(mn^3)$ where m is the number of kernel matrices. [1] Therefore, in spite of their theoretical soundness and

1. Recently, a fast and greedy approximation method was proposed (Bach et al., 2004), but the worst-case complexity does not change.

good performance, graph-based kernel methods may not be finished in a reasonable time when applied in large-scale problems.

One way to circumvent the difficulties of kernel methods is to take a learning algorithm which is directly applicable to graphs. A useful approach will be semi-supervised learning. Thanks to the inherent sparsity of a similarity matrix derived from an edge set, the solution can be obtained by solving a linear system with a sparse coefficient matrix, which is faster than SVM learning by orders of magnitude (Spielman and Teng, 2004). However, in graph-based semi-supervised learning, it has not yet been addressed how to integrate multiple graphs.

semi-supervised learning with multiple graphs

In this chapter, we describe an algorithm to assign weights to multiple graphs within graph-based semi-supervised learning. Local minima problems are avoided, since both predicting class labels and searching for weights combining multiple graphs can be formulated into one convex optimization problem. Aside from the capability of integrating all the graphs into one, the method is capable of selecting the subset of graphs critical for learning against redundant ones. In the sense of learning, a redundant graph stands for a graph which hardly affects or changes the prediction results. This will be a desirable property, especially as the number of available data sources increases. The selection mechanism is close to the way that the SVM selects support vectors (Schölkopf and Smola, 2002). The graph-combining method is applied to functional class prediction of 3588 yeast proteins. When compared with individual graphs, the combined graph with optimized weights performs significantly better than any single graph. When compared with the state-of-the-art SDP/SVM method, it shows comparable accuracy in a remarkably short time. Compared with a combined graph with equal-valued weights, our method could select important graphs for prediction without loss of accuracy, which implies the desirable property of *integration with selectivity*.

The remainder of this chapter is organized as follows. In section 20.2, we briefly introduce semi-supervised learning and review the recent literature. Section 20.3 gives a detailed explanation of the graph-combining method. In section 20.4, we show experimental results. We conclude in section 20.5 with some future challenges.

20.2   Graph-Based Semi-Supervised Learning

In this section, we briefly introduce a graph-based learning algorithm for a single graph (Zhou et al., 2004). One can have more insight from chapter 11 which provides a unified framework of various types of graph-based learning algorithms. Let us assume a weighted graph G with n nodes indexed as $1, \ldots, n$. A symmetric weight matrix, denoted as W, represents the strength of linkage. All weights are non-negative ($w_{ij} \geq 0$), and if $w_{ij} = 0$, there is no edge between nodes i and j. We assume that the first l training nodes have binary labels, $y_1, y_2, \ldots, y_l$, where

$y_i \in \{-1, 1\}$, and the remaining $u = n - l$ test nodes are unlabeled. The goal is to predict the labels $y_{l+1}, \ldots, y_n$ by exploiting the structure of the graph under the assumption that a label of an unlabeled node is likely to be similar to the labels of its neighboring nodes. A more adjacent or a more strongly connected neighbor node will more significantly affect the node.

objective
function on a
single graph in
semi-supervised
learning

Let us define an n-dimensional score vector $\hat{Y} = (\hat{y}_1, \cdots, \hat{y}_n)^\top$. In learning, we determine $\hat{Y}$ using all the available information, and in prediction, the labels are predicted by thresholding the score $\hat{y}_{l+1}, \ldots, \hat{y}_n$. It is assumed that (a) the score $\hat{y}_i$ should be close to the given label y_i in training nodes, and (b) overall, the score $\hat{y}_i$ should not be too different from the scores of adjacent vertices. One can obtain $\hat{Y}$ by minimizing the following quadratic functional:

$$\sum_{i=1}^{l} (\hat{y}_i - y_i)^2 + c \sum_{i,j=1}^{n} w_{ij} (\hat{y}_i - \hat{y}_j)^2. \tag{20.1}$$

The first term corresponds to the *loss function* in terms of condition (a), and the second term represents the *smoothness* of the scores in terms of condition (b). The parameter c trades off loss versus smoothness. Another small regularization term, $\mu \sum_{i=l+1}^{n} \hat{y}_i^2$, can be added in order to keep the scores of unlabeled nodes in a reasonable range. However, for simplicity, we degenerate this term into the smoothness term (b) by assuming $\mu = 1$. Alternative choices of smoothness and loss functions can be found in Chapelle et al. (2003). It is more prevalent to represent (20.1) with matrices

$$\min_{\hat{Y}} \ (\hat{Y} - Y)^\top (\hat{Y} - Y) + c\hat{Y}^T L \hat{Y}, \tag{20.2}$$

where $Y = (y_1, \ldots, y_l, 0, \ldots, 0)^\top$, and the matrix L is called the *graph Laplacian matrix* (Chung, 1997), which is defined as $L = D - W$ where $D = \mathrm{diag}(d_i)$, $d_i = \sum_j w_{ij}$. Instead of L, the *normalized Laplacian*, $\mathcal{L} = D^{-\frac{1}{2}} L D^{-\frac{1}{2}}$ can be used to get a similar result (Chung, 1997). The solution of this problem is obtained as

$$\hat{Y} = (\mathbf{I} + cL)^{-1} Y, \tag{20.3}$$

where $\mathbf{I}$ is the identity matrix.//

a large sparse
linear system

Actually, the score vector $\hat{Y}$ is obtained by solving *a large sparse linear system* $Y = (\mathbf{I} + cL)\hat{Y}$. This numerical problem has been intensively studied, and there exist efficient algorithms, whose computational time is nearly linear in the number of non-zero entries in the coefficient matrix (Spielman and Teng, 2004). Therefore, the computation gets faster as the Laplacian matrix gets sparser. Moreover, when the linear system solver is parallelized and distributed on a cluster system, the graph-based learning algorithm easily scales to much larger networks.

20.3   Combining Multiple Graphs

When multiple graphs are available, it is natural to incorporate them as additional information sources. For instance, proteins can be represented as graphs according to their amino acid sequences, structures, interactions, or other relationships. Selecting one graph out of m graphs would be relatively easy. One can solve the learning problem using each graph, and simply select the best one in terms of, say, the cross-validation error. However, according to a recent study (Lanckriet et al., 2004c), the integration of multiple data sources can achieve higher accuracy than any single graph alone. To incorporate all the graphs, one can straightforwardly combine the graphs with fixed uniform weights. However, as the number of available data sources increases a better approach seems to be to select important m_0 $(\leq m)$ graphs out of m. This poses the problem of deciding which combination of the graphs will be the best for prediction; examination of every possible combination of learning problems amounts to the combinatorial number $\binom{m}{m_0}$. In this section, we introduce a convex programming-based graph-combining algorithm which only selects the subset of graphs critical for learning against redundant ones. Note that, in the sense of learning, a redundant graph stands for a graph which hardly affects or changes the prediction results (e.g., a graph almost identical to another, is a linear combination of others, or which otherwise already fits well with the prediction).

Without loss of generality, the optimization problem with a single Laplacian matrix (20.2) is rewritten in a constrained form as

$$\min_{\hat{Y},\gamma} \quad (\hat{Y} - Y)^{\top}(\hat{Y} - Y) + c\gamma, \quad \hat{Y}^{\top} L \hat{Y} \leq \gamma. \tag{20.4}$$

When we have multiple Laplacian matrices, $L_1, \ldots, L_m$, the problem can be extended in order to take all of them into account,

$$\min_{\hat{Y},\gamma} \quad (\hat{Y} - Y)^{\top}(\hat{Y} - Y) + c\gamma, \quad \hat{Y}^{\top} L_k \hat{Y} \leq \gamma, \quad \forall\, k \in \{1, \ldots, m\}. \tag{20.5}$$

This amounts to taking the upper bound of the smoothness function $\hat{Y}^{\top} L_k \hat{Y}$ over all graphs and applying it for regularization. To investigate the properties of the solution of the *primal problem* (20.5), let us derive the *dual problem* in a similar way to that of Schölkopf and Smola (2002). Then, the convex optimization problem can be rewritten as the following min-max problem using Lagrange multipliers,

$$\max_{\boldsymbol{\alpha},\eta} \min_{\hat{Y},\gamma} \quad (\hat{Y} - Y)^{\top}(\hat{Y} - Y) + c\gamma + \sum_{k=1}^{m} \alpha_k(\hat{Y}^T L_k \hat{Y} - \gamma) - \eta\gamma, \tag{20.6}$$

where the Lagrange multipliers satisfy $\alpha_k, \eta \geq 0$. If the inner (minimization) problem is solved analytically, one ends up with the outer (maximization) problem with respect to the Lagrange multipliers only. The maximization problem corresponds to the dual problem of (20.5), which is easier to solve in many cases. When expressed in terms of the Lagrange multipliers, the optimal solution of the *primal problem* gains more interpretability. For example, for support vector machines, the analysis using the dual problem is effectively used for explaining the basic properties of the discriminant hyperplane (e.g., large margin and support vectors) (Schölkopf and Smola, 2002).

Now, let us solve the inner optimization problem. By setting the derivative with respect to γ to zero, (20.6) becomes

$$c - \sum_{k=1}^{m} \alpha_k = \eta. \tag{20.7}$$

Since $\eta \geq 0$, the sum of α_k is constrained as $\sum_{k=1}^{m} \alpha_k \leq c$. Substituting (20.7) into (20.6), we have

$$\max_{\boldsymbol{\alpha}} \min_{\hat{Y}} \quad (\hat{Y} - Y)^\top (\hat{Y} - Y) + \sum_{k=1}^{m} \alpha_k \hat{Y}^T L_k \hat{Y}. \tag{20.8}$$

Setting the derivative with respect to $\hat{Y}$ to zero, we get

$$(\mathbf{I} + \sum_{k=1}^{m} \alpha_k L_k)\hat{Y} = Y, \tag{20.9}$$

which leads to the optimal solution

$$\hat{Y} = (\mathbf{I} + \sum_{k=1}^{m} \alpha_k L_k)^{-1} Y. \tag{20.10}$$

Now the optimal solution of $\hat{Y}$ is written in terms of the Lagrange multipliers α_k. Comparing (20.10) with the single graph solution (20.3), one can see that the Lagrange multipliers α_k's play the role of the weights for combining graphs. Note that the role of the parameter c can also be interpreted similarly to its role in the single graph case. In the case of multiple graphs, the parameter c controls the influence of graph Laplacians in an implicit way by constraining the sum of all weights. See the Eq. 20.7.

By substituting (20.10), the Lagrangian (20.6) becomes the following dual problem,

$$\max_{\boldsymbol{\alpha}} \quad Y^\top Y - Y^\top (\mathbf{I} + \sum_{k=1}^{m} \alpha_k L_k)^{-1} Y$$
$$\sum_{k=1}^{m} \alpha_k \leq c. \tag{20.11}$$

Ignoring a constant term, the maximization problem is equivalent to the following minimization problem:

$$\min_{\boldsymbol{\alpha}} \quad Y^\top (I + \sum_{k=1}^{m} \alpha_k L_k)^{-1} Y$$
$$\sum_{k=1}^{m} \alpha_k \leq c. \tag{20.12}$$

Denote by $d(\boldsymbol{\alpha})$ the dual objective function (20.12). Due to the Karush-Kuhn-Tucker (KKT) conditions, we have $\alpha_k(\hat{Y}^\top L_k \hat{Y} - \gamma) = 0$ at the optimal solution. Therefore, $\alpha_k = 0$ iff $\hat{Y}^\top L_k \hat{Y} < \gamma$, and $\alpha_k > 0$ iff $\hat{Y}^\top L_k \hat{Y} = \gamma$. If the constraint $\hat{Y}^\top L_k \hat{Y} \leq \gamma$ is satisfied as an equality only for some of the graphs, we obtain a sparse solution for α_k, since the α_k corresponding to the other graphs are zeros. This implies *integration with selectivity*. A graph with zero weight (i.e., $\alpha_k = 0$) is considered unnecessary or redundant since the optimal score vector $\hat{Y}$ would not change even if it is removed. On the other hand, a graph with non-zero weight (i.e., $\alpha_k > 0$) satisfies $\hat{Y}^\top L_k \hat{Y} = \gamma$, and accordingly plays an essential role in determining the value of the score vector.

20.3.1   Regularized Version

The principle of combining multiple graphs, *integration with selectivity*, is a combination of two contradicting goals, *integration* versus *selection*, which needs to be balanced. In practical applications, we found the proposed algorithm too selective (i.e., the maximum weight is too dominant) leading to poorer generalization performance. To spread the weights $\{\alpha_k\}_{k=1}^{m}$, we introduce another term as follows:

$$\min_{\hat{Y},\xi,\gamma} \quad (\hat{Y} - Y)^\top (\hat{Y} - Y) + c\gamma + c_0 \sum_{k=1}^{m} \xi_k$$
$$\hat{Y}^T L_k \hat{Y} \leq \gamma + \xi_k, \quad \xi_k \geq 0, \gamma \geq 0. \tag{20.13}$$

The dual problem then leads to

$$\min_{\boldsymbol{\alpha}} \quad Y^\top (\mathbf{I} + \sum_{k=1}^{m} \alpha_k L_k)^{-1} Y \equiv d(\boldsymbol{\alpha})$$
$$0 \leq \alpha_k \leq c_0, \quad \sum_{k=1}^{m} \alpha_k \leq c. \tag{20.14}$$

The new parameter c_0 extends flexibility. When $c_0 = c$, (20.14) becomes *selection-oriented* by recovering the solution of (20.12). And at the other extreme $c_0 = c/m$, (20.14) becomes *integration-oriented* by uniformly spreading a fixed value to all weights.

20.3.2   Optimization

We can simply solve the optimization problem, for instance, with the gradient descent method. This requires the computation of the dual objective $d(\boldsymbol{\alpha})$ as well as its partial derivatives. The derivatives are

$$\frac{\partial d}{\partial \alpha_j} = -Y^\top (\mathbf{I} + \sum_{k=1}^{m} \alpha_k L_k)^{-1} L_j (\mathbf{I} + \sum_{k=1}^{m} \alpha_k L_k)^{-1} Y, \tag{20.15}$$

by means of the relation $\frac{\partial}{\partial a} B^{-1} = -B^{-1} (\frac{\partial}{\partial a} B) B^{-1}$. Although we have the inverse matrix $(\mathbf{I} + \sum_{k=1}^{m} \alpha_k L_k)^{-1}$ in the solution (20.10), the objective (20.12), and the derivative (20.15) as well, we do not need to calculate it explicitly, because it always appears as a vector form of $(\mathbf{I} + \sum_{k=1}^{m} \alpha_k L_k)^{-1} Y$, which can be obtained as the solution of sparse linear systems. Therefore, the computational cost of the dual objective and the derivative is nearly linear in the number of non-zero entries of $\sum_{k=1}^{m} \alpha_k L_k$ (Spielman and Teng, 2004).

20.4   Experiments on Function Prediction of Proteins

The graph-combining method was evaluated on the data set provided by Lanck-riet et al. (2004c). The task is to classify the function of yeast proteins into the 13 highest-level categories of the functional hierarchy (see table 20.1). The function of 3588 proteins is labeled according to the MIPS comprehensive yeast genome database (CYGD, `http://mips.gsf.de/projects/fungi/yeast.html`). Note that a protein can belong to several functional classes. We solved a two-class classification problem to determine membership or nonmembership of each functional class, and evaluated the accuracy of each classification.

Table 20.2 lists the five different types of protein graphs (or networks) used in the experiments. The graphs W_1 and W_5 are created from vectorial data, i.e., Pfam domain structure and gene expression, respectively. The graphs W_2, W_3, and W_4 are directly taken from the database in graph form, corresponding to coparticipation in a protein complex, physical interactions, and genetic interactions, respectively. See (Lanckriet et al., 2004c) for more information. The density of the Laplacian matrices (i.e. the fraction of non-zero entries) is shown in the last column of the table. All the matrices are very sparse (maximum density 0.8%), which contributes to memory-saving. If one were to try to use a diffusion kernel, it would take much more memory factor ($1/0.007 \approx 142$). In learning, each graph was transformed into a normalized Laplacian matrix $\mathcal{L}_k$.

Prediction accuracy is evaluated by fivefold cross-validation with three repetitions. For each partition of training and test nodes, the ROC (receiver operating characteristic) score is calculated, and then averaged over all the five partitions. The ROC score is calculated as the area under the ROC curve which plots true positive rate (sensitivity) as a function of false positive rate (1-specificity) for differing classification thresholds (Gribskov and Robinson, 1996). It measures the overall quality of the ranking induced by the classifier, rather than the quality of a single value of

Table 20.1   Thirteen CYGD functional classes

	classes
1	metabolism
2	energy
3	cell cycle and DNA processing
4	transcription
5	protein synthesis
6	protein fate
7	cellular transportation and transportation mechanism
8	cell rescue, defense, and virulence
9	interaction with cell environment
10	cell fate
11	control of cell organization
12	transport facilitation
13	others

threshold in that ranking. An ROC score of 0.5 corresponds to random guessing, and an ROC score of 1.0 implies that the algorithm succeeded in putting all of the positive examples ahead of all of the negatives. The value of parameter c was determined by five cross-validation searching over

$$c \in \{0.05, 0.1, 0.25, 0.5, 1, 2.5, 5, 10, 25, 50, 100\}.$$

The following values were obtained for the thirteen classes

$$(5, 5, 25, 25, 10, 10, 5, 5, 10, 10, 100, 2.5, 25),$$

respectively.

The graph-combining method was compared with individual graphs, and with the state-of-the-art SDP/SVM method based on the reported results (Lanckriet et al., 2004c). We then compared *integration by optimized weights* with *integration by fixed weights*.

20.4.1   Comparison with Individual Graphs

When compared with individual graphs ($\mathcal{L}_k$'s), the combined graph ($\mathcal{L}_{opt}$) outperformed $\mathcal{L}_k$ in terms of ROC score. To test the significance of the difference, McNemar's test was conducted. In principle, McNemar's test is used to determine whether one learning algorithm outperforms another on a particular learning task (Diet-

Table 20.2 Protein networks used in the experiment. *Density* shows the fraction of non-zero entries in the respective Laplacian matrices.

matrix	description	density (%)
W_1	Graph created from Pfam domain structure. A protein is represented by a 4950-dimensional binary vector, in which each bit represents the presence or absence of one Pfam domain. An edge is created if the inner product between two vectors exceeds 0.06. The edge weight corresponds to the inner product.	0.7805
W_2	Coparticipation in a protein complex (determined by tandem affinity purification, TAP). An edge is created if there is a bait-prey relationship between two proteins.	0.0570
W_3	Protein-protein interactions (MIPS physical interactions)	0.0565
W_4	Genetic interactions (MIPS genetic interactions)	0.0435
W_5	Graph created from the cell cycle gene expression measurements (Spellman et al., 1998). An edge is created if the Pearson coefficient of two profiles exceeds 0.8. The edge weight is set to 1. This is identical with the network used in (Deng et al., 2003).	0.0919

terich, 1998). Figure 20.3 shows the empirical p-value distribution of McNemar's test. A small p-value indicates that $\mathcal{L}_{opt}$ is better than $\mathcal{L}_k$. The total number of trials amounts to 975 ($= 3$ repetitions $\times 5$ pairwise tests $\times 5$ CVs $\times 13$ classes). In 594 (61%) trials, there is a statistically significant difference (significance level $\alpha=0.05$), which corresponds to the leftmost bar in figure 20.3. Specifically, in each pairwise comparison, $\mathcal{L}_{opt}$ significantly outperforms single L_k's in 55.31%, 58.31%, 60.03%, 68.21%, and 61.03% of the total number of trials, respectively. Figure 20.4 presents the comparison of ROC scores between $\mathcal{L}_{opt}$ and the best performing individual graph.

20.4.2   Comparison with SDP/SVM

accuracy

Figure 20.5 presents the comparison results between the graph-combining method and SDP/SVM method. The ROC score of the SDP/SVM method was obtained from Lanckriet et al. (2004c). The ROC score of the Markov random field (MRF) method from Deng et al. (2003) is also plotted in the figure. The MRF method is an early work which shares the same data sources as ours for yeast protein

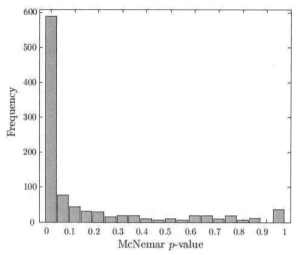

Figure 20.3 *p*-Value distribution of McNemar's test: For most of 975 McNemar's test trials, $\mathcal{L}_{opt}$ outperforms $\mathcal{L}_k$'s. Particulary, for 61% of the total number of trials, there is a statistically significant difference (at a significance level of α=0.05), which corresponds to the leftmost bar in the figure.

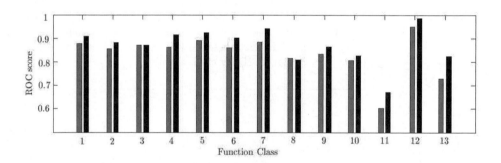

Figure 20.4 Comparing ROC scores of combined networks and the best performing individual graph. Within each group of bars, a blue bar corresponds to the best individual graph, while a black bar corresponds to $\mathcal{L}_{opt}$. Across the 13 classes, $\mathcal{L}_{opt}$ outperforms the best performing individual.

function prediction. For most classes, the graph-combining method achieves high scores, which are similar to SDP/SVM methods. In classes 11 and 13, the graph-combining method does not perform as well as SDP/SVM (but still better than the MRF method), which is an indication of the superior generalization performance of the SVM. We could not perform tests of significance since the detailed experimental results of MRF or SDP/SVM were not available.

Now, let us compare the computational time. Solving the sparse linear system, which appears in the solution (20.10), the objective (20.12), and the derivative

computational
time

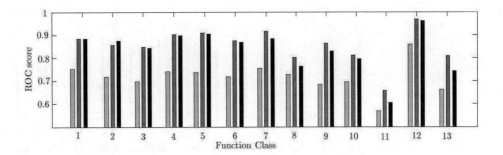

Figure 20.5   ROC score comparison between MRF, SDP/SVM, and $\mathcal{L}_{opt}$ for 13 functional protein classes: Green bars correspond to the MRF method of Deng et al. (2003); blue bars correspond to the SDP/SVM method of Lanckriet et al. (2004c). Black bars correspond to $\mathcal{L}_{opt}$.

(20.15), only took 1.41 seconds (standard deviation 0.013) with the Matlab command `mldivide` in a standard 2.2GHz PC with 1GB of memory. Solving the dual problem (20.14) that includes multiple times of computation for the sparse linear system took 49.3 seconds (standard deviation 14.8) with the Matlab command `fmincon`. In contrast, the SDP/SVM method takes several hours using a commercial SDP solver (G.R.G. Lanckriet, personal communication). Thus, in the light of its simplicity and efficiency (and hence scalability), the shorter computational time of the graph-combining method compensates considerably for the slight loss of accuracy against the SDP/SVM method.

20.4.3   Comparison with Fixed Weight Integration

A combined graph with fixed weights was defined as $\mathcal{L}_{fix} = \frac{1}{m} \sum_{k=1}^{m} \mathcal{L}_k$. Note that the fixed weights correspond to the solution of (20.14) when $c_0 = c/m = 0.2c$. The ROC scores for all functional classes are shown in figure 20.6, together with the weights for the graphs. The optimization of weights did not always lead to better ROC scores (except for classes 10, 11, 13). This can be explained using SVM theory. The graph combined with fixed weights can be regarded as an SVM decision function with all training data points, and the graph combined with optimized weights as an SVM decision function with only support vectors. There is no difference in accuracy between the two decision functions. Therefore we prefer integration with optimized weights since it has the advantage of being able to single out important graphs for learning over redundant ones without loss of accuracy. Looking at the weights of $\mathcal{L}_{opt}$ in the figure, W_4 and W_5 almost always have very low weights, which suggests that these two graphs can be redundant for learning. The capability of selecting more *important* graphs would be especially valuable as the number of available data sources increases. There was no statistically significant difference between $\mathcal{L}_{opt}$ and $\mathcal{L}_{fix}$ in performance (McNemar's test, significance level $\alpha=0.05$). Figure 20.7 presents typical ROC curves of $\mathcal{L}_{opt}$ and $\mathcal{L}_{fix}$ for class 1.

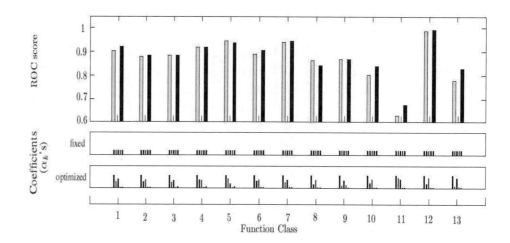

Figure 20.6 Prediction accuracy for 13 functional protein classes. The yellow bars and the blue bars in the upper panel show the ROC scores of $\mathcal{L}_{fix}$ and $\mathcal{L}_{opt}$, respectively. The middle and lower panels depict the combination weights $\mathcal{L}_{fix}$ and $\mathcal{L}_{opt}$, respectively.

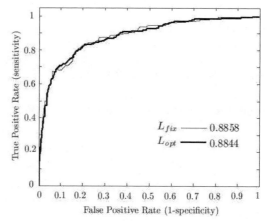

Figure 20.7 ROC curve for protein functional class 1. The thin blue and thick black curves correspond to $\mathcal{L}_{fix}$ and $\mathcal{L}_{opt}$, respectively.

20.5   Conclusion and Outlook

Summary

In this chapter, we have presented an algorithm for formulating a semi-supervised learning problem with multiple graphs. Both prediction of unknown class labels and searching for weights for combining multiple graphs are cast into one convex optimization problem. The graph-combining method showed promising results on function classification of yeast proteins, performing significantly better than any single graph, and when compared with SDP/SVM it showed comparable accuracy in a remarkably short time. When compared with fixed-weight integration it empirically proved a desirable property, *integration with selectivity*.

Future work

Although the graph-combining method provides a straightforward and principled way of combining multiple graphs, there still remain several challenges for future work. First, it will be useful to perform a more in-depth time complexity analysis. From the literature, we know that one iteration of our method is nearly linear in the total number of non-zero entries across all Laplacian matrices (Spielman and Teng, 2004). However, the analysis of the overall complexity analysis is not yet done. Second, we have to confirm whether the weights assigned by our methods are biologically meaningful or not. Third, it will be interesting to compare our method with the prediction-combination approach, where the predictions based on individual networks are combined by, e.g., majority vote.

21   Analysis of Benchmarks

In order to assess strengths and weaknesses of different semi-supervised learning (SSL) algorithms, we invited the chapter authors to apply their algorithms to eight benchmark data sets. These data sets encompass both artificial and real-world problems. We provide details on how the algorithms were applied, especially how hyperparameters were chosen given the few labeled points. Finally, we present and discuss the empirical performance.

21.1   The Benchmark

21.1.1   Data Sets

The benchmark consists of eight data sets as shown in table 21.1. Three of them were artificially created in order to create situations that correspond to certain assumptions (cf. chapter 1); this was done to allow for relating the performance of the algorithms to those assumptions. The five other benchmark data sets were derived from real data. It can thus be hoped that the performance on these is indicative of the performance in real applications.

Table 21.1   Basic properties of benchmark data sets

Data set	Classes	Dimension	Points	Comment
g241c	2	241	1500	artificial
g241d	2	241	1500	artificial
Digit1	2	241	1500	artificial
USPS	2	241	1500	imbalanced
COIL	6	241	1500	
BCI	2	117	400	
Text	2	11,960	1500	sparse discrete
SecStr	2	315	83,679	sparse binary

The purpose of the benchmark was to evaluate the power of the presented algorithms themselves in a way as neutral as possible. Thus ideally the data preprocessing should be similar for all algorithms; in particular, it should be avoided that in some cases it takes advantage of domain knowledge, when in others it does not. To prevent the experimenters from using domain knowledge, we tried to obscure structure in the data (e.g. by shuffling the pixels in the images), and even to hide the identity of the data sets (e.g. by also shuffling the data points). Also, we used the same number of dimensions (241) and points (1500) for most data sets in the same attempt to obscure the origin of the data and in order to increase the comparability of the results. However, we did provide information as to which data sets originate from images and which from text.

All data sets are available for further research at `http://www.kyb.tuebingen.mpg.de/ssl-book/`.

g241c This data set was generated such that the cluster assumption holds, i.e. the classes correspond to clusters, but the manifold assumption does not. First, 750 points were drawn from each of two unit-variance isotropic Gaussians (i.e., from $\mathcal{N}(\boldsymbol{\mu}_i, \mathbf{I})$), the centers of which had a distance of 2.5 in a random direction (i.e., $\|\boldsymbol{\mu}_1 - \boldsymbol{\mu}_2\| = 2.5$). The class label of a point represents the Gaussian it was drawn from. Finally, all dimensions are standardized, i.e. shifted and rescaled to zero-mean and unit variance. A two-dimensional projection of the data is shown on the left side of figure 21.1.

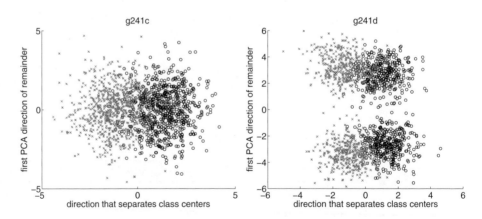

Figure 21.1 Two-dimensional projections of **g241c** (*left*) and **g241d** (*right*). Black circles, class +1; gray crosses, class -1.

g241d This data set was constructed to have potentially misleading cluster structure, and no manifold structure. First 375 points were drawn from each of two unit-variance isotropic Gaussians, the centers of which have a distance of 6 in a random direction; these points form the class +1. Then the centers of two further Gaussians for class -1 were fixed by moving from each of the former centers a distance of 2.5 in a random direction. Again, the identity matrix was used as covariance matrix, and 375 points were sampled from each new Gaussian. A two-dimensional projection of the resulting data is shown on the right side of figure 21.1.

Digit1   This data set was designed to consist of points close to a low-dimensional manifold embedded into a high-dimensional space, but not to show a pronounced cluster structure. We therefore started from a system that generates artificial writings (images) of the digit "1" developed by Matthias Hein (Hein and Audibert, 2005). The images are constructed starting from an abstract "1" implemented as a function $[0,1]^2 \rightarrow \{0,1\}$, with the main vertical line ranging from $y = 0.2$ to $y = 0.8$ at $x = 0.5$. There are five degrees of freedom in this function: two for translations ($[-0.13, +0.13]$ each), one for rotation ($[-90°, +90°]$), one for line thickness ($[0.02, 0.05]$), and one for the length of a small line at the bottom ($[0, 0.1]$). The resulting function is then discretized to an image of size 16×16. As an example, the first data point is shown in figure 21.2 (left).

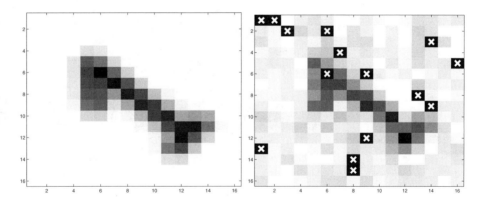

Figure 21.2   First data point from `Digit1` data set. (*Left*) Original image. (*Right*) After rescaling, adding noise, and masking dimensions (x).

We randomly sampled 1500 such images. The class label was set according to the tilt angle, with the boundary corresponding to an upright digit. To make the task a bit more difficult, we apply a sequence of transformations to the data as shown in algorithm 21.1, with σ set to 0.05. The result of this transformation (except for bias and permutation) applied to the first data point is shown in the right part of figure 21.2.

Since the data lie close to a five-dimensional manifold, SSL methods based on the manifold assumption are expected to improve substantially on supervised learning.

Algorithm 21.1 Obscure image data

Require: σ {standard deviation of random noise}
1: randomly select and permute 241 columns (features)
2: add to each column a random bias drawn from $\mathcal{N}(0, 1)$
3: multiply each column by a value from unif($[-1, -0.5] \cup [0.5, 1]$)
4: add independent noise from $\mathcal{N}(\mathbf{0}, \sigma^2 \mathbf{I})$ to each row (data point)

USPS   We derived a benchmark data set from the famous USPS set of handwritten digits as follows. We randomly drew 150 images of each of the ten digits. The digits "2" and "5" were assigned to the class $+1$, and all the others formed class -1. The classes are thus imbalanced with relative sizes of 1:4. We also expect both the cluster assumption and the manifold assumption to hold.

To prevent people from realizing the origin of this benchmark data set and exploiting its known structure (e.g. the spatial relationship of features in the image), we again obscured the data by application of algorithm 21.1, this time with $\sigma = 0.1$. Figure 21.3 illustrates the impact.

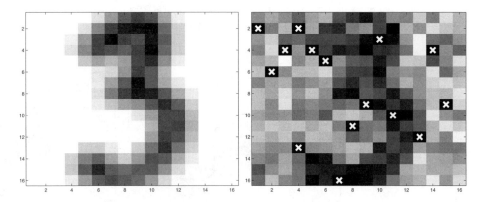

Figure 21.3   Fourth data point from the USPS data set. (*Left*) Original image. (*Right*) After rescaling, adding noise, and masking dimensions (x).

COIL   The Columbia object image library (COIL-100) is a set of color images of 100 different objects taken from different angles (in steps of 5 degrees) at a resolution of 128×128 pixels (Nene et al., 1996).[1] To create our data set, we first downsampled the red channel of each image to 16×16 pixels by averaging over blocks of 8×8 pixels. We then randomly selected 24 of the 100 objects (with $24 * 360 / 5 = 1728$ images). The set of 24 objects was partitioned into six classes of four objects each. We then randomly discarded 38 images of each class, to leave 250

---

1. at http://www1.cs.columbia.edu/CAVE/research/softlib/coil-100.html

each. Finally, we applied algorithm 21.1 (with $\sigma = 2$) to hide the image structure from the benchmark participants. Figure 21.4 gives an illustration.

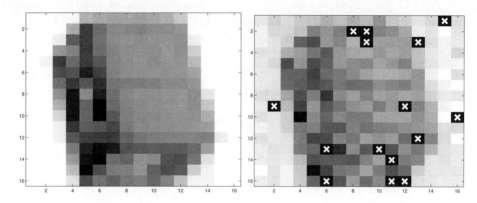

Figure 21.4 First data point from the `COIL` data set. (*Left*) Original image. (*Right*) After rescaling, adding noise, and masking dimensions (x).

BCI This data set originates from research toward the development of a brain computer interface (BCI) (Lal et al., 2004). A single person (subject C) performed 400 trials in each of which he imagined movements with either the left hand (class -1) or the right hand (class +1). In each trial, EEG (electroencephalography) was recorded from 39 electrodes. An autoregressive model of order 3 was fitted to each of the resulting 39 time series. The trail was represented by the total of $117 = 39 * 3$ fitted parameters. We thank Navin Lal for providing these data.

Text This is the 5 `comp.*` groups from the `Newsgroups` data set and the goal is to classify the `ibm` category versus the rest (Tong and Koller, 2001). We are thankful to Simon Tong for providing this data set. A tf-idf (term frequency – inverse document frequency) encoding resulted in a sparse representation with 11,960 dimensions. For the benchmark, 750 points of each class have been randomly selected and the features randomly permuted.

SecStr The main purpose of this benchmark data set is to investigate how far current methods can cope with large-scale application. The task is to predict the secondary structure of a given amino acid in a protein based on a sequence window centered around that amino acid. Our data set is based on the `CB513` set,[2] which was created by Cuff and Barton and consists of 513 proteins (Cuff and Barton, 1999). The 513 proteins consist of a total of 84,119 amino acids, of which 440 were `X`, `Z`, or `B`, and were therefore not considered.

---

2. e.g. at `http://www.compbio.dundee.ac.uk/~www-jpred/data/pred_res/`

For the remaining 83,679 amino acids, a symmetric sequence window of amino acids [-7,+7] was used to generate the input **x**. Positions before the beginning or after the end of the protein are represented by a special (21st) letter. Each letter is represented by a sparse binary vector of length 21 such that the position of the single 1 indicates the letter. The 28,968 α-helical and 18,888 β-sheet protein positions were collectively called class -1, while the 35,823 remaining points ("coil") formed class +1.

We supplied another 1,189,472 unlabeled data points. However, none of the benchmark participants chose to utilize these data in their experiments.

21.1.2   Experimental Setup

transductive
setting

We decided to carry out the experiments in the transductive setting (cf. chapter 1): the test set coincides with the set of unlabeled points. First, this is most economical in terms of the required amount of data points. Second, this poses the smallest requirements to participating methods. Otherwise it would have been necessary to develop and implement "out-of-sample extensions" (e.g. Bengio et al. (2004b)) for the inherently transductive algorithms. We expect the prediction accuracy on the unlabeled points to be similar to that achieved on out-of-sample points (after having trained on the same sets of labeled and unlabeled points). Recall, however, that transductive methods have to be retrained for every new set of test data, which may be prohibitive in some practical applications. On the other hand, the retraining offers the potential to learn from an increasing amount of unlabeled data, namely the accumulated test points. This potential is wasted when an inductive classifier is trained only once and from there on used.

numbers of
labeled points

An important question is how many labeled points are required to achieve decent classification accuracy. To shed some light on this, we equipped the benchmark data sets with subsets of labeled points of different sizes. More precisely, the number of labeled points is either 10 or 100 for all data sets except for `SecStr`, for which it is 100, 1000, or 10,000. In order to make the accuracy estimates derived from the experiments robust and independent of coincidental properties of the chosen points, we devised twelve subsets for each combination of data set and number of labeled points (ten for data set `SecStr`). When choosing the subsets of labeled points, we take care to pick at least one point from each class.

model selection

Since the unions of the sets of labeled points already cover substantial parts of the entire data sets, we provided the labels of all points to the participants of the benchmarks. This allowed for finding hyperparameter values by minimizing the test error, which is not possible in real applications; however, the results of this procedure can be useful to judge the potential of a method. To obtain results that are indicative of real world performance, the model selection has to be performed using only the small set of labeled points.

Table 21.2   TSVM results. For the linear kernel the algorithm described in chapter 6 has been used, for the nonlinear kernel the one of (Chapelle and Zien, 2005).

	g241c	g241d	Digit1	USPS	COIL	BCI	Text	
Linear	20.95	46.35	20.59	30.66		50.04	28.60	$n = 10$
Nonlinear	24.71	50.08	17.77	25.20	67.50	49.15	31.21	
Linear	18.18	23.76	18.05	21.12		42.67	22.31	$n = 100$
Nonlinear	18.46	22.42	6.15	9.77	25.80	33.25	24.52	

21.2   Application of SSL Methods

A major problem in the application of SSL methods to problems with very few labeled data points is the model selection. In the following we describe for each method how this was approached. Unless mentioned otherwise, the experiments have been conducted by the authors of the corresponding chapters.

Several authors have provided results corresponding to different variations of their algorithm. In order to keep the final results table as concise as possible, we have in these cases compared them and preselected the best one.

Finally, all the results reported on the tables below are test errors in %.

21.2.1   Transductive Support Vector Machines

Thorsten Joachims has reported results for the transductive support vector machine (TSVM) algorithm described in chapter 6 and for the spectral graph transducer (SGT) (Joachims, 2003). He used the code available on his webpage.

No model selection or parameter tuning has been performed, and according to Joachims the results are likely to be improved by appropriate preprocessing and/or model selection. For TSVM, a linear kernel was used and C was fixed to $C^{-1} = \frac{1}{n} \sum_{i=1}^{n} ||\mathbf{x}_i||^2$. For the SGT algorithm, the hyperparameters were set as in (Joachims, 2003): $C = 3200$, $d = 80$, and $k = 100$.

Since we believe that on some data sets nonlinearity might be important, we ran our own implementation of TSVM (Chapelle and Zien, 2005) with a radial basis function (RBF) kernel. Its width was chosen as the median of the pairwise distances and C was fixed to 100. Results are presented in table 21.2. The tables at the end of this chapter will refer to the nonlinear version.

21.2.2   Entropy Regularization

The method described in chapter 9 can be kernelized, but the experiments have been reported using a linear classifier. The hyperparameters (λ and weight decay) have been chosen by cross-validation. In case of a tie the smaller λ and the larger weight decay have been selected. Since the algorithm is similar to TSVM (cf. section 21.2.1)

Table 21.3 Performances of the entropy regularization method (cf. chapter 9). Because of the links with TSVM and the use of a linear classifier, the comparison with linear TSVM (see table 21.2) is relevant.

	g241c	g241d	Digit1	USPS	COIL	BCI	Text	
Entropy-Reg.	47.36	45.81	24.44	20.25	66.53	47.71	42.07	$n = 10$
Linear TSVM	20.95	46.35	20.59	30.66		50.04	28.60	
Entropy-Reg.	20.97	25.36	7.28	12.21	29.48	28.89	24.86	$n = 100$
Linear TSVM	18.18	23.76	18.05	21.12		42.67	22.31	

and a linear class of function has been used, we decided to compare the results with those of the linear TSVM. The comparison is shown in table 21.3.

21.2.3   Data-Dependent Regularization

The experiments were run using the distributed propagation data-dependent regularization, which is applicable to both relational data and data derived from a metric. The most important modeling decision in applying data-dependent regularization is the selection of the regions that bias label similarity. In the absence of domain knowledge, k-nearest neighbor regions, centered at each data point as induced by the default Euclidean distance metric, were considered.

In order to determine the number of points in each region tenfold cross-validation experiments were run. For this purpose, points that were graph-disconnected from training data were always treated as errors; this encouraged selecting a k that makes the information regularization graph connected.

The weight of labeled training data against unlabeled data, λ, was set to 0, meaning that the posterior labels of training data were not allowed to change from their given values. The regularization iteration proceeded until the change in parameters became insignificant.

As a result of data-dependent regularization, each previously unlabeled point now had a probabilistic class label. This probabilistic class label was converted to a real label by thresholding the probability. The threshold was applied as an additive term to the log probability of each class. Then the class assigned by the classifier was determined by maximizing the threshold-adjusted (log) probability.

Proper selection of the threshold requires cross-validation. However, for computational efficiency reasons the authors cross-validated only between two scenarios: the first, in which the threshold applied to each class is 0, which corresponds to treating the output of information regularization as plain probabilities; and the second, in which the threshold of each run is optimized so that the resulting class frequency on the unlabeled data matches the empirical class frequency on the labeled observations. Data sets 1, 3, 4, and 6 preferred the first algorithm for selecting the threshold (that is, no threshold), while data sets 2, 5, and 7 preferred the second algorithm.

Table 21.4   Influence of the class mass normalization (CMN, cf. chapter 11)

	g241c	g241d	Digit1	USPS	COIL	BCI	Text	
Without CMN	50.07	49.47	19.66	19.63	61.50	50.66	49.99	
With CMN	39.96	46.55	9.80	13.61	59.63	50.36	40.79	$n = 10$
Without CMN	39.37	36.42	3.17	10.65	10.01	46.92	30.54	
With CMN	22.05	28.20	3.15	6.36	10.03	46.22	25.71	$n = 100$

21.2.4   Label Propagation and Quadratic Criterion

A fully connected graph with an RBF kernel has been chosen for the algorithm described in chapter 11. More precisely, the cost function (11.11) is minimized giving the closed-form solution (11.12). The kernel bandwidth σ was selected in the following way:

- For data sets with 100 labeled examples, by cross-validation on the first split, the same σ being used on all other splits

- For data sets with 10 labeled examples, with the following basic heuristic: $\sigma = d/3$, where d is the estimated average distance between a point in the data set and its 10th nearest neighbor

The tradeoff coefficient μ was set to 10^{-6}.

As shown in table 21.4, the class mass normalization (cf. section 11.5) seemed to be very important, and later results are reported using this technique.

21.2.5   The Manifold Basis of Semi-Supervised Learning

Experiments have been conducted using the semi-supervised kernel introduced in section 12.4. This kernel was used either in an SVM or in regularized least squares (RLS; aka kernel ridge regression).

The kernel is of the form

$$\tilde{K}(x, z) = K(x, z) - \mathbf{k}_x^\top (I + rL^p G)^{-1} L^p \mathbf{k}_z,$$

where $K(x, z)$ is a base kernel, $[\mathbf{k}_x]_i = K(x_i, x)$, G is the Gram matrix (of size $l + u$), L is the normalized graph Laplacian, and r is the ratio $\frac{\gamma_I}{\gamma_A}$.

The base kernel was chosen to be an RBF with width σ. L is computed from an adjacency matrix W corresponding to a weighted k nearest neighbors graph with weights $W_{ij} = \exp\left(-\frac{\|x_i - x_j\|^2}{2\sigma_{\mathcal{G}}}\right)$ if there is an edge between x_i and x_j, and 0 otherwise. The width $\sigma_{\mathcal{G}}$ is fixed as the mean distance between adjacent nodes on this graph. The adjacency matrix is symmetrized by setting $W_{ij} = W_{ji}$ for any non-zero edge weight W_{ji}. The normalized graph Laplacian is computed as $L = I - D^{-1/2} W D^{-1/2}$ where D is a diagonal degree matrix given by $D_{ii} = \sum_j W_{ij}$.

For all data sets except `Text`, $k = 5, p = 2$ was used. For `Text`, those values are $k = 50, p = 5$. This is based on the experimental experience of the authors: relatively smaller values of k and p tend to work well for image data sets and larger values are useful for textual data sets. No further optimization on these parameters was attempted.

For the multiclass data set, a one-vs.-the-rest strategy was used. For each of the classifiers, the bias b was selected such that a sixth of the unlabeled data was classified in the positive class (because of a prior on uniform class probabilities for the six classes).

The hyperparameters were chosen by performing a search over the following grid:

1. regularization parameter $\gamma_A \in \{10^{-6}, 10^{-4}, 10^{-2}, 1, 100\}$;

2. base kernel width $\sigma \in \{\frac{\sigma_0}{8}, \frac{\sigma_0}{4}, \frac{\sigma_0}{2}, \sigma_0, 2\sigma_0, 4\sigma_0, 8\sigma_0\}$, where σ_0 is the mean norm of the feature vectors in the data set;

3. ratio $r = \frac{\gamma_I}{\gamma_A} \in \{0, 10^{-4}, 10^{-2}, 1, 100, 10^4, 10^6\}$.

For data sets `COIL` and `SecStr`, the best mean test error across splits was reported. For other data sets, the model selection criterion used was either

- fivefold cross-validation error for 100 labeled points, or
- for 10 labeled points, the normalized cut, $\frac{y^\top L^p y}{|i, y_i=1| \ |i, y_i=-1|}$, where y is the vector of predicted labels.

Data set 8 was treated differently due to its size. The linear Laplacian support vector machine/regularized least squares (SVM/RLS) was run as described in section 12.5 and (Keerthi and DeCoste, 2005). The values $k = 5, p = 4$ were set based on a crude search. Efficient nonlinear methods are currently under development and may possibly return better performance on this data set.

It is important to note that Laplacian SVM/RLS also provides out-of-sample prediction on completely unseen test points. Experimental results on data set `Digit1` are provided in chapter 12 Results are presented on table 21.5. Since LapRLS achieved slightly better performances, we consider this method for the table at the end of this chapter.

21.2.6 Discrete Regularization

This method consists in minimizing (13.12) with $p = 2$ as explained in section 13.3.1. The experiments have been carried out by Mingrui Wu. The value μ was set to 0.05. A k-nearest neighbor graph was constructed with weights on edges (i, j) computed as $\exp(-\gamma\|\mathbf{x}_i - \mathbf{x}_j\|^2)$. The values for k and γ were selected by tenfold cross-validation in the sets $\{5, 10, 20, 50, \infty\}$ and $\{\frac{1}{64}, \frac{1}{16}, \frac{1}{4}, 1, 4, 16, 64\}$ respectively. The input data are normalized such that the $\frac{1}{c^2}$ quantile of the pairwise distances equals 1, where c is number of classes.

Table 21.5   Semi-supervised kernel (chapter 12). No MS stands for "no model selection": this is the best mean test error achieved across all hyperparameter values.

	g241c	g241d	Digit1	USPS	COIL	BCI	Text	
LapRLS	43.95	45.68	5.44	18.99	–	48.97	33.68	
LapRLS – no MS	41.74	41.46	6.54	14.67	54.54	46.35	33.35	$n = 10$
LapSVM	46.21	45.15	8.97	19.05	–	49.25	37.28	
LapSVM – no MS	45.53	43.55	6.58	14.99	56.87	46.43	34.04	
LapRLS	24.36	26.46	2.92	4.68	–	31.36	23.57	
LapRLS – no MS	23.45	24.77	1.81	4.31	11.92	27.89	23.32	$n = 100$
LapSVM	23.82	26.36	3.13	4.70	–	32.39	23.86	
LapSVM – no MS	23.43	24.66	2.19	4.36	13.21	28.58	23.08	

21.2.7   Semi-Supervised Learning with Conditional Harmonic Mixing

This method is used to improve the performance of a supervised base classifier. A detailed description of its application to five of the benchmark data sets can be found in chapter 14. In a nutshell, an SVM is trained on the labeled points, and used to predict an initial (delta-) distribution on each unlabeled point. These are used to estimate conditional probability distributions that are associated to the edges of a directed graph with the data points as nodes. The authors took care to make the method essentially free of hyperparameters by averaging over a number of graphs constructed in different ways, although they conclude from their experiments that clever model selection might be able to perform better (cf. chapter 14).

21.2.8   Spectral Methods for Dimensionality Reduction

For the dimensionality methods described in chapter 16, a number k of nearest neighbors has to be chosen and the manifold dimensionality has to be estimated. k was set 3 for maximum variance unfolding (MVU), 12 for locally linear embedding (LLE), and 6 for Isomap and Laplacian eigenmaps. The dimensionality was estimated such that MVU explains 99% of the variance of the data (cf. table 21.6). After dimensionality reduction, the 1-nearest neighbor algorithm was used.

Table 21.6   First line: number of components kept in the dimensionality reduction; second line: "true" manifold dimension; third line: estimate of the manifold dimension according to the method described in (Hein and Audibert, 2005). [3]

g241c	g241d	Digit1	USPS	COIL	BCI	Text
38	33	4	9	3	8	29
241	241	5	?	1	?	?
66	63	15	4	2	9	7

Table 21.7   Nonlinear dimensionality reduction (chapter 16)

	g241c	g241d	Digit1	USPS	COIL	BCI	Text	
Isomap	47.88	46.72	13.65	16.66	63.36	49.00	38.12	
LapEig	47.47	45.34	12.04	19.14	67.96	49.94	40.84	
LLE	47.15	45.56	14.42	23.34	62.62	47.95	45.32	
MVU	48.68	47.28	11.92	14.88	65.72	50.24	39.40	$n = 10$
PCA	39.38	37.03	21.70	23.40	67.88	49.17	41.65	
None	44.05	43.22	23.47	19.82	65.91	48.74	39.44	
Isomap	43.93	42.45	3.89	5.81	17.35	48.67	30.11	
LapEig	42.14	39.43	2.52	6.09	36.49	48.64	30.92	
LLE	43.01	38.20	2.83	6.50	28.71	47.89	32.83	
MVU	44.05	43.21	3.99	6.09	32.27	47.42	30.74	$n = 100$
PCA	33.51	25.92	8.27	9.50	28.41	48.58	28.83	
None	40.28	37.49	6.12	7.64	23.27	44.83	30.77	

The performances of the different dimensionality reduction methods can be found in table 21.7. Note that principal components analysis (PCA) can achieve a very good performance on some data sets; for instance, with 100 labeled points, the test error is 17.3% on g241c, 9% on g241d, and 27.7% on Text, if, respectively, 1, 3, and 20 components are chosen. For the first two data sets, this is not really surprising given the artificial nature of the data. For Text, this can be explained by the fact that PCA performs *latent semantic analysis* (Deerwester et al., 1990). Finally, note that additional dimensions would have been helpful for the COIL data set. Indeed, with 12 components, Isomap achieve a test error of 12% (for 100 labeled points).

21.2.9   Large-Scale Algorithms

The large-scale methods described in chapter 18 use a small set of size m on which to expand the solution. m was fixed to 100, except for the large-scale data set SecStr where m was set to 1000.

The length scale σ was selected as explained in section 21.2.4, except that for ten labeled points, the distance d used in the heuristic $\sigma = d/3$ is calculated as the average distance between a point and its 10th nearest neighbor among $m + 10$ other points randomly selected.

---

3. We thank Matthias Hein for having computed those estimates.

Table 21.8   Large-scale strategies (chapter 18)

	g241c	g241d	Digit1	USPS	COIL	BCI	Text	
NoSub	39.96	46.55	9.80	13.61	59.63	50.36	40.79	
RandSub	40.11	41.93	15.21	15.64	65.11	49.96	37.37	$n = 10$
SmartSub	39.56	42.20	14.19	18.56	65.94	48.31	38.60	
SmartOnly	39.82	42.24	12.60	16.95	63.97	49.47	38.23	
NoSub	22.05	28.20	3.15	6.36	10.03	46.22	25.71	
RandSub	23.60	25.85	4.20	7.97	19.74	44.61	25.60	$n = 100$
SmartSub	22.07	26.16	4.11	7.51	22.86	44.36	25.71	
SmartOnly	22.07	25.98	3.50	6.90	15.70	44.78	25.75	

Table 21.8 presents results for the following algorithms:

NoSub: No subsampling, i.e. the results of section 21.2.4.

RandSub: Random subsampling.

SmartSub: The method described in algorithm 18.1.

SmartOnly: Training using only a subset of the data selected by algorithm 18.1. This is to be able to assess the usefulness of actually using the rest of the data in the cost (cf. matrix C_{RS} in Eq. 18.7).

21.2.10   Cluster Kernels

The kernel proposed in chapter 19 is a product of two kernels:

1. k_{orig} is a standard RBF kernel with width σ and ridge C^{-1}. Those two hyperparameters have been optimized with the code available at `http://www.kyb.tuebingen.mpg.de/bs/people/chapelle/ams/`.

2. k_{bag} resulting from repeated runs of the k-means algorithm. k has been found by tenfold cross-validation in the set $\{2, 4, 6, 8, 10, 20, 30, 40, 50\}$, the kernel k_{orig} being fixed.

Finally, the method mentioned in footnote 2 in chapter 19 was used with $\lambda = 0.5$ on data sets `COIL` and `SecStr` because it worked better.

21.2.11   Low-Density Separation

This method is not described in the book, but in (Chapelle and Zien, 2005). The code used to run the experiments is available at `http://www.kyb.tuebingen.mpg.de/bs/people/chapelle/lds/`. The hyperparameter ρ is found by cross-validation, the other hyperparameters being fixed to their default values. The reason for not optimizing on more hyperparameters is that the the model selection becomes unreliable, especially with only ten labeled points. Note that if the number k of nearest neighbors is optimized on the test error, the test error can be dramatically decreased: for instance, on `Digit1` with ten labeled points, a test error of 3.7% was achieved with $k = 5$. This has to be compared to the 15.6% achieved by cross-validation on ρ only.

21.2.12   Boosting

Ayhan Demiriz ran experiments on data set `SecStr` using the assemble algorithm (Bennett et al., 2002), which is a modified version of AdaBoost for semi-supervised learning. It turns out that the algorithm was not very well suited for a very small number of labeled points, as the algorithm stops whenever a weak learner correctly classifies all labeled points. On the other hand, it seems much better suited for large data sets, because the run time increases only linearly in the number of labeled and unlabeled points.

The weak learner was a two-level decision tree. AdaBoost and Assemble have both been run for 50 iterations. In this case, it seems that semi-supervised learning was not helpful: AdaBoost achieved 30.8% test error, while Assemble achieved 32.2%.

21.3   Results and Discussion

To compare the results of the different methods, we summarize them in tables. Tables 21.9 and 21.10 show the mean test errors and the ROC (receiver operating characteristic) scores for training with 10 labeled points; similarly tables 21.11 and 21.12 for 100 labeled points. The results for `SecStr` are presented separately in table 21.13 since the numbers of labeled points differ from the other data sets. Further, only a small number of methods competed in this benchmark.

Tables 21.9 and 21.11 contain a lot of results and might be a bit difficult to parse. For this reason, we propose to perform some clustering on the results. Concerning the data sets, we can identify two main categories:

manifold-like data sets

Manifold-like: The data lie near a low-dimensional manifold. Based on table 21.6, this seems to be the case of data sets `Digit1`, `USPS`, `COIL`, and `BCI`. For the first three, this can be easily explained by the fact the data represent images; for `BCI`, this is less obvious, but it seems plausible that the signals captured by an EEG have rather few degrees of freedom.

cluster-like data sets

Cluster-like: The data are clustered, and they tend cluster in such a way that two classes do not share the same cluster. By construction this is the case for data sets `g241c` and `g241d`. We conjecture that `Text` belongs also to this category, because cluster-based algorithms (see below) usually perform well on text data. As for the algorithms, we can also identify two categories, which correspond to the two types

Table 21.9 Test errors (%) with 10 labeled training points. Values printed in italics were obtained by performing model selection w.r.t. the test error.

		g241c	g241d	Digit1	USPS	COIL	BCI	Text
	1-NN	44.05	43.22	23.47	19.82	65.91	48.74	39.44
	SVM	47.32	46.66	30.60	20.03	68.36	49.85	45.37
21.2.8	**MVU + 1-NN**	48.68	47.28	11.92	14.88	65.72	50.24	39.40
21.2.8	**LEM + 1-NN**	47.47	45.34	12.04	19.14	67.96	49.94	40.84
21.2.4	**QC + CMN**	39.96	46.55	9.80	13.61	59.63	50.36	40.79
21.2.6	**Discrete Reg.**	49.59	49.05	12.64	16.07	63.38	49.51	40.37
21.2.1	**TSVM**	24.71	50.08	17.77	25.20	67.50	49.15	31.21
21.2.1	**SGT**	22.76	18.64	8.92	25.36	–	49.59	29.02
21.2.10	**Cluster-Kernel**	48.28	42.05	18.73	19.41	67.32	48.31	42.72
21.2.3	**Data-Dep. Reg.**	41.25	45.89	12.49	17.96	63.65	50.21	–
21.2.11	**LDS**	28.85	50.63	15.63	17.57	61.90	49.27	27.15
21.2.5	**Laplacian RLS**	43.95	45.68	5.44	18.99	*54.54*	48.97	33.68
21.2.7	**CHM (normed)**	39.03	43.01	14.86	20.53	–	46.90	–

Table 21.10 ROC scores (area under curve; %) with 10 labeled training points.

		g241c	g241d	Digit1	USPS	BCI	Text
	1-NN	–	–	–	–	–	–
	SVM	64.68	63.04	88.38	75.56	51.59	67.97
21.2.8	**MVU + 1-NN**	–	–	–	–	–	–
21.2.8	**LEM + 1-NN**	–	–	–	–	–	–
21.2.4	**QC + CMN**	64.24	62.45	96.32	90.76	49.47	70.71
21.2.6	**Discrete Reg.**	51.75	52.73	91.03	80.65	51.45	53.79
21.2.1	**TSVM**	82.41	50.65	86.98	68.21	50.92	73.42
21.2.1	**SGT**	87.41	89.40	97.58	73.08	50.70	80.09
21.2.10	**Cluster-Kernel**	61.63	77.68	89.49	74.28	51.77	73.09
21.2.3	**Data-Dep. Reg.**	63.43	56.92	96.22	84.91	50.31	–
21.2.11	**LDS**	77.35	49.70	90.10	75.88	49.75	80.68
21.2.5	**Laplacian RLS**	59.23	57.07	99.50	85.70	51.69	76.55
21.2.7	**CHM (normed)**	64.83	62.29	92.91	81.16	52.75	–

of data sets mentioned above:

manifold-based algorithms

Manifold-based: These algorithms come from parts III and IV of this book: `Discrete Reg`, `QC`, `Laplacian RLS`, `CHM`, `SDE`, `LEM`, `SGT`. Note in particular that `Discrete Reg` and `QC` minimize a similar cost function, the difference being the normalization of the Laplacian.

cluster-based algorithms

Cluster-based (or low-density separation as explained in part II of the book: There are three algorithms in this category which are expected to behave similarly: `TSVM`, `Data-Dep Reg`, `Entropy-Reg` (see section 21.2.2). Finally, `Cluster-Kernel` and `LDS` also belong to this category, but are not closely related to the former three.

A first conclusion that we can draw from these experiments is that no algorithm

Table 21.11 Test errors (%) with 100 labeled training points. Values printed in italics were obtained by performing model selection w.r.t. the test error.

		g241c	g241d	Digit1	USPS	COIL	BCI	Text
	1-NN	40.28	37.49	6.12	7.64	23.27	44.83	30.77
	SVM	23.11	24.64	5.53	9.75	22.93	34.31	26.45
21.2.8	**MVU + 1-NN**	44.05	43.21	3.99	6.09	32.27	47.42	30.74
21.2.8	**LEM + 1-NN**	42.14	39.43	2.52	6.09	36.49	48.64	30.92
21.2.4	**QC + CMN**	22.05	28.20	3.15	6.36	10.03	46.22	25.71
21.2.6	**Discrete Reg.**	43.65	41.65	2.77	4.68	9.61	47.67	24.00
21.2.1	**TSVM**	18.46	22.42	6.15	9.77	25.80	33.25	24.52
21.2.1	**SGT**	17.41	9.11	2.61	6.80	–	45.03	23.09
21.2.10	**Cluster-Kernel**	13.49	4.95	3.79	9.68	21.99	35.17	24.38
21.2.3	**Data-Dep. Reg.**	20.31	32.82	2.44	5.10	11.46	47.47	–
21.2.11	**LDS**	18.04	23.74	3.46	4.96	13.72	43.97	23.15
21.2.5	**Laplacian RLS**	24.36	26.46	2.92	4.68	*11.92*	31.36	23.57
21.2.7	**CHM (normed)**	24.82	25.67	3.79	7.65	–	36.03	–

Table 21.12 ROC scores (area under curve; %) with 100 labeled training points.

		g241c	g241d	Digit1	USPS	BCI	Text
	1-NN	–	–	–	–	–	–
	SVM	85.57	83.54	99.09	95.76	71.17	84.26
21.2.8	**MVU + 1-NN**	–	–	–	–	–	–
21.2.8	**LEM + 1-NN**	–	–	–	–	–	–
21.2.4	**QC + CMN**	86.40	82.23	99.59	91.11	56.48	84.62
21.2.6	**Discrete Reg.**	52.81	52.97	98.84	92.24	52.36	71.53
21.2.1	**TSVM**	88.55	84.18	98.02	92.74	73.09	80.96
21.2.1	**SGT**	91.74	97.48	99.76	96.72	56.79	85.22
21.2.10	**Cluster-Kernel**	93.15	98.95	99.36	94.50	70.50	85.90
21.2.3	**Data-Dep. Reg.**	87.50	74.18	99.81	97.74	54.38	–
21.2.11	**LDS**	89.37	83.13	99.23	95.62	57.22	84.77
21.2.5	**Laplacian RLS**	83.54	81.54	99.40	98.65	74.83	85.05
21.2.7	**CHM (normed)**	81.13	81.36	99.49	96.69	66.32	–

is uniformly better than the others, and that for a given semi-supervised learning problem, the algorithm needs to be selected carefully as a function of the nature of the data set. A general rule (which seems obvious a posteriori) is that manifold-based algorithms should be used for manifold-like data sets, and cluster-based algorithms should be used for cluster-like data sets.

model selection   It should be also noted that model selection was challenging for most of the competitors, especially in the case of only 10 labeled points, where the use of cross-validation can be unreliable. In this respect, the results with 100 labeled points are expected to be more reliable and to give a better indication of the strength of the different algorithms.

limits of   One of the disappointing results of this benchmark is the Text data set. Indeed,
semi-supervised   it has been shown that semi-supervised learning can be very useful for this type
learning

Table 21.13   Results for `SecStr` for different numbers of labeled points. (*Left*) Test error (%). (*Right*) ROC score (%). Values printed in italics were obtained by performing model selection w.r.t. the test error.

	100	1000	10000	100	1000	10000
SVM	44.59	33.71	–	59.09	70.86	–
Cluster Kernel	42.95	34.03	–	58.79	70.37	–
QC randsub (CMN)	42.32	40.84	–	54.77	59.99	–
QC smartonly (CMN)	42.14	40.71	–	55.59	60.25	–
QC smartsub (CMN)	42.26	40.84	–	55.35	60.08	–
Boosting (Assemble)	–	–	32.21	–	–	–
LapRLS	*42.59*	*34.17*	*28.55*	*59.02*	*70.33*	*77.95*
LapSVM	*43.42*	*33.96*	*28.53*	*58.40*	*70.54*	*77.95*

of data (Joachims, 1999; Nigam et al., 2000; Chapelle and Zien, 2005), but the results from tables 21.9 and 21.11 exhibit only a moderate improvement over plain supervised learning. The fact that the data set has been constructed in a one-vs-rest setting could be a possible explanation (cf. section 21.1.1). To test this hypothesis we tried to classify only two topics, namely `ibm` and `x`. A linear SVM achieved a mean test error of 12% (over several subsets of 100 labeled points), while a linear TSVM was able to reduce the test error to 2%. Further investigation is required to understand why such a large improvement is possible in this case.

Finally, it is worth pointing out that one should not necessarily expect an improvement with unlabeled data. The data sets `BCI` and `SecStr` seem to be examples where it is difficult to do better than standard supervised learning. At least for `SecStr`, this might be a problem of the amounts of unlabeled data that are utilized. Current approaches to protein secondary structure prediction use essentially all known protein sequences, which amount to tens or hundreds of million unlabeled data points. This is only possible due to the use of a very simple strategy: roughly speaking, each protein is represented by an average of the proteins in its neighborhood (Rost and Sander, 1993). Clearly, bringing the more sophisticated (and probably more powerful) SSL methods to this scale is an important open problem.

In all cases, we believe that there is no "black box" solution and that a good understanding of the nature of the data is required to perform successful semi-supervised learning. Indeed, in supervised learning, it seems that a good generic learning algorithm can perform well on a lot of real-world data sets without specific domain knowledge. In contrast, semi-supervised learning is possible only due to the special form of the data distribution that correlates the label of a data point with its situation within the distribution; therefore it seems much more difficult to design a general semi-supervised classifier. Instead, powerful semi-supervised learning algorithms distinguish themselves through the ability to make use of available prior knowledge about the domain and data distribution, in order to relate data and labels and improve classification. [4]

---

4. Part of this paragraph has been inspired by comments from Adrian Corduneanu.

VI   Perspectives

An Augmented PAC Model for Semi-Supervised Learning

Maria-Florina Balcan   NINAMF@CS.CMU.EDU
Avrim Blum   AVRIM@CS.CMU.EDU

The standard PAC (probably approximately correct) learning model has proven to be a useful theoretical framework for thinking about the problem of *supervised* learning. However, it does not tend to capture the assumptions underlying many *semi*-supervised learning methods. In this chapter we describe an augmented version of the PAC model designed with semi-supervised learning in mind, that can be used to help think about the problem of learning from labeled and unlabeled data and many of the different approaches taken. The model provides a unified framework for analyzing when and why unlabeled data can help, in which one can discuss both sample-complexity and algorithmic issues.

Our model can be viewed as an extension of the standard PAC model, where in addition to a concept class $\mathcal{C}$, one also proposes a compatibility function: a type of compatibility that one believes the target concept should have with the underlying distribution of data. For example, it could be that one believes the target should cut through a low-density region of space, or that it should be self-consistent in some way, as in co-training. This belief is then explicitly represented in the model. Unlabeled data are then potentially helpful in this setting because they allow one to estimate compatibility over the space of hypotheses, and to reduce the size of the search space from the whole set of hypotheses $\mathcal{C}$ down to those that, according to one's assumptions, are a priori reasonable with respect to the distribution.

After proposing the model, we then analyze sample-complexity issues in this setting: that is, how much of each type of data one should expect to need in order to learn well, and what are the basic quantities that these numbers depend on. We provide examples of sample-complexity bounds both for uniform convergence and ϵ-cover-based algorithms, as well as several algorithmic results.

22.1   Introduction

As we have already seen in the previous chapters, there has been growing interest in using unlabeled data together with labeled data in machine learning, and a number of different approaches have been developed. However, the assumptions these methods are based on are often quite distinct and not captured by standard theoretical models.

One difficulty from a theoretical point of view is that standard discriminative learning models do not really capture how and why unlabeled data can be of help. In particular, in the PAC model there is purposefully a complete disconnect between the data distribution D and the target function f being learned (Valiant, 1984; Blumer et al., 1989; Kearns and Vazirani, 1994). The only prior belief is that f belongs to some class $\mathcal{C}$: even if D is known fully, any function $f \in \mathcal{C}$ is still possible. For instance, it is perfectly natural (and common) to talk about the problem of learning a concept class such as DNF (disjunctive normal form) formulas (Linial et al., 1989; Verbeurgt, 1990) or an intersection of halfspaces (Baum, 1990; Blum and Kannan, 1997; Vempala, 1997; Klivans et al., 2002) over the uniform distribution; but clearly in this case unlabeled data are useless — you can just generate the data yourself. For learning over an unknown distribution (the standard PAC setting), unlabeled data can help somewhat, by allowing one to use distribution-specific sample-complexity bounds, but this does not seem to fully capture the power of unlabeled data in practice.

In *generative*-model settings, one *can* easily talk theoretically about the use of unlabeled data, e.g., (Castelli and Cover, 1995, 1996). However, these results typically make strong assumptions that essentially imply that there is only one natural distinction to be made for a given (unlabeled) data distribution. For instance, a typical generative-model setting would be that we assume positive examples are generated by one Gaussian, and negative examples are generated by another Gaussian. In this case, given enough unlabeled data, we could in principle recover the Gaussians and would need labeled data only to tell us which Gaussian is the positive one and which is the negative one.[1] This is too strong an assumption for most real-world settings. Instead, we would like our model to allow for a distribution over data (e.g., documents we want to classify) where there are a number of plausible distinctions we might want to make.[2] In addition, we would like a general framework that can be used to model many different uses of unlabeled data.

In this chapter, we present a PAC-style framework that bridges these positions

---

1. Castelli and Cover (1995, 1996) do not assume Gaussians in particular, but they do assume the distributions are distinguishable, which from our perspective has the same issue.
2. In fact, there has been recent work in the generative model setting on the practical side that goes in this direction (see (Nigam et al., 2000; Nigam, 2001)). We discuss connections to generative models further in section 22.5.2.

and which we believe can be used to help think about many of the ways unlabeled data are typically used, including approaches discussed in other chapters. This framework extends the PAC model in a way that allows one to express not only the form of target function one is considering but also relationships that one hopes the target function and underlying distribution will possess. We then analyze sample-complexity issues in this setting: that is, how much of each type of data one should expect to need in order to learn well, and also give examples of algorithmic results in this model.

Specifically, the idea of the proposed model is to augment the PAC notion of a *concept class*, which is a set of functions (like linear separators or decision trees), with a notion of *compatibility* between a function and the data distribution that we
main idea   hope the target function will satisfy. Then, rather than talking of "learning a concept class $\mathcal{C}$," we will talk of "learning a concept class $\mathcal{C}$ under compatibility notion χ". For example, suppose we believe there should exist a good linear separator, and that furthermore, if the data happen to cluster, then this separator probably does not slice through the middle of any such clusters. Then we would want a compatibility notion that penalizes functions that do, in fact, slice through clusters. In this framework, the extent to which unlabeled data help depends on two quantities: first, the extent to which the true target function satisfies the given assumption, and second, the extent to which the distribution allows this assumption to rule out alternative hypotheses. For instance, if the data do not cluster at all, then all functions equally satisfy this compatibility notion and the assumption ends up not helping. From a Bayesian perspective, one can think of this as a PAC model for a setting in which one's prior is not just over functions, but also over how the function and underlying distribution relate to each other.

To make our model formal, we will need to ensure that the degree of compatibility be something that can be estimated from a finite sample. To do this, we will require that the compatibility notion χ actually be a function from $\mathcal{C} \times \mathcal{X}$ to $[0, 1]$, where the compatibility of a function f with the data distribution D is $\mathbf{E}_{x \sim D}[\chi(f, x)]$. The degree of *in*compatibility is then something we can think of as a kind of "unlabeled error rate" that measures how a priori unreasonable we believe some proposed hypothesis to be. For instance, in the example above of a "margin-style" compatibility, we could define $\chi(f, x)$ to be an increasing function of the distance of x to the separator f. In this case, the unlabeled error rate, $1 - \chi(f, D)$, is a measure of the probability mass close to the proposed separator. In co-training, where each example x has two "views" ($x = \langle x_1, x_2 \rangle$), the underlying belief is that the true target c^* can be decomposed into functions $\langle c_1^*, c_2^* \rangle$ over each view such that for most examples, $c_1^*(x_1) = c_2^*(x_2)$. In this case, we can define $\chi(\langle f_1, f_2 \rangle, \langle x_1, x_2 \rangle) = 1$ if $f_1(x_1) = f_2(x_2)$, and 0 if $f_1(x_1) \neq f_2(x_2)$. Then the compatibility of a hypothesis $\langle f_1, f_2 \rangle$ with an underlying distribution D is $\mathbf{Pr}_{\langle x_1, x_2 \rangle \sim D}[f_1(x_1) = f_2(x_2)]$.

This setup allows us to analyze the ability of a finite unlabeled sample to reduce our dependence on labeled examples, as a function of the compatibility of the target function (i.e., how correct we were in our assumption) and various measures of the "helpfulness" of the distribution. In particular, in our model, we find that unlabeled data can help in several distinct ways.

- If the target function is highly compatible with D, then if we have enough unlabeled data to estimate compatibility over all $f \in \mathcal{C}$, we can in principle reduce the size of the search space from $\mathcal{C}$ down to just those $f \in \mathcal{C}$ whose estimated compatibility is high. For instance, if D is "helpful," then the set of such functions will be much smaller than the entire set $\mathcal{C}$.

ways in which
unlabeled data
can help

- By providing an estimate of D, unlabeled data can allow us to use a more refined distribution-specific notion of "hypothesis space size" such as annealed (Vapnik-Chervonenkis) VC entropy (Devroye et al., 1996), Rademacher complexities (Koltchinskii, 2001; Bartlett and Mendelson, 2002; Boucheron et al., 2005) or the size of the smallest ϵ-cover (Benedek and Itai, 1991), rather than VC dimension (Blumer et al., 1989; Kearns and Vazirani, 1994). In fact, for natural cases (such as those above) we find that the sense in which unlabeled data reduces the "size" of the search space is best described in these distribution-specific measures.

- Finally, if the distribution is especially nice, we may find that not only does the set of "compatible" $f \in \mathcal{C}$ have a small ϵ-cover but also the elements of the cover are far apart. In that case, if we assume the target function is fully compatible, we may be able to learn from even fewer labeled examples than the $1/\epsilon$ needed just to *verify* a good hypothesis! (Though here D is effectively committing to the target as in generative models.)

Our framework also allows us to address the issue of how much *unlabeled* data we should expect to need. Roughly, the "VCdim/ϵ^2" form of standard PAC sample complexity bounds now becomes a bound on the number of *unlabeled* examples we need. However, technically, the set whose VC dimension we now care about is not $\mathcal{C}$ but rather a set defined by both $\mathcal{C}$ and χ: that is, the overall complexity depends both on the complexity of $\mathcal{C}$ and the complexity of the notion of compatibility (see section 22.3.2). One consequence of our model is that if the target function and data distribution are both well behaved with respect to the compatibility notion, then the sample-size bounds we get for labeled data can substantially beat what one could hope to achieve through pure labeled-data bounds, and we illustrate this with a number of examples throughout the chapter.

22.2   A Formal Framework

In this section we formally introduce what we mean by a *notion of compatibility*, and illustrate it through a number of examples, including margins and co-training.

We assume that examples (both labeled and unlabeled) come according to a fixed unknown distribution D over an instance space $\mathcal{X}$, and they are labeled by some unknown target function c^*. As in the standard PAC model, a *concept class* or *hypothesis space* is a set of functions over the instance space $\mathcal{X}$, and we will often make the assumption (the "realizable case") that the target function belongs to a given class $\mathcal{C}$. For a given hypothesis f, the (true) error rate of f is defined as $err(f) = err_D(f) = \mathbf{Pr}_{x \sim D}[f(x) \neq c^*(x)]$. For any two hypotheses $f_1, f_2 \in \mathcal{C}$, the distance with respect to D between f_1 and f_2 is defined as $d(f_1, f_2) = d_D(f_1, f_2) = \mathbf{Pr}_{x \sim D}[f_1(x) \neq f_2(x)]$. We will use $\widehat{err}(f)$ to denote the empirical error rate of f on a given labeled sample and $\hat{d}(f_1, f_2)$ to denote the empirical distance between f_1 and f_2 on a given unlabeled sample.

We define a *notion of compatibility* to be a mapping from a hypothesis f and a distribution D to $[0, 1]$ indicating how "compatible" f is with D. In order for this to be estimable from a finite sample, we require that compatibility be an expectation over individual examples. (Though one could imagine more general notions with this property as well.) Specifically, we define:

legal notion of compatibility

Definition 22.1 *A* legal notion of compatibility *is a function* $\chi : \mathcal{C} \times \mathcal{X} \to [0, 1]$ *where we (overloading notation) define* $\chi(f, D) = \mathbf{E}_{x \sim D}[\chi(f, x)]$. *Given a sample* S, *we define* $\chi(f, S)$ *to be the empirical average over the sample.*

Remark 22.2 *One could also allow compatibility functions over k-tuples of examples, in which case our (unlabeled) sample-complexity bounds would simply increase by a factor of k. For settings in which D is actually known in advance (e.g., transductive learning; see section 22.5.1) we can drop this requirement entirely and allow any notion of compatibility* $\chi(f, D)$ *to be legal.*

Definition 22.3 *Given compatibility notion* χ, *the* incompatibility *of f with D is* $1 - \chi(f, D)$. *We will also call this its* unlabeled error rate, $err_{unl}(f)$, *when* χ *and D are clear from context. For a given sample S, we use* $\widehat{err}_{unl}(f)$ *to denote the empirical average over S.*

Finally, we need a notation for the set of functions whose incompatibility is at most some given value τ.

Definition 22.4 *Given threshold* τ, *we define* $\mathcal{C}_{D,\chi}(\tau) = \{f \in \mathcal{C} : err_{unl}(f) \leq \tau\}$. *So, e.g.,* $\mathcal{C}_{D,\chi}(1) = \mathcal{C}$. *Similarly, for a sample S, we define* $\mathcal{C}_{S,\chi}(\tau) = \{f \in \mathcal{C} : \widehat{err}_{unl}(f) \leq \tau\}$

We now give several examples to illustrate this framework:

margins

Example 1: Suppose examples are points in $\mathbb{R}^d$ and $\mathcal{C}$ is the class of linear separators. A natural belief in this setting is that data should be "well-separated": not only should the target function separate the positive and negative examples but it should do so by some reasonable *margin* γ. This is the assumption used by transductive support vector machines (SVM) (see (Joachims, 1999) and also chapter 6 in this book). In this case, if we are given γ up front, we could define $\chi(f, x) = 1$ if x is farther than distance γ from the hyperplane defined by f, and $\chi(f, x) = 0$ otherwise. So, the incompatibility of f with D is probability mass within distance γ of $f \cdot x = 0$. Or we could define $\chi(f, x)$ to be a smooth function of the distance of x to the separator, if we do not want to commit to a specific γ in advance. (In contrast, defining compatibility of a hypothesis based on the largest γ such that D has probability mass *exactly zero* within distance γ of the separator would *not* fit our model: it cannot be written as an expectation over individual examples and indeed would not be a good definition since one cannot distinguish "zero" from "exponentially close to zero" from a small sample of unlabeled data.)

co-training

Example 2: In co-training (Blum and Mitchell, 1998), we assume examples come as pairs $\langle x_1, x_2 \rangle$, and our goal is to learn a pair of functions $\langle f_1, f_2 \rangle$. For instance, if our goal is to classify webpages, x_1 might represent the words on the page itself and x_2 the words attached to links pointing *to* this page from other pages. The hope that underlies co-training is that the two parts of the example are consistent, which then allows the co-training algorithm to bootstrap from unlabeled data. For example, *iterative co-training* uses a small amount of labeled data to get some initial information (e.g., if a link with the words "my advisor" points to a page, then that page is probably a faculty member's home page) and then when it finds an unlabeled example where one half is confident (e.g., the link says "my advisor"), it uses that to label the example for training its hypothesis over the other half. This approach and several variants have been used for a variety of learning problems, including named entity classification (Collins and Singer, 1999), text classification (Nigam and Ghani, 2000; Ghani, 2001), natural language processing (Pierce and Cardie, 2001), large-scale document classification (Park and Zhang, 2003), and visual detectors (Levin et al., 2003).[3] As mentioned in section 22.1, the assumptions underlying co-training fit naturally into our framework. In particular, we can define the incompatibility of some hypothesis $\langle f_1, f_2 \rangle$ with distribution D as $\mathbf{Pr}_{\langle x_1, x_2 \rangle \sim D}[f_1(x_1) \neq f_2(x_2)]$.

graph-based methods

Example 3: In transductive graph-based methods, we are given a set of unlabeled examples connected in a graph **g**, where the interpretation of an edge is that we believe the two endpoints of the edge should have the *same* label. Given a few labeled vertices, various graph-based methods then attempt to use them to infer labels for the remaining points. If we are willing to view D as a distribution over *edges* (a uniform distribution if **g** is unweighted), then as in co-training we can define the incompatibility of some hypothesis f as the probability mass of edges that are cut by f, which then motivates various cut-based algorithms. For instance, if we require f to be Boolean, then the min-cut method of Blum and Chawla (2001) finds the most-compatible hypothesis consistent with the labeled data; if we allow f to be fractional and define $1 - \chi(f, \langle x_1, x_2 \rangle) = (f(x_1) - f(x_2))^2$, then the algorithm of Zhu et al. (2003b) finds the most-compatible consistent hypothesis. If we do not wish to view D as a distribution over edges, we could have D be a distribution over *vertices* and broaden definition 22.1 to allow for χ to be a function over *pairs* of examples. In fact, as mentioned in remark 22.2, since we have perfect knowledge of D in this setting we can allow any compatibility function $\chi(f, D)$ to be legal. We

---

3. For more discussion regarding co-training see also chapter 2 in this book.

discuss more connections with graph-based methods in section 22.5.1.

Example 4: As a special case of co-training, suppose examples are pairs of points in $\mathbb{R}^d$, $\mathcal{C}$ is the class of linear separators, and we believe the two points in each pair should both be on the *same* side of the target function. (So, this is a version of co-training where we require $f_1 = f_2$.) The motivation is that we want to use pairwise information as in example 3, but we also want to use the features of each data point. For instance, in the word-sense disambiguation problem studied by Yarowsky (1995), the goal is to determine which of several dictionary definitions is intended for some target word in a piece of text (e.g., is "plant" being used to indicate a tree or a factory?). The local context around each word can be viewed as placing it into $\mathbb{R}^d$, but the edges correspond to a completely different type of information: the belief that if a word appears twice in the same document, it is probably being used in the *same* sense both times. In this setting, we could use the same compatibility function as in example 3, but rather than having the concept class $\mathcal{C}$ be all possible functions, we reduce $\mathcal{C}$ to just linear separators.

Example 5: In a related setting to co-training, considered by Leskes (2005), examples are single points in $\mathcal{X}$ but we have a pair of hypothesis spaces $\langle \mathcal{C}_1, \mathcal{C}_2 \rangle$ (or more generally a k-tuple $\langle \mathcal{C}_1, \ldots, \mathcal{C}_k \rangle$), and the goal is to find a pair of hypotheses $\langle f_1, f_2 \rangle \in \mathcal{C}_1 \times \mathcal{C}_2$ with low error over labeled data and that agree over the distribution. For instance, if data are sufficiently "well-separated," one might expect there to exist both a good linear separator and a good decision tree, and one would like to use this assumption to reduce the need for labeled data. In this case one could define compatibility of $\langle f_1, f_2 \rangle$ with D as $\mathbf{Pr}_{x \sim D}[f_1(x) = f_2(x)]$, or the similar notion given in (Leskes, 2005).

margin notes: linear separator / graph cuts / agreement

22.3 Sample Complexity Results

We now present several sample-complexity bounds that fall out of this framework, showing how unlabeled data, together with a suitable compatibility notion, can reduce the need for labeled examples.

The basic structure of all of these results is as follows. First, given enough unlabeled data (where "enough" will be a function of some measure of the complexity of $\mathcal{C}$ and possibly of χ as well), we can uniformly estimate the true compatibilities of all functions in $\mathcal{C}$ by their empirical compatibilities over the sample. Then, by using this quantity to give a preference ordering over the functions in $\mathcal{C}$, we can reduce "$\mathcal{C}$" down to "the set of functions in $\mathcal{C}$ whose compatibility is not much larger than the true target function" in bounds for the number of *labeled* examples needed for learning. The specific bounds differ in terms of the exact complexity measures used (and a few other issues such as stratification and realizability) and we provide examples illustrating when certain complexity measures can be significantly more powerful than others. In particular, ϵ-cover bounds (section 22.3.3) can provide especially good bounds for co-training and graph-based settings.

22.3.1   Uniform Convergence Bounds for Finite Hypothesis Spaces

We begin with uniform convergence bounds (later in section 22.3.3 we give tighter ϵ-cover bounds that apply to algorithms of a particular form). For clarity, we begin with the case of finite hypothesis spaces where we measure the "size" of a set of functions by just the number of functions in the set. We then discuss several issues that arise when considering infinite hypothesis spaces, such as what is an appropriate measure for the "size" of the set of compatible functions, and the need to account for the complexity of the compatibility notion itself. Note that in the standard PAC model, one typically talks of either the realizable case, where we assume that $c^* \in \mathcal{C}$, or the agnostic case where we do not (see (Kearns and Vazirani, 1994)). In our setting, we have the additional issue of *unlabeled* error rate, and can either make an a priori assumption that the target function's unlabeled error is low, or else aim for a more "Occam-style" bound in which we have a stream of labeled examples and halt once they are sufficient to justify the hypothesis produced.

We first give a bound for the "doubly realizable" case.

Theorem 22.5 *If we see m_u unlabeled examples and m_l labeled examples, where*

$$m_u \geq \frac{1}{\epsilon}\left[\ln|\mathcal{C}| + \ln\frac{2}{\delta}\right] \quad and \quad m_l \geq \frac{1}{\epsilon}\left[\ln|\mathcal{C}_{D,\chi}(\epsilon)| + \ln\frac{2}{\delta}\right],$$

then with probability at least $1 - \delta$, all $f \in \mathcal{C}$ with $\widehat{err}(f) = 0$ and $\widehat{err}_{unl}(f) = 0$ have $err(f) \leq \epsilon$.

Proof The probability that a given hypothesis f with $err_{unl}(f) > \epsilon$ has $\widehat{err}_{unl}(f) = 0$ is at most $(1 - \epsilon)^{m_u} < \delta/(2|\mathcal{C}|)$ for the given value of m_u. Therefore, by the union bound, the number of unlabeled examples is sufficient to ensure that with probability $1 - \delta/2$, only hypotheses in $\mathcal{C}_{D,\chi}(\epsilon)$ have $\widehat{err}_{unl}(f) = 0$. The number of labeled examples then similarly ensures that with probability $1 - \delta/2$, none of those whose true error is at least ϵ have an empirical error of 0, yielding the theorem. ∎

So, if the target function indeed is perfectly correct and compatible, then theorem 22.5 gives sufficient conditions on the number of examples needed to ensure that an algorithm that optimizes both quantities over the observed data will, in fact, achieve a PAC guarantee. To emphasize this, we will say that an algorithm efficiently PAC_{unl}-learns the pair $(\mathcal{C}, \chi)$ if it is able to achieve a PAC guarantee using time and sample sizes polynomial in the bounds of theorem 22.5.

Interpretation   We can think of theorem 22.5 as bounding the number of labeled examples we need as a function of the "helpfulness" of the distribution D with respect to our notion of compatibility. That is, in our context, a helpful distribution is one in which $\mathcal{C}_{D,\chi}(\epsilon)$ is small, and so we do not need much labeled data to identify a good function among them. We can get a similar bound in the situation when the target function is not fully compatible:

Theorem 22.6 *Given $t \in [0, 1]$, if we see m_u unlabeled examples and m_l labeled examples, where*

$$m_u \geq \frac{2}{\epsilon^2}\left[\ln|\mathcal{C}| + \ln\frac{4}{\delta}\right] \quad and \quad m_l \geq \frac{1}{\epsilon}\left[\ln|\mathcal{C}_{D,\chi}(t + 2\epsilon)| + \ln\frac{2}{\delta}\right],$$

then with probability at least $1 - \delta$, all $f \in \mathcal{C}$ with $\widehat{err}(f) = 0$ and $\widehat{err}_{unl}(f) \leq t + \epsilon$ have $err(f) \leq \epsilon$, and furthermore all $f \in \mathcal{C}$ with $err_{unl}(f) \leq t$ have $\widehat{err}_{unl}(f) \leq t + \epsilon$.

In particular, this implies that if $err_{unl}(c^*) \leq t$ and $err(c^*) = 0$ then with high probability the $f \in \mathcal{C}$ that optimizes $\widehat{err}(f)$ and $\widehat{err}_{unl}(f)$ has $err(f) \leq \epsilon$.

Proof Same as theorem 22.5 except apply Hoeffding bounds (see Devroye et al. (1996)) to the unlabeled error rates. ∎

Finally, we give a simple Occam/luckiness type of bound for this setting. Given a sample S, let us define $\mathsf{desc}_S(f) = \ln|\mathcal{C}_{S,\chi}(\widehat{err}_{unl}(f))|$. That is, $\mathsf{desc}_S(f)$ is the description length of f (in "nats") if we sort hypotheses by their empirical compatibility and output the index of f in this ordering. Similarly, define ϵ-$\mathsf{desc}_D(f) = \ln|\mathcal{C}_{D,\chi}(err_{unl}(f) + \epsilon)|$. This is an upper bound on the description length of f if we sort hypotheses by an ϵ-approximation to their true compatibility. Then we can get a bound as follows:

Theorem 22.7 *For any set S of unlabeled data, given m_l labeled examples, with probability at least $1 - \delta$, all $f \in \mathcal{C}$ satisfying $\widehat{err}(f) = 0$ and $\mathsf{desc}_S(f) \leq \epsilon m_l - \ln(1/\delta)$ have $err(f) \leq \epsilon$. Furthermore, if $|S| \geq \frac{2}{\epsilon^2}[\ln|\mathcal{C}| + \ln\frac{2}{\delta}]$, then with probability at least $1 - \delta$, all $f \in \mathcal{C}$ satisfy $\mathsf{desc}_S(f) \leq \epsilon$-$\mathsf{desc}_D(f)$.*

Interpretation

The point of this theorem is that an algorithm can use observable quantities to determine if it can be confident. Furthermore, if we have enough unlabeled data, the observable quantities will be no worse than if we were learning a slightly less compatible function using an infinite-size unlabeled sample.

Note that if we begin with a non-distribution-dependent ordering of hypotheses, inducing some description length $\mathsf{desc}(f)$, and our compatibility assumptions turn out to be wrong, then it could well be that $\mathsf{desc}_D(c^*) > \mathsf{desc}(c^*)$. In this case our use of unlabeled data would end up hurting rather than helping.

22.3.2 Uniform Convergence Bounds for Infinite Hypothesis Spaces

To reduce notation, we will assume in the rest of this chapter that $\chi(f, x) \in \{0, 1\}$ so that $\chi(f, D) = \mathbf{Pr}_{x \sim D}[\chi(f, x) = 1]$. However, all our sample complexity results can be easily extended to the general case.

For infinite hypothesis spaces, the first issue that arises is that in order to achieve uniform convergence of *unlabeled* error rates, the set whose complexity we care about is not $\mathcal{C}$ but rather $\chi(\mathcal{C}) = \{\chi_f : f \in \mathcal{C}\}$ where we define $\chi_f(x) = \chi(f, x)$. For instance, suppose examples are just points on the line, and $\mathcal{C} = \{f_a(x) : f_a(x) = 1$

iff $x \leq a$}. In this case, VCdim($\mathcal{C}$) = 1. However, we could imagine a compatibility function such that $\chi(f_a, x)$ depends on some complicated relationship between the real numbers a and x. In this case, VCdim($\chi(\mathcal{C})$) is much larger, and indeed we would need many more unlabeled examples to estimate compatibility over all of $\mathcal{C}$.

A second issue is that we need an appropriate measure for the "size" of the set of surviving functions. VC dimension tends not to be a good choice: for instance, if we consider the case of example 1 (margins), then even if data are concentrated in two wellseparated "blobs," the set of compatible separators still has as large a VC dimension as the entire class even though they are all very similar with respect to D. Instead, it is better to consider distribution-dependent complexity measures such as annealed VC entropy or Rademacher averages. For this we introduce some notation. Specifically, for any $\mathcal{C}$, we denote by $\mathcal{C}[m, D]$ the expected number of splits of m points (drawn i.i.d.) from D with concepts in $\mathcal{C}$. Also, for a given (fixed) $S \subseteq \mathcal{X}$, we will denote by $\overline{S}$ the uniform distribution over S, and by $\mathcal{C}[m, \overline{S}]$ the expected number of splits of m points (drawn i.i.d.) from $\overline{S}$ with concepts in $\mathcal{C}$. Then we can get bounds as follows:

Theorem 22.8 *An unlabeled sample of size*

$$m_u = O\left(\frac{VCdim\left(\chi(\mathcal{C})\right)}{\epsilon^2} \log \frac{1}{\epsilon} + \frac{1}{\epsilon^2} \log \frac{2}{\delta} \right)$$

and a labeled sample of size

$$m_l > \frac{2}{\epsilon} \left[\log(2s) + \log \frac{2}{\delta} \right], \quad where \quad s = \mathcal{C}_{D,\chi}(t + 2\epsilon)[2m_l, D]$$

(i.e., s is the expected number of splits of $2m_l$ points drawn from D using concepts in $\mathcal{C}$ of unlabeled error rate $\leq t + 2\epsilon$) is sufficient so that with probability $1 - \delta$, all $f \in \mathcal{C}$ with $\widehat{err}(f) = 0$ and $\widehat{err}_{unl}(f) \leq t + \epsilon$ have $err(f) \leq \epsilon$, and furthermore all $f \in \mathcal{C}$ have $|err_{unl}(f) - \widehat{err}_{unl}(f)| \leq \epsilon$.

Interpretation

This is the analogue of theorem 22.6 for the infinite case. In particular, this implies that if $err(c^*) = 0$ and $err_{unl}(c^*) \leq t$, then with high probability the $f \in \mathcal{C}$ that optimizes $\widehat{err}(f)$ and $\widehat{err}_{unl}(f)$ has $err(f) \leq \epsilon$.

Proof sketch: By standard VC bounds (Devroye et al., 1996; Vapnik, 1998), the number of unlabeled examples is sufficient to ensure that with probability $1 - \delta/2$ we can estimate, within ϵ, $\mathbf{Pr}_{x \in D}[\chi_f(x) = 1]$ for all $\chi_f \in \chi(\mathcal{C})$. Since $\chi_f(x) = \chi(f, x)$, this implies we can estimate, within ϵ, the unlabeled error rate $err_{unl}(f)$ for all $f \in \mathcal{C}$, and so the set of hypotheses with $\widehat{err}_{unl}(f) \leq t + \epsilon$ is contained in $\mathcal{C}_{D,\chi}(t + 2\epsilon)$.

The bound on the number of labeled examples follows from (Devroye et al., 1996) (where it is shown that the expected number of partitions can be used instead of the maximum in the standard VC proof). This bound ensures that with probability $1 - \delta/2$, none of the functions in $\mathcal{C}_{D,\chi}(t + 2\epsilon)$ whose true (labeled) error is at least ϵ have an empirical (labeled) error of 0. ∎

We can also give a bound where we specify the number of labeled examples as a function of the *unlabeled sample*; this is useful because we can imagine our learning algorithm performing some calculations over the unlabeled data and then deciding how many labeled examples to purchase.

Theorem 22.9 *Given $t \geq 0$, an unlabeled sample S of size*

$$O\left(\frac{\max[VCdim(\mathcal{C}), VCdim(\chi(\mathcal{C}))]}{\epsilon^2} \log \frac{1}{\epsilon} + \frac{1}{\epsilon^2} \log \frac{2}{\delta}\right)$$

is sufficient so that if we label m_l examples drawn uniformly at random from S, where

$$m_l > \frac{4}{\epsilon}\left[\log(2s) + \log \frac{2}{\delta}\right] \quad and \quad s = \mathcal{C}_{S,\chi}(t + \epsilon)\left[2m_l, \overline{S}\right],$$

then with probability $\geq 1 - \delta$, all $f \in \mathcal{C}$ with $\widehat{err}(f) = 0$ and $\widehat{err}_{unl}(f) \leq t + \epsilon$ have $err(f) \leq \epsilon$. Furthermore all $f \in \mathcal{C}$ have $|err_{unl}(f) - \widehat{err}_{unl}(f)| \leq \epsilon$.

Proof   Standard VC bounds (in the same form as for theorem 22.8) imply that the number of *labeled* examples m_l is sufficient to guarantee the conclusion of the theorem with "$err(f)$" replaced by "$err_{\overline{S}}(f)$" (the error with respect to $\overline{S}$) and "ϵ" replaced with "$\epsilon/2$". The number of *unlabeled* examples is enough to ensure that, with probability $\geq 1 - \delta/2$, for all $f \in \mathcal{C}$, $|err(f) - err_{\overline{S}}(f)| \leq \epsilon/2$. Combining these two statements yields the theorem.   ∎

So, if $err(c^*) = 0$ and $err_{unl}(c^*) \leq t$, then with high probability the $f \in \mathcal{C}$ that optimizes $\widehat{err}(f)$ and $\widehat{err}_{unl}(f)$ has $err(f) \leq \epsilon$. If we assume $err_{unl}(c^*) = 0$, then we can use $\mathcal{C}_{S,\chi}(0)$ instead of $\mathcal{C}_{S,\chi}(t + \epsilon)$.

interpretation

Notice that for the case of example 1, in the worst case (over distributions D) this will essentially recover the standard margin sample-complexity bounds. In particular, $\mathcal{C}_{S,\chi}(0)$ contains only those separators that split S with margin $\geq \gamma$, and therefore s is no greater than the maximum number of ways of splitting $2m_l$ points with margin γ. However, if the distribution is nice, then the bounds can be much better because there may be many fewer ways of splitting S with margin γ. For instance, in the case of two well-separated "blobs" discussed above, if S is large enough, we would have just $s = 4$.

We finally give a stratified version of theorem 22.9 as follows:

Theorem 22.10 *An unlabeled sample S of size*

$$O\left(\frac{\max[VCdim(\mathcal{C}), VCdim(\chi(\mathcal{C}))]}{\epsilon^2} \log \frac{1}{\epsilon} + \frac{1}{\epsilon^2} \log \frac{2}{\delta}\right)$$

is sufficient so that with probability $\geq 1 - \delta$ we have that simultaneously for every $k \geq 0$ the following is true: if we label m_k examples drawn uniformly at random from S, where

$$m_k > \frac{4}{\epsilon}\left[\log(2s) + \log \frac{2(k+1)(k+2)}{\delta}\right] \quad and \quad s = \mathcal{C}_{S,\chi}((k+1)\epsilon)\left[2m_k, \overline{S}\right],$$

then all $f \in \mathcal{C}$ with $\widehat{err}(f) = 0$ and $\widehat{err}_{unl}(f) \le (k+1)\epsilon$ have $err(f) \le \epsilon$.

This theorem is an analogue of theorem 22.7 and it essentially justifies a stratification based on the estimated unlabeled error rates. We can also imagine having data-dependent bounds for both labeled and unlabeled data, and also doing a double stratification, with respect to both labeled and unlabeled error rates. In particular, we can derive a bound as follows:

Theorem 22.11 *An unlabeled sample S of size*

$$O\left(\frac{\max[VCdim(\mathcal{C}), VCdim(\chi(\mathcal{C}))]}{\epsilon^2} log\frac{1}{\epsilon} + \frac{1}{\epsilon^2} log\frac{2}{\delta}\right)$$

is sufficient so that with probability $\ge 1 - \delta$ we have that simultaneously for every $i \ge 0$, $k \ge 0$ the following is true: if we label $m_{k,i}$ examples drawn uniformly at random from S, where

$$m_{k,i} > \tfrac{8}{\epsilon^2}\left[\log(2s) + \log\tfrac{4(k+1)(k+2)(i+1)(i+2)}{\delta}\right] \quad and$$

$$s = \mathcal{C}_{S,\chi}((k+1)\epsilon)\left[2m_k, \overline{S}\right],$$

then all $f \in \mathcal{C}$ with $\widehat{err}(f) \le (i+1)\epsilon$ and $\widehat{err}_{unl}(f) \le (k+1)\epsilon$ have $err(f) \le (i+2)\cdot\epsilon$.

We can similarly derive tight bounds using Rademacher averages. For different versions of our statements using recent stronger bounds (Boucheron et al., 2000, 2005), see (Balcan and Blum, 2005).

22.3.3 ϵ-Cover-Based Bounds

The bounds in the previous section are for uniform convergence: they provide guarantees for *any* algorithm that optimizes well on the observed data. In this section, we consider stronger bounds based on ϵ-covers that can be obtained for algorithms that behave in a specific way: they first use the unlabeled examples to choose a "representative" set of compatible hypotheses, and then use the labeled sample to choose among these. Bounds based on ϵ-covers exist in the classical PAC setting, but in our framework these bounds and algorithms of this type are especially natural and convenient.

Recall that a set $C_\epsilon \subseteq 2^{\mathcal{X}}$ is an ϵ-cover for $\mathcal{C}$ with respect to D if for every $f \in \mathcal{C}$ there is a $f' \in C_\epsilon$ which is ϵ-close to f. That is, $\mathbf{Pr}_{x \sim D}(f(x) \ne f'(x)) \le \epsilon$.

To illustrate how this can produce stronger bounds, consider the setting of example 3 (graph-based algorithms) where the graph $\mathbf{g}$ consists of two cliques of $n/2$ vertices, connected together by $o(n^2)$ edges (in particular, the number of edges connecting the cliques is small compared to ϵn^2). Suppose the target function labels one of the cliques as positive and one as negative, and we define compatibility of a hypothesis to be the fraction of edges in $\mathbf{g}$ that are cut by it (so the target function indeed has unlabeled error rate less than ϵ). Now, given any set S_L of $m_l \ll \epsilon n$

examples where
ϵ-cover bounds
beat uniform
convergence
bounds

labeled examples, there is always a highly compatible hypothesis consistent with S_L that just separates the positive points in S_L from the entire rest of the graph: the number of edges cut will be at most $nm_l \ll \epsilon n^2$. However, such a hypothesis clearly has high true error since it is so unbalanced. So, we do not have uniform convergence. On the other hand, the set of functions of unlabeled error rate less than $\epsilon/4$ has a small ϵ-cover: in particular, *any* partition of $\mathbf{g}$ that cuts less than $\epsilon n^2/4$ edges must be ϵ-close to (a) the all-positive function, (b) the all-negative function, (c) the target function c^*, or (d) the complement of the target function $1 - c^*$. So, ϵ-cover bounds act as if the concept class had only four functions, and so require only a constant number of labeled examples.[4]

For another case where ϵ-cover bounds can beat uniform-convergence bounds, imagine examples are *pairs* of points in $\{0,1\}^d$, $\mathcal{C}$ is the class of linear separators, and compatibility is determined by whether both points are on the same side of the separator (i.e., the case of example 4). Now suppose for simplicity that the target function just splits the hypercube on the first coordinate, and the distribution is uniform over pairs having the same first coordinate (so the target is fully compatible). It is not hard to show that given polynomially many unlabeled examples S_U and $\frac{1}{4}\log d$ labeled examples S_L, with high probability there will exist high-error functions consistent with S_L and compatible with S_U.[5] So, we do not yet have uniform convergence. In contrast, the cover-size of the set of functions compatible with S_U is constant, so ϵ-cover-based bounds again allow learning from just a constant number of labeled examples.

In particular, we can give an ϵ-cover-based bound as follows:

Theorem 22.12 *If t is an upper bound for $err_{unl}(c^*)$ and p is the size of a minimum ϵ-cover for $\mathcal{C}_{D,\chi}(t+4\epsilon)$, then using m_u unlabeled examples and m_l labeled examples for*

$$m_u = O\left(\frac{VCdim\,(\chi(\mathcal{C}))}{\epsilon^2}\log\frac{1}{\epsilon} + \frac{1}{\epsilon^2}\log\frac{2}{\delta}\right) \quad and \quad m_l = O\left(\frac{1}{\epsilon}\ln\frac{p}{\delta}\right),$$

we can with probability $1-\delta$ identify a hypothesis which is 10ϵ close to c^*.

Proof sketch: First, given the unlabeled sample S_U, define $H_\epsilon \subseteq \mathcal{C}$ as follows: for

---

4. Effectively, ϵ-cover bounds allow one to rule out a hypothesis that, say, just separates the positive points in S_L from the rest of the graph by noting that this hypothesis is very close (with respect to D) to the all-negative hypothesis, and *that* hypothesis has a high labeled-error rate.

5. Proof: Let V be the set of all variables that (a) appear in *every* positive example of S_L and (b) appear in *no* negative example of S_L. Over the draw of S_L, each variable has a $(1/2)^{2|S_L|} = 1/\sqrt{d}$ chance of belonging to V, so with high probability V has size at least $\frac{1}{2}\sqrt{d}$. Now, consider the hypothesis corresponding to the conjunction of all variables in V. This correctly classifies the examples in S_L, and w.h.p. it classifies *every* other example in S_U negative because each example in S_U has only a $1/2^{|V|}$ chance of satisfying every variable in V, and the size of S_U is much less than $2^{|V|}$. So, this means it is compatible with S_U and consistent with S_L, even though its true error is high.

every labeling of S_U that is consistent with some f in $\mathcal{C}$, choose a hypothesis in $\mathcal{C}$ for which $\widehat{err}_{unl}(f)$ is smallest among all the hypotheses corresponding to that labeling. Next, we obtain C_ϵ by eliminating from H_ϵ those hypotheses f with the property that $\widehat{err}_{unl}(f) > t + 3\epsilon$. We then apply a greedy procedure on C_ϵ, and we obtain $G_\epsilon = \{g_1, \cdots, g_s\}$, as follows:

Initialize $H_\epsilon^1 = C_\epsilon$ and $i = 1$.

1. Let $g_i = \operatorname*{argmin}_{f \in H_\epsilon^i} \widehat{err}_{unl}(f)$.

2. Using unlabeled data, determine H_ϵ^{i+1} by crossing out from H_ϵ^i those hypotheses f with the property that $\hat{d}(g_i, f) < 3\epsilon$.

3. If $H_\epsilon^{i+1} = \emptyset$ then set $s = i$ and stop; else, increase i by 1 and go to 1.

Our bound on m_u is sufficient to ensure that, with probability $\geq 1 - \delta/2$, H_ϵ is an ϵ-cover of $\mathcal{C}$, which implies that, with probability $\geq 1 - \delta/2$, C_ϵ is an ϵ-cover for $\mathcal{C}_{D,\chi}(t)$. It is then possible to show G_ϵ is, with probability $\geq 1 - \delta/2$, a 5ϵ-cover for $\mathcal{C}_{D,\chi}(t)$ of size at most p. The idea here is that by greedily creating a 3ϵ-cover of C_ϵ with respect to distribution $\overline{S_U}$, we are creating a 4ϵ-cover of C_ϵ with respect to D, which is a 5ϵ-cover of $\mathcal{C}_{D,\chi}(t)$ with respect to D. Furthermore, we are doing this using no more functions than would a greedy 2ϵ-cover procedure for $\mathcal{C}_{D,\chi}(t + 4\epsilon)$ with respect to D, which is no more than the optimal ϵ-cover of $\mathcal{C}_{D,\chi}(t + 4\epsilon)$.

Now to learn c^* we use labeled data and we do empirical risk minimization on G_ϵ. By standard bounds (see, for instance, (Benedek and Itai, 1991)), the number of labeled examples is enough to ensure that with probability $\geq 1 - \delta/2$ the empirical optimum hypothesis in G_ϵ has true error at most 10ϵ. This implies that overall, with probability $\geq 1 - \delta$, we find a hypothesis of error at most 10ϵ. ∎

As an interesting case where unlabeled data help substantially, consider a co-training setting where the target c^* is fully compatible *and* D satisfies the conditional independence given the label property. As shown by Blum and Mitchell (1998), one can boost any weak hypothesis from unlabeled data in this setting (assuming one has enough labeled data to produce a weak hypothesis). Related sample complexity results are given in (Dasgupta et al., 2001). We can actually show that given enough unlabeled data, in fact we can learn from just a single labeled example. Specifically, it is possible to show that for any concept classes $\mathcal{C}_1$ and $\mathcal{C}_2$, we have:

Theorem 22.13 *Assume that $err(c^*) = err_{unl}(c^*) = 0$ and D satisfies independence given the label. Then using m_u unlabeled examples and m_l labeled examples we can find a hypothesis that with probability $1 - \delta$ has error at most ϵ, provided that*

$$m_u = O\left(\frac{1}{\epsilon} \cdot \left[(VCdim(\mathcal{C}_1) + VCdim(\mathcal{C}_2)) \cdot \ln\left(\frac{1}{\epsilon}\right) + \ln\left(\frac{1}{\delta}\right)\right]\right)$$

and

$$m_l = O\left(\log_{\left(\frac{1}{\epsilon}\right)}\left(\frac{1}{\delta}\right)\right).$$

Proof sketch: For convenience we will show a bound with 6ϵ instead of ϵ, 3δ instead of δ, and we will assume for simplicity the setting of example 3, where $c^* = c_1^* = c_2^*$ and also that $D_1 = D_2 = \overline{D}$ (the general case is handled similarly, but just requires more notation). We first characterize the hypotheses with true unlabeled error rate at most ϵ. Recall that $\chi(f, D) = \mathbf{Pr}_{(x_1,x_2)\sim D}[f(x_1) = f(x_2)]$, and for concreteness assume f predicts using x_1 if $f(x_1) \neq f(x_2)$. Consider $f \in \mathcal{C}$ with $err_{unl}(f) \leq \epsilon$ and let's define $p_- = \mathbf{Pr}_{x\in\overline{D}}[c^*(x) = 0]$, $p_+ = \mathbf{Pr}_{x\in\overline{D}}[c^*(x) = 1]$ and for $i, j \in \{0,1\}$ define $p_{ij} = \mathbf{Pr}_{x\in\overline{D}}[f(x) = i, c^*(x) = j]$. We clearly have $err(f) = p_{10} + p_{01}$. From $err_{unl}(f) = \mathbf{Pr}_{(x_1,x_2)\sim D}[f(x_1) \neq f(x_2)] \leq \epsilon$, using the independence given the label of D, we get $\frac{2p_{10}p_{00}}{p_-} + \frac{2p_{01}p_{11}}{p_+} \leq \epsilon$. This implies that the almost compatible hypothesis f must be one of the following four types:

1. f is "close to c^*" or more exactly $err(f) \leq 2\epsilon$.

2. f is "close to the opposite of c^*" or more exactly $err(f) \geq 1 - 2\epsilon$.

3. f "predicts almost always negative" or more exactly $p_{10} + p_{11} \leq 3\epsilon$.

4. f "predicts almost always positive" or more exactly $p_{01} + p_{00} \leq 3\epsilon$.

Now, consider f_1 to be the constant positive function, f_0 to be the constant negative function. The unlabeled sample S_U is sufficient to ensure that probability $\geq 1 - \delta$, every hypothesis with zero estimated unlabeled error has true unlabeled error at most ϵ. Therefore, by our previous analysis, there are only four kinds of hypotheses consistent with unlabeled data: those close to c^*, those close to its complement $\overline{c^*}$, those close to f_0, and those close to f_1. Furthermore, c^*, $\overline{c^*}$, f_0, and f_1 *are* compatible with the unlabeled data.

We now check if there exists a hypothesis $g \in \mathcal{C}$ with $\widehat{err}_{unl}(g) = 0$ such that $\hat{d}_{f_1,g} \geq 4\epsilon$ and $\hat{d}_{f_0,g} \geq 4\epsilon$. If such a hypothesis g exists, then we know that one of $\{g, \overline{g}\}$, where $\overline{g}$ is the opposite of g, is 2ϵ-close to c^*. If not, we must have $p_+ \leq 6\epsilon$ or $p_- \leq 6\epsilon$, in which case we know that one of $\{f_0, f_1\}$ is 6ϵ-close to c^*. So, we have a set of two functions, opposite to each other, one of which is at least 6ϵ-close to c^*. We now use labeled data to pick one of these to output, using lemma 22.14 below. ∎

Lemma 22.14 *Consider $\epsilon < \frac{1}{8}$. Let $C_\epsilon = \{f, \overline{f}\}$ be a subset of $\mathcal{C}$ containing two opposite hypotheses with the property that one of them is ϵ-close to c^*. Then, $m_l > 6\log_{\left(\frac{1}{\epsilon}\right)}\left(\frac{1}{\delta}\right)$ labeled examples are sufficient so that with probability $\geq 1 - \delta$, the concept in C_ϵ that is ϵ-close to c^* in fact has lower empirical error.*

Proof Easy calculation: if $m_l > 6\log_{\frac{1}{\epsilon}}\left(\frac{1}{\delta}\right)$, then $\sum_{k=0}^{\lfloor\frac{m_l}{2}\rfloor}\binom{m_l}{k}\epsilon^{(m_l-k)}(1-\epsilon)^k \leq \delta$. ∎

In particular, by reducing ϵ to $poly(\delta)$, we can reduce the number of labeled examples needed m_l to 1. In fact, this result can be extended to the case considered in (Balcan et al., 2004), that D^+ and D^- merely satisfy constant expansion.

This example illustrates that if data are especially well behaved with respect to the compatibility notion, then our bounds on labeled data can be extremely good. In section 22.4.2, we show for the case of linear separators and independence given the label, we can give *efficient* algorithms, achieving the bounds in theorem 22.13 in terms of labeled examples by a polynomial time algorithm. Note, however, that both these bounds rely heavily on the assumption that the target is fully compatible. If the assumption is more of a "hope" than a belief, then one would need additional labeled examples just to validate the hypothesis produced.

22.4   Algorithmic Results

In this section we give several examples of *efficient* algorithms in our model.

22.4.1   A Simple Case

We give here a simple example to illustrate the bounds in section 22.3.1, and for which we can give a polynomial-time algorithm that takes advantage of them. Let the instance space $\mathcal{X} = \{0,1\}^d$, and for $x \in \mathcal{X}$, let $\mathsf{vars}(x)$ be the set of variables set to 1 by x. Let $\mathcal{C}$ be the class of monotone disjunctions (e.g., $x_1 \lor x_3 \lor x_6$), and for $f \in \mathcal{C}$, let $\mathsf{vars}(f)$ be the set of variables disjoined by f. Now, suppose we say an example x is compatible with function f if either $\mathsf{vars}(x) \subseteq \mathsf{vars}(f)$ or else $\mathsf{vars}(x) \cap \mathsf{vars}(f) = \phi$. This is a very strong notion of "margin": it says, in essence, that every variable is either a positive indicator or a negative indicator, and no example should contain both positive and negative indicators.

Given this setup, we can give a simple PAC_{unl}-learning algorithm for this pair $(\mathcal{C}, \chi)$. We begin by using our unlabeled data to construct a graph on d vertices (one per variable), putting an edge between two vertices i and j if there is any example x in our unlabeled sample with $i, j \in \mathsf{vars}(x)$. We now use our labeled data to label the components. If the target function is fully compatible, then no component will get multiple labels (if some component does get multiple labels, we halt with failure). Finally, we produce the hypothesis f such that $\mathsf{vars}(f)$ is the union of the positively labeled components. This is fully compatible with the unlabeled data and has zero error on the labeled data, so by theorem 22.5, if the sizes of the data sets are as given in the bounds, with high probability the hypothesis produced will have error $\leq \epsilon$.

Notice that if we want to view the algorithm as "purchasing" labeled data, then we can simply examine the graph, count the number of connected components k, and then request $\frac{1}{\epsilon}[k \ln 2 + \ln \frac{2}{\delta}]$ labeled examples. (Here, $2^k = |\mathcal{C}_{S,\chi}(0)|$.) By the proof of theorem 22.5, with high probability $2^k \leq |\mathcal{C}_{D,\chi}(\epsilon)|$, so we are purchasing no more than the number of labeled examples in the theorem statement.

Also, it is interesting to see the difference between a "helpful" and "nonhelpful" distribution for this problem. An especially *non*helpful distribution would be the uniform distribution over all examples x with $|\mathsf{vars}(x)| = 1$, in which there are d components. In this case, unlabeled data do not help at all, and one still needs $\Omega(d)$ labeled examples (or, even $\Omega(d/\epsilon)$ if the distribution is nonuniform as in the lower bounds of Ehrenfeucht et al. (1989)). On the other hand, a helpful distribution is one such that with high probability the number of components is small, such as the case of features appearing independently given the label.

22.4.2   Co-Training with Linear Separators

We now consider the case of co-training where the hypothesis class is the class of linear separators. For simplicity we focus first on the case of example 4: the target function is a linear separator in $\mathbb{R}^d$ and each example is a *pair* of points, both of which are assumed to be on the same side of the separator (i.e., an example is a line segment that does not cross the target hyperplane). We then show how our results can be extended to the more general setting.

As in the previous example, a natural approach is to try to solve the "consistency" problem: given a set of labeled and unlabeled data, our goal is to find a separator that is consistent with the labeled examples and compatible with the unlabeled ones (i.e., it gets the labeled data correct and doesn't cut too many edges). Unfortunately, this consistency problem is NP-hard: given a graph g embedded in $\mathbb{R}^d$ with two distinguished points s and t, it is NP-hard to find the linear separator that cuts the minimum number of edges, *even if the minimum is 0* (Flaxman, 2003). For this reason, we will make an additional assumption, that the two points in an example are each drawn *independently given the label*. That is, there is a single distribution $\overline{D}$ over $\mathbb{R}^d$, and with some probability p_+, two points are drawn i.i.d. from $\overline{D}_+$ ($\overline{D}$ restricted to the positive side of the target function) and with probability $1 - p_+$, the two are drawn i.i.d from $\overline{D}_-$ ($\overline{D}$ restricted to the negative side of the target function). Note that our sample complexity results in section 22.3.3 extend to weaker assumptions such as distributional expansion introduced by Balcan et al. (2004), but we need true independence for our algorithmic results. Blum and Mitchell (1998) have also given positive algorithmic results for co-training when (a) the two halves of an example are drawn independently given the label (which we are assuming now), (b) the underlying function is learnable via statistical query algorithms[6] (which is true for linear separators (Blum et al., 1998)), and (c) we have enough labeled data to produce a weakly useful hypothesis (defined below) on one of the halves to begin with. We give here an improvement over that result by showing how we can run the algorithm in (Blum and Mitchell, 1998) with only *a single* labeled example, thus obtaining an efficient algorithm in our model. It is worth noticing that in the process, we also simplify the results of Blum et al. (1998)

need to assume independence for our algorithmic results

---

6. For a detailed description of the statistical query model see (Kearns, 1998) and (Kearns and Vazirani, 1994).

somewhat.

For the analysis below, we need the following definition. A *weakly useful* predictor is a function f such that for some ϵ that is at least inverse polynomial in the input size,

$$\mathbf{Pr}[f(x) = 1|c^*(x) = 1] > \mathbf{Pr}[f(x) = 1|c^*(x) = 0] + \epsilon.$$

It is equivalent to the usual notion of a "weak hypothesis"(see (Kearns and Vazirani, 1994)) when the target function is balanced, but requires that the hypothesis give more information when the target function is unbalanced; see (Blum and Mitchell, 1998).

Theorem 22.15 *There is a polynomial-time algorithm (in d and b, where b is the number of bits per example) to learn a linear separator under the above assumptions, from a polynomial number of unlabeled examples and a single labeled example.*

Proof sketch: Assume for convenience that the target separator passes through the origin, and let us denote the separator by $c^* \cdot x = 0$. We will also assume for convenience that $\mathbf{Pr}_D(c^*(x) = 1) \in [\epsilon/2, 1 - \epsilon/2]$; that is, the target function is not overwhelmingly positive or overwhelmingly negative (if it is, this is actually an easy case, but it makes the arguments more complicated). Define the *margin* of some point x as the distance of $x/|x|$ to the separating plane, or equivalently, the cosine of the angle between c^* and x.

We begin by drawing a large unlabeled sample $S = \{\langle x_1^i, x_2^i \rangle\}$; denote by S_j the set $\{x_j^i\}$, for $j = 1, 2$. (We describe our algorithm as working with the fixed unlabeled sample S, since we just need to apply standard VC-dimension arguments to get the desired result.) The first step is to perform a transformation T on S_1 to ensure that some reasonable $(1/poly)$ fraction of $T(S_1)$ has margin at least $1/poly$, which we can do via the outlier removal lemma of Blum et al. (1998) and Dunagan and Vempala (2001).[7] The outlier removal lemma states that one can algorithmically remove an ϵ' fraction of S_1 and ensure that for the remainder, for any vector w, $\max_{x \in S_1}(w \cdot x)^2 \leq poly(n, b, 1/\epsilon')\mathbf{E}_{x \in S_1}[(w \cdot x)^2]$, where b is the number of bits needed to describe the input points. We reduce the dimensionality (if necessary) to get rid of any of the vectors for which the above quantity is zero. We then determine a linear transformation (as described in Blum et al. (1998)) so that in the transformed space for all unit-length w, $\mathbf{E}_{x \in T(S_1)}[(w \cdot x)^2] = 1$). Since the maximum is bounded, this guarantees that at least a $1/poly$ fraction of the points in $T(S_1)$ have at least a $1/poly$ margin with respect to the separating hyperplane.

To avoid cumbersome notation in the rest of the discussion, we drop our use of "T" and simply use S and c^* to denote the points and separator in the transformed space. (If the distribution originally had a reasonable probability mass at a reasonable margin from c^*, then T could be the identity anyway.)

---

7. If the reader is willing to allow running time polynomial in the margin of the data set, then this part of the argument is not needed.

The second step is we argue that a *random* halfspace has at least a $1/poly$ chance of being a weak predictor on S_1. ((Blum et al., 1998) use the Perceptron algorithm to get weak learning; here, we need something simpler since we do not yet have any labeled data.) Specifically, consider a point x such that the angle between x and c^* is $\pi/2 - \gamma$, and imagine that we draw f at random subject to $f \cdot c^* \geq 0$ (half of the f's will have this property). Then,

$$\mathbf{Pr}_f(f(x) \neq c^*(x) | f \cdot c^* \geq 0) = (\pi/2 - \gamma)/\pi = 1/2 - \gamma/\pi.$$

Since at least a $1/poly$ fraction of the points in S_1 have at least a $1/poly$ margin, this implies that

$$\mathbf{Pr}_{f,x}[f(x) = 1 | c^*(x) = 1] > \mathbf{Pr}_{f,x}[f(x) = 1 | c^*(x) = 0] + 1/poly.$$

This means that a $1/poly$ probability mass of functions f must in fact be weakly useful predictors.

The final step of the algorithm is as follows. Using the above observation, we pick a random f, and plug it into the bootstrapping theorem of (Blum and Mitchell, 1998) (which, given unlabeled pairs $\langle x_1^i, x_2^i \rangle \in S$, will use $f(x_1^i)$ as a noisy label of x_2^i, feeding the result into a statistical query algorithm), repeating this process $poly(n)$ times. With high probability, our random f was a weakly useful predictor on at least one of these steps, and we end up with a low-error hypothesis. For the rest of the runs of the algorithm, we have no guarantees. We now observe the following. First of all, any function f with small $err(f)$ must have small $err_{unl}(f)$. Second, because of the assumption of independence given the label, as shown in theorem 22.13, the *only* functions with low unlabeled error rate are functions close to c^*, close to $\neg c^*$, close to the "all-positive" function, or close to the "all-negative" function.

So, if we simply examine all the hypotheses produced by this procedure, and pick some h with a low unlabeled error rate that is at least $\epsilon/2$-far from the "all-positive" or "all-negative" functions, then either f or $\neg f$ is close to c^*. We can now just draw a single labeled example to determine which case is which.   ∎

We can easily extend our algorithm to the standard co-training setting (where c_1^* can be different from c_2^*) as follows: we repeat the procedure in a symmetric way, and then, in order to find a good pair of functions, just try all combinations of pairs of functions to find one of small unlabeled error rate, not close to "all positive," or "all negative." Finally we use one labeled example to produce a low-error hypothesis (and here we use only one part of the example and only one of the functions in the pair).

22.5   Related Models and Discussion

22.5.1   A Transductive Analogue of our Model

We can also talk about a transductive analogue of our (inductive) model that incorporates many of the existing transductive methods for learning with labeled and unlabeled data. In a transductive setting one assumes that the unlabeled sample S is given, a random small subset is labeled, and the goal is to predict well on the rest of S. In order to make use of unlabeled examples, we will again express the relationship we hope the target function has with the distribution through a compatibility notion χ. However, since in this case the compatibility between a given hypothesis and D is completely determined by S (which is known), we will not need to require that compatibility be an expectation over unlabeled examples. Given this setup, from the sample-complexity point of view we only care about how much labeled data we need, and algorithmically we need to find a highly compatible hypothesis with low error on the labeled data.

Rather than presenting general theorems, we instead focus on the modeling aspect and give here several examples in the context of graph-based semi-supervised algorithms for binary classification. In these methods one usually assumes that there is weighted graph $\mathbf{g}$ defined over S, which is given a priori and encodes the prior knowledge. In the following we denote by W the weighted adjacency matrix of $\mathbf{g}$ and by $\mathcal{C}_S$ the set of all binary functions over S.

minimum cut

Minimum Cut: Suppose for $f \in \mathcal{C}_S$ we define the incompatibility of f to be the weight of the cut in $\mathbf{g}$ determined by f. This is the implicit notion of compatibility considered in (Blum and Chawla, 2001), and algorithmically the goal is to find the most compatible hypothesis that gets the labeled data correct, which can be solved efficiently using network flow. From a sample-complexity point of view, the number of labeled examples we need is proportional to the VC dimension of the class of hypotheses that are at least as compatible as the target function, which is known to be $O(k/\lambda)$ (see (Kleinberg, 2000; Kleinberg et al., 2004)), where k is the number of edges cut by c^* and λ is the size of the global minimum cut in the graph. Also note that the randomized min-cut algorithm (considered by Blum et al. (2004)), which is an extension of the basic min-cut approach, can be viewed as motivated by a PAC-Bayes sample complexity analysis of the problem.

normalized graph cuts with constraints

Normalized Cut: Consider the normalized cut setting of Joachims (2003) and for $f \in \mathcal{C}_S$ define $size(f)$ to be the weight of the cut in $\mathbf{g}$ determined by f, and let f_{neg} and f_{pos} be the number of points in S on which h predicts negative and positive, respectively. For $f \in \mathcal{C}_S$, define the incompatibility of f to be $\frac{size(f)}{f_{neg} \cdot f_{pos}}$. Note that this is the implicit compatibility function used in Joachims (2003), and again, algorithmically the goal would be to find a highly compatible hypothesis that gets the labeled data correct. Unfortunately, the corresponding optimization problem is in this case NP-hard. Still, several approximate solutions have been considered, leading to different semi-supervised learning algorithms. For instance, Joachims (2003) considers a spectral relaxation that leads to the "spectral graph transducer" algorithm; another relaxation based on semi-definite programming is considered by De Bie and Cristianini (2004b).[8]

Harmonic Function: We can also model the algorithms introduced in (Zhu et al., 2003a,b) as follows. If we consider f to be a probabilistic prediction function defined over S, then the incompatibility of f is given by $\sum_{i,j} w_{i,j} (f(i) - f(j))^2 = f^T L f$, where L is the unnormalized Laplacian of $\mathbf{g}$. Similarly we can model the algorithm introduced by Zhou et al. (2004) by noticing that the incompatibility of f is given by $f^T \mathcal{L} f$ where $\mathcal{L}$ is the normalized Laplacian of $\mathbf{g}$. More generally, all the graph kernel methods can be viewed in our framework if we consider that the incompatibility of f is given by $\|f\|_K = f^T K f$ where K is a kernel derived from the graph (see, for instance, (Zhu et al., 2003c)).

Gaussian random field and harmonic function

22.5.2 Connections to Generative Models

It is also interesting to consider how generative models fit into our model. As mentioned in section 22.1, a typical assumption in a generative setting is that D is a mixture with the probability density function $p(x|\theta) = p_0 \cdot p_0(x|\theta_0) + p_1 \cdot p_1(x|\theta_1)$ (see, for instance, (Ratsaby and Venkatesh, 1995; Castelli and Cover, 1995, 1996)). That means that the labeled examples are generated according to the following mechanism: a label $y \in \{0, 1\}$ is drawn according to the distribution of classes $\{p_0, p_1\}$ and then a corresponding random feature vector is drawn according to the class-conditional density p_y. The assumption typically used is that the mixture is identifiable. Identifiability ensures that the Bayes optimal decision border $\{x : p_0 \cdot p_0(x|\theta_0) = p_1 \cdot p_1(x|\theta_1)\}$ can be deduced if $p(x|\theta)$ is known, and therefore one can construct an estimate of the Bayes border by using $p(x|\hat{\theta})$ instead of $p(x|\theta)$. Essentially once the decision border is estimated, a small labeled sample suffices to learn (with high confidence and small error) the appropriate class labels associated with the two disjoint regions generated by the estimate of the Bayes decision border. To see how we can incorporate this setting in our model, consider for illustration the setting in Ratsaby and Venkatesh (1995); there they assume that $p_0 = p_1$, and that the class-conditional densities are d-dimensional Gaussians with unit covariance and unknown mean vectors $\theta_i \in \mathbb{R}^d$. The algorithm used is the following: the unknown parameter vector $\theta = (\theta_0, \theta_1)$ is estimated from unlabeled data using a maximum-likelihood estimate; this determines a hypothesis which is a linear separator that passes through the point $(\hat{\theta}_0 + \hat{\theta}_1)/2$ and is orthogonal to the vector $\hat{\theta}_1 - \hat{\theta}_0$; finally each of the two decision regions separated by the hyperplane is labeled according to the majority of the labeled examples in the region. Given this setting, a natural notion of compatibility we can consider is the expected log-likelihood function

how the generative models fit into our model

---

8. For a more detailed discussion on this see also chapter 7 in this book.

(where the expectation is taken with respect to the unknown distribution specified by θ). Specifically, we can identify a legal hypothesis $f_{\overline{\theta}}$ with the set of parameters $\overline{\theta} = (\overline{\theta}_0, \overline{\theta}_1)$ that determine it, and then we can define $\chi(f_{\overline{\theta}}, D) = \mathbf{E}_{x \in D}[\log(p(x|\overline{\theta}))]$. Ratsaby and Venkatesh (1995) show that if the unlabeled sample is large enough, then all hypotheses specified by parameters $\overline{\theta}$ which are close enough to θ will have the property that their empirical compatibilities will be close enough to their true compatibilities. This then implies (together with other observations about Gaussian mixtures) that the maximum-likelihood estimate will be close enough to θ, up to permutations. (This actually motivates χ as a good compatibility function in our model.)

More generally, if we deal with other parametric families (but we are in the same setting), we can use the same compatibility notion; however, we will need to impose certain constraints on the distributions allowed in order to ensure that the compatibility is actually well defined (the expected log likelihood is bounded).

As mentioned in section 22.1 this kind of generative setting is really at the extreme of our model. The assumption that the distribution that generates the data is really a mixture implies that if we knew the distribution, then there are only two possible concepts left (and this makes the unlabeled data extremely useful).

22.5.3   Connections to the Luckiness Framework

relationship to
the luckiness
framework

It is worth noticing that there is a strong connection between our approach and the luckiness framework (see (Shawe-Taylor et al., 1998; Mendelson and Philips, 2003)). In both cases, the idea is to define an ordering of hypotheses that depends on the data, in the hope that we will be "lucky" and find that not too many other functions are as compatible as the target. There are two main differences, however. The first is that the luckiness framework (being designed for supervised learning only) uses labeled data both for estimating compatibility and for learning: this is a more difficult task, and as a result our bounds on labeled data can be significantly better. For instance, in example 4 described in section 22.2, for any nondegenerate distribution, a data set of $d/2$ pairs can with probability 1 be completely shattered by fully compatible hypotheses, so the luckiness framework does not help. In contrast, with a larger (unlabeled) sample, one can potentially reduce the space of compatible functions quite significantly, and learn from $o(d)$ or even $O(1)$ labeled examples depending on the distribution (see sections 22.3.3 and 22.4). Secondly, the luckiness framework talks about compatibility between a hypothesis and a *sample*, whereas we define compatibility with respect to a distribution. This allows us to talk about the amount of unlabeled data needed to estimate true compatibility. There are also a number of differences at the technical level of the definitions.

22.5.4   Conclusions

Given the easy availability of unlabeled data in many settings, there has been growing interest in methods that try to use such data together with the (more expensive) labeled data for learning. Nonetheless, there is still substantial disagreement and no clear consensus about when unlabeled data help and by how much. In this chapter, we have provided a PAC-style model for semi-supervised learning that captures many of the ways unlabeled data are typically used, and provides a very general framework for thinking about this issue. The high-level main implication of our analysis is that unlabeled data are useful if (a) we have a good notion of compatibility so that the target function indeed has a low unlabeled error rate, (b) the distribution D is *helpful* in the sense that not too many other hypotheses also have a low unlabeled error rate, and (c) we have enough *unlabeled* data to estimate unlabeled error rates well. One consequence of our model is that if the target function and data distribution are both well behaved with respect to the compatibility notion, then the sample-size bounds we get for labeled data can substantially beat what one could hope to achieve through pure labeled-data bounds, and we have illustrated this with a number of examples throughout the chapter.

23 Metric-Based Approaches for Semi-Supervised Regression and Classification

Dale Schuurmans   DALE@CS.UALBERTA.CA
Finnegan Southey   FINNWORK@LUCUBRATIO.ORG
Dana Wilkinson   D3WILKINSON@CS.UWATERLOO.CA
Yuhong Guo   YUHONG@CS.UALBERTA.CA

Semi-supervised learning methods typically require an explicit relationship to be asserted between the labeled and unlabeled data—as illustrated, for example, by the neighborhoods used in graph-based methods. Semi-supervised model selection and regularization methods are presented here that instead require only that the labeled and unlabeled data are drawn from the same distribution. From this assumption, a metric can be constructed over hypotheses based on their predictions for unlabeled data. This metric can then be used to detect untrustworthy training error estimates, leading to model selection strategies that select the richest hypothesis class while providing theoretical guarantees against overfitting. This general approach is then adapted to regularization for supervised regression and supervised classification with probabilistic classifiers. The regularization adapts not only to the hypothesis class but also to the specific data sample provided, allowing for better performance than regularizers that account only for class complexity.

23.1 Introduction

The tradeoff between overfitting and underfitting is a fundamental dilemma in machine learning and statistics. Given a collection of data points $\mathbf{x} \in \mathcal{X}$, each associated with a dependent value $\mathbf{y} \in \mathcal{Y}$, one often wishes to learn a function or hypothesis which effectively predicts the correct $\mathbf{y}$ given any $\mathbf{x}$. If a hypothesis is chosen from a class that is too complex for the data, there is a good chance it will exhibit a large test error even though its training error is small—i.e., overfitting the training data. This occurs because complex classes generally contain

overfitting

several hypotheses that behave similarly on the training data and yet behave quite differently in other parts of the domain—thus diminishing the ability to distinguish good hypotheses from bad. Since significantly different hypotheses cannot be simultaneously accurate, one must restrict the set of hypotheses to be able to reliably differentiate between accurate and inaccurate predictors. On the other hand, selecting hypotheses from an overly restricted class can prevent one from being able to express a good approximation to the ideal predictor, thereby causing important structure in the training data to be ignored—i.e., underfitting

underfitting   the training data. Since both underfitting and overfitting result in large test error, they must be avoided simultaneously. Consequently, a popular research topic in learning is to find *automated* methods for calibrating hypothesis complexity. The work presented here exploits unlabeled data in a novel fashion to achieve this goal.

We consider two classical approaches to this problem, typically referred to as *model selection* and *regularization*, respectively (Cherkassky and Mulier, 1998; Vap-

model selection   nik, 1995, 1998). In *model selection* one first takes a base hypothesis class, H, decomposes it into a discrete collection of subclasses $H_0 \subset H_1 \subset \cdots = H$ (say, organized in a nested chain, or lattice) and then, given training data, attempts to identify the optimal subclass from which to choose the final hypothesis.[1] There have been a variety of methods proposed for choosing the optimal subclass, but most techniques fall into one of two basic categories: *complexity penalization* (e.g., the minimum description length principle (Rissanen, 1986) and various statistical selection criteria (Foster and George, 1994)); and *holdout testing* (e.g., cross-validation and boot-

regularization   strapping (Efron, 1979)). *Regularization* is similar to model selection except that one does not impose a discrete decomposition on the base hypothesis class. Instead, a penalty criterion is imposed on the individual hypotheses, which either penalizes their parametric form (e.g., as in ridge regression or weight decay in neural network training (Cherkassky and Mulier, 1998; Ripley, 1996; Bishop, 1995)) or penalizes their global smoothness properties (e.g., minimizing curvature (Poggio and Girosi, 1990)). These methods have shown impressive improvements over naive learning algorithms in every area of supervised learning research. However, one difficulty with these techniques is that they usually require expertise to apply properly, and often involve free parameters that must be set by an informed practitioner.

The contribution presented here is the derivation of *parameter-free* methods for model selection and regularization that improve on the robustness of standard approaches by using unlabeled data. As has been seen in other sections of the book, most semi-supervised learning techniques require explicit assumptions about the relationship between labeled and unlabeled data. For the methods presented here, the only assumption required is that the labeled data and the unlabeled data come from the same distribution. The methods we propose automatically differentiate

---

1. The term *model selection* has also been used to refer to other processes in machine learning and statistics, such as choosing the kernel for support vector machines or Bayesian model selection, but we restrict our attention to the classical form described above.

hypotheses based on the difference of their behavior off of the labeled training set (i.e., behavior at points not covered by the training set). Like many of the semi-supervised learning approaches proposed in this book (e.g., chapters 10 and 11), our methods regularize in a data-specific fashion rather than simply penalizing model complexity. This allows modern techniques to potentially outperform traditional fixed regularizers that penalize complexity identically across different training samples.

To begin, section 23.2 introduces the idea of metric spaces for hypotheses, allowing the geometric characterization of the supervised learning problem. Section 23.3 investigates how unlabeled data can be used to perform *model selection* in nested sequences of hypothesis spaces. The strategies developed are shown to experimentally outperform standard model selection methods and have been proved to be robust in theory. Section 23.4 considers *regularization* and shows how the proposed model selection strategies can be extended to a generalized training objective for supervised regression. Here the idea is to use unlabeled data to automatically tune the degree of regularization for a given task without having to set free parameters by hand. The resulting regularization technique adapts its behavior to a given training set and can outperform standard fixed regularizers for a given problem. Section 23.5 extends the earlier regression approach from section 23.4 to probabilistic classifiers. Finally, section 23.6 concludes with an examination of potential avenues for future research.

23.2 Metric Structure of Supervised Learning

In supervised learning, one takes a sequence of training pairs $\langle \mathbf{x}_1, \mathbf{y}_1 \rangle, ..., \langle \mathbf{x}_l, \mathbf{y}_l \rangle$ and attempts to infer a hypothesis function $h : \mathcal{X} \to \mathcal{Y}$ that achieves small prediction error $err(h(\mathbf{x}), \mathbf{y})$ on future test examples. This basic paradigm covers many of the tasks studied in machine learning research.

For model selection and regularization tasks it is necessary to be able to compare hypothesis functions. The approach we pursue in this chapter is to exploit a concrete notion of distance between hypothesis functions. Consider the metric structure on metric on space of hypotheses a space of hypothesis functions that arises from a simple statistical model of the supervised learning problem: Assume the examples $\langle \mathbf{x}, \mathbf{y} \rangle$ are generated by a fixed joint distribution P_{XY} on $\mathcal{X} \times \mathcal{Y}$. In learning a hypothesis function $h : \mathcal{X} \to \mathcal{Y}$ the primary interest is in modeling some aspect of the conditional distribution $P_{Y|X}$. Here the utility of using extra information about the marginal domain distribution P_X to choose a good hypothesis is investigated. Note that information about P_X can be obtained from a collection of *un*labeled training examples $\mathbf{x}_{l+1}, ..., \mathbf{x}_n$. The significance of having information about the domain distribution P_X is that it defines a natural *(pseudo) metric* on the space of hypotheses. That is, for any two hypothesis functions f and g, one can obtain a measure of the distance between them by computing the expected disagreement in their predictions,

$$d(f,g) \;\; \triangleq \;\; \varphi\left(\int err(f(\mathbf{x}), g(\mathbf{x}))\, d\mathrm{P}_X\right), \qquad (23.1)$$

where $err(\hat{\mathbf{y}}, \mathbf{y})$ is the natural measure of prediction error for the problem at hand (e.g., regression or classification) and φ is an associated normalization function that recovers the standard metric axioms.

For the problem of regression, prediction error can be measured by squared difference $err(\hat{\mathbf{y}}, \mathbf{y}) = (\hat{\mathbf{y}} - \mathbf{y})^2$ or some similar loss. For classification problems, prediction error can be measured with the misclassification loss $err(\hat{\mathbf{y}}, \mathbf{y}) = 1_{(\hat{\mathbf{y}} \neq \mathbf{y})}$. The standard metric properties to be satisfied are non-negativity $d(f,g) \geq 0$, symmetry $d(f,g) = d(g,f)$, and the triangle inequality $d(f,g) \leq d(f,h) + d(h,g)$. It turns out that most typical prediction error functions admit a metric of this type.

For example, in regression the distance between two prediction functions can be measured by

$$d(f,g) \;\; = \;\; \left(\int (f(\mathbf{x}) - g(\mathbf{x}))^2\, d\mathrm{P}_X\right)^{1/2},$$

where the normalization function $\varphi(z) = z^{1/2}$ establishes the metric properties. In classification, the distance between two classifiers can be measured by

$$
\begin{aligned}
d(f,g) \;\; &= \;\; \int 1_{(f(\mathbf{x}) \neq g(\mathbf{x}))}\, d\mathrm{P}_X \\
&= \;\; \mathrm{P}_X(f(\mathbf{x}) \neq g(\mathbf{x})),
\end{aligned}
$$

where no normalization is required to achieve a metric. Importantly, these definitions can be generalized to include the target *conditional distribution* in an analogous manner:

$$d(\mathrm{P}_{Y|X}, h) \;\; \triangleq \;\; \varphi\left(\int\int err(h(\mathbf{x}), \mathbf{y})\, d\mathrm{P}_{Y|x}\, d\mathrm{P}_X\right). \qquad (23.2)$$

That is, one can interpret the true error of a hypothesis function h with respect to a target conditional $\mathrm{P}_{Y|X}$ as a *distance* between h and $\mathrm{P}_{Y|X}$. The significance of this definition is that it is consistent with the previous definition (23.1) and one can therefore embed the entire supervised learning problem in a common metric space structure.

To illustrate: in regression, (23.2) yields the root mean squared error of a hypothesis:

$$d(\mathrm{P}_{Y|X}, h) \;\; = \;\; \left(\int\int (h(\mathbf{x}) - \mathbf{y})^2\, d\mathrm{P}_{Y|x}\, d\mathrm{P}_X\right)^{1/2},$$

and in classification it gives the true misclassification probability:

$$
\begin{aligned}
d(\mathrm{P}_{Y|X}, h) &= \iint 1_{(h(\mathbf{x}) \neq \mathbf{y})} \, d\mathrm{P}_{Y|x} \, d\mathrm{P}_X \\
&= \mathrm{P}_{XY}(h(\mathbf{x}) \neq \mathbf{y}).
\end{aligned}
$$

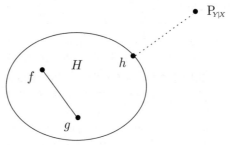

Figure 23.1   Metric space view of supervised learning: Unlabeled data can accurately estimate distances between functions f and g within H, however only limited labeled data are available to estimate the closest function h to $\mathrm{P}_{Y|X}$.

Together, the definitions in Eqs. 23.1 and 23.2 show how to impose a global metric space view of the supervised learning problem (figure 23.1). Given labeled training examples $\langle \mathbf{x}_1, \mathbf{y}_1 \rangle, ..., \langle \mathbf{x}_l, \mathbf{y}_l \rangle$, the goal is to find the hypothesis h in a space H that is closest to a target conditional $\mathrm{P}_{Y|X}$ under the distance measure (Eq. 23.2). If there is also a large set of u auxiliary unlabeled examples $\mathbf{x}_{l+1}, ..., \mathbf{x}_n$, such that $u = n - l$, then one can also accurately estimate the distances between alternative hypotheses f and g within H, effectively giving Eq. 23.1:

$$
\tilde{d}(f, g) \;\triangleq\; \varphi\left(\frac{1}{u} \sum_{j=l+1}^{n} err(f(\mathbf{x}_j), g(\mathbf{x}_j)) \right). \tag{23.3}
$$

That is, for sufficiently large u, the distances defined in Eq. 23.3 will be very close to the distances defined in Equation 23.1. In fact, below we sill generally assume that u is large enough to ensure $\tilde{d}(f, g) \approx d(f, g)$. However, the distances between hypotheses and the target conditional $\mathrm{P}_{Y|X}$ (Eq. 23.2) can only be weakly estimated using the (presumably much smaller) set of labeled training data:

$$
\hat{d}(\mathrm{P}_{Y|X}, h) \;\triangleq\; \varphi\left(\frac{1}{l} \sum_{i=1}^{l} err(h(\mathbf{x}_i), \mathbf{y}_i) \right). \tag{23.4}
$$

This measure need not be close to Equation 23.2. The challenge then is to approximate the closest hypothesis to the target conditional as accurately as possible using the available information (Eqs. 23.3 and 23.4) in place of the true distances (Eqs. 23.1 and 23.2).

This metric space perspective will be used to devise novel model selection and regularization strategies that exploit interhypothesis distances measured on an auxiliary set of unlabeled examples. The proposed approach is applicable to any supervised learning problem that admits a reasonable metric structure. In particular, all strategies will be expressed in terms of a generic distance measure that does not depend on other aspects of the problem.

23.3   Model Selection

First consider the process of using *model selection* to choose the appropriate level of hypothesis complexity to fit to data. This is, conceptually, the simplest approach to automatic complexity control for supervised learning. The idea is to stratify the hypothesis class H into a sequence (or lattice) of nested subclasses $H_0 \subset H_1 \subset \cdots = H$, and then, given training data, somehow choose a class that has the proper complexity for the given data. To understand how one might make this choice, note that for a given training sample $\langle \mathbf{x}_1, \mathbf{y}_1 \rangle, \ldots, \langle \mathbf{x}_l, \mathbf{y}_l \rangle$ one can,

empirical risk minimization

in principle, obtain the corresponding sequence of empirically optimal functions $h_0 \in H_0, h_1 \in H_1, \ldots$

$$h_k = \arg \min_{h \in H_k} \quad \varphi \left(\frac{1}{l} \sum_{i=1}^{l} err(h(\mathbf{x}_i), \mathbf{y}_i) \right) = \arg \min_{h \in H_k} \quad \hat{d}(\mathrm{P}_{Y|X}, h).$$

That is, here we assume an empirical risk minimization procedure is used to select a candidate function from each class, and moreover we assume a unique minimizer exists for each H_k.[2] The problem is to select one of these functions based on the observed training errors $\hat{d}(\mathrm{P}_{Y|X}, h_0), \hat{d}(\mathrm{P}_{Y|X}, h_1), \ldots$ (figure 23.2). However, because each hypothesis class subsumes those before it, these errors must monotonically decrease (assuming one can fully optimize in each class) and therefore choosing the function with smallest training error inevitably leads to overfitting. Some other criterion beyond mere empirical-error minimization must be invoked to make the final selection.

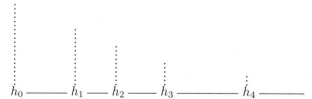

Figure 23.2   Sequence of empirically optimal functions induced by a chain $H_0 \subset H_1 \subset \ldots$ on a given training set: Dotted lines indicate decreasing optimal training distances $\hat{d}(h_0, \mathrm{P}_{Y|X}), \hat{d}(h_1, \mathrm{P}_{Y|X}), \ldots$ and solid lines indicate distances *between* hypotheses. The final hypothesis must be selected on the basis of these estimates.

---

2. This uniqueness assumption is reasonable for regression problems, but generally does not hold for classification problems under 0-1 loss; see section 23.5 below.

As mentioned, two basic model selection strategies currently predominate: *complexity penalization* and *holdout testing*. However, neither of these approaches attends to the metric distances between hypotheses, nor do they offer an obvious way to exploit auxiliary unlabeled data. By adopting the metric space view of section 23.2, however, a useful new perspective on model selection can be obtained. In our setting, the chain $H_0 \subset H_1 \subset \cdots \subset H$ can be interpreted as a sequence of hypothesis *spaces* wherein one can measure the distance between candidate hypotheses using unlabeled data. Note that it is still not possible to directly measure the distances from hypotheses to the target conditional $P_{Y|X}$, and therefore they must be estimated based on a small labeled training sample. However, the fact that there are distances *between* functions in the sequence can be exploited—this additional information being used to make a better choice (figure 23.2).

23.3.1   Strategy 1: Triangle Inequality

The first intuition explored is that interhypothesis distances can help detect overfitting in a very simple manner. Consider two hypotheses h_k and h_{k+1} that both have a small estimated distance to $P_{Y|X}$ and yet have a large true distance between them. In this situation there should be concern in selecting the second hypothesis, because if the true distance between h_k and h_{k+1} is indeed large, then both functions cannot be simultaneously close to $P_{Y|X}$, by simple geometry. This implies that at least one of the distance estimates to $P_{Y|X}$ must be inaccurate. The earlier estimate should be more trusted because it comes from a more restricted class that is less likely to overfit. In fact, if both $\hat{d}(P_{Y|X}, h_k)$ and $\hat{d}(P_{Y|X}, h_{k+1})$ really were ac-

triangle
inequality curate estimates they would have to satisfy the *triangle inequality* with the known distance $d(h_k, h_{k+1})$; that is,

$$\hat{d}(P_{Y|X}, h_k) + \hat{d}(P_{Y|X}, h_{k+1}) \geq d(h_k, h_{k+1}). \tag{23.5}$$

Since these empirical distances eventually become significant underestimates in general (because a particular h_i is explicitly chosen to minimize the empirical distance on the labeled training set) the triangle inequality provides a useful test for detecting when these estimates become inaccurate. In fact, this basic test forms the basis of a simple model selection strategy, TRI (algorithm 23.1), that works surprisingly well in many situations.

Algorithm 23.1 Triangle inequality model selection procedure.

Procedure TRI

- Given hypothesis sequence $h_0, h_1, \ldots$
- Choose the last hypothesis h_ℓ in the sequence that satisfies the triangle inequality, $\tilde{d}(h_k, h_\ell) \leq \hat{d}(h_k, P_{Y|X}) + \hat{d}(P_{Y|X}, h_\ell)$, with every preceding hypothesis $h_k, 0 \leq k < \ell$.

23.3.2   Example: Polynomial Regression

To demonstrate this method (and all subsequent methods developed here), first consider the problem of polynomial curve-fitting. This is a supervised learning problem where $\mathcal{X} = \mathbb{R}$, $\mathcal{Y} = \mathbb{R}$, and the goal is to minimize the squared prediction error, $err(\hat{\mathbf{y}}, \mathbf{y}) = (\hat{\mathbf{y}} - \mathbf{y})^2$. Specifically, consider polynomial hypotheses $h : \mathbb{R} \rightarrow \mathbb{R}$ under the natural stratification $H_0 \subset H_1 \subset \ldots$ into polynomials of degree at most $0, 1, \ldots$, etc. The motivation for studying this task is that it is a well-studied problem that still attracts a lot of interest (Cherkassky et al., 1997; Galarza et al., 1996; Vapnik, 1995, 1998). Moreover, polynomials create a difficult model selection problem that has a strong tendency to produce catastrophic overfitting effects. Another benefit is that polynomials are an interesting and nontrivial class for which there are efficient techniques for computing best-fit hypotheses.

To apply the metric-based approach to this task, define the metric d in terms of the squared prediction error $err(\hat{y}, y) = (\hat{y} - y)^2$ with a square root normalization $\varphi(z) = z^{1/2}$, as discussed in section 23.2. To evaluate the efficacy of TRI on this problem, its performance was compared to a number of standard model selection strategies, including structural risk minimization (SRM) (Cherkassky et al., 1997; Vapnik, 1998), risk inflation criterion (RIC) (Foster and George, 1994), Shibata's model selector (SMS) (Shibata, 1981), generalized cross-validation (GCV) (Craven and Wahba, 1979), Bayesian information criterion (BIC) (Schwarz, 1978), Akaike information criterion (AIC) (Akaike, 1974), Mallows' C_p statistic (CP) (Mallows, 1973), and finite prediction error (FPE) (Akaike, 1970). TRI was also compared to tenfold cross-validation (CVT; a standard holdout method (Efron, 1979; Kohavi, 1995)).

A simple series of experiments was conducted by fixing a domain distribution P_X on $X = \mathbb{R}$ and then fixing various target functions $f : \mathbb{R} \rightarrow \mathbb{R}$. The specific target functions used in the experiments are shown in figure 23.3. To generate training samples a sequence of values $(\mathbf{x}_1, \ldots, \mathbf{x}_l)$ were drawn, then the target function values $f(\mathbf{x}_1), \ldots, f(\mathbf{x}_l)$ computed and perturbed by adding independent Gaussian noise with standard deviation $\sigma = 0.05$ to each. This resulted in a labeled training sequence $\langle \mathbf{x}_1, \mathbf{y}_1 \rangle, \ldots, \langle \mathbf{x}_l, \mathbf{y}_l \rangle$. For a given training sample the series of best-fit polynomials $h_0, h_1, \ldots$ of degree $0, 1, \ldots$ was computed. Given this sequence, each model selection strategy will choose some hypothesis h_k on the basis of the observed empirical errors. The implementation of TRI was given access to u auxiliary unlabeled examples $\mathbf{x}_{l+1}, \ldots, \mathbf{x}_n$ in order to estimate the true distances between polynomials in the sequence.

The main emphasis in these experiments was to minimize the true distance between the final hypothesis and the target conditional $P_{Y|X}$. That is, the primary concern was choosing a hypothesis that obtained a small prediction error on future test examples, independent of its complexity level. To determine the effectiveness of the various selection strategies, the *ratio* of the true error (distance) of the polynomial they selected to the best true error among polynomials in the sequence $h_0, h_1, \ldots$, was measured. This means that the optimum achievable ratio was 1. The

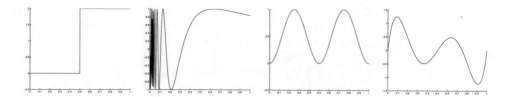

Figure 23.3   Target functions used in the polynomial curve-fitting experiments (in order): step($x \geq 0.5$), sin($1/x$), sin$^2(2\pi x)$, and a fifth-degree polynomial.

rationale for doing this was to measure the model selection strategy's ability to approximate the best hypothesis in the given sequence—not find a better function from outside the sequence.[3]

Table 23.1   Fitting $f(x) = \text{step}(x \geq 0.5)$ with $P_x = U(0,1)$ and $\sigma = 0.05$. Distribution of approximation ratios achieved at training sample size $l = 30$, showing percentiles of approximation ratios achieved in 1000 repeated trials.

$l = 30$	TRI	CVT	SRM	RIC	GCV	BIC	AIC	FPE	ADJ
25	1.00	1.08	1.17	4.69	1.51	5.41	5.45	2.72	1.06
50	1.08	1.17	1.54	34.8	9.19	39.6	40.8	19.1	1.14
75	1.19	1.37	9.68	258	91.3	266	266	159	1.25
95	1.45	6.11	419	4.7e3	2.7e3	4.8e3	5.1e3	4.0e3	1.51
100	2.18	643	1.6e7	1.6e7	1.6e7	1.6e7	1.6e7	1.6e7	2.10

Table 23.1 shows the results obtained for approximating a step function $f(\mathbf{x}) = \text{step}(\mathbf{x} \geq 0.5)$ corrupted by Gaussian noise, where the marginal distribution P_x is uniform on $[0, 1]$. The strategy ADJ (adjusted-distance estimate) in the tables is explained in section 23.3.3 below. These results were obtained by repeatedly generating training samples of a fixed size and recording the approximation ratio achieved by each strategy. The tables record the distribution of ratios produced by each strategy for a training sample size of $l = 30$, using $u = 200$ unlabeled examples to measure interhypothesis distances, repeated over 1000 trials. The initial results appear to be quite positive. TRI achieves a median approximation ratio of 1.08. This compares favorably to the median approximation ratio 1.54 achieved by SRM, and 1.17 achieved by CVT. The remaining complexity penalization strategies—GCV, FPE, etc.—all performed significantly worse on these trials. However, the most notable difference was TRI's robustness against overfitting. In fact, although

---

3. One could consider more elaborate strategies that choose hypotheses from outside the sequence; e.g., by averaging several hypotheses together (Krogh and Vedelsby, 1995; Opitz and Shavlik, 1996; Breiman, 1996). However, this idea will not be pursued further here.

Table 23.2   Fitting $f(x) = \sin(1/x)$ with $P_X = U(0,1)$ and $\sigma = 0.05$. Distribution of approximation ratios achieved at training sample size $l = 30$, showing percentiles of approximation ratios achieved in 1000 repeated trials.

$l = 30$	TRI	CVT	SRM	RIC	GCV	BIC	AIC	FPE	ADJ
25	1.02	1.08	1.34	2.80	1.89	3.16	3.67	2.80	1.08
50	1.14	1.20	4.74	12.1	9.67	14.1	15.8	13.8	1.17
75	1.30	1.63	33.2	61.5	55.2	70.1	81.6	72.4	1.30
95	1.72	23.5	306	1.2e3	479	1.3e3	1.3e3	1.3e3	1.81
100	2.68	325	1.4e5	5.2e5	1.4e5	5.2e5	5.2e5	3.9e5	9.75

Table 23.3   Fitting $f(x) = \sin^2(2\pi x)$ with $P_X = U(0,1)$ and $\sigma = 0.05$. Distribution of approximation ratios achieved at training sample size $l = 30$, showing percentiles of approximation ratios achieved in 1000 repeated trials.

$l = 30$	TRI	CVT	SRM	RIC	GCV	BIC	AIC	FPE	ADJ
25	1.50	1.00	1.00	1.00	1.00	1.00	1.00	1.02	1.01
50	3.51	1.16	1.03	1.05	1.11	1.02	1.08	1.45	1.27
75	4.15	1.64	1.45	1.48	2.02	1.39	1.88	6.44	1.60
95	5.51	5.21	5.06	4.21	26.4	5.01	19.9	295	3.02
100	9.75	124	1.4e3	20.0	9.1e3	28.4	9.4e3	1.0e4	8.35

the penalization strategy SRM performed reasonably well much of the time, it was prone to making periodic but catastrophic overfitting errors. Even the normally well-behaved cross-validation strategy CVT made significant overfitting errors from time to time. This is evidenced by the fact that in 1000 trials with a training sample of size 30 (table 23.1) TRI produced a *maximum* approximation ratio of 2.18, whereas CVT produced a worst-case approximation ratio of 643, and the penalization strategies SRM and GCV both produced worst-case ratios of 1.6×10^7. The 95th percentiles were TRI 1.45, CVT 6.11, SRM 419, GCV 2.7×10^3. Similar results for TRI are obtained for larger labeled sample sizes, such as $l = 100$ and $l = 200$. [4] For a broader selection of results see (Schuurmans and Southey, 2002).

     The results showing TRI's robustness against overfitting are encouraging, but it is further possible to prove that TRI cannot produce an approximation ratio greater than 3 due to overfitting. That is, we can bound TRI's approximation ratio under two simple assumptions. First, that TRI makes it to the best hypothesis h_m in the sequence. Second, that the empirical error of h_m is an underestimate—that

---

4. Although one might suspect that the large failures could be due to measuring relative instead of absolute error, it turns out that all of these large relative errors also correspond to large absolute errors. This is verified in section 23.4.1 below.

Table 23.4   Fitting a fifth-degree polynomial $f(x)$ with $P_X = U(0, 1)$ and $\sigma = 0.05$. Distribution of approximation ratios achieved at training sample size $l = 30$, showing percentiles of approximation ratios achieved in 1000 repeated trials.

$l = 30$	TRI	CVT	SRM	RIC	GCV	BIC	AIC	FPE	ADJ
25	7.80	1.00	1.00	1.00	1.00	1.00	1.00	1.00	1.00
50	8.58	1.01	1.00	1.00	1.01	1.00	1.00	1.08	1.00
75	9.36	1.11	1.01	1.00	1.20	1.01	1.14	2.40	1.02
95	11.0	2.59	1.42	1.13	8.92	1.35	5.46	131	1.18
100	14.2	45.3	24.1	8.00	3.1e4	11.8	9.9e3	1.4e5	13.6

is, $\hat{d}(P_{Y|X}, h_m) \leq d(P_{Y|X}, h_m)$. Note that this second assumption is likely to hold because hypotheses are chosen by explicitly minimizing $\hat{d}(P_{Y|X}, h_m)$ rather than $d(P_{Y|X}, h_m)$ (see table 23.5). The proof for the following proposition can be found in (Schuurmans and Southey, 2002).

Proposition 23.1 *Let h_m be the optimal hypothesis in the sequence $h_0, h_1, \ldots$ (that is, $h_m = \arg\min_{h_k} d(P_{Y|X}, h_k)$) and let h_ℓ be the hypothesis selected by TRI. If (i) $m \leq \ell$ and (ii) $\hat{d}(P_{Y|X}, h_m) \leq d(P_{Y|X}, h_m)$ then:*

$$d(P_{Y|X}, h_\ell) \quad \leq \quad 3d(P_{Y|X}, h_m). \tag{23.6}$$

Note that in proposition 23.1, as well as in propositions 23.2 and 23.3 below, it is implicitly assumed that the true interhypothesis distances $d(h_m, h_\ell)$ are known. This, in principle, must be measured on the true marginal P_X. This assumption will be relaxed in section 23.3.4 below.

Continuing with the experimental investigation, the basic flavor of the results remains unchanged at different noise levels and for different domain distributions P_X. In fact, much stronger results are obtained for wider-tailed domain distributions like Gaussian (Schuurmans and Southey, 2002) and "difficult" target functions like $\sin(1/x)$ (table 23.2). Here the complexity penalization methods (SRM, GCV, etc.) can be forced into a regime of constant catastrophe, CVT noticeably degrades, and yet TRI retains performance similar to the levels shown in table 23.1.

Of course, these results might be due to considering a pathological target function from the perspective of polynomial curve-fitting. It is therefore important to consider other more natural targets that might be better suited to polynomial approximation. In fact, by repeating the previous experiments with a more benign target function, $f(x) = \sin^2(2\pi x)$, quite different results are obtained. Table 23.3 shows that procedure TRI does not fare as well in this case—obtaining a median approximation ratio of 3.51 (compared to 1.03 for SRM, and 1.16 for CVT). A closer inspection of TRI's behavior reveals that the reason for this performance drop is that TRI systematically gets stuck at low even-degree polynomials (cf. table 23.5). In fact, there is a simple geometric explanation for this. The even-degree polynomials (after degree 4) all give reasonable fits to $\sin^2(2\pi x)$ whereas the odd-degree fits have a tail in the wrong direction. This creates a significant distance between successive polynomials and causes the triangle inequality test to fail between the even- and odd-degree fits, even though the larger even-degree polynomials give a good approximation. Therefore, although the metric-based TRI strategy is robust against overfitting, it can be prone to systematic underfitting in seemingly benign cases. Similar results were obtained for fitting a fifth-degree target polynomial corrupted by the same level of Gaussian noise (table 23.4). This problem demonstrates that the first assumption used in proposition 23.1 above can be violated in natural situations (see table 23.5). Consideration of this difficulty leads to the development of a reformulated procedure.

23.3.3   Strategy 2: Adjusted Distance Estimates

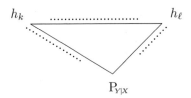

Figure 23.4   The real and estimated distances between successive hypotheses h_k and h_ℓ and the target $P_{Y|X}$. Solid lines indicate real distances, dotted lines indicate empirical distance estimates.

comparing d and $\hat{d}$

Assume for the sake of argument that $\tilde{d} = d$ (i.e., our estimate of interhypothesis distance, based on unlabeled data, is the true distance). The final idea explored for model selection is to observe that there would then be *two* metrics — the true metric d defined by the joint distribution P_{XY} and an empirical metric $\hat{d}$ determined by the labeled training sequence $\langle \mathbf{x}_1, \mathbf{y}_1 \rangle, \ldots, \langle \mathbf{x}_l, \mathbf{y}_l \rangle$. Note that the previous model selection strategy TRI ignored the fact that one could measure the empirical distance between hypotheses $\hat{d}(h_k, h_\ell)$ on the *labeled* training data, as well as estimate their "true" distance $d(h_k, h_\ell)$ on the unlabeled data. However, the fact that one can measure both interhypothesis distances actually gives an *observable* relationship between $\hat{d}$ and d in the local vicinity. This observation is now exploited in an attempt to derive an improved model selection procedure.

Given the two metrics d and $\hat{d}$, consider the triangle formed by two hypotheses h_k and h_ℓ and the target conditional $P_{Y|X}$ (figure 23.4). Notice that there are six distances involved—three real and three estimated—of which the true distances to $P_{Y|X}$ are the only two of importance, and yet these are the only two that are not available. However, the observed relationship between d and $\hat{d}$ can be exploited to adjust the empirical training error estimate $\hat{d}(P_{Y|X}, h_\ell)$. In fact, one could first consider the simplest possible adjustment based on the naive assumption that the observed relationship of the metrics $\hat{d}$ and d between h_k and h_ℓ also holds between

adjustment of error estimates

h_ℓ and $P_{Y|X}$. Note that if this were actually the case, a better estimate of $d(P_{Y|X}, h_\ell)$ could be obtained by simply rescaling the training distance $\hat{d}(P_{Y|X}, h_\ell)$ according to the observed ratio $\tilde{d}(h_k, h_\ell)/\hat{d}(h_k, h_\ell)$. Since $\hat{d}$ is expected to be an underestimate in general, because we assume the h_k are chosen by minimizing $\hat{d}$, this ratio should be larger than 1. In fact, adopting this as a simple heuristic yields another model selection procedure, ADJ, which is also surprisingly effective (algorithm 23.2). This simple procedure overcomes some of the underfitting problems associated with TRI and yet retains much of TRI's robustness against overfitting.

Algorithm 23.2 Adjusted-distance estimate model selection procedure.

Procedure ADJ

- Given hypothesis sequence $h_0, h_1, \dots$
- For each hypothesis h_ℓ in the sequence
  – multiply its estimated distance to the target $\hat{d}(P_{Y|X}, h_\ell)$ by the worst ratio of unlabeled

  and labeled distance to some predecessor h_k to obtain an adjusted distance estimate:

$$\check{d}(P_{Y|X}, h_\ell) \;\triangleq\; \hat{d}(P_{Y|X}, h_\ell) \frac{\tilde{d}(h_k, h_\ell)}{\hat{d}(h_k, h_\ell)}.$$

- Choose the hypothesis h_n with the smallest adjusted distance $\check{d}(h_n, P_{Y|X})$.

Although at first glance this procedure might seem to be ad hoc, it turns out that one can prove an overfitting bound for ADJ that is analogous to that established for TRI. In particular, if one assumes that ADJ makes it to the best hypothesis h_m in the sequence, and the adjusted error estimate $\check{d}(P_{Y|X}, h_m)$ is an underestimate, then ADJ cannot overfit by a factor much greater than 3. Again, the formal proposition is stated, but refer to Schuurmans and Southey (2002) for a proof.

Proposition 23.2 *Let h_m be the optimal hypothesis in the sequence $h_0, h_1, \dots$ and let h_ℓ be the hypothesis selected by ADJ. If (i) $m \leq \ell$ and (ii) $\check{d}(P_{Y|X}, h_m) \leq d(P_{Y|X}, h_m)$, then*

$$d(P_{Y|X}, h_\ell) \;\leq\; \left(2 + \frac{\hat{d}(P_{Y|X}, h_m)}{\hat{d}(P_{Y|X}, h_\ell)}\right) d(P_{Y|X}, h_m). \tag{23.7}$$

In this respect, not only does ADJ exhibit robustness against overfitting, it also has a (weak) theoretical guarantee against underfitting. That is, with the assumptions that the empirical distance estimates are underestimates and that the adjusted distance estimates strictly increase the empirical distance estimates, then if the true error of a successor hypothesis h_m improves the true error of all of its predecessors h_ℓ by a significant factor, h_m will be selected in lieu of its predecessors. See Schuurmans and Southey (2002) for a proof of this proposition.

Proposition 23.3 *Consider a hypothesis h_m, and assume that (i) $\hat{d}(P_{Y|X}, h_\ell) \leq d(P_{Y|X}, h_\ell)$ for all $0 \leq \ell \leq m$, and (ii) $\hat{d}(P_{Y|X}, h_\ell) \leq \check{d}(P_{Y|X}, h_\ell)$ for all $0 \leq \ell < m$. Then if*

$$d(P_{Y|X}, h_m) \quad < \quad \frac{1}{3} \frac{\hat{d}(P_{Y|X}, h_\ell)^2}{d(P_{Y|X}, h_\ell)} \tag{23.8}$$

for all $0 \leq \ell < m$ (that is, $d(P_{Y|X}, h_m)$ is sufficiently small) it follows that $\check{d}(P_{Y|X}, h_m) < \check{d}(P_{Y|X}, h_\ell)$ for all $0 \leq \ell < m$, and therefore ADJ will not choose any predecessor of h_m.

Table 23.5   Strengths of the assumptions used in propositions 23.1 and 23.2. Table shows frequency (in percent) that the assumptions hold over 1000 repetitions of the experiments conducted in tables 23.1, 23.2, 23.3, and 23.4 (at sample size $l = 20$).

	step$(x \geq 0.5)$ (Table 23.1)	$\sin(1/x)$ (Table 23.2)	$\sin^2(2\pi x)$ (Table 23.3)	poly$^5(x)$ (Table 23.4)
Prop. 23.1(i) holds	73	80	10	4
Prop. 23.1(ii) holds	87	86	99	98
Prop. 23.1 holds	61	66	9	4
Prop. 23.2(i) holds	27	32	28	67
Prop. 23.2(ii) holds	22	26	14	24
Prop. 23.2 holds	15	17	12	21

Therefore, although ADJ might not have originally appeared to be well motivated, it possesses worst-case bounds against overfitting and underfitting that are different from those that have been established for conventional methods. However, these bounds remain somewhat weak. Table 23.5 shows empirical results on the frequency with which the underlying assumptions hold on experimental data, demonstrating that both ADJ and TRI systematically underfit in the experiments. That is, even though assumption (ii) of proposition 23.1 is almost always satisfied (as expected), assumption (ii) of proposition 23.2 is only true one quarter of the time. Therefore, propositions 23.1 and 23.2 can only provide a loose characterization of the quality of these methods. However, both metric-based procedures remain robust against overfitting.

To demonstrate that ADJ is indeed effective, the previous experiments were repeated with ADJ as a new competitor. The results show that ADJ robustly outperformed the standard complexity penalization and holdout methods in all cases considered—spanning a wide variety of target functions, noise levels, and domain distributions P_X. Tables 23.1 through 23.4 show the previous data along with the performance characteristics of ADJ. In particular, tables 23.3, 23.4, and 23.5 show that ADJ avoids the extreme underfitting problems that hamper TRI; it appears to responsively select high-order approximations when this is supported by the data. Moreover, tables 23.1 and 23.2 show that ADJ is still extremely robust against overfitting, even in situations where the standard approaches make catastrophic errors. Overall, this is the best model selection strategy observed for these polynomial regression tasks, even though it possesses a weaker guarantee against overfitting than TRI (Schuurmans and Southey, 2002).

Note that both proposed model selection procedures add little computational overhead to traditional methods, since computing interhypothesis distances involves making only a single pass down the reference list of unlabeled examples. This is an advantage over standard holdout techniques like CVT which repeatedly call the hypothesis-generating mechanism to generate pseudohypotheses—which can sometimes be expensive.

Finally, note that ADJ possesses a subtle limitation: the multiplicative rescaling it employs cannot penalize hypotheses that have zero training error (hence the limiting of the degree of the polynomials to $l - 2$ in the above experiments to avoid null training errors). However, despite this shortcoming the ADJ procedure turns out to perform very well in experiments and most often outperforms the more straightforward TRI strategy.

23.3.4   Robustness to Unlabeled Data

Before moving on to regularization, a comment on the robustness of these model selection techniques to limited amounts of auxiliary unlabeled data. In principle, one can always argue that the preceding empirical results are not useful because the metric-based strategies TRI and ADJ might require significant amounts of unlabeled data to perform well in practice. However, the 200 unlabeled examples used in the previous experiments does not seem that onerous. In fact, the previous theoretical results (propositions 23.1, 23.2, and 23.3) assumed knowledge of the true marginal P_x. To explore the issue of robustness to limited amounts of unlabeled data, the previous experiments were repeated but TRI and ADJ were only given a small auxiliary sample of unlabeled data to estimate interhypothesis distances. In this experiment it was found that these strategies were actually quite robust to using approximate distances. Table 23.6 shows that small numbers of unlabeled examples were still sufficient for TRI and ADJ to perform nearly as well as before. Moreover, table 23.6 shows that these techniques only seem to significantly degrade with fewer unlabeled than labeled training examples. This robustness was observed across the range of problems considered.

Although the empirical results in this section are anecdotal, the paper (Schuurmans et al., 1997) pursues a more systematic investigation of the robustness of these procedures and reaches similar conclusions (also based on artificial data). Recently, Bengio and Chapados have also found that using a density estimate for P_x based only on labeled data allows one to dispense with unlabeled data and, surprisingly, still achieve beneficial results (Bengio and Chapados, 2003). Rather than present a detailed investigation of these model selection strategies in more serious

Table 23.6   Fitting $f(x) = \text{step}(x \geq 0.5)$ with $P_X = U(0, 1)$ and $\sigma = 0.05$ (as in table 23.1). This table gives distribution of approximation ratios achieved with $l = 30$ labeled training examples and $u = 500$, $u = 200$, $u = 100$, $u = 50$, $u = 25$ unlabeled examples, showing percentiles of approximation ratios achieved after 1000 repeated trials. The experimental setup of table 23.1 is repeated, except that a smaller number of unlabeled examples are used.

	percentiles of approximation ratios				
$l = 30$	25	50	75	95	100
TRI ($u = 500$)	1.00	1.07	1.19	1.48	2.21
TRI ($u = 200$)	1.00	1.08	1.19	1.45	2.18
TRI ($u = 100$)	1.00	1.08	1.19	1.45	2.49
TRI ($u = \ \ 50$)	1.01	1.08	1.19	1.65	7.26
TRI ($u = \ \ 25$)	1.01	1.10	1.27	2.74	64.6
ADJ ($u = 500$)	1.06	1.14	1.26	1.51	1.99
ADJ ($u = 200$)	1.06	1.14	1.25	1.51	2.10
ADJ ($u = 100$)	1.07	1.16	1.31	1.67	2.21
ADJ ($u = \ \ 50$)	1.07	1.17	1.29	1.58	3.19
ADJ ($u = \ \ 25$)	1.09	1.22	1.40	1.85	8.68

case studies, the focus now changes to a further improvement in the basic method.

23.4   Regularization

One difficulty when doing model selection is that the generalization behavior depends on the specific decomposition of the base hypothesis class into subclasses. That is, different decompositions of H can lead to different outcomes. To avoid this issue, the previous ideas need to be extended to a more general training criterion

penalizing individual hypotheses

that uses unlabeled data to decide how to penalize *individual* hypotheses in the global space H. The main contribution of this section is a simple, generic training objective that can be applied to a wide variety of supervised learning problems.

As before, assume a sizable collection of unlabeled data that can now be used to globally penalize complex hypotheses. Specifically, an alternative training criterion can be formulated that measures the behavior of individual hypotheses on both the labeled and unlabeled data. The intuition behind this criterion is simple— instead of minimizing empirical training error alone, also seek hypotheses that behave *similarly* both on and off the labeled training data. This objective arises from the observation that a hypothesis which fits the training data well but behaves erratically off the labeled training set is not likely to generalize to unseen examples.

origin hypothesis

To detect such behavior one can measure the distances of a hypothesis from a fixed simple "origin" function ϕ on both data sets. If a hypothesis is behaving erratically off the labeled training set, then it is likely that these two distances will disagree. This effect is demonstrated in figure 23.5 for two large-degree polynomials that both fit the labeled training data well but differ dramatically in their true error and their differences between distances, both on and off the training set, to the origin function. Trivial origin functions are used throughout this section—such as the zero function, $\phi = 0$, or the constant function at the mean of the y labels, $\phi = \bar{y}$. In practice, these work quite well.

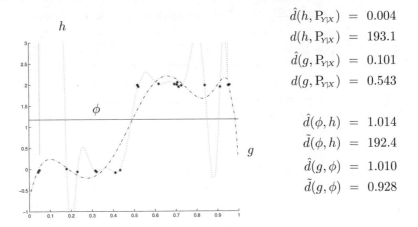

$$\hat{d}(h, \mathrm{P}_{Y|X}) = 0.004$$
$$d(h, \mathrm{P}_{Y|X}) = 193.1$$
$$\hat{d}(g, \mathrm{P}_{Y|X}) = 0.101$$
$$d(g, \mathrm{P}_{Y|X}) = 0.543$$

$$\hat{d}(\phi, h) = 1.014$$
$$\tilde{d}(\phi, h) = 192.4$$
$$\hat{d}(g, \phi) = 1.010$$
$$\tilde{d}(g, \phi) = 0.928$$

Figure 23.5 Two nineteenth-degree polynomials h and g that fit 20 given training points. Here h approximately minimizes $\hat{d}(h, \mathrm{P}_{Y|X})$, whereas g optimizes an alternative training criterion defined in (23.10). This plot demonstrates how the labeled training data estimate $\hat{d}(g, \mathrm{P}_{Y|X})$ for the smoother polynomial g is much closer to its true distance $d(g, \mathrm{P}_{Y|X})$. However, for both functions the proximity of the estimated errors $\hat{d}(\cdot, \mathrm{P}_{Y|X})$ to the true errors $d(\cdot, \mathrm{P}_{Y|X})$ appears to be reflected on the relative proximity of the estimated distances $\hat{d}(\cdot, \phi)$ to the unlabeled distances $\tilde{d}(\cdot, \phi)$ to the simple constant origin function ϕ.

To formulate a concrete training objective first requires the following tentative measures:

- empirical training error plus an additive penalty

$$\hat{d}(h, \mathrm{P}_{Y|X}) + \tilde{d}(\phi, h) - \hat{d}(\phi, h) \tag{23.9}$$

- empirical error times a multiplicative penalty

$$\hat{d}(h, \mathrm{P}_{Y|X}) \times \frac{\tilde{d}(\phi, h)}{\hat{d}(\phi, h)} \tag{23.10}$$

In each case, the behavior of a candidate hypothesis h is compared to the fixed origin ϕ. Thus, both cases will minimize empirical training error $\hat{d}(h, \mathrm{P}_{Y|X})$ plus (or times) a penalty that measures the discrepancy between the distance to the origin on the labeled training data and the distance to the origin on unlabeled data.

The regularization effect of these criteria is illustrated in figure 23.5. Somewhat surprisingly, the *multiplicative* objective (Eq. 23.10) generally performs much better than the *additive* objective (Eq. 23.9), as it more harshly penalizes discrepancies between on and off training set behavior. Consequently, this is the form adopted from now on.

Although these training criteria might appear ad hoc, they are not entirely unprincipled. One useful property they have is that if the origin function ϕ happens to be equal to the target conditional $P_{Y|X}$, then minimizing Eq. 23.9 or Eq. 23.10 becomes equivalent to minimizing the true prediction error $d(h, P_{Y|X})$. However, it turns out that these training objectives have the inherent drawback that they subtly bias the final hypotheses toward the origin function ϕ. That is, both Eq. 23.9 and Eq. 23.10 allow minima that have "artificially" large origin distances on the labeled data, $\hat{d}(\phi, h)$, and simultaneously small distances on unlabeled data, $\tilde{d}(\phi, h)$. This is illustrated in figure 23.5 for a hypothesis function g that minimizes Eq. 23.10 but is clearly attracted to the origin, ϕ, at the right end of the domain (off of the labeled training data).

Nevertheless, there is an intuitive way to counter this difficulty. To avoid the bias toward ϕ, one can use *symmetric* forms of the previous criteria that also penalize hypotheses that are unnaturally *close* to the origin off of the labeled data. That is, one could consider a symmetric form of the additive penalty (Eq. 23.9)

$$\hat{d}(h, P_{Y|X}) + \left| \tilde{d}(\phi, h) - \hat{d}(\phi, h) \right|, \tag{23.11}$$

as well as a symmetrized form of the multiplicative penalty (Eq. 23.10),

$$\hat{d}(h, P_{Y|X}) \times \max \left(\frac{\tilde{d}(\phi, h)}{\hat{d}(\phi, h)}, \frac{\hat{d}(\phi, h)}{\tilde{d}(\phi, h)} \right). \tag{23.12}$$

These penalties work in both directions: hypotheses that are much further from the origin on the training data than off are penalized, but so are hypotheses that are significantly *closer* to the origin on the training data than off. The rationale behind this symmetric criterion is that both types of erratic behavior indicate that the observed training error is likely to be an unrepresentative reflection of the true error of the hypothesis. The value of this intuition is demonstrated in figure 23.6, where the hypothesis f that minimizes the new symmetric criterion (Eq. 23.12) is not drawn toward the origin inappropriately, and thereby achieves a smaller true prediction error than the hypothesis g that minimizes Eq. 23.10. More technical justifications for this criterion are offered in (Schuurmans and Southey, 2002).

The final outcome is a new regularization procedure that uses the training objective from Eq. 23.12 to penalize hypotheses based on the given training data and the unlabeled data. In effect, the resulting procedure uses the unlabeled data to automatically set the level of regularization for a given problem. This procedure has an additional advantage—since the penalization factor in Eq. 23.12 also depends on the specific labeled training set under consideration, the resulting procedure regularizes in a data-dependent fashion. That is, the procedure adapts

symmetric
penalty

data-dependent
regularization

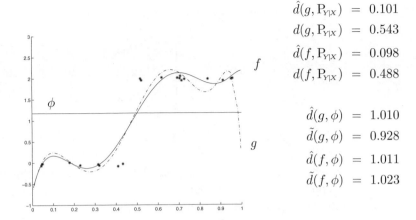

$$\hat{d}(g, \mathrm{P}_{Y|X}) = 0.101$$
$$d(g, \mathrm{P}_{Y|X}) = 0.543$$
$$\hat{d}(f, \mathrm{P}_{Y|X}) = 0.098$$
$$d(f, \mathrm{P}_{Y|X}) = 0.488$$

$$\hat{d}(g, \phi) = 1.010$$
$$\tilde{d}(g, \phi) = 0.928$$
$$\hat{d}(f, \phi) = 1.011$$
$$\tilde{d}(f, \phi) = 1.023$$

Figure 23.6 A comparison of the asymmetric and symmetrized training objectives. Here g is the nineteenth-degree polynomial which minimizes the original asymmetric criterion (23.10) on 20 data points, whereas f minimizes the symmetrized criterion (23.12). This plot shows how g is inappropriately drawn toward the origin ϕ near the right end of the interval, whereas f behaves neutrally with respect to ϕ.

the penalization to a particular set of observed data. This raises the possibility of outperforming any regularization scheme that keeps a fixed penalization level across different training samples drawn from the same problem. In fact, such an improvement can be achieved in realistic hypothesis classes on real data sets—as shown in the next section.

nonconvex optimization

One drawback with the minimization objective in Eq. 23.12 is that it is not convex and therefore local minima likely exist. Typically one has to devise reasonable initialization and restart procedures to effectively minimize such an objective. Here we simply started the optimizer from the best-fit polynomial of each degree, or in the case of radial basis function (RBF) regularization (below), we started from a single initialization point. Once initialized, a standard optimization routine (Matlab 5.3 "fminunc") was used to determine coefficients that minimized Eqs. 23.11 and 23.12. Although the nondifferentiability of Equation 23.12 creates difficulty for the optimizer, it does not prevent reasonable results from being achieved. Therefore, we did not find it necessary to smooth the objective with a softmax, although this is a reasonable idea. Another potential problem could arise if h gets close to the origin ϕ. However, since simple origins were chosen that were never near $\mathrm{P}_{Y|X}$, h was not drawn near ϕ in these experiments and thus the resultant numerical instability did not arise.

23.4.1 Example: Polynomial Regression

The first supervised learning task considered is the polynomial regression problem from section 23.3.2. The regularizer introduced above (Eq. 23.12) turns out to perform very well in such problems. In this case, our training objective can be expressed as choosing a hypothesis to minimize

$$\sum_{i=1}^{l}(h(\mathbf{x}_i)-\mathbf{y}_i)^2/l \quad \times \quad \max\left(\frac{\sum_{j=l+1}^{n}(h(\mathbf{x}_j)-\phi(\mathbf{x}_j))^2/u}{\sum_{i=1}^{l}(h(\mathbf{x}_i)-\phi(\mathbf{x}_i))^2/l}, \frac{\sum_{i=1}^{l}(h(\mathbf{x}_i)-\phi(\mathbf{x}_i))^2/l}{\sum_{j=l+1}^{n}(h(\mathbf{x}_j)-\phi(\mathbf{x}_j))^2/u}\right),$$

where $\{\langle\mathbf{x}_i,\mathbf{y}_i\rangle\}_{i=1}^{l}$ is the set of labeled training data, $\{\langle\mathbf{x}_j\rangle\}_{j=l+1}^{n}$ is the set of unlabeled examples, and ϕ is a fixed origin function (usually set to the constant function at the mean of the $\mathbf{y}$ labels). Note again that this training objective seeks hypotheses that fit the labeled training data well while simultaneously behaving similarly on labeled and unlabeled data.

To test the basic effectiveness of this approach, the experiments of section 23.3.2 were repeated. The first class of methods compared against were the same *model selection* methods considered before: tenfold cross-validation CVT, structural risk minimization SRM (Cherkassky et al., 1997), RIC (Foster and George, 1994); SMS (Shibata, 1981), GCV (Craven and Wahba, 1979), BIC (Schwarz, 1978), AIC (Akaike, 1974), CP (Mallows, 1973), FPE (Akaike, 1970), and the metric-based model selection strategy, ADJ, introduced in section 23.3.3. However, since none of the classical model selection methods performed competitively in these experiments, they are not reported here (see Schuurmans and Southey (2002) for more complete results). Instead, for comparison, results are reported for the optimal model selector, OPT*, which makes an oracle choice of the best available hypothesis in any given model selection sequence based on the test data. In these experiments, the model selection methods considered polynomials of degree 0 to $l-2$.[5]

Table 23.7 Fitting $f(x) = \text{step}(x \geq 0.5)$ with $P_X = U(0,1)$ and $\sigma = 0.05$. Absolute test errors (true distances) achieved. Results of 1000 repeated trials. This repeats the conditions of table 23.1.

		mean	median	stdev
ADA (23.12)	$\phi = \text{mean } y$	0.391	0.366	0.113
asymmetric (23.10)		0.403	0.378	0.111
REG	$\lambda = 1.0$	0.483	0.468	0.048
REG*		0.371	0.355	0.049
model sel	OPT*	0.387	0.374	0.076
	ADJ	0.458	0.466	0.112

---

5. Note that the degree is restricted to be less than $l-1$ to prevent the maximum degree polynomials from achieving zero training error which, as discussed in section 23.3, destroys the regularization effect of the multiplicative penalty.

Table 23.8   Fitting $f(x) = \sin(1/x)$ with $P_X = U(0,1)$ and $\sigma = 0.05$. Absolute test errors (true distances) achieved. Results of 1000 repeated trials. This repeats the conditions of table 23.2.

		mean	median	stdev
ADA (23.12)	$\phi = \text{mean } y$	0.444	0.425	0.085
asymmetric (23.10)		0.466	0.439	0.102
REG	$\lambda = 1.0$	0.484	0.473	0.040
REG*		0.429	0.424	0.041
model sel	OPT*	0.433	0.427	0.049
	ADJ	0.712	0.504	0.752

Table 23.9   Fitting $f(x) = \sin^2(2\pi x)$ with $P_X = U(0,1)$ and $\sigma = 0.05$. Absolute test errors (true distances) achieved. Results of 1000 repeated trials. This repeats the conditions of table 23.3.

		mean	median	stdev
ADA (23.12)	$\phi = \text{mean } y$	0.107	0.081	0.066
asymmetric (23.10)		0.111	0.087	0.060
REG	$\lambda = 5.0$	0.353	0.341	0.040
REG*		0.140	0.092	0.099
model sel	OPT*	0.122	0.085	0.086
	ADJ	0.188	0.114	0.150

The second class of methods compared against were *regularization* methods that consider polynomials of maximum degree $l - 2$ but penalize individual polynomials based on the size of their coefficients or their smoothness properties. The specific methods considered were a standard form of "ridge" penalization (or weight decay) which places a penalty $\lambda \sum_k a_k^2$ on polynomial coefficients a_k (Cherkassky and Mulier, 1998), and Bayesian *maximum a posteriori* inference with zero-mean Gaussian priors on polynomial coefficients a_k with diagonal covariance matrix λI (MacKay, 1992). Both of these methods require a regularization parameter λ to be set by hand. These methods are referred to as REG and MAP respectively.

To test the ability of the new regularization technique to automatically set the regularization level, a range of (fourteen) regularization parameters λ were tried for the fixed regularization methods REG and MAP, showing the single best value of λ obtained on the test data. For comparison purposes, the results of the oracle regularizer, REG*, is also reported. This oracle selects the best λ value for *each* training set based on examining the test data (MAP* gives similar results here (Schuurmans and Southey, 2002)). The experiments were conducted by repeating the conditions of section 23.3.2. Specifically, table 23.7 repeats table 23.1 (fitting a step function), table 23.8 repeats table 23.2 (fitting

Table 23.10   Fitting a fifth-degree polynomial with $P_X = U(0, 1)$ and $\sigma = 0.05$. Absolute test errors (true distances) achieved. Results of 1000 repeated trials. This repeats the conditions of table 23.4.

		mean	median	stdev
ADA (23.12)	$\phi = $ mean y	0.077	0.060	0.090
asymmetric (23.10)		0.110	0.074	0.088
REG	$\lambda = 10^{-1}$	0.454	0.337	0.508
REG*		0.147	0.082	0.121
model sel	OPT*	0.071	0.060	0.071
	ADJ	0.116	0.062	0.188

$\sin(1/x)$), table 23.9 repeats table 23.3 (fitting $\sin^2(2\pi x)$), and table 23.10 repeats table 23.4 (fitting a fifth-degree polynomial). The regularization criterion based on minimizing Eq. 23.12 is listed as ADA in our figures (for "adaptive" regularization). Additionally, the asymmetric version of ADA (23.10) was tested to verify the benefits of the symmetrized criterion (23.12).

The results are positive. The new adaptive regularization scheme ADA performed the best among all procedures in these experiments. Tables 23.7 through 23.10 show that it outperformed the fixed regularization strategy REG for the best fixed choice of regularization parameter (λ), even though the optimal choice varies across problems. This demonstrates that ADA is able to effectively tune its penalization behavior to the problem at hand. Moreover, since it outperforms even the best choice of λ for each data set, ADA also demonstrates the ability to adapt its penalization behavior to a specific training set, not just a given problem. In fact, ADA is competitive with the oracle regularizer REG* in these experiments, and even sometimes outperformed the oracle model selection strategy OPT*. The results also show that the asymmetric version of ADA based on (23.10) is inferior to the symmetrized version in these experiments, confirming our prior expectations.

23.4.2   Example: Radial Basis Function Regression

To test the approach on a more realistic task, the problem of regularizing radial basis function (RBF) networks for regression was considered. RBF networks are a natural generalization of interpolation and spline-fitting techniques. Given a set of prototype centers $c_1, ..., c_k$, an RBF representation of a prediction function h is given by

$$h(\mathbf{x}) \;=\; \sum_{i=1}^{k} w_i \, g\left(\frac{\|\mathbf{x} - c_i\|}{\sigma}\right), \tag{23.13}$$

where $\|\mathbf{x} - c_i\|$ is the Euclidean distance between $\mathbf{x}$ and center c_i and g is a response function with width parameter σ. In this experiment a standard local Gaussian basis function, $g(z) = e^{-z^2/\sigma^2}$, was used.

RBF networks

Fitting with RBF networks is straightforward. The simplest approach is to place a prototype center on each training example and then determine the weight vector, $\mathbf{w}$, that allows the network to fit the training labels. The best-fit weight vector can be obtained by solving for $\mathbf{w}$ in

$$
\begin{bmatrix} g\left(\frac{\|\mathbf{x_1}-\mathbf{x_1}\|}{\sigma}\right) & \cdots & g\left(\frac{\|\mathbf{x_1}-\mathbf{x_l}\|}{\sigma}\right) \\ \vdots & & \vdots \\ g\left(\frac{\|\mathbf{x_l}-\mathbf{x_l}\|}{\sigma}\right) & \cdots & g\left(\frac{\|\mathbf{x_l}-\mathbf{x_l}\|}{\sigma}\right) \end{bmatrix} \begin{bmatrix} w_1 \\ \vdots \\ w_l \end{bmatrix} = \begin{bmatrix} y_1 \\ \vdots \\ y_l \end{bmatrix}.
$$

The solution is guaranteed to exist and be unique for distinct training points and most natural basis functions, including the Gaussian basis used here (Bishop, 1995).

regularized RBF
networks

Although exactly fitting data with RBF networks is natural, it has the problem of generally overfitting the training data in the process of replicating the $\mathbf{y}$ labels. Many approaches therefore exist for regularizing RBF networks. However, these techniques are often hard to apply because they involve setting various free parameters or controlling complex methods for choosing prototype centers, etc. (Cherkassky and Mulier, 1998; Bishop, 1995). The simplest regularization approach is to add a ridge penalty to the weight vector, and minimize

$$
\sum_{i=1}^{l} (h(\mathbf{x}_i) - \mathbf{y}_i)^2 + \lambda \sum_{i=1}^{l} w_i^2, \tag{23.14}
$$

where h is given as in Eq. 23.13 (Cherkassky and Mulier, 1998). An alternative approach is to add a nonparametric penalty on curvature (Poggio and Girosi, 1990), but the resulting procedure is similar. To apply these methods in practice one has to make an intelligent choice of the width parameter σ and the regularization parameter λ. Unfortunately, these choices interact and it is often hard to set them by hand without visualization and experimentation with the data set.

This section investigates how effectively the ADA regularizer is able to automatically select the width parameter σ and regularization parameter λ in an RBF network on real regression problems. Here the basic idea is to use unlabeled data to make these choices automatically and adaptively. ADA (Eq. 23.12) is compared to a large number of ridge regularization procedures, each corresponding to the penalty in Equation 23.14 with different fixed choices of σ and λ—thirty-five in total. To apply ADA in this case a standard optimizer was run over the parameter space (σ, λ) while explicitly solving for the $\mathbf{w}$ vector that minimized Eq. 23.14 for each choice of σ and λ (this involved solving a linear system (Cherkassky and Mulier, 1998; Bishop, 1995)). Thus, given σ, λ, and $\mathbf{w}$ Eq. 23.12 could be calculated and the result supplied to the optimizer as the objective to be minimized.

A number of regression problems from the StatLib and UCI machine learning

Table 23.11   RBF results showing mean test errors (distances) on the AAUP data set (1074 instances on 12 independent attributes). Results are averaged over 100 splits of the data set.

ADA (23.12)	0.0197 ± 0.004		REG*	0.0329 ± 0.009	
REG	λ=0.0	0.1	0.25	0.5	1.0
$\sigma=$ 0.0005	0.0363	0.0447	0.0482	0.0515	0.0554
0.001	0.0353	0.0435	0.0475	0.0512	0.0554
0.0025	*0.0350*	0.0425	0.0473	0.0514	0.0555
0.005	0.0359	0.0423	0.0475	0.0516	0.0554
0.0075	0.0368	0.0424	0.0478	0.0517	0.0553

Table 23.12   RBF results showing mean test errors (distances) on the ABALONE data set (1000 instances on 8 independent attributes). Results are averaged over 100 splits of the data set.

ADA (23.12)	0.034 ± 0.0046		REG*	0.049 ± 0.0063	
REG	λ=0.0	0.1	0.25	0.5	1.0
$\sigma=$ 4	0.4402	0.04954	0.04982	0.05008	0.05061
6	0.3765	0.04952	0.04979	0.05007	0.05063
8	0.3671	*0.04951*	0.04979	0.05007	0.05069
10	0.3474	0.04952	0.04979	0.05007	0.05073
12	0.3253	0.04953	0.04979	0.05008	0.05079

repositories were investigated.[6] In the experiments, a given data set was randomly split into training (1/10), unlabeled (7/10), and test (2/10) sets. Each of the methods was then run on this split—this process being repeated 100 times for each data set to obtain results. Tables 23.11 through 23.14 show that ADA regularization was able to choose width and regularization parameters that achieved effective generalization performance across a range of data sets. The loss for ADA and REG* are given at the top of each table and the loss for each fixed parameter setting is given below. The best such setting is italicized. Furthermore, all settings that outperform ADA are shown in bold. Therefore, tables showing few bold entries indicate that ADA is outperforming most fixed regularizers.

On these data sets, ADA performs better than any fixed regularizer on every problem (except BODYFAT). This shows that the adaptive criterion is not only effective at choosing good regularization parameters for a given problem but can choose them adaptively based on the specific sample of training data given, yielding improvements over fixed regularizers.

---

6. The URLs are `lib.stat.cmu.edu` and `www.ics.uci.edu/~mlearn/MLRepository. html`.

Table 23.13   RBF results showing mean test errors (distances) on the BODYFAT data set (252 instances on 14 independent attributes). Results are averaged over 100 splits of the data set.

ADA (23.12) 0.131 ± 0.0171 | REG* 0.125 ± 0.0151

REG	λ=0.0	0.1	0.25	0.5	1.0
$\sigma=$ 0.1	0.1658	**0.1299**	0.1325	0.1341	0.1354
0.5	0.1749	**0.1294**	0.1321	0.1337	0.1352
1	0.1792	*0.1294*	0.1321	0.1336	0.1353
2	0.1837	**0.1296**	0.1322	0.1337	0.1356
4	0.1883	**0.1299**	0.1323	0.1339	0.1362

Table 23.14   RBF results showing mean test errors (distances) on the BOSTON-C data set (506 instances on 12 independent attributes). Results are averaged over 100 splits of the data set.

ADA (23.12) 0.150 ± 0.0212 | REG* 0.151 ± 0.0197

REG	λ=0.0	0.1	0.25	0.5	1.0
$\sigma=$ 0.075	0.1619	0.15785	0.1614	0.1645	0.1679
0.1	0.1624	0.15779	0.1614	0.1645	0.1679
0.15	0.1633	*0.15776*	0.1615	0.1646	0.1680
0.2	0.1642	0.15777	0.1615	0.1647	0.1682
0.25	0.1649	0.15780	0.1616	0.1648	0.1683

23.5   Classification

The regularization approach developed in this chapter can also be applied to classification problems. For classification, the label set Y is usually a small discrete set and prediction error is typically measured by the misclassification loss, $err(\hat{y}, y) = 1_{(\hat{y} \neq y)}$. With this loss function, distances are measured by the disagreement probability $d(f, g) = P_x(f(\mathbf{x}) \neq g(\mathbf{x}))$ (Ben-David et al., 1995). Using this metric, the generic regularization objective from Eq. 23.12 can be directly applied to classification problems. As it turns out, a direct application of our approach to this case gives poor results (Schuurmans and Southey, 2002). An intuitive explanation for this weakness is that classification functions are essentially histogram-like (i.e., piecewise constant), and this tends to limit the ability of unlabeled data to detect erratic behavior off the labeled training sample. A recent generalization analysis by Kääriäinen and Langford (Kääriäinen, 2005; Kääriäinen and Langford, 2005) suggests that effective model selection strategies might be achieved by using tight generalization bounds derived from unlabeled data as a complexity penalizer. This idea has yet to be investigated in detail, however. Rather than pursue modified techniques for classification here, we instead consider a straightforward regression-based approach for the remainder of this chapter.

A natural alternative to misclassification loss exists for the subset of classification methods that return a distribution over class labels instead of a single class label. With these methods, Kullback-Leibler (KL) divergence (Cover and Thomas, 1991) can be used instead of distance metrics to compare hypothesis functions with the origin function ϕ.[7] With such a distance, penalized training objectives[8] can be derived similar to Eqs. 23.11 and 23.12, the terms of which are

$$\tilde{d}(\phi\|h) = \frac{1}{u} \sum_{i=l+1}^{n} \phi(\mathbf{x}_i) \log \frac{\phi(\mathbf{x}_i)}{h(\mathbf{x}_i)} + (1 - \phi(\mathbf{x}_i)) \log \frac{1 - \phi(\mathbf{x}_i)}{1 - h(\mathbf{x}_i)}, \tag{23.15}$$

$$\hat{d}(\phi\|h) = \frac{1}{l} \sum_{i=1}^{l} \phi(\mathbf{x}_i) \log \frac{\phi(\mathbf{x}_i)}{h(\mathbf{x}_i)} + (1 - \phi(\mathbf{x}_i)) \log \frac{1 - \phi(\mathbf{x}_i)}{1 - h(\mathbf{x}_i)}, \tag{23.16}$$

$$\hat{d}(\mathrm{P}_{Y|X}\|h) = \frac{1}{l} \sum_{i=1}^{l} -\mathbf{y}_i \log h(\mathbf{x}_i) - (1 - \mathbf{y}_i) \log(1 - h(\mathbf{x}_i)). \tag{23.17}$$

Experiments were run on three classifiers that return class-membership probabilities. The ADA penalization strategy was tested on logistic regression (LR) (Hastie et al., 2001), kernel logistic regression (KLR) (Hastie and Tibshirani, 1990), and a neural network (NN) (Hastie et al., 2001). Experiments were run on the two data sets used throughout this book and on a set of UCI data sets. The LR prediction function h is

$$h(\mathbf{x}) = \frac{1}{1 + e^{-\mathbf{w}^T \mathbf{x}}} \ . \tag{23.18}$$

The prediction functions for KLR and neural networks are closely related in the experiments presented here. KLR simply kernalizes Eq. 23.18. For the neural network used here, the activation function in the first layer is $tanh()$, and the output layer uses the logistic function in Eq. 23.18. The ADA-penalized objectives for all three are therefore very similar.

In all cases, gradient descent was used to optimize the ADA objective. We compare against regularized versions of LR, using the penalty term $\lambda\mathbf{w}^T\mathbf{w}$, $0 \leq \lambda$. All experiments were repeated ten times, and the average log-loss test error reported. Ten labeled training points and 100 unlabeled points were used during training, and the remaining points were used for testing.

The results for LR on most of the book data sets (cf. chapter 21) are shown in table 23.15 for a variety of λ settings. (A binary version of COIL, called $\mathtt{COIL}_{0,1}$, was used; SecStr and Text were omitted due to excessive size and dimensionality,

---

7. Note that KL divergence is not a proper distance metric but it is frequently used in such contexts.
8. For the sake of simplicity, only binary classification is considered.

respectively.) The results show that ADA-penalized LR is competitive on `Digit1`, and beats the best fixed regularizer on the other sets. Results on six UCI data sets (AUSTRALIAN, CRX, DIABETES, FLARE, GERMAN, and PIMA) are shown in table 23.16. Again, results are competitive, coming close to the best fixed regularizer in most cases and surpassing it on two data sets.

Table 23.15 Logistic regression (LR) results for six book data sets showing mean testing error (log-loss) for ADA and regularized LR with various settings of λ.

	Digit1	USPS	$COIL_{0,1}$	BCI	g241c	g241d
ADA	0.653	0.379	0.687	0.325	0.042	0.188
$\lambda = 0$	*0.570*	1.006	18.89	2.788	0.982	1.042
0.1	**0.502**	0.621	4.765	1.607	0.692	0.734
0.5	**0.537**	0.524	4.142	1.254	0.667	0.696
1.0	**0.568**	0.494	3.878	1.120	0.660	0.684
2.0	**0.606**	0.472	3.617	1.001	0.655	0.675
5.0	0.655	*0.459*	3.278	0.874	*0.653*	0.667
10.0	0.682	0.460	*3.026*	*0.804*	0.654	*0.664*

Table 23.16 Logistic regression (LR) results for six UCI data sets showing mean testing error for ADA and regularized LR with various settings of λ.

	AUST.	CRX	DIAB.	FLARE	GERM.	PIMA
ADA	0.697	0.716	0.703	0.541	0.697	0.683
$\lambda = 0$	1.240	1.176	1.282	1.741	0.710	1.442
0.1	0.927	0.797	0.785	0.833	0.715	0.881
0.5	0.814	0.707	0.733	0.618	0.715	0.773
1.0	0.773	0.689	0.716	0.572	0.713	0.739
2.0	0.742	0.679	0.703	0.546	0.710	0.715
5.0	0.715	*0.676*	0.694	0.533	0.703	0.697
10.0	*0.704*	0.678	*0.691*	*0.531*	*0.697*	*0.692*

Similar experiments were run on kernel logistic regression using a Gaussian kernel and a variety of settings for the standard deviation, σ. Results are shown in table 23.17 for the book data sets [9] and in table 23.18 for the UCI data. Like the earlier regression results, the best fixed parameter setting is italicized and all settings that outperform ADA are shown in bold.

On the book data, the results are excellent, beating the oracle regularizer on all but `Digit1` and coming very close even there. On the UCI data, the results are more mixed but still quite positive. While the oracle is not surpassed on any data set, ADA is still better than many fixed regularizers.

Table 23.17 Kernel logistic regression (KLR) results for six book data sets showing mean testing error for ADA and regularized KLR with various settings of λ and σ.

	Digit1				ADA 0.518		USPS				ADA 0.456
$\sigma =$	0.1	0.5	1	5	10	$\sigma =$	0.1	0.5	1	5	10
$\lambda = 0$	0.693	0.691	0.572	*0.569*	0.701	$\lambda = 0$	0.693	0.693	0.691	0.478	0.480
0.1	0.693	0.692	0.636	0.690	0.723	0.1	0.693	0.693	0.692	***0.444***	0.477
0.5	0.693	0.693	0.667	0.716	0.725	0.5	0.693	0.693	0.693	0.481	0.498
1.0	0.693	0.693	0.677	0.718	0.724	1.0	0.693	0.693	0.693	0.503	0.504
2.0	0.693	0.693	0.684	0.717	0.721	2.0	0.693	0.693	0.693	0.531	0.511
5.0	0.693	0.693	0.689	0.712	0.715	5.0	0.693	0.693	0.693	0.578	0.526
10.0	0.693	0.693	0.691	0.706	0.709	10.0	0.693	0.693	0.693	0.615	0.549

	$COIL_{0,1}$				ADA 0.685		BCI				ADA 0.580
$\sigma =$	0.1	0.5	1	5	10	$\sigma =$	0.1	0.5	1	5	10
$\lambda = 0$	*0.693*	*0.693*	*0.693*	*0.693*	*0.693*	$\lambda = 0$	*0.693*	*0.693*	*0.693*	0.811	1.045
0.1	*0.693*	*0.693*	*0.693*	*0.693*	*0.693*	0.1	*0.693*	*0.693*	*0.693*	0.710	0.769
0.5	*0.693*	*0.693*	*0.693*	*0.693*	*0.693*	0.5	*0.693*	*0.693*	*0.693*	0.697	0.731
1.0	*0.693*	*0.693*	*0.693*	*0.693*	*0.693*	1.0	*0.693*	*0.693*	*0.693*	0.695	0.721
2.0	*0.693*	*0.693*	*0.693*	*0.693*	*0.693*	2.0	*0.693*	*0.693*	*0.693*	0.694	0.713
5.0	*0.693*	*0.693*	*0.693*	*0.693*	*0.693*	5.0	*0.693*	*0.693*	*0.693*	*0.693*	0.704
10.0	*0.693*	*0.693*	*0.693*	*0.693*	*0.693*	10.0	*0.693*	*0.693*	*0.693*	*0.693*	0.698

	g241c				ADA 0.513		g241d				ADA 0.514
$\sigma =$	0.1	0.5	1	5	10	$\sigma =$	0.1	0.5	1	5	10
$\lambda = 0$	*0.693*	*0.693*	*0.693*	*0.693*	0.754	$\lambda = 0$	*0.693*	*0.693*	*0.693*	*0.693*	0.736
0.1	*0.693*	*0.693*	*0.693*	*0.693*	0.701	0.1	*0.693*	*0.693*	*0.693*	*0.693*	0.697
0.5	*0.693*	*0.693*	*0.693*	*0.693*	0.695	0.5	*0.693*	*0.693*	*0.693*	*0.693*	*0.693*
1.0	*0.693*	*0.693*	*0.693*	*0.693*	0.694	1.0	*0.693*	*0.693*	*0.693*	*0.693*	*0.693*
2.0	*0.693*	*0.693*	*0.693*	*0.693*	*0.693*	2.0	*0.693*	*0.693*	*0.693*	*0.693*	*0.693*
5.0	*0.693*	*0.693*	*0.693*	*0.693*	*0.693*	5.0	*0.693*	*0.693*	*0.693*	*0.693*	*0.693*
10.0	*0.693*	*0.693*	*0.693*	*0.693*	*0.693*	10.0	*0.693*	*0.693*	*0.693*	*0.693*	*0.693*

Finally, we present results on three unregularized neural networks, with three, five, and ten hidden units respectively. Results for the book data are shown in table 23.19 and for the UCI data in table 23.20. The results against unregularized

---

9. We presume the similar scores achieved by so many of the fixed regularizes on the book data are due to some regularity in those data.

Table 23.18 Kernel logistic regression (KLR) results for six UCI data sets showing mean testing error for ADA and regularized KLR with various settings of λ and σ.

	AUSTRALIAN					ADA 0.685		CRX					ADA 1.111
$\sigma =$	0.1	0.5	1	5	10		$\sigma =$	0.1	0.5	1	5	10
$\lambda = 0$	0.851	0.772	0.748	0.708	0.710		$\lambda = 0$	1.141	1.153	**1.033**	**0.946**	**0.851**
0.1	**0.670**	**0.681**	**0.682**	0.705	0.705		0.1	**0.770**	**0.826**	**0.826**	**0.830**	**0.787**
0.5	*0.653*	**0.671**	**0.682**	0.703	0.705		0.5	**0.703**	**0.760**	**0.779**	**0.798**	**0.779**
1.0	**0.654**	**0.671**	**0.683**	0.702	0.704		1.0	**0.689**	**0.739**	**0.762**	**0.784**	**0.772**
2.0	**0.658**	**0.673**	0.685	0.701	0.703		2.0	**0.681**	**0.721**	**0.744**	**0.767**	**0.762**
5.0	**0.667**	**0.674**	0.685	0.697	0.699		5.0	*0.679*	**0.700**	**0.720**	**0.742**	**0.742**
10.0	**0.675**	**0.677**	0.685	0.694	0.696		10.0	**0.682**	**0.690**	**0.704**	**0.723**	**0.725**

	DIABETES					ADA 0.666		FLARE					ADA 0.540
$\sigma =$	0.1	0.5	1	5	10		$\sigma =$	0.1	0.5	1	5	10
$\lambda = 0$	0.683	0.897	0.933	0.744	0.694		$\lambda = 0$	0.700	0.660	0.652	0.646	**0.473**
0.1	0.683	**0.638**	0.692	0.685	0.686		0.1	0.656	0.636	0.558	*0.465*	0.474
0.5	0.688	*0.619*	**0.658**	0.680	0.687		0.5	0.667	0.656	0.592	**0.468**	**0.481**
1.0	0.690	**0.623**	**0.649**	0.678	0.685		1.0	0.675	0.667	0.616	**0.474**	**0.483**
2.0	0.691	**0.633**	**0.645**	0.675	0.681		2.0	0.682	0.677	0.639	**0.482**	**0.485**
5.0	0.692	**0.652**	**0.645**	0.669	0.674		5.0	0.688	0.686	0.664	**0.500**	**0.494**
10.0	0.693	**0.666**	**0.652**	0.666	0.670		10.0	0.690	0.689	0.676	**0.526**	**0.511**

	GERMAN					ADA 0.804		PIMA					ADA 0.680
$\sigma =$	0.1	0.5	1	5	10		$\sigma =$	0.1	0.5	1	5	10
$\lambda = 0$	0.968	1.480	1.574	0.888	**0.720**		$\lambda = 0$	**0.678**	0.906	0.818	0.714	0.684
0.1	**0.717**	0.814	0.845	**0.680**	**0.640**		0.1	0.679	0.646	0.679	0.683	0.682
0.5	**0.683**	**0.699**	**0.716**	**0.640**	**0.633**		0.5	0.686	*0.636*	0.670	0.680	0.681
1.0	**0.682**	**0.678**	**0.683**	**0.632**	**0.633**		1.0	0.688	0.641	0.666	0.679	0.679
2.0	**0.684**	**0.669**	**0.664**	*0.628*	**0.633**		2.0	0.690	0.648	0.663	0.677	0.678
5.0	**0.688**	**0.670**	**0.657**	*0.628*	**0.634**		5.0	0.692	0.661	0.661	0.673	0.674
10.0	**0.690**	**0.676**	**0.661**	**0.632**	**0.636**		10.0	0.693	0.672	0.664	0.671	0.671

neural networks are striking, dramatically reducing the tendency to overfit, even as the model complexity increases (performance on the PIMA data set with ten hidden nodes is the only notable anomaly to be found).

Overall, these results show considerable promise for the use of ADA with probabilistic classifiers, but there are clearly improvements still to be made. Adapting the technique to work with discrete classifiers also remains a key challenge.

23.6   Conclusion

A new approach to the classical complexity-control problem has been introduced that is based on the intrinsic geometry of the function-learning task. This geometry is exploited in such a way as to be able to incorporate information from both labeled and unlabeled data in a semi-supervised learning task. Unlike the majority of such

Table 23.19 Neural network (NN) results for the book data sets (except set 6) showing mean testing error for ADA and unregularized NN with 3, 5, and 10 hidden nodes.

hidden=3	Digit1	USPS	$COIL_{0,1}$	BCI	g241c	g241d
ADA	0.756	0.579	11.282	1.162	2.120	1.108
unreg NN	84.567	51.020	22.769	154.388	122.308	160.653
hidden=5	Digit1	USPS	$COIL_{0,1}$	BCI	g241c	g241d
ADA	0.829	1.422	2.998	1.324	30.349	3.108
unreg NN	77.577	47.166	41.629	165.090	151.790	139.809
hidden=10	Digit1	USPS	$COIL_{0,1}$	BCI	g241c	g241d
ADA	1.828	9.985	2.070	0.993	4.742	1.253
unreg NN	83.693	61.913	24.233	118.572	124.658	142.555

Table 23.20 Neural network (NN) results for six UCI data sets showing mean testing error for ADA and unregularized NN with 3, 5, and 10 hidden nodes.

hidden=3	AUST.	CRX	DIAB.	FLARE	GERM.	PIMA
ADA	0.90	0.78	2.45	0.64	0.64	0.93
unreg NN	34.40	79.53	13.95	40.73	0.64	8.87
hidden=5	AUST.	CRX	DIAB.	FLARE	GERM.	PIMA
ADA	1.53	1.19	1.71	0.53	0.82	0.89
unreg NN	41.13	88.43	46.47	62.41	**0.73**	58.43
hidden=10	AUST.	CRX	DIAB.	FLARE	GERM.	PIMA
ADA	1.09	1.33	2.10	0.72	1.03	11.64
unreg NN	110.13	48.96	30.23	80.88	13.89	55.94

techniques, this approach requires no assumptions about the relationship between labeled and unlabeled data other than the key assumption that they are drawn from the same probability distribution.

These new techniques seem to outperform standard approaches in a wide range of regression problems and either outperform or are competitive with standard approaches in a range of classification problems, with only one comparatively weak instance (ADA-regularized KLR). The primary source of this advantage is that the proposed metric-based strategies are able to detect dangerous situations and avoid making catastrophic overfitting errors while still being responsive enough to adopt reasonably complex models when this is supported by the data. This is accomplished by attending to the real distances between hypotheses. Standard complexity-penalization strategies completely ignore this information. Holdout methods implicitly take some of this information into account, but do so indirectly and less effectively than the metric-based strategies introduced here. Although there is "no free lunch" in general (Schaffer, 1994) and a universal improvement cannot be claimed for every complexity-control problem (Schaffer, 1993), one should be able to exploit additional information about the task (i.e., knowledge of P_X) to obtain significant improvements across a wide range of problem types and conditions. The empirical results support this view. Furthermore, ADJ remains very competitive with newer model-selection techniques (Bengio and Chapados, 2003). Additionally, ADJ has been independently extended along three lines (Chapelle et al., 2002): (i) producing excellent results on time-series data, (ii) using estimated densities in lieu of unlabeled data, and (iii) hybridizing ADJ with cross-validation.

An important direction for future research is to develop theoretical support for these strategies—in particular, a stronger theoretical justification of the regularization methods proposed in section 23.4, an improved analysis of the model selection methods proposed in section 23.3, and investigation of how to apply the technique in section 23.5 to a more general set of classifiers . It remains open as to whether the proposed methods TRI, ADJ, and ADA are in fact the best possible ways to exploit the hypothesis distances provided by P_X. A clear direction for future research is the investigation of alternative strategies that could potentially be more effective in this regard. For example, it remains for future work to extend the multiplicative ADJ and ADA methods to cope with zero training errors. Additionally, more exploration of the effects of alternative origin functions (perhaps even ensembles of origin functions) is necessary. Finally, it would be interesting to adapt the approach to model combination methods, extending the ideas of Krogh and Vedelsby (1995) to other combination strategies, including boosting (Freund and Schapire, 1997) and bagging (Breiman, 1996).

Acknowledgments

Research was supported by the Alberta Ingenuity Centre for Machine Learning, NSERC, MITACS, and the Canada Research Chair programme.

24 Transductive Inference and Semi-Supervised Learning

Vladimir Vapnik   VAPNIK@ATT.NET

This chapter discusses the difference between transductive inference and semi-supervised learning. It argues that transductive inference captures the intrinsic properties of the mechanism for extracting additional information from the unlabeled data. It also shows an important role of transduction for creating noninductive models of inference.[1]

24.1   Problem Settings

Let us start with the formal problem setting for transductive inference and semi-supervised learning.

Transductive Inference: General Setting Given a set of ℓ training pairs,

$$(y_1, x_1), ...(y_\ell, x_\ell), \quad x_i \in \mathbb{R}^d, \ y_i \in \{-1, 1\}, \tag{24.1}$$

and a sequence of k test vectors,

$$x_{\ell+1}, ..., x_{\ell+k}, \tag{24.2}$$

find among an admissible set of binary vectors,

$$\{Y = (y_{\ell+1}, ..., y_{\ell+k})\},$$

---

1. These remarks were inspired by the discussion, What is the Difference between Transductive Inference and Semi-Supervised Learning?, that took place during a workshop close to Tübingen, Germany (May 24, 2005).

the one that classifies the test vectors with the smallest number of errors. Here we consider

$$x_1, ..., x_{\ell+k} \tag{24.3}$$

to be random i.i.d. vectors drawn according to the same (unknown) distribution $P(x)$. The classifications y of the vectors x are defined by some (unknown) conditional probability function $P(y|x)$.

Below we will call the vectors (24.3) from the training and test sets the *working set* of vectors.

Transductive Inference: Particular Setting In this setting the set of admissible vectors is defined by the admissible set of indicator functions $f(x, \alpha)$, $\alpha \in \Lambda$. In other words, every admissible vector of classification Y_* is defined as follows:

$$Y_* = (f(x_1, \alpha_*), ..., f(x_k, \alpha_*)).$$

Semi-Supervised Learning Given a set of training data (24.1) and a set of test data (24.2), find among the set of indicator functions $f(x, \alpha)$, $\alpha \in \Lambda$, the one that minimizes the risk functional

$$R(\alpha) = \int |y - f(x, \alpha)| dP(x, y). \tag{24.4}$$

Therefore, in transductive inference the goal is to classify the given u test vectors of interest while in semi-supervised learning the goal is to find the function that minimizes the functional (24.4) (the expectation of the error).

Semi-supervised learning can be seen as being related to a particular setting of transductive learning. Indeed, if one chooses the function to classify the given test data (24.2) well, why not also use it to classify new unseen data? This looks like a reasonable idea.

However from a conceptual point of view, transductive inference contains important elements of a new philosophy of inference and this is the subject of these remarks.

The transductive mode of inference was introduced in the mid-1970s. It attempts to estimate the values of an unknown function $f(x, \alpha_0)$ at particular points of interest. On the other hand, inductive inference attempts to estimate the unknown function over its entire domain of definition (Vapnik, 2006). In the late 1970s the advantage of transductive inference over inductive inference was shown on real life problems (Vapnik and Sterin, 1977).

The problem of semi-supervised learning was introduced in the mid-1990s (cf. section 1.1.3) and became popular in the early 2000s (Zhou et al., 2004).

24.2 Problem of Generalization in Inductive and Transductive Inference

The mechanism that provides the transductive mode of inference with an advantage over the inductive mode in classification of the given points of interest has been understood since the very first theorems of Vapnik-Chervonenkis (VC) theory were proved.

Suppose that our goal is to find the function that minimizes the functional (24.4). Since the probability measure in (24.4) is unknown we minimize the empirical risk functional

$$R_{emp}(\alpha) = \sum_{i=1}^{\ell} |y_i - f(x_i, \alpha)| \tag{24.5}$$

instead of the risk functional (24.4).

It was shown in (Vapnik and Chervonenkis, 1991), that the necessary and sufficient conditions for consistency (as ℓ increases) of the obtained approximations is the existence of the uniform convergence of frequencies (defined by (24.5)) to their probabilities (defined by (24.4)) over a given set of functions $f(x, \alpha), \alpha \in \Lambda$:

$$P\left\{\sup_{\alpha} |R(\alpha) - R_{emp}(\alpha)| \geq \varepsilon\right\} \longrightarrow 0, \quad \forall \varepsilon > 0. \tag{24.6}$$

In 1968 the necessary and sufficient conditions for uniform convergence (24.6) were discovered (Vapnik and Chervonenkis, 1968, 1971). They are based on the so-called capacity factors. These factors will play an important role in our discussion. We now introduce them.

24.2.1 The VC Entropy, Growth Function, and VC Dimension

Given a set of indicator functions $f(x, \alpha)$, $\alpha \in \Lambda$ and set of ℓ i.i.d. input vectors

$$x_1, ..., x_{\ell}, \tag{24.7}$$

consider the value $\Delta^{\Lambda}(x_1, ..., x_{\ell})$ that defines the number of different classifications of the set of vectors (24.7) using indicator functions from the set $f(x, \alpha)$, $\alpha \in \Lambda$. This is the number of *equivalence classes*[2] of functions on which the set of vectors (24.7) factorizes the set of functions $f(x, \alpha)$, $\alpha \in \Lambda$. The number of equivalence classes has the trivial bound

$$\Delta^{\Lambda}(x_1, ..., x_{\ell}) \leq 2^{\ell}. \tag{24.8}$$

Using the value $\Delta^{\Lambda}(x_1, ..., x_{\ell})$ we define the following three capacity concepts.

---

2. A subset of functions that classify vectors (24.7) in the same way belong to the same equivalence class (with respect to (24.7)).

1. The expectation of the number of equivalence classes,

$$\Delta_P^\Lambda(\ell) = E_{x_1,...,x_\ell} \Delta(x_1,...,x_\ell),\tag{24.9}$$

where the expectation is taken over i.i.d. data (24.7) drawn according to the distribution $P(x)$.

The function

$$H_P^\Lambda(\ell) = \ln \Delta_P^\Lambda(\ell)\tag{24.10}$$

forms the first capacity concept. It is called the (annealed) *VC entropy.*[3]

The VC entropy depends on three factors:

    (a) the set of functions $f(x,\alpha)$, $\alpha \in \Lambda$,

    (b) the number of vectors ℓ, and

    (c) the probability measure $P(x)$.

The condition

$$\lim_{\ell \longrightarrow \infty} \frac{H_P^\Lambda(\ell)}{\ell} = 0\tag{24.11}$$

forms the necessary and sufficient condition for uniform convergence (24.6) *for the fixed probability measure $P(x)$.*

2. The second capacity concept is called *the growth function.* It is defined as

$$G^\Lambda(\ell) = \max_{x_1,...,x_\ell} \Delta^\Lambda(x_i,...,x_\ell).\tag{24.12}$$

The value of the growth function depends on two factors:

a. the set of functions $f(x,\alpha)$, $\alpha \in \Lambda$, and

b. the number of observations ℓ.

The condition

$$\lim_{\ell \longrightarrow \infty} \frac{\ln G^\Lambda(\ell)}{\ell} = 0\tag{24.13}$$

forms the necessary and sufficient condition for uniform convergence that is *independent of the probability measure* (for all probability measures).

3. The third capacity concept is called *the VC dimension.*[4]

We say that a set of functions $f(x,\alpha)$, $\alpha \in \Lambda$ has VC dimension h if the largest number ℓ for which the equality

$$G^\Lambda(\ell) = 2^\ell\tag{24.14}$$

holds true is equal to h. If this equality is true for any ℓ we say that the VC

---

3. The abbreviation for Vapnik-Chervonenkis entropy.
4. The abbreviation for Vapnik-Chervonenkis dimension.

dimension equals infinity. In other words

$$h = \max_{\ell}\{\ell: \; G^\Lambda(\ell) = 2^\ell\}. \tag{24.15}$$

The VC dimension depends only on one factor: (a) the set of functions. VC dimension characterizes the diversity of this set of functions.

A finite VC dimension is the necessary and sufficient condition for uniform convergence which is independent of the probability measure.

In 1968 we proved the important bound (Vapnik and Chervonenkis, 1968)

$$\ln G^\Lambda(\ell) \le h\left(\ln\frac{\ell}{h} + 1\right). \tag{24.16}$$

This bound allows one to upper-bound the growth function with a standard function that depends on one parameter, the VC dimension.

We have therefore obtained the following relationship:

$$H_P^\Lambda(\ell) \le \ln G^\Lambda(\ell) \le h\left(\ln\frac{\ell}{h} + 1\right). \tag{24.17}$$

24.3   Structure of the VC Bounds and Transductive Inference

One of the key results of VC theory is the following bound:

$$P\left\{\sup_{\alpha} |R(\alpha) - R_{emp}(\alpha)| \ge \varepsilon\right\} \le \exp\{H_P^\Lambda(2\ell) - \varepsilon^2\ell\}. \tag{24.18}$$

One can rewrite this expression in the following form: with probability $1 - \eta$ simultaneously for all α the inequality

$$R(\alpha) \le R_{emp}(\alpha) + \sqrt{\frac{H_P^\Lambda(2\ell) - \ln\eta}{\ell}} \tag{24.19}$$

holds true. Note that this inequality depends on the distribution function $P(x)$.

Since this inequality is true simultaneously for all functions of the admissible set, the function that minimizes the right-hand side of (24.19) provides the guaranteed minimum for the expected loss (24.4).

Taking into account (24.17) one can upper-bound (24.19) using the second capacity concept, the growth function:

$$R(\alpha) \le R_{emp}(\alpha) + \sqrt{\frac{\ln G^\Lambda(2\ell) - \ln\eta}{\ell}}. \tag{24.20}$$

This bound is true for any distribution function (i.e. for the worst distribution function). However it is less accurate (for a specific case $P(x)$) than (24.19).

One can also upper-bound (24.19) and (24.20) using the third capacity concept, the VC dimension

$$R(\alpha) \leq R_{emp}(\alpha) + \sqrt{\frac{h(\ln \frac{2\ell}{h} + 1) - \ln \eta}{\ell}}. \tag{24.21}$$

The good news about this bound is that it depends on just one parameter h and not on some integer function $G^\Lambda(\ell)$. However (24.21) is less accurate than (24.20) which is less accurate than (24.19).

Transductive inference was inspired by the idea of finding better solutions using the more accurate bound (24.19) instead of the bounds (24.20) and (24.21) used in inductive inference.

24.4   The Symmetrization Lemma and Transductive Inference

Bounds (24.18) and (24.19) were obtained using the so-called symmetrization lemma.

Lemma. The following inequality holds true:

$$P\left\{\sup_\alpha |R(\alpha) - R_{emp}(\alpha)| \geq \varepsilon\right\} \leq 2P\left\{\sup_\alpha \left|R_{emp}^{(1)}(\alpha) - R_{emp}^{(2)}(\alpha)\right| > \frac{\varepsilon}{2}\right\}, \tag{24.22}$$

where

$$R_{emp}^{(1)}(\alpha) = \frac{1}{\ell} \sum_{i=1}^{\ell} |y_i - f(x_i, \alpha)| \tag{24.23}$$

and

$$R_{emp}^{(2)}(\alpha) = \frac{1}{\ell} \sum_{i=\ell+1}^{2\ell} |y_i - f(x_i, \alpha)| \tag{24.24}$$

are the empirical risk functionals constructed using two different samples.

The bound (24.18) was obtained as an upper-bound of the right-hand side of (24.22).

Therefore, from the symmetrization lemma it follows that to obtain a bound for inductive inference we first obtained a bound for transductive inference (for the right-hand side of (24.22)) and then upper-bounded that.

It should be noted that since the bound (24.18) was introduced in 1968, a lot of efforts were made to improve it. However in all attempts the key element remained the symmetrization lemma. That is, in all proofs of the bounds for uniform convergence the first (and most difficult) step was to obtain the bound for transductive inference. The trivial upper bound of this bound gives the desired result.

This means that transductive inference is a fundamental step in machine learning theory.

To get the bound (24.18) let us bound the right-hand side of (24.22). Two fundamental ideas were used to obtain this bound:

1. The following two models are equivalent: (a) one chooses two i.i.d. sets:[5]

$$x_1, ..., x_\ell, \quad \text{and} \quad x_{\ell+1}, ..., x_{2\ell};$$

(b) one chooses an i.i.d. set of size 2ℓ and then randomly splits it into two subsets of size ℓ.

2. Using model (b) one can rewrite the right-hand side of (24.22) as follows:

$$P\left\{\sup_\alpha \left|R_{emp}^{(1)}(\alpha) - R_{emp}^{(2)}(\alpha)\right| > \tfrac{\varepsilon}{2}\right\} =$$
$$E_{\{x_1,...,x_{2\ell}\}} P\left\{\sup_\alpha |R_{emp}^{(1)}(\alpha) - R_{emp}^{(2)}(\alpha)| > \tfrac{\varepsilon}{2} \mid \{x_1, ..., x_{2\ell}\}\right\}. \tag{24.25}$$

To obtain the bound we first bound the conditional probability,

$$P\left\{\sup_\alpha |R_{emp}^{(1)}(\alpha) - R_{emp}^{(2)}(\alpha)| > \tfrac{\varepsilon}{2} \mid \{x_1, ..., x_{2\ell}\}\right\} \leq$$
$$\Delta^\Lambda(x_1, ..., x_{2\ell}) \exp\left\{-\varepsilon^2 \ell\right\}, \tag{24.26}$$

and then take the expectation over working sets of size 2ℓ. As a result, we obtain

$$E_{\{x_1,...,x_{2\ell}\}} P\left\{\sup_\alpha \left|R_{emp}^{(1)}(\alpha) - R_{emp}^{(2)}(\alpha)\right| > \tfrac{\varepsilon}{2}\right\} \leq$$
$$E\Delta_P^\Lambda(2\ell) \exp\left\{-\varepsilon^2 \ell\right\} = \exp\left\{H_P^\Lambda(2\ell) - \varepsilon^2 \ell\right\}. \tag{24.27}$$

This bound depends on the probability measure $P(x)$ (it contains the term $H_P^\Lambda(2\ell)$). To obtain a bound which is independent of the probability measure we upper-bound $H_P^\Lambda(2\ell)$ by $G^\Lambda(2\ell)$ (see (24.17)). Since $G^\Lambda(2\ell)$ is independent of the probability measure we obtain the bound

$$P\left\{\sup_\alpha |R(\alpha) - R_{emp}(\alpha)| \geq \varepsilon\right\} \leq G^\Lambda(2\ell) \exp\left\{-\varepsilon^2 \ell\right\} \tag{24.28}$$

on uniform convergence that is independent of the probability measure.

Therefore, from the symmetrization lemma and (24.17) we obtained the bound (24.28). Note, however, that in order to obtain this bound we twice used a rough estimate: the first time when we used the symmetrization lemma, and the second time when we used the function $G^\Lambda(2\ell)$ instead of the function $H_P^\Lambda(2\ell)$.

24.5 Bounds for Transductive Inference

The inequality (24.26) is the key element for obtaining a VC bound for transductive inference.

Indeed, this inequality is equivalent to the following one: with probability $1 - \eta$

---

5. For simplicity of the formulas we choose two sets of equal size.

simultaneously for all functions $f(x, \alpha)$, $\alpha \in \Lambda$, the inequality

$$\frac{1}{\ell} \sum_{i=\ell+1}^{2\ell} |y_i - f(x, \alpha)| \leq \sum_{i=1}^{\ell} |y_i - f(x, \alpha)| + \sqrt{\frac{\ln \Delta^\Lambda(x_1, ..., x_{2\ell}) - \ln \eta}{\ell}} \quad (24.29)$$

holds true, where probability is defined with respect to splitting the set $\{x_1, ..., x_{2\ell}\}$ into two subsets:

1. one that is used in the training set $x_1, ..., x_\ell$ and
2. one that forms the test set $x_{\ell+1}, ..., x_{2\ell}$.

Note that this concept of probability is different from the one defined for inductive inference and which requires the i.i.d. distribution of the elements $x_1, ..., x_{2\ell}$. The concepts of probability will be equivalent if an element of the working set is i.i.d. according to some unknown *fixed* probability distribution function. If it is not, then all formal claims are still correct but the concept of probability is changing. In this sense we discuss in section 24.11.1 the idea of adaptation in transductive inference.

But even in the i.i.d. case the bound for transduction is more accurate than (24.20) and (24.21) used in inductive inference. However, the main advantage of transduction over induction appears when one implements the structural risk minimization principle.

24.6   The Structural Risk Minimization Principle for Induction and Transduction

In the 1970s the structural risk minimization (SRM) principle was introduced. Its goal was to find the function that minimizes the right-hand side of inequality (24.19). In order to achieve this goal the following scheme was considered.

Prior to the appearance of the training set, the set of admissible functions is organized as a structure. The nested subsets of functions (called the elements of the structure) are specified:

$$S_1 \subset S_2 \subset ... \subset S_B \subset S = \{f : f(x, \alpha), \ \alpha \in \Lambda\}, \quad (24.30)$$

where subset S_k has a fixed capacity (say VC dimension $h = k$).

The minimization of the right-hand side of inequality (24.29) can then be performed over two terms of the inequality. One first chooses the element of the structure (controlling the second term through the value of h_k) and then the function in the chosen element of the structure (controlling the first term).

It was shown that the SRM principle is strongly uniformly consistent (Devroye et al., 1996), (Vapnik, 1998). This means that when the sample size ℓ increases, the error of the function selected by the SRM principle converges toward the best possible error. However in order to find a good solution using a finite (limited) number of training examples one has to construct a (smart) structure which reflects prior knowledge about the problem of interest. In creating such a structure transductive inference offers some additional opportunities with respect to inductive inference.

The SRM principle for transductive inference can be introduced as follows (Vapnik, 2006): *Prior to splitting the given working set $x_1, ..., x_{2\ell}$ into the two subsets that define the elements of the training and test sets, one constructs the structure on the finite number $N = \Delta^\Lambda(x_1, ..., x_{2\ell})$ of equivalence classes $F_1, ..., F_N$ that are the result of factorization of the given set of functions over the given 2ℓ vectors.*[6]

Let such a structure be

$$S_1^* \subset S_2^* \subset, ..., \subset S_B^* \subset S^* = \{F_1, ..., F_N\}, \tag{24.31}$$

where the subset S_k^* contains N_k equivalence classes of functions from $f(x, \alpha)$, $\alpha \in \Lambda$.

The opportunity to construct a "smart" structure on the elements of the equivalence classes is a key advantage of SRM for transductive inference over SRM for inductive inference.

The new development in SRM for transductive inference comes from the consideration of the different "sizes" of the equivalence classes. The idea of creating a smart structure on the set of equivalence classes due to their size remains the hierarchical Bayesian approach. In this approach one can distinguish two (several) levels of hierarchy: Suppose that we are given a priori information $P(\alpha)$ on the set of admissible functions (before the set of vectors $x_1, ..., x_{2\ell}$ appear). After these vectors appear one can calculate prior information for equivalence classes $\mu(F_1), ..., \mu(F_N)$ as an integral

$$\mu(F_k) = \int_{F_k} dP(\alpha).$$

Using this prior information one can construct a "smart" structure where the first element contains N_1 equivalence classes with the largest values $\mu(F_i), i = 1, ..., N$, the second element contains N_2 equivalence classes with the largest value $\mu(F_i)$, and so on.

Note that for transductive inference the construction of such a structure for a given working set is a prior process since we do not use both the split of our x vectors into the training and test subsets, and information about the classification of the training data.[7]

---

6. The functions that take the same values on the working set of vectors $x_1, ..., x_{2\ell}$ form one equivalence class (with respect to the working set).

7. One can unify transductive and inductive inference as follows: In both cases one is given a set of functions defined on some space. One uses the training examples from this space to define the values of the function of interest for the whole space of definition of the function. The difference is that in transductive inference the space of interest is discrete (defined on the working set (24.3)) while in inductive inference it is $\mathbb{R}^d$. One can conduct a nontrivial analysis of the discrete space but not the space $\mathbb{R}^d$. This defines the key factor of the advantage of transductive inference.

For any element S_k of the structure, simultaneously for all equivalence classes belonging to this element, with probability $1 - \eta$ the following inequality holds true:

$$\frac{1}{\ell} \sum_{i=\ell+1}^{2\ell} |y_i - F_r(x_i)| \leq \frac{1}{\ell} \sum_{i=1}^{\ell} |y_i - F_r(x_i)| + \sqrt{\frac{\ln N_k - \ln \eta}{\ell}}, \quad F_r \in S_k. \quad (24.32)$$

The probability is defined with respect to a random split of the set of vectors (24.3) into two subsets: training and test vectors.[8]

Therefore, to minimize the number of errors on the test vectors (the left-hand side of (24.32)) we have to choose the element of the structure S_k (it defines the value of the second term in the right-hand side of (24.32)) and the equivalence class belonging to this element (it defines the value of the first term in the right-hand side of (24.32)).

24.7 Combinatorics in Transductive Inference

When constructing structures on the set of equivalence classes in discrete space one can play combinatorial tricks. This is impossible when constructing a structure on the set of functions defined in the whole space.

Suppose we are given a working set of size 2ℓ which forms our discrete space. Suppose in this space we have N equivalence classes $F_1, ..., F_N$ of functions $f(x, \alpha)$, $\alpha \in \Lambda$.

Consider 2ℓ new problems described by 2ℓ discrete spaces: $S^1, ..., S^{2\ell}$, where the discrete space S^r is defined by working vectors (24.3) from which we removed the vector x_r. For each of these spaces we can construct a set of equivalence classes and a corresponding structure on this set. For each of these classes with probability $1 - \eta$ the inequality (24.32) holds true and therefore simultaneously for all $2\ell + 1$ problems the inequality (24.32) is true with probability $1 - (2\ell + 1)\eta$. Therefore with probability $1 - \eta$ simultaneously for all $2\ell + 1$ problems the inequality

$$R_1(F_i^s) \leq R_2^s(F_i^s) + \sqrt{\frac{\ln N_k^s - \ln \eta + \ln(2\ell + 1)}{\ell - 1}}, \quad F_r \in S_k \quad (24.33)$$

holds true, where the term $\ln(2\ell + 1)$ is due to our combinatorial games with one element of the working set. One can find an analogous bound for a combinatorial game with k elements of the working set.

Combinatorial games allow one to introduce a very deep geometric concept of equivalence classes (see (Vapnik, 2006, 1998) for details).

---

8. One can obtain a better bound (see (Vapnik, 1998)).

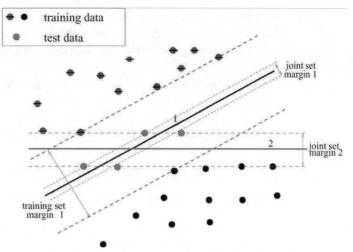

Figure 24.1   The large-margin hyperplane obtained using only the training set does not belong to the largest equivalence class defined on the working set.

24.8   Measures of the Size of Equivalence Classes

We have not yet discussed how to measure the size of equivalence classes. In this section we will discuss two possibilities. We could either

1. use a measure that reflects the VC dimension concept for the set of linear (in a feature space) indicator functions: the value of a margin for the equivalence class, or

2. measure the size of equivalence classes using the most refined capacity concept: the VC entropy.

Using the size of the margin for equivalence class.   With the appearance of support vector machines (SVMs) the important problem became the following: given a working set of vectors (24.3) construct a structure on the equivalence classes of linear functions.

Let us measure the size $\mu(F_i)$ of an equivalence class F_i by the value of the corresponding margin.[9] Any equivalence class separates working vectors (24.3) into two classes. Let us find among the functions belonging to the equivalence class one that has the largest distance (margin) to the closest vector of the set (24.3). We use this distance as the measure $\mu(F_i)$ for the size of the equivalence class F_i. This measure and how it differs from the SVM are illustrated in figure 24.1.

Using this concept of the size of an equivalence class the SVM transductive algorithms were suggested Vapnik (2006).

---

9. There is a direct connection between the value of the margin and the VC dimension defined on the set of equivalence classes (see (Vapnik, 1998, chapter 8)).

The recommendation of SRM for transductive inference would be:

To classify test vectors (24.2) choose the equivalence class (defined on the working set (24.3)) that classifies the training data well and has the largest value of the (soft) margin.

This idea is widely used in constructing transductive SVM algorithms (see chapter 6).

The universum concept: To construct a measure on the size of the equivalence class based on the most refined capacity concept, the VC entropy, the following idea was introduced in (Vapnik, 1998). Suppose that for a given working set of data (24.3) we construct additionally a new set of data,

$$x_1^*, ..., x_u^*, \quad x^* \in \mathbb{R}^d, \tag{24.34}$$

called the universum. Using the working set (24.3) we will create a set of equivalence classes of functions, and using the universum (24.34) we will evaluate the size of the equivalence classes.

The universum plays the role of prior information in Bayesian inference. It describes our knowledge of the problem we are solving. There exist, however, important differences between prior information in Bayesian inference and prior information given by the universum. In Bayesian inference, prior information is information about the relationship of the functions in the set of admissible functions to the desired one. The universum is information about a relationship between the working set and a set of possible problems. For example, for the digit recognition problem it can be some vectors whose images resemble a digit. It defines a style of digits for the recognition task.

Using the value of the VC entropy defined on the universum.   Consider now the set of equivalence classes defined by the working set (24.3). Let us measure the size $\mu(F_k)$ of the equivalence class F_r by the value $\ln \Delta^{F_r}(x_1^*, ..., x_v^*)$. This defines the logarithm of the number of different separations of the vectors from the universum (24.34) by the functions belonging to this equivalence class. This measure defines the diversity of the functions from the equivalence class. The size of the equivalence classes decreases with the index in the structure.

The recommendation of SRM for transductive inference would be:

To classify test vectors (24.2) choose the equivalence class (defined on the working set (24.3)) that classifies the training data (24.1) well and has the largest value of the VC entropy (the largest diversity) on the universum (24.34).

Using the number of contradictions on the universum.   Unfortunately it is not easy to estimate the values of the VC entropy of equivalence classes on the universum. Therefore we simplify this measure. Let us consider the vector x_i^* as one that contradicts equivalence class F_r if in class F_r there are functions that classify this vector as belonging to the first category as well as functions that classify x_i^* as belonging to the second category.

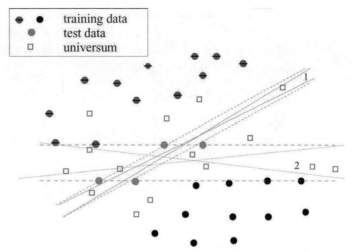

Figure 24.2 The largest number of contradictions on the universum defines the largest equivalence class.

Let us calculate the size $\mu(F_r)$ of an equivalence class F_r by the number t_r of contradictions that the universum has on this class (cf. figure 24.2).

The recommendation of SRM for such a structure would be:

To classify test vectors (24.2) choose the equivalence class (defined on the working set (24.3)) that classifies the training data (24.1) well and has the largest number of contradictions on the universum (24.34).

The idea of maximizing the number of contradictions on the universum can have the following interpretation: "When classifying the test vectors, be very specific, try to avoid extra generalizations." From a technical point of view, the number of contradictions takes into account the anisotropy of the image space, especially when input vectors are nonlinearly mapped into feature space.

24.9 Algorithms for Inductive and Transductive SVMs

One can translate the discussions of inductive and transductive methods of inference into the following SVM algorithms. In SVM algorithms one first maps input vectors x into vectors z of Hilbert space Z obtaining the images of the training data and test data:

$$(y_1, z_1), ..., (y_\ell, z_\ell), \tag{24.35}$$

$$z_{\ell+1}, ..., z_{\ell+k}, \tag{24.36}$$

and then constructs the optimal separating hyperplane in the feature (Hilbert) space.

24.9.1 SVMs for Inductive Inference

Given the images (24.35) of the training data (24.1) construct the large-margin linear decision rule (Vapnik, 1995):

$$I(x) = \theta[(w, z) + b],$$

where the vector w and threshold b are the solution of the following convex quadratic optimization problem: Minimize the functional

$$R(w) = (w, w) + C_1 \sum_{i=1}^{\ell} \theta(\xi_i), \quad C_1 \geq 0 \tag{24.37}$$

subject to the constraints

$$y_i[(z_i, w) + b] \geq 1 - \xi_i, \quad \xi_i \geq 0, \ i = 1, ..., \ell \tag{24.38}$$

(defined by the images of the training data (24.35)) where we have denoted

$$\theta(\xi_i) = \left\{ \begin{array}{ll} 1, & \text{if } \xi_i > 0 \\ 0, & \text{if } \xi_i = 0 \end{array} \right. .$$

24.9.2 SVMs for Inductive Inference Using the Universum

Given the images (24.35) of the training data (24.1), images (24.36) of the test data (24.2), and the images

$$z_1^*, ..., z_u^* \tag{24.39}$$

of universum (24.34), construct the linear decision rule

$$I(x) = \theta[(w, z) + b],$$

where the vector w and threshold b are the solution of the following convex quadratic optimization problem: Minimize the functional

$$R(w) = (w, w) + C_1 \sum_{i=1}^{\ell} \theta(\xi_i) + C_2 \sum_{s=1}^{u} \theta(\xi_s^*), \quad C_1, C_2 \geq 0 \tag{24.40}$$

subject to the constraints

$$y_i((z_i, w) + b) \geq 1 - \xi_i, \quad \xi_i \geq 0, \ i = 1, ..., \ell \tag{24.41}$$

(defined by the images of the training data (24.35)) and the constraints

$$|(z_s^*, w) + b| \leq a + \xi_s^*, \quad \xi_s^* \geq 0, \ s = 1, ..., u, \quad a \geq 0 \tag{24.42}$$

defined by the images (24.39) of the universum (24.34).

24.9.3   SVM for Large-Margin Transductive Inference

Given the images (24.35) of the training data (24.1) and the images (24.36) of the test data (24.2) construct the large-margin linear decision rule for transductive inference,

$$I(x) = \theta[(w, z) + b],$$

where the vector w and threshold b are the solution of the following optimization problem: Minimize the functional

$$R(w) = (w, w) + C_1 \sum_{i=1}^{\ell} \theta(\xi_i) + C_2 \sum_{j=\ell+1}^{\ell+k} \theta(\xi_j), \quad C_1, C_2 \geq 0 \qquad (24.43)$$

subject to the constraints

$$y_i((z_i, w) + b) \geq 1 - \xi_i, \quad \xi_i \geq 0, \ i = 1, ..., \ell \qquad (24.44)$$

(defined by the images (24.35) of the training data (24.1)) and the constraints

$$y_j^*((z_j, w) + b) \geq 1 - \xi_j, \quad \xi_j \geq 0, \ j = \ell + 1, ..., \ell + k \qquad (24.45)$$

(defined by the images (24.36) of the test data (24.2)) and its desired classifictions $y_{\ell+1}^*, ..., y_{\ell+k}^*$.

One more constraint. To avoid unbalanced solution, Capelle and Zien, following ideas of Thorsten Joachims, suggested the following constraint (Chapelle and Zien, 2005)):

$$\frac{1}{u} \sum_{j=\ell+1}^{\ell+k} ((w, z_j) + b) \approx \frac{1}{\ell} \sum_{i=1}^{\ell} y_i. \qquad (24.46)$$

This constraint requires that the test data have about the same proportion of vectors from the two classes as was observed for the training data.

24.9.4   SVM for Transductive Inference Based on Contradictions on the Universum

Given the images (24.35) of the training data (24.1), the images (24.36) of the test data (24.2), and the images (24.39) of the universum (24.34), construct the linear decision rule

$$I(x) = \theta[(w, z) + b],$$

where the vector w and threshold b are the solution of the following optimization problem: Minimize the functional

$$R(w) = (w, w) + C_1 \sum_{i=1}^{\ell} \theta(\xi_i) + C_2 \sum_{j=\ell+1}^{\ell+k} \theta(\xi_j) + C_3 \sum_{s=1}^{u} \theta(\xi_s^*), \quad C_1, C_2, C_3 \geq 0 \quad (24.47)$$

subject to the constraints

$$y_i((z_i, w) + b) \geq 1 - \xi_i, \quad \xi_i \geq 0, \ i = 1, ..., \ell \tag{24.48}$$

(defined by the images of the training data (24.35)), the constraints

$$y_j^*((z_j, w) + b) \geq 1 - \xi_j, \quad \xi_j \geq 0, \ j = \ell + 1, ..., \ell + k \tag{24.49}$$

(defined by the images of the test data (24.36)) and its desired classification, and the constraints

$$|(z_s^*, w) + b| \leq a + \xi_s^*, \quad \xi_s^* \geq 0, \ s = 1, ..., v, \quad a \geq 0 \tag{24.50}$$

(defined by the images (24.39) of the universum (24.34)).

24.9.5   Standard Implementation of the SVM Algorithms

To simplify the optimization problems of the described algorithms the step function $\theta(\xi)$ was replaced by the linear function ξ in the objective functionals (24.37), (24.40), (24.43), and (24.47). Therefore the following algorithms were obtained (Vapnik, 1995, 1998):

- *Large-margin inductive SVM:*
Minimize the functional

$$R(w) = (w, w) + C_1 \sum_{i=1}^{\ell} \xi_i, \quad C_1 \geq 0 \tag{24.51}$$

subject to the constraints (24.38).

- *Large-margin inductive SVM with the universum*
Minimize the functional

$$R(w) = (w, w) + C_1 \sum_{i=1}^{\ell} \xi_i, + C_2 \sum_{s=1}^{u} \xi_s^*, \quad C_1 \geq 0 \tag{24.52}$$

subject to the constraints (24.41) and (24.42).

- *Large-margin transductive SVM:*
Minimize the functional

$$R(w) = (w, w) + C_1 \sum_{i=1}^{\ell} \xi_i + C_2 \sum_{j=\ell+1}^{\ell+u} \xi_j, \quad C_1, C_2 \geq 0 \tag{24.53}$$

Table 24.1 Test errors of SVMs trained without and with universum.

# of train. examples.	250	500	1,000	2,000	3,000
Test Err. SVM (%)	2.83	1.92	1.37	0.99	0.83
Test Err. SVM+U_1 (%)	2.43	1.58	1.11	0.75	0.63
Test Err. SVM+U_2 (%)	1.51	1.12	0.89	0.68	0.60
Test Err. SVM+U_3 (%)	1.33	0.89	0.72	0.60	0.58

subject to the constraints (24.44) and (24.45). One can also use hint (24.46).

■ *Maximal contradictions on the universum transductive SVM:*
Minimize the functional

$$R(w) = (w, w) + C_1 \sum_{i=1}^{\ell} \xi_i + C_2 \sum_{j=\ell+1}^{\ell+k} \xi_j + C_3 \sum_{s=1}^{u} \xi_s^*, \quad C_1, C_2, C_3 \geq 0 \quad (24.54)$$

subject to the constraints (24.48), (24.49), (24.50). One can also use hint (24.46).

24.9.6 Experiments with the Universum

In the summer of 2005, R. Collobert and J. Weston conducted the first experiments on training SVMs with a universum. They demonstrated that

a. SVMs plus a universum can significantly improve performance even in the inductive mode ($C_2 = 0$ in inequality (24.54));

b. for small training sets it is very important how the universum is constructed. For large sets it is less important.

Using the NIST database they discriminated digit 8 from digit 5 using a conventional SVM and an SVM trained with three different universum environments. Table 24.1 shows for different sizes of training data the performance of conventional SVMs and the performance of SVMs trained using universums U_1, U_2, U_3. In all cases the parameter $a = .01$, and the parameters C_1, C_2 and the parameter of Gaussian kernel were tuned using the tenfold cross-validation technique.

For these experiments three different universums (each containing 5000 examples) were constructed as follows:

■ U_1 Select random digits from the other classes (0,1,2,3,4,6,7,9).

■ U_2 Creates an artificial image by first selecting a random 5 and a random 8, (from pool of 3,000 non-test examples) and then for each pixel of the artificial image choosing with probability 1/2 the corresponding pixel from the image 5 or from the image 8.

■ U_3 Creates an artificial image by first selecting a random 5 and a random 8, (from pool of 3,000 non-test examples) and then constructing the mean of these two digits.

24.10   Semi-Supervised Learning

Analyzing the problem of semi-supervised learning as the minimization of the functional (24.4) using training data (24.1) and unlabeled data (24.2), one has to create a clear *statistical* model that allows one to show where (from the formal point of view) one can expect to get an advantage using unlabeled data.

From the theoretical point of view such a statistical model for semi-supervised learning would be more sophisticated than the one described for transductive inference, since it would require additional reasoning in the style of the symmetrization lemma.

Also, from the point of view of possible mechanisms for generalization it looks restricted: Density is defined in input space. It does not depend on the mapping from the input space to the feature space. As we mentioned earlier, a nonlinear mapping can create a large anisotropy in feature space. Using the universum one can take into account this anisotropy, evaluating the size of equivalence classes and using it for classification. If the results obtained in the digit recognition experiments are more or less general, transductive inference can have a more interesting structure than just taking into account density properties.

Therefore it might be a good idea to consider the semi-supervised model as a particular transductive model described at the beginning of this chapter. As such, one first chooses the best equivalence class to perform transductive inference and then chooses from this equivalence class some function which one uses to classify new data that do not belong to the working set.

Such a position allows one to concentrate on the core problem of extracting additional information from the unlabeled data in order to classify them.

24.11   Conclusion: Transductive Inference and the New Problems of Inference

There are two reasons to consider the transductive mode of inference as we have described it above. The first reason is that it is an extremely useful tool for practical applications (see Weston et al. (2003b) and chapter 6).

24.11.1   Adaptation to the Test Data

Transductive inference also contains elements of *adaptation* to new data which we did not discuss since it is not easy to formalize. Back in the 1970s in the very first article devoted to the application of transductive inference (Vapnik and Sterin, 1977), we used data from one medical clinic to classify patients from another clinic. Transduction significantly improved performance.

Another example would be zip code recognition where transductive inference suggests *simultaneously recognizing* all digits of a zip code in contrast to recognizing every digit separately as in inductive inference. It is easy to imagine a situation where given the training data and an unknown zip code the recognition of any fixed digit of a zip code depends on recognition of the rest of the digits of the zip code. That is, the rule is constructed for the specific zip code. For another zip code one constructs another rule (which might reflect the adaptation to different handwriting). One can find many such examples.

24.12 Beyond Transduction: Selective Inference

The second reason for considering transductive inference is that it forms the simplest model of noninductive inference. These inferences are based on the same general model as inductive inference: the SRM principle. The theory of transduction describes (in the framework of the SRM principle) the mechanisms that provide the advantage of transductive inference over inductive inference.

There also exist models of inferences that go beyond transduction. In particular, *selective inference*:

Given ℓ training examples,

$$(x_i, y_1), ..., (x_\ell, y_\ell), \tag{24.55}$$

and u candidate vectors,

$$x_{\ell+1}, ... x_{\ell+u}, \tag{24.56}$$

select among the u candidates the k vectors with the highest probability of belonging to the first class. Examples of selective inference include:

- *Discovery of bioactive drugs:* Given a training set (24.55) of bioactive and non-bioactive drugs, select from the u candidates (24.56) the k representatives with the highest probability of belonging to the bioactive group.

- *National security:* Given training set (24.55) of terrorists and nonterrorists, select from the u candidates (24.56) the k representatives with the highest probability of belonging to the terrorist group.

Note that selective inference requires a less demanding solution than transductive inference: it does not require classification of the most difficult (border) cases.

Selective inference is the basis for solving high-dimensional decision-making problems. To analyze the selective inference problem one can use the same SRM principle but with a different concept of equivalence classes.

24.12.1 Transductive Inference and the Imperative for Inference in a Complex World

Lastly, the philosophy of transductive inference reflects the general imperative for inference in a complex (high-dimensional) world (Vapnik, 1995), which in fact defines an advantage of the predictive learning models (machine learning techniques) with respect to the generative learning models (classical statistics techniques) (cf. section 1.2.4):

Solving a problem of interest, do not solve a more general (and therefore worse-posed) problem as an intermediate step. Try to get the answer that you really need but not a more general one.

- Do not estimate a density if you need to estimate a function.
(Do not use classical generative models; use ML predictive models.)

- Do not estimate a function if you need to estimate values at given points.
(Try to perform transduction, not induction.)

- Do not estimate predictive values if your goal is to act well.
(A good strategy of action can rely just on good selective inference.)

25 A Discussion of Semi-Supervised Learning and Transduction

The following is a fictitious discussion inspired by real discussions between the editors of this book and a number of people, including Vladimir Vapnik. It involves three researchers; for simplicity, we will call them A, B, and C, without implying any one-to-one mapping to real persons. The topic of the discussion is: *What is the Difference between Semi-Supervised and Transductive Learning?*

A: Let me start by saying that to me, the topic of our discussion seems strange. Rather than asking for the difference, we should ask what SSL[1] and transduction have in common, if anything. SSL is about how to use information contained in unlabeled data which we have in addition to the labeled training set. Transduction, on the other hand, claims that it is powerful because it is solving a simpler task than inductive learning.

B: Exactly. In inductive learning, one learns a function that makes predictions on the whole space. Transduction asks for less — it only concerns itself with predicting the values of the function at the test points of interest. This is an easier problem, since an inductive solution implies a transductive one — by evaluating the function at the given test points — but not vice versa.

A: But couldn't you easily build an inductive algorithm from a transductive one by carrying out the following procedure? For all *possible* test inputs $\mathbf{x}$: add $\mathbf{x}$ as a single unlabeled point to the labeled training set, and use the transductive algorithm to predict the corresponding output. This gives you a mapping from $\mathbf{x}$ to y, in other words, a *function*, just like any inductive algorithm. So a transductive solution implies an inductive one, and thus transduction is no easier than induction.

---

1. We use the shorthand SSL for semi-supervised learning.

B:　As soon as we have more than one unlabeled point, this argument fails. Nevertheless, in order to retain the distinction between induction and transduction, we may want to exclude the situation. Whatever it is called, even the case of one unlabeled point is interesting: it could be viewed as induction with a function class which is not given explicitly.

Transduction works because the test set can give you a nontrivial factorization of the function class. Let us call two functions equivalent if they cannot be distinguished based on any of the given training or test examples. It is then sufficient to use only one representative of each equivalence class, and forget about all other functions. Our function class is effectively finite, and we can directly write down a generalization error bound.

By the way, the size of the equivalence classes is important for generalization: I believe that functions from large classes generalize better. Think of the notion of a margin: if you have a large margin of separation between two classes of data, then there are usually many different functions that fit into this margin, and correctly separate the data (and thus are equivalent on the data).

C:　This seems an interesting point. You said that one point is not enough for transduction — how about for SSL? Would one unlabeled point be of any use?

A:　Every unlabeled point gives me information on $P(\mathbf{x})$. Whether the point is useful or not will of course depend on whether my distribution is benign. For example, if the distribution satisfies the semi-supervised smoothness assumption,[2] then even a single point gives me information. For instance, it affects my estimate of the local density of the points, and thus it affects where I will try to enforce smoothness. As a consequence, it affects my prediction of how the class label should behave as a function of the input.

B:　For transduction to work, it is not necessary to make smoothness assumptions.

C:　But surely, the factorization of the function class which you talked about before will also depend on $P(\mathbf{x})$?

B:　Yes.

C:　I think it should be possible to construct cases where large equivalence classes generalize worse than small ones. So I would claim that transduction, the way you view it, will not always work, but only if the data are benign in some sense...

---

2. See chapter 1.

A: ... and I would argue that one notion that captures whether the data are benign *is* the semi-supervised smoothness assumption. This also makes the connection with the margin, since large-margin separation is low-density separation.

B: Maybe yes, maybe no.

C: And what happens toward the other extreme of an infinite number of points?

A: Usually, learning becomes easier if we have more points. With transduction, the more test points we have, the closer we get to inductive learning, because we will have to predict outputs for a set of points that eventually covers the whole domain. According to B, transduction would then become harder, since induction is harder. But that's absurd — how can one make a problem harder by adding more information?

C: Interesting point... However, I am tempted to defend B, albeit with an argument he may not like: In the limit of infinitely many test points, transduction should converge toward something like "induction *plus knowledge of* $P(\mathbf{x})$." This could well be statistically *easier* than standard supervised inductive learning, provided $P(x)$ contains useful information for our task. Which brings us again to the role of the smoothness assumption.

A: This seems to show that transduction relies on the same kind of assumptions as SSL. And, for increasing amounts of unlabeled points, SSL also converges to induction plus knowledge of $P(\mathbf{x})$. So where is the difference? In the limit of infinitely many unlabeled points, transduction cannot be easier than inductive SSL.

B: In the real world, we do not have infinitely many data points. Anyway, my point of view is more fundamental. It is based on what is behind the VC bounds for induction. To prove these bounds, one uses the symmetrization lemma — we upper-bound the difference between the error on the training set and the expected error by the error on the training sample and the error on a second sample — the ghost sample. This is exact transduction; it is a statement about the error on a given set of points. But the VC bounds for induction then have to take an expectation with respect to the unknown points, or even a supremum over the choice of the points. This is much worse than what one can do *knowing* the points.[3]

A: But a better bound does not necessarily imply a better algorithm..

B: True, but bounds guide us to design new algorithms. Transduction is a step on the way, which lies at the heart of induction. It looks deeper than induction.

---

3. See chapter 24 and (Vapnik, 2006).

C: But doesn't this contradict the no-free-lunch theorem?

B: There might exist distributions for which transduction can give worse results than induction.

A: If I try to sum up the arguments of B, there are two different reasons why transduction can be useful. The first one is that the bounds for transduction are tighter than the bounds for induction, and the second one is that measuring the size of the equivalence classes is an opportunity to change the ordering in the structure of our class of functions. This second reason seems closely related to the motivations in SSL.

C: Maybe we should look at a more concrete issue: Is the "transductive SVM" an example of a transductive algorithm?

A: No. It is semi-supervised and inductive. It uses unlabeled data, and it provides a function defined everywhere. Would you agree, B?

B: Maybe it is semi-supervised. My point is that transduction is orthogonal from SSL. SSL stresses new technical ideas while transduction stresses new philosophical ideas related to noninductive inference. I am convinced that in ten years the concept of noninductive inference will be much more popular than inductive inference.

A: I surely agree that the two notions are orthogonal, but for different reasons. To make my point clear let me consider two sets. One of them is a set of unlabeled data which we have for training. I don't care about the predictions on this set, I only care about how to use the information this set provides about $P(\mathbf{x})$. So I need to assume that this set actually comes from $P(\mathbf{x})$, or at least from a distribution that is related to $P(\mathbf{x})$ in some way. The other set is the actual test set. I do not care where it comes from; it could be anything. In my view, a transductive algorithm is one whose solution depends on the test points that I am given. The opposite of a transductive algorithm is an inductive one. A semi-supervised algorithm, on the other hand, is one that depends on the unlabeled set (as opposed to a supervised algorithm). It does not care which test points are used in the end to evaluate its performance.

B: This does not make sense to me. The test points need to be meaningful. Transduction is intrinsically simpler than induction: it does not make predictions for arbitrary test points.

A: Coming back to the idea of avoiding to solve a more complicated problem than necessary, what about *local learning*?[4] The idea behind it is that, given a test point, one should focus on the training points which are in a neighborhood of this test point, construct a local decision rule, and predict the label of the test point according to this ad hoc rule. Isn't it almost the same idea as in transduction?

B: Indeed, the philosophy is similar, since in both cases one solves a simpler problem. However, local learning is still inductive because there exists an implicit decision function, even though it is never explicitly constructed. The concept of local learning is actually almost the same as transduction with one test point which we were talking about earlier.

C: This local learning idea might also be present in TSVM. Indeed, I can see an advantage in using as unlabeled points the test points rather than an arbitrary set of unlabeled points: by doing so, the algorithm concentrates in the regions of the space where it is important to be accurate, as in local learning.[5]

A: The way I view them, transductive algorithms can also be designed for computational reasons. Take, for instance, the Bayesian committee machine.[6] The solution returned by this algorithm is an expansion on a set of basis functions. But for computational efficiency, only basis functions centered at the test points are considered. So the solution will depend on the test set and the algorithm is transductive according to my definition...

C: ... but not according to the definition of B, since for this algorithm the test points can be arbitrary.

A: If we cannot agree on a definition of transduction, maybe we can at least agree on some examples of transductive algorithms?

C: Graph-based algorithms[7] can be interpreted as both semi-supervised and transductive. They are transductive because there is no straightforward way of making a prediction on a test point which is not drawn from $P(\mathbf{x})$. Indeed, including that point in the graph could be harmful, since it may provide misleading information about $P(\mathbf{x})$. In transduction, the test points have to be from $P(\mathbf{x})$, or at least some distribution related to $P(\mathbf{x})$.

---

4. See (Bottou and Vapnik, 1992).
5. Some experimental evidence for this claim is presented in (Collobert et al., 2006).
6. See (Tresp, 2000).
7. See part III of the book.

A: And this shows why transductive methods are always semi-supervised: they use information contained in the test points. Otherwise there would be no reason not to consider arbitrary test points.

B: I have a typical example of transductive learning. Consider zip code recognition: since all the digits have been written by the same person, one can gain by trying to recognize all the digits simultaneously instead of one by one.

C: This is an interesting example. But it seems different from the standard i.i.d. framework: in this case, if viewed as drawn from the distribution of all possible digits, the test points are dependent, because they have been written by the same person.

B: Indeed, and it is probably in this kind of situation where transduction is most useful: when the test points have some special structure.

A: I do not think we have resolved the question we were asking. Read chapter 25 of Chapelle et al. (2006) and the references therein, and you will understand what I mean.

References

B. Abboud, F. Davoine, and M. Dang. Expressive face recognition and synthesis. In *Computer Vision and Pattern Recognition Workshop*, volume 5, page 54, 2003.

N. Abe, J. Takeuchi, and M. Warmuth. Polynomial learnability of stochastic rules with respect to the KL-divergence and quadratic distance. *IEICE Transactions on Information and Systems*, E84-D(3):299–316, March 2001.

Y. S. Abu-Mostafa. Machines that learn from hints. *Scientific American*, 272(4):64–69, 1995.

A. K. Agrawala. Learning with a probabilistic teacher. *IEEE Transactions on Information Theory*, 16:373–379, 1970.

A. Agresti. *Categorical Data Analysis*. Wiley, Hoboken, NJ, 2002.

H. Akaike. Statistical predictor information. *Annals of the Institute of Statistical Mathematics*, 22:203–271, 1970.

H. Akaike. A new look at the statistical model identification. *IEEE Transactions on Automatic Control*, 19:716–723, 1974.

B. Alberts, D. Bray, A. Johnson, J. Lewis, M. Raff, K. Roberts, and P. Walter. *Essential Cell Biology: An Introduction to the Molecular Biology of the Cell*. New York, Garland Science Publishing, 1998.

S. F. Altschul, W. Gish, W. Miller, E. W. Myers, and D. J. Lipman. A basic local alignment search tool. *Journal of Molecular Biology*, 215:403–410, 1990.

S. F. Altschul, T. L. Madden, A. A. Schaffer, J. Zhang, Z. Zhang, W. Miller, and D. J. Lipman. Gapped BLAST and PSI-BLAST: A new generation of protein database search programs. *Nucleic Acids Research*, 25:3389–3402, 1997.

Y. Altun, D. McAllester, and M. Belkin. Maximum margin semi-supervised learning for structured variables. In *Advances in Neural Information Processing Systems*, volume 18, 2005.

M. R. Amini and P. Gallinari. Semi-supervised logistic regression. In *Fifteenth European Conference on Artificial Intelligence*, pages 390–394, 2002.

J. A. Anderson. Multivariate logistic compounds. *Biometrika*, 66:17–26, 1979.

M. Anjos. *New Convex Relaxations for the Maximum Cut and VLSI Layout Problems*. Phd thesis, Waterloo University, Waterloo, Canada, 2001.

F. Bach, G. Lanckriet, and M. Jordan. Multiple kernel learning, conic duality, and the SMO algorithm. In *Proceedings of the Twenty-first International Conference on Machine Learning*, New York, 2004. ACM Press.

R. Baeza-Yates and B. Ribeiro-Neto. *Modern Information Retrieval*. ACM Press, New York, 1999.

M.-F. Balcan and A. Blum. A PAC-style model for learning from labeled and unlabeled data. In *Conference on Computational Learning Theory*, pages 111–126, 2005.

M.-F. Balcan, A. Blum, and K. Yang. Co-training and expansion: Towards bridging theory and practice. In *Advances in Neural Information Processing Systems*, 2004.

S. Baluja. Probabilistic modeling for face orientation discrimination: Learning from labeled and unlabeled examples. In *Advances in Neural Information Processing Systems 11*, pages 854–860, 1999.

A. Banerjee, I. Dhillon, J. Ghosh, and S. Sra. Clustering on the unit hypersphere using von Mises-Fisher distributions. *Journal of Machine Learning Research*, 6:1345–1382, 2005a.

A. Banerjee, S. Merugu, I. Dhilon, and J. Ghosh. Clustering with Bregman divergences. *Journal of Machine Learning Research*, 6:1705–1749, Oct 2005b.

N. Bansal, A. L. Blum, and S. Chawla. Correlation clustering. In *The 43rd Annual IEEE Symposium on Foundations of Computer Science*, pages 238–247, 2002.

A. Bar-Hillel, T. Hertz, N. Shental, and D. Weinshall. Learning distance functions using equivalence relations. In *Proceedings of the International Conference on Machine Learning*, pages 11–18, Washington, DC, 2003.

P. Bartlett and S. Mendelson. Rademacher and Gaussian complexities risk bounds and structural results. *Journal of Machine Learning Research*, 3:463–482, 2002.

S. Basu, A. Banerjee, and R. J. Mooney. Semi-supervised clustering by seeding. In *Proceedings of the International Conference on Machine Learning*, pages 19–26, 2002.

S. Basu, A. Banerjee, and R. J. Mooney. Active semi-supervision for pairwise constrained clustering. In *Proceedings of the SIAM International Conference on Data Mining*, 2004a.

S. Basu, M. Bilenko, and R. J. Mooney. A probabilistic framework for semi-supervised clustering. In *Proceedings of the tenth ACM SIGKDD international conference on knowledge discovery and data mining*, pages 59–68, Seattle, WA, 2004b.

E. B. Baum. Polynomial time algorithms for learning neural nets. In *Proceedings of the Third Annual Workshop on Computational Learning Theory*, pages 258 – 272, 1990.

S. Becker and G. E. Hinton. A self-organizing neural network that discovers surfaces in random-dot stereograms. *Nature*, 355:161–163, 1992.

M. Belkin. *Problems of Learning on Manifolds*. PhD thesis, Department of Mathematics, University of Chicago, 2003.

M. Belkin, I. Matveeva, and P. Niyogi. Regression and regularization on large graphs. In *Proceedings of the Seventeenth Annual Conference on Learning Theory*, 2004a.

M. Belkin, I. Matveeva, and P. Niyogi. Regularization and semi-supervised learning on large graphs. In *Proceedings of the Seventeenth Annual Conference on Computational Learning Theory*, pages 624–638, Banff, Canada, 2004b.

M. Belkin and P. Niyogi. Semi-supervised learning on manifolds. In *Advances in Neural Information Processing Systems*, 2002.

M. Belkin and P. Niyogi. Laplacian eigenmaps for dimensionality reduction and data representation. *Neural Computation*, 15(6):1373–1396, 2003a.

M. Belkin and P. Niyogi. Using manifold structure for partially labeled classification. In S. Becker, S. Thrun, and K. Obermayer, editors, *Advances in Neural Information Processing Systems 15*, Cambridge, MA, 2003b. MIT Press.

M. Belkin, P. Niyogi, and V. Sindhwani. Manifold regularization: A geometric framework for learning from examples. Technical Report TR-2004-06, University of Chicago, 2004c.

M. Belkin, P. Niyogi, and V. Sindhwani. On manifold regularization. In R. G. Cowell and Z. Ghahramani, editors, *Proceedings of the Tenth International Workshop on Artificial Intelligence and Statistics*, pages 17–24. Society for Artificial Intelligence and Statistics, 2005.

R. Bellman. *Adaptive Control Processes: A Guided Tour*. Princeton University Press, Princeton, NJ, 1961.

S. Ben-David, A. Itai, and E. Kushilevitz. Learning by distances. *Information and Computation*, 117(2):240–250, 1995.

A. Ben-Hur and D. Brutlag. Remote homology detection: A motif based approach. In *Proceedings of the Seventh International Conference on Intelligent Systems for Molecular Biology*, 2003.

G. M. Benedek and A. Itai. Learnability with respect to a fixed distribution. *Theoretical Computer Science*, 86:377–389, 1991.

Y. Bengio and N. Chapados. Extensions to metric based model selection. *Journal of Machine Learning Research*, 3:1209–1227, 2003.

Y. Bengio, O. Delalleau, and N. Le Roux. The curse of dimensionality for local kernel machines. Technical Report 1258, Département d'informatique et recherche opérationnelle, Université de Montréal, 2005.

Y. Bengio, O. Delalleau, and N. Le Roux. The curse of highly variable functions for local kernel machines. In *Advances in Neural Information Processing Systems 18*. MIT Press, Cambridge, MA, 2006a.

Y. Bengio, O. Delalleau, N. Le Roux, J.-F. Paiement, P. Vincent, and M. Ouimet. Learning eigenfunctions links spectral embedding and kernel PCA. *Neural Computation*, 16(10):2197–

2219, 2004a.

Y. Bengio, H. Larochelle, and P. Vincent. Non-local manifold Parzen windows. In *Advances in Neural Information Processing Systems 18*. MIT Press, Cambridge, MA, 2006b.

Y. Bengio and M. Monperrus. Non-local manifold tangent learning. In L.K. Saul, Y. Weiss, and L. Bottou, editors, *Advances in Neural Information Processing Systems 17*, Cambridge, MA, 2005. MIT Press.

Y. Bengio, J.-F. Paiement, P. Vincent, O. Delalleau, N. Le Roux, and M. Ouimet. Out-of-sample extensions for lle, isomap, MDS, eigenmaps, and spectral clustering. In S. Thrun, L. Saul, and B. Schölkopf, editors, *Advances in Neural Information Processing Systems 16*. MIT Press, Cambridge, MA, 2004b.

K. P. Bennett and A. Demiriz. Semi-supervised support vector machines. In M. S. Kearns, S. A. Solla, and D. A. Cohn, editors, *Advances in Neural Information Processing Systems*, volume 11, pages 368–374, Cambridge, MA, 1999. MIT Press.

K. P. Bennett, A. Demiriz, and R. Maclin. Exploiting unlabeled data in ensemble methods. In *Proceedings of the eighth ACM SIGKDD international conference on knowledge discovery and data mining*, 2002.

J. O. Berger. *Statistical Decision Theory and Bayesian Analysis*. Springer-Verlag, New York, 2nd edition, 1985.

R. H. Berk. Limiting behavior of posterior distributions when the model is incorrect. *Annals of Mathematical Statistics*, pages 51–58, 1966.

M. Bernstein, V. de Silva, J. C. Langford, and J. B. Tenenbaum. Graph approximations to geodesics on embedded manifolds. Technical report, Stanford University, Stanford, December 2000.

J. Besag. On the statistical analysis of dirty pictures. *Journal of the Royal Statistical Society, Series B (Methodological)*, 48(3):259–302, 1986.

A. Beygelzimer, S. Kakade, and J. Langford. Cover trees for nearest neighbor. Sumitted for publication, 2004.

M. Bilenko and S. Basu. A comparison of inference techniques for semi-supervised clustering with hidden Markov random fields. In *Proceedings of the ICML-2004 Workshop on Statistical Relational Learning and its Connections to Other Fields*, Banff, Canada, 2004.

M. Bilenko, S. Basu, and R. J. Mooney. Integrating constraints and metric learning in semi-supervised clustering. In *Proceedings of the International Conference on Machine Learning*, pages 81–88, Banff, Canada, 2004.

M. Bilenko and R. J. Mooney. Adaptive duplicate detection using learnable string similarity measures. In *Proceedings of the ninth ACM SIGKDD international conference on knowledge discovery and data mining*, pages 39–48, Washington, DC, 2003.

C. Bishop. *Neural Networks for Pattern Recognition*. Clarendon Press, Oxford, 1995.

R. E. Blahut. Computation of channel capacity and rate distortion functions. In *IEEE Transactions on Information Theory*, volume 18, pages 460–473, July 1972.

A. Blum and S. Chawla. Learning from labeled and unlabeled data using graph mincuts. In *Proceedings of the Eighteenth International Conference on Machine Learning*, pages 19–26, 2001.

A. Blum, A. Frieze, R. Kannan, and S. Vempala. A polynomial-time algorithm for learning noisy linear threshold functions. *Algorithmica*, 22:35–52, 1998.

A. Blum and R. Kannan. Learning an intersection of k halfspaces over a uniform distribution. *Journal of Computer and Systems Sciences*, 54(2):371–380, 1997.

A. Blum, J. Lafferty, M. Rwebangira, and R. Reddy. Semi-supervised learning using randomized mincuts. In *International Conference on Machine Learning*, 2004.

A. Blum and J. C. Langford. PAC-MDL bounds. In *Conference on Computational Learning Theory*, 2003.

A. Blum and T. Mitchell. Combining labeled and unlabeled data with co-training. In *Proceedings of the Eleventh Annual Conference on Computational Learning Theory*, pages 92–100, 1998.

A. Blumer, A. Ehrenfeucht, D. Haussler, and M. K. Warmuth. Learnability and the Vapnik Chervonenkis dimension. *Journal of the ACM*, 36(4):929–965, 1989.

R. Board and L. Pitt. Semi-supervised learning. *Machine Learning*, 4(1):41–65, 1989.

B. E. Boser, I. M. Guyon, and V. N. Vapnik. A traininig algorithm for optimal margin classifiers. In D. Haussler, editor, *Proceedings of the Fifth Annual ACM Workshop on Computational Learning Theory*, pages 144–152, 1992.

L. Bottou and V. Vapnik. Local learning algorithms. *Neural Computation*, 4(6):888–900, 1992.

S. Boucheron, O. Bousquet, and G. Lugosi. Theory of classification: a survey of some recent advances. *ESAIM: Probability and Statistics*, 9:323–375, November 2005.

S. Boucheron, G. Lugosi, and P. Massart. A sharp concentration inequality with applications. *Random Structures and Algorithms*, 16:277–292, 2000.

O. Bousquet, O. Chapelle, and M. Hein. Measure based regularization. In *Advances in Neural Information Processing Systems 16*. MIT Press, Cambridge, MA, 2004.

O. Bousquet and D. Herrmann. On the complexity of learning the kernel matrix. In *Advances in Neural Information Processing Systems*, volume 14, 2002.

S. Boyd and L. Vandenberghe. *Convex Optimization*. Cambridge University Press, Cambridge UK, 2004.

M. Brand. Structure learning in conditional probability models via an entropic prior and parameter extinction. *Neural Computation*, 11(5):1155–1182, 1999.

M. Brand. Nonlinear dimensionality reduction by kernel eigenmaps. In *International Joint Conference on Artificial Intelligence*, 2003.

M. Brand. From subspaces to submanifolds. In *Proceedings of the British Machine Vision Conference*, London, 2004.

L. Breiman. Bagging predictors. *Machine Learning*, 24:123–40, 1996.

S. E. Brenner, P. Koehl, and M. Levitt. The ASTRAL compendium for sequence and structure analysis. *Nucleic Acids Research*, 28:254–256, 2000.

R. Bruce. Semi-supervised learning using prior probabilities and EM. In *IJCAI-01 Workshop on Text Learning: Beyond Supervision*, August 2001.

W. L. Buntine. Operations for learning with graphical models. *Journal of Artificial Intelligence Research*, 2:159–225, 1994.

C. J. C. Burges. Geometric methods for feature extraction and dimensional reduction. In L. Rokach and O. Maimon, editors, *Data Mining and Knowledge Discovery Handbook: A Complete Guide for Practitioners and Researchers*. Kluwer, Dordrecht, the Netherlands, 2005.

V. Castelli. *The Relative Value of Labeled and Unlabeled Samples in Pattern Recognition*. PhD thesis, Stanford University, Stanford, CA, December 1994.

V. Castelli and T. M. Cover. On the exponential value of labeled samples. *Pattern Recognition Letters*, 16:105–111, 1995.

V. Castelli and T. M. Cover. The relative value of labeled and unlabeled samples in pattern recognition with an unknown mixing parameter. *IEEE Transactions on Information Theory*, 42(6):2102–2117, November 1996.

G. Celeux and G. Govaert. A classification EM algorithm for clustering and two stochastic versions. *Computational Statistics & Data Analysis*, 14(3):315–332, 1992.

O. Chapelle, B. Schölkopf, and A. Zien, editors. *Semi-Supervised Learning*. The MIT Press, 2006.

O. Chapelle and V. Vapnik. Model selection for support vector machines. In *Advances in Neural Information Processing Systems*, volume 12, 2000.

O. Chapelle, V. Vapnik, and Y. Bengio. Model selection for small sample regression. *Machine Learning*, 48(1-3):9–23, 2002.

O. Chapelle, V. Vapnik, and J. Weston. Transductive inference for estimating values of functions. In *Advances in Neural Information Processing Systems*, 1999.

O. Chapelle, J. Weston, L. Bottou, and V. Vapnik. Vicinal risk minimization. In T. K. Leen, T. G. Dietterich, and V. Tresp, editors, *Advances in Neural Information Processing Systems 13*, pages 416–422, Cambridge, MA, 2001. MIT Press.

O. Chapelle, J. Weston, and B. Schölkopf. Cluster kernels for semi-supervised learning. In S. Becker, S. Thrun, and K. Obermayer, editors, *Advances in Neural Information Processing Systems 15*, pages 585–592, Cambridge, MA, 2003. MIT Press.

O. Chapelle and A. Zien. Semi-supervised classification by low density separation. In *Tenth International Workshop on Artificial Intelligence and Statistics*, pages 57–64, 2005.

J. Cheng, D. Bell, and W. Liu. Learning belief networks from data: An information theory based approach. In *International Conference on Information and Knowledge Management*, pages 325–331, 1997.

V. Cherkassky and F. Mulier. *Learning from Data: Concepts, Theory, and Methods*. Wiley, New York, 1998.

V. Cherkassky, F. Mulier, and V. Vapnik. Comparison of VC-method with classical methods for model selection. In *Proceedings World Congress on Neural Networks*, pages 957–962, 1997.

F. R. K. Chung. *Spectral Graph Theory*. Number 92 in Regional Conference Series in Mathematics. American Mathematical Society, Providence, RI, 1997.

I. Cohen, F. Cozman, N. Sebe, M. C. Cirelo, and T. Huang. Semisupervised learning of classifiers: Theory, algorithms, and their application to human-computer interaction. *IEEE Transactions on Pattern Analysis and Machine Intelligence*, 26(12):1553–1568, 2004.

I. Cohen, N. Sebe, F. G. Cozman, M. C. Cirelo, and T. S. Huang. Learning Bayesian network classifiers for facial expression recognition using both labeled and unlabeled data. In *IEEE Conference on Computer Vision and Pattern Recognition*, 2003.

D. Cohn, R. Caruana, and A. McCallum. Semi-supervised clustering with user feedback. Technical Report TR2003-1892, Cornell University, Ithaca, NY, 2003.

R. R. Coifman, S. Lafon, A. B. Lee, M. Maggioni, B. Nadler, F. Warner, and S. W. Zucke. Geometric diffusions as a tool for harmonic analysis and structure definition of data: Diffusion maps. *Proceedings of the National Academy of Sciences*, 102:7426–7431, 2005.

M. Collins and Y. Singer. Unsupervised models for named entity classification. In *Proceedings of the Joint SIGDAT Conference on Empirical Methods in Natural Language Processing and Very Large Corpora*, pages 189–196, 1999.

R. Collobert, F. Sinz, J. Weston, and L. Bottou. Large-scale transductive SVMs. *Journal of Machine Learning Research*, 2006. In press. `http://www.kyb.tuebingen.mpg.de/bs/people/fabee/transduction.html`.

D. B. Cooper and J. H. Freeman. On the asymptotic improvement in the outcome of supervised learning provided by additional nonsupervised learning. *IEEE Transactions on Computers*, C-19(11):1055–1063, November 1970.

A. Corduneanu and T. Jaakkola. Continuation methods for mixing heterogeneous sources. In *Proceedings of the Eighteenth Annual Conference on Uncertainty in Artificial Intelligence*, 2002.

A. Corduneanu and T. Jaakkola. On information regularization. In *Proceedings of the Nineteenth conference on Uncertainty in Artificial Intelligence*, 2003.

A. Corduneanu and T. Jaakkola. Distributed information regularization on graphs. In *Advances in Neural Information Processing Systems 17*, 2004.

C. Cortes, P. Haffner, and M. Mohri. Rational kernels. *Neural Information Processing Systems 15*, 2002.

C. Cortes and V. N. Vapnik. Support–vector networks. *Machine Learning Journal*, 20:273–297, 1995.

T. Cover and J. Thomas. *Elements of Information Theory*. Wiley, New York, 1991.

T. Cox and M. Cox. *Multidimensional Scaling*. Chapman & Hall, London, 1994.

F. G. Cozman and I. Cohen. Unlabeled data can degrade classification performance of generative classifiers. In *Proceedings of the Fifteenth International Florida Artificial Intelligence Research Society Conference*, pages 327–331, Pensacola, FL, 2002.

F. G. Cozman, I. Cohen, and M. C. Cirelo. Semi-supervised learning and model search. In *Proceedings of the ICML-2003 Workshop: The Continuun from Labeled to Unlabeled Data in Machine Learning and Data Mining*, pages 111–112, 2003a.

F. G. Cozman, I. Cohen, and M. C. Cirelo. Semi-supervised learning of mixture models. In *International Conference on Machine Learning*, pages 99–106, 2003b.

M. Craven, D. DiPasquo, D. Freitag, A. McCallum, T. Mitchell, K. Nigam, and S. Slattery. Learning to construct knowledge bases from the World Wide Web. *Artificial Intelligence*, 118 (1–2):69–113, 2000.

P. Craven and G. Wahba. Smoothing noisy data with spline functions. *Numerische Mathematik*, 31:377–403, 1979.

N. Cristianini and J. Shawe-Taylor. *An Introduction to Support Vector Machines*. Cambridge University Press, Cambridge, UK, 2000.

N. Cristianini, J. Shawe-Taylor, A. Elisseeff, and J. Kandola. On kernel-target alignment. In *Advances in Neural Information Processing Systems 14*, 2002a.

N. Cristianini, J. Shawe-Taylor, and J. Kandola. Spectral kernel methods for clustering. In *Advances in Neural Information Processing Systems 14*, pages 649–655, 2002b.

L. Csató. *Gaussian Processes — Iterative Sparse Approximations*. PhD thesis, Aston University, Birmingham, UK, 2002.

J. A. Cuff and G. J. Barton. Evaluation and improvement of multiple sequence methods for protein secondary structure prediction. *Proteins*, 34(4):508–519, March 1999.

S. Dasgupta. Performance guarantees for hierarchical clustering. In *Conference on Computational Learning Theory*, pages 351–363, 2002.

S. Dasgupta, M. L. Littman, and D. McAllester. PAC generalization bounds for co-training. In T. G. Dietterich, S. Becker, and Z. Ghahramani, editors, *Advances in Neural Information Processing Systems 14*, Cambridge, MA, 2001. MIT Press.

N. E. Day. Estimating the components of a mixture of normal distributions. *Biometrika*, 56(3): 463–474, 1969.

T. De Bie and N. Cristianini. Convex methods for transduction. In *Advances in Neural Information Processing Systems 16*, pages 73–80, 2004a.

T. De Bie and N. Cristianini. Convex transduction with the normalized cut. Technical Report 04-128, ESAT-SISTA, K.U.Leuven, Leuven, Belgium, 2004b. URL `http://www.esat.kuleuven.ac.be/~tdebie/papers/TDB-NC_04b.pdf`.

T. De Bie and N. Cristianini. Kernel methods for exploratory data analysis: A demonstration on text data. In *Proceedings of the International Workshop on Statistical Pattern Recognition*, pages 16–29, 2004c.

T. De Bie, N. Cristianini, and R. Rosipal. Eigenproblems in pattern recognition. In E. Bayro-Corrochano, editor, *Handbook of Computational Geometry for Pattern Recognition, Computer Vision, Neurocomputing and Robotics*, pages 129–170. Springer-Verlag, Heidelberg, 2005.

T. De Bie, M. Momma, and N. Cristianini. Efficiently learning the metric with side-information. In *Proceedings of the Fourteenth International Conference on Algorithmic Learning Theory*, pages 175–189, 2003.

T. De Bie, J. A. K. Suykens, and B. De Moor. Learning from general label constraints. In *Joint IAPR International Workshops on Structural, Syntactic, and Statistical Pattern Recognition*, pages 671–679, Lisbon, Portugal, 2004. Springer.

V. de Silva and J. B. Tenenbaum. Global versus local methods in nonlinear dimensionality reduction. In S. Becker, S. Thrun, and K. Obermayer, editors, *Advances in Neural Information Processing Systems 15*, pages 721–728, Cambridge, MA, 2003. MIT Press.

S. Deerwester, S. T. Dumais, T. K. Landauer, G. W. Furnas, and R. A. Harshman. Indexing by latent semantic analysis. *Journal of the Society for Information Science*, 41(6):391–407, 1990.

M. DeGroot. *Optimal Statistical Decisions*. McGraw-Hill, New York, 1970.

O. Dekel, C. D. Manning, and Y. Singer. Log-linear models for label-ranking. In *Advances in Neural Information Processing Systems 16*, Cambridge, MA, 2004. MIT Press.

O. Delalleau, Y. Bengio, and N. Le Roux. Efficient non-parametric function induction in semi-supervised learning. In *Artificial Intelligence and Statistics*, 2005.

A. Demiriz and K. P. Bennett. Optimization approaches to semi-supervised learning. In M. C. Ferris, O. L. Mangasarian, and J. S. Pang, editors, *Applications and Algorithms of Complementarity*, pages 121–141. Kluwer, Dordrecht, the Netherlands, 2000.

A. Demiriz, K. P. Bennett, and M. J. Embrechts. Semi-supervised clustering using genetic algorithms. In *Proceedings of Artificial Neural Networks in Engineering*, pages 809–814, 1999.

A. P. Dempster, N. M. Laird, and D. B. Rubin. Maximum likelihood from incomplete data via the EM algorithm. *Journal of the Royal Statistical Society, Series B*, 39(1):1–38, 1977.

M. Deng, T. Chen, and F. Sun. An integrated probabilistic model for functional prediction of proteins. In W. Miller, M. Vingron, S. Istrail, P. Pevzner, and M. Waterman, editors, *Proceedings of the Seventh Annual International Conference on Computational Biology*, pages 95–103. ACM Press, New York, 2003.

P. Derbeko, R. El-Yaniv, and R. Meir. Error bounds for transductive learning via compression and clustering. In *Advances in Neural Information Processing Systems*, pages 1085–1092. MIT Press, Cambridge, MA, 2003.

L. Devroye, L. Györfi, and G. Lugosi. *A Probabilistic Theory of Pattern Recognition*, volume 31 of *Applications of Mathematics*. Springer-Verlag, New York, 1996.

I. S. Dhillon and Y. Guan. Information theoretic clustering of sparse co-occurrence data. In *Third IEEE International Conference on Data Mining*, pages 517–521, 2003.

I. S. Dhillon and D. S. Modha. Concept decompositions for large sparse text data using clustering. *Machine Learning*, 42:143–175, 2001.

T. G. Dietterich. Approximate statistical tests for comparing supervised classification learning algorithms. *Neural Computation*, 10(7):1895–1924, 1998.

B. E. Dom. An information-theoretic external cluster-validity measure. Research Report RJ 10219, IBM, 2001.

P. Domingos and M. Pazzani. On the optimality of the simple Bayesian classifier under zero-one loss. *Machine Learning*, 29(2/3):103–130, 1997.

D. L. Donoho and C. E. Grimes. When does Isomap recover the natural parameterization of families of articulated images? Technical Report 2002-27, Department of Statistics, Stanford University, Stanford, CA, August 2002.

D. L. Donoho and C. E. Grimes. Hessian eigenmaps: Locally linear embedding techniques for high-dimensional data. *Proceedings of the National Academy of Arts and Sciences*, 100:5591–5596, 2003.

P. G. Doyle and J. L. Snell. Random walks and electric networks. *Mathematical Association of America*, 1984.

H. Drucker, D. Wu, and V. Vapnik. Support vector machines for spam categorization. *IEEE Transactions on Neural Networks*, 10(5):1048–1054, 1999.

S. T. Dumais, J. Platt, D. Heckerman, and M. Sahami. Inductive learning algorithms and representations for text categorization. In *Proceedings of the ACM International Conference on Information and Knowledge Management*, pages 148–155, 1998.

J. Dunagan and S. Vempala. Optimal outlier removal in high-dimensional spaces. In *Proceedings of the Thirty-third ACM Symposium on Theory of Computing*, 2001.

B. Efron. The efficiency of logistic regression compared to normal discriminant analysis. *Journal of the American Statistical Association*, 70(352):892–898, 1975.

B. Efron. Computers and the theory of statistics: Thinking the unthinkable. *SIAM Review*, 21: 460–480, 1979.

A. Ehrenfeucht, D. Haussler, M. Kearns, and L. Valiant. A general lower bound on the number of examples needed for learning. *Information and Computation*, 82:246–261, 1989.

B. Fischer, V. Roth, and J. M. Buhmann. Clustering with the connectivity kernel. In *Advances in Neural Information Processing Systems 16*, 2004.

A. Flaxman, 2003. Personal communication.

D. Foster and E. George. The risk inflation criterion for multiple regression. *Annals of Statistics*, 22:1947–1975, 1994.

S. C. Fralick. Learning to recognize patterns without a teacher. *IEEE Transactions on Information Theory*, 13:57–64, 1967.

Y. Freund and R. Schapire. A decision-theoretic generalization of on-line learning and an application to boosting. *Journal of Computer and System Sciences*, 55(1):119–139, 1997.

J. H. Friedman. On bias, variance, 0/1-loss, and the curse-of-dimensionality. *Data Mining and Knowledge Discovery*, 1(1):55–77, 1997.

J. H. Friedman, J. L. Bentley, and R. A. Finkel. An algorithm for finding best matches in logarithmic expected time. *ACM Transactions on Mathematical Software*, 3:209–226, 1977.

J. H. Friedman, T. Hastie, and R. Tibshirani. Additive logistic regression: A statistical view of boosting. *Annals of Statistics*, 28(2):337–407, 2000.

N. Friedman. The Bayesian structural EM algorithm. In *Proceedings of the Conference on Uncertainty in Artificial Intelligence*, pages 129–138, 1998.

N. Friedman, D. Geiger, and M. Goldszmidt. Bayesian network classifiers. *Machine Learning*, 29: 131–163, 1997.

G. Fung and O. Mangasarian. Semi-supervised support vector machines for unlabeled data classification. *Optimization Methods and Software*, 15:29–44, 2001.

C. Galarza, E. Rietman, and V. Vapnik. Applications of model selection techniques to polynomial approximation. Preprint, 1996.

A. Gammerman, V. Vapnik, and V. Vowk. Learning by transduction. In *Conference on Uncertainty in Artificial Intelligence*, pages 148–156, 1998.

S. Ganesalingam. Classification and mixture approaches to clustering via maximum likelihood. *Applied Statistics*, 38(3):455–466, 1989.

S. Ganesalingam and G. McLachlan. The efficiency of a linear discriminant function based on unclassified initial samples. *Biometrika*, 65:658–662, 1978.

S. Ganesalingam and G. McLachlan. Small sample results for a linear discriminant function estimated from a mixture of normal populations. *Journal of Statistical Computation and Simulation*, 9:151–158, 1979.

A. Garg and D. Roth. Understanding probabilistic classifiers. In *Proceedings of the 12th European Conference on Machine Learning*, pages 179–191, 2001.

S. Geman, E. Bienenstock, and R. Doursat. Neural networks and the bias/variance dilemma. *Neural Computation*, 4(1):1–58, 1992.

S. Geman and D. Geman. Stochastic relaxation, Gibbs distributions and the Bayesian restoration of images. *IEEE Transactions on Pattern Analysis and Machine Intelligence*, 6:721–742, 1984.

R. Ghani. Combining labeled and unlabeled data for text classification with a large number of categories. In *Proceedings of the IEEE International Conference on Data Mining*, 2001.

R. Ghani. Combining labeled and unlabeled data for multiclass text categorization. In *Proceedings of the International Conference on Machine Learning*, 2002.

E. Giné and A. Guillou. Rates of strong uniform consistency for multivariate kernel density estimators. *Annales de l'Institut Henri Poincaré (B) Probability and Statistics*, 38(6):907–921, November 2002.

L. Goldstein and K. Messer. Optimal plug-in estimators for nonparametric functional estimation. *Annals of Statistics*, 20(3):1306–1328, 1992.

G. H. Golub and C. F. Van Loan. *Matrix Computations*. Johns Hopkins University Press, Baltimore, 3rd edition, 1996.

C. Goutte, H. Déjean, E. Gaussier, J.-M. Renders, and N. Cancedda. Combining labelled and unlabelled data: A case study on Fisher kernels and transductive inference for biological entity recognition. In *Conference on Natural Language Learning*, 2002.

T. Graepel, R. Herbrich, and K. Obermayer. Bayesian transduction. In *Advances in Neural Information System Processing*, volume 12, 2000.

Y. Grandvalet. Logistic regression for partial labels. In *Ninth Information Processing and Management of Uncertainty in Knowledge-based Systems*, pages 1935–1941, 2002.

Y. Grandvalet and Y. Bengio. Semi-supervised learning by entropy minimization. In *Advances in Neural Information Processing Systems*, volume 17, 2004.

A. G. Gray and A. W. Moore. N-Body problems in statistical learning. In T. K. Leen, T. G. Dietterich, and V. Tresp, editors, *Advances in Neural Information Processing Systems 13*, pages 521–527, Cambridge, MA, 2001. MIT Press.

M. Gribskov and N. L. Robinson. Use of receiver operating characteristic (ROC) analysis to evaluate sequence matching. *Computers and Chemistry*, 20(1):25–33, 1996.

L. Hagen and A. B. Kahng. New spectral methods for ratio cut partitioning and clustering. *IEEE. Transactions on Computed Aided Desgin*, 11:1074–1085, 1992.

J. Ham, D. D. Lee, S. Mika, and B. Schölkopf. A kernel view of the dimensionality reduction of manifolds. In *Proceedings of the Twenty-first International Conference on Machine Learning*, pages 369–376, Banff, Canada, 2004.

J. M. Hammersley and P. Clifford. Markov fields on finite graphs and lattices. Unpublished manuscript, 1971.

J. A. Hanley and B. J. McNeil. The meaning and use of the area under a receiver operating characteristic (ROC) curve. *Radiology*, 143:29–36, 1982.

W. Härdle, M. Müller, S. Sperlich, and A. Werwatz. *Nonparametric and Semiparametric Models*. Springer-Verlag, Berlin, 2004. URL http://www.xplore-stat.de/ebooks/ebooks.html.

R. Hardt and F. H. Lin. Mappings minimizing the L^p norm of the gradient. *Communications on Pure and Applied Mathematics*, 40:556–588, 1987.

H. O. Hartley and J. N. K. Rao. Classification and estimation in analysis of variance problems. *Review of International Statistical Institute*, 36:141–147, 1968.

T. Hastie and R. Tibshirani. *Generalized Additive Models*. Chapman and Hall, New York, 1990.

T. Hastie, R. Tibshirani, and J. Friedman. *The Elements of Statistical Learning*. Springer Series in Statistics. Springer-Verlag, New York, 2001.

D. Haussler. Convolution kernels on discrete structures. Technical Report UCSC-CRL-99-10, University of California, Santa Cruz, Santa Cruz, CA, July 1999.

D. Heckerman, D. M. Chickering, C. Meek, R. Rounthwaite, and C. Kadie. Dependency networks for inference, collaborative filtering, and data visualization. *Journal of Machine Learning Research*, 1:49–75, 2001.

M. Hein, J.-Y. Audibert, and U. von Luxburg. From graphs to manifolds - weak and strong pointwise consistency of graph Laplacians. In *Proceedings of the Eighteenth Conference on Learning Theory*, pages 470–485, 2005.

M. Hein and Y. Audibert. Intrinsic dimensionality estimation of submanifolds in R^d. *Proceedings of the Twenty-second International Conference on Machine Learning*, pages 289 – 296, 2005.

J. Heinonen, T. Kilpeläinen, and O. Martio. *Nonlinear Potential Theory of Degenerate Elliptic Equations*. Oxford University Press, Oxford, 1993.

C. Helmberg. Semidefinite programming for combinatorial optimization. Habilitationsschrift ZIB-Report ZR-00-34, TU Berlin, Konrad-Zuse-Zentrum Berlin, 2000.

H. Hishigaki, K. Nakai, T. Ono, A. Tanigaki, and T. Takagi. Assessment of prediction accuracy of protein function from protein-protein interaction data. *Yeast*, 18:523–531, 2001.

D. S. Hochbaum and D. B. Shmoys. A best possible heuristic for the k-center problem. *Mathematics of Operations Research*, 10(2):180–184, 1985.

T. Hofmann and J. Puzicha. Statistical models for co-occurrence data. Technical Report AI Memo 1625, Artificial Intelligence Laboratory, MIT, Cambridge, MA, February 1998.

R. A. Horn and C. R. Johnson. *Matrix Analysis*. Cambridge University Press, Cambridge, UK, 1985.

D. W. Hosmer. A comparison of iterative maximum likelihood estimates of the parameters of a mixture of two normal distributions under three different types of sample. *Biometrics*, 29: 761–770, December 1973.

P. J. Huber. The behavior of maximum likelihood estimates under nonstandard conditions. In *Proceedings of the Fifth Berkeley Symposium in Mathematical Statistics and Probability*, pages 221–233. University of California Press, Berkeley, 1967.

E. Ie, J. Weston, W. S. Noble, and C. Leslie. Multi-class protein fold recognition using adaptive codes. In *Proceedings of the International Conference on Machine Learning*, 2005.

J. Ihmels, G. Friedlander, S. Bergmann, O. Sarig, Y. Ziv, and N. Barkai. Revealing modular organization in the yeast transcriptional network. *Nature Genetics*, 31:370–377, 2002.

T. Jaakkola, M. Diekhans, and D. Haussler. A discriminative framework for detecting remote protein homologies. *Journal of Computational Biology*, 7(1-2):95–114, 2000.

T. Jaakkola and D. Haussler. Exploiting generative models in discriminative classifiers. In *Advances in Neural Information Processing Systems 11*, pages 487–493, Cambridge, MA, 1999. MIT Press.

T. Jebara, R. Kondor, and A. Howard. Probability product kernels. *Journal of Machine Learning*, 5:819–844, 2004.

R. Jin and Z. Ghahramani. Learning with multiple labels. In *Advances in Neural Information Processing Systems 15*, Cambridge, MA, 2003. MIT Press.

T. Joachims. A probabilistic analysis of the Rocchio algorithm with TFIDF for text categorization. In *Machine Learning: Proceedings of the Fourteenth International Conference*, pages 143–151, 1997. URL ftp://ftp.cs.cmu.edu/afs/cs/user/thorsten/www/icml97.ps.Z.

T. Joachims. Text categorization with support vector machines: Learning with many relevant features. In *Tenth European Conference on Machine Learning*, pages 137–142, 1998.

T. Joachims. Transductive inference for text classification using support vector machines. In *Proceedings of the Sixteenth International Conference on Machine Learning*, pages 200–209, Bled,

Slovenia, 1999. Morgan Kaufmann. URL `http://www-ai.cs.uni-dortmund.de/DOKUMENTE/joachims_99c.ps.gz`.

T. Joachims. *Learning to Classify Text Using Support Vector Machines – Methods, Theory, and Algorithms*. Kluwer, Dordrecht, the Netherlands, 2002.

T. Joachims. Transductive learning via spectral graph partitioning. In *Proceedings of the International Conference on Machine Learning*, 2003.

I. T. Jolliffe. *Principal Component Analysis*. Springer-Verlag, New York, 1986.

M. I. Jordan, editor. *Learning in Graphical Models*. MIT Press, Cambridge, MA, 1999.

M. Kääriäinen. Generalization error bounds using unlabeled data. In *Proceedings of the Annual Conference on Computational Learning Theory*, 2005.

M. Kääriäinen and J. Langford. A comparison of tight generalization bounds. In *Proceedings of the International Conference on Machine Learning*, 2005.

S. D. Kamvar, D. Klein, and C. D. Manning. Spectral learning. In *Proceedings of the International Joint Conferences on Artificial Intelligence*, pages 561–566, 2003.

T. Kanade, J. Cohn, and Y. Tian. Comprehensive database for facial expression analysis. In *Fourth IEEE International Conference on Automatic Face and Gesture Recognition*, 2000.

M. Kanehisa, S. Goto, S. Kawashima, Y. Okuno, and M .Hattori. The KEGG resources for deciphering genome. *Nucleic Acids Research*, 32:D277–D280, 2004.

N. Kasabov and S. Pang. Transductive support vector machines and applications in bioinformatics for promoter recognition. *Neural Information Processing - Letters and Reviews*, 3(2):31–38, 2004.

M. Kearns. Efficient noise-tolerant learning from statistical queries. *Journal of the ACM (JACM)*, 45(6):983 – 1006, 1998.

M. Kearns, Y. Mansour, and A. Y. Ng. An information-theoretic analysis of hard and soft assignment methods for clustering. In *Uncertainty in Artificial Intelligence*, pages 282–293, 1997.

M. Kearns and U. Vazirani. *An Introduction to Computational Learning Theory*. MIT Press, Cambridge, MA, 1994.

M. J. Kearns and R. E. Schapire. Efficient distribution-free learning of probabilistic concepts. In S. J. Hanson, G. A. Drastal, and R. L. Rivest, editors, *Computational Learning Theory and Natural Learning Systems, Volume I: Constraints and Prospect*. MIT Press, Cambridge, MA, 1994.

S. S. Keerthi and D. DeCoste. A modified finite Newton method for fast solution of large scale linear SVMs. *Journal of Machine Learning Research*, 6:341–361, 2005.

B. Kegl and L. Wang. Boosting on manifolds: Adaptive regularization of base classifiers. In *Advances in Neural Information Processing Systems*, volume 17, 2004.

D. Klein, S. D. Kamvar, and C. Manning. From instance-level constraints to space-level constraints: Making the most of prior knowledge in data clustering. In *Proceedings of the International Conference on Machine Learning*, pages 307–314, Sydney, Australia, 2002.

J. Kleinberg. Detecting a network failure. In *Proceedings of the Forty-first IEEE Symposium on Foundations of Computer Science*, pages 231–239, 2000.

J. Kleinberg, M. Sandler, and A. Slivkins. Network failure detection and graph connectivity. In *Proceedings of the Fifteenth annual ACM-SIAM symposium on Discrete algorithms*, pages 76–85, Philadelphia, PA, USA, 2004. Society for Industrial and Applied Mathematics.

J. Kleinberg and E. Tardos. Approximation algorithms for classification problems with pairwise relationships: Metric labeling and Markov random fields. In *Proceedings of the 40th IEEE Symposium on Foundations of Computer Science*, pages 14–23, 1999.

A. R. Klivans, R. O'Donnell, and R. Servedio. Learning intersections and thresholds of halfspaces. In *Proceedings of the Forty-third Symposium on Foundations of Computer Science*, pages 177–186, 2002.

M. Kockelkorn, A. Lüneburg, and T. Scheffer. Using transduction and multi-view learning to answer emails. In *European Conference on Principles and Practice of Knowledge Discovery in Databases*, pages 266–277, 2003.

R. Kohavi. A study of cross-validation and bootstrap for accuracy estimation and model selection. In *Proceedings of International Joint Conference on Artificial Intelligence*, 1995.

V. Koltchinskii. Rademacher penalties and structural risk minimization. *IEEE Transactions on Information Theory*, 47(5):1902–1914, 2001.

P. Komarek and A. Moore. Fast robust logistic regression for large sparse datasets with binary outputs. In *Artificial Intelligence and Statistics*, 2003.

R. I. Kondor and J. Lafferty. Diffusion kernels on graphs and other discrete structures. In *Proceedings of the Nineteenth International Conference on Machine Learning*, 2002.

B. Krishnapuram, D. Williams, Y. Xue, A. Hartemink, L. Carin, and M. Figueiredo. On semi-supervised classification. In *Advances in Neural Information Processing Systems*, volume 17, 2004.

M. Krogel and T. Scheffer. Multirelational learning, text mining, and semi-supervised learning for functional genomics. *Machine Learning*, 57(1/2):61–81, 2004.

A. Krogh, M. Brown, I. Mian, K. Sjolander, and D. Haussler. Hidden Markov models in computational biology: Applications to protein modeling. *Journal of Molecular Biology*, 235:1501–1531, 1994.

A. Krogh and J. Vedelsby. Neural network ensembles, cross validation, and active learning. In *Advances in Neural Information Processing Systems 7*, pages 231–238, 1995.

R. Kuang, E. Ie, K. Wang, K. Wang, M. Siddiqi, Y. Freund, and C. Leslie. Profile-based string kernels for remote homology detection and motif extraction. In *Computational Systems Biology Conference*, 2004.

S. Lafon. *Diffusion Maps and Geometric Harmonics*. PhD thesis, Yale University, New Haven, CT, 2004.

T. N. Lal, M. Schröder, T. Hinterberger, J. Weston, M. Bogdan, N. Birbaumer, and B. Schölkopf. Support vector channel selection in BCI. *IEEE Transactions on Biomedical Engineering*, 51 (6):1003–1010, 2004.

L. Lamport. How to write a proof. *American Mathematical Monthly*, 102(7):600–608, 1993.

G. R. G. Lanckriet, N. Cristianini, P. Bartlett, L. El Ghaoui, and M. I. Jordan. Learning the kernel matrix with semidefinite programming. *Journal of Machine Learning Research*, 5:27–72, 2004a.

G. R. G. Lanckriet, T. De Bie, N. Cristianini, M. I. Jordan, and W. S. Noble. A statistical framework for genomic data fusion. *Bioinformatics*, 20:2626–2635, 2004b.

G. R. G. Lanckriet, M. Deng, N. Cristianini, M. I. Jordan, and W. S. Noble. Kernel-based data fusion and its application to protein function prediction in yeast. In *Proceedings of the Pacific Symposium on Biocomputing*, 2004c.

T. Lange, M. H. C. Law, A. K. Jain, and J. M. Buhmann. Learning with constrained and unlabeled data. In *Computer Vision and Pattern Recognition*, pages 731–738, San Diego, CA, 2005.

S. Lauritzen. *Graphical Models*. Oxford Statistical Sciences. Clarendon Press, Oxford, 1996.

G. Lebanon. Learning Riemannian metrics. In *Proceedings of the Nineteenth Conference on Uncertainty in Artificial Intelligence*, San Fransisco, 2003. Morgan Kaufmann.

I. Lee, S.V. Date, A.T. Adai, and E.M. Marcotte. A probabilistic functional network of yeast genes. *Science*, 306 (5701):1555–1558, 2004.

T. I. Lee, N. J. Rinaldi, F. Robert, D. T. Odom, Z. Bar-Joseph, G. K. Gerber, N. M. Hannett, C. R. Harbison, C. M. Thompson, I. Simon, et al. Transcriptional regulatory networks in *Saccharomyces cerevisiae*. *Science*, 298:799–804, 2002.

B. Leskes. The value of agreement, a new boosting algorithm. In *Conference on Computational Learning Theory*, pages 51 – 56, 2005.

C. Leslie, E. Eskin, J. Weston, and W. S. Noble. Mismatch string kernels for SVM protein classification. In S. Becker, S. Thrun, and K. Obermayer, editors, *Advances in Neural Information Processing Systems*, pages 1441–1448, Cambridge, MA, 2003. MIT Press.

C. Leslie and R. Kuang. Fast kernels for inexact string matching. *Conference on Computational Learning Theory*, 2003.

A. Levin, P. Viola, and Y. Freund. Unsupervised improvement of visual detectors using co-training. In *Proceedings of the Ninth IEEE International Conference on Computer Vision*, pages 626–633, Nice, France, 2003.

D. D. Lewis. The Reuters-21578 data set. http://www.daviddlewis.com/resources/testcollections/reuters21578/, 1997.

D. D. Lewis. Naive (Bayes) at forty: The independence assumption in information retrieval. In

Tenth European Conference on Machine Learning, pages 4–15, 1998.

D. D. Lewis and M. Ringuette. A comparison of two learning algorithms for text categorization. In *Third Annual Symposium on Document Analysis and Information Retrieval*, pages 81–93, 1994. URL `http://www.research.att.com/~lewis/papers/lewis94b.ps`.

C. Liao and W. S. Noble. Combining pairwise sequence similarity and support vector machines for remote protein homology detection. *Proceedings Sixth Annual International Conference on Computational Molecular Biology*, 2002.

R. Liere and P. Tadepalli. Active learning with committees for text categorization. In *Proceedings of the Fourteenth National Conference on Artificial Intelligence*, pages 591–596, 1997. URL `http://www.cs.orst.edu/~lierer/aaai97.ps`.

J. Lin. Divergence measures based on the Shannon entropy. *IEEE Transactions on Information Theory*, 37(1):145–151, 1991.

N. Linial, Y. Mansour, and N. Nisan. Constant depth circuits, Fourier transform, and learnability. In *Proceedings of the Thirtieth Annual Symposium on Foundations of Computer Science*, pages 574–579, Research Triangle Park, NC, October 1989.

R. J. A. Little. Discussion on the paper by Professor Dempster, Professor Laird and Dr. Rubin. *Journal of the Royal Statistical Society, Series B*, 39(1):25, 1977.

H. Lodhi, C. Saunders, J. Shawe-Taylor, N. Cristianini, and C. Watkins. Text classification using string kernels. *Journal of Machine Learning Research*, 2:419–444, 2002.

J. Löfberg. *YALMIP 3*, 2004. `http://control.ee.ethz.ch/~joloef/yalmip.msql`.

D. MacKay. Bayesian interpolation. *Neural Computation*, 4:415–447, 1992.

J. B. MacQueen. Some methods for classification and analysis of multivariate observations. In *Proceedings of Fifth Berkeley Symposium on Mathematical Statistics and Probability*, pages 281–297, 1967.

C. Mallows. Some comments on C_p. *Technometrics*, 15:661–676, 1973.

K. V. Mardia and P. E. Jupp. *Directional Statistics*. Wiley, Hoboken, NJ, 2nd edition, 2000.

A. McCallum and K. Nigam. A comparison of event models for naive Bayes text classification. In *Learning for Text Categorization: Papers from the AAAI Workshop*, pages 41–48. AAAI Press, 1998a.

A. McCallum and K. Nigam. Employing EM and pool-based active learning for text classification. In *Proceedings of the International Conference on Machine Learning*, Madison, WI, 1998b.

A. McCallum, R. Rosenfeld, T. Mitchell, and A. Ng. Improving text classification by shrinkage in a hierarchy of classes. In *Machine Learning: Proceedings of the Fifteenth International Conference*, pages 359–367, 1998.

G. J. McLachlan. Iterative reclassification procedure for constructing an asymptotically optimal rule of allocation in discriminant analysis. *Journal of the American Statistical Association*, 70 (350):365–369, 1975.

G. J. McLachlan. Estimating the linear discriminant function from initial samples containing a small number of unclassified observations. *Journal of the American Statistical Association*, 72 (358):403–406, 1977.

G. J. McLachlan. *Discriminant Analysis and Statistical Pattern Recognition*. Wiley, Hoboken, NJ, 1992.

G. J. McLachlan and S. Ganesalingam. Updating a discriminant function on the basis of unclassified data. *Communications in Statistics: Simulation and Computation*, 11(6):753–767, 1982.

G. J. McLachlan and T. Krishnan. *The EM Algorithm and Extensions*. John Wiley and Sons, New York, 1997.

M. Meila. *Learning with Mixtures of Trees*. PhD thesis, MIT, Cambridge, MA, 1999.

S. Mendelson and P. Philips. Random subclass bounds. In *Proceedings of the Sixteenth Annual Conference on Computational Learning Theory*, 2003.

C. J. Merz, D. C. St. Clair, and W. E. Bond. Semi-supervised adaptive resonance theory (smart2). In *International Joint Conference on Neural Networks*, volume 3, pages 851–856, 1992.

D. Miller and H. Uyar. A generalized Gaussian mixture classifier with learning based on both labelled and unlabelled data. In *Proceedings of the Conference on Information Science and Systems*, 1996.

D. Miller and H. Uyar. A mixture of experts classifier with learning based on both labelled and unlabelled data. In M. Mozer, M. Jordan, and T. Petsche, editors, *Advances in Neural Information Processing Systems 9*, pages 571–577, Cambridge, MA, 1997. MIT Press.

T. P Minka. *A Family of Algorithms for Approximate Bayesian Inference*. PhD thesis, Massachusetts Institute of Technology, Cambridge, MA, 2001.

T. Mitchell. *Machine Learning*. McGraw Hill, New York, 1997.

G. D. Murray and D. M. Titterington. Estimation problems with data from a mixture. *Applied Statistics*, 27(3):325–334, 1978.

A. G. Murzin, S. E. Brenner, T. Hubbard, and C. Chothia. SCOP: A structural classification of proteins database for the investigation of sequences and structures. *Journal of Molecular Biology*, 247:536–540, 1995.

E. A. Nadaraya. On estimating regression. *Theory of Probability and Its Applications*, 9:141–142, 1964.

E. A. Nadaraya. *Nonparametric Estimation of Probability Densities and Regression Curves*. Kluwer, Dordrecht, the Netherlands, 1989.

R. M. Neal and G. E. Hinton. A view of the EM algorithm that justifies incremental, sparse, and other variants. In M. I. Jordan, editor, *Learning in Graphical Models*, pages 355–368, Cambridge, MA, 1998. MIT Press.

S. A. Nene, S. K. Nayar, and H. Murase. Columbia object image library (COIL-100). Technical Report CUCS-006-96, Columbia University, New York, February 1996.

Y. Nesterov and A. Nemirovsky. Interior-point polynomial methods in convex programming: Theory and applications. *SIAM*, 13, 1994.

A. Y. Ng and M. Jordan. On discriminative vs. generative classifiers: A comparison of logistic regression and naive Bayes. In T. G. Dietterich, S. Becker, and Z. Ghahramani, editors, *Advances in Neural Information Processing Systems*, volume 14, pages 841–848, Cambridge, MA, 2001. MIT Press.

A. Y. Ng, M. Jordan, and Y. Weiss. On spectral clustering: Analysis and an algorithm. In T. G. Dietterich, S. Becker, and Z. Ghahramani, editors, *Advances in Neural Information Processing Systems 14*, Cambridge, MA, 2002. MIT Press.

K. Nigam. Using unlabeled data to improve text classification. Technical Report doctoral dissertation, CMU-CS-01-126, Carnegie Mellon University, Pittsburgh, 2001.

K. Nigam and R. Ghani. Analyzing the effectiveness and applicability of co-training. In *Ninth International Conference on Information and Knowledge Management*, pages 86–93, 2000.

K. Nigam, A. McCallum, S. Thrun, and T. Mitchell. Learning to classify text from labeled and unlabeled documents. In *Proceedings of the Fifteenth National Conference on Artificial Intelligence*, pages 792–799, 1998.

K. Nigam, A. McCallum, S. Thrun, and T. Mitchell. Text classification from labeled and unlabeled documents using EM. *Machine Learning*, 39(2/3):103–134, 2000.

A. O'Hagan. Some Bayesian numerical analysis. In J. M. Bernardo, J. O. Berger, A. P. Dawid, and A. F. M. Smith, editors, *Bayesian Statistics 4*, pages 345–363, Valencia, 1992. Oxford University Press.

T. O'Neill. Normal discrimination with unclassified observations. *Journal of the American Statistical Association*, 73(364):821–826, 1978.

D. Opitz and J. Shavlik. Generating accurate and diverse members of a neural-network ensemble. In *Advances in Neural Information Processing Systems 8*, 1996.

M. Ouimet and Y. Bengio. Greedy spectral embedding. In *Proceedings of the Tenth International Workshop on Artificial Intelligence and Statistics*, 2005.

A. Papoulis and S. U. Pillai. *Probability, Random Variables and Stochastic Processes*. McGraw-Hill, New York, 4th edition, 2001.

J. Park, K. Karplus, C. Barrett, R. Hughey, D. Haussler, T. Hubbard, and C. Chothia. Sequence comparisons using multiple sequences detect twice as many remote homologues as pairwise methods. *Journal of Molecular Biology*, 284(4):1201–1210, 1998.

S. Park and B. Zhang. Large scale unstructured document classification using unlabeled data and syntactic information. In *Pacific-Asia Conference on Knowledge Discovery and Data Mining*, LNCS vol. 2637, pages 88–99. Springer-Verlag, 2003.

J. Pearl. *Probabilistic Reasoning in Intelligent Systems: Networks of Plausible Inference*. Morgan Kaufmann, San Mateo,CA, 1988.

F. C. N. Pereira, N. Tishby, and L. Lee. Distributional clustering of English words. In *Meeting of the Association for Computational Linguistics*, pages 183–190, Columbus, Ohio, 1993.

D. Pierce and C. Cardie. Limitations of co-training for natural language learning from large datasets. In *Proceedings of the 2001 Conference on Empirical Methods in Natural Language Processing*, pages 1–9, 2001.

J. C. Platt. Fast embedding of sparse similarity graphs. In S. Thrun, L. K. Saul, and B. Schölkopf, editors, *Advances in Neural Information Processing Systems 16*, Cambridge, MA, 2004. MIT Press.

T. Poggio and F. Girosi. Regularization algorithms for learning that are equivalent to multilayer networks. *Science*, 247:978–982, 1990.

T. Poggio, S. Mukherjee, R. Rifkin, A. Rakhlin, and A. Verri. B. In *Proceedings of the Conference on Uncertainty in Geometric Computations*, pages 22–28, 2001.

M. Porter. An algorithm for suffix stripping. *Program*, 14(3):130–137, 1980.

J. Ratsaby and S. Venkatesh. Learning from a mixture of labeled and unlabeled examples with parametric side information. In *Proceedings of the Eighth Annual Conference on Computational Learning Theory*, pages 412–417, 1995.

R. A. Redner and H. F. Walker. Mixture densities, maximum likelihood and the EM algorithm. *SIAM Review*, 26(2):195–239, April 1984.

B. Ripley. *Pattern Recognition and Neural Networks*. Cambridge University Press, Cambridge, UK, 1996.

J. Rissanen. Stochastic complexity and modeling. *Annals of Statistics*, 14:1080–1100, 1986.

J. Rocchio. Relevance feedback in information retrieval. In *The SMART Retrieval System:Experiments in Automatic Document Processing*, chapter 14, pages 313–323. Prentice Hall, Englewood Cliffs, NJ, 1971.

K. Rose, E. Gurewitz, and G. Fox. A deterministic annealing approach to clustering. *Pattern Recognition Letters*, 11(9):589–594, 1990.

K. Rose, E. Gurewitz, and G. Fox. Vector quantization by deterministic annealing. *IEEE Transactions on Information Theory*, 38(4):1249–1257, 1992.

S. Rosenberg. *The Laplacian on a Riemannian Manifold*. Cambridge University Press, Cambridge, UK, 1997.

B. Rost and C. Sander. Prediction of protein secondary structure at better than 70% accuracy. *Journal of Molecular Biology*, 232(2):584–599, July 1993.

D. Roth. On the hardness of approximate reasoning. *Artificial Intelligence*, 82(1-2):273–302, 1996.

S. T. Roweis and L. K. Saul. Nonlinear dimensionality reduction by locally linear embedding. *Science*, 290:2323–2326, 2000.

Y. Saad. *Iterative Methods for Sparse Linear Systems*. PWS Publishing Company, Boston, 1996.

H. Saigo, J. Vert, N. Uea, and T. Akutsu. Protein homology detection using string alignment kernels. *Bioinformatics*, 20:1682–1689, 2004.

Sajama and A. Orlitsky. Estimating and computing density based distance metrics. In *Proceedings of the Twenty-second International Conference on Machine Learning*. Morgan Kaufmann, San Francisco, 2005.

L. K. Saul and S. T. Roweis. Think globally, fit locally: Unsupervised learning of low dimensional manifolds. *Journal of Machine Learning Research*, 4:119–155, 2003.

C. Saunders, A. Gammerman, and V. Vovk. Transduction with confidence and credibility. In *International Joint Conference on Artificial Intelligence*, volume 2, pages 722–726, San Francisco, 1999. Morgan Kaufmann.

C. Schaffer. Overfitting avoidance as bias. *Machine Learning*, 10(2):153–178, 1993.

C. Schaffer. A conservation law for generalization performance. In *Proceedings of International Conference on Machine Learning*, pages 683–690, 1994.

B. Schölkopf and A. J. Smola. *Learning with Kernels*. MIT Press, Cambridge, MA, 2002.

B. Schölkopf, A. J. Smola, and K.-R. Müller. Nonlinear component analysis as a kernel eigenvalue problem. *Neural Computation*, 10:1299–1319, 1998.

D. Schuurmans and F. Southey. Metric-based methods for adaptive model selection and regularization. Special issue on new methods for model selection and model combination. *Machine Learning*, 48(1-3):51–84, 2002.

D. Schuurmans, L. Ungar, and D. Foster. Characterizing the generalization performance of model selection strategies. In *Proceedings of International Conference on Machine Learning*, pages 340–348, 1997.

G. Schwarz. Estimating the dimension of a model. *Annals of Statistics*, 6:461–464, 1978.

B. Schwikowski, P. Uetz, and S. Fields. A network of protein-protein interactions in yeast. *Nature Biotechnology*, 18:1257–1261, 2000.

H. J. Scudder. Probability of error of some adaptive pattern-recognition machines. *IEEE Transactions on Information Theory*, 11:363–371, 1965.

M. Seeger. Input-dependent regularization of conditional density models, 2000a. Technical Report, Institute for ANC, Edinburgh, UK. See `www.kyb.tuebingen.mpg.de/bs/people/seeger`.

M. Seeger. Learning with labeled and unlabeled data, 2000b. Technical Report, Institute for ANC, Edinburgh, UK. See `www.kyb.tuebingen.mpg.de/bs/people/seeger`.

M. Seeger. Covariance kernels from Bayesian generative models. In T. G. Dietterich, S. Becker, and Z. Ghahramani, editors, *Advances in Neural Information Processing Systems 14*, pages 905–912, Cambridge, MA, 2002. MIT Press.

E. Segal, M. Shapira, A. Regev, D. Pe'er, D. Botstein, D. Koller, and N. Friedman. Module networks: Identifying regulatory modules and their condition specific regulators from gene expression data. *Nature Biotechnology*, 34(2):166–176, 2003a.

E. Segal, H. Wang, and D. Koller. Discovering molecular pathways from protein interaction and gene expression data. *Bioinformatics*, 19:i264–i272, July 2003b.

J. A. Sethian. *Level Set Methods and Fast Marching Methods*. Cambridge University Press, Cambridge, UK, 1999.

F. Sha and L. K. Saul. Analysis and extension of spectral methods for nonlinear dimensionality reduction. In *Proceedings of the Twenty-second International Conference on Machine Learning*, Bonn, Germany, 2005.

B. Shahshahani and D. Landgrebe. The effect of unlabeled samples in reducing the small sample size problem and mitigating the Hughes phenomenon. *IEEE Transactions on Geoscience and Remote Sensing*, 32(5):1087–1095, September 1994. URL `http://dynamo.ecn.purdue.edu/~landgreb/GRS94.pdf`.

J. Shawe-Taylor, P. L. Bartlett, R. C. Williamson, and M. Anthony. Structural risk minimization over data-dependent hierarchies. *IEEE Transactions on Information Theory*, 44(5):1926–1940, 1998.

J. Shawe-Taylor and N. Cristianini. *Kernel methods for Pattern Analysis*. Cambridge University Press, Cambridge, UK, 2004.

N. Shental, A. Bar-Hillel, T. Hertz, and D. Weinshall. Computing Gaussian mixture models with EM using equivalence constraints. In *Advances in Neural Information Processing Systems 16*, pages 465–472, 2004.

J. Shi and J. Malik. Normalized cuts and image segmentation. *IEEE Transactions on Pattern Analysis and Machine Intelligence*, 22(8):888–905, 2000.

R. Shibata. An optimal selection of regression variables. *Biometrika*, 68:45–54, 1981.

V. Sindhwani. Kernel machines for semi-supervised learning, 2004. Technical Report, masters thesis, University of Chicago.

V. Sindhwani, W. Chu, and S. S. Keerthi. Semi-supervised Gaussian processes, 2006. Technical Report, Yahoo! Research.

V. Sindhwani, P. Niyogi, and M. Belkin. Beyond the point cloud: From transductive to semi-supervised learning. In *Proceedings of the International Conference on Machine Learning*, 2005.

T. Smith and M. Waterman. Identification of common molecular subsequences. *Journal of Molecular Biology*, 147:195–197, 1981.

A. Smola and R. Kondor. Kernels and regularization on graphs. In *Conference on Learning Theory*, 2003.

P. Sollich. Probabilistic interpretation and Bayesian methods for support vector machines. In

Proceedings of 1999 International Conference on Artificial Neural Networks, pages 91–96, London, 1999. The Institution of Electrical Engineers.

P. Sollich. Probabilistic methods for support vector machines. In S. A. Solla, T. K. Leen, and K.-R. Müller, editors, *Advances in Neural Information Processing Systems*, volume 12, pages 349–355, Cambridge, MA, 2000. MIT Press.

K. Sparck-Jones. A statistical interpretation of term specificity and its application in retrieval. *Journal of Documentation*, 28(1):11–21, 1972.

P. T. Spellman, G. Sherlock, M. Q. Zhang, V. R. Iyer, K. Anders, M. B. Eisen, P. O. Brown, D. Botstein, and B. Futcher. Comprehensive identification of cell cycle-regulated genes of the yeast *Saccharomyces cerevisiae* by microarray hybridization. *Molecular Biology of the Cell*, 9: 3273–3297, 1998.

D. A. Spielman and S. H. Teng. Nearly-linear time algorithms for graph partitioning, graph sparsification, and solving linear systems. In *Proceedings of the Twenty-sixth annual ACM Symposium on Theory of Computing*, pages 81–90, New York, 2004. ACM Press.

A. Stolcke and S. M. Omohundro. Best-first model merging for hidden Markov model induction. Technical Report TR-94-003, ICSI, University of California, Berkeley, 1994. URL `http://www.icsi.berkeley.edu/techreports/1994.html`.

C. J. Stone. Optimal rates of convergence for nonparametric estimators. *Annals of Statistics*, 8 (6):1348–1360, 1980.

A. Strehl, J. Ghosh, and R. Mooney. Impact of similarity measures on web-page clustering. In *Workshop on Artificial Intelligence for Web Search (AAAI 2000)*, pages 58–64, 2000.

R. Strichartz. *The Way of Analysis*. Jones and Bartlett, Sudbury, MA, 1995.

J. F. Sturm. Using SeDuMi 1.02, a Matlab toolbox for optimization over symmetric cones. Special issue on interior point methods (cd supplement with software). *Optimization Methods and Software*, 11-12(8):625–653, 1999.

J. Sun, S. Boyd, L. Xiao, and P. Diaconis. The fastest mixing Markov process on a graph and a connection to a maximum variance unfolding problem. *SIAM Review*, 2006.

M. Szummer and T. Jaakkola. Clustering and efficient use of unlabeled examples. In *Advances in Neural Information Processing Systems 14*, Cambridge, MA, 2001.

M. Szummer and T. Jaakkola. Information regularization with partially labeled data. In *Advances in Neural Information Processing Systems*, volume 15. MIT Press, 2002a.

M. Szummer and T. Jaakkola. Partially labeled classification with Markov random walks. In T. G. Dietterich, S. Becker, and Z. Ghahramani, editors, *Advances in Neural Information Processing Systems 14*, Cambridge, MA, 2002b. MIT Press.

B. Taskar, P. Abbeel, and D. Koller. Discriminative probabilistic models for relational data. In *Proceedings of the Eighteenth Annual Conference on Uncertainty in Artificial Intelligence*, 2002.

J. B. Tenenbaum, V. de Silva, and J. C. Langford. A global geometric framework for nonlinear dimensionality reduction. *Science*, 290(5500):2319–2323, 2000.

A. N. Tikhonov and V. Y. Arsenin. *Solutions of Ill-Posed Problems*. W. H. Winston, Washington, DC, 1977.

D. M. Titterington. Updating a diagnostic system using unconfirmed cases. *Applied Statistics*, 25 (3):238–247, 1976.

D. M. Titterington, A. Smith, and U. Makov. *Statistical Analysis of Finite Mixture Distributions*. Wiley Series in Probability and Mathematical Statistics. Wiley, New York, 1st edition, 1985.

S. Tong and D. Koller. Restricted Bayes optimal classifiers. In *Proceedings of the Seventeenth National Conference on Artificial Intelligence*, pages 658–664, 2000.

S. Tong and D. Koller. Support vector machine active learning with applications to text classification. *Journal of Machine Learning Research*, 2:45–66, November 2001.

V. Tresp. A Bayesian committee machine. *Neural Computation*, 12(11):2719–2741, 2000.

K. Tsuda and W. S. Noble. Learning kernels from biological networks by maximizing entropy. *Bioinformatics*, 20(Suppl. 1):i326–i333, 2004.

N. Ueda and R. Nakano. Deterministic annealing variant of the EM algorithm. In *Advances in Neural Information Processing Systems 7*, pages 545–552, 1995.

P. Uetz, L. Giot, G. Cagney, T. A. Mansfield, R. S. Judson, J. R. Knight, D. Lockshon, V. Narayan, et al. A comprehensive analysis of protein-protein interactions in *Saccharomyces cerevisiae*. *Nature*, 403(6770):623–627, 2000.

L. G. Valiant. A theory of the learnable. *Communications of the ACM*, 27(11):1134–1142, 1984.

T. van Allen and R. Greiner. A model selection criteria for learning belief nets: An empirical comparison. In *International Conference on Machine Learning*, pages 1047–1054, 2000.

C. van Rijsbergen. A theoretical basis for the use of co-occurrence data in information retrieval. *Journal of Documentation*, 33(2):106–119, June 1977.

L. Vandenberghe and S. Boyd. Semidefinite programming. *SIAM Review*, 38(1):49–95, 1996.

V. Vapnik. *The Nature of Statistical Learning Theory*. Springer-Verlag, New York, 1995.

V. Vapnik. *Statistical Learning Theory*. Wiley, New York, 1998.

V. Vapnik. *Estimation of Dependences Based on Empirical Data*. Springer Series in Statistics. Springer-Verlag, New York, 2nd edition, 2006.

V. Vapnik and A. Chervonenkis. Uniform convergence of frequencies of occurrence of events to their probabilities. *Doklady Akademii Nauk SSSR*, 181:915–918, 1968.

V. Vapnik and A. Chervonenkis. On the uniform convergence of relative frequencies of events to their probabilities. *Theory of Probability and Its Applications*, 16(2):264–280, 1971.

V. Vapnik and A. Chervonenkis. *Theory of Pattern Recognition [in Russian]*. Nauka, Moscow, 1974.

V. Vapnik and A. Chervonenkis. The necessary and sufficient conditions for consistency in the empirical risk minimization method. *Pattern Recognition and Image Analysis*, 1(3):283–305, 1991.

V. Vapnik and A. Sterin. On structural risk minimization or overall risk in a problem of pattern recognition. *Automation and Remote Control*, 10(3):1495–1503, 1977.

A. Vazquez, A. Flammini, A. Maritan, and A. Vespignani. Global protein function prediction from protein-protein interaction networks. *Nature Biotechnology*, 21(6):697–700, 2003.

S. Vempala. A random sampling based algorithm for learning the intersection of half-spaces. In *Proceedings of the Thirty-eighth Symposium on Foundations of Computer Science*, pages 508–513, 1997.

K. A. Verbeurgt. Learning DNF under the uniform distribution in quasi-polynomial time. In *Conference on Computational Learning Theory*, pages 314–326, 1990.

J.-P. Vert and M. Kanehisa. Graph-driven features extraction from microarray data using diffusion kernels and kernel CCA. In S. Becker, S. Thrun, and K. Obermayer, editors, *Advances in Neural Information Processing Systems 15*, pages 1425–1432, Cambridge, MA, 2003. MIT Press.

J.-P. Vert and Y. Yamanishi. Supervised graph inference. In *Advances in Neural Information Processing Systems*, volume 17, 2004.

P. Vincent and Y. Bengio. Density-sensitive metrics and kernels. In *Workshop on Advances in Machine Learning*, Montréal, Québec, Canada, 2003.

S. V. N. Vishwanathan and A. Smola. Fast kernels for string and tree matching. *Neural Information Processing Systems 15*, 2002.

U. von Luxburg and O. Bousquet. Distance-based classification with Lipschitz functions. *Journal of Machine Learning Research*, 5:669–695, 2004.

U. von Luxburg, O. Bousquet, and M. Belkin. Limits of spectral clustering. In *Advances in Neural Information Processing Systems 17*. MIT Press, Cambridge, MA, 2005.

C. von Mering, R. Krause, B. Snel, M. Cornell, S. G. Olivier, S. Fields, and P. Bork. Comparative assessment of large-scale data sets of protein-protein interactions. *Nature*, 417:399–403, 2002.

V. Vovk, A. Gammerman, and C. Saunders. Machine-learning applications of algorithmic randomness. In *Proceedings of the Sixteenth International Conference on Machine Learning*, pages 444–453. Morgan Kaufmann, San Francisco, 1999.

K. Wagstaff. *Intelligent Clustering with Instance-Level Constraints*. PhD thesis, Cornell University, Ithaca, NY, 2002.

K. Wagstaff, C. Cardie, S. Rogers, and S. Schroedl. Constrained K-means clustering with background knowledge. In *Proceedings of the International Conference on Machine Learning*, pages 577–584, 2001.

G. Wahba. *Spline Models for Observational Data*. Number 59 in CBMS-NSF Regional Conference

Series in Applied Mathematics. SIAM, Philadelphia, 1990.

M. J. Wainwright and M. I. Jordan. Graphical models, exponential families, and variational inference. Technical Report 649, Department of Statistics, University of California, Berkeley, 2003.

L. Wang, K. L. Chan, and Z. Zhang. Bootstrapping SVM active learning by incorporating unlabelled images for image retrieval. In *Conference on Computer Vision and Pattern Recognition*, pages 629–634, 2003.

W. Wapnik and A. Tscherwonenkis. *Theorie der Zeichenerkennung*. Akademie Verlag, Berlin, 1979.

C. Watkins. Dynamic alignment kernels. In A. J. Smola, P. Bartlett, B. Schölkopf, and C. Schuurmans, editors, *Advances in Large Margin Classifiers*, Cambridge, MA, 1999. MIT Press.

G. S. Watson. Smooth regression analysis. *Sankhya - The Indian Journal of Statistics*, 26:359–372, 1964.

K. Q. Weinberger, B. D. Packer, and L. K. Saul. Nonlinear dimensionality reduction by semidefinite programming and kernel matrix factorization. In R. Cowell and Z. Ghahramani, editors, *Proceedings of the Tenth International Workshop on Artificial Intelligence and Statistics*, pages 381–388, 2005.

K. Q. Weinberger and L. K. Saul. Unsupervised learning of image manifolds by semidefinite programming. In *Proceedings of the IEEE Conference on Computer Vision and Pattern Recognition*, volume 2, pages 988–995, Washington D.C., 2004.

Y. Weiss. Segmentation using eigenvectors: A unifying view. In *Proceedings of the International Conference on Computer Vision*, pages 975–982, Kerkyra, Greece, 1999.

J. Weston, C. Leslie, D. Zhou, A. Elisseeff, and W. S. Noble. Cluster kernels for semi-supervised protein classification. *Advances in Neural Information Processing Systems 17*, 2003a.

J. Weston, F. Pérez-Cruz, O. Bousquet, O. Chapelle, A. Elisseeff, and B. Schölkopf. Feature selection and transduction for prediction of molecular bioactivity for drug design. *Bioinformatics*, 19(6):764–771, 2003b.

H. White. Maximum likelihood estimation of misspecified models. *Econometrica*, 50(1):1–25, January 1982.

C. K. I. Williams. Prediction with Gaussian processes: From linear regression to linear prediction and beyond. In M. I. Jordan, editor, *Learning in Graphical Models*, volume 89 of *Series D: Behavioural and Social Sciences*, Dordrecht, the Netherlands, 1998. Kluwer.

C. K. I. Williams. On a connection between kernel PCA and metric multidimensional scaling. In T. K. Leen, T. G. Dietterich, and V. Tresp, editors, *Advances in Neural Information Processing Systems 13*, pages 675–681, Cambridge, MA, 2001. MIT Press.

C. K. I. Williams and M. Seeger. Using the Nyström method to speed up kernel machines. In T.K. Leen, T.G. Dietterich, and V. Tresp, editors, *Advances in Neural Information Processing Systems 13*, pages 682–688, Cambridge, MA, 2001. MIT Press.

E. P. Xing, A. Y. Ng, M. I. Jordan, and S. Russell. Distance metric learning, with application to clustering with side-information. In *Advances in Neural Information Processing Systems*, volume 15, pages 505–512, Cambridge, MA, 2003. MIT Press.

M. Yamasaki. Ideal boundary limit of discrete Dirichlet functions. *Hiroshima Mathematical Journal*, 16(2):353–360, 1986.

Y. Yang and X. Liu. A re-examination of text categorization methods. In *Proceedings of the Twenty-first International ACM SIGIR Conference*, pages 42–49, 1999.

Y. Yang and J. O. Pedersen. Feature selection in statistical learning of text categorization. In *Machine Learning: Proceedings of the Fourteenth International Conference*, pages 412–420, 1997.

D. Yarowsky. Unsupervised word sense disambiguation rivaling supervised methods. In *Meeting of the Association for Computational Linguistics*, pages 189–196, 1995.

G. Yona, N. Linial, and M. Linial. Protomap: Automatic classification of protein sequences, a hierarchy of protein families, and local maps of the protein space. *Proteins: Structure, Function, and Genetics*, 37:360–678, 1999.

K. Yu, V. Tresp, and D. Zhou. Semi-supervised induction with basis function. Technical Report 141, Max-Planck Institut, Tübingen, 2004.

A. L. Yuille, P. Stolorz, and J. Utans. Statistical physics, mixtures of distributions, and the EM algorithm. *Neural Computation*, 6(2):334–340, 1994.

S. Zelikovitz and H. Hirsh. Improving short-text classification using unlabeled background knowledge to assess document similarity. In *Proceedings of the Seventeenth International Conference on Machine Learning*, 2000.

T. Zhang and F. Oles. A probability analysis on the value of unlabeled data for classification problems. In *International Joint Conference on Machine Learning*, pages 1191–1198, 2000.

Y. Zhang, M. Brady, and S. Smith. Hidden Markov random field model and segmentation of brain MR images. *IEEE Transactions on Medical Imaging*, 20(1):45–57, 2001.

Z. Zhang and H. Zha. Principal manifolds and nonlinear dimensionality reduction by local tangent space alignment. *SIAM Journal of Scientific Computing*, 26(1):313–338, 2004.

D. Zhou, O. Bousquet, T. N. Lal, J. Weston, and B. Schölkopf. Learning with local and global consistency. In S. Thrun, L. Saul, and B. Schölkopf, editors, *Advances in Neural Information Processing Systems 16*, pages 321–328. MIT Press, Cambridge, MA, 2004.

D. Zhou, J. Huang, and B. Schölkopf. Learning from labeled and unlabeled data on a directed graph. In L. De Raedt and S. Wrobel, editors, *Proceedings of the Twenty-second International Conference on Machine Learning*, 2005a.

D. Zhou, B. Schölkopf, and T. Hofmann. Semi-supervised learning on directed graphs. In L. K. Saul, Y. Weiss, and L. Bottou, editors, *Advances in Neural Information Processing Systems 18*, pages 1633–1640, Cambridge, MA, 2005b. MIT Press.

X. Zhu and Z. Ghahramani. Learning from labeled and unlabeled data with label propagation. Technical Report CMU-CALD-02-107, Carnegie Mellon University, Pittsburgh, 2002.

X. Zhu, Z. Ghahramani, and J. Lafferty. Combining active learning and semi-supervised learning using Gaussian fields and harmonic functions. In *ICML-2003 Workshop on the Continuum from Labeled to Unlabeled Data in Machine Learning*, pages 912–912, Washington, DC, 2003a.

X. Zhu, Z. Ghahramani, and J. Lafferty. Semi-supervised learning using Gaussian fields and harmonic functions. In *Twentieth International Conference on Machine Learning*, pages 912–912, Washington, DC, 2003b. AAAI Press.

X. Zhu, J. Lafferty, and Z. Ghahramani. Semi-supervised learning: From Gaussian fields to Gaussian processes. Technical Report CMU-CS-03-175, Carnegie Mellon University, Pittsburgh, 2003c.

Notation and Symbols

Sets of Numbers

$\mathbb{N}$	the set of natural numbers, $\mathbb{N} = \{1, 2, \ldots\}$
$\mathbb{R}$	the set of reals
$[n]$	compact notation for $\{1, \ldots, n\}$
$x \in [a, b]$	interval $a \leq x \leq b$
$x \in (a, b]$	interval $a < x \leq b$
$x \in (a, b)$	interval $a < x < b$
$|C|$	cardinality of a set C (for finite sets, the number of elements)

Data

$\mathcal{X}$	the input domain
d	(used if $\mathcal{X}$ is a vector space) dimension of $\mathcal{X}$
M	number of classes (for classification)
l, u	number of labeled, unlabeled training examples
n	total number of examples, $n = l + u$.
i, j	indices, often running over $[l]$ or $[n]$
x_i	input patterns $x_i \in \mathcal{X}$
y_i	classes $y_i \in [M]$ (for regression: target values $y_i \in \mathbb{R}$)
X	a sample of input patterns, $X = (x_1, \ldots, x_n)$
Y	a sample of output targets, $Y = (y_1, \ldots, y_n)$
X_l	labeled part of X, $X_l = (x_1, \ldots, x_l)$
Y_l	labeled part of Y, $Y_l = (y_1, \ldots, y_l)$
X_u	unlabeled part of X, $X_u = (x_{l+1}, \ldots, x_{l+u})$
Y_u	unlabeled part of Y, $Y_u = (y_{l+1}, \ldots, y_{l+u})$

Kernels

$\mathcal{H}$	feature space induced by a kernel
Φ	feature map, $\Phi : \mathcal{X} \to \mathcal{H}$
k	(positive definite) kernel
K	kernel matrix or Gram matrix, $K_{ij} = k(x_i, x_j)$

Vectors, Matrices, and Norms

$\mathbf{1}$	vector with all entries equal to one
$\mathbf{I}$	identity matrix
$A^{\top}$	transposed matrix (or vector)
A^{-1}	inverse matrix (in some cases, pseudoinverse)
$\mathbf{tr}\,(A)$	trace of a matrix
$\mathbf{det}\,(A)$	determinant of a matrix
$\langle \mathbf{x}, \mathbf{x}' \rangle$	dot product between $\mathbf{x}$ and $\mathbf{x}'$
$\|\cdot\|$	2-norm, $\|\mathbf{x}\| := \sqrt{\langle \mathbf{x}, \mathbf{x} \rangle}$
$\|\cdot\|_p$	p-norm , $\|\mathbf{x}\|_p := \left(\sum_{i=1}^{N} |x_i|^p \right)^{1/p}$, $N \in \mathbb{N} \cup \{\infty\}$
$\|\cdot\|_{\infty}$	∞-norm , $\|\mathbf{x}\|_{\infty} := \sup_{i=1}^{N} |x_i|$, $N \in \mathbb{N} \cup \{\infty\}$

Functions

$\ln$	logarithm to base e
$\log_2$	logarithm to base 2
f	a function, often from $\mathcal{X}$ or $[n]$ to $\mathbb{R}$, $\mathbb{R}^M$ or $[M]$
$\mathcal{F}$	a family of functions
$L_p(\mathcal{X})$	function spaces, $1 \leq p \leq \infty$

Probability

$\mathrm{P}\{\cdot\}$	probability of a logical formula
$\mathrm{P}(C)$	probability of a set (event) C
$p(x)$	density evaluated at $x \in \mathcal{X}$
$\mathbf{E}\,[\cdot]$	expectation of a random variable
$\mathbf{Var}\,[\cdot]$	variance of a random variable
$\mathcal{N}(\mu, \sigma^2)$	normal distribution with mean μ and variance σ^2

Graphs

$\mathbf{g}$	graph $\mathbf{g} = (V, E)$ with nodes V and edges E
$\mathcal{G}$	set of graphs
$\mathbf{W}$	weighted adjacency matrix of a graph ($\mathbf{W}_{ij} \neq 0 \Leftrightarrow (i, j) \in E$)
$\mathbf{D}$	(diagonal) degree matrix of a graph, $\mathbf{D}_{ii} = \sum_j W_{ij}$
$\mathcal{L}$	normalized graph Laplacian, $\mathcal{L} = \mathbf{I} - \mathbf{D}^{-1/2}\mathbf{W}\mathbf{D}^{-1/2}$
L	unnormalized graph Laplacian, $L = \mathbf{D} - \mathbf{W}$

SVM-related

$\rho_f(x, y)$	margin of function f on the example (x, y), i.e., $y \cdot f(x)$
ρ_f	margin of f on the training set, i.e., $\min_{i=1}^{m} \rho_f(x_i, y_i)$
h	VC dimension
C	regularization parameter in front of the empirical risk term
λ	regularization parameter in front of the regularizer
$\mathbf{w}$	weight vector
b	constant offset (or threshold)
α_i	Lagrange multiplier or expansion coefficient
β_i	Lagrange multiplier
$\boldsymbol{\alpha}, \boldsymbol{\beta}$	vectors of Lagrange multipliers
ξ_i	slack variables
$\boldsymbol{\xi}$	vector of all slack variables
Q	Hessian of a quadratic program

Miscellaneous

I_A	characteristic (or indicator) function on a set A, i.e., $I_A(x) = 1$ if $x \in A$ and 0 otherwise
δ_{ij}	Kronecker δ ($\delta_{ij} = 1$ if $i = j$, 0 otherwise)
δ_x	Dirac δ, satisfying $\int \delta_x(y) f(y) dy = f(x)$
$O(g(n))$	a function $f(n)$ is said to be $O(g(n))$ if there exist constants $C > 0$ and $n_0 \in \mathbb{N}$ such that $\vert f(n) \vert \leq Cg(n)$ for all $n \geq n_0$
$o(g(n))$	a function $f(n)$ is said to be $o(g(n))$ if there exist constants $c > 0$ and $n_0 \in \mathbb{N}$ such that $\vert f(n) \vert \geq cg(n)$ for all $n \geq n_0$
rhs/lhs	shorthand for "right-/left-hand side"
$\blacksquare$	the end of a proof

Contributors

Maria-Florina Balcan
Computer Science Department
Carnegie Mellon University
ninamf@cs.cmu.edu

Arindam Banerjee
Department of Computer Science and Engineering
University of Minnesota
banerjee@cs.umn.edu

Sugato Basu
Department of Computer Sciences
University of Texas at Austin
sugato@cs.utexas.edu

Mikhail Belkin
Department of Computer Science and Engineering
Ohio State University
mbelkin@cse.ohio-state.edu

Yoshua Bengio
Département d'Informatique et Recherche Opérationnelle
Université de Montréal
bengioy@iro.umontreal.ca

Mikhail Bilenko
Department of Computer Sciences
University of Texas at Austin
mbilenko@cs.utexas.edu

Avrim Blum
Computer Science Department
Carnegie Mellon University
avrim@cs.cmu.edu

Christopher J. C. Burges
Text Mining, Search and Navigation Group
Microsoft Research
Chris.Burges@microsoft.com

Ira Cohen
Enterprise Systems and Software Lab
HP Labs
ira.cohen@hp.com

Adrian Corduneanu
Computer Science and Artificial Intelligence Laboratory
Massachussets Institute of Technology
adrianc@alum.mit.edu

Fabio G. Cozman
Engineering School
University of Sao Paulo
fgcozman@usp.br

Nello Cristianini
Department of Engineering Mathematics
University of Bristol
nello@support-vector.net

Tijl De Bie
OKP Research Group
K.U.Leuven
tijl.debie@gmail.com

Olivier Delalleau
Département d'Informatique et Recherche Opérationnelle
Université de Montréal
delallea@iro.umontreal.ca

Zoubin Ghahramani
Department of Engineering
University of Cambridge
zoubin@eng.cam.ac.uk

Yves Grandvalet
Heudiasyc
Université de Technologie de Compiègne
yves.grandvalet@utc.fr

Yuhong Guo
Department of Computing Science
University of Alberta
yuhong@cs.ualberta.ca

Jihun Ham
Department of Electrical and Systems Engineering
University of Pennsylvania
jhham@seas.upenn.edu

Eugene Ie
Department of Computer Science and Engineering
University of California at San Diego
tie@cs.ucsd.edu

Tommi Jaakkola
Computer Science and Artificial Intelligence Laboratory
Massachussets Institute of Technology
tommi@csail.mit.edu

Thorsten Joachims
Department of Computer Science
Cornell University
tj@cs.cornell.edu

Michael I. Jordan
Department of Statistics
Department of Electrical Engineering and Computer Science
University of California at Berkeley
jordan@cs.berkeley.edu

Jaz Kandola
Gatsby Computational Neuroscience Unit
University College London
jkandola@gatsby.ucl.ac.uk

John Lafferty
Computer Science Department
Carnegie Mellon University
lafferty@cs.cmu.edu

Neil D. Lawrence
Department of Computer Science
University of Sheffield
neil@dcs.shef.ac.uk

Nicolas Le Roux
Département d'Informatique et Recherche Opérationnelle
Université de Montréal
nicolas.le.roux@umontreal.ca

Daniel D. Lee
Department of Electrical and Systems Engineering
University of Pennsylvania
ddlee@seas.upenn.edu

Christina Leslie
Center for Computational Learning Systems
Columbia University
cleslie@cs.columbia.edu

Andrew McCallum
Department of Computer Science
University of Massachusetts Amherst
mccallum@cs.umass.edu

Tom Mitchell
Machine Learning Department
Carnegie Mellon University
tom.mitchell@cmu.edu

Raymond Mooney
Department of Computer Sciences
University of Texas at Austin
mooney@cs.utexas.edu

Kamal Nigam
Google
knigam@kamalnigam.com

Partha Niyogi
Department of Computer Science
University of Chicago
niyogi@cs.uchicago.edu

William Stafford Noble
Department of Genome Sciences
University of Washington
noble@gs.washington.edu

Alon Orlitsky
Department of Electrical and Computer Engineering
University of California at San Diego
alon@ucsd.edu

John C. Platt
Knowledge Tools Group
Microsoft Research
jplatt@microsoft.com

Sajama
Department of Electrical and Computer Engineering
University of California at San Diego
sajama@ucsd.edu

Lawrence K. Saul
Department of Computer and Information Science
University of Pennsylvania
lsaul@cis.upenn.edu

Dale Schuurmans
Department of Computing Science
University of Alberta
dale@cs.ualberta.ca

Bernhard Schölkopf
Department of Empirical Inference
Max Planck Institute for Biological Cybernetics
bernhard.schoelkopf@tuebingen.mpg.de

Matthias Seeger
Department of Empirical Inference
Max Planck Institute for Biological Cybernetics
matthias.seeger@tuebingen.mpg.de

Fei Sha
Department of Computer and Information Science
University of Pennsylvania
feisha@cis.upenn.edu

Hyunjung (Helen) Shin
Department of Empirical Inference
Max Planck Institute for Biological Cybernetics
shin@tuebingen.mpg.de

Vikas Sindhwani
Department of Computer Science
University of Chicago
vikass@cs.uchicago.edu

Finnegan Southey
Department of Computing Science
University of Alberta
finnwork@lucubratio.org

Koji Tsuda
Department of Empirical Inference
Max Planck Institute for Biological Cybernetics
koji.tsuda@tuebingen.mpg.de

Vladimir Vapnik
NEC Laboratories America
vlad@nec-labs.com

Kilian Q. Weinberger
Department of Computer and Information Science
University of Pennsylvania
kilianw@seas.upenn.edu

Jason Weston
NEC Laboratories America
jasonw@nec-labs.com

Dana Wilkinson
School of Computer Science
University of Waterloo
d3wilkinson@cs.uwaterloo.ca

Dengyong Zhou
NEC Laboratories America
dzhou@nec-labs.com

Xiaojin Zhu
Department of Computer Science
University of Wisconsin-Madison
jerryzhu@cs.wisc.edu

Index

An online index is availabe on the book webpage at
`http://www.kyb.tuebingen.mpg.de/ssl-book/`